www.mygrammarlab.com

Pearson Education Limited
Edinburgh Gate
Harlow
Essex CM20 2JE
England
and Associated Companies throughout the world.

www.pearsonelt.com

First published 2012

Fourth impression 2016

ISBN: 9781408299111 (with key)
ISBN: 9781408299128 (without key)
ISBN: 9781408299289 Class audio CDs

Set in Frutiger and ITC Stone Serif

Printed in China
CTPSC/04

The authors would like to acknowledge the staff and students at the following institutions for piloting the materials: Wimbledon School of English, Westminster Kingsway College, the College of North West London.

Text Acknowledgements

Article on page 45 adapted from History of Magnum, http://agency.magnumphotos.com/about/about, copyright © Magnum Photos; Extract on page 26 from "Lobster's white shade of pale puts fishmonger £20,000 in red", The Guardian, 09/12/1997 (Harding, L.), copyright © Guardian News & Media Ltd 1997; Extract on page 30 from Notes from a Small Island, published by Black Swan (Bill Bryson, 1995). Reprinted by permission of The Random House Group Ltd; Extract on page 56 adapted from The Tower of London, www.hrp.org.uk/TowerOfLondon/. Reproduced with permission; Extract on page 58 adapted from The One Hundred Stupidest Things Ever Done, Michael O'Mara Books Ltd (Ross and Kathryn Petras, 1997) copyright © Ross and Kathryn Petras 1997, all rights reserved; Extract on page 89 adapted from "Cinema audiences boom as people look to escape recession", The Telegraph, 26/05/2009 (Wallop, H.), copyright © Telegraph Media Group Limited 2009; Extract on page 123 adapted from "Solving Japan's old-age problem", The Guardian, 20/03/2010 (Collinson, P.), copyright © Guardian News & Media Ltd 2010; Extract on page 187 adapted from "How overprotective parents may harm their children's health", The Daily Mail, 24/06/1999 (Marsh, B.), copyright © Solo Syndication, 1999; Quote on page 222 from Nelson Mandela's Inaugural Speech May 1994, reproduced with permission of the Nelson Mandela Foundation; Extract on page 315 from The Good Terrorist, Jonathan Cape Ltd (Doris Lessing, 1985) pp.5,7; Extract on page 319 adapted from "Why that joke email could get you the sack", The Guardian, 02/12/2000 (Inman, P. and Wilson, J.), copyright © Guardian News & Media Ltd 2000; Extract on page 328 from Wall Games, HarperCollins (Michael Dobbs, 2011). Reprinted by permission of HarperCollins Publishers Ltd, copyright © 2011, Michael Dobbs; Extract on page 328 from Heathen, Warner (Shaun Hutson, 1992). Reproduced by kind permission of Brie Burkeman & Clarke Ltd on behalf of Shaun Hutson; and Extract on page 332 from Nice Work, Vintage Books (David Lodge, 1988), copyright © David Lodge 1988. Reprinted by permission of The Random House Group Limited, Curtis Brown Group Ltd, London on behalf of David Lodge , and Viking Penguin, a division of Penguin Group (USA) Inc.

Illustrated by Ian Baker, Kathy Baxendale, Paul Boston, Glynn Goodwin, Charlie Hill, Joanna Kerr, Garry Parsons, Roger Penwill, Ben Scruton and Lucy Truman

Picture Credits

The publisher would like to thank the following for their kind permission to reproduce their photographs:

(Key: b-bottom; c-centre; l-left; r-right; t-top
akg-images Ltd: 251, Electa 250, Erich Lessing 24, 67, North Wind Picture Archives 326; **Alamy Images:** Mike Abrahams 81, Pat Behnke 90, CuboImages srl 346, dalekhelen 177, FirePhoto 174, Paul Glendell 197, John Hopkins 277, Oleksiy Maksymenko 181r, Luke Peters 172r, Photolicensors International AG 296, Anthony Pleva 184, Frances Roberts 305, Geoffrey Robinson 359, James Royall 89, Shangara Singh 354, UrbanImages 120r, Rob Wilkinson 313; **The Art Archive:** Chopin Foundation Warsaw / Collection Dagli Orti 242bc; **Bridgeman Art Library Ltd:** Christie's Images 31, Dulwich Picture Gallery, London, UK 29, Louvre, Paris, France / Giraudon 23l, Mauritshuis, The Hague, The Netherlands 18 (Painting), National Gallery, London, UK 20, 23cr; **Corbis:** 350, Antar Dayal / Illustration Works 334, Bettmann 23c, 253, Carlos Barria / Reuters 139, John-Francis Bourke 286, Dave G. Houser 276, Francis G. Mayer 236, Heritage Images 23cl, Jeremy Horner 258, Imaginechina 164, Karen Kasmauski 123, Larry W. Kachelhofer / U.S. Navy / CNP 256, Louise Gubb / Corbis SABA 222, Gideon Mendel 330, Oberto Gili / Beateworks 23r, Ocean 124, Paul Kaye; Cordaiy Photo Library Ltd. 100, Ryan Pyle 163, Régis Bossu / Sygma 64, ML Sinibaldi 267, Steve Russell / ZUMA Press 128r, Sygma 111, Vincent Laforet / Pool / Reuters 168, Vladimir Godnik / beyond 283tr (Inset); **DK Images:** 298; **Mary Evans Picture Library:** 219; **Fotolia.com:** 119r, Mark Atkins 206, Antonio Ballesteros 242tc, Beboy 264, Deborah Benbrook 116, bobeobi 61, Zacarias da Mata 87, DMM Photography Art 18 (Frame), epridnia 94, Gatsby 249, gilmart 194, Gooseman 272, Anton Gvozdikov 112l, Hallgerd 309, Angela Hawkey 208, JackF 120l (Inset), Jenifoto 49, Jgz 279, kmiragaya 242tr, Loic Lucide 50, moshimochi 119l (Inset), philip1652 188, pinggr 281, Michael Rolands 205, Sergey Rusakov 292, Gina Sanders 65, Ivan Stanic 314, Stephen Sweet 112 (Wall), Andrea Vonblon 102r, Jason Young 59; **Getty Images:** 34, 137, 141, 146, 221, 225, 240, 316, 34, 137, 141, 146, 221, 225, 240, 316, Peter Cade 198, FilmMagic 232, Rob Gage 152, Hulton Archive 37r, 76, 226, 239, Michael & Patricia Fogden 301, New York Daily News 310, Popperfoto 242br, 181l, Redferns 339, Andersen Ross 290, Time Life Pictures 247; **iStockphoto:** Grafissimo 235, wdstock 128r (Inset); **Magnum Photos Ltd:** Robert Capa © International Center of Photography 45; **NASA:** 261, 333; **Pearson Education Ltd:** 16; Corbis 48, 191, Peter Evans 278, Photodisc. Colin Paterson 93, Photodisc. Photolink. F. Schussler 292r, Photodisc. Photolink. Tomi 283t; **Photolibrary.com:** Jose Fuste Raga 33 (Inset), Jamie Grill 112tl, Imagesource 142, 156, Manchan Manchan 79, Monkey Business Images Ltd 341, Santi Román 352, Paula Solloway 62, Jochen Tack 303, Frank Wartenberg 39, Jack Wilburn 306; **Press Association Images:** AJM / AJM / EMPICS Entertainment 230, Barratts / S&G Barratts / EMPICS Archive 244, Andrew Parsons 166, Edmond Terakopian 280; **Reuters:** Dario Pignatelli 37l; **Rex Features:** 135, Albanpix Ltd 183, Amanda Hall / Robert Harding 13, c.20thC.Fox / Everett 96, CSU Archv / Everett 106r, David Caird / Newspix 255, Everett Collection 102l, 105, 109, 112r, 252, KeystoneUSA-ZUMA 33, Alisdair Macdonald 268, Roger-Viollet 98, Frederic Sierakowski 294, Sipa Press 242bl, 322, Sylvain Grandadam / Robert Harding 182; **Shutterstock.com:** blanche 285, David Gaylor 172c (Inset), Simon Gurney 56, holbox 271, David MacFarlane 216, Alexandre Nunes 130, Bill Poon 54, snowblurred 201, Studio 37 324, Supri Suharjoto 126, tungtopgun 47; **The Kobal Collection:** 94 (Third Man); **TopFoto:** TopFoto.co.uk 242tl

All other images © Pearson Education

Every effort has been made to trace the copyright holders and we apologise in advance for any unintentional omissions. We would be pleased to insert the appropriate acknowledgement in any subsequent edition of this publication.

Contents

Introduction to MyGrammarLab

Welcome to **MyGrammarLab** – a three-level grammar series that teaches and practises grammar through a unique blend of book, online and mobile resources. We recommend that you read this introduction along with the guide on the inside front cover to find out how to get the most out of your course.

What level is MyGrammarLab?

The **MyGrammarLab** series takes learners from elementary to advanced grammar, each level benchmarked against the Common European Framework and providing grammar practice for Cambridge ESOL exams:

	Level description	CEFR level	Grammar practice for exams
Elementary	elementary to pre-intermediate	A1/A2	KET
Intermediate	pre-intermediate to upper intermediate	B1/B2	PET FCE
Advanced	upper intermediate to advanced	C1/C2	CAE IELTS

What is unique about MyGrammarLab?

MyGrammarLab offers every learner of English the opportunity to study grammar in the way that best suits their needs – and provides as much practice as necessary to ensure that each grammar point is learnt and can be used in the context of real communication.

At each level, learners have access to a variety of materials:

book

- **clear explanations** to ensure full understanding of the grammar
- **natural examples** to illustrate the grammar points, based on the Longman Corpus Network
- a topic-based approach that presents **grammar in context**
- a **variety of exercise types** – from drills to contextualised practice
- a **review section** at the end of each module to revise the key grammar points
- information on the **pronunciation** of grammar items
- information on **common errors** and how to avoid making them
- a **grammar check section** for quickly checking specific grammar points
- a **glossary** of grammar terms used in the explanations

online

- a **grammar teacher** who explains key grammar points through short video presentations
- a full **diagnostic test** to identify the grammar points that need to be learnt
- **more practice** for every unit of the book
- regular **progress tests** to check that the grammar has been understood
- **catch-up exercises** for learners who fail the progress tests – to ensure that every learner has the opportunity to master the grammar
- a full **exit test** at the end of each module
- automatic **marking and feedback**
- **pronunciation practice** of grammar items
- the option to **listen and check** the answers for practice exercises from the book
- additional **grammar practice for exams**

mobile

- downloadable exercises for **practice anywhere, any time**
- the ability to **create exercises** from a bank of practice questions
- automatic marking and **feedback** for wrong answers

What is a MyLab?

A MyLab is a Learning Management System – an online platform that enables learners and teachers to manage the learning process via a number of online tools such as automatic marking, the recording of grades in a gradebook and the ability to customise a course.

How can I get the most out of MyGrammarLab?

To the Student:

If you are using MyGrammarLab in class, your teacher will tell you which units to study and which exercises to do.

If you are using MyGrammarLab for self-study, you can work through the book from Module 1 to Module 18. Or you can choose a grammar point that you want to study and go to a specific unit. Here is a good way to study a complete module:

Each module in the book starts with a summary of intermediate grammar points that you should already know. On the facing page there is a short text which illustrates examples of the module grammar, followed by a short diagnostic test. This shows you the units you need to study in order to learn more about the main grammar points.

Go online for a full diagnostic test Look for this instruction at the bottom of the first page of each module. Take the online diagnostic test then click on the feedback button to see which unit to go to for more information and practice.

Each unit starts with one or two pages of grammar explanations. Where there is one page, the practice exercises are on the facing page. Where there are two, the practice exercises are on the following two pages.

For more information about the grammar, go online to watch the grammar videos in each unit and listen to your grammar teacher.

If you would like more grammar and listening practice, you can listen to the correct answers for some of the practice exercises in the book. Look for this symbol: 2.10 **Listen and check.** If you have the book with answer key, you can check all the answers at the back of the book.

Go online for more practice Look for this instruction at the end of the practice exercises in the book. All the online exercises are different to the exercises in the book. They are marked automatically. Your grades are recorded in your own gradebook.

Look for this symbol on the grammar information pages in the book: 1.10. This means that there is some information on a pronunciation point. Go online to hear the information and practise the pronunciation.

Go online for a progress test Look for this instruction at the end of the practice exercises in the book. The online progress tests show you if you have understood the grammar points in the units that you have studied. If your grade is low, do the catch-up exercises online. If your grade is good, you probably don't need to do these.

For practice away from your computer, download the catch-up exercises to your mobile phone. You can create your own practice tests. Go to www.mygrammarlab.com to download.

At the end of each module there is a two-page review section. The review exercises bring together all the grammar points in the module.

Go online for an exit test Look for this instruction at the end of each module. This takes you to an online exit test that will show you how much you know and if you need more practice.

To the Teacher:

If you are using MyGrammarLab with a class of students, you can either work through the book from the first to the last module, or you can select the areas that you would like your students to focus on.

You can work through a module as outlined on the previous page – but as a teacher, you are able to assign tests and view all the scores from your class in one gradebook. This will enable you to see at a glance which areas are difficult for your students – both as a group and individually.

For pronunciation and listening practice in class, audio CDs are available. The disk and track number for each pronunciation explanation and each recorded answer to a practice exercise are given in the book. Look for these symbols:
Pronunciation ➤ 1.02
1.10 **Listen and check.**

All tests (diagnostic, progress and exit) are hidden from students. Assign these when you want your class to take the test. Marking is automatic – as is the reporting of grades into the class gradebook.

Some practice exercises – such as written tasks – require teacher marking. These are hidden from your students so you should only assign these if you want them to submit their answers to you for marking. The grades are reported automatically into the gradebook.

Key to symbols

⚠	This highlights a grammar point that learners find particularly difficult and often gives common errors that students make.
ACADEMIC ENGLISH	These notes will help you to express your ideas in a style that is appropriate to formal written English.
FORMALITY CHECK	This introduces information about the formality or informality of a particular grammar point or item of vocabulary.
GRAMMAR IN USE	This indicates an exercise which practises grammar in a typical context, often a longer passage or dialogue.
Pronunciation ➤ 1.10	This indicates where you will find pronunciation practice on the audio CDs and in the MyLab.
2.10 **Listen and check.**	This indicates that there is a recorded answer online. You can check your answer by listening to the recording or, if you are using the edition with answer key, by looking in the key at the back of the book.
adverbial	Some words in the explanations are shown in purple. This indicates that they are included in the glossary on p. 11. Look in the glossary to find out what these words mean.

Glossary

adverbial a word or phrase used as an adverb to answer questions such as *How?*, *When?* and *Where?* or to link two sentences, e.g. *After that, However*

agent the person/thing that does the action of a passive verb, e.g. *The cars are produced by* **machines.**

attributive position when an adjective comes before the noun it describes, e.g. *an* ***expensive*** *meal* → predicative position

backshift changing the tense in reported speech to go one step back, i.e. present to past, past to past perfect, e.g. *'He's really nice.'* → *I told you he* **was** *really nice.*

classifying adjective an adjective which describes what type something is, e.g. *a* ***medical*** *emergency, an* ***industrial*** *estate.*

cleft sentence one simple sentence that has been 'split' into two clauses to focus on one part of it, e.g. *The book was written in 2008.* → *It was in 2008 that the book was written.*

collocation words that often go together, e.g. *to take a photo, a strong swimmer*

complement a word or phrase that follows a linking verb and describes the subject or object of the verb, e.g. *Jane seems* ***nervous.***

compound adjective an adjective formed from two words, e.g. *slow-growing, air-conditioned.*

compound noun a noun formed from two words which are related to each other, e.g. *dishwasher, sports car, mobile phone.*

coordinating conjunction a linking word (*and, but, or*), which joins two clauses of equal value, i.e. two main clauses or two subordinate clauses, e.g. *He laughed* ***but*** *she cried.* → subordinating conjunction

determiner a word which comes before a noun and specifies the noun in some way, e.g. ***the*** *food,* (article) ***our*** *food* (possessive), ***some*** *food* (quantifier), ***that*** *food* (demonstrative).

direct object a noun (phrase) or pronoun that usually follows a verb and shows who or what is affected by the action, e.g. *They sold* **their old car** *last week.* → indirect object

ellipsis leaving out a word or phrase completely; in this example, *coming* is ellipted in the answer: *'Who's coming this evening' 'I am.'*

end-weight principle the principle in writing and formal speech that means we prefer to put long phrases after the verb and will manipulate the grammar to do so.

fronting moving an element of a sentence to the beginning for emphasis, particularly an element that does not usually appear at the beginning, e.g. ***On the right of the doorway*** *is the most magnificent bay tree.*

gradable adjective an adjective which can be made stronger or weaker, e.g. *very* ***expensive****, slightly* ***small*** and has a comparative form, e.g. *more expensive, smaller* → ungradable adjective

indirect object a noun (phrase) or pronoun that follows a verb and is usually linked to it with a preposition. It shows who or what receives the action, e.g. *They sold their old car to* **my brother.** → direct object

infinitive clause a subordinate clause that contains an infinitive form of a verb. It can act as the subject or complement of the verb *be* or identify a noun, e.g. ***To win the competition*** *was his aim.* ***The first person to answer correctly*** *gets the point.*

information principle the principle in writing and formal speech that means we prefer to start a clause with known or familiar information, often from the previous clause.

inversion reversing the position of two elements of the clause for emphasis, e.g. ***Never had*** *he heard such rubbish.*

nominalisation using a noun rather than a verb either to make the clause more formal, or to enable two clauses to be expressed as one, e.g. *The committee* ***decided*** *to reject the plans, and everyone was delighted.* → *The committee's* ***decision*** *to reject the plans delighted everyone.*

noun clause a clause that replaces or acts like a noun, e.g. *I was near* ***where you live*** *yesterday.* (= I was near your house.)

participle clause a subordinate clause which begins with a present or past participle, e.g. ***Lying in the sun****, I fell asleep.* ***Treated gently****, the fabric should last for years.*

particle a preposition or adverb which combines with a verb to form a prepositional or phrasal verb, often with a new meaning, e.g. *up* → *give up, off* → *take off*

performative verb a verb that actually performs the action it describes when used in the first person present, e.g. *I apologise* means *I'm sorry*, so saying it performs the action of apologising.

predicative position when an adjective comes after the noun it describes (usually after a linking verb), e.g. *that meal was expensive; I find that news surprising.* → attributive position

question tag a short tag at the end of a statement which turns it into a question.

relative clause a clause that gives information about a noun or pronoun in a main clause. In a **reduced relative clause** we use a participle to replace the relative pronoun and verb in a defining relative clause, e.g. *She doesn't like the man who lives next door.* → *She doesn't like the man* ***living next door.***

sense verb a verb that describes a sense or perception, e.g. *see, hear, smell.*

sentence adverb an adverb that refers to a whole sentence rather than one word, e.g. ***Generally****, the children were well behaved.* Includes **comment adverbs**, which express our attitude to the information in a statement, e.g. ***Understandably****, he was disappointed with the results.*

state verb a verb that describes a state such as being, thinking, possessing or feeling, rather than an action, e.g. *be, believe, have, feel.*

stranded preposition a preposition at the end of a clause, not followed by a noun or pronoun, e.g. *What are you going to do that* ***for****?* These often appear in questions and relative clauses.

subjunctive a form of a verb which is the same as the infinitive without *to*, used after certain verbs/adjectives and in some *that* clauses to convey necessity/importance, e.g. *The judge insisted that each client* ***pay*** *his own costs.*

subordinating conjunction a linking word such as *while, although, if*, which links a subordinate clause and a main clause, e.g. *She cried* ***because*** *she was happy.* → coordinating conjunction

substitution replacing one word or phrase with another to avoid repetition, for example replacing a noun with a pronoun, e.g. *I've already met James.* ***He's*** *very pleasant.*

ungradable adjective an adjective which represents the limit of a scale and cannot be made stronger with *very*, e.g. *priceless, boiling.*

MODULE

1 Nouns, possessives and pronouns

Before you start

1 Review these intermediate grammar points and check you know them.

Types of noun

- concrete e.g. *artist, table, child, station, food, storm*
- abstract e.g. *art, responsibility, anger, efficiency, perception, photography*
- proper (the names of people, places, events, etc.) e.g. *Jane, London, August*

COUNTABLE NOUNS *a car, three cars*
UNCOUNTABLE NOUNS *oil, beauty, fruit*

We do not use *a/an* with uncountable nouns, and we do not usually make them plural.

Possessive forms

1 noun + *'s* or *'* (usually with people and animals): *One of* ***Sam's vehicles*** *has been damaged.*
noun + *of* + noun (usually with things): *There's a scratch on* ***the paintwork of his car****.*

2 If the meaning is clear from the context, we can omit the following noun:
That isn't my handwriting. It's ***Selina's****.* (= Selina's handwriting)

Personal pronouns

SUBJECT PRONOUNS	OBJECT PRONOUNS	(POSSESSIVE ADJECTIVES)	POSSESSIVE PRONOUNS	REFLEXIVE PRONOUNS
I	*me*	*my*	*mine*	*myself*
you	*you*	*your*	*yours*	*yourself/yourselves*
he	*him*	*his*	*his*	*himself*
she	*her*	*her*	*hers*	*herself*
it	*it*	*its*		*itself*
we	*us*	*our*	*ours*	*ourselves*
they	*them*	*their*	*theirs*	*themselves*

- subject pronoun: *Hockney is Britain's most famous painter.* ***He****'s from Yorkshire.*
- object pronoun: *I met Julian yesterday. I like* ***him****, don't you?* (direct object)
  Those books belong to Julian. Can you give them to ***him****, please?* (indirect object)
- possessive adjective: *Did Susie leave that here? It looks like* ***her*** *umbrella.*
- possessive pronoun: *No, it's not her umbrella. It's* ***ours****. Don't you recognise it?*
- reflexive pronoun: *Quick! The baby's burnt* ***herself****!*

Indefinite pronouns

someone/body[1]	*something*	*somewhere*	*somehow*
anyone/body	*anything*	*anywhere*	*anyhow*[2]
everyone/body	*everything*	*everywhere*	
no one/body[3]	*nothing*	*nowhere*	

[1] We use *-one* and *-body* interchangeably.
[2] *anyhow* is informal and is similar to *anyway*: *Anyhow, as I was saying …*
[3] We usually write *no one* as two words, and *nobody* as one word.

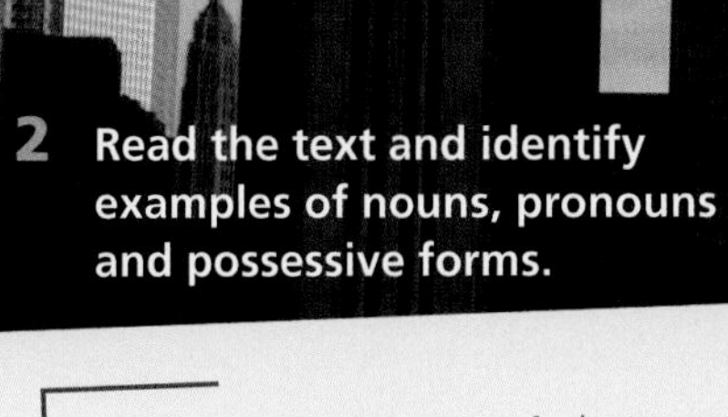

2 **Read the text and identify examples of nouns, pronouns and possessive forms.**

SINCE THE INVENTION of photography, art has been creating a new identity for itself. Movements from impressionism to abstract expressionism have widened the boundaries of what one might describe as 'art'. People's perceptions have changed and nowadays we no longer define a great work of art by its beauty but by its ability to show us something in a new way, or to challenge our perception of what it is to be human.

3 **Complete the diagnostic test below. Choose the correct words in *italics*. If both options are correct, choose both.**

1 The *chair* / *chairwoman* has just phoned to say she's been delayed in traffic. ➤ Unit 1.1
2 Have you thought about doing gymnastics? I think *it's* / *they're* very good for you. ➤ Unit 1.2
3 The society's president, against the wishes of the other founder members, *has* / *have* agreed to the sale. ➤ Unit 1.3
4 I love Adam Sandler's movies. I thought 'Funny People' *was* / *were* hilarious. ➤ Unit 1.4
5 The disabled *has* / *have* won a number of rights in recent years. ➤ Unit 1.5
6 Eliot was hit on the head by *stone* / *a stone* and had to be rushed to hospital. ➤ Unit 1.6
7 Our local delicatessen offers an enormous range of *cheese* / *cheeses*. ➤ Unit 1.7
8 The villa we're borrowing belongs to my *sister's-in-law* / *sister-in-law's* parents. ➤ Unit 2.1
9 I might be able to get you an interview; the owner's a friend of *me* / *mine*. ➤ Unit 2.2
10 Everyone's been admiring my *expensive wife's car* / *wife's expensive car*. ➤ Unit 2.3
11 Karen noticed the article in *the local paper of today* / *today's local paper*. ➤ Unit 3.1
12 We could hear the *crowd's cheers* / *cheers of the crowd* that lined the street. ➤ Unit 3.2
13 Wouldn't you agree that the processor is the *computer's main component* / *main component of the computer*? ➤ Unit 3.3
14 The class will be reading *the short stories' collection of Graham Greene* / *Graham Greene's collection of short stories* next term. ➤ Unit 3.4
15 The food in his paintings looks good enough *to eat it* / *to eat*. ➤ Unit 4.1
16 If you'd like a new tennis racket, I can get you *one* / *a one* very cheaply. ➤ Unit 4.2
17 Some elderly people have difficulty in *remembering themselves* / *remembering* what happened only a few hours before. ➤ Unit 4.3
18 On his return, Dieter and his wife had a lot to tell *themselves* / *each other*. ➤ Unit 4.4
19 In cases like these, *you* / *one* can understand the motive behind the attack. ➤ Unit 5.1
20 Can you repeat that? There was *something* / *anything* you said which I didn't quite understand. ➤ Unit 5.2

4 **Check your answers on page 384. Then go to the unit for more information and practice.**

1 Nouns

Plural forms of nouns and irregular noun plurals ➤ page 366
Differences between British and American English ➤ page 368

1 Gender

Nouns do not have grammatical gender in English. To show gender in job nouns we have to say *a female/woman doctor, a male doctor*, etc. A few nouns show gender by their suffix, usually masculine gender, such as *businessman*. A lot of people avoid these nouns now, especially if referring to a woman, and prefer a form with no obvious gender, e.g. *chair*, or to match the suffix to the person, e.g. *chairwoman*:
That's the view of Sheila Davison, chair(woman) of the Institute of Public Relations.

2 Nouns ending in *-s*

Some uncountable nouns end in *-s* but take a singular verb, for example

- some illnesses: *measles, mumps*
- sport and games: *aerobics, gymnastics, darts*
- study/abstract ideas/emotions: *mathematics, politics, news, thanks, happiness*
  ***Politics is** a topic best avoided with people you don't know well.*

 A plural subject describing a specific measurement usually takes a singular verb:
✗ ~~*Two metres aren't particularly tall these days.*~~
✓ ***Two metres isn't** particularly tall these days.*
***Twenty-four hours is** a long time in politics.* ***Ten miles is** too far to walk.*

A few nouns are more common in the plural form and take a plural verb, e.g. *goods, whereabouts, remains, stairs, proceeds*:
*The auction raised a lot of money and the **proceeds were** given to a children's charity.*

Some nouns refer to one object divided into two parts and take a plural verb, e.g. *glasses, jeans, pyjamas, scales, scissors, spectacles, trousers*:
*Special **scissors are** used to cut this fabric.*

3 Noun–verb agreement

The verb usually agrees with the subject noun even if it is separated by prepositional phrases, relative clauses, brackets or commas:
***The petrol station** across the road from the new shops **has** just cut its prices.*

However, if the verb is a long way from the subject and closer to a complement (➤ Unit 42.1/2), the verb can agree with the complement. Compare:
***The most exciting event was** the rowing finals.*
***The most exciting event** in the Sydney Olympics for most British viewers **was/were** the rowing finals.*

The same can apply after *what* used to introduce a noun clause:
***What** the Board needs to finalise now **is/are** the terms of the redundancies.*

4 Two subjects/plural subject–verb agreement

We usually use a plural verb with two subjects linked by *and* or *both ... and*:
***Mum and Dad were** hoping that you'd join them this evening.*
***Both the doctor and the surgeon have** advised me to have the operation.*

However, we use a singular verb if we consider the two items as one single concept:
✗ ~~*Fish and chips are one of the most common English dishes.*~~
✓ ***Fish and chips is** one of the most common English dishes.*

Titles of books, films, etc. take a singular verb, even if they are plural nouns:
*Hitchcock's film **'The Birds' is** based on a story by Daphne du Maurier.*

5 Collective noun–verb agreement

Collective nouns refer to a group of people, animals or things, e.g. *family, government, group, staff, team, band, class*. A large number of proper nouns fall into this category, e.g. *the United Nations, British Airways, Microsoft Corporation*. We can usually use a singular or plural verb after these nouns. The choice can depend on how we think of the noun:

	SINGULAR VERB	PLURAL VERB
collective noun seen as a whole entity	***The family has*** *a monthly income of $2,000.*	
collective noun seen as a group of individuals		***The family are*** *all gathering here for New Year.*
a + collective noun	***A team*** *of inspectors* ***is*** *visiting the prison tomorrow.*	

We always use a plural verb for

- certain collective nouns, e.g. *police, people, cattle*:
  The police are *investigating his accusation of fraud.*
- an adjective used as a collective noun (➤ Unit 12.5):
  The middle-aged have *a lot to offer employers.*
- nouns such as *the majority/a number/a couple* + *of* + plural noun:
  The majority of the people were *pleased to see the government fall.*

6 Countable and uncountable nouns

Some nouns can be countable or uncountable, but have different meanings:

COUNTABLE MEANING	UNCOUNTABLE MEANING
I'd love a ***coffee,***[1] *please.* (= a cup)	*Do you drink* ***coffee****?* (= the liquid)
I'll buy a ***chicken***[2] *for dinner tonight.* (= the whole bird)	*Would you like some* ***chicken*** *for dinner?* (= a part/the dish)
This is an amazing ***drawing***[2] *by Leonardo.* (= a picture)	*My son is very good at* ***drawing****.* (= the activity)
Someone threw a ***stone***[2] *at our window.* (= one item)	*The road crosses a flat landscape of scrub and* ***stone****.* (= the material)

[1] This applies to all drinks: *tea/a tea, cola/a cola, lemonade/a lemonade*

[2] Not all nouns of these types can be both countable and uncountable:
✗ *~~a beef~~, ~~a mutton~~* ✓ *a duck/duck, a fish/fish, a lamb/lamb*
✗ *~~an art~~, ~~a poetry~~* ✓ *a painting/painting, a sculpture/sculpture*
✗ *~~a wool~~, ~~a cotton~~* ✓ *a paper/paper, a rock/rock*

7 Quantifying uncountable nouns

We can use words like *piece* and *bit* to make some uncountable nouns countable:
The Council will remove ***two pieces of unwanted furniture*** *if desired.*

Other common nouns used in this way are: *a slice of bread/meat/cheese/cake; an item of news/furniture/clothing; a lump of sugar/coal; a cup of coffee/tea, a pair of trousers/jeans.*

We can sometimes make an uncountable noun countable to express 'different types' of the noun:
Our new skincare cream contains several essential ***oils.***
This is ***a*** *soft* ***cheese*** *from the Pyrenees.*

We can use articles with uncountable abstract nouns to refer to a specific feeling:
distrust → *a deep distrust, a distrust of lawyers*   *love* → *an everlasting love, the love of music*

When we use nouns in this way, we use a singular verb:
A ***love of fashion and music is*** *common amongst teenagers.*

Practice

1 Complete sentences 1–10 with the correct form of a suitable verb. In sentences 11–15 add *a*, *an* or *no* article (–). If two answers are possible, put both.

1 Rickets .... a disease caused by a lack of vitamin D.
2 The 10,000 kilometres .... the longest walking competition in the Olympics.
3 Hollywood classic *The Women* .... showing at the London Film Festival this week.
4 Saudi Arabia, along with most of the oil-producing nations, ... voted to raise the price of crude oil again.
5 What he'd really like us to buy him for his birthday .... some new Nike trainers.
6 Roast beef and Yorkshire pudding .... definitely still the favourite of many British people!
7 My brother thinks that economics .... really interesting. I disagree.
8 That band .... always had a reputation for performing better in the studio than live.
9 Both my brother and sister .... lived in this town all their lives.
10 The local police .... interviewing several suspects in connection with the recent attacks.
11 I first felt the desire to visit Venice when looking at .... painting by Canaletto.
12 Where can I find .... information on late Renaissance Florentine artists?
13 There's nothing more delicious than .... lamb with mint sauce.
14 We developed .... passion for Baroque music at university.
15 It isn't a lack of courage that stops me taking part in extreme sports, it is .... anxiety about getting seriously injured.

2 GRAMMAR IN USE Choose the correct words in *italics*. If both options are possible, choose both.

Snow Falling on Cedars

BY **DAVID GUTERSON**

This novel (0) *open* / *opens* in the courthouse of San Piedro, a small sleepy island off the Pacific coast of the north-west United States. Underneath the courtroom windows, four tall narrow arches of (1) *leaded* / *a leaded* glass, (2) *drama* / *a drama* which will divide the island's communities (3) *is* / *are* unfolding. The defendant stands erect in the dock; the local press and the jurors await the start of this trial. Kabuo Miyamoto is accused of the murder of Carl Heine, a young fisherman. The alleged crime by a young man of Japanese descent stirs up the emotions of the islanders and questions their beliefs and their politics. It takes place in the 1950s – not many years (4) *has* / *have* passed since the Japanese bombing of Pearl Harbour and the horrors of World War II. Although the Japanese on San Piedro (5) *was* / *were* eager to defend their adopted country against the country of their ancestors, a number of people in the community (6) *was* / *were* unable to forgive Japan its role in the war, and the trial causes their deeply-held prejudices to surface. 'Snow Falling on Cedars' (7) *is* / *are* not only one of the best mysteries of recent years, it also raises issues which affect us all. However, it ends with (8) *great* / *a great* optimism. David Guterson has succeeded in combining the best from both classic and populist American (9) *literatures* / *literature* into (10) *spellbinding* / *a spellbinding* work of art. Buy and read this beautiful novel.

3 **Complete the sentences, using the words from the box. Use each word twice. Add an article or use the plural form if necessary. 2.02 Listen and check.**

chair chicken drawing group love stone

1 Gerry threw .... into the pond and watched the water ripple outwards.
2 Who is going to be .... of the new finance committee?
3 Caleb owns a free-range farm so he allows his .... to run around wherever they like.
4 These days you don't have to be good at .... to be a successful artist.
5 Numerous .... of illegal immigrants have attempted to cross the border in the last few months.
6 Unfortunately for my waistline, I have .... of chocolate, especially in cakes!
7 For his art project, my son did .... of his pet rabbit.
8 We always have .... and chips on Monday nights.
9 The Tower of London is built of .... from Caen in Normandy.
10 They say .... is the strongest emotion.
11 Although we have a big dining table, we only have four ....
12 .... of university scientists is doing research into the causes of obesity in children.

4 GRAMMAR IN USE **Find ten more mistakes in the advertisement and correct them. 2.03 Listen and check.**

East Hamley
Adult Education Centre

ART CLASSES FOR ADULTS

~~Are~~ *Is* art your passion?
Are you interested in a drawing, painting or the sculpture?
Would you like to improve your knowledge and skills?
Would you like to experience deep sense of satisfaction you get from creating your own original work?

At East Hamley College a team of highly qualified tutors are available to help you improve your technique. We run art classes on Tuesday and Thursday evenings from 6.30 to 9.00. Each session costs £15 and lasts for two hours with a 30-minute break. We think you'll agree that £15 aren't a lot to pay for over two hours with the personal attention of our art teachers!

Both the painting and the sculpture classes takes place in the new annexe on Becton Road. This also has a relaxing café selling a coffee and a range of snacks where you can take a break and socialise with your fellow students.

You won't need to bring anything with you – we supply paint, papers and any other materials you need. But wear something that you don't mind covering in paint – a jeans and an old shirt is fine.

Every year, the work of our students are exhibited in a local gallery. So, if you're lucky, your work might get spotted – you could be the next Damien Hirst!

For details and enrolment forms contact us on 0330 676750

2 Possessive *'s*

Form rules for possessive *'s*, e.g. *boy's/boys'*
➤ page 367

According to legend, **Vermeer's** 'Girl with a Pearl Earring' shows the **artist's** maid wearing a Turkish turban and **a pearl earring of his wife's**.

1 Special rules with possessive *'s*

We can have two possessive *'s* forms together:
*We're fed up with our **neighbour's tenant's** loud music.*

If the possessive form consists of a compound noun (➤ Unit 70.1) or two or more nouns which form a single team or group, we add the *'s* to the last noun only:
*Are you coming to my **brother-in-law's** party?* (compound noun)
*I'm a great fan of **Lerner and Lowe's** musicals.* (They both wrote as a single team.)

When the nouns do not form a single group we must use *'s* with both nouns:
***Schrodinger's** and **Heisenberg's** versions of quantum mechanics had seemed different.* (two versions of the theory)

If the possessive noun is part of a prepositional phrase, we usually put the *'s* at the end of the phrase:
✗ ~~*The woman's in the corner baby began to cry.*~~
✓ ***The woman in the corner's** baby began to cry.*
(= The baby belonging to the woman in the corner ...)

2 Double possessives

We can use a double possessive – noun + *of* + noun (with possessive *'s*) – to show that the first noun means 'one of several'. We usually use the indefinite article with this pattern:
*I heard the story from **a friend of my brother's**.* (= one of my brother's friends)

We do not always include the possessive *'s* with the second noun:
*They got the information from **a friend of the owner**.*

⚠ The double possessive is common with pronouns. We always use the possessive pronoun:
✗ ~~*She's a friend of us.*~~ ~~*She's a friend of our.*~~
✓ *She's a friend of **ours**.* (= We have several friends. She is one of them.)

3 Specifying and classifying possessives

Specifying possessives show a relationship with something specific such as a person or place. They usually answer the question 'Whose ... ?':
*Marion washes **the children's clothes** on Thursdays.* (= the clothes belonging to the children)

⚠ An adjective in front of a specifying possessive only describes the noun immediately following it:
*Marion washed **the older children's clothes** in the machine.* (= the children are older)
*Marion washed **the children's older clothes** in the machine.* (= the clothes are older)

Classifying possessives describe the type of thing something is. They answer the question 'What kind of...?' and are similar to compound nouns (➤ Unit 70):
*Janice has opened a shop specialising in **children's clothes**.* (= clothes any children can wear)

⚠ An adjective in front of a classifying possessive describes the whole phrase:
*Janice's shop had a large selection of **expensive children's clothes**.*
(= The children's clothes are expensive, not the children.)

Practice

1 Choose the correct meaning, A or B.

1 Stephanie loved her beautiful daughter's sports car.
A Stephanie's daughter was beautiful. B The sports car was beautiful.
2 She inherited a wonderful wooden dolls' house.
A The dolls are made of wood. B The house is made of wood.
3 The company manufactures low-cost nurses' uniforms.
A The nurses earn low wages. B The uniforms aren't expensive.
4 Gary didn't think much of his new boss's management techniques.
A Gary has a new boss. B Gary's boss has some new management techniques.
5 Bill and Suzy found hiring a well-educated children's nanny was worth every penny.
A Their nanny was well-educated. B Their children were well-educated.
6 I managed to find a place in the 24-hour supermarket's parking lot.
A The supermarket is open 24 hours. B The parking lot is open 24 hours.
7 Dave was often embarrassed by his aggressive flatmate's comments.
A Dave's flatmate was aggressive. B His flatmate's comments were aggressive.
8 My uncle is restoring a redundant tax-inspectors' office in Newcastle.
A Some tax inspectors have been made redundant in Newcastle.
B The office in Newcastle is no longer required by the tax inspectors.

2 GRAMMAR IN USE Find nine more mistakes in the conversation and correct them. 2.04 Listen and check.

SOPHIE Who's coming with us to the exhibition on Saturday?
MAREK Well, apart from me and Kylie, there's Mike and Sandra, my ~~brother's-in-law's~~ *brother-in-law's* nephew, Paul, and Harry.
SOPHIE Harry? Is he a friend of you?
MAREK No, he's coming with Paul – he's a cousin of him.
SOPHIE What's the exhibition about, anyway?
MAREK It's an exhibition by the art's gallery's new discovery – Stephen Brewer.
SOPHIE Oh yes, I've just read an article about him in the local's paper culture section.
MAREK Yes, it was written by our next-door's neighbour's wife – she's a well-known art critic, apparently.
SOPHIE OK. It sounds like it might be interesting.
MAREK Great. I thought we might all meet up for lunch first.
SOPHIE Good idea. That French place's in Green Street reputation is excellent – a colleague mine told me about it, although I haven't been there myself.
MAREK Right, let's try that place then. By the way, will you be coming by car?
SOPHIE Why?
MAREK Well Mike's and Sandra's car is in the garage so they need a lift. Could you take them? They're neighbours of your, aren't they?
SOPHIE Yes, they are. OK, I suppose so. Shall we meet at one?
MAREK Fine. I'll tell the others.

3 Possessive with *'s* or *of*?

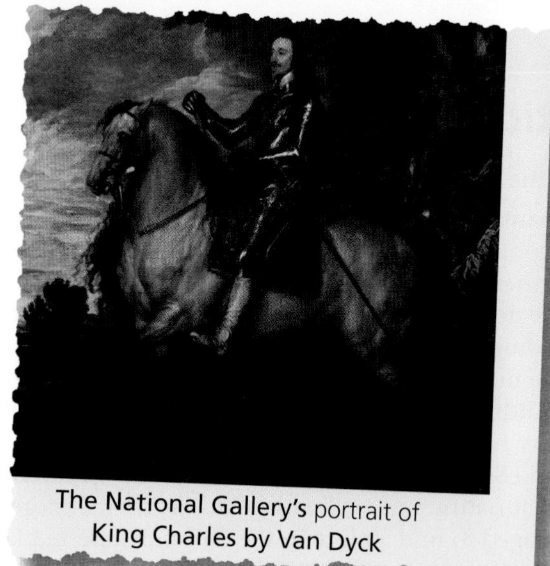

The National Gallery's portrait of King Charles by Van Dyck

1 Possessive *'s*

We usually use the possessive *'s* (and not the *of* structure):

USE	EXAMPLES
to refer to people and animals (especially with proper nouns), and to personal/professional relationships and human qualities	*Sheila is **Harold's** youngest daughter.* *Do you like **Snap's** new collar?* *Have you met the **boss's** new secretary?* ***John's** intransigence is a pain.*
to refer to general ownership, or possession of somebody's home	*Have you seen **Sheila's** new car?* *We'll be at **Mum's** soon.* (= Mum's house)
to refer to location in time (but not with dates)	*Have you seen the poem in **today's** 'Observer'?* ✗ ~~*It was in 19th December's paper.*~~
to refer to the origin of something, for example where it comes from or who made it	*Oil is **Saudi Arabia's** biggest export.* *'Hamlet' is **Shakespeare's** most famous play.* *Have you read the **committee's** report yet?*
to refer to a quantity or measure, for example of duration, distance or value	*There will be an **hour's** delay.* *The hotel was **ten minutes'** drive from the beach.*
in expressions for value/quantity with *worth*	*Could you give me a **pound's** worth of chips?*
with the names of shops, companies and people/places that provide a service	*I'm getting the Thanksgiving shopping at **Macy's**.* (= Macy's department store) *Was there anything nice at the **butcher's** this morning?* (= the butcher's shop)
in certain fixed expressions	*She was at **death's** door.* *For **pity's** sake!* *For **goodness'** sake!*

2 Noun + *of* + noun

We usually use the *of* structure (and not the possessive *'s*) in the following situations:

USE	EXAMPLES
when we refer to inanimate things and with abstract nouns (e.g. *science*)	*We set up our base camp at the bottom **of** the mountain.* *I've been studying the philosophy **of** science.*
when the noun is followed by a prepositional phrase or clause which defines it	*The players ignored the jeers **of** the people standing in the front row.*
when we refer to a specific year or date	*It was destroyed in the fire **of** 1666.*
with long or complex phrases, even when we are referring to people	*A man was sentenced to life imprisonment for the murder **of** an English tourist, Monica Cantwell.*
in certain fixed expressions and titles	*He's the President **of** the United States.* *The Prince **of** Wales is to visit Iceland.*

3 Either *'s* or *of* structure

We can usually use either the possessive *'s* or the *of* structure:

USE	EXAMPLES
with human creations such as countries, organisations, cities, institutions, machines, vehicles, buildings, etc. (The possessive *'s* is more common.)	*Plane trees are a common sight on* ***London's*** *streets.* *Plane trees are a common sight on* **the** *streets* **of** *London.*
to refer to a quality that something possesses or displays (BUT we prefer to use the possessive *'s* with human qualities)	*We were amazed by the* ***ship's*** *sheer size.* *We were amazed by* **the** *sheer size* **of** *the ship.*
to refer to the subject of something, its topic or theme (see 3.4)	*The* ***Queen's*** *portrait has caused much discussion and debate.* ***The*** *portrait* ***of*** *the Queen has caused much discussion and debate.*
to express a reason or purpose with *sake* (but note exceptions in 3.1)	*We agreed to stay together for* ***the*** *sake* ***of*** *the children/for the* ***children's*** *sake.*

ACADEMIC ENGLISH The *of* structure is much more common than the possessive *'s* in academic and formal writing.

4 Combining different possessive patterns

The possessive *'s* and the *of* structure can describe different types of relationships between nouns:

FORM	RELATIONSHIP
possessive *'s*	origin, owner or creator
of + noun	subject or topic

We can use them together to give several pieces of information in the same sentence:
One of our most popular exhibits is ***Van Dyck's portrait of King Charles.***
(*Van Dyck* = the creator of the portrait → possessive *'s*)
(*King Charles* = the subject/topic of the portrait → *of* structure)

⚠ We don't use the possessive *'s* to describe the topic of something:
✗ ~~*I wasn't convinced by the quarrel's description of the witness.*~~
✓ *I wasn't convinced by* ***the witness's description of the quarrel.***
(*the witness* = the person who made the description;
the quarrel = the topic of the description)

We can also use possessive forms with prepositions to describe a number of different relationships:

owner + *'s* | *of* + subject | preposition (e.g. *by*) + creator

Have you seen the National Gallery's portrait of King Charles by Van Dyck?

5 New information with the *of* form

We can use the *of* form to put new information at the end of a sentence.
Compare:
Nobel Peace Prize winner Aung San Suu Kyi was under house arrest for many years.
[*She is assassinated politician Aung San's daughter.*]
✓ *She is the daughter of assassinated politician Aung San.*
(The new information is the reference to Aung San.)

Practice

1 Choose the correct option, A or B, to complete the sentences. If both options are correct, choose both. 2.05 Listen and check.

1 What did you do .....
A at the course's end? B at the end of the course?
2 Have you met .....
A Sam's new assistant? B the new assistant of Sam?
3 ..... is a constant source of inspiration.
A Barcelona's architecture B The architecture of Barcelona
4 I'll wait for you outside .....
A the doctor's surgery. B the surgery of the doctor.
5 Some rubbish got caught under .....
A the conveyor belt's wheels. B the wheels of the conveyor belt.
6 Our organisation strives towards .....
A poverty's elimination. B the elimination of poverty.
7 The Ninth Symphony is arguably .....
A Beethoven's greatest work. B the greatest work of Beethoven.
8 ..... is the search for personal fulfilment in a hostile world.
A The novel's theme B The theme of the novel
9 He's taking ..... from his job at the university.
A a year's sabbatical B a sabbatical of a year
10 ..... sometimes drives me up the wall.
A My husband's impatience B The impatience of my husband
11 Throughout the flight we had to put up with .....
A the children sitting in the back row's antics.
B the antics of the children sitting in the back row.
12 The husband of the Queen of England is .....
A Edinburgh's Duke. B the Duke of Edinburgh.
13 We're going to hold the party at .....
A Michael's place. B the place of Michael.
14 ..... was an important turning point in French history.
A 1789's revolution B The revolution of 1789
15 Researchers have been amazed by the ..... to mutate when attacked.
A virus's ability B ability of the virus
16 The vet wasn't very pleased with .....
A Fido's progress. B the progress of Fido.
17 Her research investigates ..... in cattle.
A airborne disease's spread B the spread of airborne disease
18 The president must swear to uphold .....
A the country's constitution. B the constitution of the country.
19 Why can't you just hand in your notice, ...
A for goodness' sake! B for the sake of goodness!
20 ..... are generating a lot of excitement at the Paris fashion shows.
A Gaultier's latest designs B The latest designs of Gaultier

2 GRAMMAR IN USE **Write labels for these works, using the information in the chart. Each label must contain all the information.**

0 

1 

2 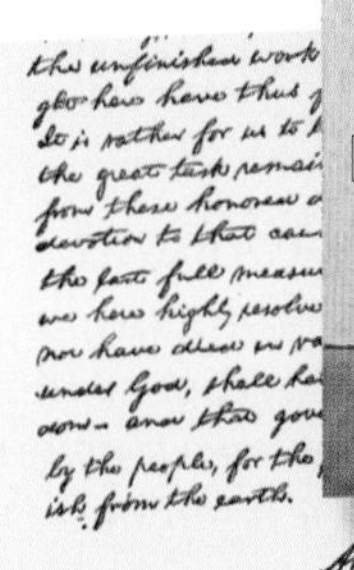

3 

4

	WORK	OWNER	CREATOR	SUBJECT
0	portrait	The Louvre	Jacques Louis David	Napoleon
1	first edition	The British Museum	Lewis Carroll	*Alice in Wonderland*
2	original copy	Cornell University Library	Abraham Lincoln	the Gettysburg Address
3	painting	The National Gallery	Vincent van Gogh	sunflowers
4	statue	The Museum of Modern Art	Auguste Rodin	Honoré Balzac

0 *The Louvre's portrait of Napoleon by Jacques Louis David*

1 ……………………

2 ……………………

3 ……………………

4 ……………………

3 **Complete the second sentence so that it has a similar meaning to the first, using the most suitable form, possessive *'s* or *of*. Make any other necessary changes, as in the example. In one sentence you will need to use both forms.** 2.06 **Listen and check.**

0 Over 200,000 people were killed in the earthquake which happened in January 2010.
Over 200,000 people *were killed in the earthquake of January 2010*.

1 I'd like some petrol. I want to spend 50 euros.
…………………… worth of petrol, please.

2 I left my jacket in the car which belongs to Uncle Stephen.
I left my jacket …………………… .

3 There's a medieval castle on the hill. It's at the top.
There's a medieval castle …………………… .

4 Clive works for a major cable TV company. He's the managing director.
Clive is …………………… .

5 A girl was trapped under the rubble. We heard her cries.
We heard …………………… .

6 *A Farewell to Arms* was written by Ernest Hemingway. It is his greatest novel.
A Farewell to Arms is …………………… .

7 Glenda described the party. It made us all laugh.
…………………… made us all laugh.

8 The flood destroyed the bridge. It happened in 2006.
The bridge was destroyed …………………… .

4 Personal pronouns

Raphael's painting of the School of Athens includes a portrait of the artist **himself**.

1 Subject and object pronouns

We do not usually omit pronouns, especially subject pronouns. Equally, we usually don't use a noun + pronoun together as the subject of a verb:

✗ ~~*Junk emails they have become a nuisance.*~~
✓ *Junk emails have become a nuisance.*

Exceptions in spoken and informal English ➤ Unit 83.2/4

We do not use object pronouns in relative clauses or infinitive phrases if the object has already appeared in the same sentence:

✗ ~~*That's the play I told you about it.*~~ ✓ *That's the play I told you about.*
✗ ~~*Those plastic cakes look good enough to eat them.*~~
✓ *Those plastic cakes look good enough to eat.*

After *as* and *than*, we use a subject pronoun with an auxiliary or modal verb:
The instructor didn't ski as well as ***I do/did/can.***

If there is no auxiliary or modal verb, we usually use object pronouns:
The instructor didn't actually ski any better than ***me.*** *They aren't as old as* ***us.***

You may hear subject pronouns in this situation, but this can sound very formal or old-fashioned: [*The instructor didn't ski any better than I.*]

FORMALITY CHECK After *It is* we use the subject pronoun in formal language, and the object pronoun in informal language and short responses:
It is ***they*** *who asked for the music to be turned down.* (formal)
It's ***them*** *who asked for the music to be turned down.* (informal)
'Who's there?' 'It's ***me.****'* (informal)

When we have a noun and pronoun, or two pronouns together, we tend to put the speaker last (possibly out of politeness):
You *and I are both invited to the pro-celebrity golf match, if you fancy it.*

However, if we have a noun and pronoun where the pronoun does not refer to the speaker, we usually put the pronoun first:
Don't you think we should let ***him*** *and his wife decide when to come?*

We usually use object pronouns after a preposition. In informal English you may hear the subject pronoun, although many people consider this incorrect:
[*They're sending the new consignment over* ***for*** *Tom and* ***I*** *to check.*]
✓ *They're sending the new consignment over* ***for*** *Tom and* ***me*** *to check.*

In some exclamations we modify object pronouns, usually with an adjective, e.g. *Silly* ***me!***

We can use a noun after a pronoun to clarify who or what we are referring to:
I want ***you boys*** *to report to the Principal after this class!*

2 Pronouns *he*, *she*, *it* and *one*

We use *he* and *she* to refer to people and often also to animals, especially domestic pets:
We had to take our cat, Rusty, to the vet yesterday. ***He's*** *got ear mites.*

Use of impersonal pronoun *they* ➤ Unit 5.1

We use *it* to refer to animals, things, ideas or actions, and not usually to people unless to refer to an unborn or young baby (if the sex is unknown):
Mary brought her new baby into the shop yesterday – ***it's*** *very cute.*

We can use *one* or *ones* to avoid repeating countable nouns:
Do you prefer the dark chocolates or the white ***ones?***

We do not use *one* to replace uncountable nouns:
✗ ~~*Do you prefer white rice or brown one?*~~ ✓ *Do you prefer white rice or brown?*

We can use *one/ones* after *the* and adjectives, but not immediately after *a/an*:
✗ ~~*I'd like a loaf of bread. Can you pass me a one from the top shelf?*~~
✓ *I'd like a loaf of bread. Can you pass me* ***one*** *from the top shelf?*
These are interesting fossil specimens. This is ***an amazing one****.*

We use *it/them*, not *one/ones* when we refer to an item that has previously been defined. Compare:
I need a cup of coffee, a large ***one****.* (= any cup of coffee)
Where's my coffee? Oh, there ***it*** *is.* (= my particular cup of coffee)

3 Reflexive pronouns

We use reflexive pronouns to refer to the subject after many verbs, including verbs with dependent prepositions (➤ Unit 66):
Politicians have to ***believe in themselves*** *if they want to convince voters.*
(= Politicians have to believe in politicians.)

We can use either the object pronoun or the reflexive to refer to the subject after *as* (*for*), *like*, *but* (*for*) and *except* (*for*):
Howard found out that everyone except ***him/himself*** *had read the report.*

Some verbs are followed by the reflexive in English where it may not seem logical, and where similar verbs in other languages are not followed by the reflexive, e.g. *acquaint yourself (with), avail yourself (of), behave yourself, commit yourself (to sth), enjoy yourself, help yourself*:
Did the children ***behave themselves*** *while we were out?* (= behave well)
Help yourself *to the food, won't you?* (= take as much as you want)

There are many verbs which take a reflexive in other languages but do not usually do so in English, e.g. *wash, dress, feel, get up, relax, remember, stand up, hurry*:
✗ ~~*I don't feel myself very well today.*~~ ✓ *I don't feel very well today.*

We can also use reflexive pronouns to emphasise the subject or object of a sentence. The pronoun can come in any one of these positions in the sentence:

myself
I ▼ *have* ▼ *used this technique* ▼ *frequently* ▼.

We can use *myself* either at the beginning or the end of a sentence and separated by a comma to mean 'as far as I'm concerned/in my personal opinion':
Myself*, I don't like the new fashion for flared trousers.*
I don't like the new fashion for flared trousers, ***myself****.*

We use *(all) by myself/yourself*, etc. to emphasise 'without any help' or 'completely alone':
The garden looks amazing. Did you do it (all) (by) ***yourself****?*
We've decided to go on holiday ***by ourselves*** *next year.*

4 Reciprocal pronouns

Compare the use of reciprocal pronouns (*each other/one another*) and reflexive pronouns:
Our cats Fluff and Bangle spend a lot of time licking ***themselves****.*
(Fluff licks Fluff and Bangle licks Bangle.)
Fluff and Bangle sometimes lick ***each other****.* (Fluff licks Bangle and Bangle licks Fluff.)

Each other usually refers to two subjects, *one another* to more than two, though we tend to use the two forms interchangeably in informal English:
He spoke fast and his words tumbled out, tripping over ***each other/one another****.*

We don't use a reflexive or an object pronoun where a reciprocal pronoun is needed:
✗ ~~*So, we'll see ourselves/us at the fountain at half past one tomorrow.*~~
✓ *So, we'll see* ***each other*** *at the fountain at half past one tomorrow.*

Practice

1 GRAMMAR IN USE **Read the article below and replace the underlined words with a suitable pronoun. 2.07 Listen and check.**

The Albino Lobster

BERNARD WARNER is a fishmonger. Mr Warner sells fish – lots of fish (0) ...it... – and Mr Warner (1) .... sometimes sells lobsters. When the lobster arrived in his shop, the lobster (2) .... didn't strike Mr Warner (3) .... as being particularly odd. The lobster (4) .... was a little paler than most others of its species, but perhaps it was just a bit old. Mr Warner left his shop to go on holiday as planned. Mr Warner's shop (5) .... was a family shop and he knew the shop (6) .... was in good hands.

'Don't sell that lobster!'
Mr Warner

En route to Majorca, Mr Warner picked up the in-flight magazine. The magazine (7) .... fell open at an article about albino lobsters. These very rare lobsters are just paler versions of a normal lobster. Albino lobsters (8) .... are also very valuable: an albino lobster (9) .... caught off the American coast was sold for £15,000; another, bigger albino lobster (10) .... was insured for £20,000.

As soon as he reached his destination, Mr Warner raced to a phone. 'Don't sell that lobster!' he told his family firm. But it was too late. The lobster (11) .... had already been sold. Mr Warner couldn't believe his bad luck. A diner somewhere had eaten the prize catch and the diner (12) .... had had no idea at all of its value. After forty years as a fishmonger Mr Warner had thought that no one knew the business better than Mr Warner (13) ...., but he had never come across an example (14) .... of those lobsters before! He said that he now knew what it felt like to gain and lose a fortune in a single day.

2 Complete the sentences, using suitable pronouns.

1 The students interviewed ...., as practice.

2 'Excuse me. That's my bag.' 'Oh, sorry. Silly ....!'

3 Alastair helped .... to an enormous slice of cake.

4 'Having another lie-in? .... students have such an easy life!'

5 'You should get that one. I haven't seen it .... but I know it's very good.'

6 All the passengers helped .... climb out of the bus to safety.

3 **Find and correct eight mistakes in these sentences. Tick (✓) the correct sentences. 2.08 Listen and check.**

1 Alicia and I left the party early; Jane and Marcia stayed longer than we.
2 Emily's had her baby – apparently it was born in the middle of the night.
3 You're suffering from too much stress. You should learn to relax yourself more.
4 Do you prefer olive oil or sunflower one?
5 I'm afraid these are the best seats I was able to find them at such short notice.
6 Dorinda and Eric have been married for ten years; they met themselves at university.
7 They didn't have that spare part I wanted in the local shop but I managed to find a one on the Internet.
8 'Who's that?' 'Hi, Steve. It's we. We've been ringing the doorbell for ages!'
9 My holiday photos are a bit disappointing. There are hardly any good ones.
10 Darren's very good with his hands. He made all the kitchen cabinets of himself.

4 **In each pair, A and B below, one or both sentences are correct. Tick (✓) the correct sentences and cross (✗) the incorrect ones. Where both sentences are correct, choose an explanation from the box. You can use the explanations more than once.**

a The pronouns refer to different people.	c There is a difference in emphasis.
b There is no difference in meaning.	d One sentence is more formal.

0 A Clare is so arrogant – she always thinks she's better than I. ....✓....
B Clare is so arrogant – she always thinks she's better than me. ....✓ d....
1 A I found those keys you wanted but I forgot to bring ones. ....
B I found those keys you wanted but I forgot to bring them. ....
2 A Ewan is thinking of bringing some work with him. ....
B Ewan is thinking of bringing some work with himself. ....
3 A We all give each other small presents at the office party. ....
B We all give one another small presents at the office party. ....
4 A Ouch! That radiator is really hot. I've burnt myself! ....
B Ouch! That radiator is really hot. I've burnt me! ....
5 A We're going to miss the bus. Quick, let's hurry ourselves! ....
B We're going to miss the bus. Quick, let's hurry! ....
6 A The paint effect you've used on the wall is great. Did you do it yourselves? ....
B The paint effect you've used on the wall is great. Did you do it by yourselves? ....
7 A Will we be able to find each other amongst all the people at the concert hall? ....
B Will we be able to find ourselves amongst all the people at the concert hall? ....
8 A The girl's coach rebuked herself for missing some very easy shots. ....
B The girl's coach rebuked her for missing some very easy shots. ....
9 A I thought the government supported GM food. Didn't the PM say that? ....
B I thought the government supported GM food. Didn't the PM say that himself? ....
10 A Most people find this painting depressing. As for me, I think it's stimulating! ....
B Most people find this painting depressing. As for myself, I think it's stimulating! ....
11 A Alicia and Charles blamed themselves for the break-up of their marriage. ....
B Alicia and Charles blamed each other for the break-up of their marriage. ....
12 A Oh, it was nothing. It is we who should thank you. ....
B Oh, it was nothing. It is us who should thank you. ....

5 Impersonal and indefinite pronouns

1 Impersonal pronouns *you, we, they, one*

When we wish to express general feelings and opinions (i.e. of people in general, not necessarily those of the speaker), we can use impersonal pronouns *you, we* or *they*:
You *can wear whatever you like to go to the theatre these days.*
You *never know!* ***You*** *bet!*

- If we wish to include ourselves, it is better to use *we*:
  We *can wear whatever we like to go to the theatre these days.*
- If we wish to exclude ourselves, it is better to use *they*:
  They *behave really badly at football matches nowadays.*

We can also use *they*

- to refer to people in authority:
  Did you know ***they'****ve put the parking charges up again?*
- if we do not know a person's gender, or do not wish to specify it:
  'Someone called you from Grant's Garage.' 'Oh, did ***they*** *leave* ***their*** *name?'*
- in written English, when we can make the subject plural:
  A doctor always makes decisions according to the best of ***his/her*** *knowledge.*
  → *Doctors always make decisions according to the best of* ***their*** *knowledge.*

Although we usually use *we* or *you*, we can use *one* in formal language to mean 'people in general', including ourselves. We very rarely use *one* in speech, especially in American English:
One *can sympathise with the sentiments behind the actions of the strikers.*

We can use *one* as a subject or object pronoun, and *oneself* as a reflexive pronoun:
One *tends to learn to fend for* ***oneself*** *if one lives alone.*

FORMALITY CHECK The use of *one* to mean 'I' is usually considered to be unnecessarily formal: [*One would like to attend the ceremony, but one is too busy.*]

Impersonal *it* ➤ Unit 44.2

2 Indefinite pronouns *someone, anything*, etc.

We use *some* compounds when we are thinking of a particular, but unspecified, person, place or thing. We use *any* compounds when we are thinking of people, places or things in general:
There's ***something*** *I would really like for my birthday.* (= a particular present)
You need someone to witness your signature. ***Anyone*** *will do.* (= any person is suitable)

We use *any + one/thing/where* to mean 'it doesn't matter who/what/where':
'Where shall I sign the card?' 'Oh, ***anywhere*** *you like.'*

If we use these pronouns and adverbs as subjects, they take a singular verb:
Everything is *going smoothly and NASA expects to launch the shuttle as scheduled.*

We can use indefinite pronouns with adjectives, or with *else*, or with a *to-* clause:
Tony decided to do ***something positive*** *about his problems.*
Something else *you become aware of all over the Basque country is the bracken.*
We need ***somewhere cheap to stay*** *for the night.*

Practice

1 GRAMMAR IN USE **Complete the two dialogues and the text with suitable pronouns. Use impersonal pronouns for the shaded gaps and indefinite pronouns for the underlined gaps. 2.09 Listen and check.**

1 ANDY Why are you so late?
MATT Oh, (1) ________ 're digging up the roads again.
ANDY I know – (2) ________ 're always doing (3) ________ around here. It's a nuisance because (4) ________ never know how long it's going to take to get (5) ________. It took me two hours to get to the station on Tuesday.

2 SANI (6) ________ called from the office this morning.
RAJ Really? Did (7) ________ say what it was about?
SANI I think it was (8) ________ to do with your presentation tomorrow.
RAJ Did (9) ________ give you their name?
SANI No, but I know it was (10) ________ from the sales team.

3 When (11) ________ looks at the work in detail (12) ________ can appreciate the superb craftsmanship with which the brushstrokes evoke the shimmering surface of the silks and satins. There is (13) ________ almost sensual about the lustrous surfaces of these rich fabrics. Every detail is perfect; there is (14) ________ in this painting which is clumsy or ill-thought-out. Of course, Van Dyck's aim is to flatter his sitter, and the accurate depiction of (15) ________ as luxurious and expensive as silk serves to emphasise the wealth and good taste of the patron.

2 **Choose the correct words in *italics*. If both options are possible, choose both.**

1 You can't have lost the tickets. They've got to be *anywhere / somewhere*!
2 I haven't got a clue where I am! Isn't there *anyone / no one* here who could direct me to the Stakis Hotel?
3 *Is / Are* everyone here now? We'll start the tour straight away then.
4 There is hardly *anybody / nobody* to be seen on the streets of the centre after dusk.
5 Peter decided that he needed to do *constructive something / something constructive* with his life.
6 The kidnap victims were blindfolded, driven into the country and thrown from the car miles from *somewhere / anywhere*.
7 It is essential that we locate *someone / somebody* who can repair this machine within the next 48 hours.
8 The mayor is caught in the city traffic. We've *somehow / anyhow* got to find a way to get her here fast.
9 'What would you like to drink?' 'Oh, *something / anything*. Whatever you're having will be fine.'
10 That new chess champion from Ukraine is amazing. *Anyone / No one* can beat him!
11 I don't know what it is exactly. But *anything / something* isn't right with the engine.
12 There was *anything / something* else I wanted to tell you, but I've forgotten what it is!

Review MODULE 1

1 **UNITS 1, 2 AND 3** **Choose the correct words in *italics*.**

1 Both my brother and my sister *is / are* tall with dark hair and blue eyes.
2 I didn't know who to believe. *Steve's / Steve* and Jane's stories were completely different.
3 A team of investigators *has / have* submitted a report to the ministry.
4 Gymnastics *is / are* very demanding for those who are not fully fit.
5 I'm fed up with the hopeless inefficiency of *the secretary of my boss / my boss's secretary*.
6 Although the other teams were faster than *we / us*, we were delighted just to get to the end of the course.
7 My *brother's-in-law's / brother-in-law's* parents have decided to emigrate to Australia.
8 Is that all the milk you've bought? Two litres *isn't / aren't* enough to last us a week!
9 The restaurant's most famous dish is *chicken / chickens* with sweet potatoes.
10 Prize winners will receive *a worth of twenty euros / twenty euros' worth* of shopping vouchers.
11 Cinemagoers have been amazed by the *battle's depiction of the director / director's depiction of the battle*.
12 Have you met Eliza? She's a good friend of *us / ours*.
13 I'm looking for some classic DVDs. Do you know where 'Twelve Angry Men' *is / are* kept?
14 Did you read about the new road scheme? It was in *the local paper of yesterday / yesterday's local paper*.
15 It was a beautiful summer's day: the sun was shining and the cattle *was / were* grazing peacefully in the meadow.
16 Nutritionists have attributed the relative longevity of the Japanese to their diet of *a fish / fish*.
17 Marshall is studying for a master's in *science's philosophy / the philosophy of science*.
18 The basis of all good science *is / are* thorough research.

2 **UNITS 4 AND 5** **Read this extract from a book and complete it with suitable pronouns. In the book, American writer Bill Bryson describes his first visit to England.**

It must be said that Dover was not vastly improved by daylight, but I liked (1) .... I liked its small scale and cosy air, and the way everyone said 'Good morning', and 'Hello', and 'Dreadful weather – but it must brighten up', to (2) ...., and the sense that this was just (3) .... more in a very long series of fundamentally cheerful, well-ordered, pleasantly uneventful days. (4) .... in the whole of Dover would have any particular reasons to remember 21 March 1973, except for (5) .... and a handful of children born that day.

I didn't know how early (6) .... could decently begin asking for a room in England, so I thought (7) .... would leave (8) .... till mid-morning. With time on my hands, I made a thorough search for a guesthouse that looked attractive and quiet, but friendly and not too expensive, and at the stroke of ten o'clock presented (9) .... on the doorstep of the (10) .... I had carefully selected, taking care not to discompose the milk bottles. (11) .... was a small hotel that was really a guesthouse, indeed, was really a boarding-house.

I don't remember its name, but I well recall the proprietress, who showed (12) .... to a room, then gave (13) .... a tour of the facilities and outlined the many complicated rules for residing there. This was all bewilderingly new to me. Where I came from, (14) .... got a room in a motel, spent ten hours making a lavish and possibly irredeemable mess of (15) ...., and left early the next morning. This was like joining the army.

3 ALL UNITS **Complete the text by writing one word only in each gap. If no word is needed, write (–).**

The da Vinci Mystery

Is this picture the work of an unknown artist or (1) .... painting by Leonardo da Vinci?

A TEAM OF ART HISTORIANS (2) .... been examining the picture at a laboratory in Paris. Tests have revealed a fingerprint near the top (3) .... the painting which is remarkably similar to (4) .... found on a da Vinci work in the Vatican. If the team (5) .... correct, the painting could be worth many millions of dollars.

The (6) .... was previously believed to be an early nineteenth-century work by an unknown German artist. (7) .... was sold at Christie's in New York in 1988 for $19,000. In 2007 (8) .... was sold again for a similar sum to Canadian-born collector, Peter Silverman. Mr Silverman knew there was (9) .... special about the painting. (10) .... wasn't convinced (11) .... was a nineteenth-century work and so, last year, (12) .... discussed (13) .... painting with Dr Nicholas Turner of the British Museum. As a result of these discussions, Mr Silverman decided to begin a thorough investigation (14) .... the picture.

Professor Martin Kemp of Oxford University, an expert on da (15) .... work, believes the picture may be a portrait (16) .... Bianca Sforza, daughter of the Duke of Milan. The (17) .... daughter was only a teenager at the time, and the picture clearly shows a teenage girl. The costume and hairstyle (18) .... those popular with the nobility (19) .... late fifteenth-century Milan. Carbon dating analysis (20) .... confirmed this date. Further scientific evidence (21) .... been provided by infra-red photography. This indicates that the picture was painted by a left-handed artist. Leonardo da Vinci, as is well known, was left-handed.

Perhaps the most convincing (22) .... of evidence is the fingerprint found on the painting. (23) .... is from the top of the middle or index finger. The matching fingerprint is on da (24) .... painting of Jerome in the Vatican collection. This is undisputedly (25) .... work by da Vinci and was painted at a time when we believe he worked by (26) ...., without assistants. There is therefore a strong probability that this is Leonardo's own fingerprint.

If it is proved that this is a painting by Leonardo then (27) .... can only speculate as to its potential value on the open market. We all know that (28) .... works by da Vinci are incredibly rare and, as (29) .... is the world's most famous old master, any work of (30) .... which does come up for sale is likely to reach a phenomenal sum.

Go online for an exit test

MODULE

2 Articles, demonstratives and quantifiers

Before you start

1 Review these intermediate grammar points and check you know them.

Articles

1 We use the indefinite article *a* before consonant sounds (*b, d, k, t, s,* etc.) and before *u/eu* when pronounced /j/: *a brainwave, a doctor, a university, a euphemism*

We use *an* before vowel sounds (*a, e, i, o, u*) and words that start with silent *h*: *an article, an engineer, an umbrella, an hour, an honest mistake, an R*

- We use *a/an* with singular countable nouns: *a garage, an opinion*
- We use *a/an* to introduce a concept: *They're building **a new block of luxury apartments** at the end of our street.*
- We use *a/an* to refer to something indefinite, i.e. any one of many, not a specific one: *I'd love to live in **a luxury apartment** one day.*

2 We use the definite article *the* with singular countable nouns (*the garage*), plural nouns (*the latest computers*) and uncountable nouns (*the purest water*).

We can omit *the* with uncountable and plural nouns: *peace, efforts*

Quantifiers

1 Quantifiers are used before a noun to specify the amount or quantity. They are words such as *some, any, much, many* and *a lot of.*

2 We use *some* and *any* for indefinite quantities, i.e. when we don't specify how much or how many of something. We usually use *some* in positive sentences, *any* in questions and negatives:

*I've got **some** money, so you don't need to bring your wallet.*

*'Have you got **any** coins for the meter?' 'Well, I've got **some** 10p and 20p coins, if that's OK.'*

*You've got **some** interesting ideas, but you haven't got **any** money to back them.*

3 We use *much* and *many* in questions and negatives, but we prefer to use *a lot of* in positive statements:

*'I haven't got **much** time. Can you hurry?'*

*'Don't hurry. I've got **a lot of** spare time today.'*

Demonstratives

1 We use the demonstratives *this/these* to refer to someone or something known or close to the speaker, and *that/those* for someone/something further away:

*'I think **these** shoes are lovely.' 'Really? I prefer **those** in the window.'*

2 Demonstratives can express closeness or distance in time as well as space:

	CLOSE	DISTANT
space	*Look at **this** MP3 player – it's tiny.* *I think **these** shoes are lovely.*	*Can I see **that** MP3 player on the top shelf?* *Look at **those** shoes at the back of the window.*
time	*What are you doing **this** weekend?* ***These** last two weeks have been difficult for me.*	*Do you remember **that** weekend in 2005?* ***Those** were the happiest years in my childhood.*

2 **Read the information and identify examples of articles, demonstratives and quantifiers.**

THE UNITED NATIONS is an international organisation founded in 1945 after the Second World War by 51 countries committed to maintaining international peace and security.

The work of the United Nations reaches every corner of the globe. Although best known for peacekeeping, conflict prevention and humanitarian assistance, there are many other ways the UN affects our lives and makes the world a better place. The UN works on a broad range of fundamental issues in order to achieve its goals and coordinate efforts for a safer world for this and future generations.

3 **Complete the diagnostic test below.**

A Complete each sentence with *a/an*, *the* or – (no article).

1 My children want me to buy them .... angora rabbit. ➤ Unit 6.2
2 New initiatives to help .... unemployed are to be announced later today. ➤ Unit 6.2
3 Next week I'll be reviewing .... stunning new film from Quentin Tarantino. .... film stars Harvey Keitel and Uma Thurman. ➤ Unit 6.3
4 Yesterday evening's programme about .... sun's future worried a large number of viewers. ➤ Unit 6.3
5 Researchers generally feel that .... yoghurt aids digestion. ➤ Unit 6.4
6 The scientist Edward Jenner was inspired by .... hope of eliminating diseases through vaccination. ➤ Unit 6.4
7 We recommend that children and teenagers are inoculated against .... meningitis. ➤ Unit 7.1
8 I learnt to play .... piano when I was a child, but gave it up in my teens. ➤ Unit 7.2

B Choose the correct words in *italics* (– = no article). If two options are possible, choose both.

1 There's *an* / *the* / – Indian restaurant in the town centre, isn't there? ➤ Unit 6.2
2 Use – / *the* / *your* thighs to take the strain when lifting something heavy. ➤ Unit 7.2
3 It costs £20 *a* / *an* / *per* hour to hire the squash court. ➤ Unit 7.3
4 *Every* / *All* / *Each* the children in the school have to take up at least one sport. ➤ Unit 8.1
5 Retailers should return *both* / *both of* / *some* the new models for a safety check. ➤ Unit 8.1
6 Advanced calculus is such a difficult subject that *a few* / *few* / *little* students have great success in it. ➤ Unit 8.2
7 My parents grew up in the 1950s. In *the* / *these* / *those* days there was far less freedom than there is now. ➤ Unit 8.3
8 This ruling only covers those *of you* / *you* / *ones* who are over eighteen. ➤ Unit 8.3
9 *This* / *That* / *A* man I'd never met before asked if he could borrow £10! ➤ Unit 8.3
10 Look at the butterfly on that flower. I've never seen one – / *this* / *that* pretty before. ➤ Unit 8.3

4 **Check your answers on page 384. Then go to the unit for more information and practice.**

Go online for a full diagnostic test

6 Articles

In 1907 **an English soldier** set up **an organisation** to educate **boys**, particularly in outdoor pursuits. **The soldier** was Robert Baden-Powell, who became Lord Baden-Powell, and **the organisation** was **the beginning** of the World Scout Movement.

1 Form

Articles (*a/an, the*) precede nouns and some other words (e.g. *few, little* and adjectives) in a noun phrase:

Can I have ***a few small paper clips****? I managed to get* ***the last gold charm bracelet*** *in the sale.*

The article is usually the first word in a noun phrase, but note

- *all/both/half + the*:
  Have you received ***all the*** *information? You've only paid* ***half the*** *outstanding amount.*
- *quite/rather/such/what/half + a/an*:
  I've got ***quite a*** *difficult problem to sort out in my maths course.*

2 Naming, describing and classifying

We use *a/an* when we name or describe something:

That's ***a*** *scarab beetle.*

'What's that?' 'It's ***an*** *enormous anthill.'*

We've just seen ***a*** *really interesting film.*

Although *a/an* is similar in meaning to *one*, it is not identical:

There's ***a*** *room available at the Marriott on Friday night.*

(= at least one room, and maybe more than one. The exact number isn't important.)

There's ***one*** *room available at the Marriott on Friday night.*

(= There is only one room available.)

We use *a/an* when we refer to one example of a group, e.g. a profession or a species:

Judith's daughter is studying to become ***a*** *solicitor.*

An *African elephant has larger ears than* ***an*** *Indian elephant.*

We usually refer to the whole group with the plural, without the definite article (➤ Unit 6.4):

✗ ~~*The African elephants have larger ears than the Indian elephants.*~~

✓ *African elephants have larger ears than Indian elephants.*

FORMALITY CHECK In more formal contexts we use *the* with a singular noun to generalise about a whole group or species:

The *African elephant has larger ears than* ***the*** *Indian elephant.*

We only use *a/an* when we talk about one example in a group or species:

An *elephant walked right past our hut yesterday evening.* (= an individual elephant)

We do NOT use *a/an* when we refer to the whole group, i.e. all members of the group:

✗ ~~*Ruthless poachers hunt an elephant for the valuable ivory of its tusks.*~~

✓ *Ruthless poachers hunt* ***the*** *elephant for the valuable ivory of its tusks.*

✓ *Ruthless poachers hunt elephants for the valuable ivory of their tusks.*

We can also use *the* with an adjective to refer to a group of people (➤ Unit 12.5):

The homeless *will be removed from the streets and placed in hostels.*

This is possible with nationality adjectives that end in *-ch, -sh, -ese* and *-s*, e.g. *the French, the Welsh, the Chinese, the Swiss*. For other nationalities, we have to use a plural noun:

The French *are known for their cuisine, but in my opinion* ***Italians*** *know better how to combine good food with a healthy diet.*

3 Known or unknown information

We use *a/an* to introduce information (i.e. a noun) that is not known to our listener/reader; but we use *the* when the information is known. Therefore, we usually use *a/an* for the first reference to something in a text, but *the* for subsequent references:
In 1907 an English soldier set up ***an organisation*** *to educate boys ...* ***the organisation*** *was the beginning of the World Scout Movement.*

We do not always have to mention something for it to be known to the listener. We consider that it is known in the following situations:

SITUATION	EXAMPLE
something is unique, i.e. there is only one of it	*The organisation was the beginning of* **the** *World Scout Movement.* **The** *BBC's funding is under threat again.*
superlatives	*Is Michael Schumacher* **the greatest** *motor racing driver ever?*
the context makes it 'known'	*'Has the last candidate arrived yet?' 'Yes, she's in* **the** *boardroom.'* (= the only boardroom in the office)
the speaker's and listener's shared knowledge makes it 'known'	*Mum's out – she's gone to* **the** *dentist.* (we both know which dentist she goes to)
a defining relative clause makes it 'known'	*Zadie Smith is* **the** *writer* ***who shot to fame with the publication of her first novel 'White Teeth'.***
a prepositional phrase makes it 'known'	*Croatia today is like* **the** *Greece* ***of thirty years ago*** *– unspoilt and not overrun by tourists.* *Meet me in* **the** *café* ***next to the bus stop.***

4 General and specific

With plural nouns and uncountable nouns we use either *the* or no article. We don't use an article when we want to refer to a group or class in general. Compare:
Tourists *are often blamed for changing the character of a town.* (= all tourists)
Did you notice what ***the tourists*** *in the castle were doing?* (= specific tourists)
It is commonly accepted today that ***brown bread*** *is good for you.*
Did you remember to get ***the brown bread*** *out of the freezer?*

 We only use an article before an abstract noun if we wish to talk about a specific type of the noun:
✗ ~~*It is impossible to live in a world without the hope.*~~
✓ *It is impossible to live in a world without* ***hope****.* (hope in general)
The hope *of finding a cure for cancer drives a lot of medical research.*
(the specific hope of finding a cure for cancer)

We do not use an article in front of nouns such as *hospital, prison, school* if we are focusing on their function, i.e. school as a place of learning or prison as a place of punishment/correction:
Can children leave ***school*** *at fourteen in your country?*
Rick's son is in ***prison*** *for burglary.*

If we focus on the physical place or building, we do use an article:
Is there ***a school*** *in the village or do the children have to go to the town?*
Joanne is an administrative officer at ***the prison****.*

ACADEMIC ENGLISH The definite article is very common in academic English, particularly with a prepositional phrase that identifies the noun:
Motorised boats harm ***the ecology of waterways****, unless their use is kept at a low level ...*

Practice

1 Match the sentences in each group with their meanings, A, B and C, as in the example.

1 0 Teachers are often blamed for failures in education. ...B....
1 The teacher is often blamed for failures in education. ....
2 The teachers were blamed for failures in the boy's education. ....
A This describes specific teachers at one school.
B This describes teachers in general.
C This describes teachers in general and is used in formal contexts.

2 1 We'll have lunch in a restaurant in Burton Street. ....
2 We'll have lunch in the restaurant in Burton Street. ....
3 We'll have lunch in the restaurant that does the two-course special. ....
A We know which restaurant – the only one in Burton Street or the one we usually go to.
B We know which restaurant because we've defined it.
C We don't know which restaurant – there are several in Burton Street.

3 1 The Swiss are known for their neutrality in times of conflict. ....
2 By winning this latest event, the Swiss has ended a magnificent year. ....
A This talks about one person.
B This talks about a group of people.

4 1 Lewis has been in hospital for several weeks. ....
2 Lewis has been at the hospital for several weeks. ....
A Lewis is a builder doing a job that is taking several weeks.
B Lewis has been ill for several weeks.

5 1 Most psychologists feel it is better to release anger than to suppress it. ....
2 I couldn't contain the anger I felt when I read the article. ....
A This talks about a feeling in general.
B This talks about a feeling on a specific occasion.

2 GRAMMAR IN USE Read this story and complete it with the correct article: *a/an*, *the* or – (no article). 2.10 Listen and check.

I FIRST EXPERIENCED terror when I was seven. My parents were living in wartime London when I was born, but my father died when I was one and my mother decided to leave (1) .... city and move to (2) .... countryside. A great-aunt of hers lived in (3) .... cottage in North Wales, and there she brought me up in (4) .... relative peace and security. (5) .... locals were all very friendly to us and accepted us without question, and I had (6) .... blissful childhood.

One day I arrived home from (7) .... school to find my mother clutching (8) .... telegram, in floods of tears. (9) .... telegram informed her that her father – my grandfather – had died. His funeral would be in three days and we had to go to London. I had never been outside (10) .... village and I was really excited at the thought of going to (11) .... capital city. So, two days later, we boarded (12) .... train to London. It was (13) .... first time I had been on a train and I was overwhelmed by (14) .... excitement of such an adventure. Several hours later we arrived. I clutched my mother's hand as we stepped down from (15) .... train. (16) .... station was full of people rushing home from (17) .... work and it was quite dark. Now (18) .... fear was starting to creep into my mind. Then, suddenly, we were in (19) .... street outside the station. I had never seen so many people, buses and cars, nor heard so much noise. I was terrified. I opened my mouth and the wail that I let escape was one of (20) .... sheer terror.

3 Find and correct the mistakes in seven of these sentences. Tick (✓) the correct sentences.

1 Training courses for several companies are held at university in the summer.
2 Have you ever seen a such beautiful sight?
3 We don't have many books on ancient history. They're on a shelf near the back.
4 New measures are being put in place to help unemployed find work.
5 Many parents say that the happiness of holding one's first child is never surpassed.
6 Could you take some more chairs into a garden? We're expecting about 20 people.
7 The children under twelve aren't allowed in to see this film without an adult.
8 The Venus flytraps are an example of a carnivorous plant.
9 Linda Gray was sentenced to three months at the prison for her role in the robbery.
10 Many elderly people value the domestic cat for its companionship.

4 GRAMMAR IN USE Read the following information about the Scout Movement. Write eleven more missing articles in the correct places. 2.11 Listen and check.

Home | Join | About | Shop | History | Contact Us | *be prepared …*

The World Scout Movement

The
Scout Movement has rich and exciting history which has led to it becoming leading global youth movement of today. Here you can find information about founder of movement, Lord Baden-Powell, and other interesting facts about scouting.

There are more than 28 million Scouts, young people and adults, male and female, in 160 countries and territories. Some 300 million people have been Scouts, including prominent people in every field.

This is impressive, considering that scouting began with twenty boys and experimental camp in 1907. It was held during first nine days of August in 1907 on Brownsea Island, near Poole in Dorset, England.

Camp was a great success and proved to its organiser, Robert Baden-Powell, that his training and methods appealed to young people and really worked.

In January 1908, he published first *Scouting for Boys*, a book issued in fortnightly parts at four pence each. It was immediate success. Baden-Powell had only intended to provide method of training boys, something that existing youth organisations could adopt. To his surprise, youngsters started to organise themselves into what was destined to become – and is today – world's largest voluntary youth movement.

7 Fixed common uses

1 No article

names and titles	*James, Chris Graham, President Obama, Mr Jones*
continents and most countries	*Europe, Africa, Asia, Japan, Argentina, Slovenia*
cities, roads, squares, parks	*Vancouver, Princes Street, Times Square, Hyde Park*
mountains and lakes	*Mount Everest, Mount Kilimanjaro, Lake Victoria*
named buildings and institutions	*Central Station, Yale University*[1]
named shops and companies	*Walmart, Harrods, Siemens, Toyota*
materials, liquids, gases	*made of silk, fry in olive oil, breathe pure oxygen*
meal(time)s	*Have you had breakfast? See you at lunch.*
sports	*She plays both tennis and squash very well.*
illnesses	*He's got lung cancer. She's had German measles.*
languages and school subjects	*He speaks Swahili. I'm studying physics and biology.*
magazines	*Cosmopolitan, Vogue, Newsweek*[2]
noun + number	*The train goes from Platform 10. See page 45.*

[1] Many large organisations include the definite article in their name:
The United Nations, The World Health Organisation.

[2] Magazine titles which express a job or function tend to have the definite article:
The Spectator, The Economist, The New Statesman.

2 Definite article *the*

some countries	*the United States* (and other plurals), *the Republic of China*
geographical names/physical environment	*the West, the Pyrenees, the Pacific Ocean, the Black Sea, the Rhone, the Thames, the city, the country*
time, date (spoken), periods	*during the day, in the morning,* (BUT *at night*), *the tenth of May, the tenth century, the Enlightenment*
the media (the form of art/entertainment)	*Let's go to the theatre at the weekend. We tend to listen to the radio for news.*[3]
measurements	*You can buy saffron by the gram.*
musical instruments	*She plays the violin.*
newspapers	*the Times, the Herald Tribune, the Daily Mirror*
in some grammatical constructions and superlatives	*the more the merrier, all the better, the most dangerous profession, the last time, the only one*
noun + *of*	*the University of California, the Gulf of Mexico*

[3] We don't use the article with *television/TV* unless we refer to the physical object:
Is there anything on ***TV*** *tonight?* (the media) *You left your keys next to* ***the TV***. (physical set)
When we think of the institution, profession or academic subject, we don't use an article:
She works in ***television***. *I'm studying* ***film*** *in my final year.*
We use *the cinema/the theatre* to refer to the experience: *We're going to* ***the cinema*** *tonight.*

We usually use a possessive adjective (not *the*) to refer to parts of the body:
✗ ~~*Put the hand up if you know the answer.*~~ ✓ *Put your hand up if you know the answer.*
We can use *the* in a prepositional phrase: *I get a sharp pain in* ***the*** *ankle when I stand up.*

3 Indefinite article *a/an*

jobs, nationalities and beliefs	*I'm a structural engineer. Fabio Capello's an Italian.*
large numbers and fractions	*a hundred thousand a million a fifth a hundredth*
prices, speeds, frequency	*two dollars a (per) kilo 20km an hour once a day*

Practice

1 Complete these sentences with *a/an, the* or – (no article). 2.12 Listen and check.

1 He's got .... asthma.
2 The ring is just a band of .... gold.
3 It prints seven pages .... minute.
4 It's the tallest building in .... United Arab Emirates.
5 Let's have a weekend in .... Pyrenees.
6 They reduced the price by .... third.
7 It's in .... Tasman Sea.
8 It appeared in .... *New York Times*.
9 What's for .... dinner?
10 I'll meet you in .... Central Park.
11 They're flying to .... Seychelles.
12 There's a list on .... page 190.
13 Can you ski on .... Mont Blanc?
14 How well does he play .... baseball?
15 We all need .... oxygen.
16 We've had over .... hundred applicants.
17 He has a job in .... television.
18 Harry worked as .... architect all his life.
19 The earlier you can get here, ... better.
20 She works for a magazine called .... *Hello*.

2 GRAMMAR IN USE Find and correct ten more mistakes with articles. 2.13 Listen and check.

MAC Oh, Carl. I've been meaning to ask you. How did your job interview go?
CARL It was fine. They offered me the job.
MAC Really? That's great. Where's it based?
CARL In their headquarters in the city centre.
MAC Oh, of course. It's the Supersave. You told me last week.
CARL Yes, that's right.
MAC Is it a big organisation?
CARL Huge – over the hundred thousand employees.
MAC Will you like that?
CARL I think so. In my last job I was manager in a really small company, but there was nowhere to go from there.
MAC And now you're back to being a salesman again – it'll be a long way up!
CARL All better! It gives me something to aim for.
MAC Is it an American company?
CARL Well, it's from Netherlands originally, but it's based here now.
MAC Where did you see the ad for the job?
CARL It was in *Herald Tribune*, but it was a smallest job ad I'd ever seen. I could easily have missed it.
MAC Maybe they didn't want hundreds of applicants! Will you have to travel much now?
CARL Yeah, probably. They said in the interview they thought I'd be away two weeks the month on average.
MAC Janey won't like that ...
CARL No, but she'll like some of the other aspects of the job, like the sports centre membership. She'll be able to play a tennis whenever she wants, free.
MAC That sounds good. Well, congratulations, let me shake the hand!

8 Quantifiers and demonstratives

1 Quantifiers: form

QUANTIFIER	+ SINGULAR NOUN	+ PLURAL NOUN	+ UNCOUNTABLE NOUN
no	*I have* **no** *idea.*[1]	*I've got* **no** *coins.*	*I've got* **no** *money.*
none of the		**none of the** *details*	**none of the** *information*
neither	**neither** *cat*	**neither of the** *cats*	
either	**either** *twin*	**either of the** *twins*	
any	**any** *document*	**any (of the)** *documents*	**any (of the)** *information*
both		**both (of the)** *awards*[2]	
few/little		**(a) few (of the)** *sweets*	**(a) little (of the)** *water*
half	**half (of) the** *task*	**half (of) the** *tasks*[2]	**half (of) the** *work*
some	**some** *chance*[3]	**some (of the)** *jewels*	**some (of the)** *jewellery*
several		**several (of the)** *episodes*	
a lot of	**a lot of the** *conference*	**a lot of (the)** *ideas*	**a lot of (the)** *time*
many/much		**many (of the)** *chairs*	**much (of the)** *furniture*
most	**most of the** *holiday*	**most (of the)** *apples*	**most (of the)** *fruit*
each	**each** *applicant*	**each of the** *applicants*	
every (one of)	**every** *page*	**every one of the** *pages*	
all	**all (of) the** *problem*	**all (of) the** *problems*[2]	**all (of) the** *trouble*

[1] For *no* + singular noun ➤ **Unit 47.1**
[2] With *both*, *all* and *half* we can omit *of* before *the*: ***Both/All (of) the*** *candidates believed they had won.*
[3] We can use *some* + singular noun: *'Has John paid you?'* ***'Some chance*** *of that! He never pays on time.'*

2 Quantifiers: use

With most quantifiers, using *of the* before a plural or uncountable noun changes the meaning of the noun from general to specific:
I'd like ***some*** *jewellery.* (general, we don't know which jewellery)
I'd like ***some of the*** *jewellery.* (specific, a particular set of jewellery)

A little/a few mean 'a small amount/number of':
There's ***a little*** *juice left in the fridge.* ***A few*** *people are interested in the new course.*

However, without the article *little* and *few* have the meaning of 'not enough'. Compare:
A few *people are interested in the new course.* (This is positive – enough to start planning it.)
Few *people are interested in the new course.* (This is negative – not enough interest.)

When we use *few* or *little* with a noun that has a negative meaning, e.g. *problems, difficulty*, the overall sense becomes positive:
There were ***few problems*** *with the implementation of the new laws.*

FORMALITY CHECK In informal and spoken English we prefer to use *very* before *little* and *few*:
There's ***very little*** *petrol in the car – we'd better get some more.*
'Are there many people in the office today?' 'No, ***very few****. It's the holiday season.'*

Each and *every* have similar meanings. Both describe 'more than one', but *each* focuses more on separate individuals, while *every* focuses on individuals as members of a group:
The contract was signed by ***each director*** *in turn.* (= individuals, one by one)
When ***every director*** *had signed the contract, it was sent off.* (= the whole group)

Each refers to two or more things, *every* to more than two:
✗ ~~*She was wearing a fine gold chain on every ankle.*~~
✓ *She was wearing a fine gold chain on* ***each*** *ankle.*
But: *She was wearing a ring on* ***each/every*** *finger.*

It is possible to use *any* + a singular countable noun, but meaning 'it doesn't matter which':
Two trucks were parked on the airstrip, making it impossible for ***any*** *plane to land.*

Some can be used in a similar way, but the meaning is more derogatory:
She probably had a row with ***some*** *kid at school.* (= I don't know which kid and I don't care.)

Some can be positive in exclamations:
That's ***some*** *car! It must have cost a fortune.*

Note that *some* has the strong pronunciation /sʌm/ when used in these ways.

Pronunciation ➤ 1.02

We can use quantifiers (except *no* and *every*) without a noun when the meaning is obvious:
The travel agent came up with two possible holidays, but we weren't keen on ***either****.*
The vote was split: ***half*** *were in favour of the motion,* ***half*** *were against it.*

When used as subjects, some quantifiers take a singular verb, and some take a plural verb:

always singular: *each either much*	***Much*** *of the research* ***has*** *already been completed.*
always plural: *both several a few many*	*Some visitors to the new gallery are enthusiastic but* ***many have*** *expressed their disappointment.*

Others take a singular or plural verb, depending on the noun they replace or modify:

singular or plural: *any half some a lot all*	***Some*** *of the information* ***is*** *considered top secret.* ***Some*** *of us* ***are*** *hiring a minibus to go to the match.*

FORMALITY CHECK *Neither* and *none* take a singular or plural verb with plural nouns; a plural verb is more informal:
None *of the students* ***is/are*** *willing to accept the increase in coursework.*

3 Demonstratives *this, that, these, those*

We can use *that/those* when we want to suggest that there is some emotional distance between ourselves and the person/thing we're talking about. We may even dislike or disapprove of the person/thing:
Are you still teaching ***that*** *Martin Bates? I never liked the way he behaved in class.*
'Do you want to keep the local newspaper?' 'What? ***That*** *old rag? No, there's nothing in it.'*

Note that *that* has the strong pronunciation /ðæt/ when used in these ways.

Pronunciation ➤ 1.03

We also use demonstratives as pronouns to refer to a noun, a thing or idea:
This *is a really nice cup of tea. What kind is it?*
Alan says he's giving up his job to travel the world. I think ***that****'s stupid.*

We can use demonstratives with a relative clause or *one/ones* or *those* + *of you/us/them*, etc. as an alternative to *the one(s)*:
Hundreds of Brixton residents turned out to welcome Tyson to their borough. ***Those*** *who had bothered were rewarded by a 40-minute walkabout.*
For ***those of you*** *interested in learning more about Picasso, I've got a list of web addresses.*

FORMALITY CHECK In informal speech we can use *this* or *these* to introduce a topic or start telling a story:
This *woman came up to me in the bank and asked if she could borrow …*

In certain expressions, we can use *this* or *that* instead of *so* to intensify an adjective:
I've never known a winter ***this*** *cold before. So you think you're* ***that*** *clever, do you?*

We use *this/that* when starting a phone call: *Is* ***that*** *Mr Oliver? – No,* ***this*** *is Mr Reynolds.*

this in academic English ➤ Unit 73.3

Practice

1 Match each sentence with the correct meaning, A or B.

1 Neither of the designs for the garden is quite right.
A There are two and I don't like them. B There are two and I like them.
2 Can you give me some of those red apples, not the green ones?
A I don't mind which apples. B I want specific apples.
3 Few organisations have really adopted the practice of job-sharing.
A I think enough organisations have done so.
B I don't think enough organisations have done so.
4 What do you think of that Lester that Ali is hanging round with?
A I like him. B I don't like him.
5 That's some house she owns! It looks like a mansion.
A It's an impressive house. B It isn't a very interesting house.
6 Can you book a meeting room for Tuesday morning? Any room will do.
A I want a specific room. B It doesn't matter which room I have.
7 Every one of you completed the challenge in time. Well done!
A I'm thinking of the group. B I'm thinking of the individual members.
8 This time it'll be a prison sentence if you're found guilty.
A I expect this to happen soon. B I think this is a remote possibility.

2 GRAMMAR IN USE Complete the conversation with demonstrative adjectives or pronouns from the box. 2.14 Listen and check.

this (x3) that (x4) these those (x2)

ROB What's on TV tonight, do you know?

JENNY No. Why don't you look in the paper you're reading?

ROB (1) .... paper doesn't have TV listings.

JENNY Oh, right. Well, try (2) .... one on the shelf, over there.

ROB OK, yes, let's see. There's nothing much on (3) .... days at all, is there? It's all soaps and detective series.

JENNY Mmm. I thought there was always a serious documentary on Tuesday evenings. (4) .... one last week on homelessness was really interesting.

ROB Yes, you're right. There's one on travellers. Listen. (5) .... is awful. 'Although landowners may lose income while travellers are on their land, there is no fast route to evicting them. (6) .... who go through the courts often have to take out more than one injunction before the matter is settled.'

JENNY Well, what do you expect? The travellers need somewhere to live, like the rest of us. The government should give them land.

ROB (7) ....'s no solution, is it? They want to travel, not to settle.

JENNY How do you know? There was (8) .... story in my magazine about travellers from years ago and the encampments they made – they were allowed to settle down then.

ROB Yes, but in (9) .... days there was more free land. Land is (10) .... valuable today, people use every bit of it and don't want travellers on their land.

JENNY Mmm, well why don't we turn the TV on and find out what the documentary says?

3 Choose the correct option, A, B or C. If two options are correct, choose both.

1 I haven't seen ..... of those films, so I don't mind which one we go to.
A any B no C either
2 You shouldn't slouch like that. It puts .... of pressure on one hip and leg.
A much B a lot C all
3 At this stage, ... information would have been a step in the right direction.
A little B some C any
4 The Fitness Room would like to invite ..... of its patrons to enter the annual fitness challenge.
A all B every C some
5 ..... witnesses responded to the police appeal after the accident.
A No B None C Any
6 ..... of the women who attended the demonstration was willing to give us an interview.
A No B None C Many
7 We would like to add that ..... medallion is inscribed with the name of its lucky owner.
A each B every C either
8 Only ..... of the news today has been about the election.
A half B a little C a few
9 We guarantee that ..... item of the dinner service will be replaceable for a period of ten years.
A each B every C all
10 We are delighted to be able to welcome ..... the competition winners to the gala evening.
A both B either C all

4 GRAMMAR IN USE Complete the information, using the words from the box. Use each word once only. 2.15 Listen and check.

all both each every many most no some these this

THE UNITED NATIONS comprises 192 member states, i.e. nearly (1) .... the sovereign states in the world, except the Vatican City, Antarctica (as it's a territory and has (2) .... government) and (3) .... states that are the subject of a dispute, such as Western Sahara and Taiwan. (4) .... wide coverage of world states gives the UN great authority.

The UN has six official languages, (5) .... of which are truly international: Arabic, Chinese, English, French, Russian and Spanish.

The UN functions in (6) .... different fields, from peacekeeping to humanitarian assistance and from environmental sustainability to counter-terrorism. (7) .... far-reaching functions mean that the UN is involved in almost every aspect of international life.

At the head of the UN is the Secretary-General. The Secretary-General is a temporary post, changed or renewed (8) .... five years at the recommendation of the Security Council. The main bodies of the UN are the General Assembly, the Security Council – resolutions are only passed with agreement from (9) .... of these, – the International Court of Justice, which presides over international disputes, and the Economic and Social Council. Voting is generally by majority, i.e. (10) .... member has one vote.

Review MODULE 2

1 UNITS 6 AND 7 **Complete this extract from a letter with *a/an, the* or – (no article).**

There are several reasons why I think I should be considered for (1) .... post of research assistant in (2) .... Faculty of Economics at your university. My first degree was in (3) .... politics and economics from (4) .... University of Warwick, (5) .... England. Then I went to (6) .... United States and took (7) .... Master's degree in international development. Since then, I have been working as (8) .... advisor to (9) .... small non-governmental organisation, and also contributing to (10) .... Independent newspaper on a regular basis.

2 UNITS 6 AND 8 **Choose the correct words in *italics*.**

1 I refer to your letter of 10th March. *A / The* letter states that I purchased a car at your showroom several weeks previously.
2 Do you remember *that / this* conversation we had three weeks ago about Kate and Geoff's wedding?
3 Please sign and date *each / all* page of the contract, then return it to the address above.
4 This packet is impossible to open. Can you pass me *the / any* scissors from the table?
5 On most nights now you'll come across *a / any* fox in an urban environment.
6 The current government has done *few / little* to alleviate the suffering of *poor / the poor*.
7 I've studied several languages but have never found one *this / much* difficult before.
8 *The fear / Fear* of losing one's teeth is a common theme in many people's dreams.

3 ALL UNITS **Match one of the options, A or B, in each pair with a continuation of the sentence or conversation. Choose from a–h in the box, as in the example.**

a Could I have a closer look at it, please?
b It's a basic human right.
c You just have to shop around.
d It's the tallest type of tree in the world.
e She took journalism and media studies.
~~f You know, the one where Chris works.~~
g You know, the one that we couldn't get last week.
h I've never come across one so demonstrative before!

0 A Let's meet in a restaurant.
B Let's meet in the restaurant. ...*B*... + ...*f*...
1 A My sister went to university.
B My sister went to the university. .... + ...
2 A The cat communicates a lot of desires and emotions.
B This cat communicates a lot of desires and emotions. .... + ...
3 A People shouldn't be denied freedom.
B People shouldn't be denied the freedom to eat meat. .... + ...
4 A A giant redwood once grew to over 70 metres.
B The giant redwood can grow to more than 70 metres. .... + ...
5 A Let's watch a DVD this evening.
B Let's watch that DVD this evening. .... + ...
6 A You can pay a lot less for a car these days.
B You could pay a lot less for a car in those days. .... + ...
7 A This is an interesting specimen.
B That's an interesting specimen. .... + ...

4 ALL UNITS **Read the article about Magnum. There are fifteen more mistakes with incorrect, unnecessary or missing words. Find and correct them, as in the example.**

MAGNUM past and present

MAGNUM IS A COOPERATIVE OF NEARLY SIXTY PHOTOGRAPHERS WITH OFFICES IN NEW YORK, LONDON, PARIS AND TOKYO.

~~A~~ The cooperative was founded in 1947 by photographers Robert Capa, Henri Cartier-Bresson, George Rodger and David Seymour. All them had been involved in the Second World War. Rodger had walked hundreds of miles to escape Japanese in Burma. And Seymour received a medal for his work in American intelligence.

However, all of founders of Magnum had been photographers for some time. Photographic work they were famous for dated back further. Capa's photos of the Spanish Civil War were called 'finest pictures of front-line action ever taken'.

They all appreciated an importance of showing the world what really happens during this major conflicts and world crises, so they decided to produce the best documentary photography at this time. Cartier-Bresson once commented, 'Some photographers tell the news step by step as if making an accountant's statement.' He and Magnum, on the other hand, felt that the news had to be shown in that way that would engage most the people who are unable to experience world-changing events at first-hand. Tragically, within a decade of the start of Magnum, the half of its original founders died while covering other wars. However, agency had started to employ other top-class photographers and its work was sure to continue.

> **"Some photographers tell the news step by step as if making an accountant's statement."**
> *Cartier-Bresson*

Today, Magnum is some goal for many young photographers. It still produces the finest documentary photographs of world events. Recent coverage has included events in Caribbean and civil wars in Africa, and while Magnum photographers cover these events, we will all be able to appreciate both best and worst of humanity. ■

Aftermath of the bombing of Madrid during the Spanish Civil War

MODULE

3 Prepositions

Before you start

1 Review these intermediate grammar points and check you know them.

Form

Prepositions can be one word only, or groups of words:

ONE WORD	MORE THAN ONE WORD
of *throughout* *within* *across*	*because of* *apart from* *according to* *by means of*

The store has opened new branches ***throughout*** *the country.*
The two atheletes rowed ***across*** *the Atlantic in record time.*
We got fewer dollars this week ***because of*** *the drop in the exchange rate.*
According to *this map, Hadrian's Wall once extended all the way to the Cumbrian coast.*

Use

1 Prepositions describe the relationship between two or more things.

The Eiffel Tower is located ***on*** *the Champs de Mars* ***in*** *the west* ***of*** *Paris.*

Visitors can go ***up to*** *the top* ***of*** *the Tower* ***by means of*** *a series* ***of*** *lifts.*

2 The three most common prepositions are *at*, *in* and *on*. They are commonly used to express relationships of place and time:

	PLACE	EXAMPLES
at	+ a specific point in space	***at*** *the bus stop* ***at*** *8 Baker Street*
in	within an area, with something that surrounds	***in*** *the wood* ***in*** *the west of Paris* ***in*** *the room*
on	+ a surface or a line	***on*** *the table* ***on*** *the river* ***on*** *the Champs de Mars*

Note ***at*** *the corner of the street* (= a point) but ***in*** *the corner of the room* (= inside).

	TIME	EXAMPLES
at	times, special periods (e.g. celebrations) and in some phrases	***at*** *five to seven* ***at*** *New Year* ***at*** *night* ***at*** *the weekend* ***at*** *the time of its opening*
in	+ parts of the day, months, seasons, years, centuries, etc	***in*** *the morning* ***in*** *December* ***in*** *1889* ***in*** *the winter* ***in*** *the twentieth century*
on	+ days and dates, including special days	***on*** *Thursday* ***on*** *(the morning of) the 31st of May* ***on*** *Labour Day*

Differences between British and American English ➤ page 368

2 **Read the information and find examples of prepositions with different uses.**

The Eiffel Tower

The Eiffel Tower was designed by Gustave Eiffel, constructed during 1887–9 and opened in 1889 for the World Fair held in Paris that year. It is located on the Champs de Mars in the west of Paris and was for many years the tallest building in the city. Many Parisians hated the structure at first but now it is a national symbol.

Visitors can go up to the top of the Tower by means of a series of lifts. There are visitor attractions and cafés/restaurants on the first two floors, and an amazing view from the third.

The Tower is open every day of the year from 9.30 in the morning until 11.00 or 12.00 at night, when it is illuminated with over 20,000 light bulbs!

3 **Complete the diagnostic test below.**

A **Choose the correct words in *italics*.**

1 The monument is *just behind* / *behind just* the petrol station. You can't miss it. ➤ Unit 9.1
2 The dispute worsened because of *that solicitors got* /*solicitors getting* involved. ➤ Unit 9.2
3 From *they said* / *what they said* on the weather forecast, we're in for a good weekend. ➤ Unit 9.2
4 Apart from *to dismantle* / *dismantling* the lighting, the band took only fifteen minutes to pack up. ➤ Unit 9.2
5 I've been offered the job in Helsinki *for that I applied* / *that I applied for*. ➤ Unit 9.3
6 I'll see you at 6.30. I'll be waiting *in* / *at* the theatre if it's raining. ➤ Unit 10.2
7 Hurry up and get *into* / *onto* the car! We're going to be late. ➤ Unit 10.5
8 The museum will close early today *due to* / *out of* staff illness. ➤ Unit 11.3

B **Choose the correct answer, A, B or C.**

1 You could hear the sonic boom of Concorde as it flew ..... the house. ➤ Unit 10.5
A above B over C across
2 The zookeeper calmly walked ..... the lion and took the bag out of its mouth. ➤ Unit 10.7
A near B up to C towards
3 Is the rank of sergeant ..... the rank of corporal in the British army? ➤ Unit 10.8
A underneath B behind C below
4 There's a new soap opera starting ..... tomorrow on BBC2. ➤ Unit 11.1
A at B – C on
5 The walking tour will have to leave right ..... time in order to cover the itinerary. ➤ Unit 11.1
A on B in C at
6 Honestly, that new manager is awful; she behaves ..... a dictator! ➤ Unit 11.4
A as B like C besides
7 Louis was unable to name one true friend ..... all his acquaintances. ➤ Unit 11.5
A between B under C among
8 The hotel's bedding is made ..... only the finest cottons and linens. ➤ Unit 11.6
A of B in C with

4 **Check your answers on page 384. Then go to the unit for more information and practice.**

Go online for a full diagnostic test

9 Prepositions and prepositional phrases

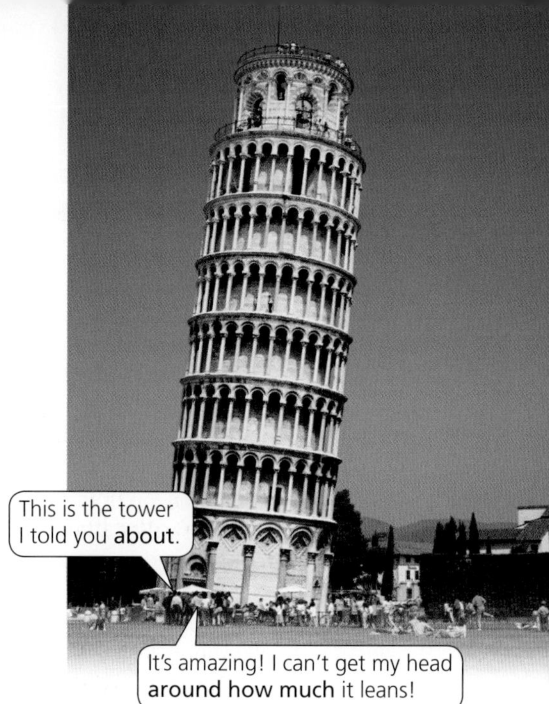

1 Prepositions and adverbs

Prepositions and adverbs are very similar, but a preposition is usually followed by an object. Compare:
*Did you ever travel **before the war**, Dad?* (preposition + object)
*I have a strange feeling that I've been here **before**.* (adverb)

We can modify prepositions by putting adverbs before them:
*The bookshop is **almost at** the end of the street, **just before** the traffic lights.*

2 Prepositional phrases

A prepositional phrase consists of a preposition and the word(s) that follow it, i.e. a noun, pronoun or noun phrase:
*People are already drawing comparisons **between** Obama and Kennedy.*
*I'll answer the phone ... it's **for** you.* *You should try to sleep **on** a firm mattress.*

We can also use *-ing* forms or *wh-* clauses after prepositions:
***As well as helping** us to move into the house, John bought us a great present.*
*Please don't interfere in any way **with what I have written** in the report.*

A prepositional phrase can include nouns, pronouns or determiners before the object:
*The head teacher doesn't approve **of our/these** arrangements with a local band.*
*The director insisted **on Ben and Chris/them/their** staying for the rehearsal.*

⚠ We don't use *that-* clauses after prepositions:
✗ ~~*The government managed to pass the bill through Parliament, despite that it had a low majority.*~~
✓ *The government managed to pass the bill through Parliament, **despite** its low majority/ **despite** having a low majority/**despite** the fact that it had a low majority.*

We can use an infinitive phrase after the prepositions *except*, *but* and *other than*, when they follow a phrase with a negative meaning:
*As you're a captive audience, you have no choice **except to pay** their inflated prices.*
*I'm afraid your action has left us no alternative **but to terminate** your contract.*

3 Stranded prepositions

A stranded preposition comes on its own at the end of a clause or sentence; its object comes earlier in the sentence. We commonly uses stranded prepositions in

- questions: *Who are you coming to the party **with**?* (object *who*)
- relative clauses: *I've been offered the job in London that I applied **for**!* (object *the job*)
- infinitive clauses: *That man is impossible to work **with**!* (object *that man*)
- the passive: *What is your coat made **from**?* (object *what*)

FORMALITY CHECK We sometimes keep the preposition and object together in more formal language:
*We are unable to offer you the position **for which** you applied.*

⚠ When we use a preposition + relative clause, we use *which* or *whom*, not *that*:
✗ ~~*We are unable to offer you the position for that you applied.*~~

More on stranded prepositions ➤ Unit 49.5
Common prepositional phrases (advanced level) ➤ page 365

Practice

1 **Complete the sentences. Put the words in brackets in the correct order. 2.16 Listen and check.**

1 Water will be made available (and crisis for hospitals schools the throughout).

....

2 The rescuers pulled the boy (a by from means of rope the well).

....

3 The journey time has been reduced (hours just three to under).

....

4 Didn't you recognise her? She was sitting (beard almost man with the opposite the).

....

5 Please have your account number to hand (mobile calling phone helpline before the).

....

6 What was the name of the TV series (in actor which appeared that) last year?

....

7 The solution the solicitors had devised (my not on depended to agreeing reveal) the total amount paid.

....

8 After she'd shut the door, she didn't move (take her hat to off except).

....

9 'I lent that book to someone else.' '(did it Who lend to you)?'

....

10 We regret to inform you that your work does not meet (which we standard the to aspire).

....

2 GRAMMAR IN USE **Choose the correct words in *italics*. If both options are correct, choose both. 2.17 Listen and check.**

Pompeii

In 79 CE Pompeii was a bustling town, the main hub (1) *of which / which* was its busy port, (2) *where from / from where* ships sailed all over the known world. The massive eruption of Mount Vesuvius in that year devastated the town, but also preserved a snapshot of Roman-era life for those who came after. Despite (3) *having / that it had* a population of about 20,000 people, (4) *about only / only about* 2,000 died in the eruption, the majority having fled because they had lived with the volcano for years and were only too aware of (5) *it / its* growling and what this meant.

Today's visitors can walk through the town's ancient streets, marvelling at the colourful frescoes (6) *with which the houses were decorated / which the houses were decorated with*; in some places it is still possible to see plaster casts of those killed in (7) *go / going* about their daily activities.

Although Vesuvius is still an active volcano, modern monitoring techniques mean that visitors can roam the ancient site with no reason to look up to the huge mountain other than (8) *enjoying / to enjoy* the view.

10 Prepositions of place and movement

... **at** the top the atmosphere was amazing, perhaps because the clouds were hanging so low **over** Machu Picchu.

1 Place *above, below, down, over, under, underneath, up*

Above and *over* have similar meanings, as do *below* and *under(neath)*:
The refuge is in the hills ***over/above*** *the town.*
Oncology departments in hospitals are often ***under(neath)*** *the ground/***below** *ground level.*

Over and *under* are more common. We use them

- when one thing covers or touches another:
  The clouds were hanging low ***over*** *the hills. The wreck lay six metres* ***under*** *the water.*
- when movement is suggested: *Are we going to fly* ***over*** *the Alps?*
- with prices, ages, speeds, distances and quantities, where we mean *more than* or *fewer/less than*: *The conference was very badly attended:* ***under*** *two hundred people came.*

Up and *down* can refer to position: *John lives a few houses further* ***up/down*** *the road from us.*

2 Place *at, in*

We usually use *in* with places that 'surround' us, such as countries, cities or towns, and with names of streets and squares, but we use *at* with specific addresses:
The trees ***in*** *Leicester Square don't look very healthy.*
Sandra lives ***in*** *Bramble Road. Sarah lives* ***at*** *36 Bramble Road.*

We use *at* when we refer to gatherings of people: ***at*** *a party,* ***at*** *a conference.*

We use different prepositions depending on how we see a place. Compare:
The group will meet at 7.30 ***at*** *the sports centre.* (= either inside or outside)
The group will meet at 7.30 ***in*** *the sports centre.* (= inside)

3 Place *against, alongside, beside, by, near, next to*

By, near, next to and *against* all express proximity; *by* and *next to* express closer proximity, and *against* suggests that something is so close that it's touching:
Stella's bought a house ***next to/by*** *the sea – she's got a wonderful view.*
Stella's bought a house ***near*** *the sea. It's only a five-minute walk to the beach.*
Don't lean ***against*** *the wall – I've only just painted it!*

We can use *right by* to make the proximity even closer: *She lives* ***right by*** *the sea.*

We use *beside* and *alongside* to express proximity along a line:
Warehouses were built ***beside/alongside*** *the motorway.*

4 Place *across, after, before, behind, in front of, opposite, over*

We use *in front of* to mean 'further forward than' and *behind* to mean 'further back than':
A is ***in front of*** *B. B is* ***behind*** *A.*

Before and *after* can refer to position in some contexts:
Karen's nephew appears ***before/in front of*** *the magistrates today.*
You'll be called first as my name is ***after*** *yours on the list.*

Opposite, across and *over* mean 'on the other side of', e.g. a road, a river:
I'll meet you in the café ***opposite*** *the theatre.* (= on the other side of the road)

With *across* and *over* we have to say on the other side of what, e.g. the road:
I'll meet you in the café ***across/over the road*** *from the theatre.*

The difference between *opposite* and *in front of* is that the items on the 'line' are not facing in the same direction, as in the diagram on page 50, but are facing each other, as in the diagram on the right:
*A is **opposite** B. A and B are **opposite** each other.*

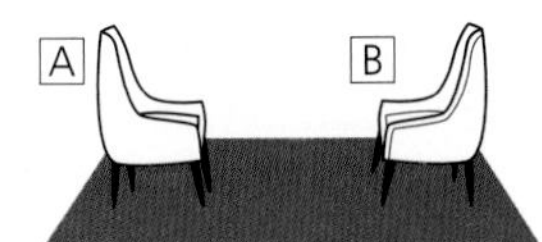

5 Movement *down, into, off, on, out of, over, up*

We use these prepositions for movement up or down:
*Look at Johnny's knee – he's just fallen **off** his bike.*
*The climb **up** the mountain was incredibly strenuous.*

We get *on* or *off* a bus, plane, train, boat and bike but *into* and *out of* a car.

We also often use *up* and *down* with roads and rivers to mean 'along':
*You walk **down** the high street and turn left at the library.*

We can use *over* for a movement across an obstacle:
*The burglar leapt **over** the garden fence as he ran away from us.*

6 Movement *across, along, over, past, through*

We use *across* for movement from one side to the other of something on a 'surface', e.g. ***across** the river/road/field.*

We use *through* for movement inside something, e.g. ***through** a room/tunnel*:
*Walk **across** the playing field to the sports centre, then go **through** the main hall …*

Over is similar to *across* (one side to the other) but it incorporates the idea of 'above':
*Are we going to fly **over** the Alps on the way to Italy?*

We use *along* for movement in a line, e.g. ***along** a river/road*:
*You can spend a pleasant afternoon strolling **along** the canals in Amsterdam.*

We use *past* for a movement from one side to the other of something, close to it:
*I was startled by a huge bird that flew **past** my window this afternoon.*

7 Movement *around, at, down (to), to, towards, up (to)*

We can use *up to* or *towards* when we approach someone or something, but we use only (*right*) *up to* if we actually reach the person/thing:
✗ ~~*Do you think I can go towards him and ask for his autograph?*~~
✓ *Do you think I can go **up to** him and ask for his autograph?*
*The scientist moved quietly **towards** the group of grazing animals.*

We can use *up* (*to*) and *down* (*to*) for movement north or south within a country, and *up to* with a major or capital city: *Are you driving **up to** London this weekend?*

We can express a circular movement with (*a*)*round*:
*We drove **(a)round** the roundabout three times before we took the correct exit.*

We can use both *to* and *at* after certain verbs, e.g. *throw, shout. To* suggests that the recipient is happy with the action but *at* that the recipient is not happy:
*Can you throw that book **to** me, please? Don't throw stones **at** the cat!*

8 Metaphorical uses

We often also use prepositions of place in a less literal way. We use *above* or *below* metaphorically to talk about 'level' or 'rank', or when we measure things on a vertical scale:
*Is the position of Managing Editor **above** or **below** that of Editorial Director?*
*His temperature rose **above** 100°.*

Similarly, we can use prepositions of movement in a less literal way:
*A system of charges has been introduced **into** the Health Service.*
*I was halfway **through** the book when my friend told me the ending!*
*We're saving all of this extra income **towards** a round-the-world trip next year.*

Practice

1 GRAMMAR IN USE **Look at the map of Paris and read the text. Complete the key to the map.**

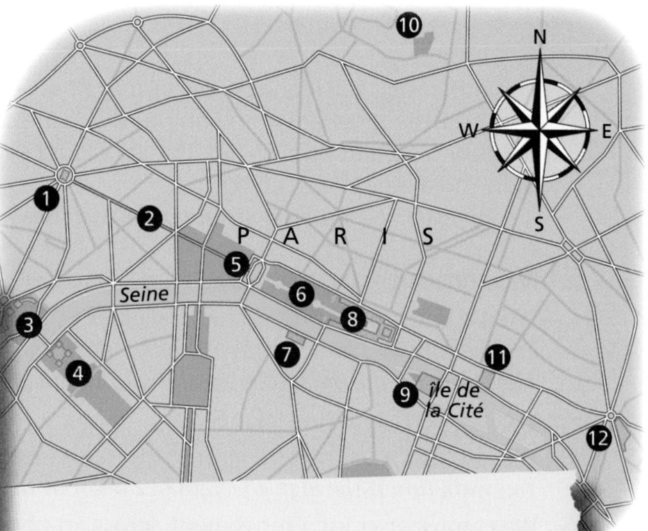

KEY

1	Arc de Triomphe	7	....
2	....	8	....
3	....	9	....
4	....	10	....
5	....	11	....
6	....	12	....

A *Quick* GUIDE TO PARIS

THE BEAUTY OF Paris is that it's a very compact city, easy to get around, and to see the sights in a relatively short time. Start your tour in the very centre of the city, on the island in the Seine (the Île de la Cité). Here you will find the impressive Palais de Justice (law courts), and north-east across the river is the City Hall of Paris. Going west from this, facing the west end of the island, you'll see the imposing east façade of the Louvre – the huge museum that sprawls alongside the river. After your visit to the Louvre, take a leisurely stroll through the lovely Tuileries Gardens to the Place de la Concorde. From there you could either go back south-east across the river and visit the stunning Musée d'Orsay, or stroll along the bustling Champs-Elysées to the magnificent Arc de Triomphe at its western end. A short distance south of this across the river you'll find the Eiffel Tower, possibly the most famous sight in Paris, and opposite this; over the river the stark Chaillot Palace (also known as Trocadero), which houses several interesting museums.

Two more sights that shouldn't be missed even on a short visit to Paris are the old Bastille prison to the east of the city, now an opera house, and to the north, on Montmartre Hill, the fascinating Place du Tertre, where artists gather to this day and will paint your portrait for a modest sum. ■

2 Choose the correct preposition. 2.18 **Listen and check.**

1 After submitting your complaint, you will be informed of a date when you will be invited to appear *after* / *before* the employment tribunal.
2 'Look at that man, Mum! ' 'Don't point *at* / *to* people, Lucy. It's very rude!'
3 Do not lean *against* / *by* the crash barriers as they're not very safe.
4 We need to limit the number of participants in each workshop to *beneath* / *under* 25 to ensure that everyone is able to join in.
5 Most of the restaurants in the town can be found *in* / *at* Lavender Road.
6 In 218 BCE Hannibal took his army of men and elephants *through* / *across* the Alps in order to fight the Roman forces in Italy.
7 There was a fire alarm while we were *in* / *at* the main auditorium at the theatre.
8 At the end of the match the contestants are expected to go *towards* / *up to* each other and shake hands.
9 The missing children were found hiding in the small park *opposite* / *across* the river from the school.
10 We were really late and only just managed to get *into* / *on* the ferry before it sailed.
11 In this cold weather we always sleep with at least two extra blankets *over* / *above* us.
12 You can put the packaging in the rubbish bin *in front of* / *opposite* the entrance – it's just outside.

3 GRAMMAR IN USE **Complete the article with the most suitable prepositions. They may consist of more than one word, and in some places more than one preposition is possible.** 2.19 **Listen and check.**

END OF THE ROAD

A tourist's tale by SUSAN HUNTER

IT WAS LATE afternoon when we drove into the little town. We had driven for (1) .... 400 kilometres that day and most of it had been (2) .... thick fog. We were tired and decided to find a hotel – we didn't know how far it might be to the next town. We parked, got (3) .... the car and stretched – a walk would be very welcome, we thought. We left our luggage (4) .... the car boot and walked (5) .... the already empty car park to a narrow but fast-flowing stream. A five-minute stroll (6) .... a tree-lined avenue (7) .... the stream took us (8) .... the town square. It was a beautiful old square with a fountain (9) .... the middle and arcades (10) .... three sides. We looked up at terraces of interesting-looking restaurants (11) .... the arcades and then back down at entrances to fascinating little shops (12) .... them.

We had no idea where to look for a hotel or a pension in this sleepy town, so we walked (13) .... an old man sitting (14) .... a bench by the fountain. He pointed us in the direction of a narrow alleyway and told us we'd find the best hotel (15) .... the little road. It seemed unlikely, but we followed his advice and sure enough, (16) .... the other end of the alleyway, (17) .... two picturesque old houses, was a sign saying 'hotel'. Just (18) .... the hotel, (19) .... the other side of the street, was a house covered in the most colourful flowers, and I immediately hoped that we might be able to see the house from our bedroom window. (20) .... the hotel reception, a cool, dark room with a coffee lounge (21) .... one corner, we asked about a room. Our satisfaction was complete when we realised that even the best room in the hotel was (22) .... $80.

We looked at the room, decided to take it and went down to the lounge, where we stopped for a delicious cappuccino. Soon dusk was falling, so we handed the room key (23) .... the receptionist and told him we'd be back with our luggage in ten minutes. As we walked (24) .... the narrow streets, we discussed what we would do the next day and how long we'd stay in the little town. Imagine our horror when we arrived (25) .... the car park to find it completely empty – our car and all of our luggage had been stolen!

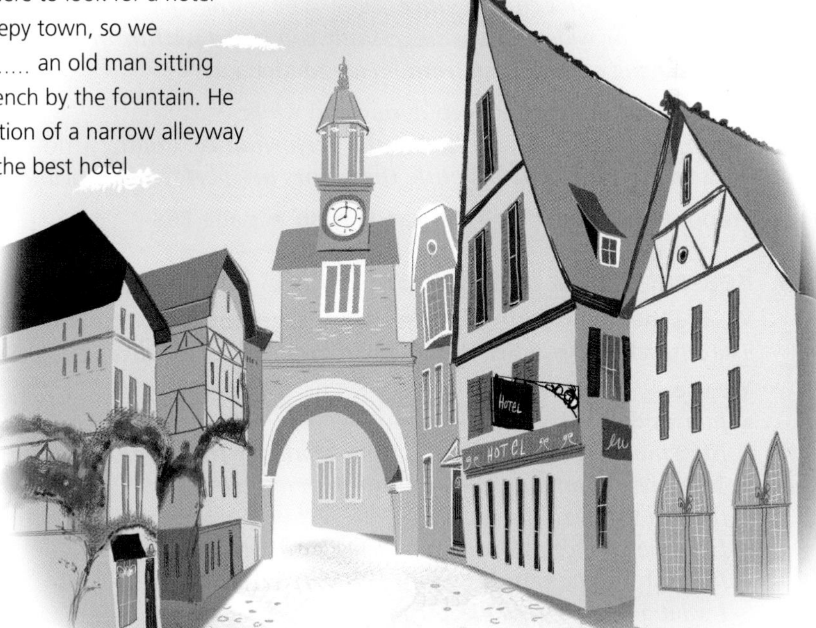

11 Prepositions of time; other meanings

1 Time *after, at, before, by, in, on, past*

These prepositions precede a specific point in time.

We can use *about* or *around* with *at* to be less specific, and in informal speech, we can omit *at* before these: *Let's meet at the station (**at**) **about** six.*

THE LONDON EYE
is open every day **from** 10.00 a.m. **until** 8.00 p.m. (winter) or 9.00/9.30 p.m. (summer).
Owing to queues at busy times, we recommend booking your ride in advance if possible.

FORMALITY CHECK In informal English, American English and news reports, we can also omit *on* before days:
Great news! The travel agent has found us a flight that leaves Wednesday.

We do not use the prepositions *at, on* or *in* immediately before adverbs or adverbial phrases such as *today, tomorrow, last/this/next week*:
✗ ~~*Our holiday starts on next week.*~~ ✓ *Our holiday starts next week.*

We use:

- *after* or *past* to mean 'later than': *Where have you been? It's **after/past** eleven o'clock.*
- *before* to mean 'before a time', and *by* to mean 'before or at a time':
  *Applications must be submitted **before** 30th November.* (= on the 29th or earlier)
  *Applications must be submitted **by** 30th November.* (= on the 30th or earlier)

The adverbial phrases *in time* and *(right) on time* have different meanings:
*The wedding car arrived **in time** but the bride wasn't ready.* (= with time to spare)
*The bride arrived right **on time** for the ceremony.* (= at precisely the right time)

2 Time *during, for, from … till/until/to, since, through(out), until/till*

These prepositions precede a period of time, or point in time (*since*):
*From next Monday, we will have to suspend flexible working arrangements **until** further notice.*
*Long hair for men was fashionable **during/through(out)** much of the seventies.*
*This volcano hasn't erupted **since** 1935. The volcano hasn't erupted **for** more than 75 years.*
*The motorway widening was successfully completed **within/in** four months.*
*I'll be staying at the Hilton **from** Friday **to** Monday.*

Note the difference between *during* and *while*:
*Please refrain from talking **during the performance**.* (*during* + noun/*-ing* form)
*Please refrain from talking **while the actors are performing**.* (*while* + clause)

Prepositions of time in American English ➤ page 368

3 Reason, means and purpose

We use the prepositions *because of, due to* and *owing to* to express a reason:
*The District Line is closed **due to/owing to/because of** engineering works.*

We use

- *from* and *out of* for cause or motive:
  *Huge numbers of people in the Third World die **from** starvation every day.*
  *They obeyed him **out of** fear rather than respect.*
- *through* to mean 'by means of':
  *He achieves success **through** patience and hard work.*
- *for* to show the purpose of an item, action, etc:
  *I want a knife that can be used **for** cutting bread.*
  *Our uncle's company manufactures lubricants **for** ball bearings.*

- *by* or *with* to introduce an instrument, i.e. what we use to do something:
  Negotiations were held ***by*** *phone between the client and his solicitor.*
  The victim was killed ***by*** *a bullet to the head/****with*** *a sawn-off shotgun.*
- *by* for the agent (or creator) of something: *It's one of the later paintings* ***by*** *Van Gogh.*

4 Comparison

We use

- *against, beside* and *contrary to* to make a contrast:
  Look at this year's sales figures ***against*** *last year's; they're so much better.*
  Beside *her sister, Laura was positively plain.*
  The Davis Cup final was won by the Croatian team, ***contrary to*** *expectations.*
- *between* to differentiate: *I can't tell the difference* ***between*** *butter and this spread.*
- *like* to make a comparison: *She behaves* ***like*** *a director, but she's really only a secretary.*
- *as* to express a role: *Speaking* ***as*** *a director of the company, I believe we should sell the shares.*

5 Inclusion and exception

We usually use *among* or *between* to show that something is part of a pair/group. *Among* usually refers to more than two:
For women, the distinction ***between work and leisure*** *is less clear-cut.*
Princes William and Harry were ***among*** *the spectators at yesterday's match.*

When we talk about one thing in addition to others, we can use *besides*:
Are there any issues remaining ***besides*** *that of the roof repairs?*

To say that something is not within certain limits, we can use *beyond, outside* or *out of*:
I'm afraid that changes to the curriculum are ***beyond/outside/out of*** *our control.*

We can use *apart from, but for* and *except (for)* to say that something is excluded:
Everyone is invited to the conference dinner, ***except (for)/apart from/but for*** *those who have bought 'day' tickets only.*

- *Except* and *except for* can both be used after phrases containing determiners such as *all, every, no*: *Julian did very well in all his exams* ***except (for)*** *geography.*
- To contradict the main idea of the sentence, we only use *except for*:
  Glock emerged from the wreckage of the car ***uninjured except for*** *a minor leg injury.*
- We can also use *but for* to mean 'if not for' (➤ Unit 38.3).

6 Material

We use

- *of* when the original material is still visible: *a dress* ***(made) of*** *Thai silk*
- *of* in metaphorical phrases: *a man* ***of*** *iron, a heart* ***of*** *gold*
- *from* when the original material has been transformed: *ice cream made* ***from*** *strawberries*
- *with* when we refer to a filling or an ingredient: *vine leaves stuffed* ***with*** *rice*

7 Other

We use

- *on behalf of* to express 'representing' someone or something:
  On behalf of *our shareholders, I'd like to thank all of you who voted in favour of the merger.*
- *for the sake of* when we do something in order to benefit someone/something else:
  I think we should move to the country ***for the sake of*** *the children.*
- *according to* to report opinions or feelings:
  The peak skiing period will be 24–25 February, ***according to*** *Chamonix tourist office.*

⚠ We do not use *according to* to report our own opinions and feelings:
✗ ~~*Holograms aren't a real art form, according to me.*~~
✓ ***According to many art critics,*** *holograms aren't a real art form.*

Prepositions of concession (e.g. *despite*) ➤ Unit 60.3

Practice

1 GRAMMAR IN USE **Read about the Tower of London and complete the information below with appropriate prepositions of time (if necessary). 2.20 Listen and check.**

CEREMONY OF THE KEYS

Tickets are free of charge but, due to the popularity of the ceremony, it is necessary to follow the correct process for applications.

PLEASE NOTE **1 April – 31 October inclusive**
groups limited to a maximum of 6 people
1 November – 31 March inclusive
groups limited to a maximum of 15 people
Visitors will be admitted to the Tower under escort at 21:30 hrs precisely. The ceremony will conclude at 22:05 hrs.

OPENING TIMES		
	Tuesday – Saturday	09:00–16:30
	Sunday – Monday	10:00–16:30
	Last admission	16:00

IN THE 1080s William the Conqueror ordered the building of a massive stone tower in London. Subsequent monarchs added to it or renovated existing buildings until a great fortress had been built. In both World Wars (1914–18 and 1939–45) the Tower was used as a prison and a place of execution, with 1941 seeing the last execution at the Tower. Today it is a major tourist attraction and a UNESCO World Heritage Site.

The Tower is open (1) .... nine o'clock (2) .... half past four. Visitors can enter the Tower (3) .... four o'clock; (4) .... that time no tickets will be sold. Visitors must arrive for the Ceremony of the Keys (5) .... half past nine; please arrive (6) .... time as latecomers will not be admitted. (7) .... winter months groups of 15 people may attend the ceremony but (8) .... the summer this will be limited to six only.
There has been a tower on the site (9) .... the 11th century. (10) .... that time the building has been extended and developed. The present Tower was used as a prison (11) .... the first part of the 20th century. It was also a place of execution; the last one was (12) .... 1941.

2 Choose the correct option in *italics*.

1 Don't forget that your final assignment must be handed to your tutor *– / on* next Monday.
2 The soldiers didn't arrive at the village *on / in* time – the rebels had already burned the remaining houses.
3 Don't be late for the Philharmonia concert – you know they always start dead *on / in* time.
4 There has been no sign of the birds *until / since* nightfall.
5 David Mamet's latest play will be showing on Broadway *while / during* the whole of December.
6 If we do not receive payment *until / by* 31st July, we shall take legal action.
7 As he was opening the shop at 7.30 in the morning, Mr Charles was attacked *by / with* a baseball bat.
8 Alexander Graham Bell spent much of his life *as / like* a teacher.
9 *Except / Apart* for a few less experienced individuals, all of the recent applicants were taken on.
10 This publication is made *of / from* paper from sustainable forests.
11 Old skyscrapers look tiny now *beside / besides* the huge towers being built today.
12 I'm calling *for the sake of / on behalf of* my elderly mother to arrange an appointment.

3 Complete the second sentence so it has a similar meaning to the first. Include one of the words in brackets in your answer, as in the example.

0 Many people stayed at home after the government increased airport taxes. ((because)/ through)
Many people stayed at home ....*because of the increase*.... in airport taxes.

1 David Bailey took many photos of his wife, Marie Helvin. (by / for)
Many photos of Marie Helvin were taken ...., David Bailey.

2 You'll find it easier to use the smaller knife to chop the vegetables. (with / for)
You'll find it easier to use the smaller knife .... the vegetables.

3 These tiny cakes contain only the best ingredients. (with / of)
These tiny cakes .... only the best ingredients.

4 My brother is the only person in my family who doesn't vote Labour. (apart / behalf)
All my family votes Labour ....

5 I'm afraid that this department does not have control over motorway maintenance. (out / outside)
I'm afraid that motorway maintenance is .... of this department.

6 In the opinion of many experts in the field, the Lightwater experiment was not conclusive. (according / contrary)
.... in the field, the Lightwater experiment was not conclusive.

7 We aren't allowed to use electronic devices while the plane is taking off or landing. (in / during)
Electronic devices must not be used ....

8 It is a common belief that clothes with vertical stripes have a slimming effect, but that is not the case. (contrary / like)
...., vertical stripes in clothes do not have a slimming effect.

4 GRAMMAR IN USE Choose prepositions from the box to complete the letter. There are five extra prepositions. 2.21 Listen and check.

among as because of between by contrary to
during except for for in like of out of since with

Dear Dr Anderson

I would like to be considered for the post of resident photographer with your magazine *Nature*.

My degree is in media studies, specialising in photography. I completed it (1) .... 2002 and I have been working (2) .... that time for various companies, including magazines, (3) .... a freelance photographer. All my work experience so far has been in the UK, (4) .... a three-month project in Poland, where I took photos of birds on the Baltic coast. (5) .... family commitments at the present time, I am seeking to move from freelance into more secure employment, and I would be very interested in working for *Nature* magazine. I have a long-standing interest in the natural world and many of my best photographs have been (6) .... wildlife and the scenery of the British Isles. (7) .... my previous employers is a small local wildlife charity, for whom I took many photos (8) .... three short-term contracts, some of which I enclose with this application. I had hoped to find a permanent position with them, but (9) .... their expectations, funding for the position was not forthcoming.

If you require further information, I am always contactable (10) .... email or phone.

Review MODULE 3

You will also need to look at pages 365–6 to complete these exercises.

1 UNITS 10 AND 11 **Complete each story with prepositions from the box above it.**

according to across between by from in to

How stupid is that?

A Bad Explorer

A man (1) .... Kentucky, USA, had a dream that would take him far away from the rolling hills of his home state. The dream: to row (2) .... the icy Bering Strait (3) .... Alaska and Russia, (4) .... a bathtub! Unfortunately, the dream was not completely fulfilled. (5) .... the explorer, '(6) .... late afternoon of the fourth day, although the sun was still high, the sea went rather thick. Next morning I was frozen in.' No problem. He abandoned the bathtub and walked (7) .... land.

at behind in into on under with

Some stupid thieves

In the town of Vang, Norway, a group of thieves were carrying out a carefully planned robbery. Everything was going smoothly. They broke into a company (8) .... night, located the safe and set up some explosives that would blow the door of the safe off, allowing them to get to the money inside. After setting the fuse, they ran (9) .... the next room, crouched (10) .... the wall and waited for the explosion.

It came a few seconds later. The safe door was blown off. So was the roof. (11) .... fact, the entire building collapsed, trapping the robbers, still crouching in the next office, (12) .... the rubble of the destroyed building. There had been just one problem they had not foreseen: the safe hadn't contained money; (13) .... the contrary, it had been filled (14) .... dynamite!

against along at between during in (x2) into off on (x2) out of to

SELF-HELP CRIME PREVENTION

A Western businessman living in Japan had been warned about pickpockets in the Tokyo subway. These notorious thieves operated (15) .... the crowded rush hour. They would grab wallets just as the subway doors were closing, leaving the victim helpless (16) .... the train while they disappeared with the loot.

One morning the businessman was (17) .... his usual subway stop when the train pulled in. He got on, and sure enough, just as the train doors were about to close, he felt a man rub (18) .... him. In a panic, the businessman reached for his wallet. It was gone! He looked up as the doors began to close and saw that a man had just got (19) .... the train.

Not wishing to let the whole situation get (20) .... hand, the businessman pushed his hands (21) .... the closing doors and grabbed the thief's jacket. The doors closed, with the thief still (22) .... the platform but with the lapels of his jacket trapped (23) .... the tight grip of the businessman. As the train began to pull away, the expression on the thief's face changed. He began screaming as he ran (24) .... the platform with the train. Finally, he held onto a post and his lapels tore away from his jacket. As the train moved (25) .... the tunnel, the businessman was satisfied that at least he had frightened the thief.

As the man hadn't got his credit card numbers (26) .... hand, he called his wife and asked her to cancel them. 'But honey,' she said, 'I've been trying to call you. You left your wallet on the dressing table when you went to work today.'

2 ALL UNITS **Choose the correct words in *italics*. If both options are correct, choose both.**

The Eden Project

a living theatre

NO, YOU'RE NOT looking at a scene (1) *from / out of* a James Bond movie! The futuristic buildings in this photo really exist. They are part of the Eden Project – one of the most spectacular of the Millennium projects.

The Eden Project is located (2) *at / in* Cornwall, England, in a former clay pit (3) *above / over* 50 metres deep. It consists of several huge domes, a large open area and a visitor centre. The Eden Project functions (4) *as / like* a 'storeroom' for a huge number of plants from all over the world. The two main domes store plants and trees (5) *from / for* the tropical and temperate regions of the world, while the open area accommodates more local species.

The Eden Project has many other functions (6) *against / besides* that of a storeroom, however. It is a centre for education, art and science, showing us ways in (7) *which / that* plants are vital to the world's existence, and promoting understanding of the delicate balance (8) *between / among* using and conserving plant life. As well as (9) *provide / providing* a focus both for scientific research and for education, the project includes exciting experiences for children, such as walking (10) *through / in* a rainforest. In addition, it hosts concerts and provides other attractions including, (11) *among / between* other things, an ice-skating rink in winter.

(12) *While / During* the final stages of its construction, at the turn of the century, the Eden Project opened its doors to visitors, (13) *contrary to / except* normal practice. (14) *For / Since* several months visitors were able to experience the challenges that lay (15) *under / behind* the building of such a project and get a taste of (16) *what / that* was to come. (17) *From / In* spring 2001 this living theatre opened fully to the public, and since then it has become a major tourist attraction. Today, for (18) *under / below* £20, everyone can experience the diversity of the world's plants.

3 ALL UNITS **Find and correct nine mistakes in these sentences. Tick (✓) the correct sentences.**

1 So, by conclusion, I would like to return to the initial question I posed.
2 The museum is open every day through the year, except from New Year's Day.
3 Did you talk to Anneka about us coming on the excursion with you?
4 Below fifty people came to the presentation of the new season's designs.
5 All sports fixtures have been cancelled owing the adverse weather conditions.
6 Hillary talks as an expert on family law, but she isn't one.
7 There will be an extra tutorial on Friday for those who missed Tuesday's.
8 The alarm sounded before just the play started, so we were all given a refund.
9 This is an interesting bag – it's made entirely from old bicycle tyres.
10 Baker Street is the road in that Sherlock Holmes is supposed to have lived.
11 All of the trainees, beyond exception, gained a distinction in one module.
12 Our next session is scheduled for two weeks' time. Within the meantime, I'd like you to do the exercises I showed you, three times a day.

MODULE

4 Adjectives and adverbs

Before you start

1 Review these intermediate grammar points and check you know them.

Adjectives

1 Adjectives are words which give extra information about nouns. They do not change their form to show number or gender:
*The hero was played by a **young** boy. Several **young** girls took the secondary roles.*

2 Many adjectives are formed from other words:
history → *historic*   *beauty* → *beautiful*   *depend* → *dependent*   *effect* → *effective*

3 We often use the past (*-ed*) and present (*-ing*) participles as adjectives to describe feelings or emotions.

We use the *-ing* form to describe a feeling that something causes:
*It was a **frightening** film.* (= It frightened us/made us feel afraid.)

We use the *-ed* form to describe a feeling that someone experiences:
*I felt **frightened** when I watched that film.* (= I was frightened/experienced fear.)

Inanimate objects cannot have feelings so we don't usually use *-ed* adjectives about feelings to describe them:
✗ ~~*The report into police behaviour during the demonstration was rather worried.*~~
✓ *The report was rather **worrying**.* (= The report made readers feel anxious.)

4 We can also combine words to make compound adjectives, e.g. *home-made, Spanish-speaking.*

Adverbs

1 Adverbs are words which modify or give extra information about verbs, adjectives, other words or whole clauses. Here are some common examples:

not formed from other words	*here just never quite soon still tomorrow too well*	
fixed phrases	*at last kind of of course*	
formed from other words	adjective + *-ly* (note spelling)	*easy* → *easily excitable* → *excitably real* → *really tragic* → *tragically*
	compounds	*some + times* → *sometimes*

2 The most common use of adverbs is to modify adjectives; the adverb usually comes before the adjective:
*I thought his answers were **pretty good** on the whole.*
*Those cars are **terribly expensive**.*

Some adverbs, e.g. *really, almost, quite, pretty,* can modify another adverb:
*The French team did **quite well** in the first round.*

2 **Read the article and identify examples of adjectives and adverbs.**

The Brink's-MAT Robbery

The biggest robbery in British history took place on 26 November 1983 when six men broke into the Brink's-MAT warehouse at Heathrow Airport, London.

They stole £3 million in cash and three tonnes of gold bullion, worth around £26 million. The armed robbers poured petrol over the terrified security guards and threatened to set them alight. The British police pursued the gang tirelessly, and in 1984 Brian Robinson and gang leader Michael McAvoy were caught and found guilty of armed robbery, receiving sentences of 25 years in prison. However, the other members of the gang are still at large, and the bulk of the gold has never been found.

3 **Complete the diagnostic test below. Choose the correct words in *italics*. If both options are correct, choose both.**

1. In view of the terrible nature of the crime, *the sentence imposed by the judge was maximum / the maximum sentence was imposed by the judge.* ➤ Unit 12.1
2. The *involved people / people involved* will be caught and severely punished. ➤ Unit 12.3
3. The rich *seem / seems* to be getting richer and the poor poorer these days. ➤ Unit 12.5
4. They're selling that *Victorian wonderful house / wonderful Victorian house* on the corner. ➤ Unit 13.1
5. Prisoners can be identified by their *grey and white / grey white* striped uniforms. ➤ Unit 13.2
6. In the eighteenth century, the Bastille was the most infamous prison *of / in* France. ➤ Unit 14.1
7. The divorce has undoubtedly made him the *unhappiest / most unhappy* man in the street. ➤ Unit 14.3
8. Our new social security scheme is *lots / far* more generous than the previous government's. ➤ Unit 14.5
9. Getting a made-to-measure suit was not nearly *more expensive than / as expensive as* I had feared. ➤ Unit 15.1
10. The more frustrated he becomes, *angrier / the angrier* he gets. ➤ Unit 15.4
11. The flavour is *more sweet / sweeter* than savoury. ➤ Unit 15.5
12. Maria worked *like / as* a shop assistant during the university vacation. ➤ Unit 15.6
13. The weather is Greece was *more boiling / much hotter* than we expected. ➤ Unit 16.1
14. Steve's sister is *absolutely / very* intelligent. ➤ Unit 16.2
15. After two months with no rain the grass is *almost / slightly* dead. ➤ Unit 16.5
16. The result of the election came as *so / quite* a shock. ➤ Unit 17.2
17. As we descended the hill the car began to go *faster / more fast.* ➤ Unit 17.3
18. I *very carefully opened the old box containing my mother's photographs. / opened the old box containing my mother's photographs very carefully.* ➤ Unit 18.1
19. I've been suffering from insomnia recently. *I only slept last night / Last night I only slept* for four hours. ➤ Unit 18.2
20. *Emotionally, Harriet / Harriet emotionally* has always been dependent on her brothers. ➤ Unit 18.5

4 **Check your answers on page 384. Then go to the unit for more information and practice.**

Go online for a full diagnostic test

12 Adjective patterns

1 Adjectives before nouns (attributive position)

Most adjectives can be used before a noun (attributive position), or after a linking verb, e.g. *be, become,* etc. (predicative position):

ATTRIBUTIVE *We've just seen an **exciting** film.*
PREDICATIVE *That film was **exciting**.*

But classifying adjectives (which describe what type of thing something is) and emphasising adjectives are normally only used BEFORE a noun:

✗ ~~*The plant they are building here is chemical.*~~ ✓ *They're building a **chemical plant** here.*
✗ ~~*The chance that they met was mere.*~~ ✓ *It was **mere chance** that they met.*

ATTRIBUTIVE POSITION	
classifying (examples)	*chemical chief criminal elder entire eventual former industrial local lone main maximum medical national nuclear only outdoor/indoor principal social sole underlying whole*
emphasising	*mere sheer utter*

ACADEMIC ENGLISH In academic writing we usually prefer adjectives in attributive position, e.g. *basic processes, experimental physics, appropriate conditions, principal causes,* etc.

2 Adjectives after verbs (predicative position)

Adjectives in predicative position are usually the complement of a linking verb, e.g. *be, become, feel, seem* (➤ Unit 42.1): *When she heard the noise Mary **became** very **uneasy**.*

However, after certain verbs of thinking and feeling (i.e. *consider, find, think*) we can omit the linking verb: *I **consider/find** him (to be) very **reliable**.*

Many adjectives beginning with the letter *a* and adjectives describing health and feelings are not usually used before nouns; instead, we use them in predicative position:

✗ ~~*Try not to disturb the asleep children.*~~ ✓ *Try not to disturb the children; they are **asleep**.*

PREDICATIVE POSITION	
beginning with *a*	*ablaze aflame afloat afoot afraid alight alike alive alone aloof ashamed askew asleep awake aware*
health and feelings	*content fine glad ill* pleased poorly ready* sorry* sure* upset* (un)well*

* There are some fixed phrases/idioms in which we use normally predicative adjectives before a noun with a special meaning, e.g. *a sure grasp, ill health, a ready wit, a sorry state, an upset stomach.*

Some predicative adjectives have equivalent words which can be used before a noun:

PREDICATIVE	*alive*	*afraid*	*alike*	*asleep*	*ill*
ATTRIBUTIVE	*live/living*	*frightened*	*similar*	*sleeping*	*sick*

*They are doing experiments on **live** animals/animals which are **alive**.*

3 Adjectives after pronouns, nouns, etc.

Adjectives always come AFTER indefinite pronouns, e.g. *something, anyone* (➤ Unit 5.2):

✗ ~~*I'm looking for cheap something.*~~ ✓ *I'm looking for* ***something cheap****.*

Some adjectives, including many that end in *-able* and *-ible*, can follow a noun after a superlative adjective or after the *first/last/next/only*:

✓ ***The only seat available*** *is in the back row.* ✓ ***The only available seat*** *is in the back row.*

Adjectives that are followed by a prepositional phrase, e.g. *interested in something, suitable for somebody*, go after, not before, a noun:

✗ ~~*The project will appeal to interested in ecology students.*~~

✓ *The project will appeal to* ***students interested in ecology****.*

This is similar to a reduced relative clause (➤ Unit 55.5). We can also use a full relative clause with the adjective in predicative position:

The project will appeal to students ***who are interested in ecology****.*

Some adjectives have a different meaning when used before or after a noun:

The meeting was full of ***concerned residents****.* (= worried)
The ***students concerned*** *were a small minority.* (= who took part/were involved)
I'm afraid we have ***opposite points of view****.* (= contrasting)
We used to live in the ***house opposite****.* (= physically facing/across from us)
The ***present director*** *is American.* (= current/existing now)
We took a vote of all ***members present****.* (= physically there)
Responsible parents *have been outraged by this show.* (= caring/conscientious)
The ***person responsible*** *will be caught and punished.* (= who did the action)
He gave us a ridiculously ***involved excuse****.* (= complicated)
The president gave medals to all ***those involved****.* (= who took part)

4 Verbs acting as adjectives

Participle forms of verbs (usually ending in *-ed* or *-ing*) can often act as adjectives. Some of these can be used on their own before or after a noun:

Please provide me with a list of the ***selected candidates/candidates selected****.*

Some participle forms can only be used AFTER a noun:

✗ ~~*Please dispose of your rubbish in the provided bins.*~~ ✓ *... rubbish in the* ***bins provided****.*

before or after a noun	*affected chosen identified infected remaining selected stolen*
only after a noun	*applying caused discussed found provided questioned taken*

When we use participles as adjectives, present (*-ing*) participles have an active meaning and past participles have a passive meaning:

I always seem to play for the ***losing team****.* (= the team which is losing)
She found the ***lost ring*** *under the sofa.* (= the ring which had been lost)

Participle forms after a noun can be part of a reduced relative clause:

I feel sorry for ***the people left behind****.* (= the people that are left behind)

More on the use of participles in clauses ➤ Unit 55

5 Adjectives acting as nouns

Adjectives can sometimes act as nouns when they describe a particular group or characteristic (➤ Unit 1.5). We usually use the definite article and a plural verb:

Old people are becoming more numerous. = ***The old are*** *becoming more numerous.*

We cannot use the possessive *'s* with adjectives used as nouns or make them plural:

✗ ~~*The government is looking at the disabled's problems.*~~

✓ *The government is looking at the problems of the disabled.*

✗ ~~*The Japaneses enjoy a high standard of living.*~~

✓ *The Japanese* (or *Japanese people*) *enjoy a high standard of living.*

Practice

1 Look at sentence A and B in each pair. Tick (✓) those which are grammatically correct and cross (✗) those which are incorrect. In some cases both sentences are correct.

1	A	Cost is the chief factor.	....	B	The cost factor is chief.	....
2	A	This is the principal argument.	....	B	This argument is principal.	....
3	A	He had an ashamed feeling.	....	B	He felt ashamed.	....
4	A	That's a ridiculous idea.	....	B	That idea is ridiculous.	....
5	A	The village has a local post office.	....	B	The village post office is local.	....
6	A	It was sheer madness.	....	B	The madness was sheer.	....
7	A	You have a ready dinner.	....	B	Your dinner is ready.	....
8	A	He had an alone sensation.	....	B	He sensed he was alone.	....
9	A	We're building an indoor pool.	....	B	The pool we are building is indoor.	....
10	A	You have very alike children.	....	B	Your children are very alike.	....
11	A	That was a silly comment.	....	B	That comment was silly.	....
12	A	She's a mere beginner.	....	B	That beginner is mere.	....
13	A	Those are afraid people.	....	B	Those people are afraid.	....
14	A	We have maximum security here.	....	B	Here the security is maximum.	....
15	A	He's my ill brother.	....	B	My brother is ill.	....

2 GRAMMAR IN USE Choose the correct words in *italics* in this article. If both options are correct, choose both.

AIRPORT MISERY

RESULTS OF a recent survey of international air travellers have revealed huge discrepancies in the levels of (1) *comfort and service provided* / *provided comfort and service* at many leading airports around the world.

A (2) *staggered* / *staggering* 75 percent of those interviewed felt that airports were failing to provide a (3) *relaxed* / *relaxing* and efficient environment. Airports in the UK and the United States came in for particular criticism. Fewer than one in ten people were fully (4) *satisfied* / *satisfying* with the service at leading airports in these countries. Airports in continental Europe received (5) *alike* / *similar* negative feedback. Perhaps the enormous growth in passenger numbers in recent years is the (6) *underlying problem* / *problem which is underlying.*

By contrast, airports in the growing economies of south-east Asia and the Pacific have received far higher satisfaction ratings. Many of the (7) *involved researchers* / *researchers involved* noted that these airports, which are generally more modern than their equivalents in the West, offered (8) *enhanced* / *enhancing* check-in facilities and (9) *pleasant somewhere* / *somewhere pleasant* in which to wait for flights.

With regard to the issues which most annoyed people, the lack of children's facilities and wireless Internet access were two of the (10) *concerns which were main* / *main concerns.* Another was the way in which airports deal with flight delays. The better airports have found ways to cope with this, ranging from television lounges to children's activity areas. (11) *Delayed* / *Delaying* passengers seem to appreciate small details such as comfortable seating and the availability of a wide range of refreshments – anything to relieve the (12) *boredom utter* / *utter boredom* of waiting for a delayed flight. (13) *Affected passengers* / *Passengers affected* were less likely to complain if their children were (14) *amused* / *amusing* and they were able to find inexpensive cafés and restaurants. The airports which came out worse seemed to have (15) *aloof staff* / *staff who were aloof,* with little interest in communicating with passengers.

3 **Indicate the correct position for the words in brackets, as in the example. The word the adjective/phrase describes is underlined. 2.22 Listen and check.**

0 There was nothing *original* in the book. (original)
1 All students should apply to the bursar's office before the end of term. (interested in the grant)
2 There was something about her behaviour. (inexplicable)
3 They gave an explanation which simply served to confuse the jury. (involved)
4 I'm afraid six o'clock is the only appointment. (available)
5 The state of affairs is unlikely to continue for much longer. (present)
6 I'm afraid the person is on holiday at the moment. (responsible for recruitment)
7 They've started having late-night parties in the apartment. (opposite)
8 Anyone would be deeply offended by that harrowing documentary. (sensitive)
9 Don't worry about getting receipts, the amounts are very small. (concerned)
10 Make sure you are wearing shoes before you set out. (suitable for a rocky terrain)

4 GRAMMAR IN USE **Some of the underlined phrases in this article contain mistakes. Find the mistakes and correct them. 2.23 Listen and check.**

NEWS

Home | World | UK | Business | Health | Politics | Education | Entertainment & Arts

More violent crime

Crime is on the rise according to a (1) worried report issued this week by the government's national statistics office.

(2) Concerned citizens are likely to be alarmed by the report's conclusions. Despite promises that the government was tackling serious crime, the report indicates a 6% rise in serious offences over the last year. The largest increase has been in assaults, especially those involving knives or other weapons. The (3) factor main in these crimes appears to be the growth of gangs in our inner cities, and many of the crimes are drug-related.

Burglaries and theft have also increased, although by a smaller percentage. The (4) publishing figures show a 3% growth since last year. Government sources claim that the (5) underlying reason for this increase is the economic situation. An opposition spokesman said there was (6) nothing surprising in the figures. He pointed at (7) causes which are social and blamed the rise in crime on the (8) present government's lack of investment in education and training. The chair of the Police Officers' Association placed responsibility for the situation on the shoulders of the Minister of Justice, the (9) responsible politician for policing. Reductions in police numbers have been a (10) factor which is principal in the growth of crime, he contends.

As usual, it is (11) old and vulnerable who are most likely to be the victims of crime. More than 38% of the (12) victims identified in the report were over the age of 65. It is certainly true that there is a fear of crime amongst the elderly, and lobbying groups are calling for (13) radical something to be done about the problem. They are asking for (14) sentences which are maximum to be given to those criminals that target (15) the elderly or disabled. They feel the (16) involved criminals should be punished more severely than others.

13 Groups of adjectives

In cartoons and movies prisoners are often shown wearing **rough grey and white striped uniforms**. In fact, these days most prisoners wear **blue or grey boiler suits** or overalls.

1 Adjective order

We often use more than one adjective to describe a noun. We put opinion adjectives, e.g. *fantastic, beautiful, useful, charming* before all others:

✗ ~~*I've bought a new fantastic MP3 player.*~~ ✓ *I've bought a* ***fantastic*** *new MP3 player.*

We put the category which is most permanent or important (usually 'type' or 'purpose') next to the noun; these are often part of the noun, e.g. *mobile phone*:

✗ ~~*We removed the gas heating old system.*~~ ✓ *We removed the old* ***gas heating*** *system.*

More on compound nouns ➤ Unit 70.1

If there are other adjectives, we usually put them in this order:

a large well-preserved eighteenth-century farmhouse

size + quality/character + age/shape + colour + origin + material

a square black box *a grey Italian leather sofa*

We don't usually use more than three or four adjectives before a noun. If we want to give more information, we can use additional clauses:

[*Elaine's just bought a beautiful well-preserved eighteenth-century French stone farmhouse.*]

Elaine's just bought ***a beautiful French*** *stone farmhouse* ***which is well-preserved and dates from the eighteenth century****.*

2 Paired adjectives

If two adjectives describe different parts of the same thing, we put *and* between them:

✗ ~~*The chrome steel door glinted in the sun.*~~

✓ *The* ***chrome and steel*** *door glinted in the sun.* (Some parts were chrome, some were steel.)

We always use *and* between two colours:

✗ ~~*They are wearing grey white uniforms.*~~ ✓ *They are wearing* ***grey and white*** *uniforms.*

We can use *and* between two adjectives which describe similar aspects of something:

The protesters are calling for more ***political and economic*** *freedom.*

When two adjectives describe contrasting aspects of the same thing (i.e. it might seem surprising that they go together) we put *but, yet* or *though* between them:

The flat was located in a ***rundown but central*** *part of town.*

Group therapy can be a ***simple yet effective*** *solution to this sort of problem.*

3 Using commas or *and*

When there are several adjectives in predicative position we usually put *and* before the last one: *I'm afraid the hotel was ancient, dirty* ***and*** *overpriced.*

With longer lists of adjectives of the same category before a noun we can use commas and put *and* before the last adjective, or we can simply list the adjectives:

I found him a ***friendly, knowledgeable and dedicated*** *guide.*

I found him a ***friendly, knowledgeable, dedicated*** *guide.*

We don't use *and* before the last adjective when the adjectives are of different categories:

✗ ~~*We enjoyed sitting in the fantastic soft grey and leather seats.*~~

✓ *We enjoyed sitting in the* ***fantastic, soft, grey leather*** *seats.*

Practice

1 Choose the correct words in *italics*. If both options are correct, choose both.

1 The colour scheme for the party is *red orange* / *red and orange*.
2 Dieter had always wanted *an expensive German* / *a German expensive* sports car.
3 The old cottage has *brick and stone* / *brick stone* walls and a charming thatched roof.
4 It was a challenging, *difficult, demanding* / *difficult and demanding* course.
5 We found the hotel to be a welcome *though* / *and* pricey haven from the noise and confusion of the surrounding streets.
6 Many of these *stone large* / *large stone* structures date from the early Bronze Age.
7 We can seat up to ten people at our *oval and mahogany* / *oval mahogany* dining table.
8 I'm fed up with these mindless, *boring and sentimental* / *boring, sentimental* TV talent shows.
9 We will never submit to their outrageous *yet* / *and* unreasonable demands.
10 Nineteenth-century novels tend to be full of *long, detailed* / *long and detailed* descriptive passages.

2 GRAMMAR IN USE Complete the article, using the words in brackets in the correct order. If necessary, add *and* or *yet*. Sometimes more than one answer is possible. 2.24 Listen and check.

Thief caught by text message

The thief of a (0) *priceless Renaissance* (Renaissance / priceless) salt cellar has been caught after a three-year hunt. The (1) .... (encrusted enamel / gold) salt cellar, known as the Saliera, is one of the most (2) .... (beautiful / famous) works of the (3) .... (sixteenth-century / Florentine / celebrated) sculptor, Benvenuto Cellini. The salt cellar, which is worth at least 50 million euros, was stolen from the Kunsthistorisches Museum in Vienna. The theft was (4) .... (simple / daring). In the middle of the night the thief climbed up some scaffolding, walked through an empty gallery and smashed the (5) .... (glass / heavy) display case containing the salt cellar. The alarm went off but the security guards assumed it was faulty and ignored it. It wasn't until four hours later that the cleaners noticed the (6) .... (shattered / glass) display case and raised the alarm.

Some time later the police received a ransom demand of 10 million euros for the return of the (7) .... (priceless / missing) sculpture. In a modern twist on a very traditional crime the thief sent his demand by text message. It was a (8) .... (stupid / fatal) mistake. The police were able to trace the mobile phone which sent the text message and the shop which had sold that particular phone. By an (9) .... (amazing / fortuitous) coincidence the shop had a surveillance camera and still had the tapes from the day on which the phone had been sold. The (10) .... (grainy / distinct) pictures of the man who had bought the phone were broadcast on TV and within days several people had phoned in with a positive identification. The suspect gave himself up to the police and led them to a forest north of Vienna. There they found the (11) .... (complete / undamaged) sculpture hidden in a (12) .... (wooden / small) box.

Detail from the Saliera

14 Comparative and superlative adjectives

1 Form and use

We use comparative adjectives to compare two (or more) things or people, and superlative adjectives to distinguish one thing or person from a number of others.

	COMPARATIVE ADJECTIVES	SUPERLATIVE ADJECTIVES
one syllable* *large*	adjective + *-er* (+ *than*): *Los Angeles is* ***larger*** *(than San Francisco).*	*the* + adjective + *-est*: *The Twin Towers Correctional Facility is* ***the largest*** *prison in the world.*
two or more syllables* *expensive*	*more* + adjective (+ *than*): *Gold is* ***more valuable*** *(than silver).*	*the most* + adjective: *Platinum is* ***the most valuable*** *metal.*
irregular adjectives *good/bad, far, old*	*better/worse, further/farther, older/elder*	*the best/worst, the furthest/farthest, the oldest/eldest*

* For exceptions ➤ 14.3 below

Spelling rules for these forms ➤ page 367

We use *than* to introduce a noun or a clause after a comparative adjective:
Los Angeles is larger ***than San Francisco.*** *Los Angeles is larger* ***than I expected it to be.***

We can use other phrases between a comparative adjective and a *than* clause:
The prisoners were more violent ***in this prison*** *than in the others we visited.*

If the object of the comparison is a pronoun without a verb we usually use an object pronoun (➤ Unit 4.1). If there is a verb we use a subject pronoun:
[*I'm taller than he.*] ✓ *I'm taller than* ***him.*** ✓ *I'm taller than* ***he is.***

When we have two or more adjectives with *more* in a list, we usually only use *more* once:
[*Lester and Graves were more hardworking and more determined than the others.*]
✓ *Lester and Graves were* ***more hardworking and determined*** *than the others.*

 After superlatives we use *in* before singular nouns (i.e. the name of a place or group), but we use *of* before plural nouns:
✗ ~~*The Twin Towers Correctional Facility is the largest prison of the world.*~~
✓ *The Twin Towers Correctional Facility is the largest prison* ***in the world.***
Mallorca is the largest ***of the Balearic islands.***

In formal English we can add an *of* phrase at the beginning of the sentence:
Of *the candidates interviewed, David Slater was the most suitable for the post.*

2 *less* and *least*

We use *less* and *least* as the opposite of *more* and *most*. We use these words with all adjectives including one-syllable adjectives:
I prefer the paisley pattern; it's ***less bold*** *than the others.*
The tuna salad is ***the least expensive*** *dish on the menu.*

FORMALITY CHECK In informal English we usually prefer to use *not as ... as*:
I prefer the paisley pattern; it ***isn't as bold as*** *the others.*

more/most/less/least with nouns ➤ Unit 57.2

3 Special rules

One-syllable adjectives ending in *-ed* and the adjectives *real, right* and *wrong* form the comparative and superlative with *more* and *most* (we do not add *-er* or *-est*):
✗ ~~*I was boreder than I was on the flight to Sydney.*~~
✓ *I was* ***more bored*** *than I was on the flight to Sydney.*

Many two-syllable adjectives ending in *-ly*, *-y*, *-ow*, *-r* and *-l*, and the adjectives *common*, *handsome*, *mature*, *pleasant*, *polite*, *simple* and *stupid* can have either *more/most* or *-er/-est*:
The photographer wanted something ***more lively*** (or ***livelier***).
The staff couldn't have been ***more friendly*** (or ***friendlier***).
Are people in the country ***more polite*** (or ***politer***) *than those in the city?*

When we add a negative prefix to two-syllable adjectives ending in *-y* (e.g. *happy – unhappy*) they can also take *more/most* or *-er* and *-est*:
She was the ***unlikeliest*** *candidate to succeed.* *He's the* ***most unhappy*** *man I've ever met.*

We sometimes omit *the* before superlatives describing titles, award, prizes, etc:
This year's prize for ***most promising*** *newcomer goes to Lizzie Gordon.*

FORMALITY CHECK In informal spoken English we sometimes use a superlative adjective when we are only comparing two things, especially if the two things make a set:
I've got two cars but the Mercedes is the ***best***.

4 Irregular adjectives

We can use *elder* and *eldest* (instead of *older* and *oldest*) to talk about people's ages, especially people in the same family, but we can't use *elder* immediately after a verb:
Their ***eldest/oldest*** *son went to Harvard.* *Mary is* ***the eldest/the oldest***.
✗ ~~*My sister is elder (than me).*~~

Note that we don't use *elder* and *eldest* to talk about the age of things:
✗ ~~*This is the eldest house in the street.*~~

We use *further* or *farther* to talk about a 'greater distance':
John's house is the ***farther*** *one.*
I've moved ***further*** *away from my parents.* (= a greater distance away)

We use *further* (not *farther*) with the meaning of 'extra' or 'more':
Let me know if you have any ***further*** *questions.* (= extra/more)

5 Intensifying and weakening; emphasis

Comparatives and superlatives can be made stronger or weaker by adding the following:

COMPARATIVES		
→ stronger	*even* *(very) much* *far* *a lot* *lots* (informal) *considerably* *significantly* *substantially* *a great deal*	*His new film's* ***even more exciting*** *than the last one.* *The issue of accountability became* ***substantially more important*** *in the weeks before the election.*
→ weaker	*a little* *slightly* *a bit* (informal) *somewhat* (formal)	*The lamb's* ***a bit cheaper*** *than the fish.* *The artist's style is* ***somewhat darker*** *than that of his contemporaries.*

We don't use *a little/a bit* when a noun follows the comparative adjective:
✗ ~~*It's a little higher price than I expected.*~~ ✓ *The price is* ***a little higher*** *than I expected.*

SUPERLATIVES		
→ stronger	*by far* *easily* (informal)	*The Twin Towers Correctional Facility is* ***by far the largest*** *prison in the world.* (much larger than all the others)
→ weaker	*one of* *some of* *among*	*New York is* ***one of the largest*** *cities in the world.* (there may be some larger)

FORMALITY CHECK Most one-syllable adjectives can also form the comparative and superlative with *more* or *most* instead of *-er* or *-est*. We usually use these forms for emphasis in spoken English:
You should be ***more proud*** *of the things you've already achieved.* (= prouder)
I think this is the award she is ***the most proud*** *of.* (= proudest)

Practice

1 **Complete the sentences, using suitable comparative and superlative forms of the adjectives in the box. Add *than* or *the* if necessary, as in the example. 2.25 Listen and check.**

bad bored dry far good keen loose pretty real scared ~~tidy~~ wet wrong

0 Since we've had a cleaner, the house has become a lot ...*tidier than*... it used to be!
1 And now we come to the award for .... actor in a leading role.
2 It's been raining non-stop. I think this will be .... July on record!
3 The authenticity of dialogue and setting often makes low-budget films seem .... the somewhat artificial version of reality in Hollywood movies.
4 In medieval times people rarely travelled far. For most peasants, ... destination would be the local market town.
5 This skirt's much too tight on the hips. I need something with a .... fit.
6 The pianist was awful! I think that's .... performance I've ever heard.
7 I don't mind the Mediterranean summer because it's a .... heat than you find in the tropics.
8 I like all Mozart's operas but I think *Don Giovanni* is the one I am .... on.
9 We've inherited two paintings. Of the two, I'd say the landscape is ....
10 I know all theft is wrong, but don't you agree that it's .... to steal from an individual than from a company?
11 .... I've ever been was when Joe and I were flying over the Himalayas and we hit a storm; it was absolutely petrifying.
12 That play was so tedious. I was .... watching that than I was when I spent three hours trapped in that lift last year!

2 GRAMMAR IN USE **Find and correct ten more mistakes. 2.26 Listen and check.**

KAREN Now we've seen all the candidates, what do you think?
TOBY It's a difficult choice, but I thought Steven was the ~~most strong~~ *strongest* of the three.
KAREN Oh? You couldn't be more wrong! Meera definitely has betterer experience.
TOBY Well of course she does, she's elder than the other two.
KAREN Yes, and she's maturer.
TOBY True. But don't you think she's a bit set in her ways? Would she really fit in here?
KAREN I don't see why not. Let's face it, the other two are very young – significantly more younger than most of our staff.
TOBY That could be a good thing. I mean younger people are adaptabler than older ones.
KAREN OK. What about Ahmed? He was the best qualified in the candidates.
TOBY I'm not sure. He seemed the less promising of the three. He was too laid-back.
KAREN Yes, he was the easily most relaxed – people are usually more nervouser at interviews.
TOBY So we come back to Steven. He was one the most ambitious candidates I've ever interviewed. I thought that was a positive thing ...
KAREN Yes. But he's very distant. Aren't we looking for someone more friendlier and approachable? Let's look at their CVs again.

3 Complete the second sentence so it has a similar meaning to the first. Use three to six words in your answer, including the word in brackets, as in the example.

0 All the other members of the family are younger than Uncle Jacob. (the)
Uncle Jacob ...*is the oldest member*... of the family.

1 I live closer to the bus stop than Ivan does. (away)
Ivan lives .... than me.

2 These apples aren't as tasty as the ones Lizzie bought. (than)
The apples Lizzie bought ....

3 The massacre was among the most despicable episodes in the regiment's history. (one)
The massacre was .... in the regiment's history.

4 The ending of the film wasn't as sentimental as I'd expected. (than)
I'd expected the ending of the film to be .... it was.

5 Mikhail's essay wasn't as bad as the others. (the)
Mikhail's essay ....

6 All the other flights were more expensive than the Easyjet one. (of)
The Easyjet flight .... the flights.

7 That was easily the most ridiculous story I've ever heard. (by)
That was .... I've ever heard.

8 Of the two sisters, Sophie and Caroline, Sophie is the elder. (than)
Sophie is .... sister Caroline.

4 GRAMMAR IN USE Study the charts; then complete the description, using the prompts in brackets. If you see <, use a suitable modifying word or phrase, e.g. *considerably*, *among* etc. as in the example.

Number of prisoners worldwide
(total 9.25 million)

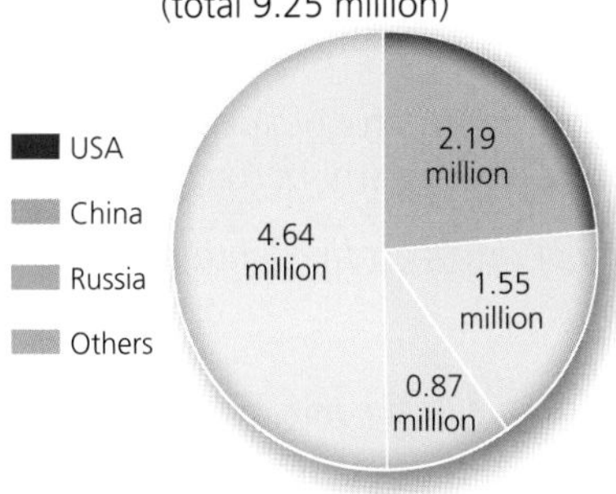

Prisoners as proportion of population
(Per 100,000 of national population)

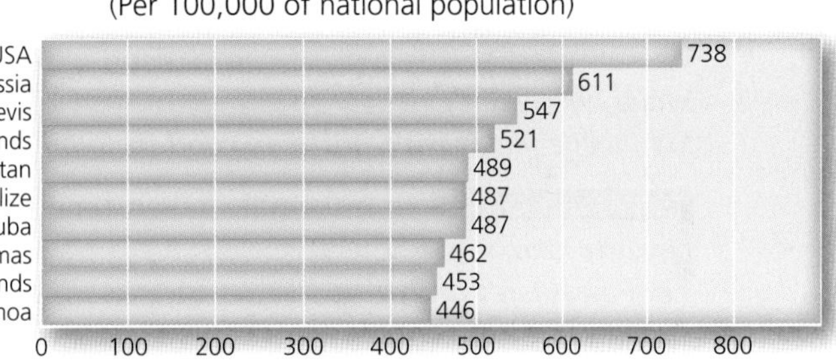

From *World Prison Population List* (seventh edition), Kings College London International Centre for Prison Studies

0 The USA has *by far the highest number of prisoners*. (< / high / number / prisoners)

1 The USA has ....
(< / large / numbers of prisoners / any other country)

2 It also has ....
of the national population. (high / number / prisoners / as a proportion)

3 .... American Samoa has (countries / the chart)
.... per 100,000 population. (low / number of prisoners)

4 China has ....
(< / great / number of prisoners / Russia).

5 St Kitts and Nevis and the US Virgin Islands are small states, but they have
....
(< / high / proportion of prisoners per population / apart from the USA and Russia).

15 Other comparative patterns

Bonnie Parker and Clyde Barrow are the most famous bank robbers in American history. In the early 1930s they carried out a string of robberies in the American mid-West. Although **they looked like an innocent young couple,** they were ruthless criminals. As they travelled, they became **more and more daring,** killing at least nine police officers. They were eventually shot dead by police in 1934. Their story was made into a film in 1967.

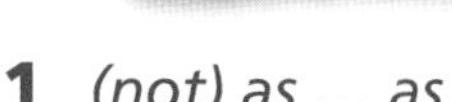

1 *(not) as ... as*

We can say that two things are equal by using *as* + adjective + *as*:
*The Spanish omelette is **as expensive as** the chicken salad. They both cost €7.99.*

We make this comparison more emphatic with *just*:
*In the American legal system, juries are **just as important as** in the UK.*

To say that things are almost equal we use *just about, about, almost, more or less* or *nearly* + *as*:
*Let's not eat here. This café's **just about as bad as** the last one.*
*My niece is **nearly as old as** me!*

We make a negative comparison with *not as/so* + adjective + *as*:
*Warsaw is**n't as large as** London.* (= London is larger.)

We can modify this type of comparison with *nearly* or *quite*:
*Motor bikes are**n't nearly so expensive as** cars.* (= Motor bikes are much cheaper.)
*My mobile phone is**n't quite as good as** Sunil's.* (= Sunil's phone is slightly better.)

FORMALITY CHECK In informal spoken English we can use *not anything like, nothing like* or *nowhere near* + *as* + adjective:
*That dress is**n't anything like as nice as** the red one.*
*This outfit's **nothing like/nowhere near as fashionable as** the one in the magazine.*

similar to, different than/from/to ➤ pages 370–1

2 *no/not any* + comparative adjective

We can use comparative adjectives to say that two things are equal.
We use *is* + *no* + comparative adjective or *is not* + *any* + comparative adjective:
*That Nokia phone **is no more expensive than/no dearer than** the Samsung.*
(= They are the same price.)
*The Nokia **isn't any cheaper than/isn't any less expensive than** the Samsung.*
(= They are the same price.)

3 Progressive comparison

We can describe how something increases or decreases in intensity by repeating *more* or the same comparative adjective, with *and* between the forms:
*As they travelled, Bonnie and Clyde became **more and more daring**.*
*Her visits to the country to see her son became **rarer and rarer**.*

4 Combined comparison

To describe how a change in one thing causes a change in another, we can use two comparative forms with *the*. Note the use of the comma after the first clause:
***The longer** you leave it, **the worse** it'll get.*

We sometimes omit the verb *be* in the clauses:
***The more sophisticated** the product, **the more substantial** the potential profit.*

5 Contrastive comparison

When we contrast two related qualities, we always use *more* (not *-er*):
✗ ~~*I'm sadder than disappointed.*~~ ✓ *I'm **more** sad than disappointed.*
✓ *Her eyes are **more** green than grey.*

We can also use *not so much ... as* or *rather than*:
*I'm **not so much** disappointed **as** sad. Her eyes are green **rather than** grey.*

6 *like* and *as*; similes and metaphors

We often describe something by comparing it to something else which has similar qualities. These comparisons are known as 'similes'. There are two forms:

- *as* + adjective + *as*: *Listening to her was **as interesting as** watching paint dry.* (In informal English we sometimes omit the first *as*: *She looks white as a sheet.*)
- *like* + noun or verb phrase: *The cruise ship was **like a skyscraper lying on its side**.*

There are many idioms in which we use these two patterns:
*You're **as white as a sheet**; I think you'd better see a doctor.*
*I feel full of energy today – I **slept like a log** last night.*

⚠ We use *like* (not *as*) before a noun to compare two things which SEEM similar:
✗ ~~*Although they looked as an innocent young couple, they were ruthless criminals.*~~
✓ *Although they looked **like** an innocent young couple, they were ruthless criminals.* (They appeared to be innocent, but they weren't.)
*When Mike puts on his dark suit he **looks like** a waiter.* (= He resembles a waiter.)
*Sometimes my boss **acts like** a dictator.* (= He behaves in a similar way to a dictator.)
*This fabric is so soft it **feels like** silk.* (= similar to silk)

⚠ We use *as* (not *like*) before a noun when we are describing someone's actual job, role or identity, or something's function:
✗ ~~*Simon's working like a waiter during the summer vacation.*~~
✓ *Simon's working **as a waiter** during the summer vacation.* (This is his job.)
*Use your payroll number **as a password** for the computer.* (This is its function.)
*Jude Law appeared **as Hamlet** in a recent production of the play.* (This was his role.)
*The SAT tests are used **as an entry test** by many American universities.* (This is their function.)

We can also describe something by comparing it with something similar without using *like* or *as*; this is known as a 'metaphor':
*The new treaty will form **a bridge** between our two nations.* (*a bridge* = metaphor for 'a link')

Metaphors are common in poetry and literary English:
*I fall upon **the thorns of life**! I bleed!* (*thorns of life* = bad experiences)

7 *as* and *such*

We can use *as* and *not such* to introduce a comparison with nouns. There are two patterns:

- *as* + adjective + *a* + noun + *as*:
  *It wasn't **as bad a result as** I'd expected.* (= better than expected)
- *not such a* + adjective + noun + *as*:
  *It was**n't such a bad result as** I'd expected.*

so dark/such a dark night that ... not light enough to, etc. ➤ Unit 59.4

Practice

1 Choose the best explanation, A or B.

1 The prices on the menu aren't nearly as expensive as I expected.
A Prices are a little cheaper than I expected.
B Prices are much cheaper than I expected.
2 It looks as if your new car isn't any more reliable than the old one!
A Both cars are equally unreliable.
B The new car is slightly less reliable than the old one.
3 I have to say that the hotel wasn't quite as luxurious as the brochure claimed.
A The hotel was much less luxurious than the brochure claimed.
B The hotel was slightly less luxurious than the brochure claimed.
4 She isn't anything like as snobbish as you said.
A She is less snobbish than you said.
B She isn't snobbish.
5 I'm afraid your figures are no more accurate than the ones Rachel gave me.
A Your figures are less accurate than Rachel's.
B Your figures and Rachel's figures are equally inaccurate.
6 As far as Daniel's job is concerned, things are about as bad as they can be.
A Daniel's job could get worse.
B Daniel's job couldn't be any worse than it is.
7 Carol's nowhere near as efficient as my last assistant, Becky.
A Carol is slightly less efficient than Becky.
B Carol is much less efficient than Becky.
8 In his new job, Gerhard is working like a slave!
A Gerhard is an actor in a film about ancient Rome.
B Gerhard has to work very hard.

2 Choose the correct words in *italics*. 2.27 Listen and check.

1 My exam results were *nearly not / not nearly* as good as Carmen's.
2 When Lucy gets dressed up she looks *as / like* a movie star.
3 It wasn't as exciting *film / a film* as his earlier ones.
4 Are you feeling OK? You're as *white as / whiter than* a sheet!
5 My new house is nothing *as / like as* big as my previous place.
6 Mobile phones seem to be getting *smaller and smaller / more small and more small.*
7 It's an unusual colour, *redder / more red* than pink.
8 When he was younger, my uncle worked *like / as* a porter in the local hospital.
9 It wasn't *such / so* a surprising piece of news as we'd expected.
10 The higher you climb, *the further than / the further* you have to fall.
11 When George tried to sing it was *like / as* a cat screeching!
12 This sweater isn't as *darker / dark* a colour as I'd wanted – can I exchange it?
13 The furnishings in the hotel rooms are comfortable rather *as / than* luxurious.
14 Carly is *nowhere / nothing* near as tolerant as her younger sister.
15 It wasn't as *easier / easy* a victory as everyone had expected.
16 As we approached the city, the roads became more *and / than* more crowded.
17 The further out you swim, *the colder / the more cold* the water gets.
18 Is it OK to use my date of birth *as / like* my PIN number?
19 I'm not as dedicated a fan of the band *than / as* I was when I was younger.
20 My bed is really comfortable, I slept *as / like* a log last night!

3 GRAMMAR IN USE **Complete the text by writing one word only in each gap.**
2.28 Listen and check.

Teenage girls cause mayhem in California street races

FOR YEARS illegal street races have been the scourge of Los Angeles. Weaving through the busy city streets in souped-up cars, amateur drivers race to win prizes of up to $3,000. Crashes and fatalities are commonplace and the police seem unable to stop the menace because (1) .... faster they chase the criminals, the (2) .... they drive, causing even more damage. The drivers call these races 'cutting up' contests and their aim is to drive (3) .... fast as possible through crowded streets, overtaking and 'cutting up' ordinary drivers. The criminals use special cars – they look (4) .... ordinary family cars to the naked eye, but in fact they have been fitted with fuel boosters. Although (5) .... nearly as powerful (6) .... professional racing cars, these vehicles can still reach high speeds and be extremely dangerous.

Ten years ago about ten people a year were killed in street races in the Los Angeles area. Now the figure is more than a hundred. As street races have grown more and (7) .... dangerous, the police have been forced to take stronger action. The crackdown has resulted in a surprising discovery – most of the racers are teenage girls rather than teenage boys, and some are as young (8) .... sixteen. But to many members of the public this isn't (9) .... a surprising revelation. Especially as many of these girls seem to be from the Asian community, perhaps modelling themselves on Nadine Toyoda, a Scottish-Japanese former street racer who has changed her ways and now works (10) .... a legitimate racing driver.

Psychologists have blamed the crime wave on the influence of computer games, many of which feature street races. Teenagers want to be (11) .... the drivers in these games. But driving in a game is fictional (12) .... than real. When you crash a car in a computer game you simply start again. In real life the consequences are rather more serious.

4 Complete the second sentence so it has a similar meaning to the first. Use the word(s) in brackets, as in the example.

0 As students get closer to their exams they become more nervous. (the more)
The closer students *get to their exams, the more nervous they become.*

1 Their summer party wasn't anything like as good as their previous one. (nothing)
Their summer party .... their previous one.

2 My test score wasn't as bad as I'd feared. (such)
It wasn't .... I'd feared.

3 I'm bored rather than tired. (not so much)
I'm ....

4 My friends claimed that the film was interesting but I found it pretty dull. (film)
It wasn't as ....

5 If you keep picking that spot it will get worse. (the more)
.... it will get.

6 She's slightly angry but she's very disappointed. (than)
She's ....

7 We noticed the sound of the police siren becoming increasingly loud. (and)
We noticed the sound of the police siren ....

8 As dogs get older they become less aggressive. (the less)
The older dogs ....

16 Gradable and ungradable adjectives

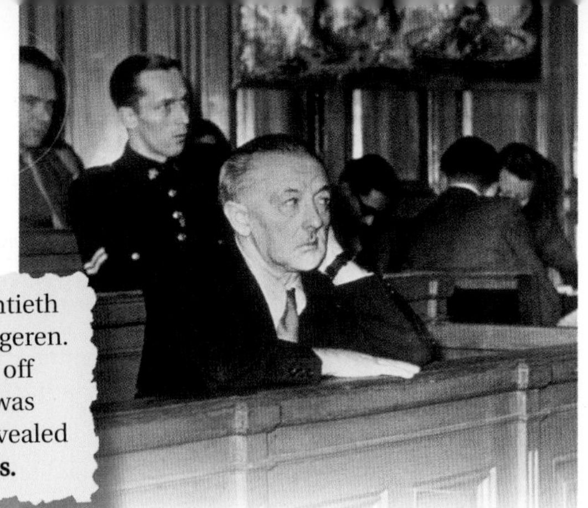

THE MOST FAMOUS art forger of the twentieth century was the Dutch artist Han Van Meegeren. He created several works which he passed off as **priceless** masterpieces by Vermeer. He was exposed in 1947 and his paintings were revealed as fakes and therefore **absolutely worthless.**

1 Gradable and ungradable adjectives

Gradable adjectives represent a point on a scale. For example, *cheap* and *expensive* are adjectives on the scale of 'how much something costs'.

Ungradable adjectives represent the limits of a scale. For example, *free* (= it costs nothing) and *priceless* (= its cost is too great to be counted) are the limits on the scale of 'how much something costs'.

ungradable adjectives	*free*	*freezing*	*vast/enormous*
gradable adjectives	*(very cheap)* *cheap* *(not very cheap)* *(a bit expensive)* *expensive* *(very expensive)*	*cold* *cool* *tepid* *hot*	*large/big* *small*
ungradable adjectives	*priceless*	*boiling*	*minute/tiny*

Most English adjectives are gradable. We can make comparative and superlative forms from all gradable adjectives (➤ Unit 14). We don't usually make comparisons with ungradable adjectives, although there are some patterns we use in spoken English:

*That was **the most delicious** meal! Her house is **even more enormous** than his!*

Some adjectives can have both gradable and ungradable meanings, depending on whether the speaker is describing an absolute quality or one which is relative to something else:

*I'm afraid there are no rooms – the hotel is **full**.* (ungradable = completely full)

*The hotel's very **full** but I think I can get you a single room for tonight.*

(gradable = has many guests but there is still some space)

Other adjectives like this are: *empty, beautiful, black, delicious, new, possible.*

2 Intensifying gradable adjectives

We can make gradable adjectives stronger with *very*, but not with the adverb *absolutely*:

✗ ~~*That new jacket looks absolutely expensive.*~~ ✓ *That new jacket looks **very expensive**.*

There are other words we use to strengthen the meaning of these adjectives:

extremely most (formal) *pretty* (informal) *rather really so terribly*

*Last night's match was **terribly exciting**. I felt **pretty upset** after the accident.* (informal)

*The chapter on the early sonnets was **most instructive**.* (formal)

We usually use *rather* with negative adjectives or when describing something unexpected:

*There was a **rather unpleasant** smell in the flat. Surprisingly, the film was **rather good**.*

More examples in spoken English ➤ Unit 81.1

We often use less common adverbs to intensify certain gradable adjectives:
*I was **bitterly disappointed** at my exam results. My brother is **painfully shy**.*
*The students in this school are **highly intelligent**.*

But note that we can often only use certain adverbs with certain adjectives.

Common adverb + adjective collocations ➤ page 369

3 Weakening gradable adjectives

Gradable adjectives can usually be made weaker by the words *fairly, slightly, a (little) bit* (informal) and *somewhat* (formal):
*I've been feeling **slightly dizzy** all morning.*
*My friend was **a bit upset**.* (informal)
*The police reported that the man was **somewhat aggressive**.* (formal)

We can use *not very* and *not at all* to weaken gradable adjectives after the verb *be*:
*The end of term test **wasn't very long** and it **wasn't at all difficult**.*

With gradable adjectives *quite* usually means 'fairly' but can have other meanings, depending on stress and intonation:
The lecture was quite interesting. (unmarked: fairly interesting)
The lecture was quite <u>interesting</u>. (stressed adjective: more interesting than the speaker expected)
The lecture was <u>quite</u> interesting. (stressed adverb: less interesting than the speaker expected)

Pronunciation ➤ 1.04

4 Intensifying ungradable adjectives

A common way to intensify the meaning of ungradable adjectives is with the adverb *absolutely*. We often use this device to add emphasis in informal English:
*I couldn't swim in the sea; the water was **absolutely freezing**.*
*The show was **absolutely fabulous**.*

We do not usually use *very* with ungradable adjectives:
✗ ~~*Entrance to the museum is very free.*~~ ✓ *Entrance to the museum is **absolutely free**.*

When we use *quite* with ungradable adjectives, it has a similar meaning to 'completely', emphasising the strength of the adjective. In speech the stress is usually on *quite*:
*The tenor's performance was **quite amazing**. You're **quite correct**.*

We can also use *a most* before an ungradable adjective + noun:
*Hilary has **a most amazing** hairstyle.* (= Her hairstyle is completely amazing.)

Although we use *absolutely* with many ungradable adjectives, there are some adjectives where we prefer to use other intensifying adverbs such as *completely, totally* and *utterly*. There are no grammar rules which explain these combinations so it is best to learn them as vocabulary items (➤ page 369).
*I'm afraid your answer is **completely wrong**.*
*Since the accident Henry has been **totally deaf** in one ear.*
*Susan was **utterly appalled** by her husband's dishonesty.*

5 Weakening ungradable adjectives (*almost, nearly*, etc.)

We use *almost, nearly, practically* or *virtually* to indicate a point close to the absolute meaning of ungradable adjectives:
*He never turns the heating on – it's **practically freezing** in there.*
*The battery in my calculator is **almost dead**.*
*After six months with the disease he was **nearly deaf** and **virtually blind**.*

We do not usually use the modifiers *fairly, slightly, a (little) bit, somewhat* or *not very* with ungradable adjectives:
✗ ~~*Their favourite possession is a slightly priceless Satsuma vase.*~~
✗ ~~*I wouldn't recommend the show; it's not very fabulous.*~~

Practice

To complete these exercises you will need to refer to page 369.

1 Put each adjective into the correct box below. Each box will contain ten adjectives.

amazing attractive cold correct dead enormous exciting expensive extinct fascinating freezing good huge interesting large minute paralysed shy sick ugly

ungradable adjectives	gradable adjectives

2 Use the words in the box below to make the adjectives in each sentence either stronger or weaker, as in the example. Use each word once only. 2.29 Listen and check.

a bit absolutely fabulously fairly highly ~~slightly~~ somewhat very virtually

Make these sentences weaker:

0 The dress I bought yesterday is damaged. *slightly damaged*
1 These days mobile phones are inexpensive. ....
2 Take care when you change gear; the gearstick's stiff. ....
3 The inscription on the tomb was indecipherable. ....
4 Many of the Inca ceremonies were bloodthirsty. ....

Make these sentences stronger:

5 Jane's flat was freezing last night. ....
6 This new computer game sounds interesting. ....
7 Hilary's husband is rich. ....
8 Victory in our next game seems unlikely. ....

3 Six of these sentences contain mistakes. Tick (✓) the correct sentences, then find the mistakes and correct them.

1 We thought the state rooms in the White House were very impressive!
2 I'm afraid there's nothing to eat; the fridge is very empty.
3 The tour bus is completely full so I've only got six seats left to offer you.
4 Come on, Lizzie. Let's get some of those Italian ice creams – I'm very famished.
5 We chose the hotel because it was very recommended by our neighbours.
6 If you were really serious about your studies, you would have given up that evening job.
7 Everyone in our class likes Jackie – she's pretty friendly.
8 Jack was a very built man with massive shoulders and a menacing stare.
9 I found the funeral ceremony absolutely moving.
10 The Ambassador would be highly delighted to accept this honour on behalf of the President.

4 GRAMMAR IN USE **Read the article and decide which word, A, B or C below, best fits each gap, as in the example. 2.30 Listen and check.**

Fakes found in major museums

OSCAR WHITE MUSCARELLA, a (0) ..... respected archeologist at New York's Metropolitan Museum, claims that more than 1,250 forgeries are on display in the world's leading museums and art galleries. In his latest book Muscarella specifically names 37 forgeries in the Louvre, 16 in the British Museum and 45 in his own museum in New York.

Muscarella's earlier claims have been heavily (1) ..... by some museum officials who are (2) ..... opposed to his arguments. But he has (3) ..... good scientific evidence for his claims, showing that over 40 percent of the objects examined by the Oxford thermoluminescence laboratory are fakes.

The reason for the quantity of forgeries is (4) ..... simple. Because many of the objects in our museums were found by amateurs and illegally exported from their countries of origin they have no official provenance or documented history. Museums are painfully (5) ..... of this embarrassing problem and as a result they have been known to overlook the lack of written records before accepting or buying antiquities.

This practice makes it (6) ..... impossible to detect forgeries, especially if they are accurate copies. But in fact many forgeries are (7) ..... obvious as they are often copied from a photograph which only shows the front of an object. When examining the back of the forgery they can look (8) ..... different from the original. But museum officials tend to be (9) ..... conservative and hate to question objects which have been sitting in their collections for many years.

Muscarella specialises in the ancient Middle East, and this is the area of archaeology in which he has found so many forgeries. But his research has had the effect of undermining the reputation of some of our most (10) ..... regarded institutions, and this should be of concern to anyone who values our cultural heritage.

0 A absolutely (B) highly C very
1 A discussed B rejected C criticised
2 A bitterly B highly C rather
3 A perfectly B absolutely C somewhat
4 A virtually B quite C a bit
5 A conscious B understanding C aware
6 A very B virtually C pretty
7 A a bit B entirely C deeply
8 A completely B absolutely C almost
9 A heavily B utterly C deeply
10 A very B highly C absolutely

17 Adverb form and use

1 Confusing forms

Some adverbs have the same form as adjectives:
close, dead (informal), *fast, fine, long, low, pretty* (informal), *short, straight, wide, wrong*

Some adverbs are formed by adding *-ward/s* or *-wise* to a noun or preposition:
home → *homeward* *after* → *afterwards* *price* → *pricewise* *health* → *healthwise*

SOME BASE ADVERBS WITH DIFFERENT MEANINGS	
close (= not far away) *closely* (= very carefully)	*He lives* ***close*** *to me.* *We watched them* ***closely****.*
direct (= without stopping) *directly* (= exactly/precisely)	*We flew* ***direct*** *from La Guardia to Houston.* *The taxi waited* ***directly*** *opposite the house.*
late (= not on time/not early) *lately* (= recently)	*The plane arrived* ***late*** *due to bad weather.* *She's been rather ill* ***lately****.*
high (= to a great height) *highly* (= extremely)	*He lifted it* ***high*** *over his head.* *Arsenic is* ***highly*** *toxic.*
hard (= with a lot of effort/severely) *hardly* (= scarcely, almost not)	*He braked* ***hard*** *when he saw the cat.* *We* ***hardly*** *know our neighbours.*
right (= direction/correctly) *rightly* (= correctly in my opinion)	*Turn* ***right*** *at the crossroads. Try to do it* ***right*** *this time!* *The tribunal* ***rightly*** *condemned the war criminals.*
free (= without paying) *freely* (= without limitation or control)	*We got into the concert* ***free****!* *Sheep roam* ***freely*** *over the hills.*
deep (= to a great depth/distance) *deeply* (= thoroughly/extremely)	*We travelled* ***deep*** *into the jungle.* *I'm* ***deeply*** *ashamed of my behaviour.*

There are a few adjectives which look like adverbs, e.g. *friendly, lonely, cowardly*.
We cannot make these adjectives into adverbs in the usual way:
✗ ~~*He left cowardlily, sneaking out the back door.*~~ ✓ *He left* ***in a cowardly way/manner*** *...*

Adjectives as adverbs in spoken English ➤ Unit 81.2 American English ➤ page 368

2 Adding information; modifying

We use adverbs to add information about the time, manner or place of an action or state:

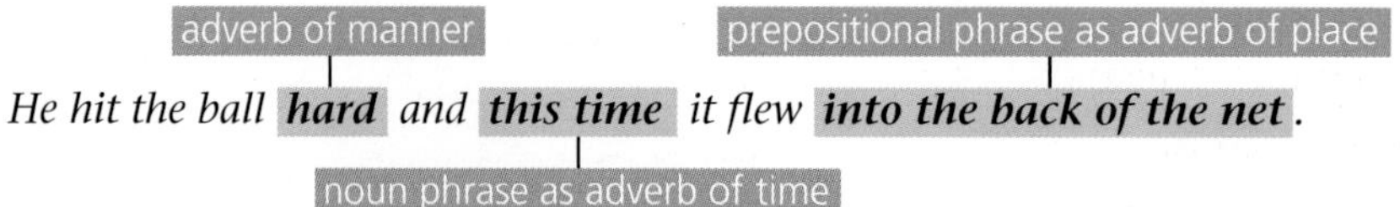

Certain adverbs, e.g. *quite (a), roughly, rather (a), about, approximately,* can be used to modify noun phrases, prepositional phrases and numbers: *Her news came as* ***quite a shock****.*
In our college ***roughly fifty students*** *have motorbikes. She made* ***rather a fuss*** *about the results.*

More on *rather* and *quite* ➤ Unit 16.2/4

We can use adverbs with *as, so, too, enough*, etc:
She performed ***so enthusiastically*** *that the judges overlooked her inexperience.*
We missed the bargains because we didn't get to the shops ***soon enough****.*

3 Using adverbs in comparisons

We can use adverbs in comparatives and superlatives, usually with *more* and *most*:
This car seems to need servicing ***more frequently*** *than our old one.*
Of all the relatives at Gran's funeral, I think Uncle Ralph felt her loss ***most deeply****.*

Adverbs which do not end in *-ly* take the same comparative and superlative forms as adjectives (➤ Unit 14):
If you tuned the engine ***more often*** *the car would go* ***faster****. Do* ***the best*** *you can.*

Practice

1 GRAMMAR IN USE **Choose the correct words in *italics*. 2.31 Listen and check.**

Prison or holiday camp?

IN A RECENT (1) *high / highly* contentious move the Prison Service has announced a decision to build three more open prisons and to close two existing 'closed' prisons. The Service says the move is prompted by the increasing numbers of low-risk prisoners. Critics are (2) *right / rightly* concerned about this move and believe it is (3) *serious / seriously* flawed. They argue the decision is a cynical cost-cutting measure which may put the public at risk.

At present open prisons are restricted to prisoners who have committed non-violent crimes and to those who are getting (4) *close / closely* to the end of their prison term. (5) *Rough / Roughly* 20% of prisoners are held in these facilities at the current time. Many open prisons are more like country hotels; prisoners can wander (6) *free / freely* around the grounds and there are no high walls or barbed wire fences. Inmates can (7) *easy / easily* walk out into the surrounding areas. And as most are positioned (8) *deep / deeply* in the countryside it would be (9) *easy / easily* for absconding offenders to disappear with little hope of recapture.

Critics of open prisons say that they do not provide the deterrent effect of traditional prisons in which prisoners have to work (10) *hard / hardly* and have few luxuries. The problem for the prison authorities is that traditional jails are (11) *high / highly* expensive to run and offer few opportunities for the rehabilitation and re-education of offenders. In open prisons offenders have the chance to experience something closer to everyday life, and this helps to prepare them for their eventual release. Whoever is (12) *right / rightly*, the public is bound to be concerned about this new development in prison policy.

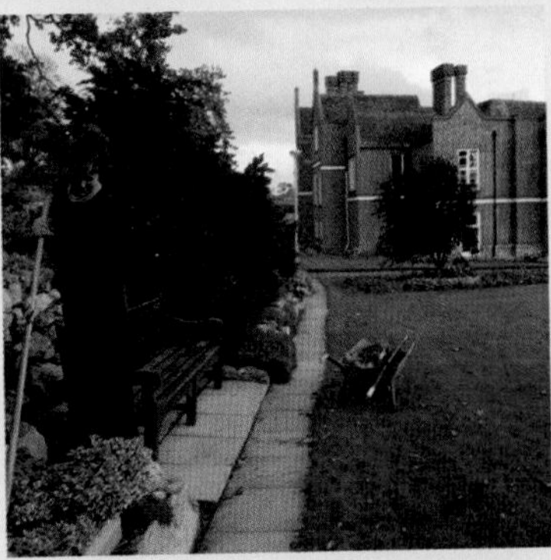

A female prisoner does the gardening, East Sutton Open Prison

2 **Complete the second sentence so it has a similar meaning to the first. Use three or four words, including the word in brackets, as in the example.**

0 Karen did really well in the test. (highly)
Karen ......*was highly successful*......... in the test.

1 The car started to accelerate as we turned the corner. (go)
As we turned the corner, the car ....

2 She really didn't expect to inherit so much money. (quite)
Inheriting so much money came .... surprise.

3 Evolution is slower during periods of climatic stability. (happens)
Evolution .... during periods of climatic stability.

4 We didn't get there in time to hear the overture. (soon)
We wanted to hear the overture but we didn't get ....

5 More or less three-quarters of our students are fee-paying these days. (roughly)
These days .... our students pay fees.

6 In the USA only a few people have heard of our products. (entirely)
Our products are .... in the USA.

7 Melinda's attempt to repair the torn curtain wasn't very successful. (rather)
Melinda's attempt at curtain repair .... failure.

8 Mr Skidmore had a deeper involvement than any of the other directors. (most)
Of all the directors, Mr Skidmore was ....

18 Adverb position

The thief entered the room **silently** and **carefully** opened the safe door.

1 The three positions

Adverbs which modify a verb or add information about how, when or where something happens can take several positions in a sentence:

front position (before subject) — end position (after object or complement)

These days *I* ***probably*** *take my health* ***much more seriously***.

mid position (next to verb)

If the object or complement of a verb is very long, we can put an end-position adverb before it:
These days I take ***much more seriously*** *all those things I used to take for granted.*

2 Front position

We usually put time and place adverbs at the end of the sentence, e.g. *I worked more than twelve hours* ***yesterday***, but we can put them at the front to form a link or contrast with information in the previous sentence:
I've been incredibly busy this week. ***Yesterday*** *I worked more than twelve hours.*

After negative adverbs (e.g. *never*), or after adverbs of time and place followed by a verb of movement or position, we can put the verb before the subject. We usually only do this in formal written English:
Never *had he seen such a disturbing sight.* ***Here*** *lies the body of our late sovereign.*

Inversion ➤ Unit 76.2/3

 We do not use adverbs of definite frequency, e.g. *daily, weekly*, in front position:
✗ ~~*Monthly I get paid.*~~ ✓ *I get paid* ***monthly***.

3 Mid position

This is the usual position for the following adverbs, and for *even* and *only*.

adverbs of indefinite frequency	*always frequently generally hardly ever never normally occasionally often rarely seldom sometimes usually*
adverbs of degree	*absolutely almost completely entirely just hardly partly quite rather really slightly totally*
adverbs of certainty	*certainly definitely probably*
most short adverbs of time	*already finally immediately no longer soon still then* (but not *today, yesterday, tomorrow*, etc.)

 With the present and past simple we put the adverb between the subject and the verb, but with simple forms of *be* the adverb goes after the verb:
✗ ~~*She arrives always by taxi and she always is on time.*~~
✓ *She* ***always arrives*** *by taxi and she* ***is always*** *on time.*

If there is a modal or auxiliary verb we put the adverb after the (first) auxiliary (+ *not*):
*We****'ve never*** *been to the Greek islands. You* ***can just*** *see the coast.*
Sea eagles ***have occasionally*** *been seen around Loch Lomond.*
They ***don't really*** *understand my point of view.*

 We put *sometimes, still, certainly, definitely* and *probably* BEFORE a negative auxiliary:
✗ ~~*I don't sometimes understand his arguments. He hasn't still convinced me.*~~
✓ *I* ***sometimes don't*** *understand his arguments. He* ***still hasn't*** *convinced me.*

FORMALITY CHECK In spoken British English, if we want to emphasise an auxiliary verb or a simple form of *be*, we can put some mid-position adverbs before it. The auxiliary/verb is usually stressed:
*'But I thought you liked him!' 'Oh, you **really** don't understand me at all!'*
*'Joe's late. That's strange' 'Not really, he **never** is on time!'*

Compare:
I don't really like him. (unmarked: I slightly dislike him.)
I really don't like him. (emphatic: I strongly dislike him.)

We do not use other time adverbs (definite time or frequency) in mid position:
✗ ~~*We yesterday bought our lunch at Joe's sandwich bar.*~~ ✗ ~~*I once a month pay my rent.*~~

But we can do this in news reports:
*The Federal Reserve **today announced** an immediate rise in interest rates.*

4 End position

This is the most frequent position for adverbs. It is the usual position for *yet, a lot, any more, any longer, too, as well*:
✗ ~~*They aren't any more selling it.*~~ ✓ *They aren't selling it **any more**.*

We usually put adverbs of manner (which describe how something is done) and adverbs of definite frequency in this position:
✗ ~~*He well plays the guitar.*~~ ✓ *He plays the guitar **well**.* ✓ *The magazine is published **monthly**.*

Adverbs of manner which end in *-ly* (except *badly*) can go in end or mid position:
*Harry **painstakingly** counted out the coins and arranged them **neatly** into piles.*
*The thief entered the room **silently** and **carefully** opened the safe door.*

We don't use *hardly ever* or *never* in end position:
✗ ~~*They watch television hardly ever.*~~ ✓ *They **hardly ever** watch television.*

If we put *often, rarely* and *seldom* in end position, we use a modifier, e.g. *very, extremely*:
✗ ~~*These days I eat desserts rarely.*~~ ✓ *These days I eat desserts **very rarely**.*

We usually avoid having too many adverbs in end position, but when this occurs we often follow this sequence:

1 manner — 2 place — 3 time

*The statue was lifted **carefully** **onto the platform** **before the ceremony**.*

5 Sentence adverbs

Sentence adverbs refer to the whole sentence, not just part of it. We usually put these adverbs at the beginning of a sentence, separated by a comma:
***Economically**, the current government has been a resounding success.*
(= The government has successfully managed the economy.)
***Generally**, the employer pays for travel expenses.* (= This is true in most cases.)

Comment adverbs are sentence adverbs such as *admittedly, frankly, indeed, understandably,* which we use to express our attitude towards the information in a statement:
***Admittedly**, these results are only preliminary.* (= This may contradict previous information.)

Pronunciation ➤ 1.05

Use of these adverbs in writing ➤ Unit 78.4, in speech ➤ Unit 81.3
Other linking adverbs, e.g. *additionally, however, therefore* ➤ Unit 61

Some adverbs, e.g. *naturally* and *clearly*, can be used as sentence adverbs and also as adverbs of manner. Note the different meanings:
*Despite being in a zoo, the animals behaved quite **naturally**.* (= in a natural way)
***Naturally**, wild animals behave quite differently in captivity.* (= of course)
*The teacher answered the question **clearly** and precisely.* (= in a clear way)
***Clearly**, the teacher didn't answer the question.* (= This is obvious.)

Practice

1 Tick (✓) all those adverbs which can complete the sentences and cross (✗) those that cannot, as in the example. In one case, none of the adverbs will fit.

0 The bank robbers ..... opened the door to the secret compartment.
A slowly ...✓... B last week ...✗... C probably ...✓...
1 We don't ..... know the identity of the masked gunman.
A still .... B really .... C certainly ....
2 You can ..... see the coast from this point.
A definitely .... B just .... C as well ....
3 Our next door neighbours go there ......
A as well .... B hardly ever .... C a lot ....
4 ..... the boss gives me a hard time.
A Every day .... B Daily .... C Sometimes ....
5 I get the feeling you haven't ..... understood my point.
A entirely .... B really .... C probably ....
6 The public don't ..... respond in the ways advertisers expect them to.
A sometimes .... B immediately .... C always ....
7 I haven't been to the cinema ......
A yet .... B often .... C very often ....
8 Signs of radiation leakage have been ..... reported at the power station.
A often .... B this week .... C always ....
9 ..... have our clients been subjected to such outrageous demands.
A Never .... B Rarely .... C Admittedly ....
10 I'm afraid the bank does not ..... permit such large overdrafts.
A generally .... B any longer .... C any more ....
11 The patient ..... reacts to any kind of bright light.
A badly .... B immediately .... C usually ....
12 He plays the saxophone ......
A too .... B quite rarely .... C never ....
13 The data from those sensors isn't ..... reliable.
A absolutely .... B sometimes .... C always ....
14 The last contestant stood up and sang the song ......
A beautifully .... B well .... C badly ....

2 Rewrite these sentences, using the words and phrases in brackets in the best order, as in the example. Note that none of these sentences is emphatic. 2.32 Listen and check.

0 My parents (allowed/hardly ever) us to (late/on weekdays/stay up).
My parents hardly ever allowed us to stay up late on weekdays.
1 Owen kicked the ball (into the net/just before half-time/skilfully).
....
2 Foxes (often/be seen/can) scavenging (on the streets of London/at night).
....
3 David (well/behaves/quite) when he is at home but he (at school/causes trouble/often).
....
4 The post (arrive/sometimes/on time/doesn't) in this part of the city.
....
5 Jennifer (immediately/didn't/recognise) the man waving (at the end of the show/ frantically/from the balcony).
....

6 Such losses (have/would/normally/avoided/been) by the use of back-up devices.

....

7 These children (never/have/had/probably) the opportunities we take for granted.

....

8 (no longer/is/unfortunately, access to the Internet) available (on weekday mornings free of charge/at our libraries).

....

9 We (unable/offer/are/usually/to) refunds on the spot, but we will examine (thoroughly before the end of the week/your claim).

....

10 Many of the old masters had assistants who would prepare the oil pigments (each morning/by hand/in their studios).

....

3 GRAMMAR IN USE **Rewrite the answers in these short dialogues to make them more emphatic. Use the adverb in brackets in a suitable position, as in the example. Make any other necessary changes. 2.33 Listen and check.**

0 'Lucy hasn't turned up yet again.' 'I know. She is unreliable, isn't she?' (really)
'I know. She really is unreliable, isn't she?'

1 'Admit it. You stole it.' 'Sorry, I don't know what you're talking about!' (really)

....

2 'They can't fit us in on Saturday.' 'That place is full on Saturday evenings!' (always)

....

3 'He never mentions his wife. Isn't that strange?' 'Yes, I've wondered about that.' (often)

....

4 'Alan won't even discuss your proposal.'
'I'm not surprised. He doesn't listen to my ideas.' (never)

....

5 'That customs officer really went through my luggage with a fine-tooth comb!'
'That's not unusual; the customs officers here are quite thorough.' (usually)

....

6 'You must have some idea of his whereabouts.'
'I'm sorry but we don't know where he is.' (honestly)

....

7 'I think you should swallow your pride and apologise to them.'
'Come off it. You can't expect me to just give in like that.' (really)

....

8 'Take a break? Give yourself space? What are you on about?'
'You don't have a clue what I'm talking about, do you?' (absolutely)

....

9 'Downloading that software seems to be taking an awfully long time.'
'I'm afraid these programs do take a long time to download.' (sometimes)

....

10 'Look. It's midday and Zoe still isn't here.'
'Well, she is in the office before twelve these days.' (rarely)

....

Review MODULE 4

1 UNITS 12,13 AND 16 **All these sentences contain one or more mistakes. Find the mistakes and correct them, as in the example. In some cases you may need to add, remove or change words; in others, you may also need to change the word order.**

0 The book is bound to appeal to ~~fascinating by crime readers~~. *readers fascinated by crime*
1 Sylvia had a warm, gentle but friendly personality.
2 They've just bought a little Persian beautiful cat.
3 This was the taken route by the original explorers.
4 The wealthies seem to have all the power in our capitalist societies.
5 Janine was absolutely upset by the behaviour of her boss former.
6 We comforted the afraid children after their terrified ordeal.
7 The injuring bird appeared to have a breaking wing.
8 Darren's new boat has an aluminium and glass-fibre unique hull.
9 The old hospital was very vast and full of rusty and decaying equipment medical.
10 No punishment is severe enough for the responsible person for these crimes.
11 Living in Scotland viewers may experience poor reception due to weather conditions.
12 Tall anyone will find these seats cripplingly uncomfortable.

2 UNITS 14 AND 15 **Match sentences 1–7 with the meanings in A–G.**

1 It's slightly cheaper.
2 It's much cheaper.
3 It isn't anything like as cheap.
4 It's just as cheap.
5 It's by far the cheapest.
6 It isn't quite as cheap.
7 It isn't as cheap.

A It's considerably more expensive.
B It's the least expensive.
C It's more expensive.
D It's somewhat less expensive.
E It's no more expensive.
F It's slightly more expensive.
G It's nothing like as expensive.

3 UNITS 17 AND 18 **Rewrite these sentences, using all the words in brackets.**

0 My boss advised me not to discuss the matter.
(before the conference / last week / publicly)
Last week my boss advised me not to discuss the matter publicly before the conference.

1 Ruined, the owner of the business agreed to sell the premises.
(reluctantly / within the month / financially / rather)

....

2 There is nothing better than collapsing.
(onto a sofa / probably / at the end of the day / lazily)

....

3 Controlled, this effective new drug can reduce blood pressure.
(amazingly / within hours / carefully / dramatically)

....

4 We seem to get the chance to talk.
(about anything / seriously / these days / rarely)

....

5 Many of my colleagues disapprove of my scheme to update the accounting procedures
(thoroughly / over the next quarter / unfortunately / in the sales department)

....

4 ALL UNITS **Choose the correct word or phrase, A, B, or C, for each gap.**

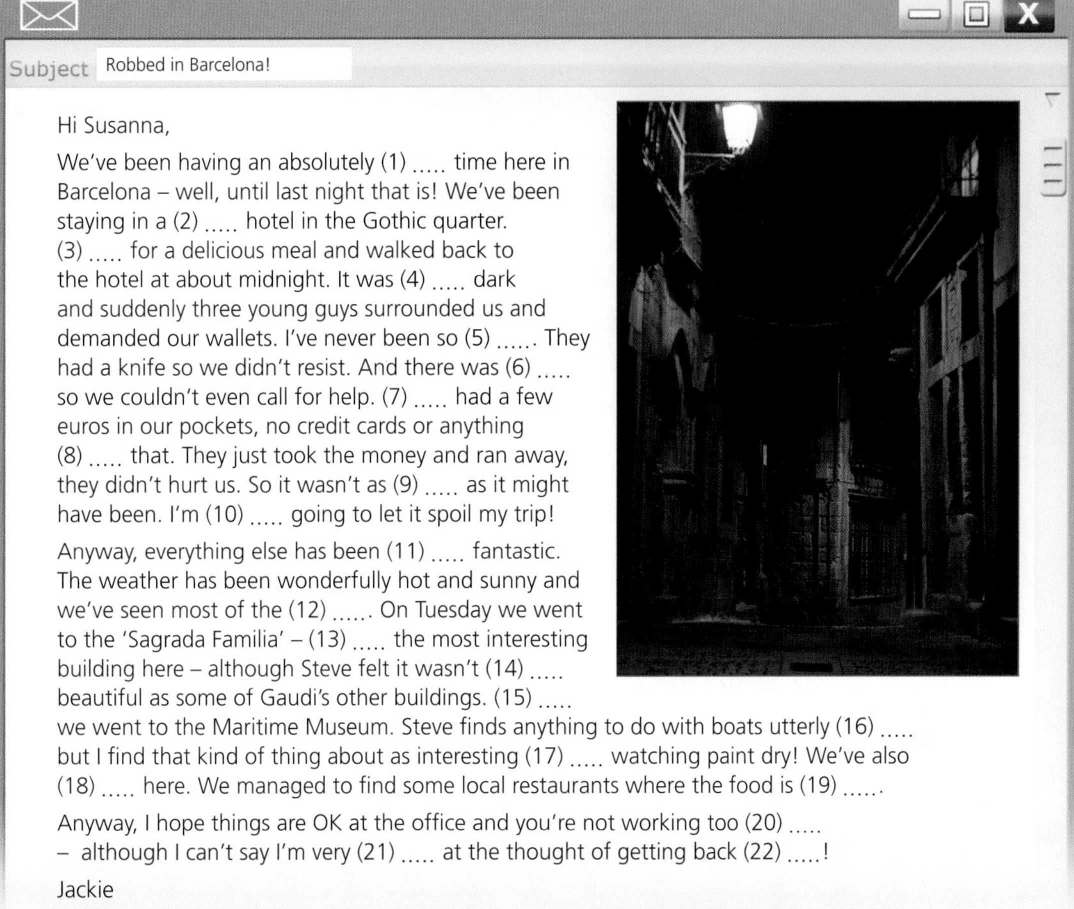

Subject Robbed in Barcelona!

Hi Susanna,

We've been having an absolutely (1) ..... time here in Barcelona – well, until last night that is! We've been staying in a (2) ..... hotel in the Gothic quarter. (3) ..... for a delicious meal and walked back to the hotel at about midnight. It was (4) ..... dark and suddenly three young guys surrounded us and demanded our wallets. I've never been so (5) ...... They had a knife so we didn't resist. And there was (6) ..... so we couldn't even call for help. (7) ..... had a few euros in our pockets, no credit cards or anything (8) ..... that. They just took the money and ran away, they didn't hurt us. So it wasn't as (9) ..... as it might have been. I'm (10) ..... going to let it spoil my trip!

Anyway, everything else has been (11) ..... fantastic. The weather has been wonderfully hot and sunny and we've seen most of the (12) ...... On Tuesday we went to the 'Sagrada Familia' – (13) ..... the most interesting building here – although Steve felt it wasn't (14) ..... beautiful as some of Gaudi's other buildings. (15) ..... we went to the Maritime Museum. Steve finds anything to do with boats utterly (16) ..... but I find that kind of thing about as interesting (17) ..... watching paint dry! We've also (18) ..... here. We managed to find some local restaurants where the food is (19) ......

Anyway, I hope things are OK at the office and you're not working too (20) ..... – although I can't say I'm very (21) ..... at the thought of getting back (22) .....!

Jackie

1 A nice B wonderful C pleasant
2 A charming little B absolutely little C little charming
3 A We yesterday went B Yesterday went we C Yesterday we went
4 A absolutely B utterly C pretty
5 A frighten B frightened C frightening
6 A nobody nearby B nearby nobody C near us nobody
7 A We only luckily B Luckily, we only C We only naturally
8 A such B as C like
9 A bad B worst C worse
10 A not certainly B certain not C certainly not
11 A very B really C such
12 A in the city sights B sights in the city C sights that in the city are
13 A by far B the most far C the farthest
14 A quite as B as quite C as quite a
15 A After B Afterwards that, C Afterwards,
16 A interesting B fascinating C nice
17 A like B to C as
18 A very well eaten B so well eaten C eaten very well
19 A inexpensive and delicious B inexpensive delicious C inexpensive, delicious.
20 A hardly B hard C much hardly
21 A exhilarated B thrilled C amazed
22 A there next week B next there week C next week there

MODULE

5 Tenses

Before you start

1 Review these intermediate grammar points and check you know them.

Auxiliary verbs

Auxiliary verbs are *be*, *have* and *do*.
We use them with main verbs to form tenses, questions and negatives. We don't use them with modal verbs:
✗ ~~*Do we must pay excess baggage on this?*~~

Forming present and past simple tenses

1 For the present simple this is the same as the infinitive, except after *he*, *she* or *it*:
I read → *he reads*   *they carry* → *it carries*

2 For the past simple we add *-ed* to the infinitive (regular verbs). The form is the same for all persons except with *be*: *I/he/she/it* **was**, *we/you/they* **were**

3 We form the negative and questions of the present and past simple with the auxiliary *do*:
Japanese cooking ***doesn't use*** *a lot of dairy food.*
Do *interest rates usually* ***go up*** *in order to reduce inflation?*
*'**Did** you **see** anything suspicious?' 'No, I **didn't see** anything.'*

Spelling rules of present simple -*s* endings ➤ page 366   Past tense -*ed* endings ➤ page 367

Forming other tenses

1

present continuous	*am/is/are* + *-ing* form of main verb	*James and Sally* ***are spending*** *the evening together.* *What* ***are*** *the children* ***doing****?*
past continuous	*was/were* + *-ing* form of main verb	*What* ***were*** *the children* ***doing*** *while you* ***were travelling****?* *It* ***wasn't raining*** *when we woke up this morning.*
present perfect simple	*has/have* + past participle, e.g. *walked, had, done*	*The printers* ***haven't finished*** *the new brochure yet.* *There* ***has been*** *a decline in applicants to the profession.*
present perfect continuous	*has/have been* + *-ing* form of main verb	*Bob Geldof* ***has been doing*** *a lot of work for charities since the mid-eighties.* *How long* ***have you been studying*** *architecture?*
past perfect	*had* + past participle	*By the end of the fundraising week we* ***had raised*** *$5,000.* ***Had*** *you already* ***seen*** *that film?*
past perfect continuous	*had been* + *-ing* form of main verb	*The lake was near bursting point as it* ***had been raining*** *heavily for weeks.*

2 Be careful not to omit *have* with the present perfect:
✗ ~~*I never been to Madame Tussaud's.*~~ ✓ *I've never been to Madame Tussaud's.*

3 *Used to* is followed by an infinitive. Notice the possible spellings in questions and negatives:
It ***used to take*** *me over an hour to get to work.* ***Did you use(d) to get*** *free milk at school?*
Supermarkets ***didn't use(d) to be*** *open on Sundays in the UK.*

Spelling rules of -*ing* forms ➤ page 367

2 **Read the information and identify examples of auxiliary verbs and different tenses.**

CINEMA AUDIENCES have jumped this year, as consumers flock to escape the recession, according to figures from the Cinema Advertising Association.

While many other entertainment venues are struggling to survive during the downturn, film fans are refusing to give up their regular trip to the cinema.

After a long period where audience figures had been falling, last year cinemas enjoyed their best summer since 1969. In the first four months of this year, 55 million tickets were sold, a 14 percent increase on the same period last year.

3 **Complete the diagnostic test below. Choose the correct words in *italics*.**

1. The city museum *is having / has* a new wing – it opened last month. ➤ Unit 19.3
2. Gary *had / had got* a powerful motorbike when he was younger, but his wife persuaded him to sell it. ➤ Unit 19.4
3. 'Sorry I haven't phoned. I lost your number.' 'Oh, *you always lose / you're always losing* my number. Why don't you put it in your mobile?' ➤ Unit 20.2
4. It *gets / is getting* easier to find people to do part-time work these days. ➤ Unit 20.5
5. By the middle of 2008 many parts of Europe *experienced / were experiencing* the worst economic recession for decades. ➤ Unit 21.2
6. The victim *came / was coming* home from work when she was attacked. ➤ Unit 21.3
7. Jim *caught / was catching* the early flight the next morning so he left the party before midnight. ➤ Unit 21.4
8. Things have certainly changed – there *would / used to* be loads of small shops around here when I was young. ➤ Unit 21.5
9. By the third month of the war rebel forces *took / had taken* most of the province. ➤ Unit 22.1
10. At the time of the takeover the company's shares *had declined / had been declining* in value for several months. ➤ Unit 22.2
11. The cat was shaking when she ran into the house; a fox *was / had been* chasing her. ➤ Unit 22.3
12. Luckily, all the boring speeches *finished / had finished* by the time we arrived at the ceremony. ➤ Unit 22.4
13. The nurses' strike *increased / has increased* the waiting time for minor surgery. We now have to wait at least a month. ➤ Unit 23.4
14. He's really much more handsome in the flesh than I *thought / have thought*. ➤ Unit 23.6
15. Street crime figures have *risen / been rising* by five percent in the last two months. ➤ Unit 24.1
16. The weather has been awful. It's *rained / been raining* for five days already this week. ➤ Unit 24.4
17. The part-time philosophy course *consists / is consisting* of twenty evening lectures and five full-day seminars. ➤ Unit 25.1
18. You can't leave a ten-year-old child on her own. What on earth *do you think / are you thinking* of? ➤ Unit 25.2

4 **Check your answers on page 384. Then go to the unit for more information and practice.**

Go online for a full diagnostic test

19 Auxiliaries and *have got*

The first 'megaplex' in the world, Kinepolis Brussels **has got** 25 screens and over 8,000 seats. It **is** part of the international Kinepolis group.

1 Uses of auxiliary verbs

We use *have* and *be* to make perfect, continuous and passive forms of tenses:
I ***haven't*** *seen her for ages.* *John* ***is*** *working very hard these days.*
The flat ***is*** *watched by the surveillance team twenty-four hours a day.*

We use *do (does/did)* to form questions and negatives in the present and past simple:
Do *you enjoy going to the theatre?* *We* ***didn't*** *go to Corfu after all.*
Doesn't *the thermostat control the heating?*

It is possible to omit the auxiliary, and sometimes the subject, in very informal English (e.g. speech, notes, postcards ➤ Unit 83.2) and in headlines:
Terrorists arrested in dawn raid. (= Terrorists were arrested ...)

do as a substitute verb ➤ Unit 73.1/2 *do* in inversion ➤ Unit 76.2

2 Use of contractions (short forms) with auxiliaries

We usually use contracted auxiliaries in speech and informal writing, either with the subject or with *not*: *she's, they've, we don't.*

Note the following exceptions and special cases.

- In spoken English (and when representing speech in writing), we can combine contracted *not* and contracted auxiliaries, e.g. *'ve*, with modal verbs:
  *He should****n't've*** *done it.*
- We don't contract *was*:
  ✗ ~~*He's watching television when she arrived.*~~ ✓ *He was watching television when she arrived.*
- In formal English we don't use contractions when there is more than one subject:
  ✗ ~~*The army and the navy've launched a recruitment drive.*~~
  ✓ *The army and the navy have launched a recruitment drive.*

Has and *is* have the same contracted form, *'s*. Similarly, *had* and *would* are both contracted to *'d*:
*He****'s*** *taken a long lease.* (= has taken) *He****'s*** *taking a holiday.* (= is taking)
*He****'d*** *known her for ages.* (= had known) *He****'d*** *know what to do.* (= would know)
You can work out the full form by looking at the main verb or from the context.

Pronunciation ➤ 1.06

FORMALITY CHECK We usually avoid using contractions in very formal English:
[*Clauses 10–15 don't apply in the case of valuables stolen from vehicles.*]
✓ *Clauses 10–15 do not apply in the case of valuables stolen from vehicles.*

Also, *ain't* (instead of *am/is/are not*) is used informally in some dialects and in popular songs. This is considered incorrect by many English speakers:
[*I ain't going to the party.*] (= I'm not going ...)

3 *be, have* and *do* as main verbs

Be, have and *do* can function as main verbs as well as auxiliaries.
be = exist, located in, behave: *They****'re*** *here!* *It****'s*** *in the bag.* *Now you're* ***being*** *silly.*
do = perform an action or complete a task: *When do you* ***do*** *the washing?*
I ***did*** *my assignment yesterday evening.* *What do you* ***do****?* (= What's your job?)

We use *have* to talk about

- possession: *The chairman of the board* ***has*** *a Gulfstream executive jet.*
- inclusion: *Our latest computer* ***will have*** *a number of upgradeable components.*
- relationships: *I* ***have*** *two older brothers.*
- experiences, e.g. illnesses/disabilities and dreams:
  This patient ***has*** *a slight limp as a result of his accident.*
  The children often ***have*** *nightmares after thunderstorms.*
- actions, e.g. eating, drinking, playing sport:
  *We****'re having*** *chicken with cashew nuts for dinner tonight.* (= We're eating chicken ...)
  The second team ***has*** *an important match on Wednesday evening.*

Sometimes we use *have* + noun when there is no single appropriate verb in English:
You ***have an appointment*** *with the accountants at four.*

In British English we can use *have* without auxiliary *do* in questions and negatives:
Has *the government any real intention of addressing the crime problem head on?*
I ***haven't*** *a clue what they're talking about.*

We don't usually use the passive of main verb *have*. When we do, it has the meaning 'be tricked or cheated': *You paid $100 for a T-shirt! You've been* ***had****!* (= You've been cheated.)

have + noun, e.g. *have a race* ➤ Unit 68.5

4 *have got*

We use *have got* as an alternative to *have* for possession and other states in the present. It is generally preferred to *have* in informal British English, especially in the negative:
[*He* ***has*** *a car but he* ***hasn't*** *a licence.*] ✓ *He* ***has/'s got*** *a car but he* ***hasn't got*** *a licence.*

FORMALITY CHECK In formal written English *have* is more usual:
Our tutors ***have*** *the highest qualifications.*

We usually use a form of *have*, not *have got*, to talk about past or future possession:
✗ *~~I had got a pet rabbit when I was a child.~~* ✓ *I* ***had*** *a pet rabbit when I was a child.*

Have got and *have* do not have continuous or passive forms when they mean 'possess':
✗ *~~He is having (got) a car.~~* ✗ *~~A car has been got by him.~~* ✓ *He* ***has got*** *a car.*

have (got) to to express obligation ➤ Unit 33.1

We also use *have/has/had got* as the present/past perfect form of the verb *get*. Compare:
*She****'s got*** *a degree in chemistry and works at the lab.* (= holds/possesses)
*She****'s just got*** *a degree and hopes to find a job in a lab.* (= has just received)
*He****'d got*** *a certificate from the doctor so he could claim sick pay.* (= had obtained)

We can use *have got* as a perfect infinitive (past form of the infinitive) with these meanings:
OBTAIN *I hope* ***to have got*** *the results by March. We expect* ***to have got*** *the keys by next week.*
RECEIVE *He's likely* ***to have got*** *the letter by now.*

We don't use *have got* in these ways:

to describe actions	✗ ~~Can you answer the phone? I've got a shower.~~ ✓ Can you answer the phone? **I'm having** a shower.
in short answers	'Do you have/Have you got anything vegetarian?' ✗ ~~'Yes, we have got.'~~ ✓ 'Yes, we **do/have**.'
in question tags (➤ Unit 79.2)	✗ ~~You've got two brothers, haven't you got?~~ ✓ You've got two brothers, **haven't you**?
with *used to*	✗ ~~We used to have got a place in the country.~~ ✓ We used to **have** a place in the country.
as a perfect infinitive expressing 'possess'	✗ ~~She has always wanted to have got a car.~~ ✓ She has always wanted **to have** a car.

have (got)/gotten in American English ➤ page 368

Practice

1 Rewrite the sentences correctly, using a suitable auxiliary verb. Whenever appropriate, use contracted forms. If two contracted forms are possible, in conversational speech for instance, write both, as in the example.

0 He could not seen them do it.
He couldn't have seen them do it. He couldn't've seen them do it.

1 I been waiting here for hours.
....

2 She will not returned by the time the show starts.
....

3 Protection under this policy not include items exceeding a value of $500.
....

4 He might not known that it was you at the door.
....

5 their boss not realise that they are under a lot of pressure?
....

6 James got better despite the fact that he not been taking his medication for weeks.
....

7 They really should told you about their decision.
....

8 The documents requested from your solicitor have not received and we are therefore obliged to cancel your contract forthwith.
....

2 Complete the sentences with a form of *be*, *do* or *have*. 2.34 Listen and check.

1 Sorry we .... late for the ceremony. Jason was .... really difficult and wouldn't get ready in time. Teenagers!
2 It is advisable to request a visit to a consultant if you .... severe stomach pain for more than two weeks.
3 I've had a letter from the head teacher because Jane has .... rude to her teachers several times this month.
4 'The accounts should have been .... by last Friday. What's happened?' 'We're .... problems making the figures add up.'
5 While Vicki enjoys .... time to relax at weekends, ... nothing isn't an option for her husband, who wants to .... active all the time.
6 You paid $5,000 for that old car? But it isn't even worth $500. You've been .... !
7 He spends half his time reading newspapers and magazines. He calls it .... research for his thesis. I call it .... lazy!
8 That evening, instead of .... dinner at home, we decided to go to the little French restaurant in the next village.
9 The weather was truly awful – freezing with driving rain – but I had to go out as I .... an appointment to keep.
10 Montague felt very depressed when the firm went bankrupt and he lost his job in Accounts. It was what he had .... all his life; he didn't know anything else.

3 GRAMMAR IN USE **Read the conversation and underline all the examples of *have*. Decide which ones can be replaced with *have got* and write the correct form of *have got*.** 2.35 **Listen and check.**

BETH Do you fancy going to the cinema at the weekend? The local Odeon ~~has~~ *has got* a good film on.

SUE I don't really like going to the cinema. I prefer to watch movies at home.

BETH Really?

SUE Yes, we have a fantastic new 3D home cinema system, so the sound and vision are both excellent.

BETH I thought you already had a state-of-the-art TV.

SUE We used to have quite a good one, yes, but our new system has much better sound than that had. Why don't you come round on Saturday evening and see it?

BETH I'm having dinner with my parents on Saturday evening. How about Friday?

SUE That's OK, but I've actually ordered the new James Bond film on DVD, and I hope to have it by Saturday. Let's make it Sunday evening, shall we?

BETH Yes, that's fine, but I need to leave a bit early as I have an interview on Monday morning.

SUE OK, come round about seven. We'll have a snack first, then watch the movie.

4 GRAMMAR IN USE **Rewrite the underlined words in the hotel brochure with forms of *be*, *do* or *have*.**

Glenforth HOTEL

THE HOTEL WEDDINGS THINGS TO DO CONTACT US SPECIAL OFFERS PHOTO GALLERY

Situated in the heart of the beautiful Scottish Highlands, the Glenforth Hotel offers the discerning guest the ultimate in luxury and gracious living.

Rooms All our rooms contain king-size beds, luxurious bathrooms and tea/coffee-making facilities. You can get extra tea, coffee and biscuits from reception at any time.

Dining We possess a Michelin-starred restaurant offering the best in cordon bleu cuisine featuring a variety of organic ingredients, all of which originate from the locality.

Leisure facilities Would you enjoy indulging in a relaxing swim or sauna? Our guests can obtain free membership of the adjacent Glenforth Health Centre, which includes a fully-equipped gymnasium, heated indoor pool and sauna/steam rooms.

Babysitting service If you have small children, you will be able to take advantage of our unique babysitting service. We employ several fully-qualified nannies who are able to take care of your children for an evening. Our nannies perform this service for a nominal fee.

Sports For those of our guests that enjoy fishing, the hotel owns the fishing rights on part of the river Glenswift, which is teeming with a large number of salmon, trout and bream.

The hotel grounds are quite famous as they have acted as the location for many movies.

0 *All our rooms have king-size beds.*
1 ....
2 ....
3 ....
4 ....
5 ....
6 ....
7 ....
8 ....

20 Present simple or continuous?

The Third Man is one of the most famous post-war films. In it, writer Holly Martins **is searching for** his friend Harry Lime in Vienna shortly after the end of World War II. When he is told that his friend has died in an accident, Martins **begins** to suspect that there is something suspicious about the death ...

1 Permanent and temporary situations

We often use the present simple to describe

- permanent situations: *A colony of Antarctic penguins* ***lives*** *in Marwell Zoo.*
- facts: *Broken bones in adults* ***don't heal*** *as fast as they do in children.*
- things which are generally true:
  British people ***drink*** *a lot of tea, while the French drink more coffee.*
- opinions: *Why don't you come with me? It* ***seems*** *silly to take two cars.*

The present continuous describes a temporary situation or action in progress at or around the time of speaking. The action is likely to continue after the time of speaking:
I'll be with you in a minute. ***I'm*** *just* ***finishing*** *something in the kitchen.*
My niece from Ireland ***is spending*** *the summer with us. She's really enjoying city life!*

Common adverbs with this form are *now, just, still, at the moment* and *currently*:
The students ***are*** *currently* ***studying*** *the writings of Günter Grass on the German course.*

We use *live, work, study* and *stay* in the continuous if the action is temporary:
✗ ~~*She stays in the Waldorf Astoria on this visit to New York, doesn't she?*~~
✓ *She's* ***staying*** *in the Waldorf Astoria on this visit to New York, isn't she?*

⚠ We can use the present simple to draw attention to someone arriving or leaving, with *here comes* and *there goes*. These are always present simple and appear before the subject:
✗ ~~*Here is coming the postman.*~~ ✓ *Here* ***comes*** *the postman.*
✗ ~~*There the last bus goes.*~~ ✓ *There* ***goes*** *the last bus.*

More on inversion ➤ Unit 76.3 State verbs and present simple ➤ Unit 25.1

2 Regular or repeated actions

We use the present simple to describe things that happen on a regular basis:
As temperatures fall with the approach of winter, the soil ***freezes*** *and* ***contracts*** *...*
Many people from the north of Europe ***take*** *their summer holiday in the warmer south.*

We often use the present simple with adverbs of frequency, e.g. *always, sometimes*, and expressions of frequency, e.g. *every day, once a week*:
Share prices usually ***change*** *on a daily basis – but often by very little.*
Our two chefs ***provide*** *an excellent choice of hot meals every day.*

It is possible to use the present continuous to talk about repeated events or actions, usually if they happen within a temporary period: ***I'm feeding*** *the neighbour's cat while she's away.*

Compare:
Alan loves sweet things. He ***eats*** *a dessert most days.* (habit over a long time)
Alan's on a diet. He ***isn't eating*** *desserts at the moment.*
(repeated action within a temporary period)

We can use the present continuous for a series of actions that are more frequent than we would normally expect: *Now that I've bought a Toyota Prius, **I'm seeing** them everywhere!*

We can use the present continuous with an adverb such as *always*, *forever* or *continually* for frequently repeated actions: *The baby**'s always making** cute little gurgling noises.*

This use is more emphatic than using the present simple for repeated actions, and, with a stressed adverb, expresses annoyance with the person who is doing the action:
*The neighbours **are continually slamming** doors and **shouting** during the night.*
***I'm always forgetting** people's birthdays. It's so annoying.*

3 Series of events/actions

We use the present simple to give directions or instructions, often with impersonal *you*:
*From here you **cross** the road, **go** through an iron gate and **follow** the path west ...*

This is similar to the imperative, but the imperative can sound more abrupt:
***Cross** the road, **go** through an iron gate and **follow** the path west ...*

We use the present simple to express the immediacy of an event, e.g. in sports commentaries, particularly when the action is over before the description finishes:
*France **kicks off**, Vieira **passes** to Henry, Henry **cuts** inside ... and it's a goal!*

Compare the use of the present continuous used in sports commentaries, when the action is in progress throughout the time of speaking:
*They**'re now entering** the back straight and Bekele **is starting** to pull away from the other runners ... he **crosses** the line two seconds ahead of his closest rival ...*

4 Describing pictures, plots and telling anecdotes

We use the present continuous to describe pictures:
*Our head of our department is the one who**'s standing** slightly apart in the college photo.*

We can use the present continuous with the present simple to give more immediacy to an anecdote. We use the continuous for actions which form a background and the simple for the actions that make up the narrative:
*There's an old woman with thick glasses who**'s serving** the hot drinks, so I **go** up to her and **ask** ...*
(She started serving before the action of the narrative.)

This is often the way that we describe the beginning of books, films or plays:
*At the start of the play, Hamlet **is walking** along the castle walls when he **hears** a strange voice.*

Newspaper headlines often use the present simple to express a past event, which again gives more immediacy to the event: *UK jobless total **climbs** to 2.4 million.*

5 Other uses

We use the present continuous to describe things which are in the process of changing, i.e. trends:
✗ ~~*British summers get hotter and winters get wetter.*~~
✓ *British summers **are getting** hotter and winters **are getting** wetter.*
*The cost of bringing up children **is increasing** all the time.*

ACADEMIC ENGLISH The use of the present continuous for trends is common in academic English:
*While it is often assumed that violent crime **is increasing**, statistics show that it **is** actually **decreasing** in most areas.*

FORMALITY CHECK We use the present simple in formal speech or writing for certain actions:
*I **note** that you referred to the National Curriculum in your speech ...*
*I **look forward** to receiving a prompt reply to my enquiry.*

Present simple for fixed future events or for future after *when*, *after*, etc. ➤ Unit 28.1
Present continuous for arrangements in the future ➤ Unit 27.3

Practice

1 Choose the correct or more suitable verb form in *italics*.

1 The Guggenheim Museum in Bilbao *houses / is housing* Spain's largest collection of Modern Art.
2 We *try out / are trying out* a new paper supplier at the moment. The old one was too expensive.
3 These animals *display / are displaying* a great deal of aggression if disturbed.
4 We *currently show / are currently showing* the film 'Mamma Mia' at all Odeon cinemas in the region.
5 Quick! Get rid of all the mess! Here *come / are coming* Mum and Dad!
6 The weather forecast says there'll be wind from the north-west tonight. That always *brings / is bringing* snow with it at this time of year.
7 You *always complain / 're always complaining* and it really gets on my nerves! Why can't you just accept things and relax?
8 Swimming *provides / is providing* exercise for more muscle groups than any other physical activity.
9 Now you've named your daughter Gemma I *hear / 'm hearing* the name everywhere! It isn't as uncommon as I thought.
10 Accessing money was very difficult last year, but banks *become / are becoming* more amenable to lending as the financial situation improves.

2 GRAMMAR IN USE Complete this description of a film, using the correct form of the verbs in brackets, either present simple or present continuous. 2.36 Listen and check.

The Day after Tomorrow

Climate change? (1) .... (you / believe) in it? This film from 2004 (2) .... (examine) the potential aftermath of a sudden and catastrophic global warming.

At the start of the film, the world (3) .... (generally / get) warmer, as is the case in reality, but climatologist Jack Hall (4) .... (discover) that a huge chunk of the Antarctic ice sheet has broken off, and realises the inevitable consequences. At the same time, his son is with some friends in New York, where it (5) .... (continually / rain), and weather-related disasters (6) .... (happen) all over the world. It soon (7) .... (become) clear that the world is about to enter a new ice age.

Implausible, perhaps, but this is above all an action film, and (8) .... (not purport) to inform its viewers about climate change. Indeed, many of the best scenes in the film (9) .... (revolve) around Jack's attempt to rescue his son from a New York that (10) .... (slowly / freeze) over. The acting is also good, though it's clear that the actors (11) .... (continually / struggle) with stilted dialogue.

The Day after Tomorrow (12) .... (currently / show) as part of the Roland Emmerich season at the Academy.

3 **Choose one verb from the box for each pair, A and B. Choose the present simple of the verb for one sentence and the present continuous for the other. If there is an adverb in brackets, write it in the correct place.**

arrive contradict open rise stay

1 A After twenty years, our local cinema .... again on a Saturday morning for Kids' Club – a morning of cartoons and adventure films.
 B The theatre .... to the public at 6.45, so I'll meet you there then.

2 A Brad Pitt and Angelina Jolie .... and are immediately swept away by their minders to the safety of the celebrity enclosure.
 B We expect the Royal Family at any moment. Yes, I think they .... (just) now. I can see the first car in the procession.

3 A Stars attending the ceremony .... (usually) at the Hilton for its luxuriousness and convenience.
 B The British contingent .... at the Hilton this year as it appears to have more secure arrangements in place.

4 A Despite the cold winter in many European countries, the milder winter elsewhere underlines the fact that temperatures .... (generally) year on year.
 B During spring temperatures .... by about a degree every two weeks or so.

5 A He .... (often) the tutor if he's made a different interpretation of the novel; I really admire his confidence.
 B I've got so fed up with his behaviour over the last few weeks – he .... (always) me, even when he knows nothing about the topic!

4 GRAMMAR IN USE **Find and correct eight more mistakes with the present simple or the present continuous in this interview.** 2.37 **Listen and check.**

SARAH Welcome to the programme. This afternoon I ~~stand~~ *'m standing* in the middle of the northern Black Forest, Germany, with Rainer Sanger, from Friends of the Forest, a pressure group which is representing people worried about the natural habitat in Europe. Rainer, you're very concerned about this area of the forest. Can you tell us why?

RAINER Yes. Much of the forest was wiped out in the storms last winter, as you can see. Many of the trees are dead, and more die because of the irreversible damage. We at *Friends of the Forest* believe that the authorities don't do enough right now to restore this beautiful forest to its former state.

SARAH But they clear the dead trees away today. I saw some men on the way here ...

RAINER Of course, but they are doing that every year. It's the normal procedure. We need more trees now, but they aren't planting any.

SARAH I see. But you have approached the authorities about this, I understand.

RAINER We have tried but they're always making excuses – usually to do with money. It gets more and more frustrating all the time! Each time, they're telling us that they haven't got enough money to restore the forest as quickly as we'd like.

SARAH But it's not just an excuse, is it? They clearly don't have enough money for everything, and the current situation is quite extraordinary.

RAINER Of course, we appreciate that, and the point is that actually, we don't ask for much money. We would just like their guidance – we have plenty of volunteers ...

21 Past simple and continuous; *used to* and *would*

The earliest films **were made** by the Lumière brothers in France in the late nineteenth century, but they **were** very different from most films today: they all **used to be** very short, black and white only, and they **didn't use to have** any sound.

1 Completed actions and situations (past simple)

We use this for completed actions in the past: *Julius Caesar **invaded** Britain in 55 BCE.*
If the context is clear, it is not necessary to give a past time reference:
*But Caesar's troops **failed** to defeat the indigenous tribes.* (in 55 BCE)

We use the past simple for

- actions happening at the same time:
  *At the junction I **took** the left turn while Micky **took** the right.*
- repeated actions: *My brother **applied** for a visa **six times** before he got one.*
- sequences of actions: *Silverman **ran** to the car, **jumped** in and **raced** off into the night.*
- one action resulting in another:
  *Wall Street traders **lost** a fortune when the Asian markets **collapsed**.*
  (The markets collapsed with the result that the traders lost a fortune.)
- states in the past: *We **lived** just outside Oxford for several years, but we **didn't like** it much.*

Common time expressions used with the past simple are *ago, last (week/month), (the day before) yesterday, the other day/week* and conjunctions such as *when, (just) as, while* and *after*:
*I heard the news hours **ago**.* *Mum called me just **after** you left this morning.*
*The door opened and the director came in (**just**) **as** I finished my presentation.*

Differences between past simple and present perfect ➤ Unit 23.6

2 Past actions and situations in progress (past continuous)

The past continuous describes an action in progress at a point of time in the past; the action began before this point of time and continued after it:
*We didn't hear the intruder because we **were sleeping** on the top floor that night.*
*At the time of our arrival the city **was going through** a period of rapid expansion.*

We often use the past continuous to show that a past action was

- temporary: *During my training I **was earning** a lot less than my wife.*
- changing or developing: *His symptoms **were becoming** more pronounced each day.*
- providing a background to completed past actions:
  *Darkness **was falling** over the city as James **hurried** back to college ...*

We can use the past continuous for two actions in progress at the same time:
*We were **watching** the sky and **listening** for the first sounds of the dawn chorus ...*

We usually use the past simple for repeated actions in the past, but we can use the past continuous if we want to emphasise that the repeated actions took place over a temporary period:
*She **received** chemotherapy on a weekly basis.* (repeated action)
*For the first three months she **was receiving** chemotherapy on a weekly basis.*
(repeated action, but only for three months)

As with the present continuous, we can use the past continuous (with *always* and other adverbs) to talk about repeated actions that happened very often, or to express annoyance (➤ Unit 20.2):
*The track was so rough that we **were continually mending** punctures.*
*They never saved their money. They **were always borrowing** cash from us.*

3 Interrupted actions

We use the past continuous to contrast an ongoing action with a single (past simple) event which interrupts it:
*Seventy cars **were crossing** the bridge when the supports **collapsed** into the river.*

We can put either clause first, and we can use *when, while* or *as* to introduce the interrupted action:
*Messengers arrived with the news of Mary's plot **when/while/as** Queen Elizabeth was hunting.*

We use *when* (not *while*) to introduce the interrupting (past simple) action:
✗ ~~*Queen Elizabeth was hunting while messengers arrived with the news of Mary's plot.*~~
✓ *Queen Elizabeth was hunting **when** messengers arrived with the news of Mary's plot.*

If the background action finishes just before the event which interrupts it, we prefer to use the past perfect continuous (➤ Unit 22.1).

4 Other uses of the past continuous

We can use the past continuous to describe past arrangements that may or may not have taken place:
*Nancy **was taking** the next flight to Paris so she had to cut short the interview.*
(Nancy had an existing arrangement to take a flight to Paris.)

We often use verbs such as *plan, expect, hope* for unfulfilled arrangements:
***Were** you **expecting** to have a meeting this morning? I'm afraid I'm too busy today.*

Future in the past and unfulfilled pasts ➤ Unit 29

We can make requests, suggestions and questions more tentative and polite by using the past continuous. We often use the verbs *think* and *wonder*:
*We **were wondering** if you would like to join us.* (= Would you like to join us ...?)
***Were** you **planning** on going somewhere else later?* (= Are you planning on ...?)

5 *used to* and *would*

Both *used to* and *would* describe actions which happened regularly in the past but no longer happen or now happen with more or less frequency:
*They **used to get paid** every three months.* (Now they get paid weekly.)
*We **would get up** early every Thursday to go to the market.* (We don't now.)

To avoid confusion with other uses of *would*, we usually mention the past time or situation:
*He **would give** her a lift to work in the days before she passed her test.*

We often continue with *would* after a past narrative has started with *used to*:
*Dad **used to** travel a lot on business. He **would** be away for weeks at a time, and he'**d** always bring presents back with him.*

We use *used to*, but not *would*, to describe past states which have changed:
*Lithuania **used to be** part of the Soviet Union.* (It isn't now.)
*There **didn't use* to be** any crime around here in the old days.* (There is now.)
✗ ~~*The capital of Nigeria would be Lagos but now it's Abuja.*~~
✓ *The capital of Nigeria **used to be** Lagos but now it's Abuja.*

We use the past simple, NOT *used to*, for
- periods of time: *They lived in Darwin for six years.* (✗ ~~*They used to live ... for six years.*~~)
- a number of times: *We visited them there three times.* (✗ ~~*We used to visit them ... three times.*~~)

Don't confuse *used to* + infinitive with *be/get used to* which means 'be/become accustomed to':
*I **used to live** alone.* (= I lived alone at a time in the past.)
*He **wasn't used to living** on his own.* (= He wasn't accustomed to it.)

* Many people now use *didn't used to* and *did (you) used to* in negatives and questions, although this was considered to be non-standard in the past.

Practice

1 Match the underlined words in 1–10 with the explanations A–J.

1. They ran the same test eight times before they found the bug in the software.
2. The soldier was trying to deactivate the land mine when it exploded.
3. While we were at university, we would often go to the capital to take part in political demonstrations.
4. Food was in short supply throughout the war.
5. Claire jumped out of her chair, ran to the balcony and grabbed the screaming child.
6. The whole time that I was talking, the one child in the audience was howling!
7. Lorenzo the Magnificent died in Florence in 1492.
8. We had a busy morning. Steve answered the phone calls and I dealt with the emails.
9. A day out for the family used to cost considerably less than it does now.
10. The fire was raging through the whole night.

A A single or completed action in the past.
B A sequence of different, completed actions in the past.
C Two actions which happened at the same time in the past.
D The same action repeated several times in the past.
E A state existing for some time in the past.
F An action in progress in the past.
G One action interrupted by another, shorter action.
H Two actions in progress at the same time in the past.
I A description of a past situation which is different now.
J A past action that happened frequently but no longer happens.

2 GRAMMAR IN USE Read the text and choose the correct verb form in *italics*. If both forms are correct, choose both. 2.38 Listen and check.

Saturday morning cinema

One of the highlights of life when I was a child (1) *was / would* Saturday morning cinema, or the pictures, as we called it then. I remember the first time my mother (2) *allowed / used to allow* me to go, when I was about ten. It (3) *was / would be* so exciting! That was with my big brother, of course; she didn't (4) *use to allow / allow* me to go on my own at that age. From then on, I (5) *would / used to* go every Saturday morning, as long as Dad (6) *earned / was earning* money at the time – his work (7) *was / used to be* a bit erratic.

My brother and I (8) *would always / always used to* meet up with a big group of friends and (9) *we'd go / we were going* to the local flea pit – it (10) *was / would be* a really old cinema, which was probably why the Saturday kids' pictures (11) *were / used to be* held there! We (12) *would always / always used to* get there about half an hour before the doors opened so we could get the best seats, and while we

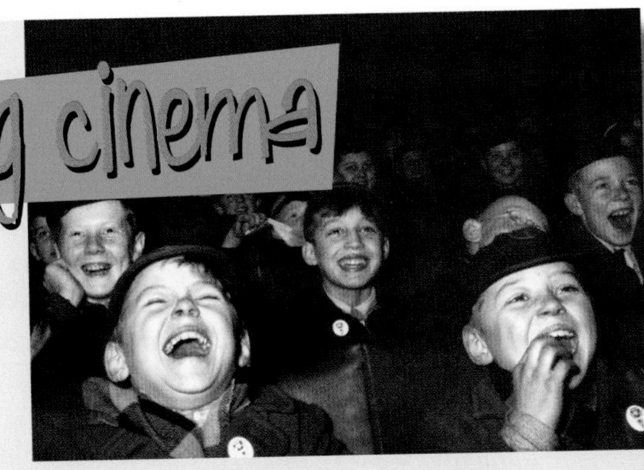

(13) *were queuing / used to queuing* some of the older children would go and buy sweets.

It's amazing to think now what a bargain it (14) *was / would be* – I can't remember how much we paid, but we (15) *used to get / were getting* about three films of different types. There'd often be a couple of parts of serials, and then a main feature. It (16) *would / used to* be really good value. Then we'd all leave the cinema hungry, despite the sweets, and troop back home for the lunch that our mothers had spent the morning making. That was the main point of course – to get us out of the house for a few hours!

3 Complete the sentences with suitable verbs from the box. Use the past simple or past continuous. 2.39 Listen and check.

announce blow collapse cook decide feel hit leave live manage mention press run into see set off settle down soar spend stand start study take

1 I .... at the bus stop when I .... the car slam into the lamp-post.
2 The icy wind .... through the trees as we .... on our journey.
3 Brad .... exhausted so he .... onto the sofa, ... the button on the remote control and .... for an evening vegetating in front of the box.
4 The twins .... the afternoon shopping because they .... for their flatmates that evening.
5 Unfortunately for us, we .... on the wrong side of Miami when Hurricane Andrew .... the city.
6 Share prices .... when the government .... record growth figures.
7 Karen and Anna first .... writing to each other about their research when they .... for their doctorates.
8 I .... early the next morning so I .... to have an early night.
9 My younger brother .... the driving test five times before he .... to pass.
10 I .... Clare at the supermarket the other day and she .... that you might be looking for work.

4 Find eight mistakes with past forms and correct them. Tick (✓) the correct sentences.

1 Lady Jane Grey used to be Queen of England for only nine days in 1553.
2 What were the children doing while their mother was visiting her sister in the hospital?
3 The huge liners doing the journey from Europe to the United States would be extremely comfortable for the first class passengers but those travelling in steerage suffered appalling conditions.
4 The victim was talking on her mobile phone while her attacker struck from behind.
5 Mary didn't join us yesterday evening because she expected a phone call from her son in Australia.
6 Before printing and literacy became widespread, people would get news from the town crier, who would shout out anything newsworthy for the whole town to hear.
7 I'm sure that children didn't use to being so undisciplined when we were at school!
8 The fox cubs were coming into our garden several times during the spring to try to get our chickens.
9 Gerald wasn't used to having such dark hair – do you think he's coloured it?
10 Sorry I'm late. I was expecting to catch the early train but I got held up in traffic on the way to the station.
11 Would your mother work when you were a child or did she stay at home?
12 I found it really difficult when I got the job on the early news programme as I really wasn't used to getting up at five o'clock in the morning!

22 Past perfect simple and continuous

Award-winning film star Grace Kelly **had been acting** on stage and in television for three years before she made her first Hollywood movie. But by the age of twenty-six, she **had given up** her film career to live as a royal princess in Monaco.

1 Actions and situations before a time in the past

We use the past perfect simple to describe a single action, or repeated actions, completed before a time in the past:
The new owners found that the timbers ***had been patched up*** *several times.*

We often include a specific time reference, such as a clause with *when* or *by the time*:
By the age of twenty-six, Grace Kelly ***had given up*** *her film career.*

We also use this form to describe a situation which existed before a past event:
At the time of her trial last year, Hinkley ***had been*** *in prison for eight months.*

We use the past perfect continuous to describe an ongoing situation or action which continued up to, or stopped just before, a time in the past, often with *before* or *by the time*:
Grace Kelly ***had been acting*** *for three years before she made her first movie.*

We often use the continuous with *for* or *since* when we want to focus on the duration of an action:
Kubrick ***had been trying*** *to get the film made* ***for more than twenty years.***
The eager fans ***had been waiting*** *in line* ***for over six hours/since the early hours of the morning.***

We don't usually use the past perfect continuous for actions and background situations still continuing at the same time as the past simple narrative. We prefer to use the past continuous:
We ***were living*** *in New York when John was made redundant.*
(an ongoing situation at the time of the redundancy)

Compare these examples:

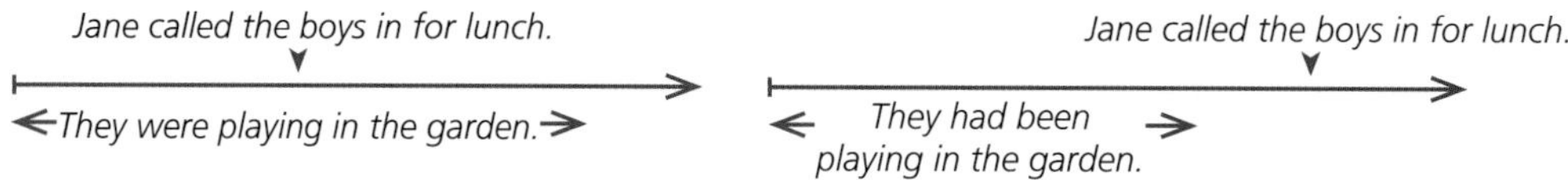

2 Completed and ongoing actions

The past perfect simple often refers to a completed action, whereas the past perfect continuous may refer to an action that was still ongoing at the time of the statement:
The leaves ***had fallen*** *from the trees early that year and they were completely bare.*
The leaves ***had been falling*** *from the trees and the ground underfoot was very slippery.*

We do not mention the number of times that we have done an action when we use the past perfect continuous:
✗ ~~*Jill had only been watching TV twice that week.*~~
✓ *Jill* ***had*** *only* ***watched*** *TV twice that week.* (repeated action: past perfect simple)

3 Past reasons

We often use the past perfect to describe the reason for a past action or situation:
*David didn't join the agency as he**'d signed up** with a rival firm.*
*The survivors looked painfully thin. They **had been living** on emergency rations since the accident.*

4 Sequence of past actions

We can use the past perfect with the past simple to make a sequence of events clear. We use the past perfect for the earlier action and the past simple for the later one:
*When we **got back**, the babysitter **had put** the children to bed.*

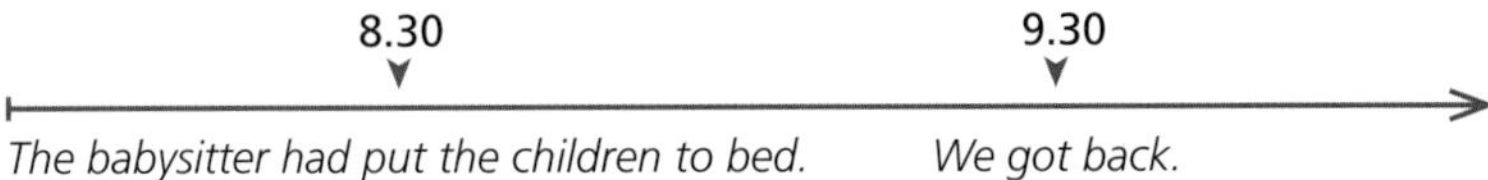

Notice the difference if both verbs are in the past simple:
*When we **got back**, the babysitter **put** the children to bed.*

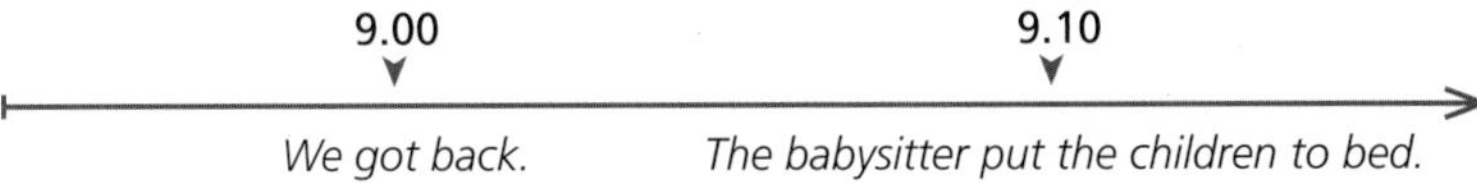

We can use *just* with the past perfect to show that the earlier action was very recent:
*We wanted to talk to the manager in charge but she**'d just left**.*

Or we can use *already* to show that the action happened sooner than we expected:
*When we got back, we were shocked to find that the babysitter **had already gone** home.*

We don't usually use the past perfect if the sequence is obvious and the first action makes the second happen:
[*I had opened the door and let him in.*]
✓ *I opened the door and let him in.* (He was able to come in because I opened the door.)

We can use either the past perfect or the past simple with time conjunctions, e.g. *after, before, as soon as, when*:
*She ushered me out of the room as soon as I **paid/had paid** my subscription.*

With *before* + past perfect the action in the past simple happens first:
*I left university **before I'd finished** the course I was taking.*

We can use this pattern for a past action which prevented a later action from happening:
*She sacked him **before he'd had** a chance to explain his behaviour.*

5 Other uses

We can use the past perfect with superlatives, ordinals (*the first, second, last,* etc.), *the only,* etc. + *ever*:
*I remember seeing 'Nightmare on Elm Street' when I was only eighteen. It was the most frightening film I**'d** ever **seen**.*
*They wanted us to go on the higher slopes but it was only the second time we**'d** ever **done** any skiing.*

We use the past perfect with verbs such as *hope, expect, want, plan, think about, wish* to describe past intentions which were unfulfilled:
*They **had hoped** to get to the summit, but Travers fell ill at base camp.*
*We**'d been planning** the merger for weeks when we received the news that it was all off.*

Remember that we don't usually use the continuous form with state verbs:
*Suzie **had wanted** to leave her job and start her own business, but then she was offered a fantastic promotion and decided to stay.*

State verbs ➤ Unit 25.1

Practice

1 Choose the best sentence, A or B, to illustrate each picture.

A I felt ill when I ate the pudding.
B I felt ill when I'd eaten the pudding.

A When I returned to my hotel room, the maid made the bed.
B When I returned to my hotel room, the maid had made the bed.

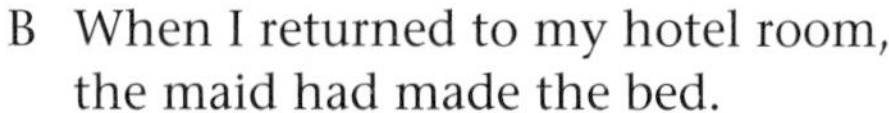

A I explained to my host that I'd been fixing the car, which had broken down.
B I explained to my host that I was fixing the car, which had broken down.

A The matinée performance started when we got there.
B The matinée performance had started when we got there.

A Carrie was excited because she was travelling to South Africa.
B Carrie was excited because she had travelled to South Africa.

A Petra had been baking a cake when we went to her new flat for tea.
B Petra had baked a cake when we went to her new flat for tea.

A I hoped to get a good result for my final exams.
B I had hoped to get a good result for my final exams.

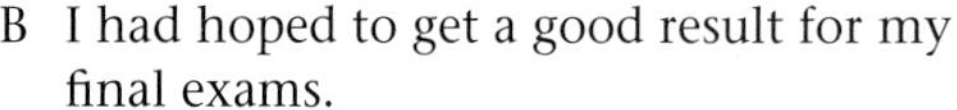

A I sat down before the doctor had told me the bad news.
B The doctor told me the bad news before I had sat down.

2 **Choose the most suitable verb form in *italics*. 2.40 Listen and check.**

1 So I *turned / had turned* on my heels and walked out of the shop in disgust.
2 Many voters were turned away from the voting stations although they *had queued / queued* for hours to cast their vote.
3 The mechanics *had been taking / had taken* the engine apart several times before they were able to locate the source of the mysterious rattle.
4 By 1280 Genghis Khan *had conquered / had been conquering* the whole of China.
5 She was surprised to find the fridge empty; the children *had eaten / had been eating* everything!
6 Our lead actor turned up and he was word perfect; apparently he *was practising / had been practising* his lines all day.
7 The children wanted to invite their friends to the circus, but their father *had booked / had been booking* tickets for just the family.
8 Debbie couldn't understand why her computer crashed; it *had been working / was working* perfectly for as long as she could remember.
9 My niece's accident was rather a setback because she *hoped / had hoped* to pursue a career as a tennis player.
10 Mrs Lawson arrived at casualty in quite a state; she *suffered / had been suffering* from severe stomach pains for hours.

3 GRAMMAR IN USE **Complete the text with the verbs in brackets. Use the past simple, past perfect, past continuous or past perfect continuous form of the verbs. 2.41 Listen and check.**

Christopher Reeve 1952–2004

KNOWN PRINCIPALLY as an actor, Reeve (1) .... (have) many other talents and interests, including directing, which he (2) .... (do) for some years at the time of his death in 2004.

Born in September 1952, Reeve was heavily influenced through his life by his novelist and poet father, F D Reeve. As a child he (3) .... (begin) acting stories with his little brother, and by the age of eight he (4) .... (already/appear) in several school plays.

He studied music and English at Cornell University, and while he (5) .... (study) in his final year, he was accepted into the renowned Juilliard School of the Performing Arts. He (6) .... (perform) both in film and on the stage for a few years when he (7) .... (accept) the part for which he is most remembered, Superman, in 1978.

Always active and a keen sportsman, Reeve (8) .... (do) all his own stunts. In sports terms, his interests focused on horse-riding, and he (9) .... (compete) in events for a few years when, in 1995, he was thrown from his horse and broke his neck. From a man who (10) .... (be) at the peak of his powers, he was now paralysed from the neck down. Perhaps because he (11) .... (be) so active, he was determined to continue making something of his life, and despite his severe injuries, he (12) .... (continue) to act and he started directing. In October 2004 Reeve (13) .... (promote) a film that he (14) .... (recently/direct) – *The Brooke Ellison Story* – when he suffered a sudden and unexpected heart attack and fell into a coma. He (15) .... (die) the following day, aged only 52, leaving a wife and three children.

23 Present perfect simple

1 Ongoing situations and actions

We use the present perfect simple to talk about situations that started in the past and are still continuing in the present:
The manor house ***has stood*** *on this spot for over two hundred years.* (It is still here.)

We often use the prepositions *for* and *since* with this use:
The centre of the island has not been inhabited ***for fifty years.*** (*for* + period of time)
The island has not been inhabited ***since*** *the earthquake of 1952.* (*since* + point in time)

When we use *since* to introduce a new clause, we usually use the past simple after it:
✗ ~~*You've been really moody ever since that letter has arrived. What's wrong?*~~
✓ *You've been really moody ever* ***since that letter arrived.*** *What's wrong?*

⚠ The present continuous + *for* expresses a present situation continuing into the future, NOT a situation that began in the past:
*We****'re staying*** *here for three months. We're going back to Chile in September.*

But note the use of either the present perfect or past simple after *It's* (*weeks/years/ages*) *since ...*, to express a period of time when we haven't done something:
It's ages since I've been/I went *to the theatre.* ***It's weeks since we've seen/we saw*** *each other.*

2 Unfinished time periods

We can use the present perfect for completed actions in the past if they may happen again, i.e. if the time period in which the actions took place has not ended:
I've only ***been*** *to Hong Kong once.* (My life is still continuing, so I may go there again.)
NASA ***has sent*** *probes to various planets.* (NASA still exists so may send more.)

Sometimes we know the time is not 'finished' because of the time expression:
This channel ***has shown*** *four wildlife documentaries* ***this week*** *and it's only Thursday!*

Compare these two sentences:
Jack Nicholson ***has won*** *three Oscars.* (He is still alive and may win some more.)
Katharine Hepburn ***won*** *four Oscars during her life.* (She is dead and can't win any more.)

British English uses the present perfect after superlatives, e.g. *the best/worst, the greatest,* ordinal numbers, e.g. *the first (second, third), the only,* often followed by *ever*:
It's the worst sports show I ***have ever seen*** *and the first I* ***have ever complained*** *about!*

Past simple with the superlative in American English ➤ page 368

3 Adverbs often used with the present perfect

These adverbs are very common with the present perfect use described in 23.2:

already always ever never often recently seldom so far still to now yet

*The Prime Minister **has seldom been put** in such a difficult position.*
*I **have never experienced** any racism in athletics.*
*We've **received** over 20,000 entries for the competition **so far**.*
*'**Have they decided** on the wedding date **yet**?' 'No, they **still haven't made up** their minds.'*

 We use *already* with the affirmative but *yet* with the negative and in questions:
✗ ~~We've yet seen the film but they haven't seen it already.~~
✓ *We've **already seen** the film but they **haven't seen it yet**.*

Past simple with these adverbs in American English ➤ page 368

4 Present results

We can use the present perfect simple to talk about an action completed in the past which has a present result:
*The avalanche **has devastated** the skiing industry in the area.*
(result: The skiing industry is still having big problems.)
*We can start the interviews now, as all the candidates **have arrived**.*

Common adverbs with this use of the present perfect are *just*, *recently* and *lately*:
***Has** the sports centre **increased** its membership fees **lately**?*
*John Barry, the composer of numerous famous film scores, **has just died**.* (= very recently)

5 Other uses

As the present perfect simple expresses relevance to the present, news reports often start with this tense, before moving into past tenses:
*The largest car plant in Detroit **has shut down**. It **closed** its doors for the last time yesterday.*

Similarly, we often use it to introduce a new topic of conversation:
*I've **heard** from Maurice – he's been in Australia for the last two months.*

In time clauses (e.g. beginning with *after*, *when*) we can use the present perfect with future reference (➤ Unit 28.1):
*We'll make a move **as soon as the rain has stopped**.*

6 Present perfect and past simple: differences

PRESENT PERFECT	PAST SIMPLE (➤ Unit 22.1)
Unfinished state/action: *France **has governed** the island of Réunion since 1642.*	Finished state/action: *France **governed** Ivory Coast from 1893 to 1960.*
Unfinished time: *I **haven't seen** Keith this morning.* (It's still morning.)	Finished time: *I **didn't see** Keith at all this morning.* (It's now afternoon/evening.)
Present result/relevance: *The Indian Government **has imposed** a ban on tiger hunting to prevent the extinction of tigers.*	No indication of present relevance: *The Indian Government **imposed** a ban on tiger hunting a few years ago.*
Indefinite time: *I've **been** to South Africa twice.*	Definite time: *I **went** to South Africa in 2009.*

We use a past or past perfect form, not the present perfect, to correct an incorrect belief or expectation, or to confirm a correct one:
✗ ~~She was just as beautiful as I have imagined.~~ ✓ *She was just as beautiful as **I had imagined**.*
✗ ~~The area is wilder than I have expected.~~ ✓ *The area is wilder than I **expected/was expecting**.*

Practice

1 Choose the correct option, A or B, to continue the text or dialogue.

1 Only halfway through the football season and Manchester United yet again leads the Premier League. The situation could easily change, however, as ...
A ... most teams played only a third of their games so far.
B ... most teams have played only a third of their games so far.

2 'I must remember to call my parents before I go away. I haven't even told them about the trip yet.'
A 'Didn't you see much of them lately, then?'
B 'Haven't you seen much of them lately, then?'

3 'What do you think of our new Finance Director?'
A 'He's even more obnoxious than I expected.'
B 'He's even more obnoxious than I've expected.'

4 We won't be able to move back into our house for a while.
A Our tenants are living there for six months.
B Our tenants have lived there for six months.

5 Today we're previewing the new album by singer-songwriter Adele, who, as I'm sure you all know, is coming to the US next month.
A She released two albums so far.
B She has released two albums so far.

6 Another earthquake has hit the Fiji region, bringing further devastation to the area, which is still suffering from the August earthquake.
A The latest tremor measured 7.2 on the Richter scale.
B The latest tremor has measured 7.2 on the Richter scale.

7 Pipeworks regrets the current inconvenience to residents of Kelvin Close.
A We have lowered the water pressure to allow for essential repairs.
B We lowered the water pressure to allow for essential repairs.

8 Investigators into the recent air crash have released their findings, which show a fault in the engine cooling system of the aircraft. All major airlines ...
A ... grounded aircraft of the same type for thorough checks.
B ... have grounded aircraft of the same type for thorough checks.

9 The seventeenth-century writer Cervantes is often considered the father of the modern novel. Most people only connect the name with *Don Quixote*, though Cervantes ...
A ... was a prolific writer.
B ... has been a prolific writer.

10 'With so much money being poured into medical research every year, you'd think that more breakthroughs would be made.' 'But breakthroughs are being made.
A Didn't a Colombian scientist discover a cure for malaria last year?'
B Hasn't a Colombian scientist discovered a cure for malaria last year?'

11 Most visitors to the prison are pleasantly surprised by the environment.
A It is far more open and greener than they have imagined.
B It is far more open and greener than they imagined.

12 My head feels really fuzzy. Concentrating has been far more difficult since ...
A I've been knocked out by that wall that has collapsed.
B I was knocked out by that wall that collapsed.

13 'Have you checked that contract again? We have to send it by lunchtime.'
A 'I've read it through twice this morning. That should be enough surely?'
B 'I read it through twice this morning. That should be enough, surely?'

14 I haven't even looked at the latest assignment for the history course yet. I'll start it once ...
A I finished going through the set book.
B I've finished going through the set book.

2 GRAMMAR IN USE **Complete the conversation, using the words from the box. Write the verbs in the present perfect or past simple. 2.42 Listen and check.**

already / watch ~~always / want~~ be ever / see he / make leave never / hear of not / finish not / see see win

ELLA Look, a DVD of *Casablanca*. (0) I *'ve always wanted* to see that.

KATE What – (1) you .... *Casablanca* – I don't believe it!

ELLA No. When did you see it, then?

KATE (2) I .... it several times. I think it's one of the best films (3) I ....

ELLA Oh, well, in that case, I'll buy it. I don't usually like old films, but (4) I .... all the new films I've got on DVD so I'll watch this tonight. Who's in it?

KATE Humphrey Bogart and Ingrid Bergman.

Humphrey Bogart (1899–1957)

ELLA Who are they? (5) I .... them.

KATE You're unreal! Humphrey Bogart (6) .... one of the greatest actors of the twentieth century, well, in my opinion, anyway.

ELLA What other films (7) ....?

KATE Oh, loads ... *The Big Sleep*, *The Maltese Falcon*, *The African Queen* – he (8) .... an Oscar for that. He died when he was in his fifties, otherwise I'm sure he'd have won more.

ELLA Well, you can tell me more about it later. Right now I've got to go because (9) I .... the children with my sister and have got to pick them up in a few minutes.

KATE You go. I'll get the bus. (10) I .... looking around here yet – there might be some more old films at good prices.

3 **Write the second sentence so it has a similar meaning to the first. Use the word in brackets, as in the example. 2.43 Listen and check.**

0 There's a cake in the oven. (baked) *I've just baked a cake.*

1 Most of the workers started here in 1996, when the factory opened.
(since) ....

2 The guest performers are all here now.
(arrived) ....

3 We visited the new theme park three times last summer and we intend to go this summer, too.
(have) ....

4 Kay and I met each other twenty years ago, when we were children.
(for) ....

5 The latest novel by Chris Cleave is stunning. It's his best to date.
(ever) ....

6 There is no decision from the panel yet about the technical irregularities.
(made) ....

7 The government last increased the rate of income tax several years ago.
(recently) ....

24 Present perfect continuous

1 Ongoing situations and actions

We use the present perfect continuous, often with *since* or *for*, to talk about an ongoing situation or action which began in the past and is still continuing, or has just finished:
*Women **have been speaking out** on this issue **for** some time, with mixed results.*
*I've **been looking into** the possibility of early retirement **since** the reorganisation.*

We do not usually use the present perfect continuous in the passive:
✗ ~~*The patient's heart rate has been being monitored continuously.*~~
✓ *The nurses **have been monitoring** the patient's heart rate continuously.*

The present perfect simple often (but not always) refers to a completed action, while the continuous usually refers to an action that is still ongoing:
*I've **read** that book by Dan Brown if you want to borrow it.* (I've finished reading it.)
*I've **been reading** that book by Dan Brown – it's really exciting!* (I'm still reading it.)

When we use the continuous we focus on duration, so we do not mention the number of times that we have done an action: ***I've been calling** you **all morning**.*

If we give a number of times, we use the present perfect simple:
✗ ~~*I've been calling you five times this morning.*~~ ✓ *I've called you five times this morning.*

2 Temporary situations

The present perfect continuous can suggest a temporary situation or action:
*We**'ve been subscribing** to one of the satellite TV companies.* (not fixed – we may change)

With *lately* or *recently*, it often refers to new developments which may be temporary:
*Helen's **been spending** a lot of time at the club **lately**.* (She didn't use to do this.)

We use the present perfect continuous + *for*, not the present continuous, to specify the duration of an activity which started in the past and is still continuing:
✗ ~~*I am learning how to play chess for three years now.*~~
✓ *I **have been learning** how to play chess for three years now.*

Verbs like *live, work, study, teach* can be used in either the simple or continuous with little difference except that the present perfect simple is seen as more permanent:
*The Montague family **has lived** in the manor house for as long as I can remember.*
*Our daughter **has been living** with us for a few weeks as she's been ill.*

3 Present result

We can use the present perfect continuous to explain a present result. The focus is on the activity rather than the result. In this case, we don't usually use time adverbs:
*I'm sorry the hall is in such a mess. We**'ve been decorating**.*

4 Present perfect simple and continuous: differences

PRESENT PERFECT SIMPLE	PRESENT PERFECT CONTINUOUS
Completion: *This country **has welcomed** several hundred refugees from Albania recently.*	Continuation: *This country **has been welcoming** refugees for many years.*
Repeated action: *She **has played** with the symphony orchestra three times this season.*	Duration of action: *She **has been playing** with the symphony orchestra all season.*
Permanent situation: *People **have eaten** a lot less meat over the last twenty years or so.*	Temporary situation: *People **have been eating** less meat recently because of the health scares.*
Focus on present result: *I've **done** the accounts – here they are.*	Focus on the activity: *I've **been doing** my accounts all afternoon.*

Practice

1 Match sentences 1 and 2 with their meanings, A or B, in each pair.

1
1 I've been reading the book you lent me on genetics.
2 I've read the book you lent me on genetics.

A I've finished the book.
B I'm still reading the book.

2
1 The firm gives company cars to junior managers.
2 The firm has been giving company cars to junior managers.

A This is the company's usual policy. It's unlikely to change.
B This isn't the company's usual policy. It may change.

3
1 Something has been killing the rabbits in the woods.
2 Something has killed the rabbits in the woods.

A There are no rabbits left in the woods.
B There are some rabbits left in the woods.

4
1 Monsanto has placed an advert in the last four *Sunday Times* newspapers.
2 Monsanto has been placing adverts in the national press.

A This was a number of repeated actions.
B This is a continuing publicity campaign.

5
1 'Hi, Fiona. What a mess! Have you been decorating?'
2 'Hi, Fiona. This room looks great! Have you decorated it?'

A Fiona is in the middle of decorating.
B Fiona isn't decorating any more.

6
1 A group of us have learnt how to play bridge.
2 A group of us have been learning how to play bridge.

A We're still learning.
B We can play it now.

2 GRAMMAR IN USE Complete the article with the present perfect simple or, if you can, the continuous form of the verbs in brackets. 2.44 Listen and check.

Kathryn Bigelow (1) .... (just / win) the Academy Award for Best Director – the first woman ever to do so. So, who is she?

Bigelow was born in California in 1951. She studied film at Columbia University and (2) .... (work) in film since the mid-1970s. She (3) .... (be) a female pioneer in the male-dominated world of film directing – she (4) .... (direct) since 1978 and in that time (5) .... (direct) eight feature films. In the last ten years, she (6) .... (also / produce) films. Some of her films (7) .... (be) modest successes, but she is best known now for *The Hurt Locker*, the film for which she won the Oscar. Only four women (8) .... (ever / be nominated) for Best Director, and of the others, Jane Campion and Sofia Coppola (9) .... (have) other Oscar awards.

As well as directing, Bigelow (10) .... (act) in one film and (11) .... (also / appear) as a model during her career. Since her success with *The Hurt Locker* she (12) .... (look) at possibilities for a new crime film set in South America.

25 State verbs

1 State verbs *believe, have, like,* etc.

There are a number of state verbs in English; we rarely use them in a continuous tense:

✗ ~~*The solicitor is doubting the credibility of his client's explanation.*~~

✓ *The solicitor* ***doubts*** *the credibility of his client's explanation.*

They often describe states of being, thinking, possessing or feeling:

existing or being	*be consist of contain exist*
possessing	*belong to have (= own) include lack own possess*
feeling or wanting	*adore desire despise detest dislike envy hate like love need pity prefer trust want wish*
thinking or believing	*believe doubt expect feel (= think) forget imagine intend know realise recognise remember see (= understand) suppose think understand*
appearance	*appear resemble seem*
other verbs	*concern cost depend deserve fit matter mean measure mind weigh*

2 Using these verbs in the continuous

It is possible to use many of the above verbs in the continuous, but the verb either has a different meaning or expresses a temporary action:

*'Is Maria ready yet?' 'No, she'****s having*** *a shower.'* (= is taking)

Santos ***is thinking of*** *getting a new Internet connection.* (= is considering now)

Here are some of the common differences in use:

VERB	USE IN SIMPLE	USE IN CONTINUOUS
be	*Your son* ***was*** *a very obedient child, wasn't he?*	*Your son* ***was being*** *very difficult at the weekend; that wasn't like him.* (= was behaving)
have	*They're very rich. They* ***have*** *three homes and a yacht.* (= own)	***I'm having*** *a really good time, thanks.* (= am experiencing)
think	***I've always thought*** *that we'd meet again.* (= have believed)	***I've been thinking of*** *contributing to Oxfam.* (= have been considering)
mean	*The sign* ***means*** *'slow down'.*	***You're*** *always* ***meaning*** *to call, but you never do.* (= are intending)
appear	*It* ***appears*** *the police haven't started the investigation.* (= seems)	*The Philharmonic* ***are appearing*** *at the Palladium.* (= are performing)
weigh	*She* ***weighs*** *70 kilos.* (= her weight is)	***I'm weighing*** *the ingredients for the cake.* (= action of weighing)

3 Sense verbs *see*, *hear*, *feel*, etc.

We do not usually use the continuous form with verbs which describe a sense or a form of perception, e.g. *hear, notice, see, smell, taste*:

✗ ~~*I'm noticing that your wife never comes to the matches. Doesn't she like cricket?*~~

✓ *I **notice** that your wife never comes to the matches. Doesn't she like cricket?*

✗ ~~*I'm hearing that you're not too happy with the management's proposal.*~~

✓ *I **hear** that you're not too happy with the management's proposal.*

We usually use the simple form or *can/could* + sense verb when we experience something without intentionally using the sense, i.e. the action is involuntary:
*I **(can) smell** the fertiliser on the fields every time I open the back door!*

We also use the simple form when the verb is intransitive:
*The fertiliser on the fields **smells** really horrible!*

With *smell* and *taste*, we can use the continuous for a deliberate action:
*I **(can) taste** cream in this.* (there is cream in the dish; involuntary action)
***I'm tasting** the cream.* (the cream might be bad; intentional action of checking)

We usually use the verbs *see* and *hear* only in the involuntary sense; we use *look at, watch* or *listen to* for an intentional action:

✗ ~~*Can you keep the noise down? I'm hearing something on the radio.*~~

✓ *Can you keep the noise down? **I'm listening to** something on the radio.*

If they have a different meaning, we can use the continuous:
***I'm seeing** a new doctor now.* (= visiting as a patient)

Some verbs of feeling can be used in both the simple and the continuous with no change in meaning:
*My wrist **hurts/is hurting** again – I must go to the physiotherapist.*
*I think those mussels may have been bad. **Do you feel/Are you feeling** OK today?*

4 Performative verbs *thank*, *apologise*, etc.

Performative verbs are verbs which can actually perform the action they describe when they are used in the first person and the present tense; they address the listener/reader directly:
*On behalf of the company, I **apologise** for any inconvenience caused.*

Common examples are:

accept agree apologise congratulate declare deny disagree forbid forgive guarantee insist invite order predict promise recommend refuse request suggest thank warn

When we use these verbs in the present, they are usually in the simple form:
*Railtrack **apologises** for the disruption to services this weekend.*
*We **recommend** the new tapas restaurant in the town centre.*

If we use these verbs to refer to the past or future, we can use them in the continuous form. Compare:

PRESENT ✗ ~~*I'm thanking you all for joining us today.*~~
✓ *I **thank** you all for joining us today.*

PAST ✓ *He **warned** the children not to swim too far from the beach.*
✓ *When we arrived, he **was warning** the children not to swim too far from the beach.*

FUTURE ✓ ***I'm inviting** about sixty people to Jenna's party – OK?*

Practice

1 Match sentences 1 and 2 with the continuations A and B in each pair.

1 1 Steven's a difficult child.
  2 Steven's being difficult.
  A He's showing off because we've got visitors.
  B He's been very demanding since birth.

2 1 This salmon weighs more than six kilos.
  2 We're weighing the salmon.
  A It will be plenty for thirty people.
  B It needs to be priced per kilo.

3 1 I invite everyone present to the opening of the new superstore.
  2 I'm inviting everyone to the opening of the new superstore.
  A And I can offer you all a 10 percent discount voucher.
  B I'll put the invitation in a letter to everyone.

4 1 The poet appears to have arrived at the theatre.
  2 The poet is appearing at the theatre.
  A There are performances every evening.
  B We don't know why she was late.

5 1 Mmm. I taste cinnamon in this. Lovely.
  2 I'm tasting it to see if there's enough cinnamon in it.
  A The recipe said one teaspoon only, but I might add more.
  B I adore the taste of cinnamon.

6 1 I think house prices will rise again next year.
  2 I'm thinking of selling my house next year.
  A At least, that's my opinion.
  B At least, that's my intention.

7 1 My sister has a baby.
  2 My sister's having a baby.
  A It's due in July.
  B He'll be six months old tomorrow.

8 1 I smell lavender.
  2 I'm smelling the lavender. It's a very strong variety.
  A Is it your perfume?
  B I know quite a lot about lavender, you know.

9 1 He's having a shower.
  2 He has a fantastic power shower in the main bathroom.
  A It cost more than 400 euros.
  B Why don't you wait in the living room?

10 1 We guarantee that your child will be supervised by experienced instructors.
  2 Mrs Knight's brother and sister-in-law are guaranteeing the loan for her.
  A The company takes full responsibility for her.
  B They believe she is entirely trustworthy.

11 1 Laura's very sarcastic sometimes.
  2 She thinks she's clever, but she's just being sarcastic.
  A It's her least attractive characteristic.
  B Take no notice of her.

12 1 What are you thinking of?
  2 What do you think about the new road layout?
  A It seems an exercise in pointless bureaucracy to me.
  B You look deep in thought.

2 GRAMMAR IN USE **Read the letter and choose the correct *italic* verb form. If both options are correct, choose both. 2.45 Listen and check.**

12 SUNNYBANK ROAD • READING • BERKS • RG2 4OX

Ms Gloria Travis
Pinetree Studios
Loughton LG12 2CO

12 February 2012

Dear Ms Travis,

Please forgive me for contacting you out of the blue. I am writing in connection with the film apprenticeships your studio offers. I (1) *noticed / was noticing* an advertisement about these in the Guardian some months ago and I have (2) *meant / been meaning* to write to you since then. My request (3) *concerns / is concerning* the film editing apprenticeship in particular.

I completed a university degree in film studies last June and I have been trying to find a position in film since then. To be honest, I (4) *have / am having* great difficulty and I (5) *feel / am feeling* rather despondent at present. My course (6) *consisted / was consisting* of most aspects of film and television production, and I specialised in film editing in my final year. I have always (7) *wanted / been wanting* to pursue a career in film and I took the degree to facilitate that, although it (8) *appears / is appearing* not to have been successful to date. I (9) *realise / am realising* that the advert for the apprenticeships was placed some months ago and you may not have any places available now. However, I am perfectly willing to work in any capacity without payment for a few weeks in order for you to see my level of commitment, in the hope that I may qualify for an apprenticeship in the future. I (10) *promise / am promising* that I won't disappoint you if you decide to employ me in any capacity.

I look forward to hearing from you.

Yours sincerely

Celia Roberts

Celia Roberts

3 **Complete the sentences, using suitable verbs from the box. Choose whether to use a simple or continuous form. 2.46 Listen and check.**

be despise forbid hurt mean see taste watch

1 I'm really annoyed you took the car without asking me. From now on I .... you to borrow the car without asking permission first!
2 That medicine .... horrible! What on earth do they put in them to make them so awful?
3 Oh, Joan, can I call you back? I .... the grand prix at the moment.
4 Hasn't Mike fixed your kitchen tap yet? I know he .... to do it for ages.
5 'What was that?' 'I don't know. I just .... something blue fly past. Was it a bird?'
6 I'm not coming to the class tonight. I've twisted my ankle and it .... a lot now.
7 What do you mean, you're leaving? Now you .... over-dramatic!
8 I can't understand why the newspapers write such awful lies about people. Everyone .... that kind of gutter journalism.

Review MODULE 5

1 UNITS 19, 20, 21 AND 25 **Choose the correct verb form in *italics*.**

Ionian Idyll

Every year more and more tourists (1) *visit / are visiting* the Ionian Islands, and most are enchanted by these lush green islands in a turquoise sea.

Many (2) *now think / are now thinking* about the possibility of owning property in this warm, unspoilt corner of Europe. Does the idea appeal to you? If so, read on! Imagine yourself standing on a wide terrace high on a cliff above the clear Ionian Sea. The sun (3) *beats / is beating* down and you (4) *hear / are hearing* the cicadas and the sound of waves lapping gently against the golden sand below. You (5) *smell / are smelling* the heady scent of jasmine. Down a steep path (6) *lies / is lying* the turquoise sea, right in front of you. We (7) *invite / 're inviting* you to share this experience with us.

We (8) *currently develop / are currently developing* a complex of luxury apartments just outside Lourdas, in the south of Cephalonia, the largest and the most varied of the Ionian Islands. Lourdas is a traditional Greek village with a variety of shops and tavernas, where local people (9) *have / have got* their long, leisurely lunches.

Behind the village the mountains (10) *rise / are rising* steeply and goats roam freely. From the village a road winds down to Lourdas Bay. The wide sweep of the bay (11) *is sheltering / shelters* a long sandy beach which is almost totally uncommercialised.

We have completed our show apartment and we (12) *now show / are now showing* prospective purchasers the apartment, either in person at the site, or online with a virtual tour.

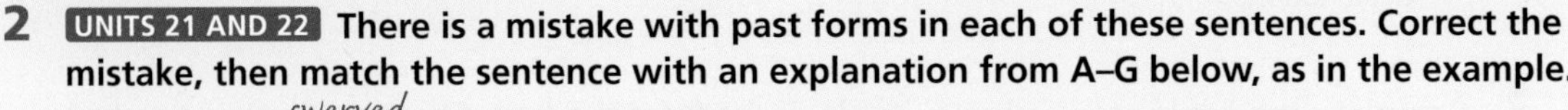

2 UNITS 21 AND 22 **There is a mistake with past forms in each of these sentences. Correct the mistake, then match the sentence with an explanation from A–G below, as in the example.**

0 The car ~~had swerved~~ *swerved* past us, then it immediately hit the lamp-post. ....*B*....

1 Julia hates working. She would be much happier when she was a student. ....

2 Almost everyone left the party when I got there. Only Alex and Mike were still there. ....

3 We all complained to our manager about Larry as he continually took two-hour lunch breaks. ....

4 Jack was exhausted when he arrived – he was running to catch the train. ....

5 Emma was waking up, was getting up, was showering as usual ... then she remembered what a big day it was. ....

6 We used to go to our son's graduation ceremony last weekend. ....

A We don't use this form for a single action in the past.

B We don't usually use this form for an action that happens immediately before another.

C We don't use this form when the action has already stopped.

D We don't use this form for a series of complete, fairly quick actions in the past.

E We don't use this form for a state in the past, only actions that are no longer happening.

F We prefer to use the continuous for actions in the past which annoyed us.

G We don't use this form when we want to show that the action happened before another action.

3 UNITS 21, 23 AND 24 **Complete the text with the phrases from the box.**

contained existed found has allowed has discovered has produced has been
has been trying have been digging have been found have unearthed were discovered

Palaeontologists in New Mexico (1) .... the remains of at least one dinosaur from the late Jurassic period. The scientists (2) .... in an unexplored part of the Morrison Formation – a vast fossil bed – for the last eight months. Last week one of the group (3) .... a section of rock which (4) .... a number of bones from one, or possibly more, large herbivorous dinosaurs. Since then, the group (5) .... to release the bones from the rock and piece them together. According to Bryce Larson, the group's leader, the bones are from a large brachiosaurus. These animals (6) .... approximately 150 million years ago. Other brachiosaurus remains (7) .... in the Morrison, but these latest bones may prove to come from the largest dinosaur anyone (8) .... to date.
For a long time the Morrison Formation (9) .... one of the most productive fossil beds in the world. Since the first bones (10) .... there in 1877, it (11) .... tonnes of material. This, more than any other fossil bed, (12) .... us an insight into the late Jurassic period in North America.

4 ALL UNITS **Complete the article by writing the verbs in brackets in the correct tense.**

Treasure Island

TREASURE ISLAND is one of the best known and most loved children's adventure stories. Published in 1883, it remains popular to this day. Recent research (1) .... (uncover) the true origin of this thrilling tale of pirates and hidden treasure. *Treasure Island*'s author, Robert Louis Stevenson, was a Scotsman born in Edinburgh in 1850. Although he (2) .... (not stay) in Scotland, in 1881 he returned to the land of his birth for a holiday. With him was his American wife Fanny, whom he (3) .... (meet) five years earlier in France, and his stepchildren from Fanny's first marriage.

The family soon settled into a relaxing routine. Each morning Stevenson (4) .... (get up) early and take them out for long walks over the hills. They (5) .... (enjoy) this for several days when the weather suddenly took a turn for the worse. Trapped indoors, Robert's stepson started painting a beautiful coloured map of a tropical island, with a large cross in the middle of the island. 'It means "Here (6) .... (lie) the buried treasure",' he told his stepfather. This was the beginning of one of the greatest adventure stories that (7) .... (ever be) written. While the rain (8) .... (beat) down on the roof of his rented holiday cottage, Stevenson sat down by the fire to write.

The story (9) .... (have got) everything necessary for a successful children's book: treasure, wild adventures at sea, a young protagonist, and a memorable villain. The story (10) .... (always stimulate) children's imaginations and (11) .... (still do) so today. Over the years film-makers across the world (12) .... (adapt) the novel for the cinema and TV. There (13) .... (be) sixteen film versions of the book, and recent rumours suggest that a famous Oscar-winning director (14) .... (work) on a new version, using the latest 3D technology.

MODULE

Future forms

Before you start

1 Review these intermediate grammar points and check you know them.

Future forms and uses

FORM	USE	EXAMPLES
future simple: *will/won't* + infinitive	general prediction	*I bet we**'ll** still **be** in this house in twenty years' time. Who **will win** the election?*
	future facts	*Next year **will be** a leap year.*
	decision made at the time of speaking	*Oh, our guests are here. **I'll sort** out some drinks and nibbles.*
be going to + infinitive	prediction based on present evidence	*Kate Atkinson's new book has already sold thousands of copies; it**'s going to be** a bestseller.*
	intention (personal or impersonal)	***Is** the management **going to accept** the current pay claim?*
present continuous	arrangements	*Next year we**'re working** on a joint project with the Frankfurt office.*
future continuous: *will/won't* be + *-ing* form	prediction of an action in progress	*By next July the economy **will be growing** at a healthy rate once more.*
	plans made in the past	*I can't make next Monday's class as **I'll be returning** from my long weekend away.*
	events that are part of a routine	*The committee **will be meeting** at the usual time on Friday.*
future perfect: *will/won't have* + past participle	prediction about a completed action in the future	***Will** you **have discussed** this with your boss before you go to the conference?*
present simple	an event that is part of a timetable	*The lecture **starts** tomorrow evening at 8.00 p.m.*
	after certain expressions of time, e.g. *as soon as*	*We will send you the books you ordered as soon as we **receive** payment.*

Using *shall, shan't*

1 The use of *shall/shan't* with *I* and *we* in the future simple is becoming dated and is rare now:
*Having learnt on an automatic car, I **shall** never **get** the hang of this manual gearbox.*

2 *Shall* is common in the question form as an offer or a suggestion:
*'I can't get this tin open.' '**Shall** I do it for you?'*
***Shall** we go out tonight?*

We do not use *shall/shan't* with *he, she, it, you, they* for predictions:
✗ ~~*He shall like the idea, I'm sure.*~~ ✓ *He **will like** the idea, I'm sure.*

2 **Read the commentary and find examples of different future forms.**

'So, who will win the election? Will the Government have done enough to calm people's fears about the economy? Is the nation going to endorse the current administration or send it into oblivion? As usual, we will be bringing you all the results and details as soon as they happen, and this year we're teaming up with Sky to bring you the best coverage ever. Our election broadcast starts tomorrow evening at 11.00 p.m. Don't miss it!'

3 **Complete the diagnostic test below. Choose the correct words in *italics*. If both options are correct, choose both.**

1 I take the 10.40 to Bristol every Friday and it's always half empty. *You'll find / You'll be finding* a seat. ➤ Unit 26.1
2 Kelly's sister *will / is going to* have a baby. It's due next month. ➤ Unit 26.2
3 I'm going away to Austria tomorrow. This time next Tuesday afternoon *I'm going to ski / 'll be skiing* down a mountain! ➤ Unit 26.3
4 'You speak very good Mandarin.' 'Thank you. It's not surprising; I'll have *lived / been living* in Beijing for eight years next month.' ➤ Unit 26.4
5 The economic forecast is really gloomy. I *don't think it will be / think it isn't* a very easy winter. ➤ Unit 26.5
6 Your driving test is next Tuesday, so *are we having / shall we have* a two-hour lesson on Monday? ➤ Unit 27.1
7 My parents have just given me 10,000 euros but I *'m not going to / don't* spend it all straightaway! ➤ Unit 27.2
8 'Have you checked my report yet?' 'No, but I'm *staying / going to stay* at home tonight. I'll look at it then.' ➤ Unit 27.3
9 The takeover is going ahead, I'm afraid, so we *will be / are* making some redundancies in the New Year. ➤ Unit 27.4
10 The Mayor of Paris is *to / about to* attend the ceremony tomorrow before leaving the city. ➤ Unit 27.5
11 These pills *will not be / are not to be* taken without food. ➤ Unit 27.5
12 The plane *is to take off / takes off* at 10.45, so we'd better check in by 8.45. ➤ Unit 28.1
13 The builder won't finish the work until you *will pay / have paid* him what you owe him. ➤ Unit 28.1
14 Mr Fellows *plays / will be playing* golf tomorrow afternoon as usual, so you can catch him on the course. ➤ Unit 28.2
15 The timetable is *due to be / on the point of being* published on 1st May. ➤ Unit 28.3
16 He's very *likely / unlikely* to accept the position as we can't match his current salary. ➤ Unit 28.4
17 The society *hopes to / envisages* expand its membership by twenty percent in the next year. ➤ Unit 28.5
18 'I'm sorry I spilt tea on your dress.' 'Don't worry. I *would / was going to* take it to the cleaners' anyway.' ➤ Unit 29.1
19 Look, I didn't put the rubbish out this morning because I thought you *would / were going to* do it! ➤ Unit 29.2
20 The new department store was to *open / have opened* on 2nd January, but the explosion prevented this. ➤ Unit 29.2

4 **Check your answers on page 384. Then go to the unit for more information and practice.**

Go online for a full diagnostic test

26 Predictions

1 Future simple *will/won't* + infinitive

We use this to talk about predictions based on opinion, analysis or judgement:
This investment from all sectors ***will bring*** *economic prosperity and continued success.*

We often use *will/won't* to predict an event which we think will happen because similar events have happened in the past:
*He'**ll be** in prison for a long time.* (Similar crimes have attracted long sentences.)
The battery ***won't last*** *forever, so you should buy a spare.* (Previous batteries haven't lasted.)

We can also use *will/won't* for future events that are certain to happen:
Aunt Charlotte ***will be*** *ninety on Thursday. It* ***won't be*** *light before 6 a.m.*

2 *be going to* + infinitive

When there is evidence in the present to justify the prediction, we use *be going to* + infinitive:
Howard's wife ***is going to have*** *a baby! Isn't it marvellous!*
*With his criminal record, there isn't a jury in the world that'**s going to believe** him.*

With *be going to* the prediction is often about the immediate future:
*Sssh! The bride's father has just got up. He'**s going to make** a speech now.*

This use of *be going to* for the immediate future often has an element of warning:
*Look out! You'**re going to spill** your coffee!*
*It's 8.30. You'**re not going to get to** school on time.*

We can use *will* for a prediction with present evidence, usually when we are giving an opinion. We often use introductory phrases such as *I think*. Compare:
That's a bad dent in the car. ***I think it'll cost*** *a lot to repair.*
(This is my opinion, maybe based on past experience.)
The mechanic has phoned. I was right – that dent ***is going to cost*** *us a lot of money!*
(This is based on present evidence given by the mechanic.)
There is often little difference between these two uses.

3 Future continuous *will/won't be* + *-ing* form

We use this form for a temporary action in progress at or around a particular point in the future:
*This time next Tuesday afternoon I'**ll be lying** on the beach!*

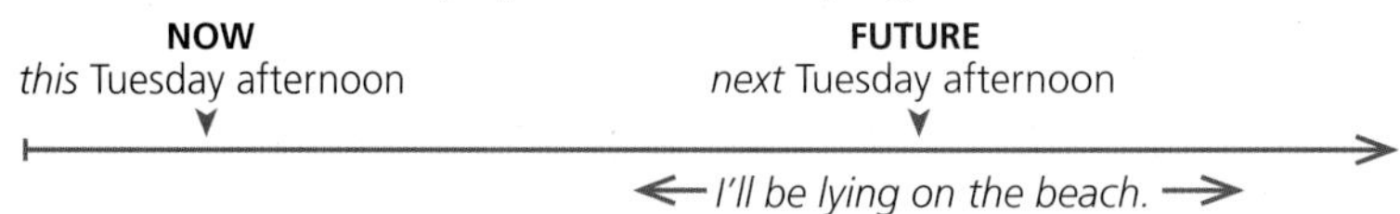

Compare this with the present continuous for a temporary action in the present:
*It's Tuesday afternoon and I'**m lying** on the beach. Aren't smartphones wonderful!*

We use this form to talk about an action that will be in progress in the future; it may have a result or make another action possible:
My mother ***will be looking after*** *the children, so we'll be able to talk.*
I ***won't be going*** *to the staff meeting tomorrow, so I'll answer the phone for you.*

We do not usually use the passive with this form, nor the verb *be*:
✗ ~~*The proposal will be being presented at the next meeting.*~~
✓ *The chairman* ***will be presenting*** *the proposal at the next meeting.*
✗ ~~*Shelley will be being in Morocco this time tomorrow.*~~
✓ *Shelley* ***will be*** *in Morocco this time tomorrow.*

We can also use *will/won't be* + *-ing* form (and *will/won't* + infinitive) to describe something we believe to be the case now:
*You can't interrupt her now. She'****ll be getting*** *ready to go on stage.*
(I think she's getting ready now.)
*'What's that noise?' 'It'****ll be*** *Ron upstairs. He's learning to play the trumpet.'*
(I think it must be him.)

4 Future perfect simple and continuous

We use the future perfect simple (*will/won't have* + past participle) to make predictions about actions which we expect to be completed before a particular time in the future:
*He'****ll have had*** *the operation by July and should be a lot fitter then.*

We usually use a time adverb/phrase (e.g. *soon, by then, within the next week*) with this kind of prediction. The times can be very close to 'now':
*I'****ll have finished*** *my report within the next hour, so you'll have a printout by lunchtime.*

We use the future perfect continuous (*will/won't have* + *been* + *-ing* form) to talk about an action which will still be in progress at a point in the future. It focuses on the duration of the action:
By 2040, people ***will have been using*** *mobile phones for over half a century.*
*We'****ll have been living*** *in this house for twenty years in December.*

With verbs such as *live, work, stay*, which contain the idea of continuity, we can also use *will/won't have* + past participle:
*We'****ll have lived*** *in this house for twenty years in December.*

We rarely use this form in the passive:
[*By July the house* ***will have been being built*** *for a year.*]
✓ *By July they* ***will have been building*** *the house for a year.*

5 Making predictions stronger or weaker

We can make predictions, intentions or decisions stronger or weaker by using certain adverbs, e.g. *definitely, certainly, probably, possibly*:
*She'****ll definitely give*** *a fantastic presentation at the conference – she always does.*
I ***certainly won't give*** *you a lift to the station – it's only down the road!*
*Call me at about 8.00. I'****ll probably have got*** *home by then.*

Note the position of the adverb:
- between *will* and the infinitive in positive sentences
- before *won't* in negative sentences.

We can show how sure we are about a future event by using an introductory verb, e.g. *think, expect, hope, doubt, suppose, promise, guarantee*:
I ***hope she'll call*** *us from the airport.*
The Club ***guarantees that tickets will be*** *sold on the day.*

With verbs like *think* and *believe* we usually show negative meaning at the beginning of the sentence (➤ Unit 47.4):
[*I* ***think I won't pass*** *the exam.*] ✓ *I* ***don't think I'll pass*** *the exam.*

Practice

1 GRAMMAR IN USE **Choose the correct words in *italics* in the conversation. If both options are possible, choose both. 2.47 Listen and check.**

DAVID Who (1) *will / 's going to* win the local election, do you think?
HANNAH Oh, it'll (2) *probably / definitely* be the Social Democrats, I've got no doubt.
DAVID How can you be so sure?
HANNAH Come on, by May the Conservatives will (3) *be / have been* running the local council for over twelve years, and they've made so many mistakes.
DAVID Quite – they've been in power for over twelve years. This area always votes Conservative. Why do you think it (4) *will / 's going to* be any different this time?
HANNAH Well, it's perfectly clear that they (5) *will / are going to* go ahead with the new railway line, so high-speed trains will soon (6) *run / be running* through the area every twenty minutes. That (7) *'s going to / will* change the landscape completely and destroy the atmosphere.
DAVID You're right, but that was more of a national government decision, wasn't it? In fact, our local politicians opposed the decision, so I (8) *don't think that will / think that won't* influence people much.
HANNAH You may be right. People (9) *probably will / will probably* vote the same way as always. It's so depressing.
DAVID It isn't so bad. Look on the bright side. You'll (10) *have / have had* plenty to complain about for the next four years!

2 **Write the second sentence so it has a similar meaning to the first, using the word in brackets. The sentence must include a future form, as in the example.**

0 We are certain of a high level of customer satisfaction with this product.
(guarantee) *We guarantee that customers will be satisfied with this product.*

1 Let's stop playing soon – our opponents have so many more points than we do.
(going) ....

2 My great-grandmother celebrates her hundredth birthday next year.
(old) ....

3 It's impossible that humans will ever be able to live on the moon, in my opinion.
(think) ....

4 It's my parents' twenty-fifth wedding anniversary next Saturday.
(married) ....

5 Come along next Monday – the band always practises on Monday afternoons.
(will) ....

6 We are one hundred percent certain of the success of our proposal.
(certainly) ....

7 Do you have any idea of your arrival time on Friday?
(arriving) ....

8 That skier is going far too fast, and those trees are very close.
(hit) ....

3 GRAMMAR IN USE **Complete the article, using suitable forms of the verbs in brackets. Sometimes more than one answer is possible.** 2.48 **Listen and check.**

Solving Japan's old-age problem

JAPAN IS AGEING FASTER THAN ANY OTHER NATION. BY THE END OF THIS DECADE THERE (0) *will be* (be) THREE PENSIONERS FOR EVERY CHILD UNDER 15 AND ONE IN SIX PEOPLE (1) .... (celebrate) THEIR 80TH BIRTHDAY ALREADY.

UNLIKE other countries, Japan has not turned to immigration to solve its problem, but to technology – manufacturers are currently working on a number of innovations, many of which (2) .... (soon be) available. Here are just a few:

CARS

The over-75s in Japan account for more than 25 percent of fatal accidents on the road. Toyota is working with Nintendo to create cars that can monitor brain activity. The car (3) .... (learn) its user's driving pattern, so when Mrs Watanabe suddenly puts her foot on the accelerator for no reason, it will know she (4) .... (have) an accident and will slow the car down automatically.

INTELLIGENT KETTLES

In the future, much of the care of the elderly (5) .... (fall) on the younger members of the family, who may live a distance away. Appliance-maker Zojurushi has developed an Internet-connected kettle which can send remote signals, so when you leave for work in the morning you will know that granny is OK because her kettle (6) .... (send) you a signal earlier that morning.

ROBOT PETS

Animals are known to be good for the elderly, but real animals are difficult to look after as their owners age. This furry white baby seal robot is being used in nursing homes to stimulate dementia sufferers, but its manufacturers hope that soon many less infirm pensioners (7) .... (care for) robot pets in their own homes.

EASY-SWALLOW FOOD

Some diseases of the elderly, such as Parkinson's, can make swallowing difficult, so the idea is that easy-swallow food, i.e. liquidised food, (8) .... (help) those people. President of Synovate Healthcare, Bill Hall, says, 'I think this (9) .... (take) the world by storm.'

SUPERMARKET AISLES

Even supermarkets are becoming more age-aware. As the population ages, more and more people (10) .... (use) motorised wheelchairs, so supermarkets are making their aisles wider to accommodate such vehicles.

What happens in Japan now (11) .... (almost certainly come) to the west as the baby-boomer generation from the 1950s and 60s reaches old age; people here will benefit from these innovations as they (12) .... (be) tried and tested in Japan.

27 Decisions, intentions and arrangements

Local student Shona Johnson **is leaving** college in June to start a career in politics. Shona **is to start** an internship at the Senate in September, where she **will be working** with the Senator for Wisconsin. Shona says she **is going to carve out** a big career for herself!

1 Future simple *will/won't* + infinitive

We can talk about spontaneous decisions with this form:
*You look tired. **I'll cook** dinner tonight.*

To ask questions about decisions, we can use *shall I/we*: ***Shall I** see you next week, then?*

We can use *will/won't* + infinitive to strengthen meaning, and to express determination:
*I **will join** you all at the festival at the weekend, whatever my parents say!*
*If you insist on lying, I certainly **won't help** you.*

In speech we usually stress *will/won't* when we use this form to express determination.

⚠ We do not usually contract *will* to *'ll* with this use, except with a stressed adverb:
*He**'ll never agree** to that!*

 FORMALITY CHECK It is possible to use this form for very formal arrangements:
*Cabinet **will meet** tomorrow to discuss the issue of identity cards.*

 FORMALITY CHECK We can also use *shall/shall not* with *I* and *we* to express determination, especially in a formal context:
*The purpose of this interview is to give my views on the economy. I **shall** therefore **not** be drawn into discussing my personal life.*

Pronunciation ➤ 1.07

2 *be going to* + infinitive

We use *be going to* + infinitive for actions that we have already decided to do:
*My nephew **is going to study** environmental law next year.* (This is his plan/intention.)
*The police **aren't going to prosecute** those youths after all.* (They have decided against it.)

We stress auxiliary *be* or *not* to express determination about something we have already decided on:
*I **am going to leave**. **I'm not going to stay** here any longer, so don't try to make me!*

Pronunciation ➤ 1.08

⚠ We usually avoid *be going to* with the verbs *go* and *come*:
[*I'm going to go home now. Are you going to come?*]
✓ ***I'm going** home now. **Are** you **coming**?*

3 Present continuous and *be going to*

We use the present continuous to describe an event in the future which has already been arranged by the time of speaking:
*We**'re seeing** a musical at the theatre next week.* (We've got the tickets.)

Compare this with the use of *be going to*:
*We**'re going to see** a musical at the theatre sometime next week.*
(It may or may not be arranged yet; the emphasis is on our intention.)

When we have made some form of commitment to an arrangement, e.g. by buying tickets or organising something with other people, we tend to use the present continuous:
I'm staying in tonight. I promised my flatmates I'd cook lasagne for them.

The emphasis here is on the 'arrangement', rather than the speaker's own intention. These two forms are often interchangeable with little difference in meaning, but the present continuous tends to 'distance' the action from the speaker and his/her choice.

We also use the present continuous for impersonal plans:
*Computer City has announced that it **is opening** four new shops next month.*

FORMALITY CHECK With impersonal uses like this, the present continuous is seen as a little more formal than *be going to*, and is more likely to be used:
[*Computer City has announced that it **is going to open** four new shops next month.*]

⚠ We cannot use this form with events which are beyond human control, e.g. the weather, because these events are predictions, not intentions or arrangements:
✗ ~~*It's snowing tomorrow.*~~ ✓ *It's going to snow tomorrow.* ✓ *It will snow tomorrow.*

4 Future continuous *will/won't be + -ing* form

We can use the future continuous to talk about events that are a result of or part of an arrangement made in the past:
*Trains **won't be running** to Upminster this weekend due to essential track repairs.*

With this structure the future event is seen as arranged, so we use this as a tactful way of refusing an invitation or asking about someone's plans:
*I'm sorry, I can't come to your wedding as **I'll be working** on that day.*
***Will** you **be staying** long?*

Compare:
Are you staying long? (more direct, less polite than *Will you be staying long?*)

There is, in fact, little difference between this and the use of the present/future continuous for arrangements. The future continuous distances the arrangement a little, making it more fixed and less open to change.

5 *be to* + infinitive

We use *be to* + infinitive in formal English to talk about official arrangements in the future:
*The President **is to hold** an official reception for the visitors.*

This construction is common in writing, especially in news articles:
*Crash investigators **are to release** their findings to the press later today.*

The verb *be* is often omitted in headlines, both for 'formal' and 'informal' topics:

PRESIDENT **TO HOLD** OFFICIAL RECEPTION

EastEnders stars to marry

We often use *be to* in *if* clauses (➤ Unit 37) when the event in the *if* clause is dependent on the event in the main clause:
*If tennis in this country **is to improve**, more money and commitment will be necessary.*
(= More money and commitment must be given first for tennis to improve.)

FORMALITY CHECK We can also use *be* (*not*) *to* + infinitive for formal commands and instructions:
*You **are not to disturb** the head teacher while the inspectors are here next week.*

It is quite common to use the passive for instructions with *be to* (without referring to the future):
*These pills **are not to be taken** with any other form of medicine.*

Practice

1 Only one sentence, A or B, is correct or appropriate in each pair. Tick (✓) the correct sentence and match the incorrect one with an explanation from 1–4 below.

1 A I'm going to fly to Thailand on Saturday if I get a standby ticket.
  B I'm flying to Thailand on Saturday if I get a standby ticket.
2 A We wouldn't have come if we'd known you were so ill. We're going to go back now.
  B We wouldn't have come if we'd known you were so ill. We'll go back now.
3 A I'm really sorry that I forgot to send the payment. I'll put it in the post tomorrow.
  B I'm really sorry that I forgot to send the payment. I am to put it in the post tomorrow.
4 A I'm afraid we aren't coming to your inaugural lecture.
  B I'm afraid we won't be coming to your inaugural lecture.

1 We don't use this structure to express a spontaneous decision.
2 This structure is direct and not polite enough.
3 This structure is too formal for the rest of the text.
4 The arrangement is not fixed so this structure is inappropriate.

2 GRAMMAR IN USE Tessa has just been elected as a representative at her university. Read her statement and choose the correct options, A, B or C. If two options are correct, choose both, as in the example.

MY FELLOW STUDENTS

Many thanks to those of you who voted for me in the student representative elections of 15 October.

I am now looking forward to our first meeting with the university council, which (0) ..... in ten days' time.

I feel that my interest in politics and my knowledge of the subject (1) ..... important factors in my representation. I am used to debating and I (2) ..... your views across clearly and firmly.

I believe strongly that student representatives should be involved in making academic decisions, and I (3) ..... for that to happen. Next year the university (4) ..... its number of degree courses to include law and medicine, which will put a strain on the existing infrastructure, i.e. buildings and facilities. I (5) ..... the authorities to ignore the problems this will bring.

My other main cause for concern is the escalating cost of transport. I can obviously do nothing about that, but I (6) ..... the university to delay the start of formal lectures and tutorials until after 10.00 a.m., to allow students to take advantage of cheaper off-peak fares.

Finally, let me remind you that all the elected student representatives (7) ..... their views in the main lecture theatre next Thursday evening at 7.00 p.m.

Tessa Pinkerton

0 (A) will be held (B) is to be held C will be being held
1 A are being B will be C are going to be
2 A will put B am putting C am to put
3 A am pushing B will push C will be pushing
4 A is going to increase B is increasing C shall increase
5 A will not allow B will not be allowing C am not going to allow
6 A am to press B will be pressing C am pressing
7 A are discussing B will be discussing C shall discuss

3 **Match the sentences 1–9 with the replies A–J, then complete the replies with the verbs in brackets, as in the example. 3.01 Listen and check.**

0 There's someone at the door. ...D....
1 Mum, my flat is being decorated. Can I come and stay with you and Dad? ....
2 Can I come round and see you this evening? ....
3 Have you got any plans for a new TV series? ....
4 Is your steak tough again? ....
5 Oh no! It's nearly half past and my train's at quarter to! ....
6 Have the management made plans to review salaries? ....
7 Does the Queen intend to address the nation? ....
8 What are Jamie's plans for the spring holiday? ....
9 Have you seen Lorna and Craig recently? ....

A No, we haven't, but we .... (have) lunch with them next Sunday.
B Yes, a speech .... (be broadcast) early next week.
C It is. This time I .... (complain) to the butcher.
D Don't get up. I 'll answer.............................. (answer) it.
E No, sorry. I .... (watch) the football highlights tonight.
F We .... (look at) salaries as usual in the end-of-year review.
G Come on then. I .... (give) you a lift to the station.
H Well, he's got exams in May, so he .... (study) for those.
I Yes. We .... (film) a new series next year. We've already found the locations and booked the actors.
J Of course, dear. How long do you think you .... (stay)?

4 GRAMMAR IN USE **Complete the conversation with verbs from the box in suitable future forms. Include the words in brackets, when given. 3.02 Listen and check.**

arrive be (x2) come have (x2) have to meet pick up send take work

PAM Can we fix a time for the next meeting? How about the 12th?
ALEX I thought something was happening on that day.
PAM Oh yes, you're right. The people from Head Office (1) .... to see us.
JOHN What time (2) .... (they)? Can we have the meeting in the morning?
PAM No, it's all arranged. I (3) .... them on a tour of the plant, followed by lunch with our suppliers, so I (4) .... available at all that day.
ALEX OK, let's have the meeting earlier in June, then. We (5) .... (all) back from the sales conference by the 3rd, won't we?
PAM Yes, but we need John's annual figures for the meeting. How are they going, John?
JOHN I (6) ....on them soon, gathering information. The sales managers (7) .... me their provisional figures in the first week of June, so I (8) .... the report ready by, oh, the 15th.
PAM So, we're looking at the week starting the 18th. How about two o'clock on that day?
ALEX Difficult. I (9) .... lunch with the sales manager of Bowman's. Could we make it three?
JOHN I can do that but I (10) .... the children that week, as the nanny's away, so I (11) .... leave here at five thirty. Is that OK?
PAM Sure. So we (12) .... at three o'clock on 18th June, in the boardroom.

28 Other ways of expressing the future

'The G8 summit ***is about to finish*** *any moment now. We* ***are expecting the ministers to go*** *straight to the press conference in the media centre, where they* ***are due to make*** *a joint statement at 2.00 p.m. The lack of agreement on environmental issues* ***is bound to disappoint*** *many people who believed this summit would deliver change.'*

1 Present simple, *be due to*, for timetabled events

We use the present simple to talk about timetabled events, usually with a time or date:
Carriageway repairs on this stretch of the motorway ***start*** *on 26th May.*

We also use *be due to* for timetabled events, usually with a time or date:
Carriageway repairs on this stretch of the motorway ***are due to start*** *on 26th May.*
'The Mousetrap' ***is due to celebrate*** *its 25,000th performance later this month.*

The present simple suggests that the timetabled event is totally fixed, but *be due to* suggests possible change, i.e. the event may change:
New measures to contain asylum seekers ***are due to come*** *into force on 1st August but a case currently before the European court may delay this until the autumn.*

When we refer to the future in subordinate clauses (starting with *after, as, before, by the time, as soon as, if, immediately, once, the moment, unless, until* and *when*), we use a present form, NOT *will/won't*:
✗ ~~*Won't the park look good once the new trees will reach maturity?*~~
✓ *Won't the park look good once the new trees* ***reach/have reached*** *maturity?*
✗ ~~*Effective penal reform will not be achieved unless the government will take it seriously.*~~
✓ *Effective penal reform will not be achieved unless the government* ***takes*** *it seriously.*

2 Future continuous for routine events

We can use *will/won't be + -ing* form to emphasise the routine nature of an event:
*We****'ll be having*** *our weekly meeting tomorrow so I'll present your proposal then.*
(future continuous: emphasis on the routine nature of the weekly meeting)

Compare this with the use of other future forms:
*We****'re having*** *our weekly meeting tomorrow instead of Friday this week.*
(present continuous: emphasis on the arrangement rather than the routine)
We ***have*** *our weekly meeting on Friday so I'll present your proposal then.*
(present simple: presents the meeting as part of a timetable)

This future continuous form can also suggest that an event is inevitable:
I'll be seeing *Mr Kennedy at the court tomorrow – he's always there on Thursdays – so we can discuss your case briefly then.*

3 Expressions for near future events

We use *be about to* to talk about an event that we intend or expect to happen in the near future. The event may or may not be planned, but evidence in the present indicates that it will happen (*be going to* ➤ Unit 26.2):
Ladies and gentlemen. Please take your seats. The performance ***is about to start.***
*Hurry up! The driver says he can't wait any longer. He****'s about to leave*** *without us.*

We can stress that the future event is very imminent by adding *just*:
Come on! The check-in desk ***is just about to close.***

We also use *be on the point of* and *be on the verge of* to talk about the near future. These both mean that something is very close to happening. They can be followed by either an *-ing* form or a noun:
Don't provoke your little brother. You can see he's ***on the point of losing*** *his temper.*
Because of the erosion of their habitats, some species ***are on the verge of extinction.***

Some adjectives contain the idea of 'in the near future', e.g. *imminent, forthcoming, impending*. We tend to use these adjectives in more formal, often written, English:
A decision from the judges is ***imminent*** *and we expect further news within the hour.*

We use *impending* only in attributive position, i.e. before the noun:
✗ ~~*The sensation of doom was impending.*~~
✓ *No one could shake off the sensation of impending doom.*

We do not usually use time adverbials (e.g. *in an hour*) with the expressions above:
✗ ~~*The President is on the point of signing an historic deal in just one hour.*~~
✓ *The President is on the point of signing an historic deal.*

4 Expressions of probability and certainty

We use *be likely/unlikely to* + infinitive to say that something in the future is probable/improbable:
The payment ***is likely to take*** *ten days. Please contact us if it does not arrive within that time.*
*They****'re unlikely to arrive*** *before six. The traffic is always awful on Fridays.*

We can use *be sure (bound/certain) to* + infinitive to say that something is going to happen or should have been expected:
The new timetable ***is sure to annoy*** *some of the teachers when they see it.*
Your application ***is bound to fail*** *if you don't get the divisional director's approval.*

FORMALITY CHECK In the negative we can put *not* after the adjective, but this can sound quite formal, so in casual speech we sometimes reformulate it:
The electrification of the west coast rail line ***is certain not to be completed*** *before 2025.*
[*Don't worry about Dad –* ***he's sure not to find out*** *about the party.*]
✓ *Don't worry about Dad –* ***I'm sure he won't find out*** *about the party.*

We can use *be sure to* and *be certain to* as imperatives but NOT *be bound to*:
✗ ~~*Be bound to give me a call when you arrive at the hotel.*~~
✓ ***Be sure/certain to give*** *me a call when you arrive at the hotel.*

5 Verbs with future meaning

Some verbs contain an implied future in their meaning; we understand that they relate to the future, even though we do not use a future form:

VERBS	STRUCTURE	EXAMPLES
decide hope promise swear intend (also + *-ing*)	verb + *to* + infinitive	*I* ***hope to see*** *everyone at the next Open Day.* ***Do*** *you* ***swear never to reveal*** *this secret?* *He* ***intends to retire/retiring*** *next year.*[1]
anticipate predict envisage	verb + noun/ *-ing* form	*We* ***anticipate congestion*** *on all routes this weekend.* *They* ***predict rain*** *tomorrow.*[2] *Do you* ***envisage making*** *any policy changes?*
arrange expect guarantee, plan undertake	verb (+ noun) + *to* + infinitive	*We****'re planning a break to get*** *a bit of sun this winter.* *We* ***expect to promote*** *trainees within three years.*

[1] The infinitive is more common after *intend* than the *-ing* form.
[2] We use *predict* with a noun or a *that* clause: *We* ***predict*** *that it will rain tomorrow.*

Some modal verbs usually express a degree of possibility in the future (➤ Units 31, 32):
Such financing opportunities ***may not be*** *so readily available in the future.*
Rankin's latest blockbuster ***might win*** *the Golden Dagger award for crime fiction.*
Given their expertise and experience, the Swiss team ***should triumph*** *in tomorrow's final.*

Practice

1 Read the sentences A and B and decide whether both are correct, one is correct, or both are incorrect. Tick (✓) the correct sentences and cross (✗) the incorrect ones.

1 A IKEA is on the point of open a new store in Bristol.
  B IKEA is about to open a new store in Bristol.
2 A All ferries will be departing one hour late because of the bad weather.
  B All ferries depart one hour late because of the bad weather.
3 A The final performance is due to take place on 15th April.
  B The final performance takes place on 15th April.
4 A Stefan is certain not to be on time – he's always late!
  B I'm certain Stefan won't be on time – he's always late!
5 A Renovations to the roof are about to begin on 2nd January.
  B Renovations to the roof are to begin on 2nd January.
6 A Will you promise taking care when you're travelling alone?
  B Be bound to take care when you're travelling alone.

2 GRAMMAR IN USE Complete the conversation with words from the box. Use each word or phrase once only. 3.03 Listen and check.

anticipate begin due to expect guarantee to hopes to intend is likely to is sure to plans to should will be

MARY When do Brian's exams start, then?
ANNA Well, they (1) .... tomorrow, actually.
MARY Do you (2) .... him to do well?
ANNA We think he will. He's taking nine subjects, and he's quite optimistic. He (3) .... pass at least six of them – he's very good at those six subjects. We think that he (4) .... pass two of the others: French and art – he's studied very hard, but he's not naturally gifted in those subjects! We've got no hopes at all for music. He (5) .... fail it. I don't know why the school entered him for it.
MARY What does he want to do next year?
ANNA That depends. If he does well, he (6) .... stay on at school for two years and study politics.
MARY Politics? That's unusual. Can he study that at his school?
ANNA Well, that's the problem. No, he can't, his school doesn't have a very good range of subjects. But we've just heard that they (7) .... opening the new sixth form college in Fareham very soon. We (8) .... being able to send him there, but we don't know for certain.
MARY Does he (9) .... to go to university afterwards then?
ANNA Yes, if everything goes OK.
MARY I see. And if he doesn't pass enough of the exams?
ANNA Well, he might leave and look for a job. Sandy – you know, my elder sister – says she (10) .... have a vacancy for a trainee in her business, but obviously she can't (11) .... take him. And he's (12) .... see the careers advisor next week anyway. We'll just have to see.

3 Write the second sentence so it has a similar meaning to the first. Use the word in brackets, as in the example. 3.04 Listen and check.

0 The result of our appeal against the parking fine will probably arrive in the post tomorrow.
(likely) *The result of our appeal against the parking fine is likely to arrive tomorrow.*

1 We expect the peace talks to take place in Helsinki on 28–29th July.
(due) ....

2 That music is so loud that it'll definitely wake all the neighbours.
(bound) ....

3 Scientists in Mexico feel that they are about to discover a new bacterium.
(discovering) ....

4 Will you swear that you won't get into debt again this month?
(to) ....

5 We think that there will be great interest in this offer.
(anticipate) ....

6 Everyone in the village lived in fear of the volcanic eruption, which was imminent.
(impending) ....

7 The designer believes that he will be able to finish by tomorrow afternoon.
(envisages) ....

8 I really don't think that the examiner will accept a handwritten script these days.
(unlikely) ....

9 P D James, recently turned ninety, is shortly going to release yet another novel.
(about) ....

10 The team meeting is to take place in Meeting Room 4 as usual.
(be) ....

11 Mr Cooper was very close to dying of hypothermia when the paramedics arrived.
(verge) ....

12 Given the current media frenzy, first-class travel for the ministers will not be approved for the foreseeable future.
(travelling) ....

4 Find and correct six mistakes in these sentences, as in the example. Tick (✓) the correct sentences.

0 We'll give you a call when we ~~will finish~~ *finish/have finished* repairing your car.

1 Letters sent second class are not likely to arrive the following day.

2 Because of repairs to the sports hall, this week's football practice takes place outside.

3 Be certain to lock your doors at night when you're alone in the house.

4 This week's rubbish collection is about to take place on Tuesday because of the public holiday on Monday.

5 You shouldn't take these pills on an empty stomach so you'd better take them after you'll eat.

6 We've got no special plans for the summer. We spend it as usual with our parents.

7 The two parties are on the verge to sign the contract.

8 Quick! That child is due to fall out of the tree – try to catch him!

29 Future in the past

1 *was/were going to* + infinitive

Sometimes we need to describe the future from a viewpoint in the past. We often use *was/were going to* to do this:
I was going to get up *early this morning but the alarm didn't go off!*

11.30 p.m. yesterday	6.00 a.m. today	9.00 a.m. today
I intend to get up early tomorrow. (this is a future plan)	*The alarm doesn't go off.*	*I wake up late.* (my plan to get up early is now in the past)

When we use *was/were going to*, the plan is not usually fulfilled (i.e. it did not happen):
The fitness club ***was going to increase*** *its annual subscription but so many members protested that it backed down.* (It didn't increase the subscription.)

We also use this form to make excuses for things we have not done:
I ***was going to buy*** *you a birthday present but I couldn't find anything you'd like.*

We can use the negative to talk about things we have done but did not intend to do:
We ***weren't going to disturb*** *you but we thought you should hear the news from us.*

However, it is possible to describe a past intention that is fulfilled. This is made clear in the context:
'Thanks for posting my letters.'
'That's OK. I ***was going to post*** *mine anyway.'* (I did post them.)

2 Other ways of expressing the future in the past

Was/were going to is a very common way of expressing the future in the past. But it is possible to transfer any form with future meaning to the past:

PRESENT/FUTURE FORM	PAST FORM	EXAMPLES
present continuous	past continuous	*They* ***were coming*** *for dinner, but in the end they didn't arrive until after midnight.*
will/shall	*would*	*The heating wasn't working so we hoped the engineer* ***wouldn't take*** *long.*
will be + *-ing* form	*would be* + *-ing* form	*Little did we know that we* ***would*** *still* ***be waiting*** *in the lounge in three hours' time!*
will have	*would have*	*The Cabinet thought the oil crisis* ***would have ended*** *before the election.*
is/are about to/due to	*was/were about to/ due to*	*As she raised her arm, he realised she* ***was about to hail*** *a taxi.*
is/are to	*was/were to*	*He* ***was to arrive*** *at the airport at nine.* *We* ***were to have been met*** *by the tour guide.*

When we transfer these forms to the past, they keep the same meaning, e.g. we use the present continuous to talk about arrangements, so the past continuous also refers to arrangements:
We ***were meeting*** *them at the concert hall, but we didn't know which entrance they were waiting at.*

With *was/were (due) to* + present infinitive, we don't know if the event happened or not:
The exam results ***were (due) to arrive*** *at the school today. We can phone to find out whether they have arrived.*

However, *was/were (due) to* + perfect infinitive (e.g. *to have done*) tells us that the event did not occur:
The exam results ***were (due) to have arrived*** *at the school today but apparently they haven't been released yet.*

Practice

1 GRAMMAR IN USE **Complete the lines of each dialogue, using a 'future in the past' form and an appropriate continuation, as in the example.** 3.05 **Listen and check.**

0 'Look, the shoe shop has closed down.' 'Oh, that's a pity. There was a pair of shoes in the window that I liked. *I was going to buy them.* '

1 'Hi, Karen. It's Graham here.' 'Graham, I don't believe it! You must be a mind reader! I ....'

2 'Where's Dad?' 'He's gone back to work. They had an emergency at the factory.' 'Oh no! I've got some really tough maths homework and he ....'

3 'Ms Sandford? This is the police. We're trying to trace Frank Simmonds. I gather he works for you.' 'Well, today was his first day. He .... at nine this morning, but he didn't turn up.'

4 'I don't think this ticket permits you to break your journey.' 'It must do. The clerk at the ticket office .... if I couldn't stop in Exeter.'

5 'What are you doing here? Aren't you supposed to be on holiday?' 'Yes, that's right. We .... yesterday, but the airline strike prevented us going.'

2 **Complete the second sentence so it has a similar meaning to the first. Use the word in brackets, as in the example.**

0 I fully intended to call you yesterday but I completely forgot! (was)
I *was going to call you* yesterday but I completely forgot!

1 In 1995 I left university and travelled to Singapore and met Tom, who I married two years later. (would)
In 1995 I left university and travelled to Singapore, where I met the man .... two years later.

2 We didn't want to reveal the designs so soon but we were forced into it. (weren't)
We .... the designs so soon but were forced into it.

3 It was expected that the shuttle would make a further voyage, but technical failure prevented it. (have)
The shuttle .... a further voyage, but technical failure prevented it.

4 The government revised its intention to increase fuel duty today as the rise in oil prices was already causing problems. (due)
The duty on fuel .... by the government today, but it didn't happen because of the problems caused by the rise in oil prices.

5 We bought the cottage twenty years ago and, amazingly, we're still living in it! (living)
When we bought the cottage, we hardly imagined that .... in it twenty years later!

6 The fire alarm went off and stopped the play from even starting! (about)
The fire alarm went off when the play ....

7 I was so late that I expected the ceremony to be over by the time I arrived. (finished)
I was so late I expected that .... by the time I arrived.

Review MODULE 6

1 UNITS 26 AND 27 **Complete the dialogues, using the cartoons and a suitable verb from the box. Use *will/won't*, *will/won't be* + *-ing* form, *will/won't have* + past participle or *be going to*.**

finish need sail shoot

'What does it say, doctor?
'Good news. .... an operation after all!'

'Is it next week that you're on holiday?'
'Yes. This time next week I .... in the Mediterranean.'

'Can you bring those to our meeting at three o'clock?'
'Sorry, but .... photocopying them by then!'

'What's happening?'
'He's got a gun. He says .... someone!'

2 UNITS 28 AND 29 **Find eight more mistakes in this email in ways of expressing the future or the future in the past. Correct the mistakes.**

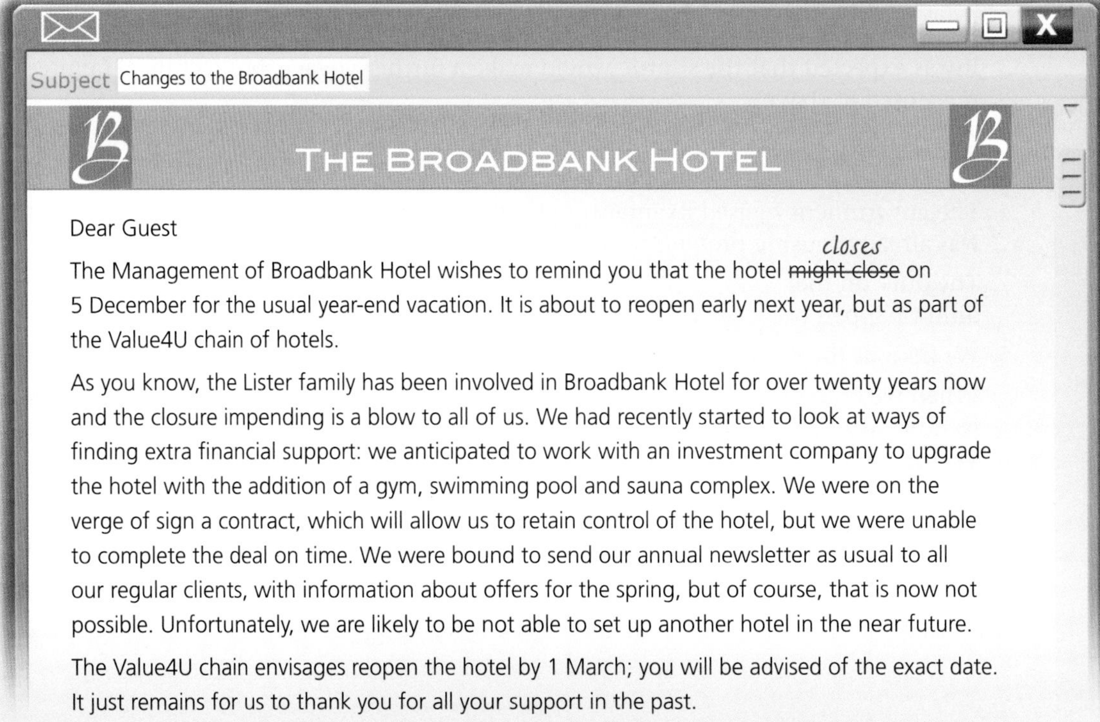
Subject Changes to the Broadbank Hotel

THE BROADBANK HOTEL

Dear Guest

The Management of Broadbank Hotel wishes to remind you that the hotel ~~might close~~ *closes* on 5 December for the usual year-end vacation. It is about to reopen early next year, but as part of the Value4U chain of hotels.

As you know, the Lister family has been involved in Broadbank Hotel for over twenty years now and the closure impending is a blow to all of us. We had recently started to look at ways of finding extra financial support: we anticipated to work with an investment company to upgrade the hotel with the addition of a gym, swimming pool and sauna complex. We were on the verge of sign a contract, which will allow us to retain control of the hotel, but we were unable to complete the deal on time. We were bound to send our annual newsletter as usual to all our regular clients, with information about offers for the spring, but of course, that is now not possible. Unfortunately, we are likely to be not able to set up another hotel in the near future.

The Value4U chain envisages reopen the hotel by 1 March; you will be advised of the exact date. It just remains for us to thank you for all your support in the past.

3 ALL UNITS **Read the article and complete it with the words and phrases from the box.**

'll be able to 'm going to definitely expects to has taken place imminent plan to sure to was going to ~~was to have~~ will attempt will be joining will be paying will extend will have spent

Historic bill passed

US PRESIDENT Barack Obama last night secured a victory for social welfare in the United States that no other administration has managed to do.

The Clinton administration of 1992–2000 (0) ....*was to have*...... introduced healthcare reform, but failed in its aim. Obama cited this as a major objective when he took office, and last night the bill to introduce reform was passed by only seven votes.

The President (1) .... sign the bill into law shortly, but Republicans (2) .... prevent this, on the basis that the bill is unconstitutional. Moments before the vote, House Speaker Nancy Pelosi said, referring to previous reforms, "We (3) .... those who established Social Security, Medicare, and now, tonight, healthcare for all Americans."

Once the President's (4) .... endorsement of the bill (5) ...., the new legislation (6) .... healthcare to nearly all Americans. It will also (7) .... end restrictive insurance practices such as refusing to cover people with pre-existing medical conditions. The bill contains some unpopular measures that Republican senators (8) .... to change, and the estimated cost of $940 billion over the next ten years is (9) .... cause controversy in many quarters.

Public opinion on the bill is divided. Corinne Murphy, a single mother of three children with severe asthma, told our reporter, "This is just amazing. I haven't been able to get reasonable insurance cover until now because of my condition, and my healthcare costs have been crippling. By the end of this year, I (10) .... over 15,000 dollars on emergency treatment. Now I (11) .... insure the family at a fraction of the cost! I (12) .... celebrate this evening." Larry Aristides, a Republican farmer, gave the opposite view: "You know, I thought Obama was great, and I (13) .... vote for him until I heard what he was planning with healthcare, so I voted for McCain instead. This is just the tip of the iceberg – the government (14) .... people to stay at home rather than work soon, like in most socialist states."

'This is just the tip of the iceberg ... '
Larry Aristides

MODULE

7 Modal verbs

Before you start

1 Review these intermediate grammar points and check you know them.

Modal forms

1 The modal verbs are *can, could, may, might, must, should, will, shall* and *would*. They differ from main verbs in several ways.

- They have the same form for all subjects: *I can, he can, they can.*
- The negative is just *not*; we do not use *do/does not*: *You* ***shouldn't*** *say that.*
- The modal verb goes before the subject in questions: ***Could*** *you come here?*
- They do not have infinitive forms (*to* ...), so to make an infinitive, we use a different verb: *I want to* ***be able to*** *sing perfectly.*
- They do not have participle forms (*-ed, -ing*), so to make continuous or perfect tenses, we change the main verb: *I* ***must be going*** *soon. She* ***might have had*** *the results by now.*
- They are followed by the infinitive without *to*: *They* ***would visit*** *you if you asked them.*

2 The verbs *need (to)* and *dare (to)* are occasionally used in two forms:

MAIN VERB FORM	MODAL VERB FORM
You ***don't need to*** *turn the computer off.*	*You* ***needn't*** *turn the computer off.*
I don't know if I ***dare to*** *tell her what's happened.* *We* ***don't dare*** *(****to****) go there after dark.*	*I don't know if I* ***dare*** *tell her what's happened.* *We* ***daren't*** *go there after dark.*

Difference between British and American English ➤ page 368

Basic uses of modal verbs

USE	MODAL VERB	EXAMPLES
ability/ lack of ability/ possibility	*can/can't* *could/couldn't*	*She* ***can speak*** *Spanish but she* ***can't speak*** *Italian.* *Mozart* ***could play*** *the piano at the age of five.* *Only amateur athletes* ***could compete****.*
possibility (present or future)	*may/might*	*Mr Andrews* ***may be*** *in his office. I'll just check.* *The shops* ***might be*** *busy tomorrow as it's a public holiday.*
obligation	*must* (strong) *should/ought to*	*The governing bodies of individual sports* ***must decide*** *who is eligible.* *We* ***should/ought to change*** *some currency soon.*
prohibition	*mustn't/can't* (strong) *shouldn't*	*You* ***mustn't/can't cross*** *the road here; it's dangerous.* *We* ***mustn't/can't use*** *the pool after 7.00 p.m.* *You* ***shouldn't eat*** *while you're driving.*
speculation	*can't/could/* *must/may/might*	*Sandra* ***must be*** *in the school; her bag's in the staff room.* *Brian* ***can't have been driving*** *the car; he doesn't drive.*
predictions/ decisions made at time of speaking	*will/won't*	*He's been found guilty of murder. He'****ll be*** *in prison for a long time.* *You must work hard for this exam. It* ***won't be*** *easy.* *I can't concentrate right now. I'****ll finish*** *this essay later.*

Has to (obligation) is not a modal verb: it is grammatically the same as a main verb: *You* ***don't have to do*** *that.*

2 Read the information and identify examples of modal verbs.

The Modern Olympic Games

The Modern Olympic Games were established by Baron de Coubertin in 1894. Athletes from countries all over the world can compete to try to prove who the best is in their sport. Until the 1970s only amateur athletes could compete, but since then the rules have been relaxed and now the governing bodies of individual sports must decide who is eligible. Only boxers have to be amateur now. In football (soccer), only three players over 23 are allowed to participate in each team – to maintain a level of amateurism.

3 Complete the diagnostic test below. Choose the correct words in *italics*. If both options are correct, choose both.

1. This console is so simple that it *is able to be* / *can be* operated by anyone. ➤ Unit 30.1
2. Helen fell off her horse last week but luckily she *managed to* /*could* get back on and ride home. ➤ Unit 30.1
3. There *can* / *may* be water on the moon's surface. ➤ Unit 31.1
4. If the weather's bad tomorrow, the race *could* / *might* not go ahead. ➤ Unit 31.2
5. My present from Alice didn't come in the post, so she *must be* / *is* delivering it by hand. ➤ Unit 32.1
6. We'd better leave soon. It's Friday evening and there *should* / *will* be a lot of traffic. ➤ Unit 32.2
7. Lewis *must* / *should* have been training very hard to develop muscles like that! ➤ Unit 32.3
8. Do you know if we *must* / *have to* have visas for South Africa? ➤ Unit 33.1
9. What a state my football shirt is in! It *needs* / *must be* washing. ➤ Unit 33.2
10. There wasn't anyone at the main gate so we *didn't need to show* / *needn't have shown* our tickets. ➤ Unit 33.3
11. We *have to* / *are supposed to* put our bags in the lockers, but most people take them into the gym. ➤ Unit 33.4
12. Polite notice: children *do not have to* / *are not allowed to* play on the grass. ➤ Unit 34.1
13. The newspaper *shouldn't* / *mustn't* have printed the rumour without evidence. ➤ Unit 34.2
14. 'I wonder where Dad is.' 'He *is* / *will be* driving to the airport, I should think.' ➤ Unit 35.1
15. 'Oh dear. The lecture starts at nine o'clock. I'm late!' 'Don't worry. This lecturer's always late. He *won't have* / *hasn't* started yet.' ➤ Unit 35.2
16. Dad *always helped us out* / *would always help us out* financially when we were at university, however difficult it was for him. ➤ Unit 35.4
17. The police interrogated the suspect for more than four hours, but she *would not reveal* / *mustn't have revealed* the names of her co-conspirators. ➤ Unit 35.6
18. Hang on a minute – *can* / *might* you repeat what you just said? ➤ Unit 36.1
19. You *won't have to* / *had better not* tell Shirley what you saw – it will only upset her and she'll blame you. ➤ Unit 36.4
20. 'It looks as though the fuel crisis is over.' 'I *wouldn't* / *won't* be too sure.' ➤ Unit 36.6

4 Check your answers on page 384. Then go to the unit for more information and practice.

Go online for a full diagnostic test

30 Ability

1 Present and future ability

We use *can* or *be able to* for ability in the present. If the ability is surprising or involves overcoming some difficulty, we often use *is/are able to*:
Despite his handicap he ***can/is able to*** *drive a car.*

We do not usually use *be able to* with a passive:
✗ ~~*This book is able to be used by beginners.*~~ ✓ *This book* ***can be used*** *by beginners.*

To emphasise difficulty or to suggest effort, we use *manage to* or *succeed in* + *-ing*:
*Do you think she****'ll manage to get*** *a visa?* (informal)
She ***succeeds in creating*** *a positive atmosphere in every meeting.* (more formal)

We use *be able to* where *can/could* is grammatically impossible:
We love ***being able to converse*** *with the local people, so I'd like* ***to be able to speak*** *the language better.* (*-ing* forms and infinitives)
I ***haven't been able to drive*** *since I dislocated my wrist.* (present perfect)

FORMALITY CHECK We can also use *be unable to* if we want to sound more formal:
The claimant has been ***unable to drive*** *since the date of the accident.*

To describe a future ability we use *will be able to*, NOT *can*:
✗ ~~*Can I speak fluently by the end of the course?*~~
✓ ***Will*** *I* ***be able to*** *speak fluently by the end of the course?*

However, we can use both *can* or *will be able to* for future arrangements:
The doctor ***can't/won't be able to see*** *you before six as he's busy till then.*

If the arrangement is less certain we use *could, may* or *might* (*be able to*):
The dentist ***might be able to*** *see you later today; I'll have to check the diary.*

2 Past ability

We usually use *could* to express past ability:
Hannah loves the water. She ***could swim*** *before she* ***could walk.***

But to talk about a specific occasion in the affirmative we use *was/were able to*, NOT *could*:
✗ ~~*Mike's car broke down yesterday but fortunately he could repair it.*~~
✓ *Mike's car broke down yesterday but fortunately he* ***was able to repair*** *it.*

It is possible to use *could*, or *was/were able to*, in questions, superlatives, and in sentences with limiting adverbs such as *only* or *hardly*:
'Could you/Were you able to fix *the computer yourself?' 'No, I* ***could only/was only able to back up*** *the important files.'*

Sorry, but this is ***the cheapest hotel*** *I* ***could/was able to find.***
She was so exhausted she ***could hardly/was hardly able to speak.***

We use *couldn't* or *was/were not able to* to describe a lack of ability/success:
Mozart ***couldn't/wasn't able to speak*** *French.*
I ***couldn't/wasn't able to find*** *those shoes in my size.*

We use *could* + *have* + past participle to describe a past ability which wasn't used or a past opportunity which wasn't taken. The meaning is similar to 'would have been able to' (➤ Unit 38.3):
She ***could have paid*** *by credit card but she preferred to use cash.*
(= She had the ability to pay by credit card but she didn't use it.)

We can use *couldn't have been* + comparative adjective when we want to emphasise a past action or feeling:
I ***couldn't have been more pleased*** *when I heard your results – congratulations!*
(= I was very pleased about your results.)

Practice

1 Choose a suitable form of *can, could, be able to, manage to* or *succeed in* to complete the sentences. Sometimes more than one form is possible. 3.06 Listen and check.

1 The manager was a bit reluctant but in the end I .... get a refund.
2 It was really annoying; I .... get on to any of the websites you recommended.
3 When does the next match start? I .... hardly hear the last announcement.
4 The new road opens next month so we .... get to the coast more quickly.
5 Most of the big hotels were full, but we .... find a room in a small guesthouse near the station.
6 The aid workers .... come home after the incident, but they decided to stay in the war zone.
7 Dr Martens finishes her surgery at 11.30, so she .... call you then.
8 After I move to the country I'm not going to .... visit you so often.
9 The government's 2004 fuel tax levy .... generating over a billion pounds in revenue in six months.
10 The shopping channel is a real boon for Liz; she adores .... buy clothes, day or night!
11 Sadly, many of the indigenous people .... resist the diseases brought by the European settlers.
12 We .... more relieved when we got the news that you were OK.

2 GRAMMAR IN USE Complete the information with the words and phrases from the box. 3.07 Listen and check.

are able to ~~can~~ can could hardly couldn't have managed to be able to were only able to won't be able to

Q Do athletes really run faster these days?

A Yes. Long-distance runners these days (0) ...*can*... complete marathons in the time that fifty years ago their predecessors (1) .... run 10,000 metres.

Q Why should this be?

A Well, technology is a factor: athletes today (2) .... use the most aerodynamic materials in their running shoes or swimsuits. But even if earlier athletes had had these innovations, they (3) .... improved their results significantly, for various other reasons. For example, athletes these days are professional; in the past they were unpaid amateurs. They had to combine their sport with paid work, so they (4) .... find enough time to train. Athletes' careers these days also last longer; they (5) .... compete until they are older. Facilities also make a difference: in the 1950s and 60s, swimmers from the US (6) .... to dominate their sport because few other nations had Olympic-sized pools. Now it's easy for swimmers everywhere (7) .... train more efficiently as they have the correct pools.

Given these conditions today, there's no reason to believe that athletes (8) .... continue to smash records.

31 Possibility

1 Present possibility

We use *can* to talk about things which are generally possible:
Health insurance ***can be*** *very expensive.* (= It is sometimes expensive.)

ACADEMIC ENGLISH We commonly use *may* in academic and scientific English:
Over-prescribing of antibiotics ***may lead*** *to the rapid development of resistant strains.*

We usually use *may*, *might* and *could* to talk about specific possibilities:
This rash ***may/might/could be*** *a symptom of something more serious.*
Mark isn't home yet – he ***may/might/could be working*** *late at the office.*
✗ ~~*There can be life on Mars.*~~ ✓ *There* ***may be*** *life on Mars.*

When we ask about possibility, we often start the question with *Do you think*:
Do you think *the shops might be open today?*

We use *may well*, *might well* and *could well* when we talk about a strong possibility:
Don't worry, the payment ***could well be*** *in the post.* (= It is probably in the post.)

To describe possibilities which depend on certain conditions we use *could* or *might* (➤ Unit 38.1): *She* ***could learn*** *much more quickly if she paid attention.*

When we think that something is POSSIBLY NOT the case we use *might not* or *may not*:
The shops ***may not/might not be*** *open today; it's a public holiday.*

When we are certain something is DEFINITELY NOT the case, we use *can't*:
You really ***can't drive*** *to Oxford in under an hour.* (I'm sure about this, it's impossible.)

2 Future possibility

We use *will/won't be able to* to talk about future possibility or impossibility:
*We'****ll be able to get*** *a coffee at the theatre but we* ***won't be able to eat*** *until after the show.*

We use *may*, *might* or *could* to talk about future actions which are less certain:
The directors ***may call*** *a stockholders' meeting.* (= Perhaps they will call a meeting.)

We usually use *could* for a weaker possibility than *may* or *might*:
You never know, she ***could find*** *a perfect job tomorrow.* (It's possible, but unlikely.)

⚠ We do not use *could not/couldn't* to say something is definitely impossible in the present or future:
✗ ~~*The shops couldn't be open today.*~~ ✗ ~~*The optician couldn't see you tomorrow.*~~
✓ *The optician* ***won't be able to*** *see you tomorrow.* ✓ *The optician* ***can't*** *see you tomorrow.*
(for future arrangements that are not possible)

We sometimes use *may/might* + *have* + past participle to talk about a possible completed action by a time in the future:
Call me next Tuesday; I ***might have finished*** *the project by then.*

3 Past possibility

We use *could* to talk about general possibility in the past (things which sometimes happened):
Teachers ***could be*** *very strict at my old school.* (= Sometimes they were strict.)

ACADEMIC ENGLISH We use *might* in the same way in academic and scientific English:
Wealthy Victorian families ***might employ*** *as many as a dozen indoor servants.*

We use *could/might* + *have* + past participle to talk about a specific past possibility:
She ***might have done*** *it; she had the opportunity and the motive.* (= Perhaps she did it ...)
John ***could have posted*** *the letter.* (I'm not sure whether he did or not.)

We also use *might have* for a past opportunity which we know was not taken:
I ***might have gone*** *to drama school, but I chose history instead.*
(= I had the opportunity but I didn't go.)

Practice

1 **GRAMMAR IN USE** **Choose the correct words in *italics*. If both are correct, choose both.** **3.08 Listen and check.**

MIKE Hi, Rob. I haven't seen you for ages! What are you doing in the gym?
ROB Trying to get fitter, of course. How are you?
MIKE I'm fine. I always thought you were super-fit because of all your cycling.
ROB Oh that. Well, you know how it is, you get a job, get married ...
MIKE But you (1) *could be* / *could have been* an Olympic cyclist – you used to be fantastic!
ROB Maybe not that good! Well, I was in a good club, and anyone (2) *could* / *may* apply to join the teams, but there were people there a lot better than me, and you know, cycling (3) *can* / *might* be very competitive.
MIKE I'm sure, but it's still a pity. Aren't you cycling at all now?
ROB Oh yeah, just not so intensively. I'm still in a club and I was thinking ... I (4) *might* / *could* try the Tour de France in a couple of years' time.
MIKE Wow! That would be awesome! It's such a long ...
ROB No, no, I certainly (5) *can't* / *won't* be able to do it all. I (6) *might* / *could* not even be able to do more than a couple of stages. It's difficult with work and everything.
MIKE Yes, but what an opportunity!
ROB Mmm, if I felt I was fit enough, then I (7) *could* / *might* ask for some unpaid leave. Anyway, why don't you come along to the club?
MIKE Really? (8) *Do you think they might* / *Might they* let me in?
ROB It's worth a try. How about next Saturday ...?

2 **Complete the second sentence so it has a similar meaning to the first. Use a suitable form of *can, could, may* or *might*, as in the example.**

0 Given some luck, our team has a good chance of winning the final next month.
With any luck *our team might win the final next month*.
1 The service in this restaurant is sometimes quite surly.
The service ....
2 Ten years ago my neighbour offered me his apartment for $30,000 but I didn't buy it.
Ten years ago I ....
3 It would be possible to issue the tickets today if you gave us your credit card number.
We ....
4 When I was at university, it was generally possible for students to have a good lifestyle.
When I was at university, ...
5 Is it possible that the disparity in the figures is due to a computer error?
Do ....
6 Perhaps the shuttle bus isn't operating at the moment – it is the low season.
The shuttle bus ....
7 Perhaps Jim took it; he was in the office all day yesterday.
Jim ....
8 It's quite possible that my sister will become an opera star – she has a lovely voice.
My sister ....

32 Speculation and expectation

1 Present speculation

When we speculate (or make deductions), we make informed guesses about an action or situation. We use a modal followed by the infinitive of a main verb in the simple or continuous form.

If we strongly believe that something is true, usually because we have evidence, we use *must* or *have got to*:
This ***must be*** *the place – it's the only restaurant in the street.*
You ***must be feeling*** *tired after your flight. Why don't you rest for a while?*

We use *have (got) to* when we want to add emphasis:
There ***has (got) to be*** *some mistake. I didn't order this furniture.*
You ***have got to be joking****! That was not a foul!*

If we strongly believe that something is NOT true, or is impossible, we use *can't* or *couldn't*:
He ***can't/couldn't be*** *the senior doctor, he's far too young.* (= I'm certain he isn't ...)
Sarah ***can't be working*** *at the moment – I see her in the garden every morning.*

We do not use *mustn't* in this sense:
✗ ~~*This mustn't be the place – there's no one inside and there are no lights on.*~~
✓ *This* ***can't be*** *the place – there's no one inside and there are no lights on.*

We also use *can* and *could* in *wh-* questions or with adverbs such as *only* or *hardly*:
✗ ~~*Who may that be at this time of night?*~~
✓ *Who* ***can/could*** *that* ***be*** *at this time of night?*
It ***can/could hardly be*** *the postman. He only comes in the morning.*
(= I don't think it is the postman.)
It ***can/could only be*** *Steve. He's the only one with a key.* (= I'm sure it is Steve.)

If we believe that something is possible or probable, we use *could, may* and *might* (➤ Unit 31.1):
He always wears smart suits. He ***could be*** *a businessman.*
'Why isn't she here yet?' 'I don't know. The train ***may be running*** *late.'*

We use *might* for tentative (less direct) questions:
Might *the losses* ***be*** *due to currency fluctuations?*

In informal speech we can make the speculation stronger by adding *well*:
Let's call the hospital. There ***may well*** *be some news now.*

We also use *couldn't* to say that something is unimaginable because we are unwilling to do it: *I* ***couldn't pick up*** *a spider; they terrify me.*

2 Present and future expectation

We use *should/shouldn't* or *ought to/ought not to* to express an expectation – we expect an action to happen now or in the future because of our prior knowledge or the current circumstances:

*The plane took off on time so it **should/ought to be landing** about now and there **shouldn't/ ought not to be** any delays.*

*There **shouldn't/ought not to be** problems with traffic at that time of the evening.*

⚠ We rarely use *should* to 'predict' a negative (unpleasant) situation. We use *will* (➤ Unit 26.1):

✗ ~~*There should be problems with traffic at that time. The roads should be awful.*~~

✓ *There**'ll be** problems with traffic at that time. The roads **will be** awful.*

3 Past speculation

We can make informed guesses about an action or situation in the past, using a modal:

*I'm not sure where Susie is. She **could have left** early.*

*Someone **might have been taking** money from the till.*

If we strongly believe that something was true because we have evidence, we use *must* + *have* + past participle (simple or continuous form):

*There was a terrific noise last night. It **must have been** an explosion.*

*I couldn't wake you this morning. You **must have been sleeping** really soundly.*

⚠ Note the difference between the two past forms *must* + *have* + past participle and *had to*:

DEDUCTION *But Lawrence is such a well-known author. You **must have read** something by him!*

OBLIGATION *Yes, I have. Unfortunately, we **had to read** several of his books on my university course.*

If we strongly believe that something was not true because of evidence, we use *can't* or *couldn't* + *have* + past participle:

*She **can't have fixed** the computer, it's still not working properly.* (= I'm sure she didn't fix it.)

*They **couldn't have been expecting** such a huge turnout at the funeral.*

We often use *can't* + *have* or *couldn't* + *have* to express surprise or disbelief:

*She **couldn't have done** it; she's such a nice woman.*

*You **can't have been waiting** for long – I only went out five minutes ago!*

⚠ We do not use *mustn't* + *have* + past participle:

✗ ~~*Susie mustn't have left yet; her bag is on the chair.*~~

✓ *Susie **can't/couldn't have left** yet; her bag is on the chair.*

If we believe that something possibly or probably happened, we use *may (not)* or *might (not)* + *have* + past participle:

*We'd better hurry – the hotel **might have given** our room away by now!*

*Students applying for this course **may have studied** maths at degree level.*

In informal speech we can make the speculation stronger by adding *well*:

*We'd better phone them, they **might well have had** some news by now.*

(= They've probably had some news.)

*We didn't interrupt because they **may well have been having** a serious conversation.*

4 Past expectation

We use *should (not)/ought (not) to* + *have* + past participle to talk about an action that we expected to happen in the past:

*I don't know where our main speaker can be. He **should/ought to have arrived** hours ago.*

(= We expected him to arrive hours ago.)

*After a long illness, his father's death **shouldn't/ought not to have come** as a surprise.*

(= The death was expected.)

We can also use this pattern with the continuous form:

*The keys **should have been hanging** outside the apartment – we couldn't get in.*

Practice

1 GRAMMAR IN USE **Write one word (or a contraction) in each gap. Do not use the same word more than once. 3.09 Listen and check.**

1 A: Is that Ayrton Senna, the racing driver, in the car over there?

B: It (1) .... be. He died in 1994. It (2) .... be his nephew, Bruno. He's driving racing cars now.

2 A: Excuse me. Is that the train to York?

B: It (3) .... be, I'll check. Yes, it says 'York' on the window!

A: How stupid! I didn't notice that. Do you know what time it leaves?

B: It (4) .... be leaving any minute now.

3 A: Have you seen my car keys?

B: No. (5) .... they still be in the car?

A: I haven't used the car today, but I need to now. I'm going into town.

B: You're kidding! On a Saturday afternoon? The town centre (6) .... be heaving with people!

4 A: Is that the phone? At this time of night? Who is it?

B: It could (7) .... Steve in Australia. It's the middle of the day there. Hello, Steve?

5 A: I'm phoning from CTC News. Would it be possible to interview the ambassador this afternoon?

B: I'm afraid the ambassador (8) .... be available at such short notice, but I'll ask his secretary.

6 A: Can you record the football match for me? I'm not sure when my meeting's going to end and I (9) .... not be home in time.

B: Of course. Do you know when you'll be back?

A: Not really. But I (10) .... be back later than nine.

2 Write four statements making deductions about each picture. Use the words and phrases in brackets, as in the example.

Mr and Mrs Hopkins are waiting for their daughter.

0 (on/train) She can't *have been on the train.*

1 (miss/it) She must ....

2 (baby/mother) She ....

3 (phone/parents) ....

4 (rain) It must ....

5 (fall/bike) The man must ....

6 (not/wife) The woman ....

7 (ambulance) Someone ....

8 (explosion) There ....

9 (earthquake) There ....

10 (terrifying) It ....

3 Match 1–6 with A–F to continue the sentences. 3.10 Listen and check.

1 He might do it –
2 He should be doing it now –
3 He must have done it –
4 He might have done it –
5 He can't have done it –
6 He should have done it by now –

A he had plenty of opportunity.
B he wasn't even in the country.
C he was the only person who stayed there.
D the deadline passed yesterday.
E he seems a very capable person.
F he usually sorts the post at this time of day.

4 GRAMMAR IN USE Read the article, then choose the best option to complete the comments below, as in the example. If two options are equally possible, choose both.

SPORTING DISASTERS

Heysel Stadium

ONE OF THE WORST disasters in the history of football took place in May 1985 at the Heysel Stadium in Brussels. It was the European Cup Final between Liverpool, UK and Juventus, Italy, and in many ways it was a disaster waiting to happen: the stadium was over fifty years old and in quite bad condition; some parts of it were said to be 'crumbling'. The Liverpool manager had wanted the Cup Final to be moved to another stadium. In addition, there was a history of violence between Liverpool and Italian teams, though not Juventus. The stadium was crowded, and although the Liverpool and Juventus fans were seated in different parts of the stadium, the 'neutral' section, where tickets were allocated to Belgian supporters, actually contained a lot of Juventus fans.

As the match was about to start, Liverpool fans charged the 'neutral' section, causing a large number of mainly Juventus supporters to flee to the back of the stand, against a wall. The wall collapsed, killing 39 fans and injuring hundreds more. Despite the awful disaster, the match went ahead after the captains appealed for calm, and Juventus won 1–0.

As a result of the disaster, twenty-seven fans were arrested, most of whom were from Liverpool, and fourteen were given three-year suspended sentences for involuntary manslaughter. English football clubs were banned from playing in Europe for five years, and Liverpool was banned for six. Measures were taken to stop football hooliganism in England and make football a safer game to watch; these measures were successful and football is now a spectator sport for families again. No more football matches took place at Heysel Stadium, although it continued to host athletics events, and it was demolished in 1994.

0 The owners of the stadium ..... its maintenance.
A should have neglected (B) must have neglected C had to neglect
1 The wall at the back of the stand ..... have been strong enough.
A can't B couldn't C shouldn't
2 The organisers ..... that there would be only Belgian fans in the neutral section.
A might think B could think C might have thought
3 The Juventus fans ..... terrified.
A must have been B could be C might well have been
4 The football teams ..... very brave to continue with the match.
A should have been B must have been C should be
5 Some of the fans who were arrested ..... from Liverpool.
A couldn't have been B didn't have to be C can't have been
6 Liverpool Football Club ..... out of European competition for a long time.
A had to stay B must have stayed C should have stayed
7 Football matches in England ..... a lot more pleasant now.
A can be B must be C should have been
8 They ..... have expected trouble at athletics meetings.
A mustn't B shouldn't C can't

33 Obligation and necessity

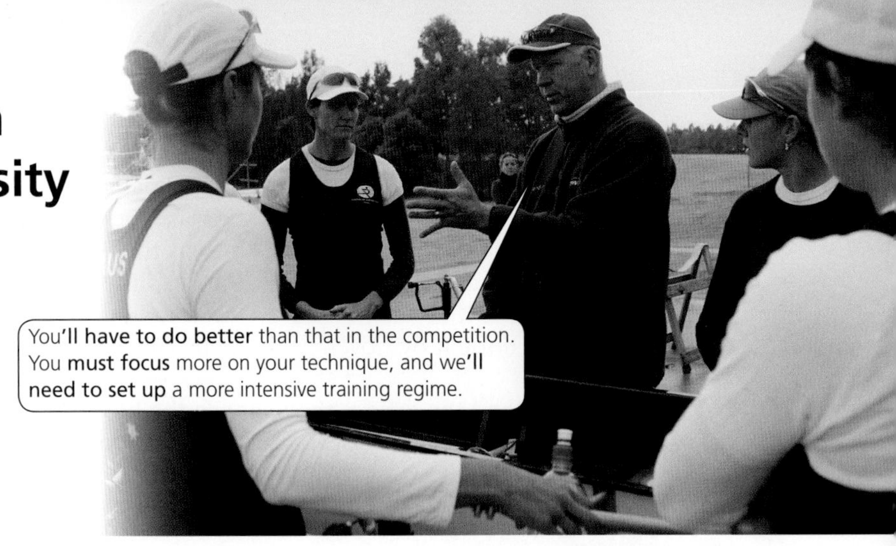

1 Present and future obligation

We usually express obligation in English with *must* or *have to*:
You ***must arrive*** *in good time for the meeting tomorrow. The Chairman will be there.*
Everyone ***has to register*** *their name and address in order to be able to vote.*

We often use *must* and *have to* with a passive verb:
Democracy ***must/has to be seen*** *to work.*

We use *have to* when it is grammatically impossible to use *must*, i.e.

- with an infinitive: *It's difficult* ***to have to stand by*** *and watch your child in pain.*
- with a participle: ***Having to listen*** *to garage music all evening is my idea of misery!*

We usually use *don't have to/don't need to* when there is no obligation:
You ***don't have to/need to pay*** *to visit most museums in the UK.* (Entrance is free.)

The difference in meaning between *have to* and *must* can be small. We usually use *have to* for obligations we see as outside our control, e.g. rules imposed by an authority:
We ***have to pay*** *if we want to put luggage in the hold.* (It's a rule of the airline.)

We often use *must* to express an obligation imposed by the speaker:
I ***must get up*** *earlier – I waste so much time in the mornings.*

Must is commonly used

- to give a strong personal opinion: *I believe people* ***must vote*** *at elections.*
- to impose an obligation on oneself: *I really* ***must try*** *to get fitter.*
- to give instructions, often in writing and often with a passive verb:
  The electricity ***must*** *always* ***be switched off*** *before repairs are attempted.*

We do not often use *you must* for obligation in face-to-face conversation as it can seem impolite:
[*You* ***must listen to*** *what I'm saying.*] ✓ *Please listen to what I'm saying.*

It is more commonly used in talking to children or by people in authority:
You ***must*** *always* ***look*** *both ways before you cross the road. You* ***must focus*** *more.*

You must in recommendations ➤ Unit 36.4

We use *have got to* for external obligation like *have to*, but it is more informal than *have to* and more common in speech than in writing. (It is rare in American English):
What time ***have*** *we* ***got to be*** *at the airport tomorrow?*
[*Claim forms* ***have got to be date-stamped*** *before payment will be made.*]
✓ *Claim forms* ***have to be date-stamped*** *before payment will be made.*

We often use *should* and *ought to* as they express a subjective (often moral) obligation felt by the speaker, but the obligation is weaker than with *must*:
You ***should treat*** *your neighbours with more respect.*

FORMALITY CHECK Questions with *ought to* are rare and formal. We prefer to use *should*:
[*Ought we to leave a tip?*] ✓ *Should we leave a tip?*

We can use *must* and *should* to express obligation in the future:
*I really **must get to** the dentist next week. You **should pay** the amount due by 25th October.*
If the obligation is external, we use *will have to* or *will need to*:
*The children **will have to stay** at home next week while the school is closed for building work.*
*We'**ll need to get** our visas sorted out or we won't be able to stop over in the States.*

We use *won't have to, won't need to* or *needn't* when there is no future obligation:
*With this food processor, you **won't have to/won't need to/needn't** peel or chop any more.*

2 Present and future necessity

We can use *need to, must* and *have to* to express a necessity that results from things other than just commands, rules or laws, or to show that something is very important:
*All living beings **need to/must/have to take** in sustenance in order to live.*
*I really **need to/must/have to be** going now. I'm meeting John in half an hour.*
*We'**ll need to set up** a more intensive training regime.*

If we want to express a necessity without suggesting who should deal with it, we can use *need* + *-ing* form:
*That poor bird – his cage really **needs cleaning**.*

This use has a passive meaning and is similar to the passive infinitive (➤ Unit 62.3):
*That poor bird – his cage really **needs to be cleaned**.*

We use *don't need to/needn't* for absence of necessity felt by the speaker:
*We **needn't/don't need to put** the heating on yet; it's not cold enough.*

3 Past obligation and necessity

We use *had to* when we talk about an obligation or necessity in the past:
*The staff and students at the university **had to evacuate** the campus.*
*Because of Steve's career we'**ve had to move** twice in the last year.*

We use *should/ought to* + *have* + past participle for an unfulfilled obligation in the past:
*You really **should have/ought to have registered** before the term started.* (But you didn't ...)

⚠ We do not use *must* to express this type of obligation (*must* + *have* ➤ Unit 32.3):
✗ ~~*The record was finally released eighteen months later than it must have been.*~~
✓ *The record was finally released eighteen months later than it **should** have been.*

We use *didn't have to/didn't need to* when there is no obligation in the past:
*You **didn't have to/didn't need to finish** the washing-up. I could have done it.*

Notice these two past forms of *need*; they have different meanings:
*We **didn't need to take** warm sweaters, as the weather was so good.*
(We don't know if the speaker took warm sweaters or not.)
*We **needn't have taken** warm sweaters. We could have used the space in our luggage for more books!* (We know that the speaker took warm sweaters.)

4 Other ways of expressing obligation

We can use *be to* for an order from a person in authority (➤ Unit 27.5):
*The members of the jury **are to report** to the judge's chambers immediately.*

We use *be supposed to* for a lesser obligation and one that is frequently ignored:
*We'**re supposed to leave** our textbooks at school, but we often take them home.*

We use *be liable to* for obligation (often in a legal context):
*Anyone causing damage **will be liable to pay for** all necessary repairs.*

FORMALITY CHECK We use *be obliged to* (*be obligated to* in American English) or *be required to* in formal contexts:
*We'**re obliged to contribute** twenty-five percent of the costs of the repairs.*
*Motorists **are required** by law **to wear** seat belts in the European Union.*

Practice

1 Read each sentence and choose the correct meaning, A or B.

1 These tablets must be taken after food.
A It is essential to take the tablets after food.
B It is advisable to take the tablets after food.

2 We needn't have taken towels and bed linen to the cottage.
A We didn't take towels and bed linen with us.
B We took towels and bed linen with us.

3 Trespassers are liable for damage to crops.
A Trespassers must pay for any damage. B Trespassers can pay for any damage.

4 Paula must study harder if she wants to pass this year's exams.
A The speaker is giving his/her opinion. B The speaker is explaining a rule.

5 The bins need emptying before we go out.
A The speaker is going to empty the bins. B The speaker may not empty the bins.

6 We're supposed to put all plastic in the recycling bin.
A This is an important rule that we always follow.
B This is a rule that we don't always follow.

7 We should have informed the bank of our change of address.
A We informed the bank of our change of address. B We didn't inform the bank.

8 Rooms must be vacated by twelve o'clock.
A The receptionist is saying this. B This is a written instruction.

2 GRAMMAR IN USE Complete the adverts with an appropriate verb or expression, as in the example. Use the information in the box to help you. 3.11 Listen and check.

REQUIREMENTS OF COURSE			
course	essential	advisable	unnecessary
A	computing skills	own computer	prior design experience
B	previous experience	computing skills	own computer
C	three GCSEs	good level of English	prior design experience/computing skills

A

WITNEY COLLEGE

WEB DESIGN COURSE

Ten-week intensive course for people interested in designing their own website. Applicants for this course (0) ....*must*...... have good computing skills but are not (1) .... to have prior design experience. If possible, applicants (2) .... bring their own computer but there are a limited number of machines available at the college.

PHONE 0690 4439868 FOR DETAILS.

B

LEARN HOW TO DESIGN THE BEST WEBSITES!

We offer Website Design courses to suit all schedules and budgets, from five-week intensive courses to year-long evening courses. You (3) .... have your own computer (on our full-time courses) but you (4) .... have some previous experience in design. You (5) .... to be able to use a computer.

CALL US ON 01202 867349

C

WEBSITE DESIGN ONE-YEAR COURSE

Applicants (6) .... have previous experience in design, as the course involves work experience with a local company. Equally, you are not (7) .... to have good computer skills as all basic training is provided. A minimum of three GCSEs is essential and all applicants (8) .... have a good level of English.

See display ad for details.

3 GRAMMAR IN USE **Complete the dialogue with words or phrases from the box. Use each word/phrase once only. 3.12 Listen and check.**

do I have to had to has to have to having to must
need to needs obliged to should supposed to will have to

BETH Hello. Reception said that you wanted a word with me.

LISA That's right. I'm interested in joining your gym. What (1) .... do?

BETH Take a seat. First, you (2) .... fill in this form. It asks for details about you and your state of health. We want to be sure that you're fit enough to use the gym.

LISA OK ... I have a slight problem with one knee. I twisted it a few weeks ago.

BETH Well, you really (3) .... tell the instructor about that, then he'll make sure that your fitness programme takes account of it.

LISA Fitness programme?

BETH Yes. If you join, you (4) .... have an induction session with one of our fitness instructors. He'll design a programme suited to your level of fitness.

LISA Oh, that's good. Now, it's £50 a month, isn't it?

BETH Well, yes, but that's the special rate if you take out an annual subscription, so you're (5) .... join for the whole year to get that rate. Otherwise it's £60 a month.

LISA I see. Yes, I think I'll join for the year. Is there anything else I should know?

BETH Let's see ... There are some rules, but they're pretty obvious. Of course, everyone (6) .... wear appropriate clothes and footwear. There are lockers outside the gym, as you're not (7) .... take anything in with you, but we don't apply that rule very strictly. You'll probably want to take a towel and a bottle of water in with you anyway: you (8) .... drink plenty of water while you're exercising, to prevent dehydration.

LISA Yes ... Are there any restrictions, like (9) .... book time ahead?

BETH No. You can use the gym whenever it's open. Obviously, if you think a piece of equipment isn't working properly and (10) .... repairing, tell an instructor. Also, for your own good, you (11) .... tell us if you feel unsure about how to use a particular machine.

LISA Of course. Now, the receptionist said I (12) .... provide proof of my address, but I'm afraid I don't have anything on me at the moment.

BETH That's OK. Bring it next time you come.

4 **Rewrite the underlined sections in the dialogues to use an appropriate modal verb or other way of expressing obligation. Sometimes more than one answer is possible.**

1 A Is it advisable to carry identification with me here? ....
  B It's imperative to carry identification. The police insist on it. ....
2 A What time is it necessary for me to arrive for the exam? ....
  B It will be necessary to get there by 9.45. ....
3 A Was it necessary to learn the language when you were in China? ....
  B Yes, it was essential to learn some as English wasn't widespread. ....
4 A Was the holiday apartment in France well-equipped?
  B Yes, it was. We took our own towels and things but it wasn't necessary. ....

Go online for more practice and a progress test

34 Prohibition and criticism

1 Present and future prohibition

We use *must not* (usually *mustn't*) to express a prohibition (something not allowed) imposed by the speaker or writer. Because *you mustn't* is so strong, it is mainly used by people in authority:

*Remember that you **mustn't remove** patient files from the surgery; they're confidential.*
*Stop it! You **mustn't pull** on people's skirts like that.* (adult to child)

To express a less strong, often moral prohibition, we use *shouldn't* or *oughtn't to*. The negative of *ought to* is *oughtn't to* or *ought not to*, but we prefer to use *shouldn't*:
*You really **shouldn't/oughtn't to speak** to your mother like that!*

To express prohibition by an external authority we often use other modal verbs or non-modal expressions. *Mustn't* may appear too strong in these situations.

GENERAL *Doctors **can't/aren't allowed to give** drugs to shorten life.*
*Smoking **is prohibited/forbidden** on the premises.*
*It **is prohibited/forbidden** to smoke here.*
FORMAL *Hotel guests **may not use** the pool after 11 p.m.*

This is similar to refusing permission (➤ Unit 36.1).

It is possible, though not common, to use *must not* + *have* + past participle for a prohibition in the present which relates to an action or situation in the past:
*This mortgage is for first-time buyers only. Applicants **must not have owned** a property previously.*
(The owning of property is in the past, but the prohibition is in the present.)

We usually use *won't be allowed to* or *can't* to express prohibition in the future:
*Let's eat before we go. We **won't be allowed to/can't take** food into the auditorium.*

2 Past prohibition and criticism

We use *couldn't* or *wasn't/weren't allowed to* for prohibition in the past:
*They **couldn't watch** the film because they were too young.*
*Journalists were shown the disused buildings but they **weren't allowed to enter** them.*

These forms are often used for laws in the past:
*In those days, women and criminals **couldn't/weren't allowed to vote**.*

We use *shouldn't/ought not to* + *have* + past participle to criticise a past action, or the affirmative form for the fact that something did not happen:
*You **shouldn't have driven** through that red light. You could have caused an accident.*
*You're late! You **should have been** here half an hour ago!*

We don't use *must* to express criticism, as this form expresses logical deduction (➤ Unit 32.3): [*You must have been here half an hour ago.*]

We can use *might/could* + *have* + past participle to make a weaker criticism:
*You **might/could have told** me about the party!*
(= You had the chance to tell me but you didn't.)

Note that we stress the past participle when we criticise. Compare:
You might have <u>told</u> me about it!
(= You didn't tell me and I would have liked to know about it.)
You <u>might</u> have told me about it. (= Perhaps you told me; I'm not sure.)

Pronunciation ➤ 1.09

Practice

1 GRAMMAR IN USE **Choose the correct words in *italics*. 3.13 Listen and check.**

MOUNT PLEASANT TENNIS CLUB

Dear New Member

We are delighted to welcome you to Mount Pleasant Tennis Club. Attached are the rules and conditions of membership. Please sign and date the final page to indicate your acceptance of the rules.

In addition to the rules above, we would like to draw your attention to the following:

- We are open all year round, though members (1) *may not / forbidden to* use the courts on tournament weekends.
- Members (2) *should / could* not normally bring guests without prior permission, but this is acceptable from November to March, when the club is less busy.
- Please remember to wear the correct footwear – you (3) *can't / won't* be allowed to play in unsuitable shoes.
- We provide lockers for personal belongings – the club (4) *must not / cannot* accept responsibility for valuables left outside the lockers.
- Members (5) *ought / may* not play competitive tennis for another club without written permission. Please note also that members who represent the club in competitions (6) *must not compete / must not have competed* for another club within the previous six months.
- Finally, may we remind you that any member who holds or has held professional status (7) *may not / must not* represent the club in a tournament. Until recently ex-professionals (8) *couldn't have joined / were not allowed to join* the club, and while we have relaxed that rule, tournaments are still for amateur players only.

2 **Complete the second sentence so it has a similar meaning to the first. Use three to six words, including the word in brackets, as in the example.**

0 We advise passengers to keep all their belongings with them at all times. (should)
Passengers ...*should keep all their belongings*... with them at all times.

1 We expected our host to pay for everyone's drinks, but he didn't. (should)
Our host .... everyone's drinks.

2 It was illegal for women to own property in many societies 100 years ago. (were)
Women .... property in many societies 100 years ago.

3 I wish you had asked me before you borrowed my camera. (might)
You .... before you borrowed my camera.

4 You are not allowed to use mobile phones in the intensive care ward. (is)
The use of .... in the intensive care ward.

5 It isn't right for people to be punished for something they can't avoid doing. (ought)
People .... for something they can't avoid doing.

6 It is essential that candidates have not applied for the same post previously. (have)
Candidates .... the same post previously.

7 The visitors weren't allowed to leave the building until the panic had subsided. (could)
The visitors .... the building until the panic had subsided.

8 It was wrong of you to leave the matches within reach of the children. (not)
You .... the matches within reach of the children.

35 Certainty, habits and willingness

1 Present and future certainty

When we believe something is certain, but we don't know it as a fact, we use *will/won't*:
*Jim's coming. He'**ll be** on his way now.*
*'It's five o'clock. Janet'**ll be** in Moscow now.'* (based on our experience of travel times)
*'I hope she's taken some winter clothes because it **won't be** warm at this time of year.'*

For something ongoing, we use *will/won't* + *be* + *-ing* form:
*Jason knows his successor **will be having** a hard time in the job.* (based on Jason's experience)

If we know something as a fact, i.e we have independent proof, we use the present simple, or, for something ongoing, the present continuous:
*Janet'**s** in Moscow. She called us from her hotel.*
*Jason has heard from his successor. He knows she'**s having** a hard time in the job.*

Sometimes we wish to make a prediction about the future that someone made in the past. For this we often use *would/wouldn't* as the past form of *will*:
*We had to hurry to get him to the hospital. It **would be** too late otherwise.*

This is similar to the use of *would* in reported speech (➤ Unit 51.5):
*'I'm sure the Lions **will win** the rugby series.'* → *She was sure the Lions **would win** the series.*

2 Past certainty

To refer to something which we feel certain has happened (but do not actually know), we use *will* + *have* + past participle:
*We sent the invitation on Monday, so they **will have received** it by now.*

This is similar to *must* + *have* + past participle (➤ Unit 32.3):
*We sent the invitation on Monday, so they **must have received** it by now.*

We use *won't* + *have* + past participle to refer to something which we feel certain has not happened:
*We sent the invitations by second-class post. They **won't have received** them yet.*

 We do not use *mustn't* in this way, but we can use *can't*:
✗ ~~*We sent the invitations by second-class post. They mustn't have received them yet.*~~
✓ *We sent the invitations by second-class post. They **can't have received** them yet.*

3 Present habits and routines

We often use *will/won't* to talk about habits and routines that have become predictable:
*Every lesson is the same: he'**ll sit down**, get his books out and then he'**ll start** giving us instructions. He **won't greet** us or show any interest in us.*

We can extend this use of *will* to talk about attitudes and characteristics:
*The public **will** always **side** with the nurses in any dispute.* (The adverb is often stressed.)
*The dominant male in this species **will not tolerate** the presence of other males.*

But when we state a simple fact, we prefer to use the present simple:
*The public always **sides** with the nurses in any dispute.*
*The dominant male in this species **does not tolerate** the presence of other males.*

We can use *will*, or the present simple, to talk about aspects of capacity or ability:
The Olympic stadium in London ***will hold/holds*** *80,000 people.*
This model ***will do/does*** *0 to 100 kilometres per hour in eight seconds.*

In speech, we use *will* (not the present simple) to describe an annoying habit or to make a criticism: *We enjoy going out with Frank and Carol, but they* ***will argue*** *in public!*

We do not contract *will* when we use it in this way – we stress it:
✗ ~~*Geoff'll leave the lights on when he's last out of the office.*~~
✓ *Geoff* ***will leave*** *the lights on when he's last out of the office!*

Similar use of present continuous ➤ Unit 20.2

Pronunciation ➤ 1.10

We often use *will/won't* to talk about inanimate objects:
Whatever I do, my car ***won't start*** *first time on cold mornings.*

4 Past habits and routines

We use *would/wouldn't* to talk about habits in the past (➤ Unit 21.5):
*Every lesson was the same: he'****d sit*** *down and get his books out, then he'****d start*** *giving us instructions. He* ***wouldn't greet*** *us or show any interest in us.*

In speech, we also use stressed *would/wouldn't* to criticise or talk about annoying habits in the past:
When Alan was a toddler he ***would cling*** *on to me whenever a stranger came into the room.*

However, if *would* is followed by an adverb, we often stress the adverb instead
*I miss Dad, even though he'****d always tell*** *me how to run my life!*
*My boss was awful: he'****d invariably find*** *something for me to do at five o'clock.*

Similar use of past continuous ➤ Unit 21.2

We can use *would/wouldn't* to talk about inanimate objects:
The car ***would*** *never* ***start*** *on winter mornings when we were in Sweden.*

5 Present and future willingness

We use *will* to express our agreement to do something. It means 'be willing to':
Jim ***will act*** *as referee today since Martin can't make it.*

We can use *will/won't* in the *if* clause of a first conditional to make a polite request:
*If you'****ll take*** *a seat for a moment, Mr Franks will be with you soon.*
(= If you are willing to take a seat ...)

Requests ➤ Unit 36.3

We use *won't/shan't* to express refusal to do something:
The Director's secretary ***won't book*** *my flights. She says it isn't in her job description.*

6 Past willingness

We use *would/wouldn't* to show willingness or refusal in the past. We use *would* (positive only) to refer to general willingness (i.e. a habit):
Dad ***would*** *always* ***help*** *us with our maths homework.*

We don't use *would* to express willingness to do something on a single occasion in the past but we can use *would not* for refusal on a single occasion in the past:
✗ ~~*The tour guide was very helpful. She would contact the Consulate for me when I lost my passport.*~~
✓ *The tour guide was very helpful. She* ***contacted/offered to contact/was willing to contact*** *the Consulate for me when I lost my passport.*
✓ *The shop assistant* ***wouldn't change*** *this jumper for me, even though I hadn't worn it.*

Practice

1 Match each sentence with A or B as the best way of continuing. (Underlined words are stressed.)

1 They will have released the exam results by now.
A Mine came in the post this morning.
B Why hasn't the school been in touch to let us know?
2 Our parents would leave all the doors open when we were children, including the front door.
A It was really annoying because we had no privacy.
B There were far fewer worries about security in those days.
3 The representatives of the transport union will always recommend strike action.
A We're expecting the result of the ballot at one o'clock.
B It's as though they can't possibly accept an amicable settlement.
4 My grandmother will act as guarantor for the loan.
A It annoys me when she meddles in my affairs.
B She's always very happy to help her grandchildren.
5 Kerry and Mike will be arriving soon.
A They left on time and there aren't any hold-ups on the motorway.
B They're parking outside right now.
6 My computer wouldn't send any emails this morning.
A This is always happening. B I don't know what went wrong with it.
7 Jack will spend every Saturday afternoon in front of the TV watching football.
A I really wish we could sometimes do something together.
B He retired last week and doesn't have to work on Saturdays any more.
8 The travel agent wouldn't give me my money back.
A She was adamant that I needn't have cancelled the flight.
B She makes a habit of being unpleasant.

2 Complete these dialogues, as in the example. Use *will, won't, would* + *have* if necessary, and a suitable form of the verbs in the box. 3.14 Listen and check.

argue be check come out go out have hold prepare say start stop work

1 A Sue says she's enjoying the job but she's putting on weight.
B Yes, that .... because of all those long business lunches.
2 A Are you having problems with your new camera?'
B Yes, the flash .... in semi-darkness, only when it's fully dark.
3 A Shop assistants used to be more polite, didn't they?
B Yes, they .... always .... 'please' and 'thank you' and smile at you.
4 A Surely there are too many people here to get on one plane?
B No, a jumbo jet .... easily .... over 300 people.
5 A I hope Josh is OK at that summer camp. He might be homesick.
B Don't worry about him. He .... a great time!
6 A Do you think that Nick will win his case in court tomorrow?
B I hope so. I'm sure that his lawyer .... a solid defence.
7 A I don't think this new secretary is as good as Janice was.
B I don't know. Janice .... always .... whenever you criticised her typing.

8 A The new horse at the riding stables seems to be working out very well.
B Quite well, but he .... and eat whenever he gets the opportunity.

9 A Oh no, I've just noticed a mistake in the headline for the front-page article!
B Phone the printers. They .... printing it yet – they don't print until early morning.

10 A What happened after the car broke down?
B Well, we knew that no breakdown service .... at that time of night, so we slept in the car.

11 A Why are you and Jack arguing so much these days?
B He takes me for granted. He .... with his friends every evening and leave me at home.

12 A I've filled in the application form and written the letter. Can you read them for me?
B Christine .... them for you. She's an editor.

3 **GRAMMAR IN USE** **Rewrite the underlined parts of this phone conversation, using *will*, *won't*, *would* and *wouldn't*, as in the example. 3.15 Listen and check.**

JAKE Hi, Alice, how nice to hear from you!

ALICE Actually, Jake, I'm phoning to ask you for some advice.

JAKE (0) I'm willing to help you (I'll help you) if I can, of course.

ALICE Your mother receives help from the Council, doesn't she? Can you tell me what (1) they agree to do and what (2) they don't agree to do for older people?

JAKE Yes, of course. Mum has a home help. She comes three times a week. (3) She's perfectly happy to do light cleaning and (4) she's willing to get the shopping, but (5) she refuses to do anything heavy.

ALICE That's fair enough. What about cooking?

JAKE Well, when she first started (6) she was happy to prepare supper when she came, but she stopped that after a few weeks.

ALICE Why was that?

JAKE You know my mum. (7) She insists on saying exactly what she thinks. Apparently, the home help used to make vegetarian food and Mum didn't like it, so (8) she refused to eat it. Why are you asking, anyway?

ALICE It's Dad. He can't move around very easily now. The neighbours are great, (9) they make a habit of popping in but (10) he's unwilling to ask them for help.

JAKE Mmm. You can understand that.

ALICE Oh, but he's so impatient. I take him to the shops once a week, but yesterday (11) the car refused to start and I was about half an hour late. (12) Was he willing to wait for me? No, (13) he insists on trying to cope by himself! He went to the shops and collapsed on the way there.

JAKE Oh dear. It's a worry, isn't it? Look, if (14) you don't mind waiting for a moment, I'll look up the phone number for the right person at social services.

36 Other uses of modals

1 Asking for and giving/refusing permission

The choice of modal verb for permission depends on the formality of the situation and how tentative or unsure the speaker is about the response.

	ASKING FOR PERMISSION	GIVING PERMISSION	REFUSING PERMISSION
less formal/ more sure	***Can** I **use** your phone?*	*Yes, of course you **can**.*	*No, I'm afraid you **can't**. No, I'm sorry.*
↓	***Could** I **leave** my coat here?*	*Yes, you **can**.*	*No, I'm sorry. I'm afraid not.*
more formal/ less sure	***May** I **interrupt**? **Might** I **ask** the court for an adjournment?*	*Yes, you **may**. Of course. Certainly.*	*No, you **may not**. No, I'm afraid not.*

- We use *can't* to refuse permission that is subject to external authority (➤ Unit 34.1):
  *You **can't smoke** in any public buildings.* (The law doesn't allow it.)
- To describe general permission in the past we use *could/couldn't*:
  *In the 1950s British children **could leave** school at the age of fourteen.*
- But we use *was allowed to* for permission on a specific occasion in the past:
  ✗ ~~*I could bring a friend with me.*~~ ✓ *I **was allowed to** bring a friend with me.*

2 Suggestions

We can make suggestions in several ways:
*We **can** try that new café. **Shall** we try that new café?*
***Let's** try that new café, (shall we?) We **could** try that new café.*

- We can use *can/could always* for an alternative, or more tentative suggestion:
  *We **could always go** to the Italian place.*
- We use *would* if we want to be more tentative or distant:
  *It **would be** a good idea to get together one evening.*
  *'Why don't you come to dinner on Sunday?' 'That **would be** nice. I'll let you know.'*
- We can use *could* to make a tentative suggestion that another person does something:
  *You **could** lose a little weight, perhaps.* (tentative)

To mean 'there is no better choice available', we can use the phrase *might as well*:
*Now the children have left, we **might as well** sell the house and get something smaller.*

To ask for suggestions (or advice), we can use *shall* with a question word (➤ Module 6 Before you start):
*What **shall** we **do** about Tom if he doesn't get into university?*

3 Offers and requests

	OFFERS	REQUESTS
less formal/ more sure	***Can** I help you?* ***I'll** help you.*	***Can/Will** you close the window, please?*
↓	*We **could** do that for you.* ***Shall** I help you?*	***Could/Would** you pass me the salt, please?*
more formal/ less sure	***May** I help you?* ***Might** I be of assistance?*	*You **might** get me some milk while you're there.*

We can use *will* or *won't* when we offer something to another person:
***Will** you **have** some more cake?* (neutral)
***Won't** you **have** some more cake?* (more encouraging)

We use the question forms of *would* or *could* to make requests tentative or polite, and *You might ...* to request things of people we do not know so well:
***Would** you **lend** me the car tomorrow night, Dad?* (tentative)
***Could** you **fill in** this form, please, sir?* (polite) ***You might ask** Mr Salmon to call me later.*

We can make a request more insistent by using *will you* as a question tag (➤ Unit 79.2):
*Come and look at this, **will you?*** (We do not expect the answer to be 'no'.)

Pronunciation ➤ 1.11

4 Recommendation and advice

We use *must/mustn't* for strong recommendations and advice:
*You really **must read** Michael Connelly's latest book. It's stunning!*
*You **mustn't blame** yourself. It wasn't your fault.*

Pronunciation ➤ 1.12

Should or *ought to* are less emphatic:
*Even people as young as twenty-five **should consider** a personal pension.*
*Children **ought not to spend** long periods in front of a computer screen.*
*The underlying shift in public opinion **ought not to be exaggerated**.*

Had better (not) expresses the best thing to do in a particular situation. It often has a sense of urgency: *Your dog **had better not dig up** my rose bush again!* (threat)
*If the burglars took your keys, you**'d better change** the locks.* (warning)

5 Orders, instructions and promises

We use *will* and *shall* for orders, formal instructions and written rules:
*The judges' decision **will/shall be** final.* *The secretary **shall minute** the proceedings.*

We use *will* to make promises:
*My government **will reduce** unemployment.*

We also use *will* when we make a spontaneous decision (➤ Unit 27.1):
*'That'll be Josie – I can't take her call now.' 'Don't worry, I**'ll tell** her you'll call back.'*

6 Expressing desires, preferences and disagreements

We often use *would* + infinitive with *to* with verbs of liking and preference (*like, love, prefer*, etc.) to express desires and preferences:
*We**'d love to come** to your wedding on 6th September. Thank you for the invitation.*
*I**'d prefer to lose** weight by a tried and tested method than by a new trendy diet.*
*I **would like you** to listen to me when I'm talking!* (use with an object)

We can use *would* with *rather/sooner* to express a preference (➤ Unit 40.4):
*Our delegates **would rather not stay** at the conference centre.*

We can use *would/wouldn't* to show disagreement in a polite way:
*I **wouldn't say** that. I **wouldn't go** that far.*

Practice

1 Choose the correct meaning, A or B.

1 Are you seeing the club chairman tomorrow? You might put in a good word for me.
A You expect the person to do this. B You're not sure the person will do this.
2 You must read the new book by Margaret Atwood – it's fantastic!
A I think you should do this. B I'm ordering you to do this.
3 Might I borrow your calculator for a moment?
A You're talking to your best friend. B You're talking to a clerk at the bank.
4 Well, we could always go on the bus.
A I don't really mind how we get there. B I really want to go on the bus.
5 I'd sooner stay at home this weekend.
A I think we should do this earlier. B I'd prefer to do this.
6 We can have a look at the shops.
A I'm making a suggestion. B I'm describing a future ability.
7 The decision made by the financial arbitrator will be accepted by all parties.
A This is a spontaneous decision by the arbitrator. B This is a formal instruction.
8 You'd better call the insurance company and tell them.
A I think this is a possible thing to do. B I think this is the best thing to do.
9 You will listen to me, young lady!
A This is talking about a future action. B This is giving an order.
10 We might as well go straight home.
A There's nothing better to do. B I really want to go home.

2 GRAMMAR IN USE Choose the correct words in *italics*. If both options are correct, choose both. 3.16 Listen and check.

ALAN OK, let's discuss next week's national championships. I can only send three reporters, so (1) *we must / we'd better* discuss who does what. Yes, James?

JAMES I'd (2) *love / rather* to cover the diving. I'm fascinated by diving.

ALAN OK, if no one else objects? Right, well, I think you (3) *should / ought to* cover the synchronised swimming as well, as it's in the pool next to the diving.

JAMES Oh, OK, if I have to ... Would anyone else like to, though?

ALAN Bad luck, James, it's yours. And (4) *you hadn't better / you'd better not* let your lack of enthusiasm show when you're there! Now, I'd like one of you (5) *focus / to focus* on the individual events in the main pool. Any takers?

EMILY I'm happy to do that, but I was going to ask, (6) *could / may* I have the Friday off? My cousin's getting married.

ALAN Probably, but let's sort out the championships first. That leaves the third reporter to cover the team events and to act as anchor for us.

KIERAN (7) *I would / I'll* do that. It sounds interesting, but there aren't many team events, are there?

EMILY We (8) *should / could* always share the main pool reporting, Kieran.

DEBBIE Er, Alan, before we go on ... I was wondering, I'm not sure, but (9) *can / might* suggest something?

ALAN Yes, what is it, Debbie?

DEBBIE Well, shouldn't we check what the Daily Herald is doing? We don't want them to get better coverage. They seem to be doing better than us at the moment.

ALAN I (10) *won't / wouldn't* say that, but they do have more money than us, I'm afraid. Debbie, call your friend on the Herald, (11) *will / won't* you, and see if you can get any information? Right, we'll go with those suggestions. (12) *Can / Shall* we go on to tomorrow's front page now?

3 **Complete the dialogues below the pictures with *will, won't, shall* or *would* and an appropriate verb. 3.17 Listen and check.**

STUDENT 1 .... me the dictionary, please?
STUDENT 2 Yes, here you are.

WOMAN .... a slice of cake?
FRIEND I won't, thanks. I'm trying to lose weight.

CADET What time do we finish these exercises? I'm exhausted.
SERGEANT Silence! You .... these exercises until I say otherwise. Do you understand?

MAN .... the minutes of the meeting?
WOMAN Oh, yes, please! We always need someone to take the minutes.

POLICE OFFICER .... with me, sir?
THIEF Come with you? No, why should I?

MAN I don't understand what you want from me!
WOMAN .... me some respect!
MAN But I do respect you!

4 **Complete the dialogues by writing one word (or a contraction) in each gap, as in the example. In some cases more than one answer is possible. 3.18 Listen and check.**

0 A It's rather hot in this meeting room. ...*Could*... I open a window, please?
B Yes, of ...*course*....

1 A Look at this rash on my arm, Mum. Do you think I .... see the doctor?
B Well, you .... to see him if it continues, but you really .... scratch it like that. You'll make it bleed.

2 A .... you have another cup of tea before you go, Grandma?
B I'd love one, thanks dear.

3 A What .... I to do about the broken windows, officer?
B .... better contact your insurance company immediately and arrange for them to be replaced. It's important to secure your home as quickly as possible.

4 A It's 3.30, Mr Curtis. Please .... I go home now?
B No, you .... not. In fact, you .... all stay until you finish your essays.

5 A .... you write me a reference letter when I leave Shiptons?
B To be honest, I'd .... not. I think your manager should do that.

Review MODULE 7

1 UNITS 30, 31 AND 32 **Find and correct the mistakes. Tick (✓) the correct sentences.**

0 Gina ~~managed~~ *succeeded* in decorating the spare room before her parents arrived for the weekend.
1 We couldn't have been more relieved when we heard that Jonny had passed his exam.
2 I'd rather not go shopping on Saturday afternoon – there should be too many people at the shops then.
3 This ebook reader is able to be read in semi-darkness because of its built-in reading light.
4 Let's have a walk through the woods. There can be some bluebells out by now.
5 I'm surprised you didn't see Bella – she should have been collecting tickets at the door.
6 At the end of the training module, can we use all the main features of InDesign?
7 What became clear after the trial was that the drugs might not always have the desired effect.
8 Mike got home OK after the party last night because he could get the last bus.
9 Honestly, the cat really mustn't have scratched the sofa – she hasn't been in all day.
10 Let's not take the ferry today. It's so windy that it couldn't be a very pleasant crossing.

2 UNITS 33 AND 34 **Write the second sentence so it has a similar meaning to the first. Use the word in brackets, as in the example.**

0 It is imperative that all visitors to the building site wear hard hats.
(must) *All visitors to the building site must wear hard hats.*
1 The obligation to observe all the health and safety rules these days is onerous.
(having) ....
2 There is no obligation to get an international licence to drive in this country.
(have) ....
3 It was stupid of the government to try to break the strike.
(should) ....
4 It would have been polite to let us know you were coming.
(might) ....
5 We booked the table but it didn't matter as the restaurant was only half full.
(need) ....
6 It is essential that you disconnect the gas supply before removing the boiler.
(disconnected) ....
7 We arrived late at the theatre and couldn't take our seats for the first ten minutes.
(allowed) ....
8 Why do we have to state ethnic origin on official forms these days?
(required) ....
9 It is essential that patients have not eaten or drunk anything for three hours before the operation.
(must) ....
10 The public are not allowed to visit the private rooms when the owner is in residence.
(may) ....

3 UNITS 35 AND 36 **Choose the correct words in *italics*.**

I'LL NEVER FORGET the day my life changed. It was a normal day – in those days I (1) *would / should* do my homework straight after school so that I could go and listen to music at Janice's after dinner.

'(2) *May / Can* I go to Janice's now, Mum? I've finished my homework.'

'No, not yet, love. Wait till your Dad's home. Remember, it's Thursday,' said Mum.

Of course. (3) *He'd / He'll* be visiting my grandmother. He did that every Thursday after work. She lived in a cold, draughty cottage on the moors. Mum and Dad wanted her to move in with us, but our house was very small, and she (4) *wouldn't / won't*. They knew that the cold winter months (5) *would have hastened / would hasten* her end, but she was a stubborn old woman who (6) *might / would* insist on her independence.

'(7) *Wouldn't / Won't* it be nice if we had some money? We could buy a big house and Granny could have a flat of her own in it. I hate being poor.'

'Oh, pet, I (8) *shan't / wouldn't* say we're poor. We've got a roof over our heads. Anyway, you (9) *might / could* as well get used to it; it isn't going to change.'

Mum (10) *won't / wouldn't* even daydream about Dad's chance of success with his inventions. It really annoyed me! But I thought I (11) *should / better* be nice, as she seemed a bit upset. '(12) *Shall / Will* I make a nice cup of tea?'

At that moment, the door opened and Dad walked in, waving a letter. 'Put on your coats, we're all going out tonight. They've bought my idea, Mary. We're rich!' ■

4 ALL UNITS **Read the article and choose words and phrases from the box to complete it. There are two extra words/phrases.**

could couldn't have didn't manage to had to might mustn't have
ought should succeeded in were unable to will have would

Twins left high and dry

IF YOU WATCHED the recent Oxford and Cambridge boat race, you (1) .... noticed the Winklevoss twins, Cameron and Tyler, in the Oxford boat. The two have always rowed together, and competed in the Beijing Olympics but (2) .... manage only sixth in their class on that occasion.

The Winklevoss brothers are very rich, as the result of a lawsuit settled out of court, but in reality they (3) .... be billionaires now. In the early 2000s, when the twins were studying at Harvard, they (4) .... often talk about setting up a social networking website for students. They (5) .... starting one, named ConnectU, but as the pair were busy studying and rowing, they (6) .... devote the time necessary to developing the site, so they decided they (7) .... employ someone else to help them. After three months Mark Zuckerberg stopped working with the twins and launched his own social networking site – Facebook – which is now worth over $4 billion.

Understandably, the twins were convinced Zuckerberg (8) .... created the site without their initial input. Although the twins have settled out of court, there are still some messy arguments going on which (9) .... continue for some time.

Did it affect their performance in the boat race? Well, the Oxford team started well but (10) .... hold out against a battling Cambridge team, who sealed an exciting victory.

MODULE

8 Conditionals, subjunctives and the 'unreal' past

Before you start

1 Review these intermediate grammar points and check you know them.

Conditionals

1 Conditional sentences usually consist of two clauses: a conditional clause (or *if* clause) and a main clause (or *result* clause) which is dependent on the conditional.

2 We usually form conditional sentences in one of two ways:

if clause	main clause	main clause	*if* clause
If I had a car,	*I would take you*.	*I would take you*	*if I had a car*.

If we put the *if* clause first, we usually separate the clauses with a comma.

3 There are four basic conditional sentence patterns where our choice of tense depends on
- the time of the condition (past, present or future)
- how possible or impossible we think the event is.

zero conditional	possible at any time, but most commonly in the present	*If your car is old, it probably needs a road test.* *If she made a new dish, she tried it out on friends straight away.*
first conditional	possible in the future	*If we don't water those plants, they'll die.*
second conditional	impossible in the present	*If my eyesight was perfect, I wouldn't need to wear these glasses.*
	possible (but unlikely) in the future	*If we were rich, we'd buy a house in the Caribbean.*
third conditional	impossible in the past	*If you had answered the door, she wouldn't have gone away again.*

4 We can make questions: *If you lost your passport, what would you do?*

5 In conversation we often use only the main clause; the *if* clause is implied:
Actually, it would be pretty difficult. (if we did as you asked)

wish/if only

1 We use *wish/if only* + past simple to express a desire for something to be different in the present. The desire can be for something which is actually impossible:
***I wish** I **knew** more about art.* (= I don't know much about it, but I would like to.)
***If only** we **were** young again.* (= We want to be young, but we know this is impossible.)

2 We use *wish/if only* + past perfect to express a regret about the past:
***If only** I **hadn't left** the car unlocked.*

The 'unreal' past

The 'unreal' past describes the use of past tenses after certain expressions, e.g. *if only, it's time*, to describe things in the present, past or future which are imagined or unreal:
*If only I **was** thin.* (= I am not thin but I would like to be thin.)
*It's time you **went** to the doctor about that cough.*

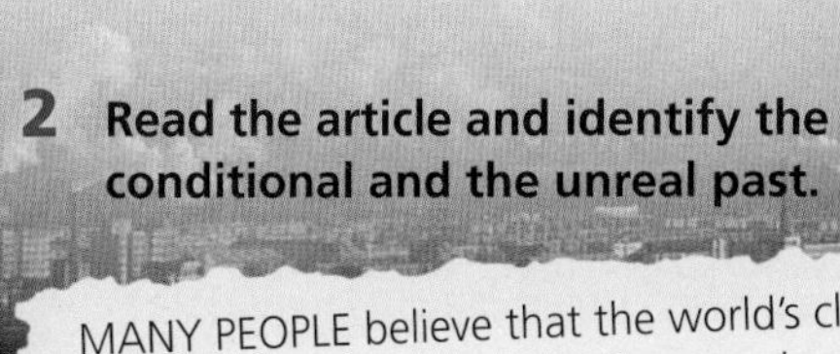

2 Read the article and identify the conditional and the unreal past.

MANY PEOPLE believe that the world's climate has started changing due to the increased carbon in the atmosphere. Some scientists estimate that levels of carbon are rising by 2.5 percent a year. If we don't do something about it now, there may be catastrophic changes in global weather patterns, leading to rises in sea level, severe storms and droughts.

If only we hadn't spent the last two hundred years chopping down forests, burning fossil fuels and filling our atmosphere with carbon from factories, power stations and cars!

3 Complete the diagnostic test below. Choose the correct words in *italics*. If both options are correct, choose both.

1 Always take a basic medicine kit on holiday *if* / *in case* you fall ill. ➤ Unit 37.1
2 If you pay for a full year's membership in advance, *then* / *that* you are entitled to a twenty percent discount on spa treatments. ➤ Unit 37.1
3 The show's next week. What are we going to do *unless the tickets turn up* / *if the tickets don't turn up* in time? ➤ Unit 37.2
4 *If* / *When* you press the 'record' button, the green light comes on. ➤ Unit 37.3
5 If the museum *will charge* / *charges* for entry, a lot of people won't be able to use it. ➤ Unit 37.4
6 There *will be* / *is* a riot if the police don't establish control over the crowd. ➤ Unit 37.4
7 *If you were* / *Were you* to listen more carefully, you might understand a little more. ➤ Unit 38.1
8 If I were you, *I'd ask* / *I asked* for a full refund. ➤ Unit 38.2
9 Had we known about the state of the hotel, we would never *book* / *have booked* it. ➤ Unit 38.3
10 The King of Belgium didn't attend the royal wedding. If he *had* / *hadn't* been there, he would have witnessed a marvellous spectacle. ➤ Unit 38.4
11 If Janice had married Nils last year, she'd *be living* / *have lived* in Gothenburg now. ➤ Unit 38.5
12 If flights to Cyprus *weren't* / *aren't* so expensive these days, they might have gone there for their honeymoon last spring. ➤ Unit 38.5
13 I was born in 1985, but I wish I *was* / *had been* alive in the 1960s. I love the music and fashion from that period. ➤ Unit 39.2
14 I wish *you stop* / *you'd stop* shouting. I'm not deaf, you know. ➤ Unit 39.2
15 *If only* / *I wish* that I had known she was vegetarian before cooking that meal! ➤ Unit 39.3
16 The regulations require that each defendant in turn *submit* / *to submit* a sworn statement to the court. ➤ Unit 40.1
17 I had to start work as soon as I left school. But I wish I *went* / *had been* to university instead. ➤ Unit 40.2
18 It is *high time* / *time for* the country were told of the Prime Minister's intentions. ➤ Unit 40.3
19 I don't like artificial fabrics. I'd rather *wear* / *wore* natural materials. ➤ Unit 40.4
20 Are you tired? You look as though you *didn't sleep* / *haven't slept* for days! ➤ Unit 40.5

4 Check your answers on page 384. Then go to the unit for more information and practice.

37 *If* and alternatives; present and future conditions

1 *if* and alternatives to *if*

There are several conjunctions we can use instead of *if*:

provided/providing (that) *so/as long as* *only if* *on (the) condition (that)*	to emphasise that the condition is necessary to the result.[1]	*Expenses will be reimbursed* ***on the condition that*** *receipts are supplied.* ***Provided*** *you pay the extra fee, we guarantee a sea-view room.*
even if	to express a condition that is unexpected in the circumstances	***Even if*** *they do go down with flu after they've had the vaccination, it's likely to be less serious.*
whether … or not	to express alternative conditions	*They'll deliver the furniture* ***whether*** *there's someone to receive it* ***or not***.[2]
In case of (+ noun)	to describe what you should do in a particular situation (usually formal, e.g. written notices)	***In case of*** *(an)* ***emergency****, pull the cord above the bath.* ***In case of fire****, do not use the elevator.*

[1] These conjunctions only refer to present or future conditions; we do not use them with the third conditional:
✗ ~~We would've had the party there so long as they'd arranged the catering.~~

[2] We can also say: *They'll deliver the furniture* **whether or not** *there's someone to receive it.*

We use *in case* to imagine a precaution necessary for a possible future situation. It is not the same as *if*. Compare:

I'll pop round later ***in case*** *you're there.* (I don't know if you'll be there, but I'll come anyway.)

I'll pop round later ***if*** *you're there.* (I'll only come if you're there.)

In conditional sentences that start with the *if* clause we can use *then* in the main clause to emphasise that the result depends on the condition being fulfilled:

If *the bill is passed by both parliamentary houses,* ***then*** *it becomes law.*

What if, suppose/supposing (that), imagine, say…, etc. ➤ Unit 82.1 *but for…* ➤ Unit 38.3

2 *unless* and negative conditions

We often use *unless* to express a negative condition. It means 'except if' and it is similar to *if … not* or *only if*:

Unless *you've got a doctor's note to say you've passed the medical, they won't allow you to go on the activity holiday.* (= If you don't have a doctor's note, they won't allow you to go.)

I wouldn't go there ***unless*** *I had to.* (= I would go there only if I had to.)

Unless is not always an alternative to *if not*, especially when the negative condition after *if* is contrary to known facts, and in most questions:

✗ ~~*You'd be happier unless you had such high expectations.*~~ (an unreal situation)

✓ *You'd be happier* ***if*** *you* ***didn't have*** *such high expectations.*

✗ ~~*What time shall we leave for the theatre unless he turns up?*~~ (a question)

We can use *unless* with *not*:
The college will offer you a place, ***unless*** *your school-leaving grade* ***is not*** *as predicted.*
(= They'll offer you a place if your grade is as predicted.)
*'Are they going to sell?' '****Not unless*** *they receive $1 million.'*
(= They won't sell if they don't receive $1 million.)

3 Zero conditional

We use the zero conditional to talk about events or situations that can occur at any time (often regularly), and their results. We often use it for actions that always have the same result, and we can replace *if* with *when* if we are referring to a regular activity:
If *you use a hot iron on nylon, it melts.*
When *I eat dairy products, I get red spots on my skin.*
If/When *you press this key, the game starts, and* ***when*** *you click here, it stops.*

We can use modal verbs (especially *can* and *may*), the present simple, present perfect or present continuous in both clauses:
If you ***can read*** *this, you****'re driving*** *too close to me!*
Prawns ***can be*** *risky to eat if they* ***haven't been kept*** *at the right temperature.*
*If/When she****'s travelling*** *abroad on business, she always* ***phones*** *me every evening.*

We can use a similar pattern to refer to the past. We use the past simple or continuous in the *if* clause and the past simple in the result clause:
When they ***went*** *to the movies, they always* ***sat*** *at the back.* (*when* for regular activity)
Karen ***got*** *a lot more done if/when she* ***was working*** *from home.*

When we give a general instruction, we use an imperative in the result clause:
If a chip pan is on fire, ***throw*** *a fire blanket on it.*

4 First conditional

We use the first conditional to describe possible future events or situations and their results:
If the result of the test is negative, you'll receive notification through the post.

We often use it for offers, suggestions and warnings:
I'll call the hotel if you don't have time.
Shall we go out tomorrow if the weather's good?
I'll call the police if you don't leave right now!

We can also use it for commands, but note that we use an imperative in the main clause:
If you get home late, ***be*** *quiet!*
Don't forget *to lock the doors if you go out.*

We can use the present simple, present continuous or present perfect in the *if* clause, and *will/shall* or *be going to* in the main clause:
*If you****'ve decided*** *to come on the motorway, you****'re going to need*** *change for the tolls.*
*If they****'re leaving*** *early, we****'ll go*** *home with Jake.*

We can use modal verbs in either clause, especially *can, could* and *may*:
If the regime ***can*** *keep the loyalty of the army, they* ***may*** *retain power.*
If global warming continues, there ***could*** *be an increase in extreme weather conditions.*

It is usually incorrect to use a future form in the *if* clause:
✗ ~~*If the weather will be good tomorrow, we'll have a picnic.*~~
✓ *If the weather* ***is*** *good tomorrow, we****'ll have*** *a picnic.*

However, it is appropriate if *will/won't* refers to willingness or refusal (➤ Unit 35.5):
The company ***will impose*** *sanctions if the workers* ***won't abandon*** *the strike.*

FORMALITY CHECK To make the first conditional more formal and the condition a little less likely, we can use *happen to*, or we can omit *if* and use *should* before the subject:
If/Should *you* ***happen to be*** *in the neighbourhood, feel free to visit our showroom.*
Should *you* ***be*** *less than delighted with our product, we will refund your money immediately.*

Practice

1 Tick (✓) the possible conditions and cross (✗) the incorrect ones. Think about the meaning as well as the grammar.

1 We'll be able to go out tomorrow evening ...
A if the babysitter will be available. B so long as the babysitter can come.
C provided the babysitter hasn't got any other plans.
2 Before we leave, we'd better turn on the automatic watering system ...
A in case it doesn't rain while we're away.
B if it doesn't rain while we're away.
C provided it doesn't rain while we're away.
3 When the weather's really hot ...
A I get a lot of headaches. B I would get a lot of headaches.
C I sometimes get a headache.
4 I'm sure you'd get a lot more business ...
A unless you charged so much. B if you didn't charge so much.
C unless you didn't charge so much.
5 Frozen chicken isn't safe to eat ...
A if it hasn't been thoroughly defrosted. B if it isn't thoroughly cooked.
C unless it has been defrosted and cooked correctly.
6 We used to walk to school ...
A when the weather was good. B whether it was hot or cold.
C even if it was raining.

2 GRAMMAR IN USE Choose the correct words in *italics*. If both options are correct, choose both. 3.19 Listen and check.

INVASION OF GIANT GRASS

There's little doubt that (1) *provided / if* we want to combat global warming and the effects of climate change, we (2) *have / would have* to find more sustainable sources of energy. Oil and gas produce harmful greenhouse gases and, of course, there is only a limited supply available. So, (3) *in case / unless* we act soon, we (4) *run out / will run out* of energy supplies. Recently, scientists have been looking at the use of fast-growing grasses as an alternative to traditional fossil fuels. These grasses can be burnt in power stations to provide a renewable source of energy. (5) *So long as / If* it is grown properly, grass (6) *will be / is* carbon neutral – that is, it does not give off more carbon than it absorbs. The idea is that farmers will grow crops for energy rather than for food. Scientists believe that if we (7) *provide / provided* sufficient subsidies, farmers will be happy to start growing these new crops.

There are several trial schemes under way at present, including two in the north of England. Local farmers are growing a variety known as elephant grass. (8) *Whether / When* it is grown in its native tropics, the grass (9) *reaches / can reach* a height of over 4 metres. It is a grass that grows happily in the cooler climates of northern Europe, forming thick forests that provide a welcome habitat for wildlife. One scheme is at the Drax power station in Yorkshire, Britain's biggest power plant. If all (10) *goes / will go* to plan, the station (11) *is / will be* able to cut its emissions of greenhouse gases by five percent. But not everyone is happy with the scheme. Local conservationists are worried about the impact of the giant grass on the countryside. (12) *Whether / If* elephant grass solves our energy needs or not, they feel it is an ugly and unwelcome blot on the landscape.

3 Write the second sentence so it has a similar meaning to the first. Use the word(s) in brackets, as in the example. Make any other changes necessary. 3.20 Listen and check.

0 If you fail to pass the medical test, we will be unable to offer you insurance cover.
(unless) *We will be unable to offer you insurance cover unless you pass the medical test.*

1 Perhaps Sophie doesn't like her parents-in-law, but she keeps it to herself.
(even) ....

2 Use the signposted exit at the rear of the building if there is a fire.
(of) ....

3 After her husband's death, Mrs Jenkins sold the house to her son but insisted that he lived in it himself.
(condition) ....
....

4 If you don't request next-day delivery, we will send the goods by normal post.
(unless) ....

5 You will be awarded marks for trying to answer all the questions; not all the answers have to be correct.
(whether ... not) ....
....

6 If you wish to apply for shares, there is a registration form on our website.
(should) ....

7 Your membership will not be renewed unless you pay your subscription within the next seven days.
(only) ....
....

8 Cars parked illegally will be towed away at the owner's expense.
(then) ....

9 You may enter the ruins but you must put on protective footwear.
(providing) ....

10 We will only achieve the deadline if you provide all the resources we have requested.
(unless) ....

11 When my parents are out of the house I can play my music as loud as I like.
(long) ....

12 The library computer can tell you about the books you have out on loan, if any.
(whether ... not) ....
....

13 You'd better take your passport because you might need proof of your identity.
(case) ....

14 You may only enter the country if you have a valid visa issued by the consulate.
(unless) ....

15 If we fail to deliver within fourteen days, we will deduct twenty-five percent from our invoice.
(should) ....

38 Unlikely, unreal and past conditions

If the sea defences **hadn't collapsed** in August 2005, New Orleans **wouldn't have been flooded**.

1 Forming the second conditional

We can use the past simple, past continuous or *was going to* in the *if* clause:
If they ***wanted*** *to make her an offer, she would listen and think it over.*
If a celebrity ***was staying*** *in the hotel, security arrangements would be tightened.*

We use *would* or a modal verb (often *might* or *could*), in the main clause:
More research funding ***could be secured*** *if people were more aware of the disease.*

We can use *should* + infinitive or *were to* + infinitive in the second conditional to emphasise that the condition is unlikely to happen:
If the printer ***should break down*** *within the first year, we would repair it at our expense.*
If you ***were to listen*** *more carefully, you might understand a little more.*

FORMALITY CHECK We can make this condition more formal in two ways:

- by using *were*, not *was*, after *I/he/she/it* in the *if* clause (➤ Unit 40.2):
  If the programmer ***were*** *familiar with this language, it would be an easy job.*
- by placing *was/were* (*to*) or *should* (➤ Unit 37.4) before the subject:
  Were *you* ***to accept*** *our offer, we could avoid the costs of a court case.*
  Were it not for *the sea walls, the city would be at risk of flooding.*
  Should *the tickets* ***fail*** *to arrive, we would arrange to have duplicates waiting at the airport.*

2 Uses of the second conditional

The second conditional has two main uses:

- to talk about an unlikely future event or situation:
  If the result of the test were positive, we would call you within two days.
  (We expect the results to be negative.)
  I wouldn't work there unless they paid me at least double. (They're unlikely to double my pay.)
  The choice between this pattern and the first conditional (➤ Unit 37) often depends on how possible we believe an event to be:

FIRST CONDITIONAL	*If Mike rings the travel agent tomorrow, he might get a cancellation.* (We believe it is likely that Mike will ring the travel agent.)
SECOND CONDITIONAL	*If Mike rang the travel agent tomorrow, he might get a cancellation.* (We believe it is unlikely that Mike will ring the travel agent.)

- to talk about an unreal current event or situation, i.e. one which is contrary to known facts. It is therefore impossible to fulfil the condition:
  If the police were confident of their case against Sykes, surely they would take him into custody?
  (The police aren't confident of their case.)

 We don't use *unless* with these unreal conditions (➤ Unit 37.2).

We can also use the second conditional for

- giving advice (with *were*): *If I were you, I would take her out of that school.*
- polite requests: *If you could deal with this matter, I'd be very grateful.*
- desires/regrets: *If we didn't have to work so hard, we could spend more time together.*

3 Forming the third conditional

We use the past perfect in the *if* clause and *would/wouldn't have* or modal verbs (usually *might have* or *could have*) in the main clause:
*If we **had paid** our cleaner more, she **wouldn't have left** us.*
*It **might have been** easier to break the news if I **had known** her a bit better.*
*If the spy had intercepted the message, he **could have averted** the crisis.*

We can use continuous forms in both clauses:
*If that taxi hadn't come along, you **would have been waiting** there for hours.*
*You wouldn't have missed the turning if you**'d been paying** attention.*

We can use a prepositional phrase (➤ Unit 9.2) instead of an *if* clause:
*Don't worry. I wouldn't have done it **without asking for permission first**.*
***But for its lack of a garden**, we might have bought that house.*

FORMALITY CHECK For a more formal or literary style, we can put *had* before the subject:
***Had** the film **been released** in the summer, it might have been more successful.*
***Had** it **not been** for his quick thinking, we would have fallen into the river.*

4 Uses of the third conditional

The third conditional describes an unreal or imagined situation or event in the past:
*If the sea defences **hadn't collapsed**, New Orleans wouldn't have been flooded.*
(But the known facts are: the sea defences did collapse and New Orleans was flooded.)
*I **would have used** your builder if I **had managed** to contact him.*
(But the known facts are: I didn't manage to contact him so I didn't use him.)

We can use the third conditional to express criticism or regret, often with *could have*:
*If you'd been driving more slowly, you **could have stopped** in time.*
*I **could have got** the job if I'd performed better in the interview.*

5 Mixed conditionals

There are several less common conditional patterns:

1 PAST CONDITION ➤ FUTURE RESULT
If + past simple | *will* + infinitive/*be going to*
*If they **left** at midnight yesterday, they **will be** here by lunchtime tomorrow.*

2 PAST CONDITION ➤ PAST/PRESENT RESULT
If + past simple | present perfect
*If you **gave** them all your money, you**'ve made** a big mistake.*

3 PAST UNREAL CONDITION ➤ PRESENT RESULT
If + past perfect (third conditional) | *would/could/might* + infinitive (second conditional)
***If** your brother **hadn't had** that promotion, he **would** still **be** working here.*
(He did have the promotion so he no longer works here.)

4 PRESENT UNREAL CONDITION ➤ PAST RESULT
If + past simple (second conditional) | *would/could/might have* + past participle (third conditional)
***If** the island **were** still a tourist attraction, more people **would have died** in the earthquake.*
(The island is no longer a tourist attraction so fewer people died.)

Differences between British and American English ➤ page 368

Practice

1 Read the statements carefully and think about the meaning. Then choose the correct words in *italics* in the explanations.

1 'If we'd missed that flight, we wouldn't be on the beach now.'
We *are / aren't* on the beach now. We *missed / didn't miss* the flight.
2 'If she wanted to see you again, she would have phoned by now.'
She *has / hasn't* phoned. She probably *does / doesn't* want to see you again.
3 'If we'd taken out the warranty, we wouldn't need to pay for these repairs.'
We *took / didn't take* out a warranty so we *have to / don't have to* pay for these repairs.
4 'I'd ask for a refund if I were you.'
I'm *talking about the past / giving advice.*
5 'We'd get a lot more light if there wasn't a huge tree in our back garden.'
There *is / used to be* a big tree in our garden.
6 'You'd be able to spend more time with the children if you changed to a part-time job.'
I think you are *likely / unlikely* to change your job.
7 'If we knew more about computers, we wouldn't have had to call the technical helpline.'
We *had to / didn't have to* call the helpline because we *didn't /don't* know much about computers.
8 'We'd have a less stressful life if we didn't live so far from the office.'
I'm expressing a regret about a *past / present* situation.

2 GRAMMAR IN USE **Read each short text and the conditional sentences that follow it. Tick (✓) the correct conditional sentences. (One or two may be correct in each case.) Put a cross (✗) by the incorrect ones. Think about the meaning as well as the grammar.**

NEWS
Home | World | UK | Business | Health | Politics | Education | Entertain
Video & Audio | Magazine | Editors' Blog | In Pictures | Also in the Ne

1 **Concorde crash**

The report into the crash of the Air France Concorde attributed the disaster to a piece of metal on the runway, apparently from a Continental Airlines DC10 which had taken off minutes before.

The metal caused one of Concorde's tyres to burst, which in turn ruptured the fuel tank on the left-hand side of the plane.

A If the runway were swept after each take-off, the disaster might have been averted.
B If the runway had been swept after the DC10 take-off, the disaster could have been averted.
C If the runway hadn't been swept after the DC10 take-off, the disaster might have been averted.

2 IN LAST WEEK'S peaceful demonstrations in Burma, one demonstrator was seriously injured when she fell and was trampled by the crowd trying to flee from the water cannons. She is still in hospital in a critical condition.

A If the demonstrator didn't fall, she might not be in hospital now.
B If the demonstrator hadn't fallen, she might not be in hospital now.
C If the demonstrator hadn't fallen, she might not have been seriously injured.

3 Over ninety-five percent of people who successfully complete our course find that they recover the course fees within a few months through income from having their work published.

A Should you not recover the fees within a year of completing the course, we would give you a full refund.
B Did you not recover the fees within a year of completing the course, we would give you a full refund.
C If you hadn't recovered the fees within a year of completing the course, we would give you a full refund.

3 **Match each *if* clause with two main clauses from A–L below. Then complete the main clauses, using the words in brackets, as in the example. Use modal verbs if appropriate. 3.21 Listen and check.**

0 If Bill Gates hadn't been in the right place at the right time, B, E
1 If athletes today didn't take their training so seriously, ...
2 If the internal combustion engine hadn't been invented, ...
3 If scientists hadn't discovered how to build an atomic bomb, ...
4 If it weren't possible for scientists to isolate individual genes, ...
5 If the printing press had not been invented, ...

A the elimination of hereditary diseases .... feasible. (not/be)
B he wouldn't be one of the richest men in the world now. (not/be)
C Hiroshima and Nagasaki .... (not/be/destroyed)
D it .... possible to extend education to most people. (not/become)
E Microsoft wouldn't have become a household name. (not/become)
F much of our history .... unknown to us. (be)
G sport .... so exciting to watch. (not/be)
H the motor car .... (never/be/developed)
I the debate around modified crops .... an issue. (not/be)
J we probably .... such a problem with carbon emissions. (not/have)
K the world .... a more secure and peaceful place. (be)
L they .... so many records in recent years. (not/break)

4 GRAMMAR IN USE **Complete the conditional sentences 1–5 from the information given, as in the example. 3.22 Listen and check.**

0 Governments would take the problem more seriously if there were more international pressure.

1 If it were to rain, ...

2 The tourist industry might ....

3 If the governments involved ....

4 There might be more ....

5 Current attempts to fight the fires would have been ....

South-East Asia faces new smog crisis

FOREST FIRES are breaking out all over south-east Asia.
(0) Governments are not taking the problem seriously because of a lack of international pressure.
(1) Only heavy rain can avert the crisis. Unfortunately, the forecast is for the weather to remain hot and dry for the foreseeable future.
(2) The government stopped releasing pollution levels in June because it didn't want to frighten off tourists. The tourist industry has not yet suffered.
(3) The governments involved didn't take positive action after the previous disaster. Environmentalists think this is why the current crisis has happened.
(4) One of the problems is that few of the countries affected have a Ministry of the Environment, so there is no serious environmental protection.
(5) The failure of governments to build reliable water supply networks in rural areas is a major reason why current attempts to fight the fires have been so ineffective.

39 *I wish* and *if only*

1 *wish/if only* + past simple and past perfect

We use *I/we wish* or *if only*

- + past simple to express a desire for something to be different in the present:
  ***I wish I had** lots of money.* (I want lots of money but I don't have it.)
  ***We wish** you **didn't have to** leave so soon.*
  (We don't want you to leave, but we know you have to.)
- + past perfect to express a wish that something different had happened in the past:
  *I feel sick. **If only I hadn't eaten** all those cakes!* (I ate them and now I regret it.)
- + *could* to describe a desire we know is impossible to achieve, often about ourselves:
  ***If only** we **could see** the situation through his eyes.* (We can't.)
  ***I wish** I **could swim** but I'm terrified of water!*

We can use *could* + *have* + past participle (➤ Unit 34.3) for a regret about the past:
***I wish** your father **could have been** there.* (Unfortunately, he wasn't able to be there.)

 Pronunciation ➤ 1.13

2 *wish/if only* + *would*

I/we wish/if only + *would* usually expresses a desire for someone to change their behaviour in the present or future. We often use it to criticise or complain about something:
***I wish** you**'d stop** looking at me like that. It's terribly distracting.*
***If only** you **wouldn't shout**. It's really irritating.*
***I wish** people **would recycle** their rubbish!*

We can also use this pattern with inanimate subjects for emphasis:
***If only** the sun **would come out** so we could take the photos.*
(The sun 'refuses' to come out. I want it to come out.)

 We cannot use this form for an impossible change, or a change to the past. For these meanings we use the past simple (for present/future time) or the past perfect (for past time):
✗ ~~*If only nuclear bombs wouldn't have been invented.*~~ (a change to the past)
✓ ***If only** nuclear bombs **hadn't been invented**.*

We can't use *would* when the subject of the wish and the subject of the change are the same. Instead we use a past tense or *could*:
✗ ~~*I wish I would be more energetic.*~~ (Subject of *wish* and *would* are the same.)
✓ *If only I **was** more energetic.* ✓ *I wish I **could be** more energetic.*

3 Differences between *wish* and *if only*

If only is often more emphatic than *I wish*. Compare these examples:
***If only** we'd seen you coming. We might have braked in time.* (a regret)
***I wish** we'd seen you coming. We would have put out the red carpet!* (a wish)

For greater emphasis we can put a subject between *if* and *only* in informal English:
***If you only** knew how much trouble you've caused!*

 *Wish* can be followed by *that*, but *if only* cannot:
✗ ~~*If only that you'd told me about it earlier.*~~ ✓ ***I wish that** you'd told me about it earlier.*

Practice

1 Write the second sentence so it has a similar meaning to the first. Use the word in brackets, as in the example.

0 I regret the fact that we didn't see the band play.
(could) *I wish we could have seen the band play.*

1 It's a pity that you didn't tell us that you were leaving.
(wish) ....

2 Unfortunately, I'm not as agile as I used to be.
(only) ....

3 Her constant criticism of me really gets on my nerves.
(stop) ....

4 I regret not going to university when I was younger.
(gone) ....

5 She would love to have a more responsible post.
(had) ....

6 I've always wanted to have the ability to speak a foreign language really well.
(could) ....

7 It's a real shame we didn't take any photos at that amazing party.
(only) ....

8 I hate having straight hair; curly hair is so much nicer.
(didn't) ....

2 GRAMMAR IN USE Complete the conversation by writing one word (or a contraction) in each gap. 3.23 Listen and check.

MARCIE Hello, Alan. I didn't expect to see you at the recycling centre!

ALAN No. I wish I (0) *hadn't* bothered – it took me hours to sort out all these things into separate bags! If (1) .... it wasn't so complicated! All these containers ...

MARCIE Well, it's great that you're recycling. I wish more people (2) .... make the effort.

ALAN You're quite 'green', aren't you? Don't you have an electric car?

MARCIE Yes, but I (3) .... I'd never bought it. It's useless. If (4) .... only knew how much trouble it's given me!

ALAN I'm sorry to hear that. They can't go very far between charges, can they?

MARCIE No – and I (5) .... they (6) .... told me that before I bought it! I have to travel a lot for my job and it just doesn't go far enough without needing to be recharged.

ALAN Can't you find places to recharge it?

MARCIE No, I wish there (7) .... more, but there's hardly anywhere.

ALAN I thought the government was giving subsidies to garages to encourage them to set up recharging stations.

MARCIE Well, I wish somebody (8) .... told them about it around here! None of the garages I know seems to have one.

ALAN No, I can't say I've seen any. Anyway, I (9) .... I (10) .... stay longer to chat but I've got to get back home.

MARCIE OK. Well, see you soon.

40 Subjunctives and the 'unreal' past

After the earhquake, the government **insisted that** each new building **have** an earthquake-resistant steel and concrete frame.

1 Subjunctives

The subjunctive form is the same as the infinitive (without *to*). It does not show any marking for tense and can be used to refer to events in the past, present or future:
*The judge insisted (that) Mr Grant **give** evidence despite his relationship to the accused.*

We use it most often in *that* clauses after certain verbs (e.g. *advise, ask, demand, insist, propose, recommend, require, request, suggest*), and after adjectives (e.g. *advisable, anxious, desirable, eager, essential, important, necessary, preferable, urgent, vital, willing*), to express the idea that something is necessary or important:
*In future cases it will be **vital** that each party **give** full disclosure prior to trial.*

We can use passive and negative forms of the subjunctive:
*Members of the committee suggested England **be excluded** from future tournaments.*
*Regulations require that officers **not enter** the crime scene without protective clothing.*

We use subjunctives
- in reported speech: *She insisted that she **pay** her own way.*
- in very formal language (e.g. legal documents):
  *We require that all receipts **be submitted** to the committee for approval.*
- in poetry: *I know not whether laws **be** right or whether laws **be** wrong.* (Oscar Wilde)

As the subjunctive is seen as rather formal or literary (it is less formal and more common in American English), British English speakers often prefer alternative forms:

subjunctive	*It is essential that every applicant* **complete** *the form in triplicate.*
should + infinitive	*It is essential that every applicant* ***should complete*** *the form in triplicate.*
present simple	*It is essential that every applicant* **completes** *the form in triplicate.*
for + subject + *to* + infinitive	*It is essential* **for every applicant to complete** *the form in triplicate.*

There are some fixed expressions which use subjunctive forms:
*If he doesn't want to see us, then **so be it**.* (= then let it happen)
*I'll take it all the way to the Supreme Court **if need be**.* (= if this is necessary)
***Long live** the republic!*

2 The 'unreal' past

After a number of expressions such as *if only, it's time, what if, assuming, say, suppose/supposing, would rather/sooner, as if/though* and *I wish* we use past tenses (active and passive) to describe things in the present, past or future which are imagined. We sometimes refer to this use of past tenses as the 'unreal' past.

We can use the past simple or the past continuous after these expressions to talk about the imaginary present and future:

PRESENT ***It's time** they **were** forced to clear up the mess.*
(They aren't being forced to clear up at the moment.)
*These kids act **as if** they **owned** the place.* (They don't own it.)

FUTURE ***I wish** I **was coming** with you tomorrow.* (I am not coming with you.)

We use the past perfect to refer to something unreal in the past:
*I wish I**'d** never **started** this course.* (I have started it.)

Many speakers prefer to use *were* for all persons when talking about the imagined present or future, especially in more formal situations and in American English. This form is sometimes called the past subjunctive and is also used in second conditional sentences:
*If I **were** you, I'd think twice before refusing that offer.* (➤ Unit 38.2)
*If only he **were** a little more convincing on the economic issues.*

FORMALITY CHECK In the above examples we can also use *was* but this is more informal.

what if, suppose + past tense ➤ Unit 82.1

3 *It's (about) time/high time (that)*

We use *it's (about) time* + past tense to say that something should be happening and isn't:
***It's time** we **left**.* (We aren't leaving and we should be.)
***It's about time** you **paid** a visit to your grandparents.* (You should visit them.)

It's high time is slightly more emphatic:
***It's high time** that the voice of the people was heard in this House.*
(Their voice isn't being heard and it should be.)

We cannot use a negative after *it's (high/about) time*:
✗ ~~*It's time we didn't stay.*~~ ✓ *It's time we **left**.*

We can also use *it's time for* + object + *to* + infinitive:
*We'd better open the gates now. **It's time for the guests to arrive.***

If we are referring to ourselves or the person we are speaking to we can also use *it's time* + *to* + infinitive:
***It's time to leave.** I'm afraid **it's time to put** your books away now, children.*

4 *would rather* and *would sooner*

We use *would rather/sooner* with the past simple to describe preferences:
*I'**d sooner** you **gave** me a cash refund. A credit note's no use to me.*
(= I would prefer a refund. / I wish you would give me a refund.)

They are often used as a polite way to refuse permission, or make suggestions:
*I'**d rather** you **didn't use** the best china.* (= Please don't use the best china.)
*I'm not keen on the idea of staying in. I'**d sooner** we **went out** bowling or something.*
(= Let's go bowling.)

If the person expressing a preference and the subject of the preference are the same, we use an infinitive (without *to*) instead of the past tense. Compare:
*We'**d sooner** you **spent** your bonus on something useful.*
(past tense: speaker and subject are not the same)
*I'**d rather spend** it on something frivolous.* (infinitive: speaker and subject are the same)

would prefer ➤ Unit 36.6

5 *as if* and *as though*

We use a past tense after *as if* or *as though* to say that how something appears now does not match with reality:
*He talks to the children **as though** they **were** imbeciles.* (We know they aren't imbeciles.)
*They are acting **as if** nothing **had happened**.* (We know something has happened.)

But we use a present tense (including the present perfect) after *as if* or *as though* when we don't know if the appearance reflects reality or not. Compare:
*You talk about her **as if** you **know** her.* (present tense: Perhaps you know her.)
*You talk about that film star **as if** you **knew** her!* (past tense: I'm sure you don't know her.)

We can use these expressions to be critical, ironic or sarcastic:
*It isn't **as if** he's in any position to pass judgement!*
(= He probably isn't in a position to do this.)

Practice

1 In four of the following extracts subjunctive forms would be appropriate for the situation. Find these four and rewrite them, using a subjunctive. You may need to use passive forms.

1 It is a requirement of this policy that all supporting documentation is submitted within 28 days of the incident.

2 and then, can you imagine, the boss insisted that I took little James to lunch. I mean, it's not my job to look after the boss's children, is it?

3 Clause 25.6 of the *Treatment of Offenders Act* suggests that each offender receives a monthly visit from a probation officer.

4 We hope the PRESIDENT will have a long life!

5 **Trudy Trouble** (7.30, BBC1)
In tonight's hilarious episode Sam suggests that Trudy visits the doctor, with predictably comical results!

6 The constitution requires that the vice president assumes immediate control of the nuclear detonation codes in the case of the sudden death of the incumbent president.

....

....

....

....

2 Rewrite these sentences using a suitable phrase from the box, as in the example. Use each phrase once only. Use subjunctive forms if appropriate. 3.24 Listen and check.

as if she | as though | I'd rather | ~~I'd sooner~~ | it is essential that | it's about time you | it's time | it was proposed that | we'd rather

0 Taking the later flight would be preferable for me. *I'd sooner take the later flight.*

1 You look awful. Have you been unwell?

....

2 If we had the choice, I think we'd prefer to sit near the front.

....

3 To comply with the regulations each new client must provide proof of identity.

....

4 We really ought to pay the bill now.

....

5 Please don't wipe your feet on the carpets.

....

6 She isn't a member of the club, but she acts like someone who is.

....

7 You should give your parents a call – they must be getting worried by now.

....

8 The company suggested giving a ten percent pay rise to all members of the sales team.

....

3 GRAMMAR IN USE **Complete the email with suitable forms of the words in brackets.**
3.25 **Listen and check.**

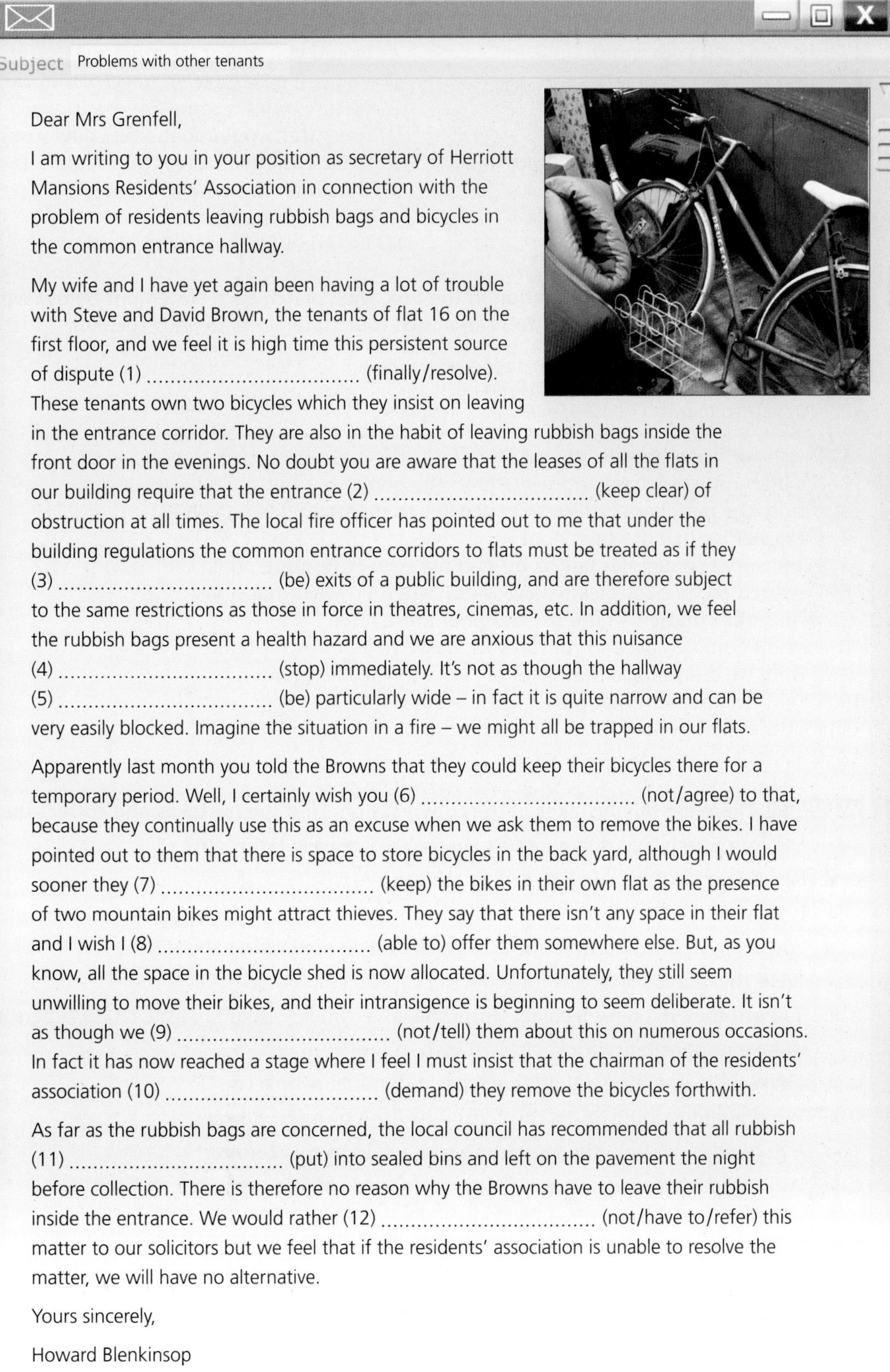

Subject Problems with other tenants

Dear Mrs Grenfell,

I am writing to you in your position as secretary of Herriott Mansions Residents' Association in connection with the problem of residents leaving rubbish bags and bicycles in the common entrance hallway.

My wife and I have yet again been having a lot of trouble with Steve and David Brown, the tenants of flat 16 on the first floor, and we feel it is high time this persistent source of dispute (1) .... (finally/resolve). These tenants own two bicycles which they insist on leaving in the entrance corridor. They are also in the habit of leaving rubbish bags inside the front door in the evenings. No doubt you are aware that the leases of all the flats in our building require that the entrance (2) .... (keep clear) of obstruction at all times. The local fire officer has pointed out to me that under the building regulations the common entrance corridors to flats must be treated as if they (3) .... (be) exits of a public building, and are therefore subject to the same restrictions as those in force in theatres, cinemas, etc. In addition, we feel the rubbish bags present a health hazard and we are anxious that this nuisance (4) .... (stop) immediately. It's not as though the hallway (5) .... (be) particularly wide – in fact it is quite narrow and can be very easily blocked. Imagine the situation in a fire – we might all be trapped in our flats.

Apparently last month you told the Browns that they could keep their bicycles there for a temporary period. Well, I certainly wish you (6) .... (not/agree) to that, because they continually use this as an excuse when we ask them to remove the bikes. I have pointed out to them that there is space to store bicycles in the back yard, although I would sooner they (7) .... (keep) the bikes in their own flat as the presence of two mountain bikes might attract thieves. They say that there isn't any space in their flat and I wish I (8) .... (able to) offer them somewhere else. But, as you know, all the space in the bicycle shed is now allocated. Unfortunately, they still seem unwilling to move their bikes, and their intransigence is beginning to seem deliberate. It isn't as though we (9) .... (not/tell) them about this on numerous occasions. In fact it has now reached a stage where I feel I must insist that the chairman of the residents' association (10) .... (demand) they remove the bicycles forthwith.

As far as the rubbish bags are concerned, the local council has recommended that all rubbish (11) .... (put) into sealed bins and left on the pavement the night before collection. There is therefore no reason why the Browns have to leave their rubbish inside the entrance. We would rather (12) .... (not/have to/refer) this matter to our solicitors but we feel that if the residents' association is unable to resolve the matter, we will have no alternative.

Yours sincerely,

Howard Blenkinsop

Review MODULE 8

1 UNITS 37 AND 38 **Here are some lines from songs. Each line is a conditional. Match the two parts of the conditional sentence to make the complete line.**

1 If I could read your mind,
2 If I had a bell,
3 Where would you be,
4 If I ruled the world,
5 If I were a carpenter, and you were a lady,
6 If I were a rich man,
7 If you're going to San Francisco,
8 If you don't know me by now,

A would you marry me anyway?
B you will never, never, never know me.
C be sure to wear some flowers in your hair.
D every day would be the first day of spring.
E what a tale your thoughts would tell.
F if you weren't here with me?
G I'd ring out a warning.
H I wouldn't have to work hard.

2 UNITS 39 AND 40 **Read the information in the box, then match each statement below with Ali (A), Marcela (M) or Teresa (T). You can match four statements to each speaker.**

A – Ali loves swimming but he doesn't have a pool in his house.
M – Marcela has a swimming pool in her house.
T – Teresa used to own a house with a swimming pool.

1 I wish we had a house with a pool. ....
2 It's high time we changed the water in the pool. ....
3 If only the pool hadn't been so expensive to maintain. ....
4 I'd rather we had our own pool. ....
5 People say I sometimes talk as if I had my own swimming pool. ....
6 I insisted the pool be cleaned every day when I owned that house. ....
7 If only the children would use our pool more often. ....
8 I wish I could go back to the days when we had our own pool. ....
9 If only we didn't have that great big pool in the back garden. ....
10 I'd sooner we used solar power to heat our pool. ....
11 I wish we could have used our pool more. ....
12 It's about time we built a pool. ....

3 ALL UNITS **There are ten mistakes in the conversation. Find the mistakes and correct them.**

SAM Did you watch that documentary on global warming last night?

CARL Yes, it was terrifying. I almost wish I didn't see it.

SAM If we would go on destroying the atmosphere like this, the effects will be catastrophic.

CARL You're right. It's high time the government does something about it.

SAM Well, they have set targets for reducing carbon emissions, haven't they?

CARL Yes, but they're pretty feeble. I think the government should insist that each person to take responsibility for their own carbon footprint.

SAM That's a bit sweeping. I don't see what individual people can do.

CARL What about turning down the central heating by a few degrees?

SAM A good idea – if only the winters aren't so cold in this country!

CARL Well, what about cars, then? If everybody used smaller cars, there was a huge reduction in carbon emissions. Take your car, for instance – don't you think it's time you sell that big four-wheel-drive thing?

SAM No, absolutely not! If I won't have that car, I wouldn't be able to take all the kids to school. And it's useful to have a big car in case of some of their friends need a lift.

CARL I guess so. Things must be pretty tough with four children …

SAM Yes. Life would be a lot easier unless I had so many kids!

4 ALL UNITS **Complete the speech bubbles for the pictures, using expressions from Units 37–40.**

1

2

3

4

5

6

7

8

MODULE

9 Word order and verb patterns

Before you start

1 Review these intermediate grammar points and check you know them.

Sentence word order

1 Normal word order is

subject | verb | object

Pete's dog **bit** *Mike*.

This has a different meaning from: *Mike bit Pete's dog.*

2 In questions and after certain adverbs we usually place a verb (*be*, auxiliary or modal) before the subject.

Did *Pete's dog bite Mike? Rarely* ***have*** *I seen such an aggressive dog!*

Introductory *there*

1 We can use all forms of the verb *be* after *there*, including modal forms:
There were *just a few customers in the store at that hour of the morning.*
There must have been *a thousand applicants for the post.*

2 The form of *be* agrees with the following noun. If there is more than one noun, the form of *be* agrees with the first noun in the list:
There ***was a table*** *and two chairs in the room. There* ***were two chairs*** *and a table in the room.*

In informal speech we sometimes use *there is* with a plural noun:
There's two ways *we can do this.*

Introductory *it*

1 *It* is always singular: ***It's*** *Alan and Margaret at the door.*

2 We use *it* + *be* to introduce information about
- weather/environment: *It'll be cold at this time of year. It's a nice day today.*
- time/dates: *It's nearly eight o'clock. It's Friday today.*
- conditions/situations: *It's peaceful there. It was getting dark as I drove home.*
- distance: *It's a long way from here. It's about twenty miles away.*

-ing forms

1 We can use *-ing* forms of verbs in the same way that we use nouns – as the subject, object or complement of a verb. We sometimes refer to *-ing* forms used in this way as 'gerunds':
Flying *is sometimes cheaper than land travel. The whole family has taken up* ***cycling****.*
Her worst habit is ***lying****.*

2 We can make a negative with *not* + *-ing*:
Not getting *a refund on faulty goods is what really annoys me.*

But we use *no* + *-ing* to explain that something is impossible or not allowed:
✗ ~~*There's not smoking in this office.*~~ / ~~*There isn't smoking in this office.*~~
✓ *Could you go outside? There's* ***no smoking*** *in this office.*
There's ***no skiing*** *here in the summer season.* (Skiing is impossible.)
No parking. (Parking is not allowed here.)

2 Read the text and identify examples of *there*, *it* and *-ing* forms.

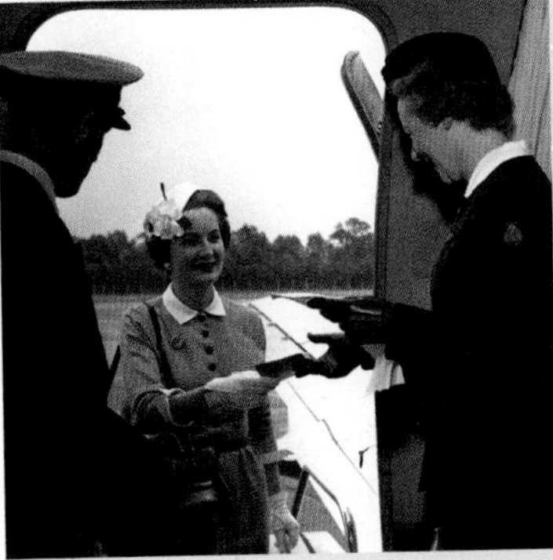

How International Travel has Changed

ONCE THE preserve of the wealthy and privileged, flying is now available to almost anyone. The emergence of budget airlines has made international travel affordable to the masses. There were just a few hundred thousand flights per year in the 1950s, now there are something like 25 million. As a result, mass tourism has become a major economic factor for many countries. Wealth has been brought to a number of poorer nations, but there has been a downside. It has become increasingly common to see coastlines disfigured with concrete hotels, to see ancient monuments damaged by the sheer weight of visitor numbers, and to witness the destruction of natural environments.

3 Complete the diagnostic test below. Choose the correct words in *italics*. If both options are correct, choose both.

1. Passengers stumbled and luggage flew from the racks as the driver suddenly *stopped the train* / *stopped*. ➤ Unit 41.1
2. The children came into the kitchen and were delighted when their mother *put on the table a freshly-baked cake* / *put a freshly-baked cake on the table*. ➤ Unit 41.3
3. Surely you don't always want to remain *to be an outsider* / *an outsider* here? ➤ Unit 42.1
4. Dilip called his boss *dishonest* / *a liar*. ➤ Unit 42.2
5. Can you show *to us the way to the motorway* / *us the way to the motorway*? ➤ Unit 42.3
6. The never-ending care and devotion of the nurses in the hospital helped *to overcome cancer my father* / *my father to overcome cancer*. ➤ Unit 42.4
7. Can you explain how *operate* / *to operate* the new software? ➤ Unit 42.5
8. It's a great hotel. There's *a* / *the* huge flatscreen TV in every room! ➤ Unit 43.1
9. The army doesn't anticipate there *being* / *be* much resistance in the area. ➤ Unit 43.2
10. We thought *was a pity* / *it a pity* that they left the party so early. ➤ Unit 43.4
11. Look at her performance. *There's* / *It's* no doubt that she should get the prize. ➤ Unit 44.1
12. *It* / *There* looks as though our team's going to win, after all. ➤ Unit 44.2
13. We were furious when the judge ordered *to pay* / *us to pay* compensation. ➤ Unit 45.3
14. We got there only *finding* / *to find* that the concert had been cancelled. ➤ Unit 45.4
15. You're welcome *help* / *to help* yourself to anything from the fridge. ➤ Unit 45.5
16. The *dispensing* / *dispensing of* medical aid is the main activity of the Red Cross. ➤ Unit 46.1
17. It's strange that you didn't mention *resigning* / *your husband resigning*. ➤ Unit 46.2
18. Despite budget constraints, the BBC continues *to make* / *making* innovative programmes. ➤ Unit 46.3
19. Dean's so sorry; he really didn't mean *to hurt* / *hurting* you. ➤ Unit 46.4
20. As the plane flew over, we saw the workers *build* / *building* the new opera house. ➤ Unit 46.5

4 Check your answers on page 384. Then go to the unit for more information and practice.

41 Verb patterns (1)

1 Transitive and intransitive verbs

Transitive verbs need a direct object:
*We spent **all our money**.*

Intransitive verbs do not have a direct object:
*They've **arrived**! The children **are sleeping**.*
Some common intransitive verbs are *arrive, come, fall, go, happen, lie, sleep, swim, wait.*

Some verbs can be intransitive or transitive, for example:

begin break change close continue dry finish hang hurt move separate stand start stop tear turn

Only the most skilled pilots are allowed to steer large passenger ships into Venice's small harbour.

Compare:
*The door **opened**.* (intransitive) *He **opened** the door.* (transitive)
*The meat **burnt**.* (intransitive) *The cook **burnt** the meat.* (transitive)

Sometimes the two uses of a verb can have very different meanings:
*He **ran** to catch the bus.* (intransitive = moved quickly)
*He **ran** the new software to show us how it worked.* (transitive = operated)

In modern usage, some transitive verbs are used as intransitive verbs:
*I don't know why you're bothering with those brands – they won't **sell**.*
And some intransitive verbs are used as transitive verbs:
*In order to survive we need to **grow** the business by fifty percent within two years.*

2 Verb + object patterns

Transitive verbs have a direct object, which can be a noun phrase or an *-ing* form (with *or* without a prepositional phrase):

subject	verb	object	
We	***discussed***	*the problem/it*	*(at great length).*
Karl	***suggested***	*practising*	*(on the nursery slopes first).*

We can omit the object after some transitive verbs if the context is clear:
*Geoff was disappointed to find that he **had failed** (the test) again.*

Some common verbs that can be used like this are: *answer, ask, drink, eat, enter, fail, leave, pass, play, practise, sing, study, wash, win* and *write.*

3 Verb + prepositional phrase

We can use a prepositional phrase after intransitive verbs:

subject	verb	prepositional phrase		
The train	***departed***	*from platform 9*	*– but we **were waiting***	*on platform 5.*

We can also use prepositional phrases after a transitive verb + object:

subject		verb		object	prepositional phrase
He	*carefully*	***removed***		*the egg*	*from the nest.*
Pilots		***are allowed***	*to steer*	*large passenger ships*	*into Venice's small harbour.*

We do not usually change the order of transitive verb + object + prepositional phrase, unless the object is very long:

✗ ~~*He carefully removed from the nest the egg.*~~
✓ *He carefully removed from the nest the three fragile blue-speckled eggs and the one chick that had already hatched.*

Practice

1 **In each pair either one or both sentences are correct. Tick (✓) the correct sentences and cross (✗) the incorrect ones.**

1 A James read his text messages while he waited the bus.
  B James read his text messages while he waited at the bus stop.
2 A The government denied access to the world's press.
  B The government denied to the world's press access.
3 A When exactly did it happen?
  B When exactly did it happen the event?
4 A Please don't disturb me, whatever happens.
  B Please don't disturb me, whatever happens during the night.
5 A She carefully placed the 24-carat gold, diamond-encrusted engagement ring that her fiancé had just bought her onto her finger.
  B She carefully placed onto her finger the 24-carat gold, diamond-encrusted engagement ring that her fiancé had just bought her.
6 A Investment is necessary in order for the company to grow.
  B You need to invest in order to grow the company.
7 A The security cameras monitor everybody entering.
  B The security cameras monitor people entering the building.
8 A The rough seas made it impossible to stand the floor of the deck.
  B The rough seas made it impossible to stand.

2 GRAMMAR IN USE **Find ten more mistakes in the article and correct them.**
3.26 **Listen and check.**

NEWS

Ash cloud disrupts European travel

FOR THE LAST WEEK a cloud of volcanic ash has been causing havoc with Europe's aviation industry. ~~Flights as a safety precaution~~ *As a safety precaution flights* have been grounded, leaving thousands of passengers stranded. This couldn't have happened it at a worse time as this is the final week of the Easter holidays and holidaymakers across the continent have been trying to fly them home.

The source of the cloud of ash is the Eyjafjallajökull volcano in Iceland. A few days after the eruption started it, the ash cloud arrived Europe. At first the cloud was confined to the skies over the British Isles and Scandinavia, but it over the European mainland has now spread. The fine particles of ash can enter jet engines and damage the internal parts, leading to catastrophic results.

Fortunately, flights to airports in southern Europe are continuing them. Some intercontinental flights originally destined for London, Amsterdam or Frankfurt have been re-routed to Madrid, which is still open the airport. Passengers arriving them there will be able to travel on to their final destination by road or rail.

The aviation industry is hoping that the wind direction will change it, taking the ash away from Europe. In the meantime, scientists are running test flights to assess the density of ash in the clouds. Depending on their findings, certain flight routes in the next few days may be reopened.

42 Verb patterns (2)

With its policy of affordable flights, JetBlue quickly **became one of North America's most popular airlines**.

1 Verb + complement

Some verbs are followed by complements (not objects). A complement is usually a noun phrase or an adjective that identifies, describes or gives information about the subject:

subject — verb — complement

Alexander Grant ***is*** *our new head of marketing*.

JetBlue quickly ***became*** *one of North America's favourite airlines*.

Verbs which introduce complements often describe states, e.g. *be, appear, feel, look, keep, remain, seem, sound, taste, make*, or changing states, e.g. *become, get, grow*.
We can usually use an adjective or a noun phrase to describe the subject after these verbs:

The whole group ***seemed*** *very keen*. *Marie's new outfit* ***looked*** *fantastic!*

That ***sounds*** *a wonderful idea!* *Your suggestion* ***seems*** *the best solution*.

You don't want to ***remain*** *a shop assistant all your life, do you?*

However, there are some differences in the way we use complements with these verbs:

- We only use an adjective after *make* if there is an object: *Shellfish make* ***me*** *ill.*
- If we use a noun phrase after *taste* and *smell* it describes an action, not a state. Compare:
  I tasted ***the food****.* (= an action)
  The food tasted ***delicious****.* (= information about the subject)
- If we use a noun phrase after *keep* it is an object, not a complement. Compare:
  He kept ***quiet****.* (complement = information about the subject)
  He keeps ***his money*** *under the bed.* (= object)
- When we use a noun phrase after *seem* or *appear* to identify (rather than describe) the subject, we have to use *to be* to introduce the noun phrase:
  ✗ ~~*Surprisingly, the young fresh-faced boy seemed the managing director.*~~
  ✓ *Surprisingly, the young fresh-faced boy* ***seemed to be*** *the managing director.* (identifying)

2 Verb + object + complement

A complement can also describe the object of a verb. In this case, the object comes before the complement:

subject — verb — object — complement

The journey ***made*** *the children irritable*. ✗ ~~*The journey made irritable the children.*~~

We often use verbs of naming, e.g. *name, call, elect*, with this pattern:
The members ***elected*** *Geraldo* ***treasurer of the society****.*
My nephew finally decided to ***call*** *his new rabbit* ***Snowy****.*

We can use a noun or an adjective as the complement after verbs such as *think, keep, consider, prove, call, find*:
Although he was twenty, Katherine still ***considered*** *him* ***a child/childish****.*
The judge ***found*** *Sam's evidence* ***unreliable****.* *The judge* ***found*** *Sam* ***an unreliable witness****.*

We can use an adjective as a complement in the same pattern in a number of idiomatic phrases after verbs such as *drive* and *turn*:
The noise of the planes flying over us at night ***drives me crazy****!*
Did you see his expression? It could ***turn milk sour****!*

3 Verbs with two objects

Some verbs can take two objects, e.g. *give, bring, buy, show*. These verbs take a direct object and an indirect object (often a person or thing that receives something).
There are two possible patterns. The first pattern is more common:

subject | verb | indirect object | direct object

1 *The judges* ***gave*** *Jason's painting/it* *first prize*.

subject | verb | direct object | indirect object

2 *The judges* ***gave*** *first prize* **to** *Jason's painting*.

If we put the direct object first, we put a preposition in front of the indirect object. The preposition depends on the verb. Here are some common examples:

to + indirect object	*award give hand lend offer owe pass show teach*
	You should offer your seat **to** *that old lady.*
for + indirect object	*book build buy catch choose cook fetch find make order save*
	Lauren cooked supper **for** *her grandfather.*
to and/or *for* + indirect object	*bring leave pay play post read sing take write*
	The sales manager brought the latest figures **to** *the meeting.* *Dave bought a present* **for** *his host.*

We prefer to put a pronoun before a noun phrase object:
[*The advertising campaign brought a huge increase in sales to us.*]
✓ *The advertising campaign brought* ***us*** *a huge increase in sales.*
If both objects are pronouns we prefer to put the direct object first:
[*He gave me it.*] ✓ *He gave* ***it*** *to me.*

4 Verb + verb

Many verbs can be followed by either an *-ing* form or an infinitive (➤ Units 45, 46):

subject | verb | verb

Can *you* *really* ***imagine*** ***lying*** *on a beach all day?*

The consultant ***refused*** ***to take*** *responsibility for the decision.*

With some verbs we can use a direct object between the two verbs:

subject | verb | direct object | verb

Can *you* ***imagine*** *your father* ***lying*** *on a beach all day?*

We ***require*** *all students* ***to attend*** *the pre-sessional English course.*

5 Verb + clause

We often use *that* clauses after verbs of speaking and thinking. (We can omit *that* after these verbs):

subject | verb | clause

The staff ***agreed*** *(that) redundancies were the only course of action*.

Some verbs of speaking and thinking can be followed by *wh-* clauses (those which start with a question word), e.g. indirect questions (➤ Unit 79.1):

subject | verb | object | clause

I couldn't meet you. *You* ***didn't tell*** *me* ***when*** *you were arriving*.

Wh- words can be followed by (object) + *to* + infinitive after verbs such as *show, explain, teach*: *Is it common for people to* ***teach their children how to drive*** *here?*

Practice

1 Rewrite the words and phrases in the correct order. 3.27 Listen and check.

1 named / Samantha / their first daughter / the couple

....

2 to stand / when he arrives / visitors / expects / His Excellency

....

3 brought / to the team / Amanda / all her expertise

....

4 brought / the team / Amanda / all her expertise

....

5 has become / a very inexperienced salesman / the Sales Manager

....

6 his grandmother / to / for / Tim / the hospital / therapy / took

....

7 so her daughter / the bracelet / bought / for her / Susan liked / it

....

8 an easy programme / trying / first / recommended / the trainer

....

9 of destruction / all sick / the scenes / us / made / in the film

....

10 require / to take / the regulations / before the competition / all athletes / a drugs test

....

2 GRAMMAR IN USE Choose the correct or most appropriate words in *italics*. 3.28 Listen and check.

SADIE I hear your trip to Prague was a bit of a disaster. What exactly went wrong?

MALIK Well, everything (1) *OK seemed / seemed OK* at first. We got on the plane and sat in our seats. Then suddenly there was an announcement. Apparently, there was some kind of mechanical fault with the engines and the captain considered (2) *unsafe / it unsafe* for the plane to take off. So we all had to get off the plane and go back to the terminal. Then we just sat there and waited. Nobody gave (3) *us any information / any information us*. There didn't seem (4) *anyone / to be anyone* in charge. They certainly didn't tell (5) *when we would be leaving us / us when we would be leaving.*

SADIE Didn't they offer (6) *to you any food or drink / any food or drink to you*?

MALIK Well, after a couple of hours someone came from the airline and handed (7) *us / to us* some vouchers for tea and coffee.

SADIE I can imagine (8) *sitting you / you sitting* there for four hours – how boring!

MALIK Yes, but eventually one of the ground crew appeared and asked (9) *us to go / to go us* to a different departure gate. They'd arranged a replacement plane.

SADIE And that took you to Prague?

MALIK No, I'm afraid not. It seems there was fog at Prague and air traffic control ordered (10) *the plane to divert to Bucharest / to divert to Bucharest the plane.*

SADIE So how did you get to Prague?

MALIK By bus. The airline managed to arrange some buses to take us. But of course they kept (11) *waiting us / us waiting* for hours before they arrived.

SADIE What a nightmare! That would have driven (12) *me mad / mad me*!

3 Each sentence below contains one mistake with word order. Rewrite the sentences correctly.

0 Most of the passengers considered crowded and uncomfortable the airport.
Most of the passengers considered the airport crowded and uncomfortable.

1 When he made out his will, Mr Smithson refused to leave anything his estranged son.

....

2 We require to supply photo identification before check-in all passengers.

....

3 The Management recommends that you keep safe your valuables by handing them in at Reception.

....

4 The invitation doesn't tell what we should wear at the reception us.

....

5 The new head teacher has been elected Mrs Henderson.

....

6 Prizes can be claimed by sending the form and proof of purchase us, at the address below.

....

4 GRAMMAR IN USE Choose the best phrase from A–O to complete each gap, as in the example. There are six extra phrases.

Children at risk from mental illness

A recent study has shown that levels of mental illness in children are rising.

THE STUDY claims (0) ..*F*.. are affecting one in five youngsters. One of the reasons given for this is the current obsessive preoccupation of parents with their children's safety. Parents today consider (1) ....., so children are driven to school and back, and their parents rarely let them go out on their own, keeping (2) ..... under parental supervision. This preoccupation has two causes: fear of traffic accidents and anxiety about child molesters and murderers on the streets. Parents' fears make (3) ..... about the outside world and children in turn miss the normal adventures of everyday life. In addition, nobody teaches (4) ..... with other children. Over-anxious children often become (5) ..... and their fears are therefore realised and even increased. It is a vicious circle. It (6) ....., however, that children are experiencing these fears unnecessarily. While parents may think a child molester lurks round every corner, this is not supported by statistics: very few children are attacked by people they don't know.

There are, however, critics of this study. Many child psychologists believe (7) ..... is not enough to cause mental problems. They consider (8) ..... a result of family breakdown in modern society.

A anxious their children
B of this lack of independence
C them at home
D the streets too dangerous for their children
E the problems to be
F ~~that mental problems such as depression and anxiety~~
G their children anxious
H victims of bullies
I that this lack of independence
J at home them
K them how to form relationships
L likely seems
M the problems be
N too dangerous for their children the streets
O seems likely

43 Introductory *there* and *it*

1 Introductory *there* and *it*

We use *there* and *it* as 'empty' subjects. They have no real meaning but we use them as grammatical devices to introduce or identify things.

We use *there* + a form of *be* to introduce new information and/or to say that something exists or happens:
*If you're looking for a café; **there's** one opposite the station.* (new information)
***There are** fifty-one states in the USA.* (= Fifty-one states exist in the USA.)

We often use this form to introduce or describe a character or place, or to 'set the scene':
*At the top of the hill **there's** a small café with wonderful views over the bay.*
***There's** an Englishman, an Irishman and a Scotsman who are on a boat …*

⚠ We don't use *the* after *there* + *be* when we are introducing NEW information:
✗ ~~*In the hotel lobby there is the cash machine.*~~
✓ *In the hotel lobby **there is a cash machine**.*

We use *it* to introduce or identify something or someone later in the phrase:
*'Who's that?' '**It**'s Alan.' 'Hello, **it**'s Steve here. Could I speak to Jane?'*
*'What's worrying you?' '**It**'s the children.'*

⚠ We don't use introductory *it* to say that something exists or happens:
✗ ~~*In the centre of town it's a nice restaurant where it's a great choice of dishes.*~~
✓ *In the centre of town **there's** a nice restaurant where **there's** a great choice of dishes.*

2 Patterns after *there* + *be*

There + *be* can be followed by a noun + participle clause (➤ Unit 55):
***There's a man** sitting in the corner. **There are two scales of temperature** used in science.*

FORMALITY CHECK In formal English, verbs with future meaning, e.g. *anticipate, expect, envisage, intend* can be followed by *there* + *to be/being* (verbs + infinitive or *-ing* ➤ Unit 46):
*The organisers didn't **expect** (**there to be**) quite such an overwhelming response.*
*We **don't anticipate** (**there being**) any resistance from the anti-hunting lobby.*

3 Common words and expressions after *there* (+ *be*)

quantifiers (➤ Unit 8.1/2) *any, some, much, many, several,* etc.	*Are **there any more** issues outstanding?* ***There are several** ways we can tackle this.*
indefinite pronouns (➤ Unit 5.2) *somebody, nothing,* etc.	*I've had a good look and **there's nothing** to report.* ***Isn't there somebody** here who can help us?*

As well as forms of *be*, we can use the following verbs after *there*:

there + appear(s)/happen(s)/ seem(s)/tend(s)/used + to be	***There used to be** a house at the end of the common.* *Researchers noticed that **there tends to be** a higher number of influenza cases in warm winters.*

FORMALITY CHECK In formal written English we can use *there* + *arise/arrive/come/emerge/ enter/exist/follow/live/occur/remain/result/sit/stand/take place*:
*Deep inside her **there arose** a desperate hope.*
*At the crime scene **there remained** little in the way of physical evidence.*
***There follows** a full list of our current terms and conditions of trading.*

ACADEMIC ENGLISH We can use *there* + a passive reporting verb (e.g. *is/are said to be, is/are thought to be*) + an indefinite noun phrase to describe a general feeling or belief.
***There are thought to be** several contributory factors in genetic mutation.*
*According to reliable sources, **there are believed to be** a million sufferers of the disease.*

4 *it* as an empty object

We use *it* as an 'empty' object after certain verbs to introduce a following clause:

like/hate/love + *it* + *when/that* clause (This is used to describe likes and dislikes.)	*I **hate it when** people stare at me. We **love it when** the grandchildren come over.*
would appreciate it + *if* clause (This is used to make a polite request.)	*I **would appreciate it if** you would keep your seat belts fastened until I switch off the seat belt signs.*
owe/leave it to somebody + infinitive clause	*We **owe it to him to** try and find a resolution. We **leave it to you to** suggest a suitable date.*
think/find/consider/feel + *it* + adjective/noun/preposition phrase + *that* clause*	*I **find it intolerable that** we have no recourse in law. He **thought it a pity that** they hadn't qualified.*
accept/regard/see/take/view + *it* + *as* + noun/adjective + clause	*We **regard it as inevitable that** some participants will not complete the course.*

* We don't usually use *it* as an 'empty' object when the main verb is not followed by an adjective or by a noun or preposition phrase:
✗ ~~*She thought it that he had resigned.*~~ ✓ *She thought that he had resigned.*

5 Impersonal *it*

We can use *it* + *be* with adjectives and nouns that describe our attitudes, feelings and opinions, e.g. *a pity, wonderful, surprising*. This allows us to describe our feelings and opinions in an impersonal way. Compare:
I'm not surprised (that) she left you. (speaker's opinion)
It isn't surprising that she left you. (impersonal statement)

There are several patterns we use:

it + *be* + adjective + *-ing* form (We use this in informal English.)	***It was lovely meeting** you at last. **It's wonderful sitting** out here in the sun.*
it + *be* + adjective/noun + infinitive clause	***It's lovely to meet** you. **It's wonderful to sit** out here in the sun. **It would be a shame to miss** this opportunity.*
it + *be* + adjective + *that* clause	***It isn't surprising that** she left you.*
it + *be* + adjective + *wh-* clause	***It was amazing how** she recovered so quickly.*

ACADEMIC ENGLISH The following patterns with *it* are common in academic and scientific English because they allow us to present information in an impersonal way.

- *it* + *be* + adjective/noun + infinitive clause:
  ***It was possible to recognise** regularities in the patterns of soil distribution.*
  ***It is difficult not to be influenced** by the work of these early philosophers.*
- *it* + *be* + adjective + *that/wh-* clause:
  ***It is significant that** so few of the patients suffered side effects.*
  ***It isn't clear how** this process begins.*
- *it* + verb phrase (usually passive) + *that* clause:
  ***It has been shown that** most of the patients improved noticeably.*
  ***It should be noted that** the majority of the responses were positive.*
  ***It is said that** economic factors were significant in a majority of the cases.*
  ***It has been argued** that many of the cases are the result of faulty diagnosis.*

Pronoun *it* ➤ Unit 4 *it* to introduce cleft sentences ➤ Unit 75.2
More expressions with *there* and *it* ➤ Unit 44

Practice

1 Insert *there* or *it* in the correct position, as in the example. 3.29 Listen and check.

0 She found *it* strange that he'd never heard of such a famous historical character.
1 Was really such a long wait between trains?
2 We always have lots of visitors but tend to be more in the summer months.
3 The director leaves to the viewer to decide who is guilty and who is innocent.
4 They assured us that would be no trouble getting a refund if the goods were faulty.
5 You know, really gets on my nerves when she talks like that.
6 What's incredible is that might have been so many more fatalities.
7 I find impossible to believe that someone with his track record would be so careless.
8 In 1666 was a fire which destroyed a large part of London.
9 We would appreciate if you submitted your estimate to our head office.
10 Grandpa loves when the children ask for his advice.

2 Rewrite the sentences, using *it* or *there*, as in the examples. 3.30 Listen and check.

0 When people don't give tips – I hate that! *I hate it when people don't give tips.*
00 Such a strong reaction was not anticipated by the protesters.
The protesters did not expect there to be such a strong reaction.
1 More than a million species of insects exist in the world.
....
2 A grandfather clock was ticking in the background.
....
3 They didn't give you a refund – I find that outrageous.
....
4 Meeting that movie star in person was thrilling.
....
5 A statement by the Prime Minister now follows.
....
6 They regard the eventual collapse of the currency as inevitable
....
7 Present in the compound were two forms of amino acid.
....
8 Does Osaka have an underground railway?
....
9 People think at least two leading politicians are involved in the scandal.
....
10 Why the landing wheels failed to descend isn't clear.
....
11 Perhaps you left your cash card in the machine.
....
12 Is nobody here able to help us?
....

3 GRAMMAR IN USE **Improve this text by rewriting the underlined clauses or sentences with *there* or *it*, as in the example.**

Book of the week

The Beach

BY ALEX GARLAND

(0) People say that somewhere in the tropical waters of Asia lies an uninhabited island with a perfect beach. Rich in animal and plant life, surrounded by virgin jungle and watered by sweet underground springs, the beach could be the setting for an idyllic and easy life.

The Beach is the story of a young man who yearns for, seeks out and eventually finds just such a place. (1) But to discover that, far from being the source of contentment and inner fulfilment that he expects, the beach turns out to be a place of savage violence, terror and death, comes as a shock.

Alex Garland takes the reader on an exotic journey from the steaming tourist-packed hostels of the Khao San Road in Bangkok to the laid-back islands of the remote seas around Thailand. (2) Not to be impressed by the author's skill in describing the unfamiliar oriental locations and his ability to empathise with the obsessions of today's young backpacking 'new-age' travellers is difficult.

Taking in personal memories of the Vietnam war, jealousy, shark-infested waters, the psychological dynamics of communal living and the clash of cultures, Garland spins a tale which both enchants and shocks the reader. (3) What gives the novel its haunting sense of unease and horror is the author's unique blend of these disparate elements.

(4) It contains all the traditional ingredients that make up a successful thriller: an exotic location, a central mystery, good versus evil, and dangers around every corner. (5) In the book is a strong sense of good and evil, (6) but to decide who is right and who is wrong Garland leaves to the reader. (7) Few moral certainties exist in this exotic corner of the world.

Events unfold at great speed, and be warned, (8) to put this book down once you have started it is impossible. With an international cast of well-observed characters Garland creates a nail-biting narrative that keeps the reader hooked until the final bloody climax.

0 *It is said that somewhere in the tropical waters of Asia lies an uninhabited island with a perfect beach.*

1 ....

2 ....

3 ....

4 ....

5 ....

6 ....

7 ....

8 ....

44 Common expressions with *there* and *it*

1 Common words and expressions after *there* (+ *be*)

We use *there* to introduce a number of phrases connected with certainty and expectation, followed by *to be*:

bound certain expected likely supposed sure	*If the government goes ahead* ***there's sure to be*** *an outcry from the miners.* *Hang on,* ***there was supposed to be*** *a television in the room.*

There also introduces a number of negative phrases, followed by the infinitive with *to*:

no alternative but *no choice but* *no need no reason*	***There's no alternative but to call*** *for a vote and face the consequences.* ***There wasn't any reason to doubt*** *the evidence.*

Some negative phrases beginning with *there* are followed by an *-ing* form:

no problem no difficulty *no trouble no hope of* *no point in no question of* *no chance of*	***There won't be any trouble getting*** *back.* ***There's no point in arguing*** *about it.* *You haven't got your receipt so* ***there's no question of getting*** *a refund.*

We can use *no knowing* followed by *wh-* words or *if/whether*:
There's ***no knowing what*** *she'll do now her husband's left her.*
The tests were inconclusive so there's ***no knowing whether*** *he'll survive the operation.*

Some phrases are followed by a *that* clause:

no denying no/any doubt	***There's no denying that*** *he's lost the company several contracts due to his incompetence.* ***There really isn't any doubt*** *that she's guilty.*

2 Common expressions after *it*

We use *it* + *seems as if/though* to describe our impressions:
It seems as if *we've known each other for years.*

We use *it* + *looks as if/though* to talk about probability:
It looks as though *I'm going to fail the test.*

We use *it* to introduce a number of negative phrases followed by a *that* clause:

no secret no surprise *no wonder no coincidence* *no accident*	***It isn't any secret*** *that she's leaving the city to start a new career.* *Clara didn't do any revision –* ***it's no surprise*** *(that) she failed the exam.*

After *it's no use* and *it's no good* we use an *-ing* form:
It's no good phoning *– the office is closed today.*
I've made up my mind so ***it's no use nagging*** *me about it.*

We can use *it's no longer* + adjective + *to* infinitive:
In the UK ***it's no longer necessary to get*** *a licence to keep a dog.*
They've closed the caves permanently so ***it's no longer possible to see*** *the prehistoric paintings.*

Practice

1 Rewrite the sentences, using *it* or *there*. Sometimes more than one answer is possible.

0 I think I'm probably going to get a promotion.
It looks as if I'm going to get a promotion.

1 People are bound to react badly to the news.
....

2 Getting a visa won't be difficult.
....

3 A massive sell-off of high-tech shares is likely in the next few days.
....

4 Carol leaving her job is not surprising.
....

5 In this bad weather a poor turnout for the election is certain.
....

6 Brian's dislike of his mother-in-law isn't a secret.
....

7 They didn't have any reason to question her motives.
....

8 I've got the impression we've got a lot in common.
....

2 GRAMMAR IN USE Choose words from the box to complete the conversation. There are three extra words/phrases. 3.31 Listen and check.

bound denying it looks as though no good no longer no need
no point in no surprise seems as if supposed to be sure to be there

PURSER Welcome on board the *Golden Seas*. You must be Sarah and Danny Frobisher. I'm your purser. Is everything OK with your cabin?

DANNY It's fine. But (1) .... was (2) .... a safe in the cabin ...

PURSER Oh, it's inside the wardrobe.

SARAH And my mobile phone isn't working. It (3) .... there's no signal.

PURSER You're right. There's no signal out at sea, so there's (4) .... trying to use your phone until we get closer to the shore.

SARAH I see. Er, the sea's very calm, are we expecting good weather? I hate rough seas!

PURSER Yes. It (5) .... it's going to be fine for the next five days. So there's (6) .... to worry about bad weather. Is there anything else?

DANNY Yes. Can you reserve seats for the evening show for us?

PURSER I'm afraid not. It's (7) .... possible to reserve seats in advance.

SARAH Perhaps we should get there early.

PURSER No, it's (8) .... doing that, they won't let you in. But don't worry, there are (9) .... plenty of spare seats.

SARAH Good. Will there be some nice places to buy souvenirs when we arrive at Aruba?

PURSER Oh yes. There are (10) .... to be plenty of good shops there.

45 Infinitive patterns

In the 1960s Spain **decided to promote** itself as the world's first mass-market tourist destination. **To cater for tourists,** the government invested huge sums in new airports and roads.

1 Infinitive forms

Infinitives with *to* can be the subject, object or complement of a verb:
***To give** is better than **to receive**. Everyone loves **to win**.*

There are also perfect (e.g. *to have given*), continuous (e.g. *to be giving*) and passive (e.g. *to have been given*) forms.

Infinitive clauses ➤ Unit 56 Passive infinitives ➤ Unit 62.3

FORMALITY CHECK *-ing* forms (➤ Unit 46.1/2) can often be used in similar ways, but they tend to be less formal than infinitive forms:
***Giving** is better than receiving. Everyone loves **winning**!*

⚠ We make a negative with *not* + infinitive:
✗ ~~*I tried to not look at the accident.*~~ ✓ *I tried **not to look** at the accident.*

An infinitive can have its own subject, introduced with *for*:
***For** evil **to succeed** it is only necessary **for** the good **to do** nothing.*

FORMALITY CHECK In informal English we sometimes put an adverb between *to* and the infinitive. This is known as a 'split infinitive' and can give emphasis to the adverb:
*Not only am I going to win – I'm going **to totally destroy** the opposition!*

We usually avoid split infinitives in formal English by moving the adverb:
[*The doctor started to carefully remove the bandages.*]
✓ *The doctor started **to remove** the bandages **carefully**.*

2 Verb + infinitive without *to*

After some verbs we use the infinitive without *to*, for example, modal verbs, auxiliary verbs, semi-modals *need* and *dare* (➤ Module 7 Before you start), and *make* and *let*:
*He **daren't leave** early without my permission.*
***Let the dish stand** for at least a minute after removing it from the microwave.*

We can use the verb *help* with or without *to*:
*The volunteers **helped** (to) **provide** support and comfort to the refugees.*

More on infinitives after *let, make, see, hear, know* and *help* ➤ Unit 63.3

3 Verb + infinitive with *to*

Certain verbs can be followed by an infinitive with *to*, but not by an *-ing* form:

afford agree aim appear arrange[1] ask[2] beg[2] campaign[1] care choose[2] claim consent dare[2] decide demand deserve expect[2] fail fight forget guarantee happen help[2] hesitate hope long[1] manage need[2] neglect offer pause plan[1] prepare pretend promise propose prove refuse seem swear tend threaten trouble[2] undertake vow wait[1] want[2] wish[2] yearn[1]

[1] With these verbs we use *for* before the object + infinitive: *We spent ages waiting* **for them to arrive**.
[2] These verbs can also have an object before the infinitive:
I **begged Alison not to leave**. *He doesn't really* **expect her to pass** *the exam.*

✗ ~~*She's decided applying for the job.*~~ ✓ *She's **decided to apply** for the job.*

Some verbs are followed by an infinitive only when they have an object (➤ Unit 46.4):

advise allow cause command compel encourage forbid force get instruct invite leave oblige order permit persuade recommend remind request teach tell tempt urge warn

✗ ~~*They forced to open our suitcases.*~~ ✓ *They* ***forced us to open*** *our suitcases.*

We use *to* + infinitive after *would like, would love* and *would hate*:

✗ ~~*When we arrive, I'd like taking a nap.*~~ ✓ *When we arrive,* ***I'd like to take*** *a nap.*

4 Infinitives of purpose and result

We can use an infinitive to describe the purpose or reason for an action:

Cover the turkey in silver foil ***to keep the meat moist.***

To cater for tourists, *the government invested huge sums in new airports and roads.*

We use *for* before the infinitive only when the subject of the infinitive is DIFFERENT from the subject of the sentence:

✗ ~~*She went to WalMart for to get some groceries.*~~

✓ *She went to WalMart* ***to get*** *some groceries.* (same subjects)

We bought a cage ***for*** *John* ***to keep*** *his hamster in.* (different subjects)

FORMALITY CHECK To make the meaning clear and in more formal English we can use *in order* or *so as* + infinitive of purpose:

Interest rates have been raised ***in order to reduce*** *inflationary pressures.*

We have removed the warning signs ***so as not to alarm*** *members of the public.*

The infinitive can also describe a result or something surprising, especially with *only* and verbs such as *find, discover, realise*, etc:

They queued for hours at the box office ***only to discover*** *that the show was sold out.*

We also use infinitives after *too* and *enough* (➤ Unit 59.4) to talk about results:

That blue outfit was ***too informal to wear*** *to the reception.*

There ***isn't enough (food) to go around,*** *I'm afraid.*

5 Infinitives after adjectives and nouns

Many adjectives, especially those describing feelings, can be followed by *to* + infinitive.

able/unable afraid anxious ashamed bound careful certain crazy curious due eager fit happy impossible likely lucky pleased prepared right shocked stupid sure surprised thrilled welcome wrong

We're ***thrilled to welcome*** *this year's prizewinner onto the podium.*

The Bensons are ***lucky to be having*** *such good weather.*

We also use *to* + infinitive after some nouns:

attempt bid decision desire fool incentive need nuisance opportunity place pleasure reason time willingness wish

She's finally made ***a decision to leave.*** *Clare would be* ***a fool to marry*** *him.*

We can use a noun + *to* + infinitive after *there is/are* and *have (got)* to express an obligation:

Don't disturb me – I've ***got a report to write*** *this evening.* ***There are some bills to pay.***

Practice

1 Write sentences from the prompts, as in the example. 3.32 Listen and check.

0 they / decide / change / hotels / when / see / room
They decided to change hotels when they saw the room.

1 tourists / not permit / take photos / museum
....

2 Mrs Grimble / threaten / call police / if / boys / not stop
....

3 doctor / urge / Henry / go on / diet / immediately
....

4 Alison / arrive / station / only / find / train / already / leave
....

5 we / promise / reduce / taxes / radically/ in order / help / small businesses
....

2 Write the second sentence so it has a similar meaning to the first. Use the words in brackets, as in the example.

0 I really don't want to see him again. (desire) *I have no desire to see him again.*

1 I'd like to ask my boss for a pay rise but I'm too scared.
(daren't) ....

2 You can't join the army because you aren't sufficiently fit.
(enough) ....

3 He was very worried that he would arrive late.
(anxious not) ....

4 Right now I'm afraid I can't give you an answer.
(able) ....

5 The government closed the borders with the aim of catching the criminals.
(order) ....

6 Closing the office was something the manager decided this morning.
(decision) ....

7 I learnt that Amanda was going to marry Ronald, which was surprising.
(surprised) ....

8 They didn't publish the news because they didn't want to frighten the public.
(so as) ....

9 Checking the balance on my account was my reason for visiting the bank this morning.
(to check) ....

10 When we got there they had already closed the store for stocktaking!
(only) ....

3 GRAMMAR IN USE **Read the text and find fifteen more places where the word *to* is missing. 3.33 Listen and check.**

Flying is bad for your health

THE DEATH of Emma Christofferson from deep-vein thrombosis allegedly caused by a twenty-hour plane journey has led to calls for an enquiry into so-called 'economy class syndrome'. The cabin crew were shocked *to* find the previously healthy 28-year-old in a state of collapse at the end of a long-haul flight from Australia to London. A blood clot had spread from her legs to her lungs with fatal results. Experts believe her death is just the latest example of the growing danger posed by sitting for extended periods of time in cramped aircraft seats.

Farol Khan, director of the Aviation Health Institute, claims have evidence that more than 6,000 passengers a year die of deep-vein thrombosis (DVT) as a result of long-haul flights. Unfortunately, as symptoms often take some time appear, the link between the condition and flying is not always apparent. But there seems be a clear relationship between the occurrence of DVT and the steady reduction in the amount of leg room between seats in economy-class cabins. In a bid increase the number of passengers carried and their consequent profitability, many airlines have squeezed more and more seats into their planes, at the cost of comfort and leg room. And our willingness put up with these uncomfortable conditions is simply based on the fact that we know more seats means lower prices. But with limited opportunities stretch or move around, the blood circulation in passengers' legs tends slow down, and blood clots can easily develop. Most at risk are elderly people, sufferers from heart conditions and smokers. But as Emma Christofferson's case shows, even the young and healthy can do little prevent blood clots occurring under these circumstances.

> … recommend moving the legs and feet regularly, and advise taking walks up and down the aisle at least once an hour.

Promoting a 'caring, sharing' image is something many airlines are keen on, and some of these have finally promised take the problem more seriously, for instance by issuing health advice to passengers 'trapped' on their long-haul flights. They usually recommend moving the legs and feet regularly, and advise taking walks up and down the aisle at least once an hour. But, as any experienced traveller knows, the aisles on most planes are only just wide enough for the trolleys get through. It is often impossible walk down the aisle get to the toilets, let alone allowing enough space take any exercise.

The truth is that until we are all prepared give up paying rock-bottom prices for long-distance travel, the airlines will have no incentive improve conditions. And a return to exclusive and expensive air travel is something nobody would contemplate advocating.

46 Verb *-ing* forms; verb + *-ing* form or infinitive?

Flying to another continent usually **means spending** hours trapped in a plane, bored stiff. But this is their first long-haul flight and they **mean to enjoy** it.

1 Verb *-ing* forms

Sometimes *-ing* forms can have their own subjects and objects:

- subject + *-ing* form: *I'm looking forward to* ***my wife returning****.*
- *-ing* form + object: ***Meeting new people*** *is one benefit of taking evening classes.*

We can use determiners, possessives, possessive adjectives or object pronouns before *-ing* forms:

All this complaining *won't get you anywhere, you know.* (determiner)
Peter's complaining *didn't do him any good.* (possessive)
Exorbitant tax rates led to ***him leaving*** *the country.* (object pronoun)

FORMALITY CHECK In formal English we prefer to use possessive adjectives rather than object pronouns before *-ing* forms: *Exorbitant tax rates led to* ***his leaving*** *the country.*

When we use the + *-ing* form and we want to link it with an object, we use *of*:
✗ ~~*The giving presents is a traditional part of the naming ceremony.*~~
✓ ***The giving of presents*** *is a traditional part of the naming ceremony.*

Many adjectives and nouns are followed by a preposition + *-ing* form (➤ Unit 65):
Lara isn't ***capable of lying*** *and she has* ***no reason for not telling*** *the truth.*

2 Verb + *-ing* form

The verbs below can be followed by an *-ing* form, but NOT by an infinitive:

admit appreciate avoid* burst out can't help* consider contemplate defer delay deny detest* dislike* endure* enjoy* escape excuse* face* fancy* feel like finish give up imagine* involve* justify* keep (on) leave off mention* mind* miss* postpone practise prevent* put off put sb off recall* recommend resent* resist* risk* save suggest tolerate* understand**

* With these verbs we can also put an object before the *-ing* form. Compare:
Can you **imagine wearing** *that dress!* (verb + *-ing* form)
Can you **imagine Jemima wearing** *that dress!* (verb + object + *-ing* form)

✗ ~~*I avoid to travel in the rush hour.*~~ ✓ *I* ***avoid travelling*** *in the rush hour.*

Certain verbs (particularly sense verbs) are only followed by an *-ing* form when they have an object:

catch discover feel find hear leave notice observe see spot watch

✗ ~~*In 'Hamlet' the prince discovers hiding behind the curtains.*~~
✓ *In 'Hamlet' the prince* ***discovers Polonius*** *hiding behind the curtains.*

3 Verb + *-ing* form/infinitive

Some verbs can be followed by an *-ing* form or an infinitive, with no difference in meaning:

attempt begin bother can't bear can't stand cease continue deserve fear hate intend like (= enjoy) love prefer start

I ***can't stand to see/seeing*** *animals in pain.*

We usually avoid putting two infinitives or two *-ing* forms together:
[*He intended starting taking lessons.*] ✓ *He intended* ***to start taking*** *lessons.*

4 Verb + *-ing* form or infinitive?

Some verbs can be followed by an *-ing* form or by *to* + infinitive, but there is a difference in meaning:

VERB	MEANING + *-ing* FORM	MEANING + *to* + INFINITIVE
remember/ forget	think about an event or situation before the time of speaking: *Do you* ***remember going*** *to school for the first time? I'll never* ***forget meeting*** *him.*	think of something you have done or should do: *Did you* ***remember to collect*** *the dry cleaning this morning? Don't* ***forget to lock*** *the back door.*
go on	continue: *They* ***went on playing*** *despite the bad weather.*	stop one action and change to another: *After opening the hospital the Prince* ***went on to meet*** *the staff.*
mean	involves or will result in: *Flying to another continent usually* ***means spending*** *hours in a plane.*	intend to do something: *But this is their first long-haul flight and they* ***mean to enjoy*** *it!*
need	requires something to be done to it: *That floor is filthy. It* ***needs washing.***	feel it necessary to do something: *I feel sick and I* ***need to see*** *a doctor.*
regret	feel sorrow about something you did/didn't do in the past: *I really* ***regret not learning*** *to swim when I was young.*	say sorry that something has/hasn't happened, in formal situations: *We* ***regret to inform*** *you of delays in today's service.*
stop	finish an action: *They* ***stopped making*** *fax machines about ten years ago.*	finish one action in order to do another one: *We* ***stopped to get*** *petrol.*
try	do something as an experiment (to see what will happen): ***Try using*** *a screwdriver to get the lid off.*	make an effort to do something difficult: *We* ***tried to get*** *tickets but the show was sold out.*

The verbs *advise, allow, forbid* and *permit* are followed by an *-ing* form when they have no object, but by an infinitive when they have an object:

✗ ~~*The doctor advised him taking a course of antibiotics.*~~

✓ *The doctor* ***advised taking*** *a course of antibiotics.*

✓ *The doctor* ***advised him to take*** *a course of antibiotics.*

5 Sense verbs

Sense verbs (➤ Unit 25.3) can be followed by an object + *-ing* form when we are describing an action in progress or an action that is repeated:

As I walked past the house I ***heard someone playing*** *Brahms' Lullaby on the piano.*
(The person was in the middle of playing when I walked past.)
I ***saw a young mother slapping*** *her child.* (She slapped him several times.)

However, when we are describing a single action or the action is complete, we use an object + infinitive (without *to*) after sense verbs:

We ***saw a young mother slap*** *her child in the supermarket.* (She slapped once.)
Last week I ***heard them play*** *the fifth symphony.* (I heard the complete symphony.)

With this meaning we use *to* + infinitive if the sense verb is passive:

The young mother ***was seen to slap*** *her child.*

Note we use an object pronoun, not a possessive adjective, after sense verbs:

✗ ~~*Have you seen our performing yet?*~~ ✓ *Have you seen* ***us*** *performing yet?*

Practice

1 Choose the correct or most likely explanation, A or B.

1 I'm looking forward to Sally cooking my favourite dish this evening.
A I'm cooking this evening. B Sally's cooking this evening.
2 Alastair forgot to lock the door.
A He should have done this but he didn't.
B He can't remember whether he locked the door or not.
3 The airline strike delayed my taking up my new position in the Los Angeles office.
A This is a person speaking. B This is an extract from a formal letter.
4 I heard a famous actor read *Treasure Island* on the radio last week.
A I heard the entire story. B I heard part of the story.
5 After the lesson ended we went on chatting.
A We had been chatting during the lesson.
B We hadn't been chatting during the lesson.
6 Why don't you try giving Tom some herb tea?
A Tom hates herb tea. B It might make him feel better.

2 Choose the correct form in *italics*.

1 Darling, did you remember *packing/to pack* some extra memory cards for the video camera yesterday?
2 I really regret *leaving / to leave* school so young, it's ruined my career prospects.
3 We tried *pressing / to press* the 'escape' key but the program just wouldn't respond.
4 A suspicious young man was seen *enter / to enter* the building shortly before the incident.
5 As we drove over the river we noticed local women *washing / wash* their clothes in the water.
6 Nothing will stop their enquiries, they mean *getting / to get* to the bottom of this strange business.
7 Transglobe Airlines regrets *announcing / to announce* the cancellation of today's service to Istanbul due to air traffic restrictions.
8 Do you remember *seeing / to see* that film last summer?
9 That wound's quite deep. You really need *putting / to put* some antiseptic on it.
10 We were all exhausted so we stopped *getting / to get* some rest at a motel.

3 Complete the second sentence so it has a similar meaning to the first. Use the word in brackets, as in the example. 3.34 Listen and check.

0 Clarissa said she hadn't used my laptop. (denied) ......*Clarissa denied using*.... my laptop.
1 I'm sorry that I gave up my job in the civil service. (regret)
.... in the civil service.
2 Make sure you top up your mobile phone credit before we leave. (forget)
.... before we leave.
3 Because of his injury, Stephen can't drive at the moment. (capable)
At the moment, Stephen .... because of his injury.
4 As part of the ceremony, the president lays flowers on the soldier's grave. (the)
.... on the soldier's grave by the president is part of the ceremony.
5 Although she was pregnant, Julia didn't stop work. (went)
Despite her pregnancy, Julia ....
6 To help with his insomnia, the doctor suggested Pedro give up drinking coffee. (advised)
To help with his insomnia, the doctor .... drinking coffee.

7 If you accept this job you will have to take on a lot of responsibility. (means)
Accepting this job ....

8 There are a lot of mistakes in this letter. Please retype it. (needs)
This letter ....

9 Is it all right with you if my brother comes to the party? (coming)
Do you .... to the party?

10 Hilary laughed out loud when she heard the joke. (burst)
Hilary .... the joke.

4 GRAMMAR IN USE **Complete the article with suitable forms of verbs from the box, as in the example. 3.35 Listen and check.**

catch close come exploit ~~go~~ hear install over-fish see take wear

JELLYFISH INVADE TOURIST BEACHES

IF YOU FEEL LIKE (0) ....*going*...... FOR A SWIM IN THE MEDITERRANEAN THESE DAYS YOU MIGHT BE IN FOR A SHOCK – IN MORE WAYS THAN ONE!

Beaches from the Costa del Sol to the French Riviera have been invaded by shoals of stinging jellyfish. The main culprit is *Pelagia noctiluca*, or the 'mauve stinger'. Its sting can cause painful injuries even to healthy humans. And, if anyone suffering from an allergy is stung, they will probably need (1) .... a doctor immediately. Medical experts advise (2) .... the usual basic precautions such as only swimming at beaches with lifeguards on duty. Those who wish to swim in more remote locations should remember (3) .... a wetsuit, as this offers considerable protection.

One tourist who was stung said, 'I don't regret (4) .... here but I think they should have warned us about the jellyfish. I (5) .... our holiday rep saying something about it but I wasn't really listening. I mean, you don't expect jellyfish in the Med, do you? It's something you associate with the tropics.'

Some scientists blame the problem on global warming. Rising sea temperatures mean jellyfish can live in parts of the sea that were previously too cold. (6) .... of tuna and turtles, which are natural predators of jellyfish, is thought to be another major cause. As the numbers of these predators have declined, so the number of jellyfish has increased. Environmentalists believe that until we stop (7) .... the limited stocks of tuna the problem will only get worse.

Tourism authorities have promised to take action against the problem, even if it means (8) .... huge nets around popular beaches. They certainly want to avoid (9) .... any beaches to the public, as this would be disastrous for the tourist industry. In some areas authorities are trying (10) .... the jellyfish before they approach the coast by sending out fishing boats to hunt for the creatures in deeper water.

OUR ADVICE IS – STAY IN THE SWIMMING POOL!

Review MODULE 9

1 UNITS 41 AND 42 **Nine of these sentences contain mistakes. Find the mistakes and correct them. Tick (✓) the correct sentences.**

1 The wind knocked the vase off the table and it broke thousands of pieces.
2 The attitude of some shopkeepers today makes me absolutely furious!
3 The children seemed content to remain to be tenants in their parents' house.
4 I can't understand what's happened. There appears some mistake.
5 The whole teaching staff found the new head teacher very inefficient and positively offensive.
6 I really find unacceptable your manager's comments.
7 The winning team proudly showed to their gathered fans their trophy.
8 The voice over the loudspeaker explained us the problem.
9 I don't know the way to the library. Can you tell me to go?
10 The young boy looked around and gingerly placed back in its correct position the gold watch. He wouldn't steal it after all.
11 Can you imagine your parents living to be over a hundred years old?
12 The smell of fish cooking drives absolutely wild my cats!

2 UNITS 43 AND 44 **Write the second sentence so it has a similar meaning to the first. Use *it* or *there* and the word in brackets, as in the example. Make any other changes necessary.**

0 I think Steve might win the race. (though) *It looks as though Steve might win the race.*
1 Such an overwhelming demand for tickets wasn't anticipated by the organisers.
(being) ....
2 She may well marry him.
(seems) ....
3 People think many other top executives are involved in the fraud.
(thought) ....
4 I would like you to send me your up-to-date retail price list.
(appreciate) ....
5 Fifty students applied for the scholarship.
(applicants) ....
6 They say he hates publicity.
(said) ....
7 We're not surprised that their children are so badly behaved.
(surprising) ....
8 In this paper we will demonstrate that DNA strands can be replicated.
(demonstrated) ....
9 We are selling twelve detached houses with double garages on this estate.
(sale) ....
10 To be nominated for this award makes me feel greatly honoured.
(honour) ....

3 UNITS 45 AND 46 **Complete the sentences with the correct form of the verbs in brackets.**

1 Please don't hesitate .... (call) if you have any problems.
2 The doctor recommended .... (avoid) strenuous activity for the first few weeks.
3 The sales team aims .... (exceed) its target by at least five percent this year.
4 Did you happen .... (notice) whether there was a cash machine there?
5 How on earth do they justify .... (keep) three cats in such a small flat?
6 Misha desperately tried .... (swim) to the shore but the current was too strong.
7 Jeremy was furious – he threatened .... (leave) unless we apologised.
8 You really can't help .... (feel) sorry for the poor guy.
9 Sometimes you have to pretend .... (like) people that you detest.
10 The judge will defer .... (pass) sentence until the psychiatric reports have been submitted.

4 ALL UNITS **Complete the text from an Internet forum by writing the words in brackets in the correct order. Use appropriate forms of the verbs, as in the example.**

Shareyourstories.com

new topic | post | reply |

AUTHOR	MESSAGE
Jake posted July 9	Has anyone here been the victim of a tourist scam while they were on holiday? I'd (0) *love to hear your stories* (your stories / love / hear).
Dieter posted July 10	This happened when I was in South America. I was driving in a rental car when a car with flashing blue lights came up behind me and (1) .... (me / stop / force). A policeman got out and (2) .... (my driving licence and passport / see / ask). Unfortunately I'd forgotten (3) .... (bring / with me / them). So he gave me a massive on-the-spot fine which I had to pay in cash. When I got back to the city I went to (4) .... (get / a police station / a receipt) and they told me there were no police cars on that road, but they'd had reports of criminals dressed as police officers demanding fines from drivers. So (5) .... (be / it / a hoax)!
Jennifer posted July 11	I think (6) .... (dishonest taxi drivers / be / there / everywhere), but this happened to me in South-East Asia. It was quite a remote place and I convinced (7) .... (me / a taxi driver / take) from the bus station to a small beach resort miles away. I (8) .... (in the boot / put / my bags) and the taxi set off into the night. We stopped at a red traffic light and suddenly I felt someone open the boot of the taxi. I looked around and two local guys had lifted out my bags and were running off into the side streets. It was all very suspicious because I (9) .... (remember / the taxi driver / ask) to lock the boot, and he said he had, but the thieves were able to open it without any trouble. I thought it was a scam and the thieves were friends of the taxi driver, but of course the taxi driver (10) .... (anything wrong / deny / do) and I didn't really have any evidence, so the police couldn't do anything about it.

Go online for an exit test

MODULE

10 Negatives and question forms

Before you start

1 Review these intermediate grammar points and check you know them.

FORM	POSITIVE	NEGATIVE	QUESTION
imperative	*Talk to me!*	***Don't talk** to me!*	
be	*He's outside.* *We're waiting for you.*	*He's **not**/He **isn't** outside.* *We're **not**/We **aren't waiting**.*	*Where **is** he?* ***Are** you **waiting** for us?*
present/ past simple	*I like Kenyan coffee.* *They finished early.*	*I **don't like** Kenyan coffee.* *They **didn't finish** early.*	***Do** you **like** Kenyan coffee?* *When **did** they **finish**?*
perfect tenses	*They have arrived.* *They had seen the film.*	*They **haven't arrived**.* *They **hadn't seen** the film.*	***Have** they **arrived**?* *What **had** they **seen**?*
modal verbs*	*We must leave soon.*	*You **mustn't leave** yet.*	***Must** you **leave** now?*
infinitives	*I told you to go.* *To stop now would be silly.*	*I told you **not to go**.* ***Not to stop** now would be silly.*	
participles	*Having seen the film,* *I understand the hype.*	***Not having seen** the film,* *I don't understand the hype.*	

* We don't use *does/do/did* with modal verbs:
*Children **shouldn't** be allowed to watch violent films.* ***Could** you lay the table before dinner?*

Negatives

1 We use *not/n't* with verbs to make the meaning of a sentence negative. We usually contract subject + *be* (*I'm not, they're not*) but with *have* and *do/did*, we contract the auxiliary verb + *not* (*I haven't, they didn't*).

2 In short answers with verbs of thinking and believing, e.g. *think, hope, believe, imagine*, we can put *not* after the verb. This use is quite formal and rare, except with *hope*:
'Has Susannah decided to call her daughter Brittany after all?'
✗ ~~*'I don't hope!'*~~ ✓ *'I hope not!'*

Questions

1 Closed questions start with a form of main verb *be*, an auxiliary verb or a modal auxiliary verb, e.g. *can, may, will*. We use them when we want a simple *yes/no* answer:
*'Does your sister still live in Canada?' '**Yes**, she does./**No**, not any more.'*

2 Open questions start with a question word, e.g. *who, what, where, how*. We use them when we want to find out more information:
*'**Why** did she leave Canada then?' '**She couldn't stand the cold winters.**'*

3 When we use more than one auxiliary verb in a sentence, e.g. *We've **been** waiting for ages*, we put *not* after the first auxiliary:
✗ ~~*We've been not waiting long.*~~ ✓ *We **haven't been** waiting long.*

4 In questions, only the first auxiliary comes before the subject:
✗ ~~*Have been you waiting long?*~~ ✓ ***Have you** been waiting long?*

2 **Read the information and identify examples of negatives and question forms.**

Colchurch Ballooning Club

Have you ever flown in a hot-air balloon?
If not, why not? It's an experience unlike any other. Join Colchurch Ballooning Club and experience it for yourself. Or, if you don't feel able to commit to a club, come along and have a trial flight.

Have you flown in a hot-air balloon and loved the experience?
Then why don't you join our regular flyers group? We don't expect too much – just agree to take a flight six times a year and you can become a full member.

Click here for more details.

3 **Complete the diagnostic test below. Choose A, B or C. If two answers are possible, choose both.**

1 The film was dreadful! The leading man may be a good singer but ..... ➤ Unit 47.1
A he's no actor! B he's not an actor! C he's any actor!

2 Your perfume smells lovely! Mmm, it's ..... the smell of damp roses. ➤ Unit 47.2
A not unlike B unlike C like

3 I've talked to the caretaker, sir, and he says he ..... about the robbery. ➤ Unit 47.3
A knows nothing B doesn't know nothing C knows anything

4 That woman in the photo ..... to be very happy. ➤ Unit 47.4
A seems not B doesn't seem C isn't seem

5 Hannah ..... tell the rest of the family what they had just seen. ➤ Unit 47.4
A begged her sister don't B begged her sister not to
C didn't beg her sister

6 'Didn't you attend the photography club meeting?' '.....' ➤ Unit 48.1
A No, I did. B No, I didn't. C Yes, I didn't.

7 There were ..... bookings for the new restaurant on its opening night. ➤ Unit 48.2
A any B few C no

8 Most of my students .... bother to revise for exams these days. ➤ Unit 48.2
A don't hardly B hardly don't C hardly

9 I've asked the manager to change this room, so we'd better ...... ➤ Unit 48.4
A unpack B not pack C not unpack

10 You shouldn't eat while you're driving. It ..... but it's quite dangerous. ➤ Unit 48.4
A is illegal B isn't illegal C isn't legal

11 'Would you prefer to travel on the 7.00 a.m. or 8.00 a.m. flight?' '.....' ➤ Unit 49.1
A The 8.00 a.m. one, please. B Yes, please. C I don't mind.

12 This dictionary's useless! What ....., do you know? ➤ Unit 49.2
A means heliotrope B does heliotrope mean C does mean heliotrope

13 I've just taken these biscuits out of the oven. Who .....? ➤ Unit 49.2
A wants one B does want one C want one

14 'Does your new car go very fast?' 'Yes, it can go at ......' ➤ Unit 49.3
A 200 kph fast B 200 fast C 200 kph

15 'I've chosen my course options.' 'Really? ..... are you going to take?' ➤ Unit 49.4
A Which subjects B What subjects C How subjects

16 'May I mention the recent article in *Scientific American*?' 'Yes, is this the one .....' ➤ Unit 49.5
A to which Adam contributed? B which to Adam contributed?
C which Adam contributed to?

4 **Check your answers on page 384. Then go to the unit for more information and practice.**

Go online for a full diagnostic test

47 Negative forms and meanings (1)

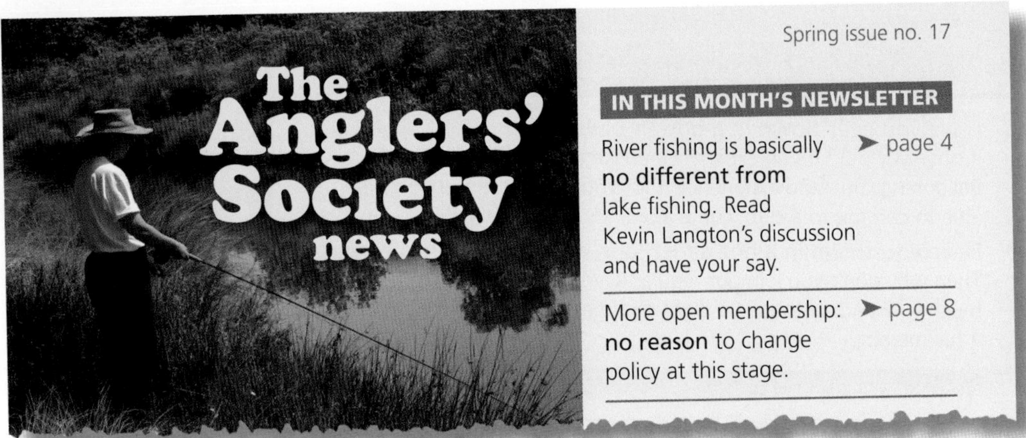

1 Uses of *no* and *not*

We use *no* to introduce negative replies: *'Have you been here before?'* ***'No**, I haven't.'*
We do not combine *no* with a verb to make a negative statement; we use *not*:
✗ ~~*I have no been here before.*~~ ✓ *I have* **not** *been here before.*

We can use *not* + *any* with a noun to express an absence or lack of something:
They ***won't*** *get* **any** *help from Janice.*

However, we can use *no* in front of nouns, instead of *not ... any* or *not ... a/an*:
They'll get **no** *help from Janice.*

We can usually use either *no* + noun or *not ... a/any* + noun, although *no* can be more emphatic:
*There is**n't any** reason to change policy at this stage.* (neutral statement)
There's **no** *reason to change policy at this stage.* (more formal/emphatic statement)

While *not ... a/any* is neutral, using *no* can sometimes express the speaker's attitude:
She's ***not an*** *artist.* (statement of fact about her job)
She's **no** *artist!* (statement of opinion about her ability to paint/draw)

We use *no* + noun in a number of set phrases, e.g. *no idea, no point, no good, no use, no harm*:
I've got **no idea** *what he was talking about!*
There's **no point** *in trying to persuade me; my mind is made up.*
There's **no harm** *in calling her.*
It's ***no use/no good*** *repeating yourself more loudly. She can't understand you.*

We can use *no* with *different* and with comparatives:
River fishing is basically ***no different from*** *lake fishing.* (= very similar to)
Next-day courier is ***no faster than*** *first-class post.* (= isn't [any] faster than)
Come on! This café is ***no more expensive than*** *the one down the road. Let's eat!*
(= This café charges the same prices as the café down the road.)

2 Uses of *not* with quantifiers and adjectives

We can use *not* in front of positive quantifiers (e.g. *much, many, a lot of*) to make the meaning of a clause or phrase negative:
Not many *people want to be referees – it's a lot of hassle and* ***not much*** *money.*

We can use *not* (+ adverb) with adjectives to make the meaning negative:
*Those new ferries are**n't** as* ***basic*** *as they used to be, but they are**n't exactly luxurious*** *either.*

 Putting *not* before an adjective weakens the adjective, but it does not have the same strength as an adjective with the opposite meaning, e.g. *not difficult* is weaker than *easy*, particularly if we add an adverb after *not* like *too* or *particularly*:
The maths exam was ***easy****.* (I am confident that I passed it.)
*The maths exam was****n't too difficult****.* (I am less confident that I passed it.)

We can also use *not* before an adjective with a negative prefix (➤ Unit 48.4):
Spanish has a tense system ***not dissimilar*** *to that of English.* (= a bit similar to)
The people here ***aren't unfriendly****, but they're so busy that it's difficult to get to know them.*

The descriptions above are much less definite than these:
Spanish has a tense system ***similar*** *to that of English. The people here are* ***friendly****.*

3 Other negative expressions

There are a number of adverbs and expressions which we use to give negative meaning to a sentence, e.g. *never, neither ... nor, none, not only, not ... for, no sooner ... than*:
The English village is ***neither*** *as pleasant* ***nor*** *as unchanging as it is believed to be.*
*The infantry assault would have lasted longer if it had****n't*** *been* ***for*** *the harsh winter conditions.*

 English rarely uses a double negative, i.e. two words with a negative meaning in the same clause, as most people consider this to be incorrect:
✗ ~~*Sorry, but I don't know nothing about that!*~~
✓ *Sorry, but I* ***don't*** *know* ***anything*** *about that! / I know* ***nothing*** *about that!*

But double negatives are possible if we intend to make a positive statement:
It wasn't very expensive, but it certainly didn't cost ***nothing****.* (= it cost something)
When I said I didn't want a lot of fuss for my birthday, I didn't mean ***no*** *effort at all!*
(= I meant some effort.)
In these examples, the meaning is positive, but the double negative emphasises it.
In spoken English, *nothing/no* (or other negative) is stressed in this kind of sentence.

 Pronunciation ➤ 1.14

In formal English, we can put *not only* at the beginning of sentences for emphasis. Notice that we change the word order when we use *not only* in this way.
Not only did they monitor *the landings, they also recorded all their dates and times.*

not only ... (but also), no sooner ... than ➤ Unit 76.2

4 Negative introductory verbs

When we use verbs like *think, suppose* and *believe* to introduce a negative idea, we prefer to make the introductory verb negative, not the verb in the *that* clause:
[*I think the later train won't be cancelled.*]
✓ *I* ***don't*** *think the later train will be cancelled.*

If we make the verb in the *that* clause negative, it can express surprise or appear emphatic:
I thought that you ***didn't*** *eat meat! When did you start?*

 We do NOT use *hope* and *wish* in this way:
✗ ~~*We don't hope that the reunion will be too painful for you.*~~
✓ *We hope that the reunion* ***won't*** *be too painful for you.*
✗ ~~*I don't wish I ate meat.*~~ ✓ *I wish I* ***didn't*** *eat meat.*

With verbs such as *seem, expect, appear,* we use either of these patterns; the meaning does not change:
He ***doesn't appear to be*** *interested. He* ***appears not to be*** *interested.*

With introductory verbs such as *ask, beg, persuade, tell, urge* + infinitive, we change the meaning when we make the introductory verb negative:
The doctor told me ***not to*** *take the pills.* (= He said I must not take the pills.)
The doctor ***didn't*** *tell me to take the pills.* (= He didn't mention taking the pills.)

Practice

1 Read each pair of sentences and choose the correct answer, A, B or C, as in the example.

A Both sentences have the same meaning.
B Both sentences have the same meaning but differ in emphasis, intensity or formality.
C Each sentence has a different meaning.

0 The airline staff weren't able to give us any information about the delay.
The airline staff were able to give us no information about the delay. ....B....
1 The waiter didn't persuade us to try the fish of the day.
The waiter persuaded us not to try the fish of the day. ....
2 Judge Phillips didn't believe that the accused had stabbed the officer.
Judge Phillips believed that the accused hadn't stabbed the officer. ....
3 Photocopying a whole book is no cheaper than buying it.
Photocopying a whole book is the same price as buying it. ....
4 That new teacher isn't very strict with us, is she?
That new teacher's lenient with us, isn't she? ....
5 Losing your temper isn't the answer to coping with difficult children.
Losing your temper is no answer to coping with difficult children. ....
6 Well, that article on the new political system told me precisely nothing!
Really? It didn't tell me nothing. ....
7 It seems that the championship won't be decided until the last race.
It doesn't seem that the championship will be decided until the last race. ....
8 The only thing is that the sea isn't very warm at the beginning of the summer.
The only thing is that the sea is quite cold at the beginning of the summer. ....

2 GRAMMAR IN USE **Read the blog and choose the correct word or phrase for each gap, A, B or C (see next page). If two options are possible, choose both.**
3.36 **Listen and check.**

posted September 18 2011

Well, here I am at university. I bet you (1) ..... get here, with all the recent problems! Arriving here was a bit of a shock – it (2) ....., but it's an old industrial town and it's pretty run-down. (3) ..... my parents nor I had expected the student rooms to be right in the middle of the town, but that will probably have its advantages.

It was the university societies and clubs 'bazaar' yesterday – you know, where new students can go and join clubs for things to do in their spare time (yeah, right!). I thought it (4) ..... different from school – history club, badminton club, etc. but someone had told me that you could find every type of club under the sun – well, that (5) ..... exaggeration! The clubs ranged from finance to skydiving! I thought there was (6) ..... in joining a club that was the same subject as my course, so I steered away from the film club and the photographic society. I thought about the psychology society, but (7) ..... students were showing an interest in that one, so I thought better of it. There was one society I (8) ..... to think twice about – folksoc – you know I love bluegrass music. Then I thought that maybe I ought to do something physical, so I looked at the rowing club. It (9) ..... to be terribly popular, but I decided to have a go. So now I'm officially a member of the university rowing club!

Well, better go. I (10) ..... bored with my ramblings today. Next one tomorrow or the day after.

Judy Q

1 A thought I wouldn't B thought I not C didn't think I'd
2 A is exactly unpleasant B isn't exactly unpleasant C isn't pleasant
3 A Nor B Both C Neither
4 A wouldn't be any B would be no C wouldn't be no
5 A wasn't no B wasn't any C was no
6 A any point B no point C not a point
7 A not many B no many C no any
8 A needed not B had not need C didn't need
9 A appeared not B didn't appear C appeared no
10 A don't hope you got B don't hope you didn't get C hope you didn't get

3 These sentences do not make sense as they are. Rewrite the underlined part of each one to make a negative sentence, as in the example. Where there are two lines, the sentence can be rewritten in two ways. 3.37 Listen and check.

0 I'll accept interruptions from you or anyone else while I'm speaking.
I'll accept no interruptions.......................... *I won't accept any interruptions*................

1 We hope that the soldiers experience a lot of resistance when they enter the city.
....

2 Because of the financial crisis, the Minister urged employers to give big pay increases.
....

3 In English, the subjunctive is usually different from the past tense.
....

4 My brother's only just started his electronics degree, so he tried to repair the TV himself when it went wrong last week.
....

5 A great number of songbirds are seen these days, owing to the erosion of their natural habitats.
....

6 In this modern city you get an impression of life in the pre-capitalist era.
....

7 I was willing to help the children, as they had to take responsibility for the schoolwork they brought home.
....

8 War crimes should be both commonplace and accepted in times of conflict.
....

9 The estimated fee for the project was unreasonable, but I decided to negotiate further.
....

10 I think that our company will be offering aid to the disaster zone this time.
....

11 Sarah has only had a few lessons on the guitar so she's a good guitarist.
....

12 The new twin-turbo engine generates a lot of noise but is especially powerful.
....

48 Negative forms and meanings (2)

1 Negative questions

Negative questions are formed by adding *n't* to a form of *be* or to the auxiliary, or using a negative adverb:
***Wasn't** Kate at the meeting last week?*
***Haven't** you seen Owen Wilson's new film yet?*
***Why hasn't** Stella contacted her solicitor yet?*
***Why will** you **never** give me a straight answer?*

FORMALITY CHECK To be more formal, we can use *not*. We put this after the subject:
***Why has** Ms Gibbons **not** contacted the duty solicitor yet?*

We often use negative questions to check or confirm that something we believe or expect is correct; we expect a positive *(yes)* answer:
*'I'd like to volunteer for a wildlife charity.' '**Aren't** you a member of a wildlife organisation?'*
(I believe that you are.)

We also use negative questions if we suspect that something we believed is not correct; in this case we expect a negative *(no)* answer:
*I didn't expect to see you here this evening. **Didn't** your visitors come after all?*
(I don't think they came.)

We can answer negative questions with *yes* or *no*:
*'Hasn't the weather been dreadful recently?' '**Yes**, (it has/it has been dreadful).'*
*'Wasn't the hairdresser busy?' '**No**, (she wasn't/she wasn't busy).'*

We can also give the opposite response to what the speaker expects, but we would then soften the response with an explanation:
*'Hasn't the weather been dreadful recently?' 'Well, **no**, I think it's been OK.'*
*'Wasn't the hairdresser busy?' '**Yes**, she was actually, but she's very fast!'*

We use negative questions
- to try to persuade someone to do something:
  ***Won't** you **come** with us to the beach tomorrow? It'll be fun.*
- to give an opinion which expects agreement:
  ***Don't** you **think** that the new shopping centre is really ugly?*
- to express surprise that something isn't correct:
  ***Haven't** astronomers **discovered** a tenth planet?* (= I thought that they had.)
- to express criticism or complaint, often with *why*:
  ***Didn't** you **remember** to post the letter? Honestly, I can't trust you to do anything!*
  ***Why haven't** you **finished** your homework?*
  ***Why didn't** you **tell** me you'd taken up golf?*

2 Restrictive adverbs and quantifiers

Many English words, such as *few*, *little* or *rarely*, have a negative or restrictive meaning (i.e. they reduce the amount, frequency or degree of the word they qualify):

TYPE	EXAMPLES	EXAMPLE SENTENCES
quantifiers	*few, little*	*There are* ***few*** *people who believe you.* *Teachers have* ***little*** *time to watch TV.*
adverbs of frequency	*rarely, seldom, hardly ever*	*The urban fox* ***seldom*** *ventures out during the day.*
adverbs of degree	*hardly, scarcely, barely*	*It is* ***hardly*** *likely that a criminal will wait politely for the police to arrive!*

The meaning of *few* and *little* is restrictive only without *a/an*. Compare:
Water the fruit frequently as ***little*** *rain falls at this time of year.* (almost none)
Take an umbrella with you; there's always ***a little*** *rain at this time of year.* (a small amount)
As these restrictive words are negative in meaning, we use a positive verb with them:
✗ ~~*Many managers don't hardly prepare for meetings at all.*~~
✓ *Many managers* ***hardly prepare*** *for meetings at all.*

We also use a positive question tag with these words (➤ Unit 79.2):
Higher-ranking police officers ***rarely*** *meet the public these days,* ***do they?***

We can put restrictive adverbs of frequency before the verb for emphasis, usually in writing (➤ Unit 76.2):
Rarely *did the old man come down the mountain to the village ...*

3 Verbs with negative meaning

Some verbs contain a negative meaning, e.g. *fail, deny, avoid*:
I ***fail*** *to understand your motivation for doing this.* (= I don't understand ...)
Joe ***denied*** *copying the essay from his best friend.* (= He said he hadn't copied it ...)

These verbs can be made negative and they can take a negative question tag:
The boy ***didn't deny*** *copying the homework.* (= He didn't say that he hadn't copied it.)
Fran ***failed*** *her driving test again,* ***didn't she?***

4 Negative prefixes

We can make verbs, nouns and adjectives negative, with a negative prefix:
Incomplete *information will delay payment of any benefit due.*

PART OF SPEECH	PREFIX	EXAMPLES
verbs	*dis- mis- un- de-*	*dislike disconnect misinform misbehave unlock unpack uncover deregulate defrost devalue*
nouns	*anti- non- in- dis- de-*	*anti-freeze anti-perspirant nonsense non-smoker non-fiction injustice inconvenience disadvantage dishonesty disinfectant decentralisation decriminalisation*
adjectives	*anti- in- (il- ir- im-) dis- non- un-*	*anti-inflammatory anti-social incomplete incredible (illegal irregular impossible) dishonest disobedient non-violent non-toxic uncomfortable unavailable unfair*

We can use verbs, noun and adjectives with a negative prefix with verbs in the negative form.

- Negative verb: *He reached down to the window, but* ***didn't unlock*** *it when he heard the cry from outside.* (= didn't open it)
- Negative noun: *It* ***isn't anti-freeze****, it's anti-perspirant!*
- Negative adjective: *Salaries here are* ***not unlike*** *those in the United Kingdom.* (➤ Unit 47.2)

Practice

1 Make negative questions with suitable forms of the verbs from the box. Some of the questions start with *Why* and you may need to add other words. Then match each question to one or two of the functions A–D below, as in the example.
3.38 Listen and check.

belong buy do give ~~hear~~ join take tell think

0 'What's Paolo Nutini's new single like?'
'*Haven't you heard it* yet? I'm amazed – it's on the radio every five minutes!' ....*B*....

1 'Alice has just applied to join the college choir.'
'.................................... to it? I thought she joined last year.' ....

2 'Mr Soames from Brent Trading is coming in on the 6th for a lunchtime meeting.'
'Really? .... your holiday in that week?' ....

3 'Oh, you're back. I was just about to do the washing-up.'
'.................................... yet? I've been out for three hours!' ....

4 'Joe and I are going to the food festival on Sunday. .... us?'
'I'm busy on Sunday, I'm afraid, but thanks for asking.' ....

5 'Sorry, but I can't come to your dinner party tomorrow. I'm double-booked.'
'.................................... earlier? I've already bought all the food!' ....

6 'We need to get some flowers or something to take with us to the hospital.'
'Oh, ... then? You were going to do it in your lunch break.' ....

7 '.................................... those hair extensions look awful on older women?'
'No, actually, I don't. In fact, I'm thinking of having some put in.' ....

8 'Harriet Ellis may arrive late for the conference on Thursday.'
'.................................... the opening talk? That's a problem.' ....

A asking for confirmation of an opinion
B expressing surprise
C expressing criticism
D inviting / trying to persuade someone

2 GRAMMAR IN USE Complete the article, using suitable words from the box in a negative form.

advantage available convenience courteous cover credible intelligent legal possible usual

Strange but true

THIS RATHER (1) .... story from yesterday's news may have escaped your attention.

Customs officials last night (2) .... an attempt at (3) .... entry into Britain by an (4) .... group of immigrants: fleas. The fleas belong to the Cardoso Flea Circus of Australia, who are due to perform this evening at the Edinburgh Festival. The troupe (or the human part of it at least) feels that this is a highly (5) .... way to treat artists. They feel that it is (6) .... for them to cancel the show at this late stage, so despite the (7) .... of having lost their star performers, the show must go on. The flea trainer, Wyman Leung, is currently working with an alternative cast of fleas provided by Cambridge and Bristol Universities, although it is a huge (8) .... to have to work with ordinary cat fleas, rather than the elite strain of crossed cat and kangaroo fleas that were sent back to Australia. The circus didn't even bother trying to train the somewhat (9) .... *pulex irritans* – the human flea.

Home Office spokespeople were all (10) .... for comment.

3 GRAMMAR IN USE **Complete the conversation with one word only (or a contraction) in each gap. 3.39 Listen and check.**

PAUL Where's Ricky tonight?

LEE He's still at school. It's the first meeting of the film club or something.

PAUL Another club? (1) .... he joined enough clubs and societies? He's (2) .... ever here now.

LEE Well, he just wants to be with his friends ...

PAUL But we hardly ever see our son! He treats this place like a hotel. (3) .... he like his home any more?

LEE (4) .... don't you ask him? No, I'm sure he (5) .... trying to avoid us or anything. You know, I was reading an article about this the other day. It seems that (6) .... of us are comfortable with our own company and we need the security of like-minded people around us.

PAUL Like-minded?

LEE Yes, you know, (7) .... dissimilar in opinions and attitudes. So we join clubs to be with other people. That's why he's joined the film club.

PAUL But that's (8) .... sociable, is it? Sitting and watching films with other people. Why (9) .... he join something where he has to interact with other people? Though that's a bit difficult for teenagers, isn't it?

LEE Oh, that really isn't fair! You should be nicer to your son.

PAUL I don't think it's (10) .... at all, it's true!

4 **Write the second sentence so it has a similar meaning to the first. Use the word in brackets, as in the example.**

0 Sending someone to prison for defending their own property isn't fair.
(injustice) *Sending someone to prison for defending their own property is an injustice.*

1 Phil claimed that he had no involvement in the pensions scam.
(denied) ....

2 If no payment is forthcoming, we will be obliged to remove your connection to the electricity supply.
(disconnect) ....

3 Hardly anyone from the housing cooperative showed any interest in joining the Neighbourhood Watch scheme.
(few) ....

4 It isn't really possible to understand what the parents of seriously ill children must go through.
(hardly) ....

5 It appears that the director deliberately gave the investigators incorrect information.
(misinformed) ....

6 It's best not to talk about topics like politics at dinner parties.
(avoid) ....

7 It isn't often that singers make it as actors, but Christina Aguilera has done so.
(rarely) ....

8 Applications in which we are unable to read the writing will be automatically rejected.
(illegible) ....

49 Questions and question words

1 Question types

Most questions are closed (*yes/no* questions) or open (with a question word). There is a third type of question: an alternative question asks the listener to make a choice between two or more options:
'Would you prefer to see the doctor on Thursday or Friday?' 'Friday, please.'
'I'm sorry. Did you ask for French fries, steamed potatoes or rice?' 'Rice, please.'

Pronunciation ➤ 1.15

In conversation, we can use statement word order with closed questions, but not with open questions, to check something we think we know or to express surprise. We usually give them a rising intonation:
***You've sent** the tickets (↗)? **You haven't sent** the tickets (↗)? Why not (↘)?*
✗ ~~*Why you haven't sent the tickets?*~~ ✓ *Why **haven't you** sent the tickets?*

When we ask questions about opinions and feelings, we often omit *that*:
Do you think (that) the nursery will give me a refund for when Elly was ill?

2 Subject questions

Who, *what*, *which* and *whose* can be the subject of a verb, as well as the object:

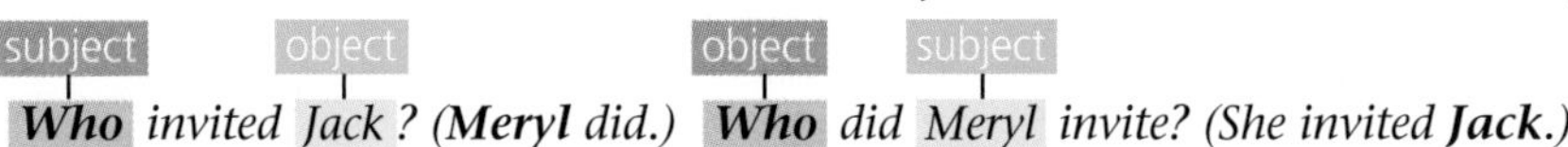

***Who** invited Jack? (**Meryl** did.) **Who** did Meryl invite? (She invited **Jack**.)*

If the question word is the subject, the word order is the same as in a statement:
***Who** made these two vases?*
***What** happened at the end of the film?*
***Whose mobile phone** is ringing?*

Be careful not to confuse subject and object questions:
✗ ~~*What said she?*~~ ✓ *What did she say?*

We use question word order with a subject question word when we are keen to return to a topic earlier in the conversation and want to get an answer:
*Well, **what <u>did</u> happen** at the end of the film?*

When we use *who*, *what* and *which* as subjects, we use a singular verb in the question, even if they refer to a plural subject:
*'**Who lives** in that amazing chateau?' 'The old **Count and Countess live** there.'*

3 *how* (+ adjective/adverb)

How asks about manner (the way something is done), progress, health or opinion:
***How** are things going with the building?* (= How is it progressing?)

Note the difference between *How's X?* and *What's X like?*:
How's Christine? (asks about Christine's health)
What's Christine like? (asks about Christine's appearance/personality)

⚠ We do not use *like* with *how*:
✗ ~~*How's Neil like?*~~ ✓ *What's Neil like?*
✗ ~~*How's the weather like at the moment?*~~
✓ *What's the weather like at the moment?* ✓ *How's the weather at the moment?*

When we form questions with *how* + adjective/adverb, we don't usually repeat the adjective/adverb in the answer: *How far is it from the station?*
✗ ~~*It's 500 metres far from the station.*~~ ✓ *It's 500 metres from the station.*

But with adjectives describing how big/large/wide/high/tall/deep/long, etc. we DO repeat it:
The new bed is ***1.8 metres wide****. The pool is only* ***1.5 metres deep****. The track is* ***10 km long****.*

4 *what* and *which*

We use *what* to ask about one (or more) of many things:
What languages *is it best to learn if you want to be an interpreter?*

We usually use *which* when the answer is one of a limited number of alternatives:
Which *cake do you want to try first?* (limited choice of cakes)
Compare with *what*:
What *cakes do you like best?* (of all cakes; unlimited choice)

We can use *what* and *which* without a noun if it is clear what we are talking about:
*'****What****'s for dinner this evening?' 'Well, we've got a chicken or burgers.* ***Which*** *do you fancy?'*

There are several common expressions in questions with *what*:
What else *did the police officer say? Are they going to prosecute?* (*What* = what other things)
What's the point in *arguing with Maisie? She's always right.*
(= This course of action is pointless.)
What's the use of *saving money when interest rates are so low?*
(= This course of action is pointless.)
The conference dinner is at the Central Hotel. ***What about*** *staying overnight?* (suggestion)

5 *wh-* words + prepositions

We usually put the preposition at the end of a *wh-* question:
Who *are you buying the bracelet* ***for****?* ***Which*** *station will you be arriving* ***at****?*

FORMALITY CHECK In more formal speech and writing, we put the preposition before the question word, and change *who* to *whom* (➤ Unit 9.3):
To which *letter are you referring?* ***From whom*** *did the defendant accept the payment?*

6 Rhetorical questions

A rhetorical question has the form of a question but it does not require an answer.
We use these

- to make an assertion about someone/something: *Haven't you grown?*
- to draw attention to something, usually negative:
  What is your bag doing in the hall? Put it away.
- to introduce a new topic: *Do you remember my friend Elena from Paraguay? Well, it turns out that she's going back there in a few weeks.*

ACADEMIC ENGLISH In formal writing and speeches, rhetorical questions are often used to draw the audience's attention to something, and the writer/speaker usually answers the question:
What does the public want from their government? They want openness and fairness, obviously, but also the ability to manage the economy ...

Question tags, reply and indirect questions ➤ Unit 79

Practice

1 Complete B's questions with suitable verbs and/or question words, and any other words necessary. The questions should ask about the underlined parts of A's statements.
3.40 Listen and check.

0 A Come on! I've been waiting out in the cold for ages!
  B Oh, really? ..*How long*... exactly have you been ...*waiting*....?
1 A Someone told me that you've decided to give up the course.
  B Oh, ... that?
2 A I've just been offered two jobs!
  B That's great! .... to take?
3 A We could just paint the walls or we could put wallpaper up – what do you think?
  B .... that thick soundproofing paper up? Then we won't hear next door's music!
4 A The roads round here are in a terrible state. I'm going to complain to someone.
  B Good idea, but ....?
5 A We went to a comedy night yesterday, and saw some really good comedians.
  B Oh, ... see?
6 A Jenna's decided to stop eating breakfast because she's putting on weight.
  B Really! What's .... giving up breakfast when she spends all her evenings in front of the TV with crisps and chocolates?

2 GRAMMAR IN USE Find seven more mistakes in the conversation and correct them.
3.41 Listen and check.

SEAN I've just joined the local wildlife trust.
GILL Is that some kind of club ~~and~~ *or* is it a society?
SEAN Well, neither, really. It's a charity. The idea is that it protects local wildlife.
GILL What's the point to join that?
SEAN What's the point? Honestly! What a crazy question!
GILL Why you think it's crazy?
SEAN Well, we're in danger of losing a lot of our wildlife as the area becomes more built-up. So we need to create safe spaces for local species.
GILL Oh, I see. And who create the spaces?
SEAN The people who run the charity.
GILL How much does it cost to join?
SEAN Oh, it only costs a few pounds much.
GILL To who do you pay that, then?
SEAN To the charity, of course.
GILL Can you visit the safe spaces they create?
SEAN Yes, we went to their main one last weekend.
GILL How was it like?
SEAN Interesting, very peaceful, just a nice, large wooded area. In fact, they held an introductory barbecue for new members.
GILL Who did organise that?
SEAN The people who run the charity. It was great, a lot of people came.

3 Complete the questions with one word only in each gap.

1 .... car did you decide to buy, the Toyota or the Volkswagen?

2 Who .... after your cats when you go on holiday?

3 We appreciate your extensive experience, Ms Wise, but what .... can you bring to our company?

4 '.............. action can the police take about this?' 'Well, we can give the offender a formal warning, and apprehend him or her if the warning is ignored.'

5 I haven't seen Isobel for ages. .... was she when you saw her yesterday?

6 One final question before commencing discussion of the contract – with .... in your company will the negotiations be taking place?

7 Everyone in the office seems really quiet today. ....'s happened?

8 .... phone is ringing? Could you please turn phones off during the lesson?

9 You look thoughtful. What are you thinking ....?

10 You didn't finish telling me about your missing jewellery. Who .... take it? Did the police ever find out?

4 Write the question for each reply, as in the example. Use the prompts in brackets and add a question word where necessary.

0 (own / white Cadillac / drive / around here)
'*Who owns the white Cadillac that drives around here?*'
'Oh, I think the Americans from Harding Road own it.'

1 (applicant / think / be / suitable?) '..'
'Well, I think they're both reasonable, but Stephen Wrigley seems to be the best for this post.'

2 (give / cattle / that type of feed?) '..
....'
'We'd only been giving them that particular type of feed for about two months.'

3 (tell / you / the divorce?) '..'
'I think it was Susan who told me about it, but most people at college seem to know.'

4 (else / do / holiday?) '..'
'We didn't really do much else on the holiday – it was a really small resort.'

5 (persuade / David / stay / team?) '..
....'
'No, I don't think we could have persuaded him to stay. The counter-offer was far too attractive.'

6 (be / point / complain / faulty goods?) '..
....'
'There's every point in complaining! How else will shops know that their goods are faulty?'

7 (watch / be / better / scuba-diving?) '..'
'Both of the watches are suitable for scuba-diving, but I think you'll find that the Timepiece is more reliable at greater depths.'

8 (the accused / steal / getaway car?) '..
....'
'Your honour, we believe that he stole the getaway car on behalf of Seamus Presley, the leader of the Presley gang.'

Review MODULE 10

1 **UNITS 47 AND 48** **Find twelve more mistakes in the conversation and correct them, as in the example.**

LOUISA Hi, Martin. What's wrong? You look awful.

MARTIN Oh, I've had that horrible flu. It lasted for ages.

LOUISA Didn't you go to the doctor?

MARTIN ~~No~~ Yes, I did. I went last week, but my doctor doesn't know nothing. I asked for that new flu drug – what's it called?

LOUISA You mean Defrenol?

MARTIN That's it. I asked but he wouldn't give me none.

LOUISA Why?

MARTIN He said that the tests haven't hardly proved that it works. Not for did he refuse to give me Defrenol, but he wouldn't give me none other medicine. I think it's because the surgery is over-budget and he doesn't want to spend any more money!

LOUISA If that's the case, it's really unhonest! Have you thought about complaining?

MARTIN No, what's the use? Complaints about doctors rarely have an effect, don't they? Anyway, I suppose there's not much you can do about a virus. He said I should drink plenty of fluids and he didn't tell me to go out until I felt better.

LOUISA How are you feeling now?

MARTIN Well, I've still got chest problems. It might be from the fumes at the factory, though they're meant to be no-toxic.

LOUISA Have you left that place? I thought you'd moved to a different job.

MARTIN No, not till next month.

LOUISA I see. Anyway, it lasts a long time, this flu. Not many people don't appreciate that. You think it's gone and you try to get back to normal, then it hits you again.

MARTIN Yes, you're right. I still can't taste anything ...

LOUISA Look, I must be going. I don't hope it lasts much longer. Bye!

2 **UNITS 48 AND 49** **Complete each sentence with a suitable word or phrase.**

1 What's .... in arguing with people who hold very strong opinions?
2 'Mmm, ... makes your pastry so tasty?' 'I use different herbs in it, that's all.'
3 .... you finished the quarterly accounts yet? I need them for the board meeting later.
4 I've got a couple of paint samples here. .... colour do you prefer?
5 What's .... of buying all this expensive equipment when you don't know if you'll enjoy the sport?
6 These sitcoms are so formulaic. This one is .... any different from that one we watched yesterday, is it?
7 By .... of the available methods did your client pay for her purchases?
8 .... you join us on the school committee? You'd be a real asset with your background.
9 Oh, come on, tell us. Who .... send you those amazing flowers?
10 'We've got an apartment for four people for the week. It seems silly to go by ourselves.' 'You're right! .... inviting Dave and Matt? They're good fun.

3 ALL UNITS **Read this interview. Complete gaps 1–5 with questions formed from the prompts in the box.**

belong / the Society / today	else / it / do	~~exactly / be / it~~
found / the Society	it / be / in existence	the Society / contribute / to science

PRES Good morning. This morning I'm talking to Professor Andrew Lyons, a Fellow of the Royal Society. Professor Lyons is going to tell me something about the Royal Society. First of all, welcome.

PROF Thank you. It's good to be here.

PRES Let's start straightaway. (A) A lot of people don't know much about the Royal Society. (0) *What exactly is it*..................?

PROF Well, basically, the Royal Society is an academy of the sciences, (B) like the American National Academy of Science. It's a charitable institution whose aim is to promote excellence in science, and to make it accessible to lay people.

PRES I see. (1) ....?

PROF It's the oldest scientific academy in the world. It started in 1660, but (C) it received its royal status two years after that.

PRES So (2) ....?

PROF It was started by the eminent scientists of the day. A group met to listen to a lecture on astronomy by Sir Christopher Wren, and it grew from that.

PRES Oh, it was started by someone as famous as Christopher Wren?

PROF Indeed, and most other well-known British scientists have belonged to it. Newton, naturally, Faraday, and (D) as well as British scientists, others such as Einstein.

PRES And (3) ....?

PROF Well, the membership is made up of Fellows – 44 are elected each year and eight others from outside Britain are invited to join. Current members include Stephen Hawking, Tim Berners-Lee and Richard Dawkins. But, of course, the majority aren't famous.

PRES No, of course. (4) ....?

PROF Mmm, in a lot of respects it is no different from many funding agencies that support young scientists with grants, but we also have an education programme to encourage schoolchildren to take up science and to support science teachers.

PRES (5) ....? Anything in the community for example?

PROF Well, yes. We organise (E) a significant number of lectures and activities for people who aren't involved in the scientific world. We want to encourage (F) lay people to get involved with science, and to understand the importance of science in all of our lives.

4 ALL UNITS **Rewrite the underlined sections A–F from Exercise 3 using a negative structure, word or phrase with a similar meaning. In some cases more than one answer is possible.**

A *Not many people know*.................... D ....

B .... E ....

C .... F ....

MODULE

11 Reported speech

Before you start

1 Review these intermediate grammar points and check you know them.

Reporting speech directly

1 We report speech directly in writing by using the exact words between inverted commas, i.e. we quote the original words. We do not use *that* to introduce direct speech:
He leaned towards them and whispered, 'Be sure to lock your door tonight.'

2 The reporting verb (*said, replied*, etc.) can go in any of these positions:
***Lovell said**, 'Houston, we have a problem.'* *'Houston, we have a problem,' **Lovell said**.*
*'Houston,' **said Lovell/Lovell said**, 'we have a problem.'*

3 When we put the reporting verb after direct speech, it can go before the subject, unless the subject is a pronoun:
✗ ~~*'The operation was a success,' said she.*~~
✓ *'The operation was a success,' **she said**.* ✓ *'The operation was a success,' **said the surgeon**.*

Tense changes in reported (indirect) speech

	TENSE IN DIRECT SPEECH	TENSE IN REPORTED SPEECH
present to past	present simple: *'The concert **starts** at eight.'*	past simple: *He said the concert **started** at eight.*
	present continuous: *'**I'm leaving** in ten minutes.'*	past continuous: *She decided she **was leaving** in ten minutes.*
	present perfect: *'We**'ve been living** here for years.'*	past perfect: *He revealed they**'d been living** there for years.*
past to past perfect	past simple: *'It **rained** heavily today.'*	past perfect simple: *Sarah mentioned that it **had rained** heavily that day.*
	past continuous: *'We **were waiting** for hours.'*	past perfect continuous: *They complained that they **had been waiting** for hours.*
modal verbs	*'I **can** pick the parcel up.'*	*I said I **could** pick the parcel up.*
	*'Spike **will** call you tomorrow.'*	*She promised Spike **would** call me the next day.*

Reporting questions, commands, etc.

1 The most common verbs for reporting questions are *ask* and *want to know*:
*She **asked** what piracy was.*
*Laura **wanted to know** if anybody had seen the incident.*
We do not use a question mark in reported questions.

2 We also use *enquire* for formal questions and *wonder* for 'ask ourselves':
*The receptionist **enquired** whether we would be requiring breakfast.*
*The concert was boring and Karl **wondered** when he could leave.*

3 To report commands, requests, advice, etc., we use a reporting verb + *to* + infinitive:
*The guard **told** us **to hand over** our cameras.*
*My boss **advised** me **not to apply for** the job.*

2 Read the information and identify examples of reported speech.

IN ONE OF the most famous speeches ever made, Martin Luther King urged his audience not to lose hope. He told them that he had a dream that day, August 28th, 1963. He said he had a dream that the sons of former slaves and the sons of former slave owners would be able to sit down together at the table of brotherhood; and that his four little children would one day live in a nation where they would not be judged by the colour of their skin.

3 Complete the diagnostic test below. Choose the correct answer, A, B or C. If two options are correct, choose both.

1 He replied ..... had gone up by twenty percent in the last two years. ➤ Unit 50.2
A that the price B the price C that it the price

2 He ..... that his mobile phone had been out of action all day. ➤ Unit 50.2
A told me B said C told

3 The doctor advised ..... drink more water. ➤ Unit 50.4
A me that I should B that me I should C me to

4 The President ..... 1st March 2000 as a great day for the nation. ➤ Unit 50.4
A promised to commemorate B promised that he would commemorate
C promised commemorating

5 Even under great pressure O'Brien denied ..... taken part in the attack. ➤ Unit 50.6
A having B to have C not having

6 Lyn hates the idea of growing old. She said yesterday that she wished she ..... young. ➤ Unit 51.1
A had still been B is still C was still

7 Frank said ..... a fantastic new job, but it wasn't true. ➤ Unit 51.2
A he'd got B he's got C he has

8 Laura was so certain last night that she ..... here by now. ➤ Unit 51.3
A would be B is C will be

9 The specialist told Malcolm that he ..... lose at least 20 kilos. ➤ Unit 51.5
A must B had to C have to

10 Your ..... Jodie was 'dispensable' was extremely unkind. ➤ Unit 51.6
A remark B remarked that C remark that

11 Sonya's advice that ..... early was pretty useless! ➤ Unit 51.6
A we arrived B we should arrive C we arrive

12 Maureen ..... if anybody had reported a missing person to the police yet. ➤ Unit 52.1
A wanted to know B said C asked

13 At the interview, they asked what ..... about hard selling techniques. ➤ Unit 52.1
A did I know B do I know C I knew

14 We asked the travel agent ..... there was a swimming pool at the villa. ➤ Unit 52.1
A if B if or not C whether or not

15 'Isn't that expensive!' → She ..... expensive. ➤ Unit 52.2
A complained that it was B asked if that wasn't C exclaimed if it was

16 I ..... the sofa to be delivered the next Monday. ➤ Unit 52.2
A asked that B asked for C wanted to know that

4 Check your answers on page 384. Then go to the unit for more information and practice.

Go online for a full diagnostic test

50 Patterns in reported speech

'We understand it still that there is no easy road to freedom. We know it well that none of us acting alone can achieve success. We must therefore act together as a united people …'

1 Direct and reported speech

It is possible, though rare, to quote words directly in speech. We may do this if we want to focus on the exact words spoken: *But did he actually say 'I miss you'?*

We usually report words using indirect speech in conversations as we do not have punctuation to clearly signal what is the reported speech:
*But did he actually **tell** you **that he missed you**?*

2 Common reporting verbs

There are a number of common verbs (reporting verbs) used to report statements. They are often followed by *that*, e.g. *say, tell, add, answer, reply, mention, remark, shout*:
*For the third time that day, the minister **replied that** it was out of the question.*

We can omit *that* after most reporting verbs, especially in conversation, but we prefer not to after *reply*, *respond* and *answer*, and we rarely omit it after *shout*:
✗ ~~*I shouted they were barred from the club.*~~
✓ *I **shouted that** they were barred from the club.* ✓ *I **said** they were barred from the club.*

⚠ There are differences in use between *say* and *tell*:
✗ ~~*He said us that his phone wasn't working.*~~
✓ *He **said that** his phone wasn't working.* ✓ *He **said to us that** his phone wasn't working.*
✗ ~~*He told that his phone wasn't working.*~~ ✗ ~~*He told to us that his phone wasn't working.*~~
✓ *He **told us that** his phone wasn't working.*

When we are reporting more than one sentence, it is not necessary to repeat the reporting verb:
*Tom **insisted that** he hadn't been there. He had worked late, and had then gone straight home.*

We can also report our thoughts using verbs such as *think, decide, dream* or *imagine*:
*She never **imagined that** it would be so difficult to run for the Senate.*

When we report a negative statement we usually make the verbs within the statement negative: 'He hasn't arrived yet.' → *She said that he **hadn't arrived** yet.*

But with some verbs, e.g. *think, expect, plan, intend*, the reporting verb itself is usually negative: 'She won't be on time.' → *I **didn't expect that** she'd be on time.*

3 Using different reporting verbs

A large number of reporting verbs are 'functional'; they indicate the purpose of the original speech:
'You should stop smoking.' → *He **advised** her to stop smoking.* (advice)
'If you do that again, I'll call the police.' → *He **threatened** to call the police.* (warning)

FORMALITY CHECK In informal conversation we usually report speech with the verbs *say* and *tell*. In more formal speech and in writing, we use a greater variety of reporting verbs:

'I think you should inform the judge.' → *Dad **told** me he thought I should inform the judge.*
*The lawyer **advised** me to inform the judge.*

4 Reporting verbs (+ clause)

VERB ONLY (+ PRONOUN)

'I'm really sorry.' → *She apologised.*

EXAMPLES *agree apologise refuse*

VERB + (*that*) CLAUSE

'I hacked into the accounts system.' → *He* ***admitted (that)*** *he had hacked into the system.*

EXAMPLES *accept acknowledge add admit agree announce answer* argue assert assume believe boast comment complain concede conclude confess continue* decide declare deny doubt exclaim expect explain feel foresee imagine imply insist know mention notice observe point out predict promise propose* protest recommend remark repeat reply* report respond reveal say shout* state suggest suppose vow whisper*

* *that* is obligatory

Some of these verbs can be followed by an infinitive or *-ing* form. (See the charts below.) Some of these verbs can be followed by the subjunctive (➤ Unit 40.1).

VERB + OBJECT + *that* CLAUSE

'Don't worry. You'll arrive on time.' → *She* ***reassured me that*** *I would arrive on time.*

EXAMPLES *advise assure inform reassure remind tell warn*

5 Reporting verbs + infinitive

VERB + *to* INFINITIVE

'We'll collect the children, if you like.' → *They* ***offered to collect*** *the children.*

EXAMPLES *agree demand guarantee offer promise propose refuse swear threaten volunteer vow*

VERB (+ OBJECT) (+ *not*) + *to* INFINITIVE

'Please can I use the car?' → *She* ***asked to use*** *the car.*

'Please let me stay.' → *She* ***begged us to let*** *her stay.*

EXAMPLES *ask (somebody) beg (somebody) expect (somebody) want (somebody)*

VERB + OBJECT (+ *not*) + *to* INFINITIVE

'You shouldn't say anything.' → *I* ***advised him not to say*** *anything.*

EXAMPLES *advise allow challenge command compel encourage forbid force implore instruct invite order permit persuade remind request tell urge warn*

VERB + OBJECT + (*to* INFINITIVE) + COMPLEMENT

'Michael Schumacher is the greatest racing driver ever.'

→ *She* ***considers Michael Schumacher (to be)*** *the greatest racing driver ever.*

EXAMPLES *acknowledge assume believe consider declare expect feel find presume suppose think understand*

6 Reporting verbs + *-ing* form

VERB + *-ing* FORM

'I didn't do it.' → *He* ***denied doing*** *it.*
He ***denied having done*** *it.*

EXAMPLES *admit apologise for decide on deny mention propose recommend regret report suggest*

VERB + OBJECT+ PREPOSITION + *-ing* FORM

'You forged the cheques, didn't you?' → *They* ***accused me of forging*** *the cheques.*

EXAMPLES *accuse somebody of blame somebody for congratulate somebody on thank somebody for*

Practice

1 Use the words to write reported statements. Start with the underlined word or phrase.

1 that informed she was ill the photographer us

....

2 assumed Gemma's brother be the young man everyone to

....

3 justice to the guilty person to vowed Inspector Stanford bring

....

4 on Thursday the leaflet that the collection be would said

....

5 Sally having from the cupboard the biscuits taken admitted

....

6 did extra tell have to the guide for lunch not we'd us pay

....

7 closed the museum not imagine we today that did be would

....

8 our director through a difficult year us working for thanked so hard

....

2 Report each of these statements, using a suitable verb from the box, as in the example. There are five extra verbs. 3.42 Listen and check.

accuse admit apologise blame consider deny encourage persuade reassure ~~refuse~~ regret remind reply suggest warn

0 Lily: 'I will not take part in the new play.'

Lily refused to take part in the new play.

1 My friend Tina: 'Don't you ever tell anyone about my problems again!'

....

2 My manager: 'It was your fault that we lost the Siemens contract.'

....

3 The art critic: 'Picasso was definitely the most exciting artist of the twentieth century.'

....

4 The reporter: 'I'm terribly sorry about getting the Minister's name wrong.'

....

5 The police officer: 'We believe that you have been making threatening phone calls.'

....

6 My friends: 'Come on – you can do the marathon with us. You're just as good as us.'

....

7 The team manager: 'I feel terrible now about contradicting Julie in front of the team.'

....

8 My wife: 'Don't worry about the arrangements. They're all under control.'

....

9 My mother: 'You had your tonsils taken out at the age of nine, remember?'

....

3 GRAMMAR IN USE **Read this summary. Choose the correct reporting verb in 1–8. Write one word only in the gaps A–H. 3.43 Listen and check.**

Key points in the President's speech

INTRODUCTION

President Obama started by (1) *thanking / blaming* his predecessor (A) .... providing service to the nation, and he reminded the audience (B) .... 44 Americans had now taken the presidential oath, in prosperity and peace, or other conditions.

THE ECONOMY

He went on (C) .... say that the country was in the middle of a crisis. He (2) *urged / explained* that this took the form of both war and a failing economy. He stated that these problems (D) .... not be met easily, but he (3) *encouraged / insisted* that they would be met. The President (4) *promised / assured* (E) .... act in order to create new jobs, improve health care and explore renewable energy.

INTERNATIONAL AFFAIRS

With regard to defence, he (5) *apologised / denied* that America had to make a choice between safety and ideals, and he insisted (F) .... the country is a friend to all nations who seek peace. He (6) *added / expected* that earlier generations had used conviction and alliances to overcome enemies.

CONCLUSION

He concluded by (7) *suggesting / encouraging* his citizens (G) .... remember the words of George Washington and meet whatever may come with hope and virtue. He (8) *urged / guaranteed* them (H) .... to be disheartened and to carry the gift of freedom to future generations.

4 **Eight of these sentences contain mistakes in grammar or punctuation. Find and correct the mistakes, as in the example. Tick (✓) the correct sentences.**

0 'These traffic-calming measures have been put into place for a very good reason,' ~~said he~~ he said.
1 The doctor reminded me to not take the tablets before meals.
2 Delia commented that fresh coriander could be found in any good supermarket now.
3 The child shouted he wanted to go home to his mother.
4 And then the interviewer actually said that's a lie, Minister.
5 My accountant advised to me keep all my receipts and give them to him.
6 A lot of older people regret not to have gone to university when they were younger and had the opportunity.
7 Alicia implored her eldest son not to join the army.
8 The doorman at the entrance demanded being shown proof of my age.
9 When Jason asked about the source of the meat at the restaurant, the waiter answered "it was all sourced locally".
10 The runner-up congratulated the new champion winning the most prestigious tournament of the year.

51 Changes in reported speech

'Friends and Comrades, the light has gone out of our lives and there is darkness everywhere. I do not know what to tell you and how to say it. ... And so the cremation will take place on Saturday in Delhi city by the side of the Jamuna river ...'

NEHRU SPOKE eloquently earlier today about the assassination of Mahatma Gandhi. He started by telling his people that the light **had gone** out of their lives. He added that there **is** darkness everywhere. He said he **didn't know** what to tell the people and how to say it. He finished by announcing that the cremation **will take place** on Saturday in Delhi ...

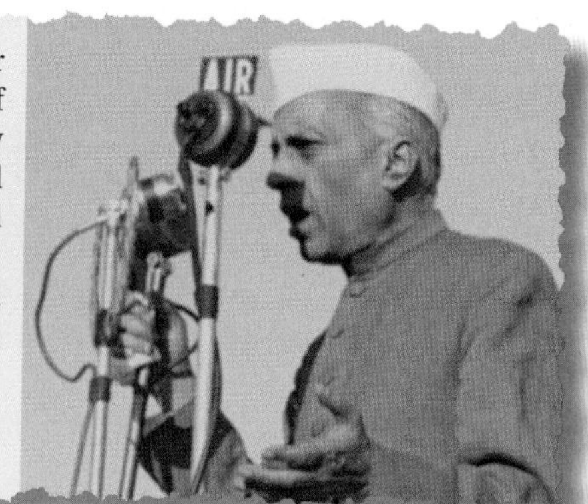

1 No backshift

Although we often change the tense of the original words in reported speech (backshift), we do not when

- the reporting verb is in a present tense:
  He says that these fish ***do not survive*** *in salt water.*
- the reported verb is in the past perfect:
  'They'd arrived an hour early.' → *I said they'****d arrived*** *an hour early.*
- the direct speech includes an 'unreal' past (➤ Unit 40):
  'I wish I were younger.' → ✗ ~~*Janice said that she wished she had been younger.*~~
  ✓ *Janice said that she wished she* ***were*** *younger.*

2 Obligatory backshift

We always change the tense if we no longer believe the direct speech statement is true:

'Where's Tom this evening?' ✗ ~~*'He said he's going to join us, but I don't think he will.'*~~
✓ *'He said* ***he was going to join*** *us, but I don't think he will.'*

*Kim just called. She said she'****s going*** *on holiday with Paula.* (still true)
She said she ***was going*** *with Paula, but Paula can't get time off work.* (no longer true)

3 Optional backshift

In some cases we can choose to change the tense or not. This often depends on the relationship of the reported event to the time of reporting it. For example, if we report 'I'm going to Rome tomorrow morning' on the day it is said, we are likely to say:
*Susanna said she'****s going*** *to Rome tomorrow morning.*

But reported a few days later, we are more likely to say:
Susanna said she ***was going*** *to Rome the next morning.*

We don't usually change the tense when

- the reported action is still happening or going to happen:
  'I am working on a tentative settlement.'
  → *The negotiator said* ***he is working*** *on a tentative settlement.* (still working on it)
  'There is darkness everywhere.' → *Nehru said there* ***is*** *darkness everywhere.*
  (That is still the situation at the time of reporting the speech.)
- the reported verb expresses a fact or situation that cannot or is unlikely to change:
  He explained that these animals ***roamed*** *the earth millions of years ago.*
  He told us that counselling ***is not*** *the answer for everyone.*
- the verb comes after a time conjunction, e.g. *when, after*:
  Martin replied that he had started the job immediately ***after*** *he* ***left*** *school.*

Note that in all of these cases, it is also possible, and correct, to change the tense:
The negotiator said ***he was working*** *on a tentative settlement.*
Martin replied that he had started the job immediately after he ***had left*** *school.*

4 Changes and additions with adverbs

If the place or time of reporting is significantly different from that in the original speech, we often need to make changes to adverbs of place and time:

now → *then* *here* → *there* *today* → *that day* *tomorrow* → *the next day*
yesterday → *the day before* *ago* → *before* *last Monday* → *the last/previous Monday*

*Alex said, '**I'll meet you here** again **tomorrow** at 3.30.'*
*Alex said **she would** meet **us there** again **the next day** at 3.30.*

But if the statement is reported on the same day and in the same place, we would say:
*Alex said **she will/would** meet **us here** again **tomorrow** at 3.30.*
*He finished by announcing that the cremation **will take place** on Saturday in Delhi ...*

We often use adverbs in reported speech to indicate HOW the original words were said:
'Jewellery is not allowed!' → *She told us **very sharply** that jewellery wasn't allowed.*
'Oh, add my name if you must.' → *Dad **reluctantly** agreed that we could add his name.*

5 Modal verbs

Ought to, used to, could, might, would, need and *should* do not change in reported speech:
'You ought to listen to your father.' → *Mum told me that I **ought to** listen to my father.*
'You needn't stay if you don't want to.' → *My boss said I **needn't** stay if I didn't want to.*

But we need to make changes to other modal verbs:
'The new law will be in place soon.' → *She said the new law **would** be in place soon.*
'Publication may be delayed.' → *The editor said that publication **might** be delayed.*
'Julian can't have written the letter.' → *I told them Julian **couldn't have** written the letter.*

Shall becomes *would* when it refers to the future, but *should* when it is a suggestion:
'I shall tell them everything.' → *I decided I **would** tell them everything.*
'Shall we tell the manager?' → *She suggested that they **should** tell the manager.*

We can use both *must* and *had to* in reported speech:
'You must lose twenty kilos!' → *The doctor said that I **must/had to** lose twenty kilos.*
'They must have finished.' → *We thought that they **must/had to** have finished.*

6 Reporting with nouns

As well as reporting speech with a reporting verb, we can use a noun + *that* to report someone's words when we want to add more information:

PRIME MINISTER *The recession will soon be over.*
→ *The Prime Minister **said** that the recession would soon be over.*
→ *The Prime Minister's **statement that the recession would soon be over** was ridiculed by the Opposition.*

KENNY *You should try the new Chinese restaurant. It's excellent.*
→ *Kenny **recommended** that we try the new Chinese restaurant.*
→ *What did you think of Kenny's **recommendation that we try the new Chinese restaurant**?*

We do not usually leave out *that* after reporting nouns:

MORE EXAMPLES *admission advice allegation announcement answer argument assertion claim comment complaint denial explanation forecast point remark response suggestion*

✗ ~~*The Prime Minister's statement the recession would soon be over was ridiculed by the Opposition.*~~

More on use of nouns (nominalisation) ➤ Unit 78.1

Practice

1 GRAMMAR IN USE **Read the conversation and choose the correct words in *italics*. If both options are possible, choose both.** 3.44 **Listen and check.**

SUE Sorry I'm late – I got held up in traffic. Have I missed Len?

MIA Yes, he left after lunch. He made a lovely speech. It was short, but very good. He started by saying that he (1) *has / had* really enjoyed his twenty years in the firm, and he wished he (2) *can / could* stay longer, but that his health (3) *isn't / wasn't* really good enough any more.

SUE Mmm, I think his heart is the main reason he's retiring.

MIA Yes, that's right. He said he'd never forget the day he started. He said he thought (4) *he'd made / he's made* a terrible mistake when he (5) *left / had left* at five – his boss called him back and told him that he (6) *must / had to* work to five thirty. Nobody had told him that in the interview – stupid, isn't it?

SUE Yes, awful! But he (7) *can / could* have asked someone to be sure, really. Did he say what he (8) *intends / intended* to do in the future?

MIA Well, he let us into a little secret. He explained that he (9) *came / had come* into quite a lot of money recently, and that he and his wife are going to Australia for six months to see their son, and that they (10) *may / might* decide to stay there.

SUE Really? So that's the real reason he's leaving.

MIA He says not. He insisted that he (11) *will / would* stay at the company if it weren't for his health, but I don't believe him. Anyway, he finished by thanking all of (12) *them / us* for being such good colleagues for the last twenty years.

2 GRAMMAR IN USE **Report these voicemail messages, as in the example. Change the tenses, pronouns and adverbs as necessary.**

"Hi, Mum. It's Lucy here, just phoning to say Happy Birthday. I'm going to be out all afternoon but I'll try you again later."

1 Lucy phoned to say *Happy Birthday. She said she's going to be out all afternoon but she'll try you again later.*

"Elaine, hi. It's Rosemary here. I didn't get to Spanish last night as I'd been out all day and I got home late. I'll ring again to find out what the homework is."

2 Rosemary called a couple of days ago. She said ....

....

....

"Oh, er, hello. This is Christine Reynolds. I'm phoning to find out the results of my blood test. I'm going on holiday tomorrow morning so I'd be grateful if you could ring me back later."

3 Doctor, Christine Reynolds left a message earlier today. She said ....

....

....

"Good afternoon. This is Tim at Barrett's Supermarket Delivery Service. I'm afraid that we can't fulfil your order, as you didn't include credit card details on your website order form. We must have these details, or payment in advance, to fulfil an order. I'll await your instructions."

4 Someone called from Barrett's a few days ago. He said ....

....

....

3 **Rewrite these sentences in reported speech, as in the example. Decide whether to change the tenses and adverbs of time and place. 3.45 Listen and check.**

0 'The London Eye is now the most popular tourist destination in London.'
The guidebook states *that the London Eye is now the most popular tourist destination in London.*

1 'I've decided to stay another week as the research is going so well here.'
Professor Jones rang from Vancouver. He said ....

2 'We've got tickets for the opera this weekend.'
Gerry and Louisa told me last week that ....

3 'The smaller islands are mostly uninhabited and very peaceful.'
There are so many people here! But that TV programme a few weeks ago said ....

4 'Mum's really ill. I wish we didn't live so far away from her.'
Georgia was really depressed last night. She told me that ....

5 'The house is in a very pleasant cul-de-sac, and there aren't many children there.'
Here's the road. Oh no – it's awful! But the estate agent insisted that ....

6 'The accused first met the Wilsons when he decorated their living room.'
In court, the lawyer claimed that ....

7 'Shall we switch to an online banking system?'
My husband suggested that ....

8 'You mustn't leave your car in these parking bays for more than twenty minutes.'
The traffic warden explained ....

4 **Use the verbs in brackets to complete each sentence. Change one verb into a reporting noun and use the other to complete the statement, as in the example.**

0 We were all astonished by the pilot's *announcement* that the smooth landing *had been* entirely on autopilot. (be / announce)

1 The official's .... that he .... the documents on the train created a stir in the Department of Defence. (admit / leave)

2 Frankly, at this newspaper no one believes Riley's .... that he .... money to allow his opponent to win the snooker championship. (accept / deny)

3 The defendant's .... that the accused .... her over a period of twenty months needs to be carefully considered. (allege / stalk)

4 What about Amanda's lack of concentration at work? Did you believe her .... that she .... from stress-induced headaches? (suffer / explain)

5 'Did you query the solicitor's bill?' 'Yes, I did, but I wasn't impressed by his .... that the extra charges .... because we had withheld information!' (be applied / respond)

52 Reported questions, commands and requests

'Today I want to talk about piracy and music. What is piracy? Piracy is the act of stealing an artist's work without any intention of paying for it.'

COURTNEY LOVE addressed the conference today. She chose to talk to us about piracy and music – first she asked what piracy was, and then defined it for us as the act of stealing an artist's work without any intention of paying for it.

1 Reported questions

Reported question word order is the same as in statements:

if/whether/wh-word	subject	verb (+ object/complement)
He asked if	we	were feeling hungry.
She asked what	piracy	was.

The word order above is fixed:
✗ ~~*She asked what was piracy.*~~

We do not use auxiliary *do*, *does* or *did* in reported questions:
✗ ~~*They asked the driver where did the bus stop.*~~ ✓ *They asked the driver* ***where the bus stopped.***

We introduce indirect closed (*yes/no*) questions with *if* or *whether*:
Lester wondered ***if/whether*** *there was anything better in life.*

We can present alternatives with *whether/if ... or not*. We can put *or not* immediately after *whether* but NOT immediately after *if*:
Deborah asked ***whether or not*** *there was a lift in the apartment block.*
Deborah asked ***whether/if*** *there was a lift in the apartment block* ***or not.***

In indirect open questions we use a question word:
The nurse asked ***when*** *exactly the pain had started.*

We report negative questions which express surprise or criticism with a 'functional' verb (➤ Unit 50.4):

'Wasn't the play fantastic?' → ✗ ~~*She asked if the play hadn't been fantastic.*~~
✓ *She* ***exclaimed that the play had been fantastic.***

'Isn't the rule stupid?' → ✗ ~~*He asked if the rule wasn't stupid.*~~
✓ *He* ***complained that the rule was stupid.***

2 Reported commands, requests, etc.

In indirect commands we use a reporting verb, e.g. *tell, order, command, forbid* + *to* + infinitive:
When the vet had finished, he ***told*** *them to let the animal sleep.*
He ***forbade*** *us to pass on any of the information to the authorities.*

We use *ask* for reporting requests, and *beg* or *urge* with urgent requests:
'Please come back later.' → *His secretary* ***asked*** *me to come back later.*

We can use *ask for* + passive infinitive if *ask* has no object:
The cinema manager ***asked for*** *the culprit* ***to be brought*** *to his office.*

Note that to report a negative command or request, we put *not to* before the verb (except with *forbid*, which already has a negative meaning):
Several members of the royal family ***urged*** *Edward VIII* ***not to abdicate.***
I asked you ***not to bring*** *a present.* (= I said 'Please don't bring a present.')
This is different from: *I didn't ask you to bring a present.* (no request made)

We can report statements that fulfil other functions in the same way:
'Come on. I'll give you a lift.' → *Geoff* ***offered to give*** *me a lift.*

For other verbs with *to* + infinitive ➤ Unit 50.5

Practice

A ⁰Come in. ¹Did you have a good journey? ²Would you like to freshen up before dinner? ³Now, do you like spicy food or not?

1 **GRAMMAR IN USE** **Complete these reports, using the information in the speech bubbles.** **4.01** **Listen and check.**

B ⁴What's going on? ⁵Oh no, those two Harris children aren't bullying the others again, are they? ⁶OK, bring them to the office. ⁷Louisa, call their parents for me, will you?

C Oh, James. ⁸Where are you going? ⁹Please, please, don't go rock climbing again this weekend. ¹⁰Don't you realise how worried I get?

D Good morning. Thanks for coming at such short notice. ¹¹Would you like a cup of tea? OK. ¹²Please take a seat. ¹³Have you considered our offer? ¹⁴Are you ready to join the elite team?

A When we arrived at the address, our new landlady asked (0) ...*us to come in*..., and she wanted to know (1) .... a good journey. She asked (2) .... before dinner. Then she enquired (3) ....

B The head teacher asked (4) ...., then, when he investigated the source of the noise, he (5) .... that the two Harris children were bullying the others again. He asked (6) .... to the office, then he (7) .... their parents for him.

C James's wife was really upset when he came downstairs with his overnight bag. She (8) .... She (9) .... rock climbing again that weekend and she (10) ....

D The leader of the team thanked me for coming at such short notice. She (11) .... a cup of tea and (12) .... Then she got to the point and asked (13) .... their offer, and (14) .... to join the elite team.

2 **There is a mistake in each of these reported questions, commands and requests. Find the mistake and correct it, as in the example.** **4.02** **Listen and check.**

0 The police ordered the onlookers ~~to not~~ *not to* go near the crime scene.
1 Andy was really excited about the new job and asked if could he start straightaway.
2 The prime minister asked for the new crime bill to draft as soon as possible.
3 The builder told us let the plaster dry completely before we paint it.
4 The neighbours asked if or not we had heard anything during the night.
5 Dad asked me where I'd been all night?
6 Carol was running as fast as she was able to, wondering how possibly could she get away from this maniac.
7 The salesperson wanted to know what is the problem with the new fax machine.
8 Sandra begged to her landlord not to evict her before she had found somewhere else to live.
9 'Please don't tell the others about this.' → Harriet didn't beg us to tell the others about it.
10 'Doesn't the bride look lovely!' → She asked whether the bride looked lovely.

Go online for more practice and a progress test

Review MODULE 11

1 UNITS 50 AND 51 **Complete this report. For 1–8, write the verb in brackets in the correct form. For A–F, use a verb from the box in the correct form (which may be a noun).**

add assert explain joke quote thank

NEWS

Home | World | UK | Business | Health | Politics | Education | Entertainment & Arts

Last night at the Emmy Awards

On receiving the first Bob Hope Humanitarian Award, Oprah Winfrey started by (A) .... everyone for voting for her.

She stated that nothing (1) .... (be) more important to her than striving to be a good human being and (B) .... that receiving the first award was beyond expression.

Oprah went on to describe her childhood in Nashville and her father, who owned a barber's shop. Smiling fondly, she recalled his stubbornness and her (C) .... that he still (2) .... (own) it because she (3) .... (not/can) get him to retire raised a laugh. Her (D) .... that she (4) .... (learn) her sense of humanity from her father was very moving: she (E) .... that he (5) .... (always/invite) the local transients to dinner because they 'wanted the same from life as everyone else – to be fed'.

She finished by (F) .... Maya Angelou: 'When you learn, teach. When you get, give', and she emphasised that the award (6) .... (mean) that she (7) .... (continue) to give back to the world what it (8) .... (give) to her.

2 UNIT 52 **Write the reported questions, commands and requests, using the verbs given.**

1 Student: 'Does the university library open on Sundays or not?'
(wanted) ....

....

2 Julie's mother: 'Julie, please don't talk with your mouth full – it really isn't polite.'
(urged) ....

....

3 Manager: 'Could someone take the minutes and type them up afterwards?'
(asked for) ....

....

4 Becky: 'Mike, whatever you do, please don't let the children leave the garden.'
(begged) ....

....

5 Jeremy: 'Wasn't the meal awful? It was cold and had far too much salt in it.'
(complained) ....

....

3 ALL UNITS **What did these people say? Rewrite the reported versions of some quotations by famous people in direct speech.**

1 Pablo Picasso once claimed that age only mattered when one was ageing. He said that as he had arrived at a great age, he might just as well be twenty.

....

....

2 Writer George Bernard Shaw once said that the liar's punishment was not that he was not believed, but that he could not believe anyone else.

....

....

3 Groucho Marx once asked a club to accept his resignation because he didn't want to belong to any club that would accept him as a member.

....

....

4 President John F Kennedy once told the American people to ask not what their country could do for them, but to ask what they could do for their country.

....

....

4 ALL UNITS **Read the article and choose the correct word or phrase, A, B or C, for each gap.**

Worries about Internet use

A RECENT SURVEY into Internet use has thrown up some worrying results. The Stanford University survey asked respondents how much time (1) ..... on the Internet and (2) ..... Internet use had affected the amount of time they spent with family and friends. It also enquired whether their Internet use (3) ..... the time respondents spent working, either at home or in the office. The answers were interesting, but not unexpected. Two-thirds of the people surveyed responded that (4) ..... fewer than five hours a week on the Internet. The survey concludes that the behaviour of these people (5) ..... little. However, a quarter of those people who do use the Internet for more than five hours a week claimed that they spend less time with their family and friends. One in four of the total respondents also said that the time they spent working at home (6) ....., benefiting their employers.

Professor of Political Science at Stanford, Norman Nie, (7) ..... that we are moving from a world where we know and see neighbours and friends to one where interaction (8) ..... place at a distance. He asked rhetorically whether (9) ..... a hug or hear a warm voice over the Internet. It seems that the results of the survey prove that the Internet (10) ..... people into solitary beings who can't be bothered to call their mother on her birthday.

1 A did they spend B they did spend C they spent
2 A whether B what C if or not
3 A had increased B was increased C have increased
4 A they still spending B 'I still spend ... C they still spent
5 A changed B had changed C has changed
6 A increased B had increased C increases
7 A explains us B says us C tells us
8 A takes B had taken C took
9 A or not B could we get C we could get
10 A is turning B was turning C had turned

MODULE

12 Relative, participle and other clauses

Before you start

1 Review these intermediate grammar points and check you know them.

Relative clauses

1 Relative clauses identify or give information about someone or something in the main clause. They are introduced by relative pronouns, such as *that*, *which* or *who*:

which statesman?

*Garibaldi was the statesman **who united Italy** in the nineteenth century.*

what name?

*The Risorgimento is the name **which historians give to the movement led by Garibaldi**.*

2 The relative pronoun is the subject or object of the relative clause, so we don't repeat the noun from the main clause or introduce a personal pronoun to replace it:

✗ ~~*Garibaldi was the statesman who he united Italy in the nineteenth century.*~~

✓ *Garibaldi was the statesman **who united Italy** in the nineteenth century.*

Participle clauses

1 Participle clauses use participle forms e.g. *living, broken* to give more information about someone or something in the main clause. We usually use a comma to separate the participle clause from the main clause:

***Living in isolated villages**, peasants in Tsarist Russia rarely learned to read or write.*

***Broken by years of warfare**, Britain was almost bankrupt in the late 1940s.*

2 Participle clauses have active and passive forms but they do not have a tense. Their time reference is usually clear from the verb in the main clause:

***Not having a ticket**, I won't be able to go to the concert tomorrow.* (present/future)

***Not having a ticket**, I wasn't able to go to the concert yesterday.* (past)

Infinitive clauses

1 An infinitive clause can act as the subject or complement of the verb *be* or identify a noun:

***To win the championship** is our aim. Our aim is **to win the championship**.*

*The first person **to finish the race** will be the winner.*

2 Infinitives can be active or passive, but they do not have a tense. Their time reference is shown by the context or by the tense of the verb in the main clause:

*The tax bill will be the first item **to be debated** in the next parliament.* (future)

*Their proposal was the first one **to be debated** at yesterday's planning meeting.* (past)

3 We make infinitives negative by putting *not* in front of them:

***Not to be selected** for the team was Trudi's greatest disappointment.*

Noun (*wh-*) clauses

1 A *wh-* clause can replace a noun or noun phrase:

***Their actions** were inexcusable → **What they did** was inexcusable.*

*I don't remember **his clothing**. → I don't remember **what he was wearing**.*

2 We usually use these clauses more often in spoken and informal English.

2 Read the information and identify examples of relative and other clauses.

SIMON BOLIVAR
Born in 1783, Simon Bolivar grew up in the city of Caracas, Venezuela. As a young man from a wealthy family, he had a series of private tutors, several of whom were admirers of the new revolutionary ideas sweeping Europe and the Americas. What Bolivar learnt from these men was to have a profound effect on his political views.

Joining a prestigious military academy in 1797, Bolivar developed a love and mastery of military tactics and in 1813 he joined the campaign to restore the Venezuelan Republic. He led a series of nationalist rebellions, which liberated many of the countries that had previously been under Spanish rule. He is one of the very few people to have a country named after him – Bolivia.

3 Complete the diagnostic test below. Choose the correct words in *italics*. If both options are correct, choose both. In one case both are grammatically correct but only one is appropriate.

1. If you're in Edinburgh, *remember to visit the famous castle, which is the capital city of Scotland. / which is the capital city of Scotland, remember to visit the famous castle.* ➤ Unit 53.1
2. I'd like one of those chocolate bars *has / that has* toffee in the middle. ➤ Unit 53.2
3. The book, *that / which* is rather long, covers the politician's entire life. ➤ Unit 53.3
4. The charity event raised over £1,000 for St Andrew's *Hospice which / Hospice, which* opened last year. ➤ Unit 53.4
5. Our manager gave a two-hour presentation, *which / that* was very tedious. ➤ Unit 53.5
6. All cows over 30 months *who / which* may have been exposed to the disease will be destroyed. ➤ Unit 54.1
7. This document may only be opened by the legal representative of the company *to which it is addressed / which it is addressed to.* ➤ Unit 54.2
8. The novel is set in the period *where / when* the divide between rich and poor was much more marked than it is today. ➤ Unit 54.3
9. I'd always wanted to take Giselle to the city where I grew *up in / up.* ➤ Unit 54.3
10. You can put the photo *whichever / wherever* you think it looks best. ➤ Unit 54.6
11. *Servicing / Serviced* regularly, the engine should last for 200,000 kilometres. ➤ Unit 55.1
12. Writing in the 'Evening Standard', an *article / author* complained about the lack of facilities for the disabled on the Underground. ➤ Unit 55.2
13. 'It's only me!' she said, *opening / she opened* the door. ➤ Unit 55.3
14. *Because he hadn't / Not having* kept his word, John felt ashamed. ➤ Unit 55.4
15. Objects *bought / buying* in junk shops can often be quite valuable. ➤ Unit 55.5
16. Their long-term plan was *the company / for the company* to expand into Asia. ➤ Unit 56.1
17. We often find that the larger sizes are the first ones *to sell / that sell.* ➤ Unit 56.2
18. Jim got to the station only *finding / to find* that the train had already left. ➤ Unit 56.3
19. 'Why don't you tell the police *which / what* you told me yesterday?' ➤ Unit 57.1
20. Now that we have Internet search engines, it *takes less time / doesn't take as long* to get information on obscure subjects. ➤ Unit 57.2

4 Check your answers on page 384. Then go to the unit for more information and practice.

Go online for a full diagnostic test

53 Relative clauses

Napoleon Bonaparte, **who was born in Corsica**, was France's greatest military leader.

1 Relative clauses and alternatives

A relative pronoun can be the subject or object of a relative clause:
Last week I saw that film ***which*** *won all the Oscars.* (subject = the film won the Oscars)
Last week I saw the film ***which*** *you made at college.* (object = you made the film)

To make the meaning clear, we usually put the relative clause as close as possible to the noun it refers to:
✗ ~~*You can buy this dish from your local supermarket, which is made from organic wheat.*~~
✓ *You can buy this dish,* ***which is made from organic wheat****, from your local supermarket.*

Relative clauses are not the only way to define or add information. Alternatives include:
People who have a complaint → people ***with a complaint*** (prepositional phrase ➤ Unit 54.4)
The man who lives downstairs → The man ***living downstairs*** (participle clause ➤ Unit 55.1/2)
The first person who helped me → The first person ***to help me*** (infinitive clause ➤ Unit 56.1)

2 Defining relative clauses

A defining relative clause identifies or classifies a noun or pronoun in the main clause.
IDENTIFYING *Is this the book* ***that you were looking for****?*
CLASSIFYING *Would all those* ***who have booked dinner*** *please go into the restaurant?*

The defining relative clause gives information which is necessary for the sense of the sentence. In the first example above, *Is this the book?* does not convey the full meaning of the whole sentence, i.e. the specific book that you were looking for.

We often use these clauses to describe an important quality of someone or something:
Van Gogh was an artist ***who used a lot of bold, vibrant colours****.*

⚠ In defining relative clauses we can omit the relative pronoun when it is the object of the relative clause, but NOT when it is the subject:
✗ ~~*I saw the film won all the Oscars.*~~ ✓ *I saw the film you made at college.*

In American English *that* is more common than *which* or *who* in defining relative clauses.

Relative clauses with introductory *it* ➤ Unit 75.2

3 Non-defining relative clauses

A non-defining relative clause gives extra information about a noun or pronoun in the main clause (or about the whole clause), but it doesn't define or classify; the main clause still makes sense without it:

Napoleon Bonaparte was France's greatest military leader.
\+ EXTRA INFORMATION *Napoleon Bonaparte was born in Corsica.*
→ *Napoleon Bonaparte,* ***who was born in Corsica****, was France's greatest military leader.*

Napoleon lost the Battle of Waterloo in 1815.
\+ EXTRA INFORMATION *The fact that he lost the battle led to his exile.*
→ *Napoleon lost the Battle of Waterloo in 1815,* ***which led to his exile****.*

We can also use non-defining relative clauses to show consecutive actions:
*Heskey passed the ball to Owen, **who scored a magnificent goal**.*

We always use a relative pronoun, e.g. *which, who,* to introduce non-defining relative clauses:
✗ ~~*Last year's winner presented the cup, each holder keeps for the year.*~~
✓ *Last year's winner presented the cup, **which** each holder keeps for the year.*

However, we don't use *that* in the same way:
✗ ~~*This offer, that will not be repeated, must end next week.*~~

4 Defining or non-defining relative clause?

Compare:

DEFINING *The natives who traded with the settlers retained their land.*
This answers the question 'Which natives retained their land?' The answer is 'the ones who traded with the settlers'. It identifies or defines particular natives and this means that some of the natives probably didn't trade with the settlers and therefore lost their land.

NON-DEFINING *The natives, who traded with the settlers, retained their land.*
This sentence means 'The natives retained their land.' It doesn't identify particular natives, so it means that all the natives retained their land.

In written English the use of commas shows these differences.

- In non-defining clauses we use a comma to separate the relative clause from the rest of the sentence.
- In defining relative clauses we don't use commas at all.

 Pronunciation ➤ 1.16

The use of commas also reflects the way we say the two types of relative clause. In defining relative clauses, there is no pause between the main clause and the relative clause:
We asked for the lovely double room which had a sea view.

Although we don't often use non-defining relative clauses in speech, when we do there is usually a falling intonation at the end of the main clause:
We asked for the lovely double room (↘), which had a sea view.

5 Comment clauses

We can add a non-defining relative clause to the end of a sentence to make a comment about the information (not the noun) in the main clause. Unlike most non-defining relative clauses, comment clauses are common in spoken English.

FACT *Winston Churchill lost the 1945 election.*
COMMENT *People didn't expect this.*
→ *Winston Churchill lost the 1945 election, **which was rather unexpected**.*

In conversation, we can use a comment clause to add our opinion:
A *We had to wait for over an hour to see the doctor.*
B ***Which is outrageous!***

⚠ We use *which*, NOT *who, whose, that* or *it* to introduce a comment clause within a sentence:
✗ ~~*Harold never phones before visiting, that is annoying.*~~
✓ *Harold never phones before visiting, **which is annoying**.*

In writing we always put a comma before *which*, and in speech there is usually a falling intonation at the end of the main clause.

Practice

1 Choose the correct or most likely meaning, A or B.

1 I read a book while I was waiting at the airport, which was very boring.
A The book was boring. B Waiting at the airport was boring.
2 The members of the team, who had sponsors, flew to the championships in Ottawa.
A All the members of the team flew to Ottawa.
B Some of the members of the team didn't fly to Ottawa.
3 It's the only hotel in the town that has free wireless Internet access.
A There are several hotels in the town. B There is only one hotel in the town.
4 I had a plate of pasta at the new pizzeria restaurant, which was enormous.
A The plate of pasta was enormous. B The restaurant was enormous.
5 The students who passed the test received a prize.
A All the students received a prize. B Some of the students didn't receive a prize.
6 My flatmate, who is unemployed, often struggles to pay the rent.
A I have one flatmate. B I have several flatmates.

2 Match each headline 1–6 with a sentence from A–G. Using each pair, write one sentence containing a relative clause, as in the example. Use the present perfect tense in the main clause and add commas where necessary.

A They were grounded by the cloud of volcanic ash.
B They have been studying cancer genes for years. → 0
C It was held in The Hague.
D They oppose the current prime minister.
E It was in danger of closing through lack of funds.
F The man jumped off the Severn Bridge.
G It is threatened by oil from the leaking underground well in the Gulf of Mexico.

0 **Scientists discover new wonder-cure for cancer**
1 **BODY OF MAN FOUND IN RIVER SEVERN**
2 **Bangkok protesters bring city to a standstill**
3 GLOBAL WARMING CONFERENCE ENDS WITHOUT AGREEMENT
4 **US President visits area of Louisiana coastline**
5 **Flights across northern Europe resume**
6 **London Zoo remains open**

0 Scientists *who have been studying cancer genes for years have just discovered a new wonder-cure for cancer.*
1 The body of a man ……………………………………
2 In Bangkok, protesters ……………………………………
3 The global warming conference ……………………………………
4 The president of the United States ……………………………………
5 Flights across northern Europe ……………………………………
6 London Zoo ……………………………………

3 Combine the sentences, using relative clauses, as in the example. Omit the pronoun if possible. 4.03 Listen and check.

0 Craig's parents made him promise to be home by midnight. They are very strict.
Craig's parents, *who are very strict, made him promise to be home by midnight.*

1 The boss refused to discuss our grievances. I think that's outrageous.
The boss ....

2 Sunil's parents made him marry a distant relative. He'd never met her before.
Sunil's parents ....

3 One of my brothers lives in Los Angeles. I'm going to stay with him.
I'm going ....

4 We bought lots of furniture at IKEA. Some of it wouldn't fit in the car so we asked the shop to deliver those pieces on Friday.
On Friday, IKEA is going to deliver ....

5 Sue had seen a great dress in a magazine. She spent hours at the shops trying to find it.
Sue spent hours ....

6 Samantha Davis has started her own Internet company. She used to work in our London office.
Samantha Davis, ...

4 GRAMMAR IN USE Complete the text, using suitable relative pronouns. Then add six more missing commas, as in the example. 4.04 Listen and check.

The Iron Duke

Arthur Wellesley, first Duke of Wellington, is a leading military and political figure of the nineteenth century. He is best known as the commander of the British forces (1) .... helped to defeat Napoleon Bonaparte at the battle of Waterloo in 1815.
Wellesley, who was born in Ireland joined the British army in 1787. At first he worked for the Lord Lieutenant of Ireland, (2) .... was a friend of his brother Richard Wellesley. He also began a political career when he was elected as a member of parliament for Trim, (3) .... was a constituency in Ireland two years later.
Wellesley saw his first active military service in 1794 in the Netherlands. In 1796 he went to India to fight in the fourth Anglo-Mysore war which culminated in the battle of Seringapatam. But the most significant phase of Wellesley's career began in 1808, when he sailed to Portugal to lead the British army in the campaign against the French occupation of the Iberian peninsula. In 1813 he defeated Napoleon's brother Jacob, the man (4) .... had proclaimed himself king of Spain, at the battle of Vitoria. It was a significant victory (5) .... effectively liberated Spain from French occupation. As a reward for this success, Wellesley was given the title of Duke of Wellington by the British government.
Wellington's greatest victory came in Belgium in 1815. Together with Gebhard von Blücher who was the general leading the Prussian forces he finally defeated Napoleon at Waterloo, in Belgium. The victory brought an end to the war (6) .... had ravaged Europe for almost twenty years. Wellington returned to London as a national hero and resumed his political career serving as prime minister from 1828 to 1830.

54 Pronouns, adverbs and prepositions in relative clauses

Although gangster Al Capone was responsible for a number of murders and extortion rackets in 1930s Chicago, the crime **for which he was eventually tried and imprisoned** was tax evasion.

1 Relative pronouns

This chart lists relative pronouns and how they can be used:

PRONOUNS	USED FOR	SUBJECT	OBJECT	DEFINING	NON-DEFINING
who[1]	people, animals	✓	✓	✓	✓
whom[2]	people	✗	✓	✓	✓
which[3]	objects, animals	✓	✓	✓	✓
that[4]	people, objects, animals	✓	✓	✓	✗
whose	relationships, possessions	✓	✓	✓	✓
no pronoun[5]	people, things, animals	✗	✓	✓	✗

[1] We can use *who* to refer to animals when they are known individuals, e.g. domestic pets: *Is Sheba the cat* **who** *was run over and nearly killed last year?*
[2] *Whom* is formal and we rarely use it in speech. We now mainly use *whom* after prepositions (see **54.2**).
[3] We always use *which* (not *who*) to refer to inanimate objects. (For *which* to introduce a comment clause ➤ Unit 53.5).
[4] In spoken English we can use *that* or *who* to refer to people.
[5] (For information on omitting pronouns in object defining relative clauses ➤ Unit 53.2).

ACADEMIC ENGLISH In formal and academic English we use *which* rather than *that* in defining relative clauses:
This report is based on the survey **which** *was conducted by Shering and Beecham.*

We can also use *whose* to refer to inanimate objects:
It would only be possible to colonise planets **whose atmosphere** *contained enough oxygen to sustain human life.* (= the atmosphere of which)

2 Relative clauses with prepositions

We can use prepositions with relative pronouns. Their position depends on formality:

	INFORMAL / NEUTRAL	FORMAL
My grandparents **lived in** *the house but they didn't own it.*	*My grandparents didn't own the house (***which / that***) they lived* **in**.	*Our clients, Mr and Mrs Thompson, did not own the house* **in which** *they lived.*
I'd like some information about an insurance claim. I **referred to** *it in an email.*	*Do you have any information about the insurance claim (***that / which***) I referred* **to** *in my email?*	*The insurance claim* **to which** *you referred does not appear to be in our records.*

We do not put a preposition before the relative pronoun *that*:
✗ ~~*They didn't own the house in that they lived.*~~

If we put a preposition before *who*, the pronoun always becomes *whom*:
The patients, **among whom** *there were several immigrants, had to undergo a series of tests.*

Compare:
The people **who this report is addressed to** *will have to consider its proposals carefully.*
The people **to whom this report is addressed** *will have to consider its proposals carefully.*

3 Relative clauses with *where*, *when*, and *why*

We can use these adverbs to introduce or replace relative clauses about places, times, etc:

ADVERB	USE IN RELATIVE CLAUSES	EXAMPLES	
*where**	instead of *which/that* + a preposition to describe places	*The house **that** Dickens wrote his later novels **in** is now a school.* *This is the line **on which** you sign your name.*	*The house **where** Dickens wrote his later novels is now a school.* *This is the line **where** you sign your name.*
when	instead of *that* or *on which* to describe times, days, years, etc.	*I remember – it was the day **that/on which** the heatwave started.*	*I remember – it was the day **when** the heatwave started.*
why	instead of *for* + *which*, (usually with the noun *reason*)	*High taxation is often the main reason **for which** governments fall.*	*High taxation is often (the main reason) **why** governments fall.*

* In informal English we also use *where* with the meaning *in which* to describe a situation:
*Have you seen the episode **where** the Hoppers' farm is destroyed in a fire?*
*I once saw an accident on the motorway **where** three people ended up going to hospital.*

It is possible to use *where*, *when* and *why* without the noun to which they refer:
*It's (the place) **where** that music festival is held every year.*
*I can't remember (the time) **when** I got home last night.*
*She's hyperactive. That's (the reason) **why** she can't concentrate.*

We don't include a preposition in *when* or *where* clauses:
✗ ~~*That's the house where I grew up in.*~~

4 Prepositional phrases

In some cases we can use prepositional phrases to replace relative clauses:

with	instead of *that/which/who* + *have* to describe possession	*Passengers **who have first-class tickets** can board now.*	*Passengers **with first-class tickets** can board now.*
in/at/on, etc.	instead of *which/that* + *be* + preposition to describe position	*I've never seen the furniture **which is in the attic**.*	*I've never seen the furniture **in the attic**.*

what to introduce noun clauses ➤ Unit 57.1

5 Modifying relative pronouns

We often use modifiers such as *all of* and *many of* before *which* or *whom* in a non-defining relative clause to refer to the subject or object of the clause:
*The supermarket withdrew all of its jars of tomato puree, **several of which** were found to contain fragments of glass.*
*The renewable energy grants, **half of which** are provided by local government, will be available from September.*
*The college entered over a hundred students for the exam, **all of whom** passed.*
*We interviewed fourteen applicants for the post, **none of whom** we thought suitable.*

6 *whichever*, *whenever*, etc.

In defining relative clauses we can modify the pronoun or adverb with *-ever* to give the meaning of *anything*, *anyone*, *anywhere*, etc:
*Use **whichever phone** you want – they all have outside lines.* (= any phone that)
*Invite **whoever** you like to the party.* (= any person who)
*You can put the photo **wherever** you think it looks best. I don't mind.* (= in any place where)

Practice

1 Choose the correct words in *italics*. Sometimes two or three options are possible.

1 This is the palace *in which* / *that* / *where* King Philip II lived and died.

2 Julius Caesar was the Roman general *whom* / *which* / *who* conquered Gaul.

3 Queen Victoria is the only British monarch *who had* / *with* / *whose* nine children.

4 9th November 1989 was the day *on which* / *when* / *that* the Berlin Wall fell.

5 Delfina Potocka was the Polish noblewoman *for whom* / *for who* / *which* Chopin wrote his famous Minute Waltz.

6 Genghis Khan was a ruler *of whom* / *which his* / *whose* empire stretched from China to the Middle East.

2 Rewrite the underlined parts of each sentence, using a word or phrase from the box and any other words necessary.

into which ~~at which~~ many of which none of which whichever when whenever why where

0 There are several delightful hotels in the area <u>that you may wish to stop at</u>. ......*at which you may wish to stop.*......

1 All the towels are clean so you can use <u>any of the towels that you like</u>. ....

2 Do you know the reason <u>for her disappearance</u>? ....

3 This is the spot <u>at which Lady Jane Grey was executed</u>. ....

4 We looked at five or six second-hand cars, <u>but there weren't any that were suitable</u>. ....

5 The children had no idea of the adventure <u>that their curiosity would lead them into</u>. ....

6 In Scotland, December 31st is a day <u>on which everybody has a party</u>. ....

7 You can come and visit us <u>any time you want</u>. ....

8 They have a great range of designer jackets – <u>many of them are quite inexpensive</u>. ....

3 GRAMMAR IN USE **Complete the article with suitable relative pronouns or adverbs, as in the example. Use one word only. 4.05 Listen and check.**

> TV CHOICE >

JACK OF HEARTS

9.00 p.m., BBC 1

Jack of Hearts is a new six-part drama series (0) ...*that*.... comes to our screens this week. It has been given the prime Wednesday evening slot, (1) .... shows that the network has faith in its latest creation. The first episode opens to a scene (2) .... a young man is being chased. He stops at a phone box and makes a desperate call. This calls wakes up a man (3) .... most viewers will recognise as Keith Allen – an actor (4) .... characters are usually villains on the wrong side of the law. This time, however, he is playing a hard-pressed probation officer with a complicated professional and personal life, both of (5) .... form the main themes of the series. The writers have managed to find a different angle on his personal problems. At the centre of these problems is his stepdaughter, for (6) .... he attempts to keep the household together. His relationship with his wife, (7) .... seems to be a short-tempered, moody woman, is further threatened later in the series (8) .... she joins the staff of a college at (9) .... she is faced with a problem from her past. Thus the ground is prepared in this first episode for a series (10) .... may help to lift British summertime TV out of its regular slump.

4 GRAMMAR IN USE **Find thirteen more mistakes in the text and correct them, as in the example. 4.06 Listen and check.**

Table of Contents EDIT | SAVE | PRINT | E-MAIL | A+ A-

tourism

- **Tourism today** is an industry *which* has grown so much in recent years that in many countries it provides the greatest single contribution to the country's revenue. But is it always a good thing? Mass tourism which is a relatively recent phenomenon, brings with it a whole raft of problems. First, it means that a country's economy may rely on an industry who is wholly seasonal, with the consequence that the huge numbers of people work in tourism during the season have no income during the rest of the year. Some find wherever work they can, but others may look for support from a government is already receiving lower revenues.
- **Second**, it is true that in many countries tourists are destroying the very sights where they flock to see. They take home pieces of an ancient monument or of a coral reef which will gradually result in erosion of the attractions and therefore of the industry. While this kind of destruction may be wholly unintentional, a certain type of tourist which wants only a 'good time' can be very destructive in a different way: they behave badly, pick fights and often damage the hotel rooms where they are staying in. Obviously, it is then this behaviour by that the local community judges all members of that nationality, creating enmity rather than fostering empathy, whose should be one of the main advantages of tourism.
- **Finally**, there are many places tourism is threatening a well-established way of life: people that whose livelihoods traditionally come from older industries, such as agriculture or fishing, are finding new jobs and wealth in the overdeveloped tourist regions, but at what cost? It is sometimes difficult to understand the reasons which for countries become involved with tourism.

55 Participle clauses

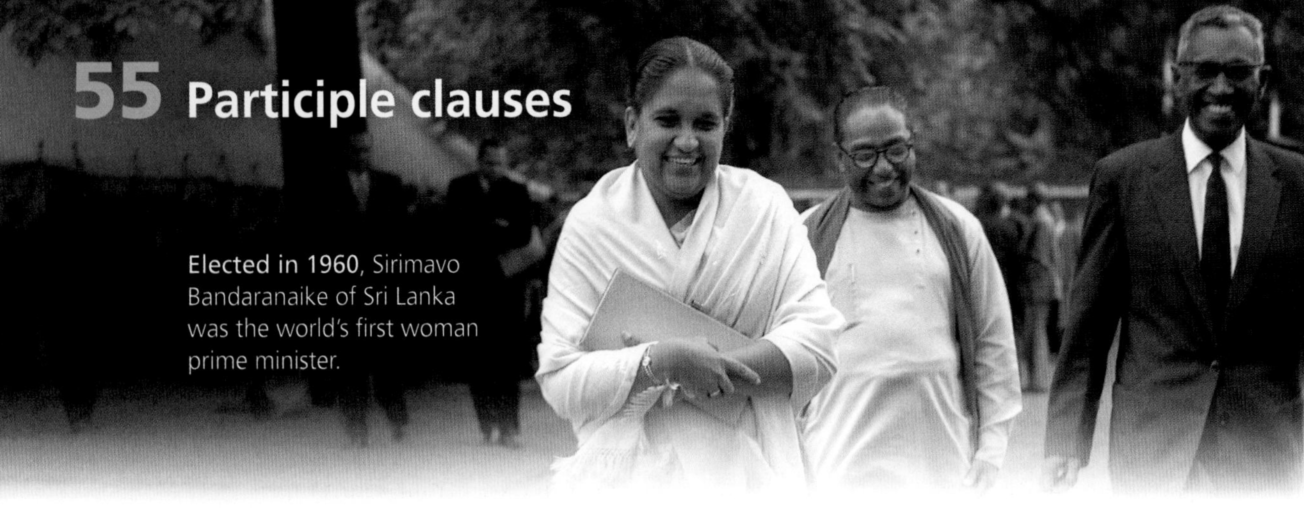

Elected in 1960, Sirimavo Bandaranaike of Sri Lanka was the world's first woman prime minister.

1 Forms

There are several different participle forms in participle clauses:

	ACTIVE PARTICIPLE	PASSIVE PARTICIPLE
simple		*(not) repaired*
continuous	*(not) repairing*	*(not) being repaired*
perfect	*(not) having repaired*	*(not) having been repaired*

***Using** a password, I opened the email application.* (Active: I used a password.)
***Used** with a password, the application offers complete security.* (Passive: the application is used by someone.)

State verbs, e.g. *be, own, possess* (➤ Unit 25.1), can be used in participle clauses:
✗ ~~*Yolanda is rich and is owning six homes.*~~ ✓ *Yolanda is rich, **owning six homes**.*

2 Positioning and relationship with the subject

Participle clauses give information about a noun in the main clause, so they do not usually contain a subject. The subject of the main clause acts as the subject of the participle clause:
***Moaning with pain**, the victim was examined by a young doctor.* (The victim was moaning.)

 A participle clause at the beginning of a sentence cannot refer to the object of the main clause:
✗ ~~*Moaning with pain, a young doctor examined the victim.*~~
(This would mean that the young doctor was moaning, not the victim.)

In formal written English the participle clause can have a subject which is related to the subject of the main clause, but which isn't exactly the same:

***Horns locked**, the two stags struggle for supremacy.* (The horns belong to the stags.)
*I crouched in the alleyway, **my eyes straining** in the darkness.* (My eyes are part of me.)

For rules about subjects and objects in reduced relative clauses ➤ Unit 55.5

3 Clauses of time and sequence with *-ing* participle

We usually use these clauses when two actions happen at around the same time:
***Turning the corner**, we saw the hospital in front of us.*
(= As we were turning the corner we saw the hospital in front of us.)

In written English an *-ing* participle clause often describes the setting or background:
***Living in Los Angeles**, Brad was one of those ever-optimistic movie wannabes.*
***Standing alone in the desert**, the huge pyramid dominated the landscape.*

If one action happened before another, we usually use a perfect participle clause for the earlier action. This can go before or after the main clause:
Having finished his coffee, *Versace began to walk back to his house.*
= *Versace began to walk back to his house,* ***having finished his coffee***.

We can also use prepositions in front of *-ing* participles:
On entering *the darkened room, we noticed a strange figure huddled in the corner.*
(= As we entered the room ...)
After swallowing *the pill, Edward lay down and tried to get some rest.*

4 Participle clauses for reason, condition and result

Provided that the subject of BOTH clauses is the same, we can use participle clauses to replace clauses of reason, condition and result. We often do this in writing:

	FULL CLAUSE	PARTICIPLE PHRASE
reason[1]	*She will be unable to answer your queries because she is not qualified.* *As I hadn't been asked, I didn't really want to interfere.* *I had to borrow a set of keys from my landlord because I'd forgotten to take mine.*	***Not being qualified***, *she will be unable to answer your queries.* ***Not having been asked***, *I didn't really want to interfere.* ***Having forgotten to take my keys***, *I had to borrow a set from my landlord.*
condition	*If you treat it gently, the fabric should last for years.*	***If treated/Treated gently***, *the fabric should last for years.*
result[2]	*The corporation shut down the plant, with the result that many workers were left unemployed.*	*The corporation shut down the plant,* ***leaving many workers unemployed***.

[1] We often use the perfect participle because a reason or cause usually comes before a result.
[2] Note that the result is often not intended: *I stayed at work rather late, missing my last train home.*

5 Reduced relative clauses

Participle clauses are an efficient way of giving more information about a noun and can often be used to replace a defining relative clause (➤ Unit 53.2). We call these reduced relative clauses. Compare these examples:
The man ***who lives upstairs*** *is very noisy.* (defining relative clause)
→ *The man* ***living upstairs*** *is very noisy.* (active participle phrase)
They haven't identified the body ***which was found in the Thames***. (defining relative clause)
→ *They haven't identified the body* ***found in the Thames***. (passive participle phrase)

Unlike participle clauses, in reduced relative clauses we put the noun we are describing in front of the participle and we do not use commas to separate the clause from the rest of the sentence.

We can only use participles in this way when the subject of the main clause and the relative clause is the same. We cannot use a reduced relative clause if there is another subject between the relative pronoun and the verb:
✗ ~~*The house living in is really old.*~~ ✓ *The house* ***which we live in*** *is really old.*

In reduced relative clauses we only use an *-ing* form when we are describing a continuing action or situation. We can't use an *-ing* form for a single completed action or with state verbs:
✗ ~~*The thief taking her bag has been arrested.*~~
✓ *The thief* ***who took*** *her bag has been arrested.* (single completed action)
✗ ~~*The police are investigating the man owning the burnt-out factory.*~~
✓ *The police are investigating the man* ***who owns*** *the burnt-out factory.* (state verb)

We use commas around reduced non-defining relative clauses:
The college, ***founded in the nineteenth century***, *became a university in the 1930s.*

 Pronunciation ➤ 1.17

Practice

1 Choose the best participle forms from A–G to complete the sentences. There is one extra form. 4.07 Listen and check.

A giving	C not giving	E being given	G given
B not having been given	D having been given	F having given	

1 The best part ..... to another actor, Josh felt unwilling to continue in the show.
2 I've always treasured the watch ..... to me on my eighteenth birthday.
3 The police officers stood at either end of the hallway, ... Ray no chance of escape.
4 ..... our tickets to the attendant, we were ushered into the antechamber of the tomb.
5 We are dividing up the grant according to need, the largest amount ..... to the homeless.
6 ..... one month's notice by the landlord, the tenant was able to stay on in the house.

2 Use the information in the chart to write sentences, using a participle clause, as in the example.

	action/reason	result/further information
0	Hilary got a job in a café.	She was able to make lots of new friends.
1	I wasn't very fit.	I was unable to finish the marathon.
2	I left my keys at the office.	I couldn't get into my flat last night.
3	Manuela hasn't got a visa.	She can't travel to the USA.
4	They got home early.	They found the place had been burgled.
5	The old house had been restored by experts.	It regained its former glory.
6	Dave and Maria's children had left home.	They felt they should move to a smaller house.

0 *Having got a job in a café, Hilary was able to make lots of new friends.*
1 ....
2 ....
3 ....
4 ....
5 ....
6 ....

3 Rewrite the following sentences, replacing the underlined phrase with a suitable participle clause, as in the example.

0 As they hadn't been arrested, they were able to leave the police station.
Not having been arrested, they were able to leave the police station.

1 She fell asleep while she sat in the armchair.
....

2 Because I can speak Finnish I managed to follow their conversation.
....

3 So far nobody has claimed the money which we discovered under the floorboards.
....

4 After he had moved out, Danny found it difficult to find a nice place to stay.
....

5 If you leave it for too long, oil paint will form a skin.

....

6 The sea was very rough, which made me feel sick.

....

7 As I am not very good with figures I'll let you do the accounts.

....

8 This is a house which has been built to last forever.

....

4 GRAMMAR IN USE **Complete the text with participle clauses, using the words in brackets. If a participle clause is not possible, use a relative clause. 4.08 Listen and check.**

Amelia Earhart

AMELIA EARHART GREW UP IN KANSAS, in a middle-class family. (0) *Graduating from high school in 1916* (graduate / from high school in 1916), she began her first job at Spadna Military Hospital, (1) .... (work / as a nursing assistant). Most of the patients were soldiers (2) .... (wound / in World War I). In 1918 she contracted Spanish influenza and became a patient herself. Later, (3) .... (recover), she travelled to California to join her parents, (4) .... (move there). (5) .... (visit / an airfield) in Long Beach in 1920, Amelia was offered a ten-minute flight with her father and she fell in love with the idea of becoming a pilot. (6) .... (work / as a photographer), a truck driver and stenographer, she managed to save up the $1,000 that it cost to take flying lessons. On May 15th, 1923, she was granted a pilot's licence.

On June 17th, 1928, Amelia flew from Newfoundland and arrived at Burry Port in Wales 20 hours later, (7) .... (become / the first woman) to fly across the Atlantic Ocean. When Earhart and her companions returned, they were given a reception by the President, (8) .... (receive them) at the White House. Earhart was determined to do the flight again, but this time on her own. On May 20th, 1932, at the age of thirty-two, she set off from Newfoundland, (9) .... (land / at Culmore), Northern Ireland fifteen hours later.

Early in 1937, (10) .... (buy / a Lockheed Electra 10E), Earhart started planning a round-the-world flight. She left Miami on June 1st, (11) .... (head / south-east). After stops in South America and elsewhere the plane landed in New Guinea on June 29th, (12) .... (cover about 35,000 kilometres). The final part of the journey would be over the Pacific Ocean. (13) .... (leave / New Guinea) on July 2nd, Earhart and her navigator Fred Noonan headed for Howland Island in the Pacific. But their plane failed to arrive and no trace of Earhart was ever found. For years people have advanced theories about her disappearance but the most likely is that the plane, (14) .... (run out / of fuel), simply crashed into the sea.

Famous Aviators

56 Infinitive clauses

1 Form and use

An infinitive clause can act as the subject or complement of the verb *be*:
***To reach the top** is their aim. Their aim is **to reach the top**.*

We use *for* with an infinitive clause if the subject of the infinitive is not the same as the subject of the sentence:
✗ ~~*Jack's aim is his team to win.*~~ ✓ *Jack's aim is **for his team to win**.*

We can use the following infinitive forms:

	ACTIVE INFINITIVE	PASSIVE INFINITIVE
simple	*(not) to mend*	*(not) to be mended*
continuous	*(not) to be mending*	*(not) to be being mended*
perfect	*(not) to have mended*	*(not) to have been mended*

We use the perfect infinitive for an event that happened before the event in the main clause:
*Her greatest claim to fame is **to have been chosen for the last Olympic squad**.*
(She is famous now because she was chosen in the past.)

Sentences with an infinitive clause as their subject can sound rather formal. In speech we usually prefer impersonal *it* (➤ Unit 43.5) or an *-ing* form (➤ Unit 46.1):

To keep up a friendship is difficult. → ***It's** difficult to keep up a friendship.*
***Keeping up** a friendship is difficult.*

FORMALITY CHECK In spoken English we can also use some specific expressions followed by an infinitive clause to comment on the information in the main clause:
***To tell the truth**, I found the exhibition disappointing. I'm not keen on spicy food, **to be honest**.*
***To cut a long story short**, he's left home.*

2 Defining clauses

We can use an infinitive clause to identify or classify a person or thing in the main clause, in a similar way to a defining relative clause (➤ Unit 53.2). We can do this after a superlative, an ordinal number (e.g. *first*), or *one, next, last* and *only*:
***The youngest person to enter the programme** was just fourteen.*
(= The youngest person that entered ...)
*The window seat is usually **the first one to be taken**.* (= the first one which is taken)
*Linda was **the only one to stay for the whole performance**.* (= the only one who stayed ...)

We don't usually use an infinitive clause to replace relative clauses containing modal verbs, because the meaning would not be clear:
[*He's the only player to save the team from defeat.*] (could mean 'who saved' or 'who will save')
✓ *He's the only player **who might save** the team from defeat.*

3 Purpose and result clauses

We often use an infinitive clause to describe a deliberate purpose or aim. This is the infinitive of purpose (➤ Unit 45.4):
*Davy took a year out **to travel and see the world**.*

ACADEMIC ENGLISH Infinitives of purpose are common in academic English:
*Dickins ended each episode with a cliffhanger **to encourage readers to buy the next edition**.*

We can use an infinitive to describe a result or something unexpected, especially with *only* and verbs such as *find, discover, realise*, etc. (➤ Unit 45.4):
*Mike rushed out, **only to realise he'd forgotten his keys**.*
*Lizzie rejoined her friends, **only to discover that Mr Darcy had left**.*

Infinitives after verbs, nouns and adjectives ➤ Units 45 and 46

Practice

1 Complete the famous quotations, using suitable infinitive forms of verbs from the box, as in the example.

not be do forgive ~~love~~ live not take

0 'It is better ......*to have loved*...... and lost than never to have loved at all.' (Lord Tennyson)
1 'To err is human, ..., divine.' (Alexander Pope)
2 'To be, or ...., that is the question.' (William Shakespeare)
3 'One never notices what has been done; one can only see what remains ....' (Marie Curie)
4 'One should eat ...., not live to eat.' (Molière)
5 'An intelligence test sometimes shows a man how smart he would have been .... it.' (Laurence J Peter)

2 GRAMMAR IN USE Find and correct five more mistakes in this text which should be replaced with infinitive forms. 4.09 Listen and check.

In the middle of the seventeenth century Louis XIV decided to build a vast new garden ~~surround it~~ *to surround* his new palace at Versailles. The first person to be asking to look at the site was his favourite architect, Andre Le Nôtre. Le Nôtre arrived at Versailles only he discovered a thick forest with uneven ground and an inadequate water supply. It was a great honour to had been choose for such a task, but it is not difficult to understand Le Nôtre's reluctance to take on such a challenge – the main water basin alone is 1.5 kilometres long, and there are dozens of fountains, statues and avenues. It was the first garden that designed on such a large scale, and took more than forty years for building. When Le Nôtre died, in 1700, the garden was still incomplete.

3 Complete the second sentence so it has a similar meaning to the first, using appropriate infinitive forms. 4.10 Listen and check.

1 The first person that arrives in the office in the mornings is usually Gary.
Gary is usually .... in the mornings.
2 Celia's major regret is that she had never made more of her musical abilities.
Never .... is Celia's major regret.
3 The company launched an advertising campaign with the aim of increasing its market share.
The company .... its market share.
4 Finding the old house in such a derelict state came as a great shock.
It came as .... in such a derelict state.
5 They will probably sell the ground floor flat first.
They expect the ground floor flat ....
6 The town hall was one of the few buildings that hadn't been destroyed in the earthquake.
The town hall was one of the few .... in the earthquake.

57 Noun clauses and other noun structures

Machiavelli is a well-known character from Italian political history, although he is more famous for **what he wrote** than for **what he did**.

1 Noun clauses

A noun clause can start with *that*, *if/whether* or a *wh-* word.
The clause acts like a noun:
Did you notice ***that she left early?*** (= Did you notice her early departure?)
He asked ***if I intended to leave.*** (= He asked my intentions.)
I'll never understand ***why he did it.*** (= I'll never understand his reasons [for doing it].)

These clauses are common in spoken English as noun phrases can sound rather formal:
Please inform us of your final decision. (formal)
Let us know ***if you want to go ahead.*** (informal)

Because a noun clause acts like a noun, it can be the subject or object of a verb:
What they did *doesn't interest me. I'm not interested in* ***what they did.***

We can use *what, where, when, why, who* and *how* to introduce a *wh-* noun clause:

noun phrase	*wh-* clause
I was quite shocked by his behaviour.	→ *I was quite shocked by what he did.*
The school isn't far from our home.	→ *The school isn't far from where we live.*
The label doesn't say the name of the painter.	→ *The label doesn't say who painted it.*

More on clauses with *where*, *when*, etc. ➤ Unit 54.3

What usually means *the thing(s) (that)*. We can use a *what* clause to replace a noun + defining relative clause if the noun we are referring to is clear from the context:
Tell us about ***the event (that) you witnessed.*** → *Tell us about* ***what you saw.***
I'm afraid ***the dish (that) I like*** *isn't on the menu.* → *I'm afraid* ***what I like*** *isn't on the menu.*

We don't include the noun in a *what* clause:
✗ ~~*It was the money what I wanted, not the fame.*~~
✓ *It was the money (that) I wanted, not the fame.*
OR *The money was* ***what I wanted,*** *not the fame.* (= the thing that I wanted)

2 Comparison clauses with nouns

We can compare nouns which refer to amounts by using *more, less* and *fewer*. A clause beginning with *than* can be added after the noun:
Now that we've built the extension, our house has a lot ***more space than*** *it used to.*
Property taxes usually produce ***less income than*** *customs duties do.*
Due to the congestion charge there are ***fewer cars*** *in central London than there were previously.*

We can also make superlative forms using *the most/the least/the fewest* + noun:
The most time *you should spend on the running machine is twenty minutes.*
The exam papers with ***the fewest mistakes*** *will gain the highest marks.*

We use *fewer/fewest* with plural nouns and *less/least* with uncountable nouns, although in casual speech ***less*** is sometimes used with both:
This checkout is for customers with ***fewer than*** *five* ***items.***
It would taste better if you used ***less salt than*** *you did this time.*
[*It doesn't seem very busy. Do you think there are* ***less people*** *here today* ***than*** *there are usually?*]

More on *less* ➤ Unit 14.2 More on *few* ➤ Unit 8.2

Practice

1 Complete each sentence with one word only. Do not use the same word more than once.

1 Modern cars use .... fuel than the old ones did.
2 I don't know her address – I've got no idea .... she lives these days.
3 If you want to pass the test, you'll have to make .... mistakes next time.
4 .... they did with the money is still a mystery.
5 Do you know .... the boss wants to see me?
6 Caroline never explained .... she made all that money.
7 Since his retirement Silvio has had .... time to spend in the garden.
8 I only voted for him because he was the .... irritating of the candidates.

2 GRAMMAR IN USE Replace each <u>underlined</u> phrase with a *wh-* noun clause, using the words in brackets, as in the example. 4.11 Listen and check.

Isaac Newton

In 1687 the English scientist Sir Isaac Newton published a book entitled *Mathematical Principles of Natural Philosophy*. At the time few people fully understood (0) <u>the suggestions in the book</u> (what/suggest). Nonetheless, the book was hugely influential and made Newton famous around the world, although fame was not (1) <u>his intention</u> (what/want). Newton's theories were based on mathematics and (2) <u>his observations of</u> (what/see) in the world around him. He noticed that all objects, heavy or light, fell to the ground. He wanted to explain (3) <u>the reasons for this</u> (why/happen). His theory of gravity provided a revolutionary explanation of (4) <u>the movement of different objects</u> (how/different objects / move). (5) <u>The ideas in his book</u> (what/write) became the basis for much of our understanding of physics and the processes which govern relationships between physical objects.

0 *what the book suggested*
1 ....
2 ....
3 ....
4 ....
5 ....

3 Find and correct six mistakes in these sentences. Tick (✓) the correct sentences.

1 It's raining so there are less children in the park than usual.
2 I couldn't believe the ridiculous reason what they gave for their behaviour.
3 I'll only accept that promotion if it pays more money than I'm getting now.
4 We weren't very close so we didn't hear that she said very clearly.
5 You should see where she lives – it's amazing!
6 It's quite a good novel, but very similar to the one what he published two years ago.
7 Who she married hardly matters any more, does it?
8 Darren won because he took the fewest time to complete the task.
9 The explanation what the suspect gave didn't convince the detective.
10 Let's meet at the Luna café – it's close to where I work.

Review MODULE 12

1 UNITS 53 AND 54 **Correct the mistakes in these sentences.**

1 Emperor Charles V who ruled over Spain in the sixteenth century had only one son.
2 That's the vintage car she's spent so much money on it.
3 I've thrown away most of the clothes wore when I was a teenager.
4 Do you know the woman who her children are always playing football in the street?
5 That's a question which for the company has no answer, I'm afraid.
6 The director refused to take my call which was really annoying.
7 What you need is the cable, that connects the computer to the printer.
8 You can collect the new bag, when you see my sister, which cost a lot of money.
9 It isn't very clear to who you are referring in this recent correspondence.
10 Do you have any idea for why she hasn't responded to our various offers?

2 UNITS 55 AND 56 **Use infinitive and/or participle clauses to rewrite this extract from a TV listings magazine in a more natural way. Change the underlined parts, as in the example. You may have to change the word order.**

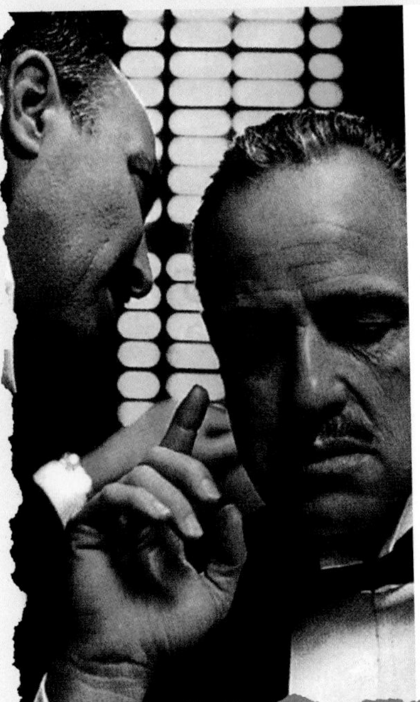

Movie of the week

The Godfather

(0) It dates from 1971 and (1) was directed by Francis Ford Coppola, *The Godfather* won three Oscars. (2) The film lasts almost three hours and is Shakespearean in its scope and ambition. It is the story of a New York mafia family (3) which is headed by Marlon Brando as the 'godfather'.

Although Brando has the title role it is Al Pacino, (4) who plays his troubled son and heir Michael, who steals the show in a masterly performance.

(5) As he struggles to reconcile his distaste for crime and brutality with his sense of family honour and duty, Pacino's character embodies the moral dilemma at the heart of the movie.

(6) The director intersperses long scenes of family life with shorter sequences of extreme violence in order to achieve his aim of taking the audience on an emotional rollercoaster ride.

(7) Because it was shot in explicit detail, this violence may shock some viewers. But anyone (8) who is prepared to put up with this will enjoy a unique dramatic experience. In fact, for many people *The Godfather* is the greatest American film (9) which had been made in the 1970s.

Dating from 1971 ....

3 UNITS 55, 56 AND 57 **Complete the second sentence so it has a similar meaning to the first. Use three to six words, including the word in brackets.**

1 Martin is always a great asset at any party because he is so charming. (being)
.... always a great asset at any party.

2 This is the only hotel in which they don't charge for Internet access. (to)
This is the only hotel .... for Internet access.

3 I took a short computing course following my graduation from college. (having)
.... a short computing course.

4 I'll never forget the things that I saw that night. (what)
.... is impossible to forget.

5 As she threw open the windows, Mary said, 'There's nothing like fresh air! (throwing)
'There's nothing like fresh air!' .... the windows.

6 There wouldn't be as many accidents if traffic was reduced. (less)
If there was .... as many accidents.

4 ALL UNITS **Choose the correct word or phrase, A, B or C, for each gap.**

TalkingAboutHistory.org
The forum for history students

Posts | Search | Contact Us

Amanda

I'm writing an essay on Catherine the Great. Can anyone give me any information? I know she was one of Russian's greatest rulers, but was she the first woman (1) ..... Russia?
14.30 Wednesday 9 May

Carlos

Catherine wasn't Russian, she was German, (2) ..... is rather surprising. She married The Grand Duke Paul, (3) ..... was the grandson of Peter the Great. Her husband became Tsar in 1762 but died shortly afterwards, (4) ..... Catherine as the ruling empress.
15.21 Wednesday 9 May

Tasmin

I've been to the palace (5) ..... she lived – the Catherine Palace in Tsarskoye Selo. It certainly gives you an idea of (6) ..... powerful she was. Catherine was a great patron of the arts. The huge art collection (7) ..... during her lifetime is now the basis of the Hermitage Museum in St Petersburg.
17.15 Wednesday 9 May

Leo

Catherine was a very important political figure in the eighteenth century. She started as a liberal, (8) ..... more conservative as she grew older. She made important changes to the system of government but (9) ..... Russia's borders was her main ambition. Catherine wasn't the only woman (10) ..... Russia; there were several other powerful women leaders in Russian history.
09.42 Thursday 10 May

1 A ruling B ruled C to rule
2 A that B which C what
3 A whom B who C that
4 A leaving B who left C that left
5 A which B where C that
6 A what B how much C how
7 A built up B building up C build up
8 A became B becoming C to become
9 A expanding B the expansion C expanded
10 A governing B governed C to govern

MODULE

13 Conjunctions and linking expressions

Before you start

1 Review these intermediate grammar points and check you know them.

Sentences and clauses

1 A sentence consists of one or more clauses; in writing, it starts with a capital letter and ends with a full stop:

2 In the example above, clause 1 is an independent or main clause – it has meaning of its own and can stand alone. Clause 2 is a dependent or subordinate clause – it has meaning only in relation to the main clause it accompanies.

Ways of linking

1 We link sentences and clauses with conjunctions (linking words that join two things). Coordinating conjunctions (*and, but, or*) link clauses of equal value, usually main clauses:
We can pay in one lump sum. We can pay in instalments.
→ *We can pay in one lump sum* **or** *we can pay in instalments.*
We can put either of the clauses first:
We can pay in instalments **or** *we can pay in one lump sum.*

2 We often want to link clauses that are not of equal value, i.e. a main clause and a subordinate clause. A subordinate clause always starts with a subordinating conjunction, e.g. *when, if, although*. The conjunction indicates the type of relationship between the main and the subordinate clause:

	MAIN CLAUSE	SUBORDINATE CLAUSE	
time	*Call me*	*when*	*you get home.*
condition	*Wait here*	*if*	*you want to see a supervisor.*
concession	*He passed*	*although*	*he'd hardly studied.*

Some subordinating conjunctions, e.g. *since*, can express different relationships, such as
- time: *We've lived here* **since** *we got married.*
- reason: *We've postponed the meeting* **since** *you're so busy this week.*

3 When we want to show a relationship between two sentences rather than two clauses within one sentence, we use a linking adverbial. We usually put this at the start of the second sentence, followed by a comma separating it from the sentence:
There was an unprecedented response to our advert. ***Therefore****, I am afraid we are taking your application no further.*
We can use linking adverbials to show different relationships such as
- time: *Our next stop is the island of Lefkas, where you have two hours to visit the port and have lunch.* ***After that****, we will be sailing to the smaller Ionian island of Ithaki ...*
- contrast: *Several students didn't obtain the required 40 percent in the exam needed for an overall pass.* ***Nevertheless****, they were awarded a pass grade on second marking.*

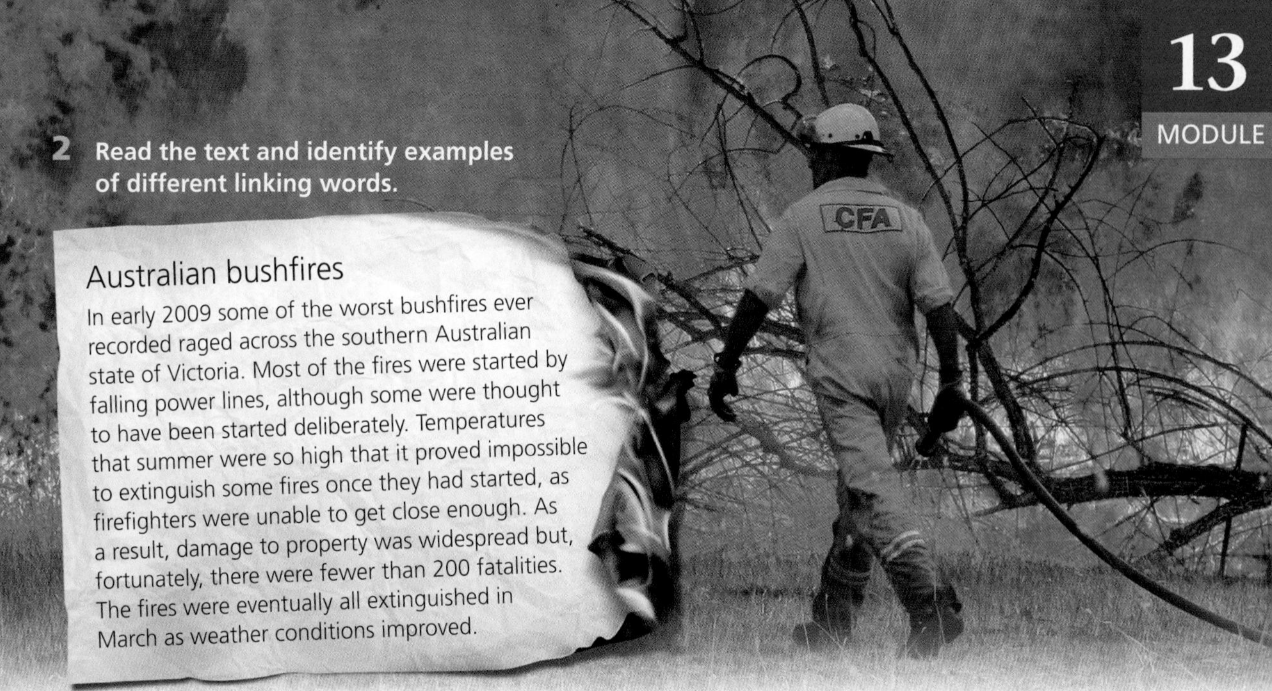

2 Read the text and identify examples of different linking words.

Australian bushfires

In early 2009 some of the worst bushfires ever recorded raged across the southern Australian state of Victoria. Most of the fires were started by falling power lines, although some were thought to have been started deliberately. Temperatures that summer were so high that it proved impossible to extinguish some fires once they had started, as firefighters were unable to get close enough. As a result, damage to property was widespread but, fortunately, there were fewer than 200 fatalities. The fires were eventually all extinguished in March as weather conditions improved.

3 Complete the diagnostic test below. Choose the correct words in *italics*. If both options are correct, choose both.

1. The college neither acknowledged my application nor *did / didn't* they invite me for interview. ➤ Unit 58.1
2. Will you let me know *immediately / as soon as* the hospital contacts you? ➤ Unit 59.1
3. 'I don't understand why the interview was cancelled.' 'It was *since / because* the director was unable to attend.' ➤ Unit 59.2
4. The flag is raised *so that / so as to* indicate that the monarch is present. ➤ Unit 59.3
5. Is this package *enough light / light enough* to send by normal post? ➤ Unit 59.4
6. We will exchange sale goods *if / as long as* they are returned within seven days. ➤ Unit 59.5
7. Nick hardly knows Al but he talks about him as if they *are / were* friends. ➤ Unit 59.6
8. Visitors to tropical resorts still stay out in the sun too long, *even though / even* they have had plenty of warning about the dangers of the sun's rays. ➤ Unit 60.2
9. *Ideal / Ideal though* it may appear, always obtain a structural survey on a property. ➤ Unit 60.2
10. *Despite / Though* she was a woman, Marie Curie made a successful career for herself in a male-dominated world. ➤ Unit 60.3
11. *In spite of / Although* the fact that the machine was under guarantee, the company refused to replace it. ➤ Unit 60.3
12. The flight took over eight hours. *Then, / After,* we had a three-hour coach transfer. ➤ Unit 61.2
13. All the actors seem totally relaxed when they come onto the stage, but *beforehand, / before that,* they are almost sick with anxiety. ➤ Unit 61.2
14. The number of skiers on the slopes contributed to last season's avalanche. *Consequently, / For this reason,* numbers will be restricted this year. ➤ Unit 61.4
15. The plumber charged $100 for an hour's work. He did a good job, *mind you / still.* ➤ Unit 61.5
16. The experiment was concluded after thirty days. *In / To* summarise, the results we achieved were not really comprehensive enough to merit publication. ➤ Unit 61.6

4 Check your answers on page 384. Then go to the unit for more information and practice.

58 Linking sentences and clauses

The year 2005 was a particularly bad year for hurricanes in North and Central America. Several major hurricanes **not only** caused over 100 billion dollars' worth of damage, **but also** claimed over 2,200 lives. **Although** most of the damage was sustained in the southern United States, there was also extensive damage in Central America.

1 Linking two main clauses

In speech and writing we usually prefer to link two short main clauses to create a longer sentence:

MacMahon leapt out of the way of the car. He rolled to safety at the side of the road.

→ *MacMahon leapt out of the way of the car **and** (he) rolled to safety at the side of the road.*

We join main clauses with the coordinating conjunctions *and*, *but* and *or*. The most common coordinator is *and*, especially in speech. We use

- *and* for addition: *I cooked the starter **and** laid the table.*
- *but* for contrast: *I cooked the starter **but** I didn't lay the table.*
- *or* for choice: *Do you want me to cook the starter **or** lay the table?*

We always put the coordinating conjunction between the two clauses:

✗ ~~*But I wanted to see you I was too busy.*~~ ✓ *I wanted to see you **but** I was too busy.*

When we want to emphasise that two things happened (or didn't happen), we can also use the 'two-part' conjunctions *both ... and*, *either ... or*, *neither ... nor* and *not only ... but (also)*:

*At the French Open, Federer **both** proved his return to form **and** won the only Grand Slam title to have evaded him.*

*Several major hurricanes **not only** caused over 100 billion dollars' worth of damage, **but also** claimed over 2,200 lives.*

*To take part you can **either** register as an individual **or** enter a team of up to eight challengers.*

The conjunction *neither ... nor* is negative (and therefore uses a positive verb) and we invert the subject and auxiliary verb after *nor* (➤ Unit 76.2):

✗ ~~*I neither don't know about his wedding, nor I don't care about it.*~~

✓ *I **neither** know about his wedding, **nor do I** care about it.*

2 Linking a main and a subordinate clause

There are several different types of subordinate clause, for example:

- *that* or *wh-* clauses: *Didn't the notice say **when the water was going to be cut off?***
- adverbial clauses of time, using conjunctions such as *when*, *before* and *after* (➤ Unit 59.1):
  *The state of the company's finances only became clear **after the Finance Director had left.***
- adverbial clauses of condition, using conjunctions such as *if* and *unless* (➤ Unit 37.1/2):
  *There may well be more accidents in future **if air traffic continues to grow.***
- adverbial clauses of contrast, using conjunctions such as *although*, *while* (➤ Unit 60.1/2):
  ***Although the Aztecs were rich and powerful,** the Spanish conquistadors overpowered them.*
- relative clauses, introduced by pronouns, e.g. *who*, *which*, *that* (➤ Units 53 and 54):
  *It was surprisingly not their latest CD **that went platinum**, but the one before.*

We usually put the subordinate clause after the main clause:

The price of our holiday increased because a new green tax was imposed on all flights.

We can reverse the order of the clauses if we want to emphasise the information in the subordinate clause. In this order, we usually put a comma between the clauses:

Because a new green tax was imposed on all flights, the price of our holiday increased.

More on clause order and emphasis ➤ Unit 76.2/4

Practice

1 Match the clauses to make sentences as in the example, and choose the most suitable linking word from the box to join them. Decide if each sentence contains two main clauses or a main clause and a subordinate clause, and write M + M or M + S.

after although and if or that unless ~~when~~

0 Did the doctor say exactly *when* — → B
1 It was the finest portrait ....
2 Our car broke down last week ....
3 Your order will be cancelled ....
4 The policeman was rushed to hospital ....
5 We can either go camping ....
6 Usain Bolt won the gold medal ....
7 I'm not going to play this game ....

A we'd just had it serviced. ....
B you'll be able to go back to work? *M + S*
C we can stay in a cheap hotel. ....
D he smashed the World Record. ....
E you follow the rules properly. ....
F the artist had ever painted. ....
G we don't receive payment by the due date. ....
H he had been stabbed in the park. ....

2 GRAMMAR IN USE Read the story and find the relevant underlined conjunction. Cross it out, and write it in the appropriate place, as in the example. 4.12 Listen and check.

WITNESS: I WAS THERE Posts | Search | Contact Us

A disaster remembered

The only natural disaster I've witnessed was several years ago, before (0) *when* I was staying with relatives in Istanbul. It was a hot summer and we'd felt a few tremors, ~~when~~ (1) .... they had been minor ones. One evening, we'd been out for a meal and had spent another couple of hours chatting before we went to bed. I must have fallen asleep, so (2) .... I was suddenly awakened by a violent rattling. I realised at once that it was an earthquake. My thoughts immediately turned to my son, sleeping in the room next door with his cousin. As (3) .... I'd got to the door of my room, it opened. It was my son, checking that I was OK. The shaking was so strong by now that we could both (4) .... stand still nor move very easily. We knew we had to get out of the house, in case the building started to collapse.

By now it was chaos in the house. My brother took control or (5) .... shouted to us all to get outside and go down to the sea. (Luckily, the house was on the outskirts of the city, by the sea.) As soon as (6) .... we were running down to the beach, something fell from a nearby building, and we realised how lucky we were. There were hundreds of people on the beach – in an earthquake zone everyone knows that you get away from buildings although (7) .... you can. It was a bizarre night after that – neither (8) .... frightening and strangely calm at the same time. It was frightening because no one knew whether there would be another tremor, but we were all far from the buildings now because (9) .... we didn't feel in immediate danger.

The next night we didn't know whether to carry on as normal and (10) .... sleep outside again in case of aftershocks. My family has a small boathouse on the beach, so we all slept in that unless (11) .... it seemed more sensible. Eventually, we realised that there would be no aftershocks and that we were safe to go home. It was awful to find out later that thousands of people had been killed further east, closer to the epicentre, where hundreds of buildings had collapsed. This kind of tragedy will keep happening while (12) .... more stringent building regulations are applied.

59 Subordinate clauses (1) time, reason, result, etc.

On 26 December 2004 a huge earthquake took place in the Indian Ocean and caused one of the deadliest tsunamis ever. Over 200,000 people were killed, and **because** it was the peak holiday season, that figure included several thousand tourists. In fact, it was **such** a powerful tsunami **that** two people were killed as far away as South Africa!

1 Time

The most common conjunctions of time are *when, as, after, before, while, until* and *since*:
Rosemary waited ***until*** *her children were at school* ***before*** *she started studying again.*

Other, less common conjunctions are *as soon as, once, whenever, now (that), the minute/moment (that), immediately* and *by the time (that)*:
It was such a pity you didn't contact us ***immediately/the moment*** *you got back.*
Hurry up! ***By the time*** *you're ready, all the tickets will be sold out!*

2 Reason

We usually give a reason with the conjunction *because*:
We've kept the company at five people simply ***because*** *the office is too small to take any more.*
Several thousand tourists were killed ***because*** *it was the peak holiday season.*

In speech, *because* is often shortened to *'cos* /kɒz/.

Other conjunctions of reason are *since, as* and *for*. Whereas *because* can be used in all circumstances, *since* and *as* both introduce reasons that are already known:
Terence, ***since/as*** *you raised the subject, perhaps you could start by telling us your concerns.*

FORMALITY CHECK In formal speech and writing, we often use *given that* to introduce a reason that is already known:
Given that *there are so few women in powerful positions in commerce, the number in politics is quite surprising.*
For is quite old-fashioned now and rarely used in conversation and informal writing:
She decided not to move to a seaside resort, ***for*** *they were full of old, retired people.*
In informal English, we would use *because* or *as*:
She decided not to move to a seaside resort, ***as*** *they were full of old, retired people.*

3 Purpose

The most common conjunction of purpose is *so that ... (not)*. We often omit *that*:
Would you mind turning the monitor round ***so (that)*** *other people can't see the screen?*

A more formal alternative is *in order that ... (not)*:
Please leave all bins outside your property ***in order that*** *rubbish collectors can access them easily.*

We can use *for fear that* when we don't want something to happen. It is also possible to use *lest* + subjunctive in this way, although this is quite old-fashioned:
We didn't go in daylight ***for fear that*** *we would be recognised/****lest*** *we* ***be*** *recognised.*
(= so that we wouldn't be recognised)

We can also use infinitive clauses after *in order* and *so as*:
The school will be holding a number of events ***in order to/so as to*** *raise money for repairs.*

Infinitive of purpose ➤ Unit 45.4

4 Result

The most common conjunction expressing result is *so*:

The baby was crying for half of the night ***so*** *I'm feeling exhausted today.*

Note the difference between *so* and *because*:

Joe hated the new job, ***so*** *he resigned last week.* (*so* + result of hating the job)

Joe resigned last week ***because*** *he hated the new job.* (*because* + reason for resigning)

We can describe the result of a particular quality or characteristic using these patterns:

so + adjective/adverb + *(that)* clause	*I'm afraid it was* ***so dark (that)*** *I couldn't see her face.* *Sally stayed with us* ***so often that*** *we invited her to move in.*
such + (adjective +) noun + *(that)* clause	*I'm afraid I can't identify her. It was* ***such a dark night (that)*** *I couldn't see her face.*[1]
too + adjective (+ *for*) + infinitive clause	*It was* ***too dark*** *(for me) to see her face.*
(not) adjective + *enough* (+ *for*) + infinitive clause	*It wasn't* ***light enough*** *(for me) to see her face.*[2]

[1] Note the article after *such* with a singular noun:
✗ ~~*It was such dark night.*~~ ✓ *It was* **such a** *dark night.*

[2] *Enough* always follows the adjective:
✗ ~~*It wasn't enough light.*~~ ✓ *It wasn't* **light enough**.

We can use *so much … that* after a verb to express the result of an action:

Dave shouted ***so much*** *at the football match* ***that*** *he had a sore throat the next day.*

We do not combine *so much* + adjective:

✗ ~~*Sorry, I was so much busy that I forgot to call you.*~~

✓ *Sorry, I was* ***so busy that*** *I forgot to call you.*

FORMALITY CHECK A more formal alternative is *so* + adjective + *as* + infinitive clause:

It was ***so dark as to*** *make it impossible to see her face.*

5 Condition

The most common conjunctions expressing condition are *if* and *unless*:

Emotions cannot be true ***unless*** *they are spontaneous.*

Other conjunctions expressing condition are *as long as, providing,* and *in case* (➤ Unit 37.1):

You can go to the party on Saturday ***as long as*** *you book a taxi home. Take a couple of numbers of cab firms with you* ***in case*** *the usual one is booked up.*

FORMALITY CHECK More formal alternatives are *on (the) condition that* and *provided (that)*:

A widow has left £135,000 to an animal charity ***on (the) condition that*** *her cats are looked after for the rest of their lives.*

6 Other conjunctions

We can use the conjunctions *as if* and *as though* to say how someone behaves or does something:

The Minister continues to act ***as though*** *he's unaware of the serious complaints against him.*

Note the difference between present and past forms after these conjunctions (➤ Unit 40.5):

She behaves ***as if she can*** *afford expensive things.* (Maybe she can; we don't know.)

She behaves ***as if she could*** *afford expensive things.* (We know that she can't afford them.)

We use *except that/when/where/if* to express exception:

What can I say ***except that*** *I'm sorry? I didn't intend to offend you.*
(= The only thing I can say is ...)

I keep my room locked ***except if*** *I'm only away for a couple of minutes.*
(= The only time I don't lock it is when ...)

Preposition *except* ➤ Unit 11.5

Practice

1 Complete the second sentence so it has a similar meaning to the first. Use the conjunction in brackets, as in the example. 4.13 Listen and check.

0 The voting station will remain open in order to allow all votes to be cast. (so that)
The voting station will remain open *so that all the votes can be cast.*

1 Angela's worried about being asked difficult questions so she won't appear on expert panels. (for fear that)
Angela won't appear on expert panels ……………………

2 The restaurant only accepts group bookings if a deposit is paid. (except if)
The restaurant does not accept group bookings ……………………

3 The photo was awarded first prize because it embodies the concept of solitude. (so)
The photo embodies the concept of solitude, ……………………

4 We can settle your claim out of court if you undertake not to reveal the sum agreed. (provided that)
Your claim may be settled out of court ……………………

5 It is impossible to approve the building plans before we have seen the details. (after)
We can only approve the building plans ……………………

6 The conditions of the contract were too restrictive for me to accept the job. (such ... that)
The contract imposed ……………………

7 You talk about law in such a way that it seems you've had legal training. (as if)
You talk about law ……………………

8 The meeting was so noisy that I missed the most important announcement. (so much ... that)
There was ……………………

2 Complete the sentences with a suitable subordinating conjunction from the box. There are four extra conjunctions.

as long as | as though | by the time | except if | except that | for fear that
given that | in order that | so as to | so much that | that | the moment

1 It shouldn't matter what our employees look like, …………… they can do the job.

2 …………… the dispute has already been resolved in principle, a formal agreement should be forthcoming in the next day or two.

3 Darren is so involved in his psychology studies that he analyses people …………… they start talking to him!

4 Many wealthy business people employ accountants …………… they can find all the legal ways of not paying tax.

5 The new model is hardly any different from the last, …………… it can reach 60 kph in under eight seconds.

6 The instructions for this task are so confusing …………… it's a wonder that any students understand it at all!

7 Is Mrs Hardwick the owner of the hotel? She certainly behaves …………… she is.

8 That comedian at the club last night was hilarious. I laughed …………… my sides were hurt.

3 GRAMMAR IN USE **Complete the article with subordinate clauses from A–I below, as in the example. 4.14 Listen and check.**

End of a space-age era

The United States space shuttle programme has now been brought to a close. For thirty years, the space shuttles, part rocket, part plane, have travelled back and forth into space and supplied the International Space Station tirelessly and safely, apart from two major disasters. The most recent of these happened in 2003 (0) *F* the external shell of *Columbia* (1) ___ and hit the outside of the spaceship. Had this floated away from the shuttle, it wouldn't have been a problem, but (2) ___, the orbiter burnt up as it re-entered the Earth's atmosphere. No human could sustain the temperatures encountered on re-entry without sufficient protection, (3) ___. NASA engineers guessed this would happen but limited their investigations during the shuttle's flight (4) ___ there was little they could do to save the crew. As a result of this and the ensuing investigation, construction of the International Space Station was put on hold (5) ___, some two years later.

The *Columbia* disaster was the second to befall the shuttle programme – it took place some 17 years.(6) ___. This disaster received more publicity than the second (7) ___: Christa McCauliffe was the first non-astronaut to take part in a shuttle flight, on the 'Teacher on Board' programme, (8) ___ as it lifted off, and millions watched the disaster unfold.

Despite these two disasters, the space shuttle programme has been a success, and these space-age workhorses can only pave the way to better – and safer – transportation into space.

A so all seven astronauts on board were killed
B while it was lifting off
C so the nation's eyes were on the spacecraft
D as they knew
E after *Challenger* had broken up on lift-off
F ~~when a small piece of foam insulation broke off~~
G because a lay person was on board
H because it damaged part of the shuttle's heat shield
I until shuttle flights resumed

4 Find and correct five more mistakes in these sentences, as in the example. Tick (✓) the correct sentences.

0 The rules at that school were so strict ~~as to it was~~ *that it was* inevitable to break them occasionally.
1 The match went to penalties, and Inter-Milan lost so their top striker missed the first one.
2 The medical insurance is valid for one year on condition that we are immediately informed of any change in the insured person's circumstances.
3 Tarantino's latest film has a so violent scene as the censors refused to pass it.
4 Honestly, Jim, you talk as though you've been to law school, but we all know you haven't!
5 Please initial each page of the document as indicated, except where a full signature is required.
6 You'll have to meet Wendy at the station tonight. I won't be home enough early to get to the station in time.
7 Laurence's explanation for his behaviour at the ceremony was so ridiculous as to we laughed out loud.
8 This government will increase payments to the disabled and the elderly in order that they may have a comfortable and dignified life.

60 Subordinate clauses (2) contrast and concession

1 Contrast

The conjunctions *but, while, whereas* and *whilst* express a contrast:
Reds and yellows are warm colours, ***whereas*** *blues and greens are cool.*

While is more informal than *whereas; whilst* is very formal. We often put the subordinate clause with *while* or *whilst* before the main clause:
While/Whilst *only 84 people died on the railways last year, more than 5,000 died on the roads.*

2 Concession

The conjunctions *although, (even) though* and *yet* indicate that the information in the main clause is somehow surprising or unexpected:

CONJUNCTION	WHEN USED	EXAMPLES
although	in neutral contexts	*We now know there were over 3000 fatalities,* ***although*** *only 376 were reported at the time*
though/much as	in informal contexts	*I enjoyed the exhibition,* ***though*** *I thought it was rather badly organised.* ***Much as*** *it pains me to say this, we'll have to cancel the trip.*
yet[1]	in formal contexts	*These exclusive villas are only a five-minute walk from the resort,* ***yet*** *they are a haven of peace and tranquillity.*
even though[2]	to add emphasis	*Psychosis is also part of this debate,* ***even though*** *problems arising from it affect a relatively small number of people.*

[1] We do not start a statement with *yet*:
✗ ~~Yet they arrived on time, their plane took off an hour late.~~

[2] We do not use *even although*, or *even* by itself:
✗ ~~*She loves him, even although he is selfish.*~~ ✗ ~~*She loves him, even he is selfish.*~~
✓ *She loves him,* ***even though*** *he is selfish.*

Compare *even though* and *even if* (➤ Unit 37.1):
I'm going to apply for the job, ***even though*** *it pays very little.* (I know that it pays very little.)
I'm going to apply for the job, ***even if*** *it pays very little.* (I don't know what it pays.)

We can use these conjunctions with an adjective instead of a clause:
The necklace, ***even though*** *(it was) staggeringly expensive, would match the dress perfectly.*
Though *exhausted after the drive home, Shelley cooked a meal for them all.*

We can use *though* after an adjective, with linking verbs such as *be, look* and *seem*:
Beautiful ***though*** *she is/may be* (= although she is beautiful), *you must be sure of her character, too.*

It is also possible to use *however* + adjective/*much/many* in this way:
However exhausted *she felt after the drive home, Shelley cooked a meal for them all.*
We've got to get these plans approved, ***however difficult*** *it may be.*
(= though it may be difficult)
You won't change my mind, ***however much*** *you argue!*

3 Prepositions of concession

Despite and *in spite of* are prepositions; they can be followed by a noun or an *-ing* form:
In spite of *the depressed gold price, mine production rose in most areas last year.*
Despite *often* ***offering*** *basic salaries, charities rarely have problems in recruiting staff.*

- We do not introduces a clause with *despite* or *in spite of*; we have to use a conjunction:
  ✗ ~~*Despite the plane left an hour late, we arrived at our destination on time.*~~
  ✓ ***Though*** *the plane left an hour late, we arrived at our destination on time.*
- If we want to introduce a clause with *despite* or *in spite of*, we add *the fact that*:
  In spite of the fact that *the rehearsal had gone so badly, the first night was a great success.*

Practice

1 Choose the clause, A or B, that provides the best ending for each sentence. 4.15 Listen and check.

1 Many people believe that capital punishment is a deterrent to serious crime, even though
A it actually makes little difference to the crime rate.
B the crime rate has decreased in some places where it is used.

2 We usually consider it healthy to eat lots of fruit, but
A it's one of the best food groups in terms of vitamins.
B too much can produce an excess of acid in the stomach.

3 I enjoy having people to stay, though
A I always appreciate the peace when they've gone.
B I always feel unhappy when they've gone.

4 Iain Banks' early novels were considered quite strange, while
A his later ones also seem to be quite weird.
B his later works are more mainstream and accessible.

5 The patient had the nurses running round and they quickly lost patience, much as
A they tried to sympathise with her. B they got annoyed with her.

6 Global warming is often considered the main factor in current climate fluctuations, yet
A it appears to be having a real effect on phenomena such as hurricanes.
B periods of warming have long been a feature of the Earth's development.

2 Write the second sentence so it has a similar meaning to the first. Use the words in brackets, as in the example.

0 Although the earthquake appeared horrific at the time, there were few fatalities.
(though) *Horrific though the earthquake appeared at the time, there were few fatalities.*

1 Warnings of the flood were given well in advance, yet people didn't leave their homes.
(spite) ....

....

2 Very little of the remaining stock sold, despite the low prices in the sale.
(even though) ....

....

3 The magazine had tried introducing several new features. Nevertheless, circulation continued to drop.
(although) ....

....

4 The Scots won the battle, even though they had a far smaller force.
(despite) ....

....

5 Although this may seem difficult now, you'll soon wonder why it caused so many problems.
(though) ....

....

6 I adore children but I can't accept that kind of behaviour from any child.
(much as) ....

....

61 Adverbial linking expressions

THE DESTRUCTION OF THERA
Approximately 3,500 years ago, there was a huge volcanic eruption in the Aegean Sea, which devastated the island of Thera (Santorini). **In addition**, it destroyed the successful Minoan civilisation on the island of Crete. **However**, it now seems that the heaviest fall of volcanic ash was to the north-east, over what is now Turkey.

1 General points

Adverbial linking expressions can be single-word adverbs, e.g. *therefore, however*, or they can be adverbial phrases, e.g. *as a result, in conclusion.*

- They are not conjunctions: they are generally more formal than conjunctions and are used mainly in writing.
- They are usually separated from the sentences they link by punctuation.
- We usually place the adverb at the beginning of the second sentence of the pair we are linking, but we can sometimes also insert it into the sentence it introduces, separating it out with commas:
  *There was an unprecedented response to our advert. I am afraid, **therefore**, we are not taking your application further.*
- We can also insert it before the verb (or after *be* or an auxiliary):
  *There was an unprecedented response to our advert. I am afraid we are **therefore** not taking your application further.*
- Some adverbial expressions can be placed at the end of the sentence:
  *The director didn't come to the launch. It was a success, **nevertheless**.*

2 Time and sequence

We use adverbials of time to describe sequences or stages in a process:

LINKING WORDS	MEANING	EXAMPLES
*afterwards, beforehand**	one action happening after/before another	*Dinner will be served at 8.00. **Afterwards**, the Mayor will give a speech.* *I had a blood test last week and had to fast for 12 hours **beforehand**.*
after that, then, next, following that	a stage in a process	*Put a plastic cup in the holder, **then** select the drink you want and insert the correct coins.*
eventually, finally, in the end	last stage in a long process	*The police interviewed every male in the street and **finally** charged Jim Murphy with assault.*
first(ly), second(ly), third(ly), finally	sequence of events	***First**, a verbal warning is given; **second**, two written warnings are given; **third**, a final warning is given, and **finally** the employee may be dismissed.*
	to number points in an argument	*The medical trial had to be abandoned: **firstly**, there weren't enough volunteers, and **secondly**, the company withdrew one of the drugs.*

* We usually only put *beforehand* at the end of a clause, not the beginning:
✗ ~~*I had a blood test last week. Beforehand, I had to fast for 12 hours.*~~

3 Addition

We use *in addition, similarly, furthermore, what is more* and *moreover* to add something:
*Approximately 3,500 years ago, a huge volcanic eruption devastated the island of Thera. **In addition**, it destroyed the successful Minoan civilisation on the island of Crete.*

In conversation we prefer to use *also*:
*Can you post this letter when you go to the shops? **Also**, can you get me a bar of chocolate?*

4 Result and reason

In formal English, we use *therefore, consequently, accordingly, as a consequence/result* to express a result. In conversation we often use *so*:

These drugs heal most ulcers but they do not cure the underlying disease. ***Consequently****, ulcers tend to recur after treatment has stopped.*

The computer crashed yesterday evening ***so*** *I've spent all day today trying to sort it out.*

We can use *for this/that reason* to show a relationship of reason:

We do not believe that the officers behaved inappropriately in the circumstances. ***For that reason****, we welcome the independent inquiry.*

5 Contrast and concession

We use *however, nevertheless/nonetheless, on the other hand, even so* and *on the contrary* to make a contrast:

A pet may be a good companion for the elderly. ***However****, its need for exercise may be a problem.*

The new software is not problem-free. ***Nevertheless****, it is still an improvement on previous versions.*

Even so expresses a particularly surprising contrast:

The last attempt to swim the Channel ended in disaster. ***Even so****, more swimmers than ever are training to achieve this difficult feat.*

Last year the government turned away more asylum seekers than ever before.	***Nonetheless****, the public considers that too many are allowed to stay.* *The public,* ***however****, considers that too many are allowed to stay.* *The public considers that too many are allowed to stay,* ***even so****.*

FORMALITY CHECK In speech we often use these more informal adverbs of concession:

I know it's not late. I have to go, ***all the same****.*

The new programme on dinosaurs is a bit far-fetched. ***Still/Mind you****, it's a lot more interesting than most of the other programmes on TV right now.*

We haven't had much success with the garden. This year has been much drier than usual, ***though****.*

The adverb *still* can appear at the beginning of the sentence, but not the end; *though* usually appears at the end, and *all the same* and *mind you* are common in both positions:

I know it's far too expensive for someone on my income.	***Still****, it's worth it!* ***All the same****, it's worth it!* ***Mind you****, it's worth it!* *It's worth it,* ***all the same****! It's worth it,* ***mind you****! It's worth it,* ***though****!*

6 Other linking adverbials

We use *in conclusion, in brief, overall* and *all in all* to summarise:

In conclusion*, the survey indicated that the local population would welcome a cycle lane.*

ACADEMIC ENGLISH The adverbials *To summarise* and *To conclude* are common ways of introducing a conclusion in an academic paper:

To conclude*, hotels large and small have a real need for dependable communication systems.*

Many adverbials introduce a comment on the previous sentence by

- giving an example – *for example, for instance, such as*:
  We specialise in office services, ***such as*** *payroll and bookkeeping.*
- naming/explaining something – *notably, namely* (formal):
  This affects one of the principles of political economy, ***namely*** *the free market in labour.*
- restating a point – *in other words, to put it another way, that is (to say)*:
  The position is paid pro rata. ***In other words****, your salary is calculated according to how many hours you work in comparison with a full-time employee.*

Some adverbials can mark a transition from one topic to another in speech, e.g. *by the way, come to think of it, incidentally* (➤ Unit 81.3):

I did enjoy my trip to Stratford. ***By the way****, if you're ever there, do look up Aunt Joan. She'd love to see you.*

Practice

1 Write the linking adverb or expression in brackets in an appropriate position. Make any other changes necessary, as in the example. Sometimes more than one position is possible. 4.16 Listen and check.

0 The new satellite navigation system contains all the major road maps of Europe. ~~It~~ *In addition, it* receives updates automatically on a regular basis. (in addition)

1 Most people who haven't had training in typing start out by using two fingers only. They learn how to touch type purely by practice. (eventually)

2 Rob wants us to visit his sister in Canada later this year. I'm still not sure that I want to fly after all the problems with the volcanic ash. (though)

3 He does what novelists have always tried to do, to depict the world in which they live. (namely)

4 *The King's Speech* was a low-budget British film. It won four Oscars at the 2011 ceremony. (nevertheless)

5 We recognise that all of our clients have different and individual needs. We offer a tailor-made programme at no extra cost. (therefore)

6 We were really hoping that we'd have good weather for the day we visited the golf tournament, but it poured down. We made the most of it and enjoyed ourselves as much as we could. (still)

2 Each pair of sentences contains one formal and one informal sentence. Complete each sentence with an appropriate linking expression, as in the example.

1 A We decided on the course of action we should take, ...*then*... we put it into action.
B An appropriate plan was discussed and organised. ...., it was put into action.

2 A We've almost finished the plans for the evening. We've booked the main act and we're .... talking to a possible support act now.
B The arrangements are almost complete. The main act has been booked. ...., discussions with a supporting act are in train.

3 A You know, we never trusted Jason's business partner; he seemed a bit shifty. .... we didn't expect him to get mixed up with those robberies.
B The defendant was never entirely trusted by his colleagues. ...., his involvement in the series of bank robberies came as a complete surprise to them.

4 A They got it wrong last year and too many of us failed, ... this year's exam is supposed to be much easier.
B The failure rate in last year's examination was considered to be too high. ...., this year's paper is considerably easier.

5 A If you're new to gardening, you should stick to plants that are hardy and grow easily to begin with, ... pansies and violas.
B Newcomers to gardening would be wise to focus on some of the simpler hardy annuals, ... pansies and violas.

6 A I don't think that I'd change my life much if I came into money. I know people say that suddenly having a lot of money always changes your life, ...
B Many of those who are accustomed to living on a small income believe that their lives would not be significantly altered by a major change in income. ...., that is rarely the case.

3 GRAMMAR IN USE **Read the text and complete it with suitable linking words from the box, as in the example. Use appropriate punctuation where necessary.**
4.17 Listen and check.

As a result consequently first following that Furthermore However in addition Nevertheless ~~therefore~~

IT IS COMMON knowledge that much of the Netherlands is land that is reclaimed from the sea. Flooding is (0) ...*therefore*... a constant fear near the coast of Holland, particularly in these days of global warming. Technology today allows for strong sea defences and early warnings. (1) ...., it was not always the case.

On 14 December 1287 a violent storm gathered strength in the North Sea and the English Channel, causing problems in the south-east of England and the north-west of Holland. (2) ...., a massive storm tide followed and hit the coast of Holland. There were of course sea walls in place to protect the land from such tides. (3) ...., the sea breached these defences and a huge flood ensued, now known as St Lucia's Flood. (4) ...., over 50,000 people were killed.

The human cost was not the only consequence of the flood; (5) ...., the shape and development of the country were altered forever in a number of ways: (6) ...., the sea broke through the man-made defences, then it flooded a huge area and created a large inlet which became known as the Zuider Zee (South Sea), and later Ijsselmeer, and (7) ...., allowed sea access to Amsterdam, which (8) .... developed as an important port city.

4 **Eight of these sentences contain a mistake in word order or formality caused by an inappropriate linking word. Correct the mistakes, as in the example, and tick (✓) the two correct sentences.**

0 I know Darren is a pain in class and he really gets on your nerves. ~~Nevertheless~~ *Still*, we've got to do our best by him.
1 I think that I did quite well in the computing exam. It was more difficult than though I expected.
2 We'd love to come to your birthday party. Is it OK if we in addition bring the children?
3 The jury spent a long time deliberating, but came to a unanimous decision after four hours finally.
4 We were expecting a basic but pleasant apartment. However, what we got was little more than a hovel.
5 Strictly no pets are allowed in the hotel rooms. Mind you, guide dogs for the blind may be permitted with prior permission from the management.
6 I was frozen to the bone when I got in after our walk in the snow yesterday, as a consequence I had a really long, hot bath.
7 I know you'd like us to look after your horse next week. We'd rather all the same not.
8 Our party believes that equal rights are essential in a modern democracy. We therefore promise to create strict legislation should we be returned to government.
9 Over forty percent of marriages end in divorce today, nearly one in every two, that is to say.
10 First, you put the disc in the disc drive and wait for the menu to appear on the screen then.

Review MODULE 13

1 UNITS 58 AND 59 **Choose the correct option in *italics*. If both options are correct, choose both.**

1 We can *either / or* use long-life bulbs here or save money by using the ordinary ones.
2 We looked after the children *until / while* John visited his mother in the hospital.
3 Martin dropped out of university after a year but he behaves as though he *has / had* a degree.
4 *As / Since* your insurance covers flight cancellation, you will receive a full refund.
5 The bank neither informed its customers of the account changes, nor *apologised / didn't apologise* for the inconvenience it caused.
6 Please photocopy on both sides of the sheet *so that / in order not to* waste paper.
7 Members may not bring guests except *that / if* the management is notified in advance.
8 It was *so sad / such a sad sight* that no one was able to hold back their tears.

2 UNITS 60 AND 61 **Complete the article with the linking words from the box, as in the example.**

~~although~~ consequently despite firstly for these reasons
however moreover nevertheless secondly though while

The Elgin Marbles

THE ELGIN MARBLES are statues which date back to the fifth century BCE. (0) ..*Although*.. they were created in Greece and were located in the Parthenon in Athens until the late eighteenth century, they are now exhibited in the British Museum, London.

The statues were bought in 1799 by the Englishman Lord Elgin, who wanted to bring them back to Britain as part of his personal art collection. (1) ...., on the sea voyage back to England, the ship carrying them was sunk and the 'Marbles' were temporarily lost. It would be an incredibly expensive operation to recover them. (2) ...., Elgin did so, and (3) .... placed himself in enormous debt. (4) .... his own desires, he had to sell them to the British Government and they were housed in the British Museum, where they have been ever since.

More recently, the statues have become the subject of debate between Britain and Greece and, indeed, among British historians and archaeologists. (5) .... the Greek authorities have requested their return on many occasions, the request has always been refused. One of the main arguments for not returning them, valid (6) .... the Greek request may have been, was because of the pollution that is affecting the Parthenon and the possibility of earthquakes in Greece. This argument is less valid now, since the completion of the new Acropolis Museum.

There are of course compelling arguments for their return: (7) ...., it cannot be denied that the statues are part of the Greek heritage and belong in their original environment; (8) ...., with the opening of the new Acropolis Museum, these works of art would now be as accessible to the public in Athens as they are now in London. (9) .... the Greek authorities have already received parts of the Parthenon statues back from other sources. (10) ...., spaces have been left in the new museum for the return of the rest of the statues, and it would seem churlish not to let them go home now.

3 ALL UNITS **Do sentences A and B have the same or different meanings? Write S or D for each pair.**

0 A In spite of the fact that this computer costs less, it's as good as the other one.
B Despite its lower price, this computer is as good as the other one. ...S...

1 A Despite the awful weather, the parade was a success.
B Although the weather was awful, the parade was a success. ....

2 A Patsy was late getting ready to leave, so we gave her a lift.
B Patsy took her time getting ready so that we'd have to give her a lift. ....

3 A Even though I went to the party, I didn't see her.
B Even if I went to the party, I wouldn't see her. ....

4 A The new museum is extremely popular. It hasn't made any money yet.
B The new museum is extremely popular, yet it hasn't made any money. ....

5 A The old phone had over 100 downloadable applications, but this one doesn't.
B The old phone had over 100 downloadable applications, whereas this one doesn't. ....

6 A Always number the pages first so that you don't lose their order if dropped.
B Always number the pages first in order not to lose their order if dropped. ....

7 A We were at the Norfolk Hotel, while the rest of the group was at the Grange.
B While we were staying at the Norfolk Hotel the rest of the group moved to the Grange. ....

8 A 'Mary threatened to leave last night. She's still here now.'
B 'Mary threatened to leave last night. Still, she's here now.' ....

4 ALL UNITS **Read the conversation and choose the correct or most appropriate linking words, A, B or C. If two options are correct, choose both.**

A This oil spill in the Gulf of Mexico is a complete catastrophe, isn't it? It's going to upset the ecology there for years.

B I know, it'll (0) ..... affect the economy (1) ..... many jobs will be lost.

A It's awful. They must be able to find a way to stop it, but (2) ..... the scientists ..... the politicians seem to know what to do. How did it start?

B There was a huge explosion, don't you remember? (3) ..... only eleven workers were killed.

A Oh yes, that's right, (4) ..... the whole rig sank. It's leaking something like 5,000 barrels of oil a day into the sea, isn't it?

B Yes, and when you think that we're running out of fossil fuels, all that waste.

A (5) ....., the coastlines for miles around will be destroyed, and take years and years to recover. Actually, I can't understand why they can't stop it.

B I think what they're trying to do is drill another well, (6) ..... capture the oil in a controlled way, but that's going to take another few weeks, so, in the meantime, they're trying all kinds of other things, (7) ..... trying to pump mud and other things into the leak to stop the oil coming.

A Mmm, I think they've just succeeded in almost stopping it. It's taken them long enough, (8) .....!

0 A furthermore (B) also C in addition
1 A so B so that C for that reason
2 A either ... or B both ... and C neither ... nor
3 A But B Nevertheless C Even so
4 A even if B even though C though
5 A Also B What's more C Furthermore
6 A in order that B to C so as to
7 A such as B namely C that is to say
8 A all the same B mind you C still

MODULE

14 The passive

Before you start

1 Review these intermediate grammar points and check you know them.

Passive forms of tenses

1 These are more common in writing than in spoken English.

2 We make the passive form of verbs in all tenses by using *be* in the appropriate tense plus the past participle of the main verb:
A password ***is used*** *to access the site.* (The customer **uses** a password to access the site.)
My bag ***was stolen.*** (A thief **stole** my bag.)
The murder ***is being investigated.*** (The police **are investigating** the murder.)
The show ***has been cancelled.*** (The organisers **have cancelled** the show.)
Drinks ***will be served*** *in the interval.* (The waiters **will serve** drinks.)

3 It is possible to make passive forms of the perfect continuous tenses, but we prefer to use an active form and an impersonal subject, e.g. *they/one*:
[*By next month the murder* ***will have been being investigated*** *for over a year.*]
✓ *By next month they* ***will have been investigating*** *the murder for over a year.*

Passive modals

FORM	ACTIVE	PASSIVE
modal verbs: verb + *be* + past participle	*Candidates* ***must answer*** *all the questions.* *They* ***have to take*** *a test.*	*All the questions* ***must be answered.*** *A test* ***has to be taken.***
modal perfects: verb + *have been* + past participle	*Someone* ***might have stolen*** *it.* *The jury* ***ought to have convicted*** *him.*	*It* ***might have been stolen.*** *He* ***ought to have been convicted.***

Subjects and agents

1 In this active sentence *the judge* is the subject of the active verb and *the names of the winners* is the object:

subject — active verb — object
The judge ***will read out*** *the names of the winners in alphabetical order.*

In the passive equivalent *the names of the winners* becomes the subject of the passive verb and *the judge* becomes the agent (the person or thing that causes the action of the passive verb):

subject — passive verb — agent
The names of the winners ***will be read out*** *in alphabetical order (by the judge).*

2 We often don't mention the agent in the passive, but if we do it is introduced with *by*.

2 **Read the information and identify the passive forms and uses.**

CHICHEN ITZA

THE GREAT stepped pyramid at Chichen Itza is one of the most impressive ancient monuments in the Americas. It was built by the Mayan people in the sixth to ninth centuries. From the size and quality of the structure it is clear that it must have been one of the most important centres in the Mayan empire, which covered much of Central America in ancient times.

Chichen Itza is a UNESCO World Heritage site and was chosen as one of the seven wonders of the world in a recent popular vote. The monuments have been owned by the Mexican government since 1972 and are now open to the public.

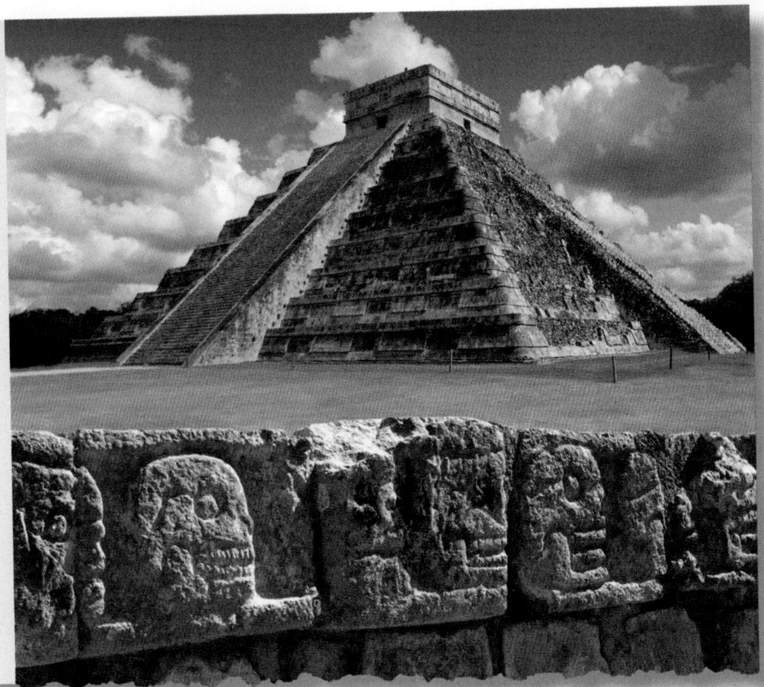

3 **Complete the diagnostic test below. Choose the correct words in *italics*. In some cases both options are possible, but only one is appropriate in the situation.**

1 Has all the evidence been taken *by the police away* / *away by the police?* ➤ Unit 62.1
2 Advice having *been* / *being* taken, the committee decided not to proceed. ➤ Unit 62.2
3 My greatest ambition for the future is to *have been* / *be* given my own TV chat show. ➤ Unit 62.3
4 An honorary degree was given *to the eminent scientist* / *the eminent scientist* by the university. ➤ Unit 62.4
5 The post *has been* / *has* arrived at last. ➤ Unit 62.5
6 Before shaving, *a shower is usually had by Steve* / *Steve usually has a shower.* ➤ Unit 62.5
7 *This programme was recorded* / *The camera operators recorded this programme* in front of a live audience. ➤ Unit 62.6
8 *'The Tempest' is thought to be* / *Some people think 'The Tempest' is* Shakespeare's final play. ➤ Unit 63.1
9 It has been argued *that carbon emissions are* / *carbon emissions to be* the main cause of global warming. ➤ Unit 63.1
10 Twenty percent of the world's oil *gets* / *is* owned by Saudi Arabia. ➤ Unit 63.2
11 They made the contestants *dress* / *to dress* in ridiculous outfits. ➤ Unit 63.3
12 Alice is going to get *repaired her car* / *her car repaired* free of charge as the other driver caused the damage. ➤ Unit 64.1
13 Unfortunately, James has just *had* / *got* his expansion proposals rejected by the board. ➤ Unit 64.1
14 When you receive the contract, please have your clients *sign* / *signed* each page. ➤ Unit 64.2
15 After years of complaining, we eventually *had* / *got* our neighbours to repair their broken fence. ➤ Unit 64.2

4 **Check your answers on page 384. Then go to the unit for more information and practice.**

Go online for a full diagnostic test

62 The passive: form and use

The stone circle at Stonehenge is the greatest monument **to have been built** by the ancient Britons. It **is regarded as** England's most important archaeological site.

1 Passive multi-word verbs

If a phrasal verb has an object, we can usually make it passive. We never separate the parts of the verb in the passive form:

They ***took*** *the company* ***over*** *in 2010.* → ✗ ~~*The company was taken by them over in 2010.*~~
✓ *The company* ***was taken over*** *(by them) in 2010.*

ACADEMIC ENGLISH There are several prepositional verbs and phrases which are commonly used in the passive, especially in writing:

*be aimed at   be applied to   be based on   be considered as   be found in   be known as
be referred to (as)   be regarded as   be related to   (can) be seen as   be thought of (as)   be used as*

The agency's new outreach scheme ***is aimed at*** *unemployed graduates.*

2 Passive -*ing* forms

We can use -*ing* forms in the passive:

ACTIVE	PASSIVE
-ing form: *I don't like people* ***bullying*** *me.*	*being* + past participle: *I don't like* ***being bullied****.*
having + past participle: ***Having signed*** *the deal, we went out to celebrate.*	*having been* + past participle: *The deal* ***having been signed****, we went out to celebrate.*

We can use either *having been* + past participle or *being* + past participle to refer to the past after certain verbs which are followed by an -*ing* form, e.g. *regret, remember*:
We regret ***not having been shown/not being shown*** *the Acropolis.*
(= We regret the fact that the tour guide didn't show us the Acropolis.)

3 Passive infinitives

There are several passive infinitive forms.

- *to be* + past participle (to refer to the present or future):
  Children like ***to be praised*** *when they do well at school.*
  James was hoping ***to be accepted*** *on the engineering course.*
- *to have been* + past participle (to refer to the past):
  Stonehenge is the greatest monument ***to have been built*** *by the ancient Britons.*
  This ascent is the first ***to have been achieved*** *without the aid of oxygen.*
- in reported speech with *ask for* + object:
  Inspector Pascoe ***asked for the prisoners to be held*** *in the cells overnight.*

We can use the passive infinitive (or an active -*ing* form ➤ Unit 46.4) after *need*:
That cage really ***needs to be cleaned****.* (= That cage really needs cleaning.)

4 Verbs with two objects

Some active verbs have a direct and an indirect object:

They offered the customer a refund.

Either object can become the subject of the passive verb:

The customer ***was offered*** *a refund. A refund* ***was offered to*** *the customer.*

If the object of the passive verb is the indirect object of the active verb it is usually introduced with a preposition, e.g. *to the customer* (➤ Unit 42.3).

5 Verbs not used in the passive

Verbs with no direct object (intransitive verbs)	✗ ~~*The visitors were arrived early.*~~ ✓ *The visitors* ***arrived early****.* ✗ ~~*The plane has been landed.*~~ ✓ *The plane* ***has landed****.*
Certain verbs followed by (object +) *to* + infinitive verb, such as *want (him to leave), refuse (to answer)*	✗ ~~*He was wanted to leave.*~~ ✓ *She* ***wanted him to leave****.* ✗ ~~*Your questions are refused to answer.*~~ ✓ *I* ***refuse to answer*** *your questions.*
Certain verbs describing states, such as *have* (= own), *be, belong, lack, resemble, pretend* and *seem*	✗ ~~*A Ferrari is had by John.*~~ ✓ *John* ***has*** *a Ferrari.* ✗ ~~*Marilyn Monroe is resembled by her.*~~ ✓ *She* ***resembles*** *Marilyn Monroe.*
have + noun to describe an action e.g. *have a shower, have lunch*	✗ ~~*Lunch is being had by John.*~~ ✓ *John's* ***having*** *lunch.*

For *make/let* ➤ Unit 63.3

6 Reasons for using the passive

We often use the passive

- when the agent is not relevant, or not known:
  Wars ***have been fought*** *throughout history.* (Who fought them is not important here.)
  I think the old house ***has been demolished****.* (We don't know who did it.)
- when the agent is obvious from the context or from general knowledge:
  The parcel's ***being delivered*** *at midday.* (obviously by the delivery company)
- when we want to be less direct, or more polite in a formal situation. Compare:
  Will you grant our application for planning permission? (direct question)
  Will *our application for planning permission* ***be granted****?* (more polite/less direct)
- when we want to describe general feelings, opinions and beliefs (➤ Unit 63.1):
  Rio de Janeiro ***has been described as*** *the most beautiful city in the Americas.*
  São Paulo ***is said to be*** *the fastest-growing city in South America.*

Sometimes we know the identity of the agent, but we don't want to mention it because we don't want to blame a specific person, or we want to avoid personal responsibility:

I see the washing-up ***hasn't been done****. Oh dear, look, the vase* ***has been broken****.*

7 Using passives in writing

ACADEMIC ENGLISH In written English we often use the passive to

- focus on the issues rather than on the people involved:
  The research ***was carried out*** *over a period of six months.*
- describe rules and procedures:
  Answers ***must be written*** *in ink. Candidates* ***will be interviewed*** *in alphabetical order.*
- describe commercial, industrial and scientific processes:
  Minutes ***are taken*** *and then* ***submitted*** *to the chair for approval.*
  Components ***are electronically tagged*** *and* ***transported*** *to the production line.*
- describe historical, economic and social processes:
  Tribal lands ***were sold*** *years ago. The currency* ***has been devalued*** *twice since 1980.*

Using the passive to order information ➤ Unit 77.5

Practice

1 Rewrite these sentences in the passive, using the words in brackets. 4.18 Listen and check.

0 Harold remembered that his parents had taken him there when he was very young.
(having) *Harold remembered having been taken there when he was very young.*

1 I don't like people phoning me late at night.
(being) ....

2 You should complete the form in black ink.
(be) ....

3 We have not tested this product on animals.
(has) ....

4 Having paid for the tickets, we had no choice but to continue.
(been) ....

5 Ibrahim regrets the fact that his parents didn't send him to a better school.
(having) ....

6 You need to wash those sheets.
(washing) ....

7 It was the first palace that the Egyptians built on the east bank of the Nile.
(to) ....

8 The judge ought to have sent him to prison for life.
(been) ....

2 GRAMMAR IN USE Choose the correct words in *italics*. Not all the correct answers are passive. 4.19 Now listen and check.

The story of Icarus

The story of Icarus is one of the most famous myths (1) *to have/ to have been* preserved from ancient Greek times. Icarus and his craftsman father, Daedalus, were summoned to Crete to work for King Minos. Minos was the wealthiest king in Greece but (2) *had/was had* a great rival in Theseus, King of Attica.

Having (3) *arrived/been arrived* in Crete, Daedalus started constructing the famous maze or Labyrinth which contained the terrifying Minotaur, a creature that was half-man and half-bull. Years later, the Labyrinth (4) *having been/ to be* completed, King Minos asked for fourteen Athenian youths (5) *to be/ being* sacrificed to the Minotaur. As Daedalus was himself an Athenian, he was offended by this and (6) *Theseus was decided to help by him/ he decided to help Theseus* to kill the Minotaur.

King Minos was furious to discover that Daedalus had helped his arch enemy and (7) *soldiers were sent to arrest him/to be arrested soldiers were sent*. But Daedalus and his son had escaped to a secret workshop that (8) *was had by them/they had* on the cliffs overlooking the sea. There they hatched a plan to escape by flying away. Daedalus made two pairs of wings from eagle feathers. But he made a serious mistake – the feathers were (9) *holding/held* together by wax. Icarus put on his wings and jumped off the cliff, flying high into the sky. But as he flew higher the heat from the sun melted the wax and Icarus (10) *was plunged/plunged* to his death in the sea below.

3 A passive verb form would be more suitable for twelve of the sentences 1–20. Tick (✓) the eight sentences which should not be changed. If you think a sentence should be changed, choose the correct reason(s) (A–D) from the box, then rewrite the sentence. The first two (0 and 00) have been done as examples.

The passive form is more appropriate because:
A the agent is unknown or unimportant
B the agent is obvious from the context or general knowledge
C we are describing rules, processes or procedures
D we are describing a general feeling or opinion

0 You must dry clean this garment. A/B This garment must be dry cleaned.

00 That baby really resembles her mother. ✓

1 The area sales manager wants Clara to move to the Barcelona office.

2 The builders built the bridge in 1450.

3 My parents are staying with us over the weekend.

4 Flight BA 783 departs from Gate 98 at 6.30 p.m.

5 They collect the information from retail outlets and they enter it on the database.

6 An unidentified person has vandalised the lift in our block.

7 The ancient Egyptians were superb stonemasons.

8 People hardly ever see foxes in daylight.

9 Sarah was having a bath when the phone rang.

10 The jury convicted the man and the judge sentenced him to fifteen years in jail.

11 The machines heat the milk to 110°C and then rapidly cool it to produce the final pasteurised product.

12 They've given the twins a kitten for their birthday.

13 There seem to be two answers to this question.

14 People must sign and submit their application forms by the end of January.

15 Johnny pretends to like classical music to impress his friends.

16 They say China is the world's fastest growing economy.

17 We will send you an invoice after we have delivered the final consignment of goods.

18 They are carrying out an investigation of the circumstances surrounding the kidnapping.

19 The local authorities refused to give us any assistance.

20 We divide up the tips and share them equally amongst the staff.

63 Other passive structures

Hisarlık in modern-day Turkey **is believed to be** the site of the ancient city of Troy.

1 Passive reporting structures

When we want to describe an impersonal or general feeling (not something said by a particular person), or we don't want to mention the person whose words are being reported, we can use a passive form of the reporting verb. For example:

- subject + passive verb + *to* + infinitive:
  He was said to be *innocent.* ***He was asked to leave.***
- *It* + passive verb + *that* clause: ***It was said that*** *he was innocent.*

We can use these passive patterns as an alternative to using an impersonal subject like *they*:
They *said he was innocent.*

More on structures with impersonal *it* ➤ Unit 44

We can use the same pattern with *it* when reporting specific decisions or opinions:
It was decided/agreed/felt that *it would be too costly to take the case to trial.*

ACADEMIC ENGLISH We can use these structures with verbs such as *assume, argue, believe, demonstrate, know*, etc:
Hisarlık ***is believed to be*** *the site of ancient Troy.*
It is often argued that *rapid deforestation is the cause of most soil erosion.*

be regarded as/considered as, etc. ➤ Unit 62.1

We can also use the pattern with *it* to report specific opinions, conclusions, etc:
In 'The Selfish Gene' ***it is suggested that*** *genes control almost every aspect of human behaviour.*

2 Passives with *get*

In informal English, *get* can be used instead of *be* in passive forms which describe actions. We often use *get* to describe accidental, negative, unusual or unexpected actions:
How did he ***get hurt****?* (= How was he hurt?)
His hand ***got trapped*** *in the car door.* (= His hand was trapped ...)
Hurry up or you'll ***get caught*** *in the storm.* *Some of the workers* ***are getting laid off****.*
Apparently there was a power cut – Jane ***got stuck*** *in the lift for over an hour!*

⚠ We cannot use *get* to describe states:
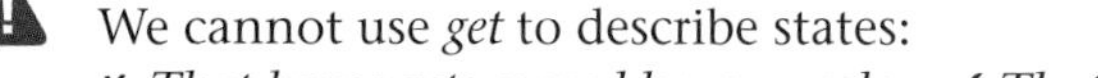
✗ ~~That house gets owned by my uncle.~~ ✓ *That house* ***is owned*** *by my uncle.* (state)

3 *make, let, help*, etc.

With the verbs *make* (meaning *force* or *require*), *see, hear* and *help* we make active sentences with verb + object + infinitive without *to*:
The boss ***made me work*** *late.* *I* ***saw her take*** *it.* *We* ***helped them unpack****.*

But in the passive form we use the infinitive with *to*:
→ *I was* ***made to work*** *late.* *She* ***was seen to take*** *it.* *They* ***were helped to unpack****.*

The verb *let* (meaning *allow*) has no passive form so we use a passive form of *allow/permit* or *give permission* + infinitive with *to*:

The teacher ***let us leave*** *early.* → ✗ ~~We were let to leave early.~~
✓ *We* ***were allowed/permitted/given permission to leave*** *early.*

Practice

1 Complete the second sentence so it has a similar meaning to the first, using the word in brackets.

1 The customs officer insisted that I open my suitcases. (made)
I .... the customs officer.

2 A farmer let us park the caravan in his field overnight. (permission)
We .... the farmer's field overnight.

3 A lot of people think the government is out of touch with public opinion. (felt)
It .... out of touch with public opinion.

4 Some people believe that the proposed legislation is unworkable. (considered)
The proposed legislation ....

5 A witness saw the man hide something in his carry-on bag. (seen)
The man .... in his carry-on bag.

6 There's a risk of a large multinational taking over our small company. (getting)
Our small company is at risk of ....

2 GRAMMAR IN USE Read the newspaper extract and the dialogue below. Then use the words in the box to complete both. 4.20 Listen and check.

be taken over   forced to make   got criticised   has been suggested   have criticised
interested   it is reported that   made to cut down on   they say   think   thought   to be

Bad news for history fans

THE POPULAR Ancient History TV channel is (1) .... to be in danger of closing down. The channel is said (2) .... losing a million dollars a week. Despite reasonable viewing figures, it has been unable to attract sufficient advertising, and investors (3) .... the company's chief executive for failing to trim expenses. Last month the channel was (4) .... redundancies in its production team, but the savings have not been sufficient to stave off the impending financial crisis. It (5) .... that a larger channel might be interested in taking over, but NBC, CNN and HBO have all denied having any interest. However, (6) .... the BBC may wish to buy some of the channel's award-winning documentaries.

DENISE You like watching the Ancient History channel, don't you?

ANDREA Yes, I really like it.

DENISE Well, people (7) .... it might be closing down. (8) .... it's losing millions of dollars every week.

ANDREA That's a pity. I know the boss (9) .... for not making enough cuts last year. And weren't they (10) .... their programming?

DENISE I don't know. But it seems they just don't get enough advertising.

ANDREA Perhaps it could (11) .... by another channel ...

DENISE I don't think any of them are (12) ....

ANDREA What about those documentaries? Someone like the BBC might want them ...

64 *have/get something done*

The pharaohs of ancient Egypt **had their tombs built** while they were still alive, as the work took many years to complete.

1 *have/get something done*

We use *have* + object + past participle (known as the causative) to describe something which is done for the subject by someone else. We can use it in all tenses.
The pharaoh ***had the pyramid built*** *while he was still alive.* (Slaves built it for the pharaoh.)
Have *you just* ***had your hair done****? It looks lovely.* (Has the hairdresser done it for you?)
We'll *probably* ***have the roof repaired*** *in the spring.* (Builders will do it.)

In informal English we can use *get* instead of *have*:
Do you ***get your hair done*** *at Ebony's?* *I'm going to* ***get the keys copied****. Do you want a set?*
Harry ***got himself moved*** *to the New York office.*

In imperatives it can be the person spoken to or someone else who will do the action:
Have/Get that mess cleaned up *at once!*
Please ***have those spreadsheets faxed*** *over to the New York office this afternoon.*

We can use the causative in future statements as commands or promises. Here it can be the subject of the sentence or someone else who will do the action:
Make sure you ***have those keys back*** *on my desk tomorrow morning.*
Don't worry. ***I'll have the report finished*** *before the meeting.* (I will do it or I will get it done.)
We're going to get it fixed *as soon as the insurance money comes through.*

We can also use this pattern to describe something which is done to the subject by someone else without them asking for it, often something unpleasant or unexpected:
Liz ***had her passport stolen****.* (= Her passport was stolen.)
John ***got his tyres slashed*** *by some hooligans.*
Darryl argued with the police officer and ended up ***getting himself arrested****.*
Out of the blue, Mark ***had his plan approved*** *by the board yesterday.*

 With this meaning, we can only use *have*, not *get*, in the present perfect:
✗ ~~*I'm afraid Alicia has got her visa application refused.*~~
✓ *I'm afraid Alicia* ***has had her visa application refused****.*

2 *have somebody do something*

There is an 'active' version of the causative which means 'cause someone to do something'. The object is the person who does the action. There are two patterns:

- *have* + object + infinitive:
  I ***had the mechanic repair*** *my washing machine.*
  *They****'re having the architect draw up*** *a set of plans for the new extension.*
  This pattern is more common in American English.
- *get* + object + *to* + infinitive: *I'll* ***get the hairdresser to do*** *my hair this afternoon.*
  We ***get the gardener to mow*** *the lawn once a fortnight in the summer.*

In British English we can use the *get* + object + *to* + infinitive pattern with the meaning of 'persuade or force someone to do something':
After numerous letters from our solicitor we finally ***got them to give*** *us a refund.*

Practice

1 Choose the word or phrase, A, B, C or D, which best completes each sentence.

1 After waiting for ages for a plumber we ..... the leaking tap fixed.
A get B had C have D having
2 They are getting their uncle ..... them his cottage in the country.
A lend B lending C to be lending D to lend
3 The judge had the prisoner ..... down to the cells after the verdict.
A take B to take C taken D taking
4 I ..... my secretary retype the memo.
A got B get C had D having
5 Abigail ..... her husband to put up some shelves in the kitchen.
A got B had C have D is having
6 The minister will have his press officer ..... the news tomorrow.
A announce B announced C to announce D being announced
7 We'll ..... the builders to move the skip tomorrow morning.
A get B have C be having D getting
8 No problem. I'll ..... the figures printed out and on your desk by lunchtime.
A having B getting C have D to get

2 GRAMMAR IN USE Complete the text with suitable forms of the verbs *have, get, bury, copy* or *make*. 4.21 Listen and check.

The Terracotta Army

In 1974, Chinese farmers digging a water well near the city of Xi'an discovered several terracotta statues buried in the earth. Senior archaeologists were called in and (1) .... a large pit dug in the surrounding area. What they discovered made headlines around the world – it was the fabled terracotta army of China's first emperor, Qin Shi Huang.

According to the ancient historian, Sima Qian, Emperor Qin had (2) .... an enormous underground necropolis, or city of the dead, constructed around the year 200 BCE. The emperor (3) .... his servants to fill the necropolis with carved soldiers whose purpose was to protect him in death. For years people thought Sima Qian's account was simply a myth, but we now know it to be true.

Excavations continue at the site but archaeologists believe there to be around 8,000 soldiers and over 500 horses. The emperor (4) .... each soldier (5) .... separately, so that no two soldiers look exactly the same. Because of the huge number of statues required, a certain amount of mass production was necessary. But the emperor (6) .... his artists to carve a different face on each statue. Some people believe he made the artists (7) .... the faces of real soldiers, but this seems unlikely. Because the emperor wanted his army to last, he (8) .... his carved soldiers (9) .... from terracotta, which, unlike wood, does not rot or disintegrate with time.

Emperor Qin (10) .... himself (11) .... in a mausoleum close to the site of the terracotta army. It is likely that in the coming years the Chinese government will (12) .... its archaeologists to excavate the tomb. It may turn out to contain even greater treasures than those found in the tomb of Tutankhamun in Egypt. For it is certain that an emperor as powerful as Qin would have (13) .... his most valuable treasures (14) .... close to his own body.

Review MODULE 14

1 UNITS 62 AND 63 **This text would be improved if at least seven of the verbs were passive. Underline the phrases that should go into the passive and rewrite those sections of the text below. The first one has been done as an example.**

Solving the Mystery of Hieroglyphics

For almost two thousand years the symbols and inscriptions which people had carved onto the great monuments of ancient Egypt were a complete mystery. They were obviously a kind of writing, but nobody knew what they meant.

Then, in 1799, a French officer discovered a strange stone in the small Egyptian town of Rosetta. It had three types of writing carved into its surface. One of the languages was Greek but the other two were unknown. A year later the British seized the stone and the British moved it to the British Museum in London.

For twenty years the stone lay gathering dust in the museum. Then in 1822 somebody asked a French scientist named Jean François Champollion to look at the stone. He immediately recognised that some of the symbols matched those he had seen on monuments in Egypt. By comparing the Greek words with the Egyptian symbols he was able to work out their meaning. The Egyptian symbols were hieroglyphs, a type of writing in which pictures represent sounds and meanings.

Once somebody had solved the puzzle of their written language it became possible for scholars to decipher the inscriptions on all the great monuments. Thus people finally unlocked the mysteries of Egypt's fabulous history and culture.

0 *which had been carved*
1 ....
2 ....
3 ....
4 ....
5 ....
6 ....
7 ....

2 UNITS 63 AND 64 **Match 1–3 with the correct continuation, A, B or C, in each group.**

1
1 She is thought to have left
2 She was made to leave
3 Her boss let her leave

A as she was feeling sick this morning.
B but nobody seems to know for sure.
C as a result of the disciplinary enquiry.

2
1 Several members of the local force were said
2 It has been suggested in the press
3 A leading police officer got

A that bribery is common amongst junior police officers.
B caught receiving bribes.
C to be receiving bribes from the criminals.

3
1 Have him report to me
2 I had him reported
3 I had him report to me

A because I was his line manager.
B when you see him later.
C to his commanding officer.

4
1 We got the computer repaired
2 Get the computer repaired
3 We got the engineer to repair the computer

A before we do the presentation.
B after he had fixed the printer.
C because it had broken down.

3 ALL UNITS **Complete the text, using suitable forms of the words in brackets, as in the example.**

Highlights of China

The Forbidden City

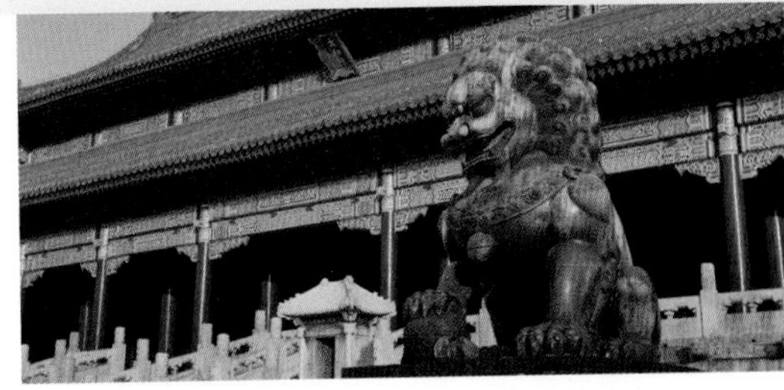

LOCATION OF THE PALACE

The ancient palace of the emperors of China, known as the Forbidden City, is situated in the heart of modern-day Beijing. The palace (0) ....*can easily be reached*..... (can / easy / reach) by bus or metro. However, you can also (1) .... (get / your travel agent / arrange) a private guide to collect you from your hotel.

HISTORY AND DESCRIPTION OF THE PALACE

Emperor Yongle (2) .... (have / the palace / build) at the centre of his new capital, Beijing. (3) .... (it / believe / be / construct) early in the fifteenth century. The complex covers more than 74 hectares and (4) .... (surround) by 10-metre-high walls. (5) .... (it / say) that more than one million workers were involved in its construction. After being used by successive emperors for five centuries, the palace (6) .... (abandon) in 1924 when the last emperor left.

VISITING THE FORBIDDEN CITY

Tickets to visit the palace (7) .... (can / purchase) at the entrance. Be aware that the complex contains 980 buildings spread over a huge area. If you are short of time, (8) .... (have / your hotel / arrange) an organised tour so that you can focus on the highlights.

4 ALL UNITS **Complete the second sentence so it has a similar meaning to the first, using the word in brackets. In some cases more than one answer is possible.**

1 There is a general feeling that the new government is unlikely to last long. (said)
It .... is unlikely to last long.

2 The unruly football fans were arrested because of their bad behaviour. (got)
As a result of their bad behaviour, the ....

3 We regret that we weren't given the chance to buy shares in our company. (having)
We .... to buy shares in our company.

4 Make sure someone cleans up this mess by the time I get back. (cleaned)
.... by the time I get back.

5 Sasha was delighted that they had accepted him on the degree course. (been)
Sasha was delighted .... on the degree course.

6 The guard wouldn't let us take photos of the exhibits. (to)
We .... of the exhibits.

7 I'm organising someone that can drive the kids to the airport. (getting)
.... the kids to the airport.

8 After they had completed the audit, the company published its report. (having)
The audit .... published its annual report.

MODULE

15 Word combinations

Before you start

1 Review these Intermediate grammar points and check you know them.

Dependent prepositions

In English there are many verbs, nouns and adjectives which are used with particular or dependent prepositions. For example, we *accuse* someone *of* a crime, not *at* a crime, *by* a crime or *for* a crime. Examples include:

VERB + PREPOSITION	NOUN + PREPOSITION	ADJECTIVE + PREPOSITION
to ***succeed in*** *something*	*to have* ***a fear of*** *something*	*to be* ***keen on*** *something*

Multi-word verbs

1 Multi-word verbs are formed from a verb, e.g. *grow*, plus a preposition, e.g. *on, off, up*, or/and an adverb, e.g. *away, back, out*. The combination sometimes creates a new meaning which is different from the meaning of the original verb.

2 There are four types of multi-word verb:

TYPE	EXAMPLES	SENTENCE
prepositional verbs	*cope with something* *rely on somebody*	*How does she* ***cope with*** *all those kids?*
intransitive phrasal verbs* (two-part phrasal verbs)	*come back* *grow up*	*Make sure you* ***come back*** *before midnight.*
transitive phrasal verbs (two-part phrasal verbs)	*put something off* *turn somebody down*	*We****'re putting*** *the party* ***off*** *because of the awful weather.*
phrasal–prepositional verbs (three-part phrasal verbs)	*look forward to something* *catch up with somebody*	*They****'re looking forward to*** *the holidays.*

* As intransitive phrasal verbs do not have an object, they cannot be made passive:
✗ *~~Have the children been come back yet?~~* ✓ ***Have*** *the children* ***come back*** *yet?*

3 Multi-word verbs form tenses, and are used in questions, negatives and (apart from intransitive phrasal verbs) in the passive, in the same way as other verbs:
Will *you* ***be putting*** *the party* ***off****?* (future continuous question)
The party ***has been put off*** *until next month.* (present perfect passive)

Collocations

Collocations are words that often go together. There are different patterns:

adjective + noun	*a strong swimmer a heavy smoker a great success*
verb + noun	*take a photo take turns run a race run a business fail a test*
verb + noun + preposition	*make friends with somebody take care of somebody* *make the most of something*

2 **Read the information and identify examples of different multi-word verbs and other word combinations.**

ADVERTISEMENT FEATURE

CLIVE'S REPAIR SHOP

THESE DAYS WE ALL RELY ON OUR COMPUTERS, MOBILE PHONES, SAT-NAVS AND DIGITAL TVS. BUT WHAT HAPPENS WHEN THEY BREAK DOWN?

How can you run a business or a home without functioning equipment? Many people just throw things away and buy replacements because previous experience of repair shops has put them off using them. That was before **CLIVE'S REPAIR SHOP** opened!
Clive's is different. First, we guarantee all our repairs for twelve months and offer insurance against any future breakdowns. Then, if anything goes wrong during this period, we give you A FULL REFUND.
And if we don't succeed in repairing your equipment, we won't charge you a penny.

Try our service. We GUARANTEE you'll be satisfied.

3 **Complete the diagnostic test below. Choose the correct words in *italics*. In two cases both options are possible, but only one is appropriate in the situation.**

1 The supervisor said I shouldn't have shouted at the clients so I had to *apologise to* / *apologise to them* at the next meeting. ➤ Unit 65.1
2 The company has no interest in *if* / *whether* I speak any foreign languages. ➤ Unit 65.1
3 Sunil managed to visit his relatives in New Zealand despite his fear *of flying* / *flying*. ➤ Unit 65.2
4 The auditors initially issued a demand for full repayment but then changed their minds and simply *demanded for* / *demanded* a token contribution. ➤ Unit 65.2
5 Donna's son has come out of hospital at last. I'm so glad *of* / *for* her. ➤ Unit 65.3
6 Did you agree *with helping* / *to help* Caroline with the cooking? ➤ Unit 66.1
7 Sylvia was astonished at *that her colleague had behaved so atrociously* / *her colleague behaving so atrociously*. ➤ Unit 66.2
8 Can you explain *me the solution* / *the solution to me*? ➤ Unit 66.4
9 I blame the government *for* / *of* the terrible state of our roads. ➤ Unit 66.4
10 There are few people *for whom* / *whom for* he cares so deeply. ➤ Unit 66.5
11 I've just seen Lucy. I ran *her into* / *into her* at the supermarket. ➤ Unit 66.5
12 I presented my proposal to the board but they turned *down it* / *it down*. ➤ Unit 67.1
13 The government *brought recently in* / *recently brought in* some legislation to deal with the problem. ➤ Unit 67.1
14 It is a condition of receiving this credit card that you do not *reveal* / *give away* your confidential PIN number to any third party. ➤ Unit 67.2
15 Could you *turn on* / *activate* the kettle, darling? I'm dying for a cup of tea. ➤ Unit 67.2
16 Are you looking forward *the party to* / *to the party*? ➤ Unit 67.4
17 I love my children so I put *up willingly* / *willingly up* with their bad behaviour. ➤ Unit 67.4
18 There's a *light* / *faint* smell of gas. Have you left the cooker on? ➤ Unit 68.1
19 As part of her doctorate, Helena is *making* / *doing* some research in the British Library. ➤ Unit 68.4
20 It isn't fair to *have* / *take* risks with other people's savings. ➤ Unit 68.5

4 **Check your answers on page 384. Then go to the unit for more information and practice.**

Go online for a full diagnostic test

65 Dependent prepositions (1)

1 General rules

Prepositions after verbs, nouns and adjectives always have an object. The object can be a noun, pronoun or verb *-ing* form. (Note that *to* can be a preposition):

I apologised ***to my boss/her/the managing director****.* *I apologised* ***for arriving*** *late.*

The *-ing* form can have its own subject. This can be a noun phrase, an object pronoun or, in more formal English, a possessive adjective:

I'm looking forward ***to*** *my wife* ***returning****.* *Dad insisted* ***on*** *us* ***apologising****.*

The detective insisted ***on*** *our* ***leaving*** *the crime scene.* (formal)

We use *whether*, not *if*, after prepositions:

✗ ~~*That depends on if you pass the test.*~~ ✓ *That depends* ***on whether*** *you pass the test.*

2 Noun + preposition

Some nouns are followed by dependent prepositions:

Please indicate your preferred ***method of*** *payment.*
The policy will provide ***insurance against*** *damage to your vehicle.*
She has a wonderful ***relationship with*** *her children.*

If a noun is related to a prepositional verb (➤ Unit 66.5), the noun often has the same preposition:

He ***succeeded in*** *winning the Palme d'Or.* (*to succeed in* something)
We congratulated him on his ***success in*** *winning the Palme d'Or.* (a *success in* something)

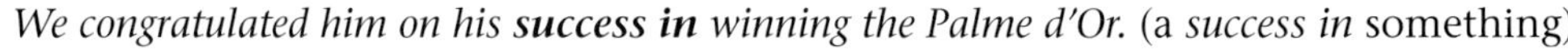

However, some nouns with dependent prepositions have a different preposition from the verb, or have a preposition where the related verb doesn't have one:

a demand for something (to demand sth)
a discussion about something (to discuss sth)
a fear of something (to fear sth)
an influence on/over something/somebody (to influence sth/sb)
a relationship with somebody (to relate to sb)

The members had a ***discussion about*** *the subscription charges.*

✗ ~~*We discussed about the subscription charges.*~~ ✓ *We* ***discussed*** *the subscription charges.*

There are some noun + preposition forms which can only be followed by a noun:

✗ ~~*The court issued a demand for repaying of the debt.*~~
✓ *The court issued a* ***demand for repayment*** *of the debt.*

Preposition + noun, e.g. *at hand*, *without delay* ➤ page 365

3 Adjective + preposition

A lot of adjectives describing feelings and opinions have dependent prepositions:

My grandfather's very ***keen on*** *trout fishing.* *I've never been* ***afraid of*** *flying.*
People are becoming increasingly ***worried about*** *climate change.*

If an adjective is related to a verb or noun which takes a preposition, the adjective usually takes the same preposition:

We ***depend on*** *his generosity.* → *We are* ***dependent on*** *his generosity.*
I expressed my ***gratitude for*** *their assistance.* → *I was* ***grateful for*** *their assistance.*
He's always had an ***interest in*** *art.* → *He's always been* ***interested in*** *art.*

Some adjectives can be followed by different prepositions, depending on the meaning:

Debbie's been promoted. I'm so ***glad for*** *her.* (= pleased for her)
I was so exhausted, I was ***glad of*** *a break.* (= grateful for it)
A lot of people are ***concerned about*** *global warming.* (= worried)
Don't ask Mike, he wasn't ***concerned with*** *the decision.* (= involved)

For lists of the nouns and adjectives described in this unit ➤ pages 370–1

Practice

To complete these exercises you may need to refer to page pages 370–1

1 Match the sentence beginnings 1–10 with the endings A–J.

1 Although I had a lot of questions I was afraid
2 The passengers' relatives were anxious
3 It's not a matter
4 We have to face the possibility
5 My parents expressed surprise
6 We tend to be scared
7 As I stepped onto the boat I suddenly felt anxious
8 Danny takes great pleasure
9 The committee sees no problem
10 Ever since that experience at the zoo she's been afraid

A of large animals.
B at the fact that I'd finally found a job.
C of whether you want to do it or not, it's an order.
D in criticising his classmates.
E of asking them.
F in approving your application for planning permission.
G of things we know little about.
H for news of their loved ones.
I about the absence of life jackets.
J of them not getting here in time.

2 GRAMMAR IN USE Complete the article with suitable prepositions. 4.22 Listen and check.

Phone networks on brink of collapse

By Jeremy Iston

THE EVER-GROWING demand (1) .... smartphones has placed an unexpected strain on the world's mobile phone networks.

Smartphones are full of applications designed to send and receive emails, surf the Internet, watch online videos and access social networking sites. Although the mobile phone network has been upgraded to deal with the task (2) .... transmitting this kind of data, it was originally made (3) .... the transmission of basic phone calls and text messages, and is therefore struggling to find a way (4) .... dealing with these increasing demands.

It is the sophisticated applications on the new smartphones which are responsible (5) .... most of this increase (6) .... cellular traffic. To ensure that the information available (7) .... their users is kept constantly up to date, some of these applications connect to the network every eight seconds. Others continuously stream information or stay logged on for hours while downloading videos or messages. This has the effect (8) .... monopolising the network and slowing down speeds for other users. Phones crowded (9) .... these data-hungry applications are selling at a phenomenal rate and

are popular (10) .... many young people. In the UK over 60,000 phones that use the Android wireless system are sold every day.

If demand continues to grow at this rate the entire system is in danger (11) .... collapsing. What is the solution (12) .... this problem? The latest LTE (Long Term Evolution) technology can deal with much larger volumes of traffic, but requires new phone masts and new handsets. The expense (13) .... installing the new network and producing new handsets means that the prospect (14) .... such a system being adopted worldwide is unlikely in the immediate future. The alternative is to build more transmitters. We may be fond (15) .... our mobile phones, but do we really want more of these eyesores cluttering up our cities and countryside?

66 Dependent prepositions (2)

1 Preposition or *to* + infinitive

Many adjectives describing feelings and emotions can be followed by a preposition or *to* + infinitive:

*We were **annoyed at finding** our places taken. He's **keen on learning** archery.*
*We were **annoyed to find** our places taken. He's **keen to learn** archery.*

Some verbs can also be followed by a preposition or *to* + infinitive, but there may be a change of meaning:

*They don't **agree with** the government's policy.* (= They have a different opinion.)
*I **agreed to** help him fill out the forms.* (= I said that I was willing to ...)

More on verbs + infinitive ➤ Units 45 and 46.3/4

2 Preposition or *that* clause

Many of the words which describe or report what we say, think or feel are followed by a preposition + *-ing* form. Some of these words can also be followed by a *that* clause:

*The judge **insisted on** the jury **disregarding** the doctor's testimony.*
*The judge **insisted that** the jury disregarded the doctor's testimony.*

We can't put a *that* clause after a preposition, except with expressions such as *the fact that* or *the idea that*:

✗ ~~*My parents disapproved of that my brother left school at sixteen.*~~
✓ *My parents **disapproved of the fact that** my brother left school at sixteen.*

Reporting verbs ➤ Unit 50 Subjects with *-ing* forms ➤ Unit 65.1

3 Verb + object + preposition

After certain verbs, e.g. *accuse, prevent,* we use object + preposition + *-ing* form to link the verb with the person it affects and the action it refers to:

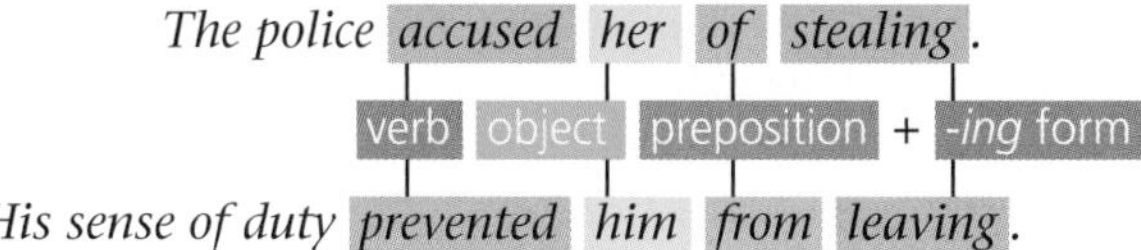

These verbs can be made passive:

*She **was accused** of stealing (by the police).*
*He **was prevented** from leaving (by his sense of duty).*

4 Verbs with two objects

Some verbs with dependent prepositions have two objects, e.g. *explain something to somebody, discuss something with somebody*. We usually use the pattern below with a direct object (usually a thing) and an indirect object (usually a person):

The tour guide ***discussed*** *the day's schedule* ***with*** *us*.

verb | direct object | preposition + indirect object

Can you ***explain*** *it* ***to*** *me*?

Unlike other verbs used with two objects, e.g. *give*, with these verbs we cannot omit the preposition: *He gave it to me. He gave me it.*

✗ ~~*He explained me it.*~~ ✗ ~~*He explained it me.*~~ ✓ *He* ***explained*** *it* ***to*** *me.*
✗ ~~*He discussed us it.*~~ ✗ ~~*He discussed it us.*~~ ✓ *He* ***discussed*** *it* ***with*** *us.*

In the passive, only the direct object can become the subject of the passive verb:

My teacher ***explained*** *it to me.* → ✗ ~~*I was explained it by my teacher.*~~
✓ ***It was explained*** *to me (by my teacher).*

With some verbs we can change the order of the objects, but we use different prepositions:
I ***blame*** *our schools* ***for*** *the poor standard of education.* (= blame somebody for something)
I ***blame*** *the poor standard of education* ***on*** *our schools.* (= blame something on somebody)

Common verbs with prepositions and two objects ➤ page 371

5 Prepositional verbs

Prepositional verbs consist of a verb, e.g. *look*, plus a preposition, e.g. *into, at, for*. The combination of the verb and preposition often creates a new meaning which can sometimes, but not always, be worked out from the parts:
She ***looked for*** *her missing passport.* (= searched, tried to find)
Would you mind ***looking into*** *his complaint?* (= investigating, researching)

Prepositional verbs are transitive – they always have an object. We put the noun or pronoun object after the preposition:
We didn't ***fall for his story****. We didn't* ***fall for it****.*

The rules for object position are different for phrasal verbs (➤ Unit 67.3).

With prepositional verbs we cannot put an adverb between the preposition and object, but we can put an adverb between the verb and preposition:
✗ ~~*She parted with reluctantly her money.*~~ ✓ *She* ***parted reluctantly with*** *her money.*

FORMALITY CHECK In formal English we sometimes prefer to avoid a preposition at the end of a sentence. With prepositional verbs we can put the preposition in front of (but NOT after) the relative pronouns *whom* or *which*:
These are the principles (which) our party ***stands for.***
→ ✗ ~~*These are the principles which for our party stands.*~~
✓ *These are the principles* ***for which*** *our party* ***stands.***
That's the type of client (whom) I'm ***dealing with.***
→ *That's the type of client* ***with whom*** *I'm* ***dealing.***

Pronunciation ➤ 1.18

ACADEMIC ENGLISH Some prepositional verbs are mainly used in the passive form (➤ Unit 62.1), especially in written English:
The marketing strategy ***is aimed at*** *a target audience of eighteen- to twenty-five-year-olds.*

Common prepositional verbs ➤ page 372
Differences between prepositional and phrasal verbs ➤ Unit 67.3

Practice To complete these exercises you may need to refer to page 372.

1 What are the people saying in the pictures? Complete each sentence, using a suitable form of a verb from box A, a preposition from box B and the words in brackets, as in the example. There are two extra verbs and prepositions.

A call deal fall go get (x2) ~~look~~ look put take

B about after ~~for~~ for out over round through with (x2)

0 'I'm *looking for a new computer*. Can you give me any advice on the different models?' (a new computer)

1 'I'm sorry my assistant wouldn't give you a refund. I'll .... straightaway.' (it)

2 'Your little boy's so cute. I think he .... !' (you)

3 'You can't wear that top with that skirt. It doesn't ....' (it)

4 'You need a lot of strength and stamina to ....' (this course)

5 'I can't seem to .... I've had it for two weeks now.' (this cold)

6 'I think he's hurt. I'll ....' (an ambulance)

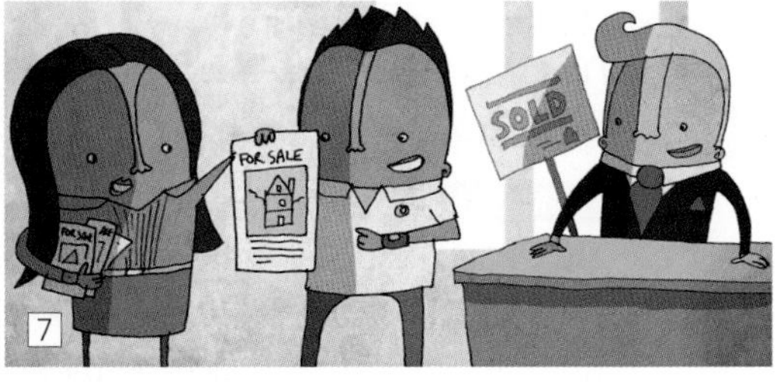

7 'This house looks interesting. Can we make an appointment to .... ?' (it)

2 GRAMMAR IN USE **Choose the correct words in *italics*.** 4.23 **Listen and check.**

NEWS

Home | World | UK | Business | Health | Politics | Education | Entertainment & Arts

New technology catches liars

A team at Cornell University in New York has developed software (1) *aimed / designed* at detecting lies in emails and text messages.

Traditional lie detectors work by measuring a person's heartbeat. They (2) *look / rely* on (3) *that / the fact that* a person's pulse gets faster when they are nervous or stressed – a strong indicator that they are not telling the truth. The new software is much more subtle. It scans electronic messages and looks (4) *for / like* various clues which indicate lies are being told.

Researchers have identified a number of these clues, or 'falsehood indicators', ranging from overuse of the third person to frequent use of negative adjectives and verbs. A team of volunteers provided (5) *with the researchers / the researchers with* both truthful and dishonest emails. By comparing them they came (6) *across / over* a number of characteristics. They noticed, for instance, that truthful emails were usually short and written in the first person, with lots of use of 'I' to start sentences. Dishonest emails were on average 28 percent longer than honest ones because people (7) *consider / worry* about not sounding convincing, so tend to give more detail when lying. And because liars want people to fall (8) *at / for* their stories, they tend to use more sense verbs such as 'see' and 'feel', perhaps in an attempt to gain the reader's sympathy.

There has been a lot of interest from law enforcement agencies, insurance companies, welfare agencies and banks – all of which are struggling to cope (9) *for / with* the growing tide of fraud. They hope the new program will be effective in protecting (10) *from the public / the public from* the ever-increasing threat posed by Internet crime.

3 Complete each sentence with the correct form of a suitable verb from box A and a preposition from box B. Use each verb once only. Some of the prepositions will be needed more than once. You will need two prepositions in 8–12. 4.24 **Listen and check.**

A: accuse agree blame convince cure depend disagree explain present prevent quarrel rely

B: about for from to of on over with

1 Somehow I managed to .... my parents .... my innocence.
2 The immigration authorities couldn't .... the refugees .... entering the country.
3 Do you honestly think this treatment will .... him .... his stutter?
4 The Chief Constable is going to .... Harold .... this year's award for bravery.
5 In my opinion we can .... today's unemployment problem .... the previous government.
6 I'm rather confused; you'd better .... that procedure .... me again.
7 I wouldn't dare .... him .... stealing, although I certainly don't trust him.
8 Congress is bound to .... the President .... the increase in federal taxes.
9 Since the accident he's had to .... his mother .... everything.
10 I'm happy to report that the unions .... us .... the need for wage controls next year.
11 In the event of a power cut you will have to .... the emergency generator .... electricity.
12 Look, just give me the car keys; I don't want to .... you .... this any longer.

67 Phrasal verbs

In the old days, if somebody wanted to **look something up**, they'd open an encyclopaedia – now they just log on to the Internet.

1 Grammar of phrasal verbs

Phrasal verbs consist of a verb plus a particle, usually an adverb. They can be transitive or intransitive. Intransitive phrasal verbs are sometimes used in imperatives:
Watch out *– that floor's not very safe.* ***Come on!*** *I can't wait all day!*

Some phrasal verbs have a transitive use with one meaning, and an intransitive use with a different meaning. Compare:
The plane ***took off*** *on time.* (*take off*, intransitive = become airborne)
The man ***took off*** *his coat.* (*take something off*, transitive = remove)

Note the correct word order in these sentence patterns:

transitive phrasal verb + noun object	✓ *I made that story up.* ✓ *I made up that story.*
transitive phrasal verb + pronoun object	✗ ~~*I made up it.*~~ ✓ *I made it up.*
transitive phrasal verb + adverb	✗ ~~*I paid early back the loan.*~~ ✗ ~~*I paid back early the loan.*~~ ✓ *I paid the loan back early.* ✓ *She never pays me back.*
transitive phrasal verb + relative pronoun	✗ ~~*That's the room which up I did.*~~ ✗ ~~*That's the room up which I did.*~~ ✓ *That's the room which I did up.*
transitive phrasal verb + passives	✗ ~~*That story was made by a resentful employee up.*~~ ✓ *That story was made up by a resentful employee.*

We can form nouns from some multi-word verbs (➤ Unit 70):
The car ***broke down*** *five kilometres from home.*
→ *The* ***breakdown*** *happened five kilometres from home.* (noun)

2 Meaning of phrasal verbs

Phrasal verbs usually have a meaning which is different from the meaning of the parts:
Are you taking a suitcase? (*take* = carry)
The power's off. (*off* = not connected)
After the argument, he ***took off*** *without a word.* (*take off* = leave unexpectedly)

The same phrasal verb can have more than one meaning:
That music's too loud. ***Turn it down.*** (= reduce the volume)
They offered her the job but she ***turned it down****.* (= didn't accept the job)

In some cases it is possible to get an idea of the meaning of a multi-word verb from its particle, but note that these particles do not always have the meanings shown here:

up	completion/finality/maintaining sth	*give up break up eat up keep up*
down	collapse, movement downwards/writing	*fall down break down note down*
out	removal/thoroughness	*take out work out see out mark out*
on	starting/continuing/progressing	*turn on carry on take on get on*
off	stop connection/departure	*turn off break off set off*

FORMALITY CHECK Where a multi-word verb has no exact synonym, e.g. *grow up*, we can use it in formal and informal contexts. However, when there is a single verb with an equivalent meaning (e.g. *think about* = *consider*), the multi-word verb tends to be used in informal contexts while the single verb is more formal. Compare:
The bank will ***consider*** *your application for a loan in due course.* (formal)
Honestly, how can you ***think about*** *money at a time like this!* (informal)

3 Differences between phrasal and prepositional verbs

The main difference between phrasal and prepositional verbs is the way we use them with objects. Because prepositions are always followed by an object, with prepositional verbs we have to put an object (noun or pronoun) after the preposition:

I won't ***stand for*** *this behaviour any longer. I won't* ***stand for*** *it any longer.*

Phrasal verbs are formed from a verb + adverb particle. As adverbs do not need to be followed by an object, we can put a noun object before or after the particle:

We couldn't ***work out*** *the answer. We couldn't* ***work*** *the answer* ***out.***

When the object of a phrasel verb is a pronoun we always put it between the verb and particle:
✗ ~~*We couldn't work out it.*~~ ✓ *We couldn't* ***work*** *it* ***out.***

Learner dictionaries indicate which type a verb is by showing a noun object with the verb:

put sb/sth off phr v [T] to arrange to do something at a later time or date, especially because there is a problem, difficulty, etc. *They've put the meeting off till next week.*

ACADEMIC ENGLISH Phrasal verbs are not common in formal written English, unlike prepositional verbs.

4 Phrasal-prepositional verbs

These verbs are formed by combining a verb with an adverb and preposition. The combination creates a new meaning which cannot usually be understood from the meanings of the individual parts:
We ***look forward to*** *hearing from you.* (= anticipate with pleasure)

They are transitive and can be made passive:
All her staff ***looked up to*** *her.* (active) *She* ***was looked up to*** *by all her staff.* (passive)

We usually put noun or pronoun objects after the second particle:

I can't ***put up with*** *this treatment any longer. I can't* ***put up with*** *it any longer.*

We cannot usually put the object immediately after the verb or between the particles:
✗ ~~*I can't put this treatment up with any longer.*~~ ✗ ~~*I can't put it up with any longer.*~~
✗ ~~*I can't put up this treatment with any longer.*~~ ✗ ~~*I can't put up it with any longer.*~~

However, if the verb has two objects, e.g. *let somebody in on something, take somebody up on something*, we can put a noun or pronoun object immediately after the verb:

We ***let*** *James* ***in on*** *the plan. We* ***took*** *her* ***up on*** *her offer.*

We can put an adverb between the two particles, but not before the first particle or after the final particle:
✓ *He* ***stands up strongly for*** *his principles.* (particle + adverb + particle)
✗ ~~*He stands strongly up for his principles.*~~ (adverb + particle + particle)
✗ ~~*He stands up for strongly his principles.*~~ (particle + particle + adverb)

For a list of the verbs described in this unit ➤ page 372

Practice To complete these exercises you may need to refer to page 372.

1 Rewrite the parts of the sentences in brackets. Put the words in the correct order, as in the example.

0 Computers don't have floppy disk drives any longer.
(away / they've / them / done / with).
They've done away with them. ....

1 We have a wireless network in the office. (by / it / our / was / set /IT engineer / up).

....

2 The architect (old barn / beautiful house / the / into / turned / a).

....

3 Fog at JFK airport (up / held / for several hours / them).

....

4 Don't (tomorrow / put / until / off / it); do it now.

....

5 This calculation is so complicated! (help / it / can / out / you / me / work)?

....

6 Silvio's coming for the weekend. We (him / put / in the spare room / can / up).

....

7 I can get the machine started but I don't know (off / to / it / how / turn).

....

8 You don't have to complete the form; the computer (it / automatically / out / fill / will).

....

2 Rewrite the verb phrases in these sentences using a suitable phrasal or prepositional verb from the box. Use a pronoun (*it*, *him*, *her*, *them*) to replace the underlined object, as in the example.

carry out fix up get over ~~give up~~ look into pick up
point out run down run into sort out take after

0 Alan's managed to quit smoking. .... *to give it up* ....
1 Would you mind organising the removal yourself? ....
2 I met Steve quite by chance at the supermarket this morning. ....
3 I've arranged the meeting for ten o'clock tomorrow. ....
4 You're always criticising your colleagues. ....
5 I'm sure the police will investigate the burglary. ....
6 The builders undertook the job very professionally. ....
7 Could you collect the children from school tonight? ....
8 Has Perry recovered from the flu yet? ....
9 They really resemble their mother, don't they? ....
10 Would you highlight the advantages for me? ....

3 GRAMMAR IN USE **Complete the text with multi-word verbs, using no more than three words for each gap. The words in brackets will help you. 4.25 Listen and check.**

Anger management

MANDY DICKSON has (0) ....*set up*..... (set) a one-day anger workshop which helps people learn about and (1) .... (deal) their anger. It is (2) .... (aim) ordinary people who don't feel able to control their tempers. She (3) .... (point) that anger is natural and nothing to be ashamed of, but we should recognise it and (4) .... (look) its true causes. Then we can (5) .... (face) it, and begin to do something positive. Participants (6) .... (fill) a questionnaire about things that make them angry. They compare their responses and often (7) .... (find) that the causes are other feelings such as fear or grief.

But in our culture it isn't acceptable to (8) .... (act) these feelings in public. Men, in particular, are supposed to (9) .... (cover) these feelings. Once we know the causes of anger, we must learn how to (10) .... (keep) situations which will induce them. When we are angry we want other people to understand us, but we often make the mistake of (11) .... (run) those around us. Anger is often caused by the feeling that you have been (12) .... (let) by other people. But we can't always expect other people to know our feelings. So the most important way to (13) .... (cut) the number of anger-producing situations is to tell people exactly how we feel. It really all (14) .... (come) communication.

4 GRAMMAR IN USE **There are ten more mistakes with phrasal and phrasal-prepositional verbs in the dialogue (incorrect word order, use of objects and particles). Correct the mistakes, as in the example. 4.26 Listen and check.**

GAVIN Is that a new laptop?

ANDY Yes. My old one ~~broke it down~~ *broke down* a few weeks ago.

GAVIN It looks like a good one. How are you getting with on it?

ANDY Not great. It's completely different from my old one.

GAVIN Let me have a look. Oh, I think it uses a different operating system. They should have pointed out it to you when you bought it.

ANDY Well, they didn't. It's so confusing – the manufacturers are always coming over with new systems for computers. Why don't they stick to the ones everybody's familiar with?

GAVIN It all comes down with economics, I suppose. If they didn't keep changing the systems, nobody would spend money on new software!

ANDY That's true. Look, I hate to bring up it but didn't you say you were a bit of an expert on computer programs? Could you give me a hand with this one?

GAVIN Of course. No problem. But I'm a bit busy right now. I have to get back of the office in a few minutes.

ANDY Sorry. I don't want to hold up you. Can we fix up another time?

GAVIN Sure. I'll be here for lunch tomorrow. We can catch up each other with then and set up it. Well, I ought to be going.

ANDY Yes, I'd better get down at my work. I've got a big report to finish …

68 Common collocations

Young people are often the first to **take advantage of** new technology. If a product **does well** with teenagers, there is usually a **strong possibility** it will succeed with the rest of the public.

1 Adjective + noun

We often use specific adjectives with particular nouns. For example, we can describe *rain* as *light* or *heavy* but we can't say *strong rain* or *weak rain.*

✗ ~~*Strong rain is predicted this evening.*~~ ✓ ***Heavy rain** is predicted this evening.*

These are some common adjective + noun collocations. Sometimes the meaning changes:

ADJECTIVE	NOUN
light	*clothes colour drinker meal punishment rain sleeper smoker wind work* (= not physically demanding)
heavy	*burden casualties demands drinker industry* (= large scale) *losses meal punishment rain smoker traffic work* (= physically demanding)
weak	*argument coffee currency joke point ruler signal swimmer taste*
strong	*accent argument* (= convincing) *case* (= good reasons) *coffee feelings influence leader position possibility sense signal smell swimmer taste wind*
faint	*chance hope possibility smell*
little/great	*difficulty interest pleasure success time*
good/bad	*behaviour habit luck news person time word*
poor	*health memory performance relation* (= less successful than others)

*The lawyer presented a **strong argument** but failed to win the case.*
*Don't go by car, the **traffic**'s really **heavy** today.*
*Karl's very strong so **heavy work** doesn't bother him.*

 Combinations from other languages do not often translate directly. It's always best to check in a dictionary first.

2 Verb + noun

There are many verb + noun collocations that we use to describe particular actions, e.g. *take a bath, tell a story, make a mistake*. In many cases the meaning of the verb does not change, but in some cases it has a new meaning:

miss the point (= not understand an argument) *miss a bus/train,* etc. (= arrive too late)
pass an exam (= succeed in) *pass a law* (= the act of officially creating a new law)
run a business (= manage a business) *run a bath* (= fill a bath with water)

We make most of these combinations with the verbs *make, do, have* and *take*. See opposite.

3 Verb + noun + preposition

A few verbs combine with a noun and a preposition:

have	*keep*	*make*	*run*	*take*
faith in *confidence in* *trust in*	*account of* *an eye on* *faith with*	*a success of* *the most of* *a fool of*	*the risk of* *rings round*	*account of a dislike to* *pity on pleasure in* *the form of*

*Make sure you **keep an eye on** Terry – I don't trust her.*
*The company lets Heinrich make all their purchasing decisions, they **have faith in** his judgement.*
*If you wait until later, you**'ll run the risk of** missing your train.*

4 Collocations with *make* and *do*

Here are some common collocations with *make* and *do*. (Note that in the charts below *sb* = somebody and *sth* = something):

make			
an appearance	*a decision*	*a gesture*	*a profit (on sth)*
an appointment (= arrange)	*a difference*	*a good/bad job of sth*	*progress (with sth)*
arrangements	*a discovery*	*a habit of sth*	*a promise (to sb)*
an attempt	*an effort*	*a journey*	*a remark (about sth)*
a bed	*an enemy (of sb)*	*a list*	*a sound*
(sth) better/worse	*an enquiry*	*a living*	*a speech (on/about sth)*
a (phone) call	*an exception*	*a mess (of sth)*	*a start (on sth)*
a change	*an excuse (about sth, for sb)*	*a mistake*	*a suggestion*
a charge (for sth)	*a fire*	*money*	*time (for sth/sb)*
a choice	*a fortune*	*a noise*	*trouble*
a comment	*friends (with sb)*	*an offer (for sth, to sb)*	*oneself understood*
a confession	*a fuss (about sth)*	*a plan*	*war*
a contribution (to)		*a point (about sth)*	*a will*

do			
your best (= try hard)	*an/some exercise*	*homework*	*an operation*
business (with sb)	*an experiment*	*the housework*	*research*
the cleaning/cooking/ironing/washing (-up)	*sb a favour*	*yourself an injury*	*right/wrong*
a course	*good* (= help other people)*/evil*	*a job*	*the shopping*
some damage (to sth)	*sb some good* (= make sb better/healthier)	*justice*	*sport*
the dishes	*your hair/face/nails*	*a kindness*	*your teeth* (= brush/clean)
your duty	*harm (to sb)*	*the laundry*	*well/badly* (= be successful/unsuccessful)
an exam/a test		*military/jury service*	

5 Collocations with *have* and *take*

We use some nouns with either *have* or *take*, e.g. *have/take a guess*; in other cases we only use one of these verbs:

have			
an appointment (= an existing arrangement)	*a dance*	*lunch/dinner/a meal*	*a say*
an argument	*a drink*	*a problem (with)*	*something to eat*
a baby	*an effect (on sth)*	*a quarrel*	*a talk*
a care	*a fall*	*a race (with/against sb)*	*a think*
a chance (to do sth)	*a fit*	*a/the right (to)*	*(no/the) time*
a chat	*a go (at sth)*	*a row*	*a wash*
	an/no/any idea		

take			
action	*effect*	*a photo(graph)*	*root (in)*
advantage (of)	*exception (to)*	*place*	*sides (with sb)*
a breath	*medicine*	*power*	*a step/steps*
care (of)	*a message*	*precedence (over)*	*turns*
a chance (on)	*offence (at sth)*	*responsibility (for)*	*the trouble (to)*
control (of)	*part (in)*	*a risk*	*years/months/weeks/days/hours*, etc.
a decision			

have or *take*					
a bath/shower	*an exam/test*	*a holiday/a vacation*	*a nap*	*a seat*	*a stroll*
a break	*a guess*	*a look (at)*	*a rest*	*a sip*	*a swim*

Practice

1 **GRAMMAR IN USE** **Choose the correct words in *italics*.**
4.27 Listen and check.

LINDY Carla. You're good with machines. Could you (1) *make / do* me a favour? I need to (2) *do / make* a phone call and my mobile doesn't seem to be working.

CARLA Let me (3) *have / do* a go. Ah. There's a very (4) *weak / light* signal here. We should go into the garden, the signal might be (5) *stronger / heavier* there.

LINDY But it's raining.

CARLA That's OK. It's only (6) *light / weak* rain. Right. Let's go … Great, it seems to be OK now.

LINDY Thanks. Actually, I've never been very happy with that phone. It's probably time I (7) *did / made* a change and bought a new one – it's always had pretty (8) *faint / poor* performance and the battery is useless. It can't even (9) *take / make* photographs!

CARLA Well, the new models are much better, and cheaper …

LINDY Which one do you suggest? You know I have faith (10) *of / in* your judgement. And I'm sure I'd (11) *make / do* a mess of it if I tried to buy one on my own!

CARLA This one I've got is good. These phones (12) *do / run* rings around most of the competition. Why don't we go out and look at what's available?

LINDY We'd have to drive to the high street and the traffic's pretty (13) *heavy / strong* at this time of day.

CARLA What about tomorrow then? We could go in the late morning and (14) *do / have* some lunch afterwards, just something (15) *light / weak* – there's that nice café by the park.

LINDY That sounds great.

2 **Complete the sentences with a suitable form of *have, take, make* or *do*.**
4.28 Listen and check.

1 In many countries women still .... less money than men for the same work.
2 Unless a cheque is received by return of post we will have no option but to .... steps to recover the disputed sum through the courts.
3 You should always .... the most of every opportunity you're given.
4 Be careful with that heavy machine, Grandad. You'll .... yourself an injury.
5 I've never done this before but I'm willing to .... a go at it.
6 Why don't you .... a chat with her about it, if she's worried?
7 And what makes you think you .... the right to lecture me on morality?
8 This just isn't good enough. You must .... more of an effort next time.
9 Latest reports confirm that the rebel army .... control of the southern provinces.
10 I can't think why you're so reluctant to go. Come on, ... a risk for once!
11 I'm worried about Keira, I don't really .... much confidence in her abilities.
12 The residents insist on .... their say; they're going to demand a public meeting.
13 Karl forgot to water the plants but it didn't seem to .... them any harm.
14 I hear your daughter is .... really well at school this year.
15 Leave everything to me. I .... all the arrangements.

3 GRAMMAR IN USE **Replace the underlined phrases with a suitable form of *make* or *do*, and the highlighted phrases with a suitable form of *have* or *take*. You will also need to add a word or phrase from the box, and any other necessary words, as in the examples.**

bad job ~~best~~ chance charge decision fuss a go good hours and hours journey laundry mistake place promise problem research shopping stroll trouble ~~vacation~~

HIGHLAND HORRORS

This month Jeremy Vegal's 'Hotel Road Test' is the **Trent Castle Hotel** in Scotland.

IN THE BAD OLD DAYS, some country hotels had a reputation of being cold, draughty and dour places which (0) tried hard to make their guests feel as unwelcome as possible – people (00) going on holiday there often regretted it. Well, the tourist industry has moved on and we felt it was time to see if the winds of change blowing through the British hotel world had yet reached our northern extremities. From the catalogues and brochures, it seems that every castle in Scotland has turned itself into a hotel, and it was difficult to (1) reach a conclusion about which one to try. In the end we (2) risked things and settled for a little-known but promising place deep in the Highlands.

So, full of optimism, I (3) travelled north on the overnight sleeper, a trip that seemed to (4) last for a very long time, jumped into a cab and headed east to the Trent Castle Hotel. I had (5) investigated and I knew that the place had been converted from a sixteenth-century fortress about five years ago. From the outside it certainly looked the part with tall granite walls and looming turrets overlooking the dark waters of Lochtrent. Clearly, many bloody battles had (6) occurred there in the past. But the owners had (7) committed an error with their work on the interior. Rather than warm and welcoming, it was just as grim and forbidding as the outside.

I got to my room on the third floor, and despite (8) experiencing difficulties with the hot water, managed to have a shower. Always eager to test a hotel's efficiency, I called room service and asked for my (9) clothes to be washed. It took forty-five minutes for the chambermaid to arrive, and when she did, she happily informed me that the hotel would (10) impose a fee for each item of clothing I wished to have cleaned. Never one to (11) complain, I politely declined the offer of instant bankruptcy and decided to ask the woman about the possibility of an extra blanket or ten, as the temperature in my room was hovering around zero and it was only the middle of the afternoon. She (12) guaranteed to bring one straightaway, and that was the last I was to see of her for my entire visit.

Anxious to find some warmth, I decided to (13) make an attempt at finding the hotel sauna, sure that some dry heat would (14) be healthy for me. But when I asked the receptionist about the location of this facility, she looked at me as though I had invented it. 'It's been closed for months,' she announced. 'If you want something to do you could always (15) go for a walk and (16) buy some things, there's a lovely souvenir shop six miles down the road.' The prospect was deeply unexciting.

'Look,' I said, 'I don't want to (17) cause difficulties, but the sauna is advertised in your brochure.'

'Oh, that thing's full of mistakes,' she replied, 'The printers really (18) messed it up.'

Rather like the owners, I thought to myself ... .

0 *did their best*
00 *taking a vacation*
1 ...
2 ...
3 ...
4 ...
5 ...
6 ...
7 ...
8 ...
9 ...
10 ...
11 ...
12 ...
13 ...
14 ...
15 ...
16 ...
17 ...
18 ...

Review MODULE 15

To complete these exercises you may need to refer to pages 370–2.

1 UNITS 65, 66 AND 68 **Write one word only in each gap.**

Nuclear Fusion

For years it has been mankind's most cherished dream – a source of energy that is clean and inexhaustible and does not (1) .... on our ever-diminishing stocks of fossil fuels. Now a laboratory in America has (2) .... the first step towards making that dream a reality.

The source of this energy is nuclear fusion – the energy that is created when two atoms combine or 'fuse'. This is the reaction that powers the stars and our own sun. It is very different (3) .... nuclear fission, which is when atoms are split. Nuclear fission is the source of energy used in nuclear power stations and atomic bombs.

The National Ignition Facility (NIF) in California is designing a system in which 192 powerful laser beams are aimed (4) .... a small pellet of tritium and deuterium, attempting to replicate the intense pressure and heat found at the centre of stars. The brief pulse of intense energy should force the atoms together to create helium, releasing huge amounts of energy in the process. Some scientists are worried (5) .... how this energy might be used and critics have (6) .... the American project of being a thinly-veiled attempt at developing more sophisticated nuclear weapons.

Teams in France and the UK are engaged (7) .... similar research, but using different technology. The French project plans to use magnetic fields rather than lasers. Of course, even if scientists (8) .... in creating these reactions, they have not yet developed a method (9) .... converting this energy into a form that can be used for everyday purposes. If they (10) .... a mistake, there is a (11) .... possibility that they run the (12) .... of creating explosive energy that cannot be controlled.

2 UNITS 66 AND 67 **Rewrite John's half of this unnatural telephone conversation in a more natural, informal style. Use the multi-word verbs in the box to replace the underlined verbs and phrases. Make any other necessary changes, as in the example.**

do sth up   finish sth off   get on with sb   go with sth   look at sth   look down on sb
~~pull sth down~~   put sb up   put sth up   put up with sb   sit down   sort sth out
stay up   take sth off   talk about sth   turn sth into sth   turn sth down

JOHN (*to neighbour*) Yes, that's glass from the conservatory, I've just (0) demolished the conservatory [pulled it down]. Excuse me. (*phone is ringing, he goes inside*) Hello?

DAVE John. It's Dave. How are things?

JOHN Sorry, I can't hear you. I'll just (1) reduce the volume on the radio. That's better.

DAVE How are things? Still working on the house?

JOHN Yes. We've (2) completed the work on the kitchen and we're (3) renovating the dining room. We're (4) transforming the room into a second bedroom. I've just (5) mounted the wallpaper but I've been having trouble getting it to (6) remain vertically attached. It's a nice colour: it (7) matches the paintwork. Anyway, it's all got to be (8) organised and ready by Saturday. Jane's mother is coming and we're (9) providing accommodation for her for a few days.

DAVE I thought you didn't like her.

JOHN We don't (10) interact in a friendly way with each other but I can (11) tolerate her for a few days, especially if we don't (12) discuss politics!

DAVE Why do you dislike her so much?

JOHN I'm sure she (13) regards me as inferior to her. And she's so lazy, I mean she comes in, (14) removes her coat, (15) assumes a seated position and expects us to wait on her hand and foot! And she spends the whole time (16) observing everything, trying to find things to criticise!

DAVE Mmm. I see what you mean ... .

3 ALL UNITS **Write the second sentence so it has a similar meaning to the first. Use the word(s) in brackets, as in the example.**

0 She finds new technology rather frightening.
(of) *She is rather scared of new technology.*

1 Lizzie's going to use her inheritance to establish a charity.
(up) ....

2 We found the quality of her singing voice quite astonishing.
(astonished) ....

3 It's important to defend the rights of minorities.
(stand) ....

4 Can you watch the children while I'm at the shops?
(an eye) ....

5 Do you think his behaviour influenced the outcome of the election?
(an effect) ....

6 I don't mind if you sleep on the sofa.
(objection) ....

7 The new legislation covers deregulation of the airline industry.
(concerned) ....

8 Have you considered your parents' reaction?
(account) ....

9 The daily swim seems to be beneficial to his health.
(good) ....

10 I couldn't see the details until the guide highlighted them.
(pointed) ....

11 My brother is working on an exciting renewable energy project.
(engaged) ....

12 She felt sorry for all the homeless children.
(took) ....

13 Ramon finds it difficult to cope with stress.
(difficulty) ....

14 The current political situation is full of danger.
(fraught) ....

15 Admiring sports stars is a common trait amongst teenagers.
(looking) ....

16 I really enjoy helping people less fortunate than myself.
(pleasure) ....

MODULE

16 Word formation and words often confused

Before you start

1 Review these intermediate grammar points and check you know them.

Use of prefixes and suffixes

1 Prefixes are short additions that go in front of words, e.g. *im-*, *un-*, *dis-*.
We often add them to adjectives, verbs and nouns to change their meaning.
Most of these prefixes make words negative:
possible → ***im**possible* *tie* → ***un**tie* *approval* → ***dis**approval*

2 Suffixes are short additions that go at the end of words, e.g. *-er*, *-ment*, *-ify*.
We add them to words to change their meaning:
work → *work**er***
and to change their class :
occur → *occur**rence*** (verb → noun)
solid → *solid**ify*** (adjective → verb)

Compound nouns and adjectives

1 Compound nouns and compound adjectives are words which have been created by combining two words which are related to each other.

2 They can be written
- as a single word: *dressmaker*
- as two separate words: *fashion magazine*
- occasionally as two words joined by a hyphen: *waste-bin*

It is best to check the formation in an up-to-date dictionary.

3 Compound nouns and adjectives are very useful because they give a lot of information in a short space:
It's a place where you can park your car. → *It's a **car park**.*
Does the hotel have any staff who speak English?
→ *Does the hotel have any **English-speaking** staff?*

Verbs which are often confused

Some verbs, e.g. *borrow/lend*, act as 'mirror images' of each other. They describe the same event from different points of view.

- If you want to use something that belongs to someone else you can *borrow* it from them. The owner of something can *lend* it to you for a certain period:
*'Dad, could we **borrow** your electric drill?'*
*'Sorry. I've already **lent** it to Michael.'*

2 **Read the information and identify examples of prefixes, suffixes, compound nouns and compound adjectives.**

City invaders

UNTIL RECENT TIMES A RACCOON ROAMING AROUND CITY STREETS WAS A RARELY SEEN PHENOMENON. NOW IT IS AN ALMOST NIGHTLY OCCURRENCE.

The continuing expansion of our cities and the resulting destruction of their natural habitat has made life in the countryside impossible for many raccoons. As a result, thousands of the unfortunate creatures have migrated to the back gardens and scraps of wasteland found in many cities. Rather than hunting small animals, they simply steal from waste-bins and rubbish dumps, scavenging from the carelessly discarded human waste that lies all around them. Most people regard these urban raccoons as a nuisance, but few know what to do about them. For as soon as one is captured or destroyed, several more appear to take its place.

3 **Complete the diagnostic test below. Choose the correct words in *italics*.**

1 I'm interested in your keep-fit class. What qualifications does the *trainee* / *trainer* have? ➤ Unit 69.1
2 Learning to touch-type can take some time. But, if you are *persistence* / *persistent*, you will eventually master it. ➤ Unit 69.2
3 I noticed your *ex-* / *pre-* employee working at the supermarket yesterday. ➤ Unit 69.3
4 It's shocking. Some of the children leaving our schools are only *half-literate* / *semi-literate*. ➤ Unit 69.3
5 There are some great *record* / *records* shops in the High Street. ➤ Unit 70.1
6 I'd like a cheese salad, a burger and two *coffee cups* / *cups of coffee*, please. ➤ Unit 70.1
7 There aren't any waiters – it's a *self-service* / *serve yourself* restaurant. ➤ Unit 70.2
8 Interest in Latino music is no longer confined to *speaking Spanish* / *Spanish-speaking* audiences. ➤ Unit 70.2
9 That old curtain fabric has *done* / *made* a marvellous evening gown. ➤ Unit 71.1
10 Darling, can you *bring* / *fetch* my mother from the station on Tuesday? ➤ Unit 71.2
11 Sorry I'm home so late, I *took* / *brought* the car to work today and I got stuck in a traffic jam. ➤ Unit 71.2
12 The prime minister *spoke* / *talked* at the climate change conference in Copenhagen. ➤ Unit 71.3
13 Our old cat doesn't do much. It just likes to *lie* / *lay* in the sun all day. ➤ Unit 71.4
14 What do you think of that plan to *rise* / *raise* the Titanic from the seabed? ➤ Unit 71.4
15 They *robbed* / *stole* my purse in broad daylight! ➤ Unit 71.5

4 **Check your answers on page 384. Then go to the unit for information and practice.**

Go online for a full diagnostic test

69 Word formation

1 Using suffixes to change meaning

SUFFIX	COMMON USES	EXAMPLES
-er -ee[1] *-or -ant -ent -ist*	to change a word describing a thing, place or action to a noun describing a person connected with it, or the name of the job[2]	*teacher Londoner employer/employee director consultant artist*
-ese - ian -an -ish	to change the name of a country to the language/the nationality adjective[3]	*Japanese Hungarian Polish*
-ian -ician -ist	to change the name of a subject to the person studying/connected with it	*historian statistician mathematician economist*
-ism -ist/ite	we use *-ism* to create a noun describing a belief or movement, and *-ist* to describe a person who follows that movement or belief	*Impressionism/Impressionist communism/communist Thatcherism/Thatcherite*
-ie -y	to make a familiar or pet version of a name	*doggie mummy Sammy*

[1] Nouns ending in *-er* have an active meaning and nouns ending in *-ee* have a passive meaning, e.g. an *interviewer* asks questions and an *interviewee* answers them; a *trainer* teaches and a *trainee* learns.

[2] Note there are some exceptions, e.g. a *processor* is an electronic component, not a person.

[3] Some nouns that end in *(-i)an* and *-ese* can also be used to describe a person:
Italian → ***an Italian*** *Chinese* → ***a Chinese***

2 Using suffixes to change word class

CHANGE	SUFFIXES	EXAMPLES
adjective → noun	*-ness -ity -ance -ence*	*laziness density endurance difference*
noun/verb → adjective	*-al -ful -less -able -y -ous -ent -ive*	*central spiteful careless suitable scary continuous persistent elusive*
noun/adjective → verb	*-ise/ize -(e)n -(i)ate -(i)fy*	*standardise harmonise heighten differentiate solidify*
verb → noun	*-al -ance -ence -ment -tion -ure*	*arrival ignorance dependence argument education closure*

Pronunciation ➤ 1.19

3 Using prefixes to change meaning

PREFIX	MEANING	EXAMPLES
auto-	*self*	*autobiography auto-immune autonomous*
bi-	*two*	*bilingual bi-annual bisect*
co-	*together/joint*	*co-signatories co-directors co-owners*
ex-	*former/previous*	*ex-husband ex-president ex-teacher*
inter-	*among/between*	*international inter-state intermarriage*
in-/im-	*into inside*	*insert income import*
mega-	*huge/a million*	*megastar mega-structure megabytes*
mono-	*one only*	*monolingual monopoly monophonic*
over-	*superior too much*	*overlord overdrive overstate*
re-	*again*	*repay reorganise restate*
semi-	*half*	*semi-literate semicircle semi-independent*
sub-	*below*	*substandard sub-zero sub-prime*
under-	*inferior too little*	*underclass underperform undervalue*

Prefixes with a negative meaning, e.g. *dislike, unfair* ➤ Unit 48.4

Practice You may find it helpful to use a dictionary when completing these exercises.

1 GRAMMAR IN USE **There are ten more incorrectly formed words in the text. Find the words and correct them. 4.29 Listen and check.**

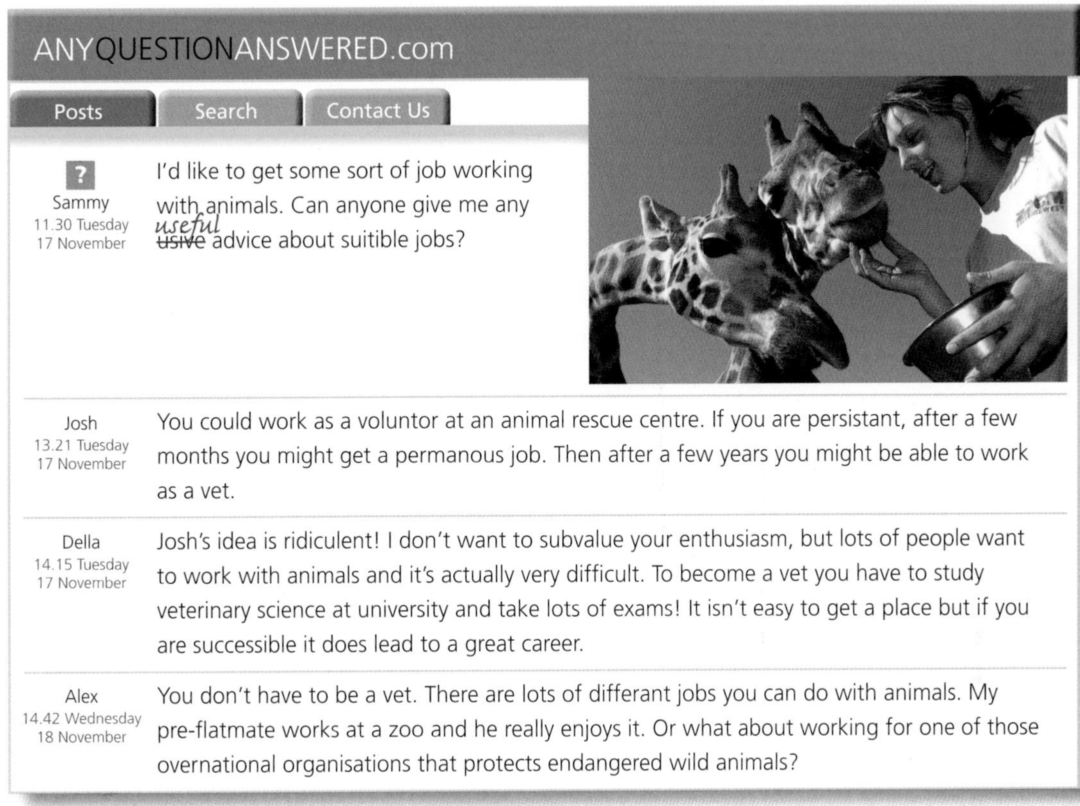

ANYQUESTIONANSWERED.com

Posts | Search | Contact Us

Sammy
11.30 Tuesday
17 November

I'd like to get some sort of job working with animals. Can anyone give me any ~~usive~~ *useful* advice about suitible jobs?

Josh
13.21 Tuesday
17 November

You could work as a voluntor at an animal rescue centre. If you are persistant, after a few months you might get a permanous job. Then after a few years you might be able to work as a vet.

Della
14.15 Tuesday
17 November

Josh's idea is ridiculent! I don't want to subvalue your enthusiasm, but lots of people want to work with animals and it's actually very difficult. To become a vet you have to study veterinary science at university and take lots of exams! It isn't easy to get a place but if you are successible it does lead to a great career.

Alex
14.42 Wednesday
18 November

You don't have to be a vet. There are lots of differant jobs you can do with animals. My pre-flatmate works at a zoo and he really enjoys it. Or what about working for one of those overnational organisations that protects endangered wild animals?

2 **Complete each sentence, using a suitable form of the word in brackets, as in the example.**

0 A long-term aim of the European Union is to *harmonise* rules and regulations among the member states. (harmony)

1 Even experienced .... failed to predict the banking crisis of 2008. (economy)

2 The existence of an .... at the very bottom of society has long been recognised by sociologists. (class)

3 Badgers are .... creatures, rarely appearing in daylight. (elude)

4 Most of the .... in our San Diego factory work part-time. (employ)

5 Although she is ...., Maria prefers to write in Spanish rather than English. (language)

6 .... in the face of continuous setbacks is the mark of true determination. (persist)

7 We really must try to reduce our .... on fossil fuels. (depend)

8 .... between tribes is rare in this part of the Amazon. (marriage)

9 Local readers are protesting at the .... of the public library. (close)

10 The liquid compound will tend to .... if subjected to temperatures below zero. (solid)

70 Compound nouns and adjectives

1 Compound nouns

In compound nouns the first word usually 'classifies' the second word – it describes it or tells us its purpose:

wasteland (= land that has no use) *a fashion magazine* (= a magazine about fashion)

The first word is usually singular:

✗ ~~*a dressesmaker*~~ ✓ *a dressmaker* ✗ ~~*a cars park*~~ ✓ *a car park*

Compound nouns are formed in several ways:

noun + noun	*headache cash card bathroom database*
noun + verb form	*windsurfing fire-eater Thanksgiving screwdriver*
verb + noun	*cookbook stepping stone filing cabinet swimsuit*
adjective + noun	*highway blackbird real estate mobile phone*
preposition/adverb + verb/noun	*overview outsourcing upkeep income*
verb + preposition/adverb	*flyover fallout make-up feedback*

The main stress is usually on the first part of the compound noun:

Karl is a German teacher. (compound noun = He teaches German.)

Karl is a German teacher. (= He is a teacher who comes from Germany.)

Some compound nouns are formed from multi-word verbs (➤ Units 66 and 67). They usually follow the same order as the verb, but there are a few exceptions:

break out → *outbreak* *spill over* → *overspill* *put in* → *input*

Pronunciation ➤ 1.20

Some compound nouns describe containers. The compound form only describes the container itself, not its contents. Compare:

- in a shop: *I'd like six Royal Doulton* ***teacups****.*
  (compound noun = cups designed to hold tea)
- in a café: ✗ ~~*I'd like a teacup and a slice of cake, please.*~~
  ✓ *I'd like a cup of tea and a slice of cake, please.* (= tea in a cup)

2 Compound adjectives

Compound adjectives can be formed from adjectives, adverbs, nouns, verbs and prepositions. They usually have a hyphen when they are used before a noun:

adjective + noun	*high-status low-maintenance full-time large-scale*
noun + adjective	*user-friendly air-conditioned tax-free lifelong*
verb + preposition/adverb	*drive-in worn-out built-up slowed-down walk-in*
self + verb/adjective/noun*	*self-raising self-conscious self-confident self-service*

* We also make compound nouns with *self*: *self-confidence*, *self-awareness*, etc.

Many are formed by adding an *-ed* or *-ing* participle to an adverb, adjective or noun:

He's a ***well-known*** *actor and the author of a* ***best-selling*** *novel.*

This Japanese maple is a particularly ***slow-growing*** *variety.*

The marines made a ***death-defying*** *leap over the cliff edge.*

We often use compound adjectives to describe time, quantity and measurement:

a ***three-week*** *holiday a* ***four-hour*** *delay a* ***ten-minute*** *drive a* ***five-year-old*** *child*

The noun is usually singular:

✗ ~~*A ten kilometres journey*~~. ✓ *A* ***ten-kilometre*** *journey.*

Compound adjectives formed with participles can often replace relative clauses:

The impact of recent legislation is an issue ***which commentators frequently ignore****.*

→ *The impact of recent legislation is a* ***frequently-ignored*** *issue.*

Pronunciation ➤ 1.21

Practice

1 Complete each sentence with a suitable compound noun. Part of the word has been given in brackets.

1 All my correspondence is kept in the metal .... next to my desk. (filing)
2 Apparently the company's .... contains over two million names. (base)
3 Clarisse doesn't wear ...., she prefers the natural look. (up)
4 You can't drive that vehicle on the public .... without a licence. (way)
5 Tourist agencies have warned of an .... of cholera in northern Thailand. (out)
6 It's great to have a vintage car but the .... can be prohibitively expensive. (keep)

2 Rewrite these sentences, using compound adjectives to replace the underlined words, as in the example. Use suitable forms of one word from each box and make any other changes necessary. 4.30 Listen and check.

car home fast rare ~~rapid~~ self three	confident ~~expand~~ hour manufacture make move visit

0 São Paulo is a city <u>which is getting bigger very quickly</u>. *São Paulo is a rapidly-expanding city.*
1 Eleanor is attractive and a person <u>who has confidence in herself</u>. ....
2 The Midlands is Britain's main region <u>that produces automobiles</u>. ....
3 They were soon engulfed by the water, <u>which was flowing very quickly</u>. ....
4 Each new member of staff must take part in a training session <u>which lasts three hours</u>. ....
5 Northumberland is a part of England <u>which people don't go to very often</u>. ....
6 <u>The desserts, which are produced by ourselves</u>, are the main feature of our restaurant. ....

3 GRAMMAR IN USE Complete the article with compound nouns and compound adjectives, using the clues in brackets, as in the example.

Hypoallergenic cats

A (0) *California-based* (based in California) company has come up with a (1) .... (engineered by genetics) solution for those (2) .... (people that love animals) that have an allergy to cats. In Britain alone there are 2.6 million (3) .... (people who suffer from asthma) who are allergic to cats.

These allergies are caused by a protein in the cat's skin which causes coughing, sneezing and skin irritation in sufferers. (4) .... (scientists who do research) have now identified the genes that produce this protein. By examining the (5) .... (extracted with care) DNA of different cats they have produced a breed that looks exactly like an ordinary cat, but does not trigger allergic reactions in humans. Allerca Lifestyle Pets of San Diego has been breeding the (6) .... (free of allergens) cats and are now offering them for sale around the world.

71 Verbs often confused

Beavers **bring** twigs and branches from surrounding areas to build a dam. They start by building vertical poles, then **lay** branches across them to form a wall.

1 *make* and *do*

Make has a number of uses:
Aunt Alice ***is going to make*** *the bridesmaids' dresses.* (= create)
Gouda cheese ***is made*** *in Holland.* (= is produced)
This multinational ***makes*** *a lot of products in Sri Lanka.* (= manufactures)
The spare bedroom ***has made*** *a wonderful office for Deirdre.* (= has become)
Those new drugs seem ***to make*** *him very lethargic.* (= cause him to be)

- *make* + object + infinitive (without *to*) means 'force' or 'command' (➤ Unit 63.3):
  The police officer ***made me empty*** *my pockets.*
- idiomatic meanings such as 'earn' and 'keep an appointment':
  He ***makes*** *$1,000 a week on the oil rigs. I can't* ***make*** *it on Friday – I'm out all day.*

We often use *do* to describe an activity or to mean 'carry out/complete a task':
What ***are*** *we* ***going to do*** *for your birthday?* (= take part in an activity)
*You can go out after you****'ve done*** *your homework.* (= you've completed)

We can use *do* + determiner + *-ing* form to describe regular tasks at home or at work:
There isn't much in the fridge as I ***haven't done the shopping*** *yet.*
We ***do the stocktaking*** *every Wednesday morning.*

Collocations with *make* and *do*, e.g. *make an effort, do research* ➤ Unit 68.3

2 *bring* and *take, fetch*

Bring and *take* have opposite meanings:

bring	*take*
to take someone or something with you to the place you are now, to your home, or to the place/event you have been talking about: ***I've brought*** *the pliers you said you needed – here they are.* *When are you* ***going to bring*** *your new friend to meet us?* (to our house)	to move someone or something away from the place you are now, away from your home or away from the place/event you have been talking about: *I can't find the cheque book – Dennis* ***must have taken*** *it when he left this morning.* *When are you* ***taking*** *me to meet your parents?* (away from here to their home)

The choice of verb depends on the situation of the speaker:
Are you ***bringing*** *your scuba gear?* (on our holiday)
Are you ***taking*** *your scuba gear?* (on your holiday)

Fetch means to collect someone or something from another place and bring it to the place you are now, to your home or to the place you are talking about. We don't use *bring* with this meaning of 'collecting':
✗ ~~*Could you bring the kids from school tomorrow?*~~
✓ *Could you* ***fetch*** *the kids from school tomorrow?* (= go to the school and bring them home)

3 *speak* and *talk*

Speak and *talk* have very similar meanings and are often equally appropriate:
*I'm going to **talk/speak** to my teacher about it after the lesson.*

- We usually use *speak*, not *talk*, for formal speeches:
  ✗ ~~*Before the election the President talked to the nation on television.*~~
  ✓ *Before the election the President **spoke** to the nation on television.*
- We use *speak*, not *talk*, to refer to languages:
  ✗ ~~*Anatoly talks English with an accent.*~~ ✓ *Anatoly **speaks English** with an accent.*
- We use *talk* for long conversations:
  ✗ ~~*We were up half the night speaking!*~~ ✓ *We were up half the night **talking**!*

There are a number of expressions with *speak* or *talk*:
*Could you **speak up**?* (= talk louder) *I'd like **to talk about** our plans.* (= explain/discuss)
*You're **talking nonsense**.* (I strongly disagree with what you are saying.)

4 *lay* and *lie*, *raise* and *rise*

INFINITIVE	PAST TENSE	PAST PARTICIPLE	PRESENT PARTICIPLE
lay (= action)	*laid*	*laid*	*laying*
lie (= state)*	*lay*	*lain*	*lying*
lie (= tell lies)*	*lied*	*lied*	*lying*
raise	*raised*	*raised*	*raising*
*rise**	*rose*	*risen*	*rising*
*arise**	*arose*	*arisen*	*arising*

* these verbs are intransitive (cannot have an object)

Lay expresses an action; *lie* describes a state or position:
*First, **lay** all the parts on a clean work-surface.* (action = place them flat on something)
*I think I'll just **lie** on the sofa until my headache goes.* (state/position)
*We've **been laying** artificial grass on the new pitch.* *We found these photos **lying** in a drawer.*
*That child **lies** all the time.* (= says things which are not true)

Raise refers to the action of someone or something lifting, increasing or moving something else (i.e. an object) in an upward direction. *To rise* only refers to the movement itself:
*The government has been urged to **raise** corporation tax rates to match those in other European Union states. Rates are predicted to **rise** by ten percent.*
✗ ~~*Fares will raise next year*~~. ✓ *They will **raise the fares** next year.*
✗ ~~*They will rise the fares next year.*~~ ✓ ***Fares will rise** next year.* (no object)

FORMALITY CHECK In formal English we sometimes use *arise* to refer to difficulties occurring, or something caused or started by a situation. It does not have an object:
*Tissue rejection is a problem which can **arise** in this procedure.*
*We will contact you, should the need **arise**.*
✗ ~~*Let's hope nobody arises that issue.*~~ ✓ *Let's hope that issue **doesn't arise**.*

5 *rob* and *steal*

Rob refers to the person or place that suffered the crime; *steal* refers to what was taken:
✗ ~~*Thieves stole my uncle.*~~ ✓ *Thieves **robbed** my uncle.* (*rob* + victim)
✗ ~~*A gang stole the head office.*~~ ✓ *A gang **robbed** the head office.* (*rob* + place)
✗ ~~*They robbed his gold watch.*~~ ✓ *They **stole** his gold watch.* (*steal* + object taken)

We can use the preposition *from* to link *steal* to a person or place and we can use the preposition *of* to link *rob* with the thing which was taken:
*Colonel Blood **stole** the crown jewels **from the Tower of London in 1665**.*
*No man has the right to **rob** another **of his freedom**.*

say/tell ➤ Unit 50.2

Practice

1 Choose the correct words in *italics*. 4.31 Now listen and check.

1 Is there any chance of you *bringing / fetching* Clarissa from her piano lesson?
2 We'd better order a taxi to *bring / take* us to the airport next week.
3 Apparently the ambassador will *talk / speak* at the full assembly tomorrow.
4 Five modern masterpieces have been *stolen / robbed* from a gallery in Paris.
5 Since this government came into office, inflation has *raised / risen* four times.
6 After *lying / laying* the cloth on the ground, they leave it to dry in the hot sun.
7 My neighbour is such a chatterbox – she never stops *speaking / talking*!
8 I'll be able to join you once I've *made / done* these reports for my boss.
9 Whatever problems *raise / arise*, I'm sure you can deal with them.
10 Can you *take / bring* me a screwdriver? I need to change the fuse in this plug.
11 Some politicians would like to *rob / steal* us of our right to free speech.
12 My aunt says the vase is Victorian, but she isn't sure exactly when it was *done / made*.

2 GRAMMAR IN USE Complete the article with suitable forms of words from the box, as in the example.

bring (x2) do lie (x2) ~~make~~ raise rise rob speak steal take (x2)

Animal smuggling on the rise

WITH THE GROWING interest in exotic pets, unscrupulous criminals (0) *have been making* huge sums of money by illegally smuggling animals into many countries. As the number of these incidents (1) ...., customs authorities and ecological organisations are becoming more worried about the effect on local wildlife.

(2) .... animals from their natural habitat is always a questionable practice because once non-indigenous animals (3) .... into a foreign country, they can easily escape and cause devastation to local animal populations. Many species (4) .... diseases to which indigenous animals have no defence. The ecological balance can be permanently upset, threatening the most vulnerable species with extinction.

The animals come from various sources. Some are captured in the wild, others (5) .... from their rightful owners (often zoos or nature reserves), but many are sold by illegal breeders. One of the most serious problems is the theft of eggs from the nests of rare birds. The adult birds are frightened off and thieves simply (6) .... the eggs (7) .... at the bottom of the nest. Eggs are obviously much easier to smuggle than live birds and (8) .... nests is an easy way to acquire birds which are difficult to catch when fully grown.

Methods of smuggling range from the ingenious to the ridiculous. In 2007 a smuggling racket between the UK and Australia was smashed when customs officials discovered snakes and lizards hidden inside plastic garden statues. In December 2009 Gypsy Lawson arrived in Los Angeles with a rhesus monkey hidden under her shirt. When questioned about the suspicious lump under her clothing, she (9) .... to customs officers and claimed that she was pregnant. And last year a 23-year-old man was caught at Melbourne Airport in Australia with two racing pigeons inside his trousers, strapped to his legs.

What can be (10) .... about this problem? (11) .... at a conference last week, a leading ecological campaigner called on governments to (12) .... the fines and prison sentences given to animal smugglers. Increased penalties will deter many criminals, she believes. ■

3 GRAMMAR IN USE **The three news items below contain incorrect or inappropriate verbs. Underline them and write them correctly, as in the example. 4.32 Listen and check.**

0 ....raised....
1 ....
2 ....
3 ....

US RATE RISE

THE CHANCELLOR returned from this month's meeting of the 'Group of Six' with news that interest rates are to be rised by an average of half a percentage point in the United States. While the Chancellor has been in Dallas, city markets have been feverish with rumours of even higher increases. The US dollar has been laying at an all-time low for several weeks and the American trade deficit has been arising steadily. The Chairman of the Federal Reserve has gone to Tokyo to discuss the problems which have arose from pressure in Congress to tackle the deficit. He will be in Japan until next Tuesday.

4 ....
5 ....
6 ....
7 ....
8 ....

Priceless treasure disappears

THE BENTON HOARD, a priceless collection of ancient Roman silver, has disappeared from its display cabinet in the British Museum. At today's emergency press conference, museum director Alan Woods talked of his theory that the treasures had probably been robbed by a professional gang on behalf of a specific collector as the silver is too well-known to be sold on the open market. Ten museums have been stolen in the last six months and the number has been raising steadily over the last few years. The Benton Hoard is one of Britain's most important collections of Roman silver. It was found in 1926, having laid undiscovered for almost sixteen centuries beneath a Sussex field.

9 ....
10 ....
11 ....
12 ....
13 ....
14 ....

NEW PETTING ZOO TO OPEN

A GROUP of local naturalists has done a successful proposal to open a new petting zoo in Brigstowe. Talking at a recent press conference, organiser Stephanie Fenton told reporters that the zoo will be aimed at young children. Teachers will be able to fetch children to the zoo, where they will have the chance to interact with the animals in a natural environment. Arising attendances at similar zoos in recent years have shown that this type of 'petting' zoo, where children can actually touch animals, can make a lot of good in helping to rise early awareness of natural history.

Review MODULE 16

1 UNITS 69 AND 70 **Use the words in brackets to form one word for each gap in the article. Some of the words are compounds. (You may use hyphenated words, as in example 00.)**

Pets for Patients

PETS FOR PATIENTS is an organisation which provides small pets for those suffering from certain mental and physical illnesses. It believes it is time to (0) ......*reconsider*...... (consider) our (00) ......*long-held*...... (long hold) belief that animals should be kept out of hospitals and away from sick people.

For years medical experts have considered animals to be a source of dangerous (1) .... (infect), completely (2) .... (suit) for an environment containing vulnerable and sick people. Now new research has shown that rather than posing a risk to patients, pets can promote recovery and have (3) .... (benefit) psychological effects. Patients suffering from (4) .... (severe disable) conditions, such as those which prevent them from leaving their beds and moving around, have been given small pets to look after.

(5) .... (continue) monitoring has shown that while stroking or grooming pets, patients' blood pressure and heart rates have been (6) .... (low). Because of this, their (7) .... (depend) on drugs has been reduced, and feedback from the medical trials has shown (8) .... (consider improve) recovery times for a large number of patients.

Doctors have noted that the effect on patients' (9) .... (psychology) states has been (10) .... (remark). It appears that the stimulus provided by looking after pets has given patients a (11) .... (height) sense of (12) .... (response) and improved their general (13) .... (self confide). According to the researchers, it is almost impossible to (14) .... (state) the positive effects of 'pet therapy'.

Pets for Patients is currently raising money to (15) .... (able) it to provide small pets to all the long-term care centres in the country.

2 UNITS 70 AND 71 **Choose the best explanation, A or B.**

1 Are you taking your own skis?
 A You are about to go on holiday with your friends.
 B You are about to go on holiday with me.
2 They each work ten-hour shifts.
 A They work for one hour at a time, but ten times each day.
 B They work for ten hours continuously.
3 Could we have six coffee cups, please?
 A We are in a shop. B We are in a café.
4 A gang of thieves stole the cash machine.
 A They took the whole machine. B They took the money from the machine.
5 Look at those men laying the pavement.
 A The men are relaxing. B The men are working.

6 The elderly patient in the end bed is self-conscious.
A The patient is shy. B The patient is awake.
7 Send us the feedback as soon as possible.
A We want our food to be returned. B We want to know what you think.
8 The bank offered us a tax-free savings account.
A We won't have to pay for the account. B We won't have to pay tax on the account.
9 Steve, could you fetch my car from the garage?
A Steve is my flatmate. B Steve works at the garage.
10 Are you done yet?
A Have you finished a task? B Have you produced something?

3 ALL UNITS **Choose the correct word(s) in *italics*.**

1 I need my glasses. Could you *fetch* / *take* them from my bedside table?
2 Everyone's afraid the government is going to *rise* / *raise* income tax next year.
3 Kiaran's the author of a best- *sold* / *selling* guidebook.
4 If there's one thing I can't stand it's *lazyness* / *laziness*.
5 You'll have to *talk* / *speak* up – grandpa's slightly deaf.
6 I've just read a fascinating *selfbiography* / *autobiography*.
7 The insurance policy covers *stolen* / *robbed* goods up to the value of $10,000.
8 Some of the key components of the Airbus are *done* / *made* in Spain.
9 The contents of the grave had *laid* / *lain* undisturbed for over eight centuries.
10 The new drug has been subject to several *controlled-carefully* / *carefully-controlled* trials.
11 I enjoyed the fitness class but the *trainer* / *trainee* wasn't very experienced.
12 Residents have been complaining about the *closement* / *closure* of the local library.
13 I've *brought* / *taken* you a paper. Do you want to read it now?
14 Complications can *rise* / *arise* if the correct clinical procedures are not followed.

4 ALL UNITS **Complete each sentence, using a suitable form of the word in brackets, as in the example.**

0 The oak is a ......*slow-growing*...... tree which takes many years to reach maturity. (grow)
1 The machinery detects .... or faulty parts and automatically ejects them. (standard)
2 Marathons are a feat of .... rather than of speed. (endure)
3 Caroline has given up her job and become a freelance .... (consult)
4 I prefer .... plants – I can't be bothered to spend all my time pruning and watering! (maintain)
5 Uncle David is a famous ....; in fact he's a professor at the local university. (mathematics)
6 Unemployment in the town has increased due to the .... of jobs to cheaper areas. (source)
7 One way to keep your house warmer is to have a roll of insulation .... in the roof space. (lay)
8 My local doctor operates a .... surgery; you don't need to make an appointment. (walk)
9 People with colour-blindness often find it hard to .... between brown and green. (differ)
10 We've agreed to .... the loan after six months. (pay)
11 According to recent research, people with .... jobs tend to live longer than ordinary workers. (status)
12 Children can be surprisingly .... to those they dislike. (spite)

MODULE

17 The grammar of formal English

Before you start

1 Review these intermediate grammar points and check you know them.

Avoiding repetition

1 To avoid unnecessary repetition of words or phrases in speech or writing, we can use

- substitution, when we replace one word or phrase with another, such as a pronoun: ***Instructions** are given on each machine. We ask customers to read **them** carefully before exercising.*
- ellipsis, when we leave out words or phrases altogether: *Mike left at about the same time as Jane (left).*

2 We can leave out or replace nouns, verbs and entire clauses which have previously been mentioned:

The managers in our company have often adopted production processes which give rise to unsatisfying jobs because it is cheaper for them to do so.

(*them* = managers; *do so* = adopt production processes ...)

Emphasis and focus

We show emphasis in writing in many different ways. They include

- fronting, or bringing a word or phrase to the beginning of a sentence: *The bell rang. **Almost at once** the old man appeared at the door.*
- making one simple sentence into two clauses or a cleft sentence: *The Berlin Wall fell in 1989. **It was in 1989** that the Berlin Wall fell.*

Jackson published the book himself.

What Jackson did was publish the book himself.

- inversion (reversing the position of two things): ***Hardly had she** written one book before she started another.*

We usually invert the subject and the auxiliary, modal or main verb that follows it:

Harry did not offer once to take Norma home to visit her elderly parents.

Not once did Harry offer to take Norma home to visit her elderly parents.

Nominalisation

We use nominalisation (making nouns from other parts of speech) to be more concise in writing. We can form nouns from verbs

- by adding a suffix: *educate → educa**tion** establish → establish**ment** teach → teach**er***
- by using a verb as a noun (more informal): *Can't you open that? Shall I give it **a try**? I'll take you to the station if you give me **a shout** when you're ready.*
- by combining the verb and particle in multi-word verbs. The particle often (but not always) comes before the verb in the noun form:
  *The epidemic first **broke out** in Guinea. → The first **outbreak** of the epidemic was in Guinea.*
  *The plane **took off** very smoothly. → The **takeoff** was smooth.*
  *The car **broke down** not far from home. → The **breakdown** happened not far from home.*

⚠ Not all verbs can be used as nouns. It is best to check in a good dictionary.

✗ ~~*He made a speak on the theatre in Ireland.*~~ ✓ *He made **a speech** on the theatre in Ireland.*

2 **Read the text and identify a cleft sentence and examples of substitution and nominalisation.**

What is generally understood by the term 'literature'?

Most people readily accept that great historical plays and novels are part of it, but what about other types of writing, such as short stories, or other media, such as works published on the Internet? This topic is much debated in academic circles. What particularly concerns those involved in education is the type of literature taught in schools. Should the subject of literature also include contemporary works by little-known authors, which children may find more accessible, or is this just 'dumbing down'?

3 **Complete the diagnostic test below.**

A Choose the most suitable words in *italics*. If both options are suitable, choose both.

1 I really don't like these modern paintings. I much prefer *those* / *the paintings* over there. ➤ Unit 72.2
2 We didn't complete the obstacle course as quickly as the other team *completed it* / *did*. ➤ Unit 73.1
3 It was agreed that three staff volunteers would help with the stocktaking and that they would be paid extra to *do it* / *do so*. ➤ Unit 73.2
4 We wish to apologise to viewers for the loss of transmission yesterday. *It* / *This* was caused by an incident involving a low-flying helicopter. ➤ Unit 73.3
5 Jones failed to complete the 400 metres because *he tore* / *tore* a muscle. ➤ Unit 74.1
6 Doris Lessing's new novel failed to make the shortlist, but most critics felt it *should have done* / *should have*. ➤ Unit 74.2
7 The President was unable to put through all the reforms that he had *wanted to put through* / *wanted to*. ➤ Unit 74.3
8 We learnt that Chinua Achebe was not after all attending the conference, but *we had come to see the novelist* / *it was the novelist we had come to see*. ➤ Unit 75.2
9 The scientists have made a breakthrough. *What they're doing is* / *It is* approaching the problem from a different angle. ➤ Unit 75.3
10 *All* / *The only thing* they want is a second chance. ➤ Unit 75.4
11 Our policy is quite clear. Under no circumstances *refunds can* / *can refunds* be given. ➤ Unit 76.2

B Choose the best sentence or continuation of the sentence.

1 A Beside the river bank stands a gnarled old oak tree. ➤ Unit 76.3
B Beside the river bank a gnarled old oak tree stands.

2 One of Ian McEwan's best novels was *On Chesil Beach*. ➤ Unit 77.1
A The film of the novel also received much critical acclaim.
B Much critical acclaim was also given to the film of the novel.

3 Kington staggered from the remains of the building. ➤ Unit 77.2
A The damage wrought by the earthquake and its aftermath appalled him.
B He was appalled by the damage wrought by the earthquake and its aftermath.

4 It took Louis de Bernières several years to write *Birds Without Wings*. ➤ Unit 78.1
A It was published in 2004 and people anticipated it keenly.
B Its publication in 2004 was keenly anticipated. ➤ Unit 78.2

5 All we asked for was a bed to sleep in, a fire to cook by and water … .
A for washing B to wash with

4 **Check your answers on page 384. Then go to the unit for more information and practice.**

Go online for a full diagnostic test

72 Substitution (1) nouns and noun phrases

'Many years later, as **he** faced the firing squad, Colonel Aureliano Buendia was to remember that distant afternoon when his father took **him** to discover ice.'

from *One Hundred Years of Solitude* by Gabríel Garcia Márquez

1 Making reference in text

A key feature of continuous text is the use of reference words to bind sentences together:
Guest speaker Professor John Doherty gave the lecture this morning.
[*Professor John Doherty's theme was endorphin production in mammals.*]

Better alternatives:
✓ *... **Doherty's** theme was endorphin production in mammals.*
✓ *... **His/The professor's** theme was endorphin production in mammals.*
In some cases we can omit the repeated information (➤ Unit 74.1).

It is very common in written English to use different ways of referring to the same noun in texts; it avoids repetition and provides variety. We can use synonyms (words with similar meaning) or longer/shorter/more general forms of the noun:
***Officers Mike Cornish and Jackie Trent** arrived at the scene. **The officers** stopped short at the carnage before them. This was the first time **Trent** had attended a motorway accident and **the policewoman** found the sight disturbing. **Her superior officer**, however, was more experienced ...*

Most reference in text refers back to a previously mentioned item:

***The museum**'s lifelike new dinosaur will surely enhance **its** status amongst younger visitors.*

We can use substitution to refer back to a previous sentence, as long as there is no ambiguity:
*She had a vast collection of antique clocks, which she kept in a small room devoted to her hobby. While most of **them** dated from the Victorian era, she had a few smaller **ones** which dated back to the early nineteenth century.*

Occasionally we use a substitute word to refer forward in the text. This has the effect of creating suspense and is often used in dramatic or literary language:

*Many years later, as **he** faced the firing squad, **Colonel Aureliano Buendia** was to remember ...*

2 Replacing a noun or noun phrase

SUBSTITUTIONS	EXAMPLE
a personal pronoun (➤ Unit 4)	***John** came into the room. **He** was wearing a blue silk suit.*
adjective/demonstrative + *one/ones* (➤ Unit 4.2)	*Davis appeared in numerous **films** but practically no great **ones**. When faced with **two contradictory theories** one has to ask 'Do I find **this one** or **that one** more convincing?'*
demonstrative pronouns (➤ Unit 8.3)	*It is possible to respect both your own **opinions** and **those** of other people.*
quantifiers, e.g. *some, all, each, none, either, neither, both, a few* (➤ Unit 8.1/2)	*The **boys** went out and **some** did not return until the morning. The doctor suggested I should try **aspirin or ibuprofen**, but **neither** worked.*

We don't use *one* for uncountable nouns; instead, we omit the noun:
✗ *~~I really like white rice but my husband prefers brown one.~~*
✓ *I really like white rice but my husband prefers brown (rice).*

Practice

1 GRAMMAR IN USE **Substitutions in this text are shown in *italics*. Find the word or phrase that each one refers to and write it below, as in the example.**

The clock on the platform was showing midnight as the train drew in. Tessa checked (0) *her* ticket against the sign on the window, opened the door to Coach H, climbed in and shut (1) *it* gently behind her.

The train was already reaching (2) *its* highest speed, thundering across country towards Warsaw, when Tessa dropped (3) *her* bags in the correct compartment. She thought briefly of the few kilometres already behind her and (4) *the many* ahead, then she bent to her luggage. She tried to lift the two heavy bags onto the rack, but she could hoist (5) *neither* over her head. She pulled the lighter (6) *one* onto the seat, and sat down, pulling the (7) *other* close to her.

Alone in the carriage, she contemplated her future. She hadn't expected (8) *this* so soon, but the job opportunity in Warsaw had come up unexpectedly. She'd always wanted to return to (9) *the city* of her birth and (10) *that* of her parents, but hadn't thought she would do it within two weeks of leaving college. At first she had discounted (11) *the position*, so far away from the town that had become home, but she had spoken to her prospective employers at length on the phone, after which all her concerns were laid to rest. Tessa closed her eyes and allowed the rhythm of the speeding (12) *locomotive* to lull her to sleep.

0 ......Tessa...... 4 .... 7 .... 10 ....
1 .... 5 .... 8 .... 11 ....
2 .... 6 .... 9 .... 12 ....
3 ....

2 GRAMMAR IN USE **Some changes have been made to these extracts from a novel. Decide the best substitutions for the words in *italics* and write them below. Use one word only each time. 4.33 Listen and check.**

Alice and Jasper are looking at a house they are about to go into.

'I should think, 1910,' said Alice. 'Look at how thick the walls are.' (0) *The thickness of the walls* could be seen through the broken window just above (1) *Alice and Jasper* on the first floor. She got no response, but nevertheless shrugged off her backpack, letting (2) *the backpack* tumble onto a living rug of young nettles that was trying to digest rusting tins and plastic cups. (3) *Alice* took a step back to get a better view of the roof. (4) *The step back* brought Jasper into vision. (5) *Jasper's* face, as she had expected (6) *his face* would be, was critical and meant to be noticed. For her part, she did not need to be told that she was wearing (7) *Alice's* look, described by him as silly. 'Stop (8) *that look*,' he ordered. His hand shot out, and her wrist was encircled by hard bone. (9) *Her wrist* hurt. …

Without referring to him, she ran up the stairs and he followed slowly, listening to how she banged on doors, and then, hearing nothing, flung (10) *the doors* open. On the first-floor landing (11) *Alice and Jasper* stood looking into order, not chaos. (12) *On the first-floor landing*, every room had sleeping bags, one, two or three. Candles or hurricane lamps. Even chairs with little tables beside (13) *the chairs*. Books. Newspapers. But no one was in. There were other rooms on this floor, but (14) *no other room* was used. …

0 ......This...... 4 .... 8 .... 12 ....
1 .... 5 .... 9 .... 13 ....
2 .... 6 .... 10 .... 14 ....
3 .... 7 .... 11 ....

73 Substitution (2) verbs and verb phrases

When Terry Pratchett started writing his Discworld fantasy novels, his intention was **to combine the fantasy with fun and engage people** in his fantasy world. With sales of over 45 million books, it is very clear that he **has done so**!

1 Substituting a verb with *do*

If we do not want to repeat a verb, we either substitute the main verb with a form of *do* or omit the main verb and repeat the auxiliary verb only (ellipsis ➤ Unit 74.2):

The bride wore pink, as ***did*** *her four bridesmaids.* (*did* = wore pink)

Management has agreed to resume negotiations although the union ***hasn't*** *yet.* (*agreed* is omitted)

We do not leave out the verb altogether:

✗ ~~The bride wore pink, as her four bridesmaids.~~

We use *do* to avoid repeating a present simple or past simple verb in the second of two clauses joined by *and, but* or *or*:

He lived according to his principles and he believed everyone else ***did****, too.*

(*did* = lived according to their principles)

The chef seems to expect all his customers to enjoy raw food, but I certainly ***don't****.*
(*don't* = don't enjoy raw food)

We can also use *so/neither* + *do/does/did* + subject:

Sara really enjoys the thrill of the open road, and ***so does*** *her husband.*

The younger children in the villages don't learn the official language. ***Neither do*** *older children, at least not until their last years of school when it is clear they may need it for work.*

We also substitute *do* for a main verb in subordinate clauses, e.g. those starting with *that, where, if, whereas,* and in comparison clauses:

At the time, the Farmer family lived very near to where I ***did****.*

The young princess and her sister had dark hair, whereas their brother ***didn't*** *– he had ginger hair.*

The average son doesn't help in the home as much as a daughter ***does****.*

2 Substituting a verb or verb phrase with *do it/that/so*

We often use *do it/that* to replace a verb phrase which describes a single, specific action:

Margaret had been trying to pluck up the courage to confront her son about the money, and she was just about to ***do it*** *when the doorbell rang.*

We can also use *do it* or *do that* when the subject of the verb changes:

I was unable to contact the barrister about the trial date. Can the clerk ***do it/that*** *tomorrow?*

We use *that* (and not *it*) to emphasise an action or make a contrast with a preceding statement:

Many people exaggerate the value of items claimed on insurance forms.

✗ ~~I really couldn't do it.~~ ✓ *I really couldn't do* ***that****.*

In speech, we stress *that*.

We prefer to use *do so* (and not *do it/that*) when we refer to an activity or a series of actions rather than a single, specific action:

Anyone wishing to interrupt with questions should feel free to ***do so.***

When you plan to get fit, you should only ***do so*** *within a planned exercise programme.*

Do so tends to be more formal than *do it/that.*

✗ ~~*Schools should encourage teachers to attend conferences and give them time off to do it.*~~

✓ *Schools should encourage teachers to attend conferences and give them time off to* ***do so.***

3 Substituting clauses with *it*, *this* or *that*

We use the pronouns *it, this* or *that* to refer back to an action in a previous clause/sentence:

I broke his camera and he was really upset about it. (*it* = breaking his camera)

This and *that* are more emphatic than *it*; they bring the focus onto the action they refer to:

Many of the latest models have been recalled because of a fault in the steering. ***This*** *has caused embarrassment to the manufacturers.*

ACADEMIC ENGLISH *This* and *these* are very common in academic English, where they usually refer to a previous statement/statement(s):
... they may improve the impact resistance of some materials. ***This*** *still requires confirmation ...*

4 Substituting clauses with *so* and *not*

To avoid repetition, we can use *so* rather than a *that* clause after these verbs:

appear assume be afraid believe expect guess hope
imagine presume remain seem suppose suspect think

Was that a tear in the defendant's eye as he described the incident?
[*She believed that it was.*] ✓ *She believed* ***so.***

With most other verbs we do not use *so*:

The officer asked Martina if the door was open. → ✗ ~~*She remembered so.*~~ ✓ *She remembered that it was.*

We usually form the negative by adding *not* to the auxiliary *do*:
They hoped that the hotel would have a restaurant but they ***didn't*** *presume* ***so.***

More formally, we can use *not* with all of these verbs (except *remain*), without using the auxiliary:
Would the average person intervene in a violent incident? From this report it appears ***not.***
They queried whether the document had been countersigned by two witnesses, but I ***believed not.***
✗ ~~*The child appeared agitated when his father entered the room, but he remained not for long.*~~
✓ *The child appeared agitated when his father entered the room, but he* ***didn't remain so*** *for long.*

We do not use a *that* clause after *so*:
✗ ~~*The interviewer asked if respondents believed ministers were taking green issues seriously and 61 percent replied that they thought so that they were.*~~
✓ *The interviewer asked if respondents believed ministers were taking green issues seriously and 61 percent replied that they* ***thought so.***

We can substitute *if* clauses with *if so* (positive) and *if not* (negative):
Please check ***that the amendments to your policy are correct. If so****, you need take no action.*
(*if so* = if the amendments are correct)
We hope that all your dealings with the bank are satisfactory. ***If not****, please see the enclosed leaflet outlining our complaints procedures.*
(*if not* = if your dealings with the bank are not satisfactory)

Practice

1 GRAMMAR IN USE **Complete the text with the words and phrases from the box.**
4.34 Listen and check.Listen and check.

did did so do do it does done that if not so do that thought so

Diary of an aspiring novelist

DO YOU DREAM of being the next J K Rowling? The large print in the advert caught my eye as the train picked up speed. We've all (1) ...., haven't we? I couldn't make out the rest of the advert before it disappeared from sight, and I don't pass through that station regularly. But a good friend (2) ....! So I asked him to find out what it was about when he next used the train. A few days later he (3) ...., and he sent me the website address of a distance-learning creative writing course.

I thought about it, I hesitated, but eventually I sent off for the details and then read them voraciously when they arrived. Did I really want to commit my time to doing this course? I (4) ...., but I wondered if I was being silly. I mean, why should a 65-year-old retired accountant study creative writing? Who starts a new career at that age? 'Mary Wesley (5) ....,' said my friend, 'and she published several novels before she died. Apply for it – you have to (6) ...., I think. (7) ...., you'll regret it for the rest of your life.'

(8) .... was all the encouragement I needed. The next day I phoned the college and enrolled for the next course, starting after the summer in late September, just two weeks from now. The course materials arrived in August. I think they look really good, and (9) .... my children, both of whom have been to university. I can't wait to start working on the assignments, and getting my tutor's comments, and when I (10) ...., I'll know whether I'm likely to be the next J K Rowling or not!

2 **Read the sentences below and underline the parts that are unnecessary repeats of verbs or clauses. Then rewrite these parts, using a substitute phrase, as in the example. Sometimes more than one answer is possible.**

0 There is little point in starting out early to avoid the traffic, as everyone else starts out early, too. ....*does / does so*....
1 Harris maintained that he had had no involvement in the publication of the photographs, but very few of the other editors believed that he had had no involvement. ....
2 If the player answers the question correctly, he/she moves his/her piece according to the number on the dice. If he/she doesn't answer the question correctly, the turn passes to the next player. ....
3 Such light skin wounds do not generally hurt a cat as much as they hurt a human, since the cat has much tougher skin. ....
4 The management understands the wish to applaud during play but we ask you to refrain from applauding during play as it distracts the players. ....
5 I know that some days I push myself too hard. I've pushed myself too hard all my life. ....

6 There has been an increased number of burglaries in the area in recent months. The increased number of burglaries has resulted in a greater police presence. ....

7 Everything pointed to a one-sided match. The press photographers certainly thought it would be a one-sided match, with thirty lenses behind the Lithuanian goal. ....

8 Though many historians agree about the origin of the letter, several prominent historians do not agree. ....

9 The manager appealed to me to help them. I helped them, and afterwards, he asked me to take over the manufacturing for them. ....

10 The new government promised to hold a referendum on currency reform. If they haven't held a referendum by midway through the term, they will lose the voters' confidence. ....

3 GRAMMAR IN USE **Improve the text below by using substitution for the words in *italics*, as in the example. 4.35 Listen and check.**

It's no joke when you email

HAVE YOU EVER sent an email to a friend from work? Well, we all (0) *send them* sometimes, don't we? Or have you sent a joke to a colleague on the office computer? (1) *If you have*, you might like to think again. This is exactly what Rupert Beverly and David Pennington (2) *sent* and now they wish they hadn't. They were sacked from an engineering company in the north of England for (3) *sending a joke email*.

Hang on – you may think – this is one small company in the UK. However, (4) *sacking people for sending emails* happens not only in less-regulated small companies but in large multinational ones, too. Eight sales staff at Cable and Wireless lost their jobs after sending a slightly risqué email. Someone made a complaint about the email and by (5) *making a complaint*, brought it to the attention of the management, who claimed that the email could be construed as offensive. The sacked workers didn't think (6) *that it could be offensive* themselves and they insisted that it wasn't really provocative, as they knew it was a sackable offence to download material of that sort.

Big Brother really is watching you now!

Regulations governing this area vary from country to country: at present the law in the USA allows companies to monitor staff emails and while that in the UK is currently not so strict, it looks as though it will follow the US model. In Germany, however, the law does not allow 'spying' on employees' personal email, but at least one multinational based there is (7) *spying on people's email* by sending all emails to the UK to be monitored.

Civil rights organisations are concerned that monitoring emails infringes personal liberty and that it also undermines trust in the working environment. They want management to (8) *monitor emails* only when necessary, and to be able to prove that it was indeed necessary to (9) *monitor the emails*.

And what of Rupert and David? Well, their claim for unfair dismissal was rejected: the tribunal found that the company was within its rights to sack employees for sending joke emails, and also, more worryingly, for the time wasted in (10) *sending joke emails*. Watch out, Big Brother really is watching you now!

0 ......*do it*...... 3 .... 6 .... 9 ....
1 .... 4 .... 7 .... 10 ....
2 .... 5 .... 8 ....

74 Ellipsis

1 Omitting a noun/pronoun

We often omit nouns or pronouns in the second of two clauses joined by *and*, *but* or *or* (➤ Unit 58.1):

Lucy went up to the counter and (she) asked for a coffee.

We needed information about the interviewees' professions and (information) about their educational background.

We do not leave out pronouns in subordinate clauses, e.g. those starting with a conjunction such as *that*, *if*, *when* or *although*:

✗ ~~*That night she was so tired that fell asleep as soon as got into bed.*~~

✓ *That night she was so tired that* ***she*** *fell asleep as soon as* ***she*** *got into bed.*

But we can leave out subject pronouns at the beginning of short sentences in informal speech (➤ Unit 83.2).

2 Omitting a verb

We can often omit a verb to avoid repeating it:

She writes for a magazine and he (writes) for a daily newspaper.

We do not generally leave out the auxiliary or modal.

FORM	CHANGE	EXAMPLE
present/ past simple verb	omit main verb in *and* clauses	*She clearly* ***liked*** *the students, and they (liked) her.*
auxiliary + main verb	omit main verb	*Over 40 percent of those on benefits* ***are looking*** *for a job, or claim that they* ***are*** *(looking for one).*
modal + main verb	omit main verb	*Students working on doctorates* ***may apply*** *for funding from our organisation. Other researchers* ***may*** *(apply for funding) as well; we will consider all applications.*
compound verb forms	omit second/third auxiliary or only the main verb	*The problem was one that had been observed in other vessels and the crew should have been told about it, or at least the captain* ***should*** *(have been told)/****should have*** *(been told)/* ***should have been*** *(told).*

In coordinated clauses, where the second clause is very similar in pattern to the first, we can leave out the auxiliary as well as the main verb:

Since the divorce I've lived in London and my wife (has lived) in Cambridge.

We can introduce a new modal to add interpretation, but still not repeat the main verb:

It wasn't clear at first whether the house owners had been away for long but the letters on the doormat indicated that they ***must have*** *(been away).*

It is possible to omit both auxiliary and modal verbs in comparison clauses:

House prices ***have dropped*** *much less than share prices (have done)/than share prices* ***have*** *(done).*

Sally ***could play*** *the piano much better than her sister (could).*

3 Omitting infinitives or *wh-* clauses

We can omit an infinitive phrase when the meaning is clear, but we keep the *to*:

He didn't win the competition even though he had expected ***to*** *(win it).*

After most verbs which are followed by an infinitive with *to*, such as *ask*, *forget*, *promise*, *want* and *would like* in *if* or *wh-* clauses, we can also omit *to*:

The new 'freedom pass' allows anyone over sixty to use the buses and trains free of charge ***whenever they want*** *(to).*

In questions and embedded questions, we often use the question word only and omit the clause: *Dr Angelo said he was going on a call but he didn't say* ***where*** *(he was going).*

Practice

1 In each of these pairs of sentences, at least one of the choices is correct, and both may be. Tick (✓) the correct ones.

1 A The invigilator came in and he sat down without acknowledging the candidates.
B The invigilator came in and sat down without acknowledging the candidates.

2 A The orchestra's temporary musician plays the piano much better than the usual pianist.
B The orchestra's temporary musician plays the piano much better than the usual pianist plays.

3 It was thought that the suspect had also targeted a late-night shopper, but it transpired that ...
A he couldn't have. B he couldn't have done it.

4 The newcomers resented our presence at the celebrations ...
A and we resented. B and we theirs.

5 A The tests didn't yield conclusive results, although they had been expected to.
B The tests didn't yield conclusive results, although they had been expected.

6 A The instructions explain clearly how to grow the plants but not when to grow them.
B The instructions explain clearly how to grow the plants but not when to.

2 Delete the words in these sentences that can or should be omitted. Delete as many words as you can.

1 The students could either take the exam in June or they could take it in December.
2 The children were delighted with the party lights and they wanted to see them turned on again.
3 We enquired whether the new restaurant would be open on Sunday evenings, like the one it replaced, but the new owners could only tell us that it might be open on Sunday evenings.
4 The casual labourers didn't earn much money during the summer, though they had expected to earn some.
5 The young woman plays the violin superbly and her brother plays the cello equally well.
6 Baxter's sick tonight, which is unfortunate as he can play better than all the others can.
7 We thought that the old woman had been looking after the house, but she can't have been looking after it as she was in hospital at the time.
8 The task states that candidates should not write more than the number of words given, but it doesn't state how many words that is.

3 GRAMMAR IN USE **Improve this short text, using ellipsis where possible. You should be able to shorten it in five places. 4.36 Listen and check.**

CONTEMPORARY CLASSICS

This popular course examines literature from the last twenty years and it examines literature from a variety of countries across the English-speaking world. It was due to be replaced this year, but because of its popularity it has not been replaced; instead, it will run for two more years.

- The course is a compulsory Level 3 component in Literature degrees and the course forms an optional part of the English language degree.
- For this course you are required to have studied at least two previous literature courses at Level 2 and you are required to have passed them with Grade 3 minimum. If registering for this course from another educational institution, you may be asked to provide proof of previous study and you may be required to take an internal test.

75 Emphasis (1) cleft sentences

The 2006 Nobel Prize for Literature was awarded to the Turkish author Orhan Pamuk. **It was his exploration of the clashes and interactions of different cultures that** brought him the award.

1 Form and use of cleft sentences

In a divided or cleft sentence, information which could be given in one clause is divided into two parts, each with its own verb:

Vanessa has made the greatest impact. (normal sentence: single clause, one verb)

*It **is** Vanessa who **has made** the greatest impact*. (cleft sentence: two clauses, two verbs)

We use this pattern to emphasise new information, give explanations or make a contrast with a previous statement:

*All of the Redgrave family are gifted actors. But it is **Vanessa** who has made the greatest impact in the world of feature films.*

2 *It* cleft sentences

It cleft sentences have this pattern:

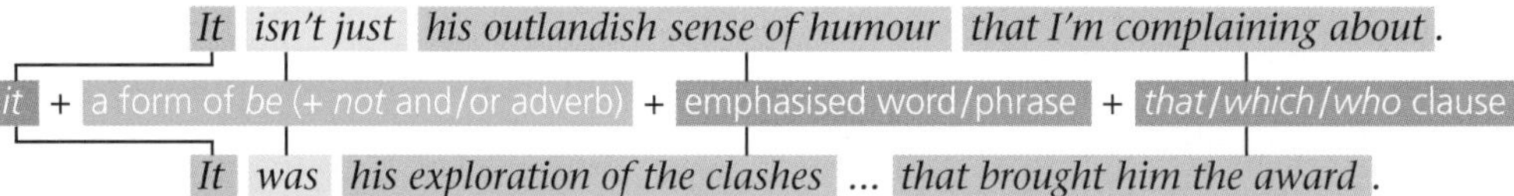

We can use *it* to emphasise the following:

(neutral)	→ *Tom saw Will Smith at the awards party last night.*
subject	→ *It was **Tom** who saw Will Smith at the awards party last night.*
object	→ *It was **Will Smith** that Tom saw at the awards party last night.*
adverbial phrases	→ *It was **last night** that Tom saw Will Smith at the awards party.* *It was **at the awards party** that Tom saw Will Smith last night.*

We can use *when* and *where* (instead of *that*) in subordinate clauses of time and place:

*It was **in January when** the test results were published.*

*It's **in Green Street market where** the best bargains can be found.*

We do not use *how*, *why*, or *what* in this way:

✗ ~~*It was greed why he did it.*~~ ✓ *It was because of greed that he did it.*

✗ ~~*It is using a calculator how he does it.*~~ ✓ *It is by using a calculator that he does it.*

✗ ~~*It is the speed of the ride what is so thrilling.*~~ ✓ *It is the speed of the ride that is so thrilling.*

We can reverse *it* + verb and the emphasised element in *it* clefts, but only in a very formal, literary style:

*And thus **Cézanne it was** who took the first steps towards Impressionism.*

Less literary: *And so it was Cézanne who took the first steps towards Impressionism.*

ACADEMIC ENGLISH The *it* cleft is very common in academic prose, where it presents information as known:
One of the main effects of publication is the enhancement of the researcher's profile. It is ***this*** *that makes writing for journals so essential in the academic world.*

3 *Wh-* cleft sentences

We can use this pattern to highlight the action in a sentence:

wh- clause + a form of *be* (+ *not*) + emphasised word/phrase

What the manager did | *was* | *(to) change the formation of the team*.

In these sentences *what* means 'the thing(s) that'. The *wh-* clause always contains a verb, which is usually a form of *do*. The emphasised phrase contains an infinitive with or without *to*. If the emphasised verb is in the continuous or perfect, the form of *do* matches it:

The boys aren't leaving Sandy at home. They are taking him to the beach with them.

→ *What the boys are doing is taking Sandy to the beach with them.*

Old members are absent but the new members have taken their seats in the assembly.

→ *What the new members have done is taken their seats in the assembly.*

We use *wh-* clefts, not *it* clefts, to highlight the action (verb) in a sentence:

✗ ~~*It is totally undemocratic that these actions are.*~~

✓ *What these actions are is totally undemocratic.*

We can reverse the order of the parts in *wh-* cleft sentences and put the emphasised part at the beginning:

The man appeared to be engrossed in his book, but he wasn't reading. ***Watching the factory opposite*** *was what he was really doing.*

4 Other types of cleft sentence

We can use *wh-* clauses with *when, where, why* and *who* to highlight a time, a place, a reason or a person, but we usually use an introductory noun phrase (highlighted below).
The *wh-* clause acts like an ordinary relative clause:

We forgot to invite Ian. → ✗ ~~*Who we forgot to invite was Ian.*~~
✓ *The one/person (who) we forgot to invite was* ***Ian****.*

person	***The guy*** *who told me about the new club was Zack.*
place	***The house*** *where I used to live is near here.*
time	***The day*** *(when) we left was the saddest day of my life.*
reason	***The reason*** *(why) they never told me is they don't trust me.*

We can emphasise a noun phrase or a verb phrase with *the* (*only/last*) *thing, something* or *all*:

The thing (that) I most disliked about the movie was ***the scene in the graveyard****.*

The only thing (that) they want is ***a chance to air their grievances****.*

The last thing (that) we did was ***(to) pack the kettle****.*

Something the surveyor neglected to mention was ***the damp in the kitchen****.*

All (that) we're asking for is ***to be given a chance****.*

We can also use *the one/only thing/person* with a negative verb:

The one thing (that) this shop ***won't do*** *is* ***repair goods bought in other shops****.*

The only thing (that) we ***didn't find*** *was* ***the key to the cellar****.*

The one person (that) ***I didn't want*** *to see just then* ***walked into the room****.*

More on relative clauses ➤ Units 53 and 54

Practice

1 GRAMMAR IN USE **Read the review and complete the article with phrases from A–L below (not all the phrases are needed). There is one place where two phrases can be used.** 4.37 **Listen and check.**

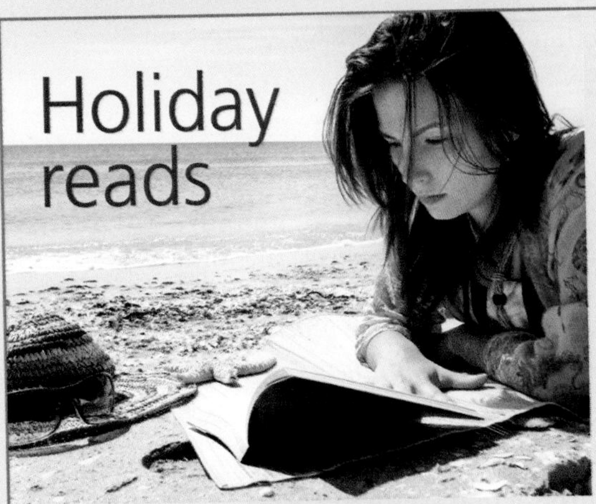

Holiday reads

IF YOU'RE LOOKING for some good books to take on holiday and you like a good detective thriller, you can't do better than the Stieg Larsson *Millennium* trilogy. The three books centre around an unlikely heroine – an anti-social egotistic young woman called Lisbeth Salander. (1) ..... is make this anti-hero a vulnerable and therefore not entirely unlikeable character, which is no mean feat. While the writing (or at least the translation) is fairly mediocre, (2) ..... hooks the reader – these books are fast-moving, sometimes shocking journeys into the criminal underworld in the company of Salander and investigative journalist Mikael Blomqvist. It is through the Blomqvist character (3) ..... with one of the protagonists – he is a hard-bitten journalist but remains sympathetic and keeps his integrity through a series of misadventures.

The characters and general feel of the novels are introduced in *The Girl with the Dragon Tattoo*, and developed through the series. (4) ..... is the graphic violence, although this is kept to a minimum and is never gratuitous.

This trilogy has enjoyed enormous success, and the one thing (5) ....., one has to conclude, is the untimely death of its author, himself an investigative journalist who delved into organised crime and neo-Nazism in Sweden. This, of course, led to endless conspiracy theories – was Larsson murdered? Had he uncovered some awful criminal organisation at the heart of Swedish political life? (6) ..... is the entirely natural, albeit tragic, cause of death – a massive heart attack.

A the thing that some readers might find off-putting
B it is the pace that
C it makes these theories unlikely that
D that has helped fuel its success
E it is the pace what
F that the reader can identify
G why it has been so popular
H what makes these theories highly unlikely
I how the reader can identify
J what some readers might find offputting
K it is what Larsson manages to do
L what Larsson manages to do

2 Read the information below then correct the sentences. Each correction must contain a cleft sentence. 4.38 **Listen and check.**

Nick turned up late for work on Monday because he got stuck in a traffic jam on the ring road. Nick had a hands-free mobile phone in his car so he was able to call his manager and warn her that he would be late. She was furious but managed to reschedule an important meeting for the afternoon.

0 The manager arrived late for work on Monday.
No, it was *Nick who arrived late on Monday.*

1 Nick was late because he had overslept.
No, it was .... that he was late.

2 Nick sent his manager a text message to let her know he'd be late.
No, what Nick .... from his hands-free phone.

3 Nick was late on Wednesday morning.
No, ... that he was late.

4 Nick's manager had to start the meeting without him.
No, what she .... the afternoon.

5 Nick got stuck in a traffic jam in the town centre.
No, not the town centre; it .... got stuck.

6 The manager had to reschedule the meeting because a client was unable to come.
No, it .... had to reschedule the meeting.

7 Nick called his manager to give her the sales figures.
No, it .... that he rang her.

8 Nick's manager felt a little annoyed with him for being late.
No, she didn't feel a little annoyed. What ....

3 Write the second sentence so it has a similar meaning to the first. Use the word in brackets, as in the example.

0 Sebastian left the job because of the long working hours.
(why) *The reason why Sebastian left the job was the long working hours.*

1 The union representative called the strike.
(person) ....

2 Political analysts do not question his dedication.
(isn't) ....

3 These criminals are totally ruthless.
(what) ....

4 Dickens used to live around the corner.
(place) ....

5 It was the next-door neighbour who complained.
(one) ....

6 The children inherited everything except the house.
(only) ....

7 The climbers reached the peak at six o'clock.
(was) ....

8 They engaged two au pairs to look after the children.
(did) ....

9 Before leaving we switched off the power supply.
(last) ....

10 The company has imposed a ban on private emails.
(done) ....

11 The only thing the customers wanted was to get their money back.
(all) ....

12 The managing director informed the staff of the news.
(it) ....

13 Our mechanics just need five minutes to change the tyres.
(all) ....

14 The introduction of stamp duties led to the loss of the American colonies.
(that) ....

76 Emphasis (2) inversion and fronting

Charles Dickens started his literary career by writing for magazines. Indeed, his first novel, *The Pickwick Papers*, was serialised in a magazine before being published as a book. **Only later did Dickens produce** full novels to be published as complete books.

1 Reasons for inversion and fronting

Inversion and fronting are both ways of changing the normal word order of a sentence.

- Normal statement word order is subject + verb (Before you start ➤ page 180). Inversion is the word order in questions *(Are you ready?)*, but we also use it for emphasis in statements. Compare:
  NON-INVERTED ***He was** late and he didn't apologise.*
  INVERTED *Not only **was he** late, but he didn't (even) apologise.*
  The inverted statement emphasises the inverted action more.
- Fronting brings adjectives and adverbs to the beginning of the sentence. Compare:
  NON-FRONTED *The actors were a mixed bunch. Pacino was **the least inspiring** of the lot.*
  FRONTED *The actors were a mixed bunch. **Least inspiring** of the lot was Pacino.*
  The fronted statement places more emphasis on the adjective phrase *least inspiring*.

2 Subject–auxiliary inversion

We invert the auxiliary/modal verb (*do, have, should,* etc.) and subject after these phrases:

after adverbs with 'restrictive'/ negative meaning (e.g. *hardly, scarcely, rarely, little, never, seldom*)	***Little** did we realise the true extent of his involvement.* ***Never** had they experienced such behaviour.* ***Hardly** had the guests arrived **when** the bell for supper was rung.*
only + time expression or prepositional phrase	***Only later** did Dickens produce full novels ...* ***Only with a great deal of effort** was he able to escape.*
only + conjunction (inversion in main clause)	***Only if** the weather improves **will** the golf tournament **take place**.*
in no way, at no time, under no circumstances, on no account	***At no time** during the operation did the patient regain consciousness.* ***Under no circumstances** can refunds be given.*
not + *only*/time expression/ person or thing	***Not only** is he late, he hasn't even brought a present.* ***Not since** records began has youth unemployment been so high.* ***Not a single stone** was left unturned in the search.*
no sooner ... than	***No sooner** had we set out than the skies opened.*
clauses beginning with *neither* or *nor*	*They have no intention of paying and **neither** have we.* *We couldn't face the customers and nor could the boss.*
clauses beginning with *may* which describe a strong wish	***May** he live to regret this decision!*
after fronted comparisons, *also, such* and *so**	*The captain is refusing to play under these conditions and **so** are the rest of the team.*

* See also 76.4 opposite.

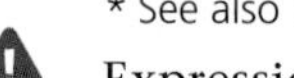

Expressions with *no, not,* etc. not listed above (e.g. *no doubt*) cannot be inverted:
✗ ~~*No doubt will he give us a key.*~~ ✓ ***No doubt** he will give us a key.*

We do not invert the subject and auxiliary after *only* if there is no time expression or prepositional phrase immediately after it:
✗ ~~*Only can members park there.*~~
✓ ***Only** members can park there.* ✓ ***Only on Sundays** can members park there.*

3 Subject–verb inversion

We occasionally invert a main verb and subject after prepositional phrases (e.g. *between the trees*) or adverbs of place (e.g. *here, there, outside*) and adverbs of time (e.g. *next, then, first, now, finally*). We can use a form of *be* or verbs of place and movement (e.g. *stand, sit, lie, come, go, climb, run, sail, fly*) before the subject.

- place adverbs/prepositional phrases + *be* or verbs of place/movement:
  Here lies *the body of our late lamented sovereign.*
  All along one wall climbed *a beautiful rambling rose.*
- time adverbs + *be* or verbs of place/movement: *For the first hour the teams seemed evenly matched.* ***Then came*** *the turning point in the game as Ed scored.*
  That was the final instalment of the book of the week. ***Next is*** *the news.*

We often use this pattern to form a link with the information in the previous sentence, and it is common in formal literary English.

We don't use inversion if the subject of the clause is a pronoun:

Here comes the bus. → ✗ ~~*Here comes it.*~~
✓ *Here **it** comes.*

We can also use inversion in *as* and *than* clauses in formal English:
Mr Slater is expecting a pay rise, ***as are*** *several other salesmen in the team.*
Social security officials are far more vigorous in handling suspect benefit claimants ***than is*** *the Inland Revenue in dealing with suspected tax evasion.*

Inversion is common in certain fixed expressions, often with subjunctives (➤ Unit 40.1):
So be *it.* ***Long live*** *the king!*

4 Fronting adjective and adverbial phrases

We can place the following at the beginning of the sentence with inversion of the subject and a form of the verb *be*:

comparative and superlative adjectives*	*The first act was dire.* ***Much more exciting*** *was the play's second act.* *Many of the monuments are truly awesome.* ***Best of all*** *is the Colosseum.*
so + adjective + *that* clause	***So intense*** *was the heat (that) the firefighters were unable to enter the building for two hours.*
also + adverbial phrase	*Members of the royal family attended the funeral.* ***Also at the service*** *were several ambassadors.*
such	*They led a life of poverty.* ***Such*** *is the fate of most orphans in this area.*
adverbial phrases describing position and participle verbs of position and movement (e.g. *stand, attach, lie*)	*After showing us around the house, the agent took us outside.* ***At the back of the house*** *was an untidy garden, much of which was taken up by a large and unkempt lawn.* ***Standing in the corner of the garden*** *was a massively overgrown silver birch tree, which towered over the roof of the garage.* ***Attached to the roof*** *was an unsightly FM aerial.*
infinitive clauses	*For years I have been writing to the President.* ***To meet him*** *is my most fervent wish.*
infinitive without *to* (if it 'echoes' an earlier verb)	*He said he would arrive on time. And* ***arrive*** *on time he did.*

* We can front verbs and adjectives using *as* and *though* (➤ Unit 60.2):
Try as *she might, she simply couldn't open the jam jar.* ***Battered though*** *he was, he never lost his will to succeed.*

5 Fronting objects and complements

In literary language, we also front previously mentioned objects or complements:
The house was large and sprawling, with two wings and a dark attic. Hilary spent most of her time in the drawing room or the garden. ***The attic*** *she rarely visited.*

Ben awaited his new roommate anxiously. He hoped that he was intelligent and talkative. Then Oliver arrived. ***Intelligent*** *he certainly was, but in every other way Ben was disappointed.*

Practice

1 GRAMMAR IN USE **Choose the best option, A, B or C, to complete these short extracts. Sometimes more than one option may be possible.** 4.39 **Listen and check.**

1 Mrs Sugden meant no harm to anyone, but ..... the intelligence to be really kind.

From *Enigma Variations* by Irene Young

A neither she had B neither had she C she had neither

2 He could hear the pursuers getting closer. They were almost upon him, reaching out for him, the pounding of their boots ringing in his ears, yet ..... his legs would not respond.

From *Wall Games* by Michael Dobbs

A try as hard as he might B try as hard as might he C as hard as he might try

3 ..... when the spectators began to return to the slope above the melon beds, coming in greater numbers than ever before.

From *The Siege of Krishnapur* by J G Farrell

A The rains had hardly stopped B Hardly had the rains stopped
C Hardly the rains had stopped

4 In the first bedroom a door opened onto a short flight of rickety steps that led to an attic. Ward had often threatened to have it converted into a work room but, ... with most attics, it remained nothing more than a storehouse for junk that wasn't wanted elsewhere in the cottage.

From *Heathen* by Shaun Hutson

A the case is B as the case is C as is the case

5 There were three of them. Roberta — she was always called Bobbie, and was the oldest. ....., who wanted to be an engineer when he grew up. And the youngest was Phyllis, who was always trying to be good.

From *The Railway Children* by E Nesbitt

A Peter next came B Came next Peter C Next came Peter

6 'That was despicable.' 'You were not sick unto death,' retorted Joan. 'And since ..... the prince's heart, how could I have stolen it from you?'

From *The Child Bride* by Philippa Wait

A at no time have you possessed B at no time you have possessed
C at no time possessed you

7 It appeared that, despite the age gap, they'd become quite good friends. And then, since her father's fatal heart attack eighteen months ago, ... to come to terms with his loss, to face the grief and despair at the thought of never seeing him again, than her mother's letters and telephone calls had begun to fill her with stunned horror. Abseiling, at fifty-eight?

From *Calypso's Island* by Rosalie Ash

A no sooner she had slowly started B no sooner that she had slowly started
C no sooner had she slowly started

8 And now, her face straight, her lips seeming to quiver, she went into the song; and ....., so touching the cadences, so tender with longing the words, that she seemed transformed before their eyes.

From *My Beloved Son* by Catherine Cookson

A so beautiful her rendering of it was B so beautiful was her rendering of it
C her rendering of it so beautiful was

2 **In ten of the following sentences there are mistakes with word order and missing auxiliaries. Find and correct the mistakes, changing the verb form if necessary. Tick (✓) the correct sentences.**

1 The team is going to complain about this and so is the referee.
2 Little we knew the full extent of his involvement in the fraud.
3 The sales director is resigning, as most of the marketing team.
4 Over in the corner stood the three-metre tall statue of Lenin.
5 The embassy refuses to intervene. Well, so it be.
6 The council promised to put on a great display. And put they on a great display.
7 Under no circumstances will latecomers be admitted to the auditorium.
8 Now the time is for wise investors to think seriously about buying Treasury Bonds.
9 Rarely the early explorers had encountered such friendly and positive attitudes.
10 Not since Kubrick's *2001* has a director made such an intellectually challenging sci-fi movie.
11 The government's proposals are unrealistic, as those are of the opposition.
12 Opposite this house did the old city walls run.
13 Only after climbing onto the roof he managed to escape from the rising flood waters.
14 No doubt didn't he realise the consequences of his actions.

3 **Make these sentences more emphatic by 'fronting' part of them. Do not use any additional words. 4.40 Listen and check.**

0 I can tolerate criticism but I can't stand hypocrisy.
I can tolerate criticism but hypocrisy I can't stand!
1 Though he was exhausted, he managed to reach the finishing line.
....
2 Selim's life's ambition is to make the pilgrimage to Makkah.
....
3 *The New Confessions* is Boyd's most complete work.
....
4 The school governors really can't accept that proposal.
....
5 An enormous flower display was placed on the table.
....
6 The Cresta Run is much more challenging for the dedicated skier.
....
7 Several sharp criticisms of ministerial conduct were also included in the report.
....
8 An elderly man was lying in the shop doorway.
....
9 It proved impossible to get to the bottom of the mystery.
....
10 The damage was so severe that the pilot couldn't regain control.
....

77 Organising information in writing

J K Rowling's **first Harry Potter manuscript** was rejected by twelve publishing houses. **It** was finally accepted by a small company in London called Bloomsbury.

1 The information principle

In English we usually move from something known (already mentioned or obvious from the context) at the beginning of the sentence to something new at the end. This is called the information principle:

information obvious from the context — already mentioned

The door opened and John walked in. He was holding a black leather briefcase.

new information — new information

Starting sentences with information which relates back to something already mentioned helps the text to 'flow' more smoothly and makes it easier for the reader to understand:

J K Rowling's first Harry Potter manuscript was rejected by twelve publishing houses. It was finally accepted by a small company in London called Bloomsbury. The chairman of the company gave the first chapter to his eight-year-old daughter, Alice, to read. She read it quickly and immediately demanded the next chapter.

We do not usually put new information at the beginning, unless we want to focus on it (see 77.3/4).

2 The end-weight principle

In English we prefer to put long and complex phrases or clauses at the end of a sentence. These also often contain new information, so this principle – the end-weight principle – and the information principle reinforce each other:

A striking feature of the central areas of the capital are ***the elegant classical squares which were originally laid out by aristocratic developers in the eighteenth century.***

Sentences with a heavy clause at the beginning can seem clumsy and be difficult to understand:

[*The elegant classical squares which were originally laid out by aristocratic developers in the eighteenth century are a striking feature of the central areas of the capital.*]

We give more importance to the information principle in text, so we can put a heavy clause at the beginning of a sentence if it contains familiar information linking it to the preceding text:

London has many public parks and squares which date from previous centuries. ***The elegant classical squares which were originally laid out by aristocratic developers in the eighteenth century*** *are a striking feature of the central areas of the capital.*

If the subject of a sentence is a long clause we can use *it* as an 'empty' subject so that we can put the long subject at the end:

It *was hard to believe* ***that he had behaved so appallingly.***

(= That he had behaved so appallingly was hard to believe.)

It can also be an 'empty' object, anticipating a later clause. This allows us to combine several pieces of information into one sentence, again putting new information at the end:
We leave ***it*** *to the reader* ***to appreciate what this will mean.***
(= The reader can appreciate what this will mean. We leave the reader to do this.)
She thought ***it*** *a pity/sad* ***that he hadn't joined in the festivities.***
(= He hadn't joined in the festivities. She thought that was a pity.)

We don't use *it* as an 'empty' object when the main verb is followed immediately by a *that* clause:
✗ ~~*She thought it that he hadn't joined in.*~~ ✓ *She thought that he hadn't joined in.*

3 Focus

In English we can show which part of a sentence or clause contains the most important point or 'focus' by placing the important point at the beginning or end of the sentence – these are the two positions which appear most important to a reader or listener:
Sandra *invited Lucy to* ***her dinner party.***

If we want to put the focus on an item that doesn't naturally come at the beginning or end of the sentence (e.g. *Lucy* in the example above) we have to manipulate the grammar to bring the item to the front focus position. For example, we can use cleft sentences (➤ Unit 75):
It was Lucy *that Sandra invited to her dinner party.*
Lucy *was the girl that Sandra invited to her dinner party.*

Similarly, we can give focus to something by moving it into the end focus position:
The girl that Sandra invited to her dinner party was ***Lucy.***

4 Contrast and emphasis

Because word order in English is usually fixed, we can emphasise or contrast something by moving it to an unfamiliar position. We often do this with adverbial expressions and infinitive clauses (➤ Unit 76.4) and objects and complements (➤ Unit 76.5):
The facade of the house was blank and austere. But it was ornate and luxurious ***inside.***
→ ***But inside*** *it was ornate and luxurious.*
I may be ***old****, but I'm not stupid.*
→ ***Old*** *I may be, but I'm not* ***stupid****!* ***Old*** *I may be, but* ***stupid*** *I'm not!*
Priscilla invariably rejected impoverished suitors. Her only ambition was ***to marry for money.***
→ ***To marry for money*** *was her only ambition.*

5 Manipulating grammar and vocabulary

In order to follow the ordering principles above when writing, we have to choose suitable vocabulary and grammar. As the subject usually comes at the beginning of a sentence in English, the simplest way to organise a sentence is to choose a subject which links with the previous information:
Whenever possible, we pack all our furniture in ***flat packages.*** *[****Transport*** *becomes cheaper because less space is taken up by a* ***flat pack*** *than a bulky one.]*
→ ***A flat pack*** *takes up less space than a bulky one, which means that transport becomes cheaper.*

Alternatively, we may change the grammar or vocabulary:

using a different verb or a passive verb (➤ Unit 62)	*Our neighbours got a good price for their* **car**. *They* **sold it** *to a local garage. /* **It was bought** *by a local garage.*
using introductory *it* (➤ Unit 43.1/5)	*Fleming's behaviour was inexplicable.* **It was hard to believe** *that he had become this savage with a bare knife.*
using participle or infinitive clauses (➤ Units 55 and 56)	*Steve went home.* **Walking towards his door,** *he noticed a piece of paper left on the doorstep.* *Anatole walked away from the discussion.* **To argue with such a person** *was fruitless.*

Practice

1 GRAMMAR IN USE **Read the novel extracts below and study the underlined phrases. Match each one with a reason A–E for placing it in this position in the sentence. One reason can be matched with two phrases.**

A FOCUS – putting an adverbial phrase of reason at the beginning of the sentence. ....
B END-WEIGHT – putting a long clause or phrase after the verb. ....
C FOCUS – placing a time or place adverbial at the beginning of the sentence. ....
D CONTRAST – fronting an adverbial to make a contrast with what has gone before. ....
E INFORMATION FLOW – starting a sentence with known information. ....

(1) Ten days later, at eight-thirty in the morning of Wednesday, 22nd January, Robyn Penrose set off in a snowstorm and an ill humour to begin her stint as the University of Rummidge Faculty of Arts Industry Year Shadow, or URFAIYS as she was designated in memoranda emanating from the Vice-Chancellor's Office. (2) One of these documents had informed her (3) that she was to be attached to a Mr Victor Wilcox, Managing Director of J. Pringle & Sons, for one day a week during the remainder of the winter term, and she had chosen Wednesdays for this undertaking since it was the day she normally kept free from teaching. By the same token it was a day she normally spent at home, catching up on her marking, preparation and research, and she bitterly resented having to sacrifice it. (4) For this reason above all others she had come very close to declining Philip Swallow's proposal to nominate her for the Shadow Scheme.

The nursemaid was also in the kitchen. ... Her contradictory statements about the blanket were to make her a suspect.

(5) Outside, the servants and a growing gaggle of villagers began to search for traces of the murderer and the weapon. (6) Daniel Oliver, the jobbing gardener, showed Urch some footmarks on the lawn near the drawing-room windows.

2 **Choose the best option, A or B, according to text ordering principles.**
5.01 **Listen and check.**

1 Della Jones, one of our best-loved singers, is well known for her opera repertoire.
A Her greatest operatic roles have included Rosina in *Il Barbiere di Siviglia* and the title role *in La Cenerentola.*
B Rosina in *Il Barbiere di Siviglia* and the title role in *La Cenerentola* are included among her greatest operatic roles.

2 One of the great comic stars of the 1960s was Walter Matthau,
A particularly noteworthy was Jack Lemmon's film work with him.
B his film work with Jack Lemmon being particularly noteworthy.

3 If you're looking for a quiet holiday, forget about Ibiza.
A It may be sun-drenched and beautiful but it isn't peaceful!
B Sun-drenched and beautiful it may be, peaceful it isn't!

4 The elderly man expressed no regrets about the years he spent in the army.
A On the contrary, he thought it an honour that he'd been able to serve his country.
B He'd been able to serve his country and he thought that was an honour.

5 Potential residents will find everything they need in the Dinglewood rest home.
A Among its features are luxurious private rooms and twenty-four-hour nursing care.
B Luxurious private rooms and twenty-four-hour nursing care are among its features.

6 The Tower of London is one of the oldest landmarks in the city.
A Today its main claim to fame is the recently built Jewel House containing the fabulous crown jewels of Great Britain.
B The recently built Jewel House containing the fabulous crown jewels of Great Britain is its main claim to fame today.

7 Birch trees can reach 30 metres in height and have a very vigorous growth pattern.
   A Damage can be caused to drains and house walls if they are close to the particularly fast-growing roots.
   B The roots are particularly fast-growing and can cause damage if they are close to drains and house walls.
8 Recycling has recently become an important issue in local politics and recycling facilities are becoming more common.
   A Receptacles for glass, paper, board, plastics, old clothes and books can now be found in the centre of most towns.
   B You can now find receptacles for glass, paper, board, plastics, old clothes and books in the centre of most towns.

3 GRAMMAR IN USE **In the following text the underlined parts do not conform with the principles of ordering information. Rewrite these sentences appropriately, changing the grammar as necessary. 5.02 Listen and check.**

The Hubble Space Telescope

THE HUBBLE SPACE Telescope was put into orbit by the American space shuttle Discovery in April 1990. (0) The Earth is orbited by it at an altitude of 610 kilometres. (1) The light from space is not affected by interference from the Earth's atmosphere at this height. As a result the Hubble telescope is at least ten times more accurate than telescopes on the ground and has a much greater range. (2) In our search for distant stars and planets this makes it the most useful tool.

The telescope is named after the most influential astronomer of the twentieth century, Edwin Hubble. Working at the Mount Wilson Observatory in Pasadena, (3) his close observation of the Andromeda Galaxy was used by the American astronomer to develop the theory that the universe is expanding.

The Hubble Space Telescope has not had a smooth history. (4) Scientists at NASA discovered that the main mirror had become distorted and could not be used with any accuracy only two months after it went into orbit. Rather than abandon the project, NASA decided to find a way to resolve this problem. (5) COSTAR (corrective optics space telescope axial replacement) was the name of the solution. This was a device which contained ten smaller mirrors designed to compensate for the distortion in the telescope's main mirror. It cost $360 million to develop the technology and more than 30 hours of spacewalks by astronauts to fix the device. (6) The Hubble Space Telescope is now working correctly and sending its astonishing data back to Earth, the repairs were completed in January 1994.

0 *It orbits the Earth at an altitude of 610 kilometres.*
1 ....

....
2 ....
3 ....

....
4 ....

....
5 ....
6 ....

....

78 Other text features

Since the early eighteenth century literary critics and academics have queried whether Shakespeare wrote all of the works attributed to him, or indeed, whether Shakespeare was in fact just one person. **This controversy** still continues today.

1 Nominalisation

It is sometimes more concise and elegant, especially in written English, to use noun phrases rather than verb phrases to express an idea, as this can combine two sentences into one:

VERB PHRASE ***The committee decided*** *to open the playground to all children. This was welcomed by the local schools.*

NOUN PHRASE ***The committee's decision*** *to open the playground to all children was welcomed by the local schools.*

The noun phrase is often made up of two nouns linked by a preposition:

VERB PHRASE	NOUN PHRASE
They released the video in 1998.	*The release* **of** *the video in 1998 …*
The law was amended last week.	*The amendment* **to** *the law last week …*
The war drained the country's resources.	*The war was a drain* **on** *the country's resources.*

An adverb in a verb phrase changes to an adjective if the verb is nominalised:
The girl shouted ***loudly*** *and attracted the attention she wanted.*
The girl's ***loud*** *shouts attracted the attention she wanted.*

We can use nominalisation to summarise information from a previous sentence. This is useful for developing an explanation or argument:
The rioters threw petrol bombs at the embassy. ***The situation*** *was getting out of hand.*

The judges have considered at great length the six novels in the shortlist, and we have reached agreement. ***Our decision*** *is unanimous. This year's prize goes to ...*

We can often use *have* + noun to combine information about an event into one sentence rather than two:
They raced up the hill. The race was exhausting. → *They* ***had an*** *exhausting* ***race*** *up the hill.*

2 Using parallel structures

Although we try to avoid repeating words when we are writing a text, a useful way of making a text cohesive is to use similar grammar in different sentences, for example, using the same verb form, similar word order or repeating a particular grammatical form:
She is probably going to *fail the exam. And* ***she is probably going to*** *blame her teacher.*

Your own home. ***To live*** *and sleep in.* ***To cook*** *and eat in.* ***To watch*** *TV or maybe do some work in.*

We avoid sudden changes in grammar as this often looks clumsy and unclear:
[*I can't wait to lie on the sand. Swimming in the sea is great. To sunbathe is something I would love to do as well.*]
✓ *I can't wait to be* ***lying*** *on the sand,* ***sunbathing*** *and* ***swimming*** *in the sea.*

If we want to create a dramatic effect or make a strong contrast, we can repeat an unusual grammatical pattern. But we usually only use this device in narrative and fiction; in less literary contexts it can seem inappropriate:
Rarely had I *seen such a ramshackle boat. And* ***never had I*** *actually been expected to board one.*

Repetition, particularly in sets of three, is a common rhetorical device, i.e. used in giving speeches. We call this 'tripling':
America, at its best, *matches a commitment to principle with a concern for civility. ...* ***America, at its best,*** *is also courageous. ...* ***America, at its best,*** *is compassionate.*

(Barack Obama, inaugural address, 2009)

3 Levels of formality

A key feature of the use of language which is appropriate to its context is the choice of vocabulary. Most English words are 'neutral' and we can use them in any situation. But some words are only appropriate, for example, in a formal situation and others only in an informal one. Compare:

*The **show starts** at nine o'clock.* (neutral)
*The **performance commences** at nine o'clock.* (formal)
*The **show kicks off** at nine.* (informal)

We often use phrasal verbs in informal contexts and formal equivalents in formal speech and writing (➤ Unit 67.2). However, the formal equivalents can be too formal for most speech and writing:

*Do you usually use an alarm clock to help you **wake up** and **get up** in the morning?*
[*The Sunburst alarm clock allows you to **awake** and **arise** in the most natural way possible.*]
✓ *... allows you to **awake/wake up** and **get up** in the most natural way possible.*

The choice of grammatical patterns can also indicate a particular level of formality:

*Everyone **has to** remove their shoes **before they enter** the chamber.* (neutral)
***Prior to entering** the chamber, all visitors **are required to** remove footwear.* (formal)
*Looks like we**'ve got to** take off our shoes **before we go in**.* (informal)

Certain forms and grammatical patterns are more suitable for formal situations:

impersonal pronouns (➤ Unit 5.1)	***One** might prefer a four-star hotel.*
passives (➤ Unit 62.7)	*Non-reflective glasses **should be worn** at all times.*
subjunctives (➤ Unit 40.1)	*I demand that **she apologise** in writing.*
infinitive clause subjects (➤ Unit 56.1)	***To interrupt your elders** is very rude.*
non-defining relative clauses (➤ Unit 53.3)	*The Law Society, **to which he had appealed,** rejected his argument at once.*

 In written English we usually do not mix formal and informal language in the same text unless we want to create a comic or ironic effect:

[*The Minister was unable to attend the reception because he was a bit tied up.*]
✓ *The Minister was unable to attend the reception **due to a prior engagement**.*

4 Adverbs

Adverbs are used a lot in written English, for example, to describe a particular aspect of something we are commenting on:

***Economically**, the current government has been a resounding success.*
(= The government has successfully managed the economy.)

We can also use an adverb to modify an adjective or a participle. The adverb can come before or after the participle:

*Although **successful economically**, the government is starting to lose popularity.*
***Financially speaking**, few of the dot.com companies have a good track record.*

Some adverbs make a comment; for example, the adverbs *definitely, probably, in fact,* comment on the truth of the statement:

*Hardback sales held up; paperback sales were **definitely** down.*

Some comment on the limitation of the statement, for example, *in most cases, generally*:

*The term 'art' is **generally** used to denote painting and sculpture.*

ACADEMIC ENGLISH These adverbs are common in academic writing, which is often concerned with the certainty or probability of the information it gives:

*In the remaining fourteen patients, symptoms resolved, **apparently** spontaneously, after a median of four weeks.*

Practice

1 **Each sentence below can be improved using one of the text features in this unit. Decide which text feature in A–D could apply to each sentence. Then rewrite the underlined section, as in the example.**

A Nominalisation B Parallel structures C Formality D Adverbs

0 Ladies and gentlemen, please take your seats quickly as the next poetry reading is gonna kick off in five mins exactly.

C will start/commence in precisely five minutes

1 Despite being successful in a commercial sense, Grisham's last novel failed to receive critical acclaim.

....

2 To write a successful first novel is surprising, to write a second is astonishing, but writing a third is near impossible!

....

3 Arnold Makepeace was selected as the new Professor of Literature, which surprised everybody.

....

4 Only once in a while does a biography this good come along: it's a truthful account, it's a sympathetic perspective, the story is also gripping.

....

5 It appears that the government is considering the extension of VAT to books.

....

6 Several biographies of Princess Diana were published very soon after her death. This was considered tasteless by many people.

....

7 As handling the books while consuming food and drink can damage them, customers mustn't bring food and drink into the shop.

....

2 GRAMMAR IN USE **Each extract either contains incorrect or inappropriate vocabulary or grammar, or would be more appropriate if nominalised. Correct each extract, using the clues in brackets to help you.** 5.03 **Listen and check.**

0 (formality)

Dave – I'm off to Mum's for the weekend. Don't forget to ~~activate~~ switch on the burglar alarm if you go out! See you Monday. Love Jane

1 (adverb)

THE ARCHAEOLOGICAL excavations have revealed some facts that were previously unknown about the Roman city. We've heard that even the smallest of houses had some kind of weapon store.

2 (parallel structures)

- Swimming in the morning and skiing in the afternoon.
- Dining on seafood in the evening and to fall asleep to the sound of lapping waves at night.

There's nowhere like Andalucia!

CALL NOW FOR OUR BROCHURE.

3 (nominalisation)

When we arrived in the centre of Athens, there was a large crowd of strikers and riot police. The crowd and the riot police seemed quite threatening, so we got back on the metro and went back to the hotel.

(parallel structures)

4

To make a recording first insert a blank tape into the machine. Then select the track you wish to record and set the counter to zero. You ought to press the red 'record' button and at the same time press the 'play' button.

(nominalisation)

5

Professor Mills explained at length the principles behind the theory of gravity to the students, which made them all feel rather more confident about the forthcoming examination.

(formality)

6

Policyholders wishing to make a claim under **Section 3** should be prepared to provide receipts of purchase for all items. Items for which receipts cannot be provided will not be eligible for reinstatement other than in really special circumstances and at the absolute discretion of the insurers.

(formality)

7

We moved into the new house today. Everything went pretty smoothly. The furniture van arrived with exceptional punctuality at ten and an exhausting period of three hours was spent unloading. At last, at one o'clock we were able to sit down on our own sofa in our own new living room!

3 GRAMMAR IN USE **Read this draft text, then complete the rewritten sections of the article below with a noun/noun phrase or adverb.** 5.04 **Listen and check.**

St Andrew's Hospital Trust has recently confirmed that a fresh wave of food poisoning has broken out in the Scottish resort, and this has alarmed everyone who lives in the town. A spokesperson stated that the illness was not serious and could be easily treated. This appeased community leaders but they requested further reassurances that the authorities were doing everything within their control to contain the spread. The hospital authority has announced that it will investigate fully the causes of this epidemic. As a recent investigation into a similar outbreak concluded that the cause was poor meat hygiene in a local butcher's shop, it isn't surprising that local shopkeepers are concerned about what will come out of the pending investigation. The leader of the Shopkeepers' Association, Len Murphy, suggested that the source of the epidemic might be hospital kitchens, which has angered hospital staff. The kitchen staff at the hospital have now called for a strike of hospital auxiliaries across the region, which has concerned the health authority. The financial consequences of this action are likely to be extremely severe for the health authority.

(0) *The recent confirmation* by St Andrew's Hospital Trust of an (1) .... of food poisoning in the Scottish resort has alarmed (2) .... A (3) .... that the illness was not serious and could be easily treated appeased community leaders, but they requested further reassurances that the authorities were doing everything within their control to contain the spread. The hospital authority has announced a (4) .... into the causes of this epidemic. As the (5) .... of a recent investigation into a similar outbreak cited poor meat hygiene in a local butcher's shop, (6) ...., local shopkeepers are concerned about the (7) .... of the pending inquiry. A (8) .... by the leader of the Shopkeepers' Association, Len Murphy, that the source of the epidemic might be hospital kitchens has angered hospital staff. A (9) .... by kitchen staff at the hospital for a strike of hospital auxiliaries across the region has concerned the health authority. (10) ...., this is likely to have severe consequences for the health authority.

Review MODULE 17

1 UNITS 72, 73 AND 74 **Read the draft article below. Identify three more places where ellipsis is possible and delete the words. Then find nine more places where a substitution would be better than the given text.**

The Inuit system of child adoption, although ~~it is~~ archaic, appears much more humane than our ~~system~~ *own* in the so-called civilised world, where childless couples must apply through faceless agencies for the opportunity to adopt. Childless couples must undergo a series of intrusive interviews and examinations and, if they are successful, will then be put on a waiting list for an unspecified period of time. An Inuit couple wanting to adopt simply makes the fact that they want a child known and soon enough the couple will receive a call from a woman who is prepared to give up her child. She may want to give up her child because she already has too many children and she does not want another child, or the call may come from a relative or friend who wishes to help someone less fortunate than themselves. Traditionally, the couple would be asked if the couple would like the child and, if they do, a simple handover would take place. Today, however, the handover system has been replaced by bureaucracy in the form of civil registration, although the tradition itself has not been replaced. The tradition survives even in the twenty-first century.

2 UNITS 75 AND 76 **Complete the second sentence so it has a similar meaning to the first, but is more emphatic. Use three to six words, including the word in brackets.**

0 The position demands quick-thinking and analytical skills. (what)
What the position demands is quick-thinking and analytical skills.

1 Rick entered the room and his eyes alighted on the note on the table. (sooner)
No .... than his eyes alighted on the note on the table.

2 It's no big secret – any aspiring actor wants the chance to make an impression. (all)
It's no big secret – .... is to have the chance to make an impression.

3 Kerry was devastated – the vegetation was really sparse and the once-lush area resembled a desert. (so)
Kerry was devastated – .... that the once-lush area resembled a desert.

4 Imagine my surprise when the chief inspector himself met me at the front desk. (it)
Imagine my surprise when .... himself who met me at the front desk.

5 The children didn't enjoy the traditional exhibits. They found the interactive displays very interesting. (much)
The children didn't enjoy the traditional exhibits. .... the interactive displays.

6 The decadence of the Roman civilisation eventually led to its downfall. (was)
.... of the Roman civilisation that eventually led to its downfall.

7 Their attitude was all the more surprising as we had hardly ever been treated with anything but courtesy. (seldom)
Their attitude was all the more surprising as .... with anything but courtesy.

8 Anastasia didn't want him to feel like a prisoner. (last)
.... for him to feel like a prisoner.

3 UNITS 77 AND 78 **Read the text about Paul Robeson and match the underlined clauses and sentences 1–6 with the text features in A–F.**

PAUL ROBESON was the first African American to gain international success in the 'white' world of Hollywood movies. He was born in 1898, the son of a runaway slave. (1) Highly intelligent, he won a scholarship to Columbia University, where he qualified as a lawyer. But there were few opportunities for black lawyers then and Robeson decided to pursue a career on the stage, where he soon became one of the biggest stars on Broadway. (2) Applauded for his acting ability and acclaimed for his remarkable physical presence on stage, Robeson went on to show the world his greatest talent, his superb deep bass singing voice, in Jerome Kern's hit musical *Show Boat* in 1927.

(3) Success on Broadway inevitably led to Hollywood and Robeson made his screen debut in 1933, before moving to England, where he starred in *King Solomon's Mines*.

Back in America Robeson returned to *Show Boat*, singing his famous song, Ol' Man River. (4) A recording and singing career followed with Robeson popularising traditional songs developed by black slaves in the American South. In the 1950s Robeson made a visit to the Soviet Union. It was an era of strong anti-communist feelings in the United States and when Robeson returned home his passport was cancelled. (5) He was blacklisted by Hollywood and was unable to find work. (6) Robeson left the States in 1958 and began a new career as a concert performer in Europe. But he became seriously ill in the sixties and returned to New York. He died in Harlem in 1976.

A Putting familiar information at the beginning by using a noun. ....
B Giving extra focus to information by putting it at the front of the sentence. ....
C Repeating a grammatical structure to give extra emphasis (parallelism). ....
D Familiar information at the beginning, new information at the end (the information principle). ....
E Putting familiar information at the beginning by using the passive. ....
F Long and complex phrases at the end (the end-weight principle). ....

4 ALL UNITS **Complete the text with one or two words in each gap.**

Publishing pitfalls and how to avoid them

So, you've written your masterpiece and (0) ......*it's*...... the best thing since sliced bread. Now what do you do? The last (1) .... you should do is copy it fifteen times and send it to every publishing house you know. The scattergun approach is not appreciated in publishing, (2) .... is it effective!

Think carefully about which publishers to approach – you clearly need to identify (3) .... known for publishing the type of book you've written. List the appropriate publishing houses and then find the names of the relevant editors. Call the switchboard of each (4) .... and request the name of the person responsible for your type of book.

When you have a few relevant contacts – and only a few – (5) .... you should consider is calling each initially to find out how (6) .... like to receive unsolicited manuscripts. (7) .... only is it courteous to do (8) ...., but it may save you time as some editors may require only a phone call to register interest. But remember – do be patient, do listen to the editor and (9) .... consider his/her suggestions carefully. After all, you're talking to the expert.

(10) .... always a good idea to consider an agent. Costly though it (11) .... be, as an agent will take a percentage of your future earnings, (12) .... thorough is a good agent's knowledge that it will be money well spent.

Read More

MODULE

18 The grammar of spoken English

Before you start

1 Review these intermediate grammar points and check you know them.

Question tags

1 We can add a question tag to the end of a statement to turn it into a question. We use

- *do/does/did* (in the present/past simple tense): *You already **know** Harriet, **don't you?***
- a form of *be*: *There **weren't** many people at the concert, **were there?***
- an auxiliary verb: *She **hasn't had** the baby yet, **has she?***
- a modal verb: *Tax returns **can** be submitted online now, **can't they?***

In most cases, if the sentence is positive, we use a negative form in the question tag. If the sentence is negative, we use a positive form.

2 We answer these questions in the following way:

POSITIVE TAG	*John isn't experienced enough to do this job, **is he?***
ANSWER	*No, **I don't think he is.*** (agreement) *Actually, **yes, he is.*** (contradiction)
NEGATIVE TAG	*You're staying away for two weeks, **aren't you?***
ANSWER	***Yes, that's right.*** (agreement) ***No, it's three weeks.*** (contradiction)

Indirect questions

1 An indirect question is one question within another question or a statement:

introductory phrase — indirect question

Can you tell me *how long I'll have to wait to see the doctor?*

2 Other common introductory phrases are *I'd like to know …*, *Do you know …*, *I wonder …* :

I'd like to know *if that car is abandoned or not.*

Do you know *where the cash machine is?*

Making adjectives and adverbs stronger

In spoken English we can use the adverbs *really* and *pretty* to make the meaning of adjectives stronger:

*That film was **really exciting**.*

*It's **really freezing** in here!*

*I think their songs are **pretty good**.*

In informal American English *real* can be used instead of *really*:

*That watch looks **real expensive**.*

Stance and sentence adverbs

1 Adverbs such as *clearly, honestly, obviously, surprisingly, understandably* can express our attitude towards an action:

*You've **obviously** been eating too many sweets, young man!* (This is a logical deduction which is clear to anybody.)

2 We can also use these adverbs in conversation to introduce, extend, or make a comment on a topic or opinion:

***Obviously**, I had absolutely no idea of how expensive it would turn out to be.*

2 **Read the dialogue and see how many features of spoken English you can identify.**

A There's nothing on TV tonight, is there?
B No. Just those really boring talent shows. I can't stand them.
A No, neither can I.
B Let's go out somewhere, shall we?
A OK. How about that new French restaurant? Sheryl went there last week.
B Did she?
A Yeah. She said it was pretty good. Obviously, it's a bit expensive.
B Oh, that's OK. Do you know if it's open tonight?
A Mmm, think so.

3 **Complete the diagnostic test below. Choose the correct words in *italics*. If both options are appropriate in spoken English, choose both.**

1 Can you tell me where *did they put / they put* the spare keys to the garage? ➤ Unit 79.1
2 She doesn't need to pay for the whole course in advance, *does she / needn't she*? ➤ Unit 79.2
3 'I'm going to the Greek islands next summer.' '*Aren't / Are* you? How exciting!' ➤ Unit 79.3
4 'Have you seen my new kitten? He's worth £500.' 'He's lovely. He's a rare breed, then, *is he / isn't he*?' ➤ Unit 79.3
5 'They've stopped giving discounts for students.' 'So *they have / have they*. What a pity.' ➤ Unit 79.4
6 'The battery's flat. You didn't turn the lights off, did you?' 'Yes, I *turned / did turn* them off, I remember it distinctly.' ➤ Unit 80.1
7 How *the point / on earth* will you get there? The buses have all been on strike for a week. ➤ Unit 80.2
8 I don't believe you. *What / How* a ridiculous story! ➤ Unit 80.3
9 Dave's headache was *so / such* severe he just had to go straight to bed. ➤ Unit 80.3
10 'The new registrar is handsome and really friendly.' 'Handsome *is he / he may be*, but he certainly isn't friendly!' ➤ Unit 80.4
11 The film was brilliant! The car chase was *dead / a bit* exciting! ➤ Unit 81.1
12 I wasn't very impressed by the actress. *She gave a bit unconvincing performance. / Her performance was a bit unconvincing.* ➤ Unit 81.1
13 Hurry up! Why do you always drive so *slowly / slow*? ➤ Unit 81.2
14 I really enjoy organic food. Although, *fortunately / admittedly*, it is rather expensive. ➤ Unit 81.3
15 Suppose I *missed / 'd missed* the train. I would never have met you. ➤ Unit 82.1
16 Come on, it's 8.30. It's high time we *leave / left* for the airport. ➤ Unit 82.2
17 We'd better take some candles with us *if / in case* there's a power cut. ➤ Unit 82.3
18 'Hey. This is the wrong road!' 'Oh no. I knew I *shouldn't've / should not have* taken the left turning.' ➤ Unit 83.1
19 'Hi Jake. How are you?' '*I'm fine / Fine*, thanks. How are you?' ➤ Unit 83.2
20 Did you see that film on TV last night, *you know / well*, the one with Tom Cruise? ➤ Unit 83.3

4 **Check your answers on page 384. Then go to the unit for more information and practice.**

79 Spoken questions and responses

1 Indirect questions

We usually use indirect questions to make a question more polite or more tentative. We often use them when we are in a formal situation, when we are talking to strangers, or when we are not sure whether the person we are asking knows the answer.

In indirect questions we use statement word order; the subject always precedes the verb or verb phrase. This is similar to reported questions (➤ Unit 52):

✗ ~~*Do you know where is the nearest bank?*~~ ✓ *Do you know where **the nearest bank is**?*

✗ ~~*Could you tell me when did he leave?*~~ ✓ *Could you tell me when **he left**?*

In indirect questions we can use *whether (or not)* instead of *if (or not)* (➤ Unit 52.1):

*I wonder **whether or not** Mum's back? I wonder **whether** Mum's back **or not**?*

2 Question tags

There are a number of variations in the form of the verb in question tags:

TAGS AFTER ...	EXAMPLES
I am	*I'm still part of the team, **aren't I**?*
need (negative)	*He doesn't need to repeat the year, **does he**?* (or: *He needn't repeat the year, **need he**?*)
may/might	*It may/might be fine tomorrow, **mightn't it**?*
must/can't + have	*He must have taken it, **mustn't he**?* *They can't have seen it, **can they**?*
ought to	*We really ought to leave now, **oughtn't we**?/**shouldn't we**?*
Let's	*Let's try that new restaurant, **shall we**?*

If a positive sentence contains a negative or 'restrictive' adverb, e.g. *scarcely, hardly* (➤ Unit 48), it takes a positive tag:

*There **was hardly** enough food for everyone at the wedding, **was there**?*

Differences between British and American English ➤ page 368

Generally, the pronoun in the tag matches the subject of the sentence:

***This** is a good example, isn't **it**?* (*This* and *it* are both singular.)

***Those** are the flowers for Mum, aren't **they**?* (*Those* and *they* are both plural.)

***Nothing** ever happens when I'm away, does **it**?*

But notice these exceptions:

***Someone**'s been taking my food again, haven't **they**?*

***Nobody** has phoned, have **they**?*

We can use question tags for several purposes, and we say them differently.

- to ask for information (we don't know the answer), we use a rising intonation (↗):
  *You haven't talked to Jim yet, **have you**?*
- to confirm something we think we already know, we use a falling intonation (↘):
  *It's the first of May today, **isn't it**?*
- to make a request, we use a falling intonation (↘):
  *You'll bring me back some of those lovely oranges, **won't you**?*

We also use question tags with imperatives. The form of the tag depends on the purpose:

*Pick me up at eight, **could you**?* (request)

*Stay another night with us, **won't you**?* (invitation)

*Turn the TV off, **will you**? Don't annoy Rufus, **will you**?* (polite command)

We can also use a positive statement with a positive tag when we seek confirmation:

'I'm sorry, but I'm going to have to cancel this evening. I'm really busy and I'm still at work.'

*'Poor you. Things **are** still really hectic, **are they**?'* (to express sympathy)

 Pronunciation ➤ 1.22

3 Reply and echo questions

We use 'follow on' or reply questions to show interest and to make a conversation 'flow':
'We went to a really interesting play last night.' ***'Did you?'*** (↗)

We form reply questions in the same way as tag questions, using auxiliary verbs, *do did*, etc. But, unlike tag questions, if the statement is positive, the reply question is positive and if the statement is negative, the reply question is negative:
'I'm going to Malaysia on business next week.' ***'Are you** (really)?'*
'They didn't give the concert after all last night.' ***'Didn't they?*** (↗) *Why not?'* (↘)

Reply questions can often express surprise, especially with the word *really* or an exclamation:
'Great news: Jim's just been promoted.' ***'Has he really?'/'Has he? How fantastic!'***

We use negative reply questions to show emphatic agreement with the speaker. Here we use a falling intonation:
'That was the best holiday we've ever had!' 'Yes, ***wasn't it****?'* (↘)

When we want to clarify something that the speaker has said or asked, we can use an echo question:
'I went to Stacy's yesterday.' 'You went ***where****?'*
'Have you been to the Earth Centre?' 'Have I been to ***what****?'/'Have I been* ***where****?'*

4 Short responses

If we want to agree with the speaker or say something is the same, we use these patterns:

positive statement	*so* + *be*/auxiliary or modal verb + subject	*'I saw Jane yesterday.' 'Oh, yes,* ***so did I****.'*
	subject + *be*/auxiliary or modal verb + *too*	*'I saw Jane yesterday.'* ***'I did too.'***
negative statement	*neither/nor* + *be*/auxiliary or modal verb + subject	*'I didn't have enough money'.* ***'Neither/Nor did I.'***
	subject + *be*/auxiliary or modal verb + *either*	*'I didn't have enough money'.* ***'I didn't either.'***

To disagree or say something is different we can use a form of *be*, an auxiliary or modal verb:
'I love French movies.' 'Oh, ***I don't****.' 'I haven't seen that one.' 'Oh,* ***I have****.'*

In informal speech we can just use the object pronoun, usually with *too*, *neither* or *nor*:
'I saw Jane yesterday.' ***'Me too!'***
'Julian's coming with us.' ***'Him too?'***
'I didn't want to go.' ***'Me neither.'/'Nor me.'***

We can use *so* at the beginning of a short answer to express a certain amount of surprise. With this meaning we use *so* + subject + *be*/auxiliary verb, etc:

'They've put a new statue in front of the palace.' → ✗ *'~~So have they!~~'*
✓ *'**So** they have!'*

To express a negative response to a question or prediction we make the verb negative and use *so* in informal spoken English:

'Are you coming to the party tomorrow?' → ✗ *'~~I think not.~~'*
✓ *'I **don't think so**.'*

An exception to this is *hope*. We do not use the *not … so* pattern but use *hope not*:

'It's going to rain!' → ✗ *'~~Oh, I don't hope so!~~'*
✓ *'I **hope not**.'*

For a more emphatic negative response we can use *no way* + auxiliary + subject:
'It's going to rain!' ***'No way is it*** *going to rain!'*
'It's $25.' ***'No way am I*** *paying $25 for that!'*

Practice

1 Complete the indirect questions, as in the example. 5.05 Listen and check.

0 Who is responsible for street cleaning in this area?
Could you tell me *who is responsible for street cleaning in this area?*

1 Why did it take you so long to deliver this parcel?
I'd like to know ....

2 Has Harriet finished the minutes of the meeting yet or not?
Can you tell me whether ....

3 When will the new curtains for the hotel suites be ready?
Please let me know ....

4 How often is the bed linen in the villas changed?
Does the brochure say ....

5 Which metro station should we go to for the Eiffel Tower?
Do you know ....

6 Did Vettel win yesterday's race or not?
I wonder whether ....

2 Complete each question with an appropriate question tag. 5.06 Listen and check.

1 'I hope you're not doing anything tonight. I've just booked tickets for the circus.'
'Oh, there were tickets left, ...? I thought it would have sold out.'

2 We needn't register before the first talk, ...?

3 Be a good girl and pop to the shops for me, ...? We need some cheese.

4 How can you think of marrying her? You've hardly known her five minutes, ...?

5 No one was staffing the west turnstile at the time of the accident, ...?

6 Put some decent trousers on, ...? They won't let you in wearing jeans.

7 It seems to me, Minister, that the government has broken all its pre-election promises regarding the health service, ...?

8 'I'll help you with your homework.' 'Oh, you can do calculus, ..., Dad?'

9 Mrs Allison did say that we could take dictionaries into the exam with us, ...?

10 'Ryan didn't go to work yesterday because he was ill.' 'Oh, he was ill, ...?
I thought he was watching the football.'

3 Match each sentence 1–10 with a response A–J. 5.07 Listen and check.

1 I can't stand cold weather.
2 I heard that they're going to put up the train fares.
3 I'd love another coffee.
4 Dorian didn't come to the party.
5 We've just bought a new high definition TV.
6 Are you going to see Carol later?
7 Would you like to come bungee jumping with us?
8 That was a lovely concert.
9 We took the kids to the zoo last weekend.
10 Wow. They've just scored another goal!

A Yes, wasn't it?
B Have you?
C Neither can I.
D So they have!
E Me too.
F Really? So did we.
G Didn't he?
H I hope not.
I No way am I doing that!
J I don't think so.

4 **GRAMMAR IN USE** **Complete the questions and the short responses in the conversation below. Write one word or a contraction in each gap. 5.08 Listen and check.**

MS MARCH Excuse me. Do you know (1) .... this is the flat advertised for rent in the local shop?

LANDLADY Yes, it is. I'm the landlady.

MS MARCH I'm Eleanor March. I think we spoke on the phone a few days ago.

LANDLADY (2) .... we? I don't remember. Well, come in, (3) .... you? This is the living room. It's not looking at its best right now, I'm afraid.

MS MARCH (4) .... it? It looks fine to me.

LANDLADY It's a bit untidy. That's one of the reasons I'll be pleased to see the back of the current tenants. Now, come through. This is the master bedroom.

MS MARCH Mmm, it's nice. But there's no radiator in here ...

LANDLADY Er, no, but it's got an electric heater.

MS MARCH It's got a (5) ....?

LANDLADY An electric heater.

MS MARCH Oh, I see. But aren't electric heaters quite expensive?

LANDLADY Oh, I don't think (6) .... – they're very economical. Now, through here is the second bedroom ...

MS MARCH Oh, there are two bedrooms, (7) .... there?

LANDLADY Yes. And it's very large for a second bedroom in a flat of this type.

MS MARCH Yes, (8) .... it is! It's an excellent size. Oh dear, someone's broken the window in here, (9) .... they?

LANDLADY Oh, don't worry about that. I'll get that fixed. This is the bathroom.

MS MARCH Mmm. It's a bit dingy. I don't suppose you could paint it, (10) .... you?

LANDLADY Well, we can discuss that later. This is the kitchen. I designed it myself.

MS MARCH Did you (11) ....? It's great!

LANDLADY Yes, though it is in a bit of a mess. Now, let's go back to the living room, (12) .... we?

MS MARCH Yes. Well I'm quite interested in renting the flat. Nobody else has been to see it, have (13) ....?

LANDLADY No. Would you like to see any of the rooms again?

MS MARCH I don't (14) .... so. But I'd just like to check the rent. I think the advert said it was £650 a month, (15) .... it?

LANDLADY (16) .... it? I thought I'd put £750.

MS MARCH Well, £650 plus bills.

LANDLADY Oh yes, so (17) .... did – £650 plus bills.

MS MARCH Are there any particular rules?

LANDLADY Well, I don't like loud music.

MS MARCH Oh, (18) .... do I. I always play my music very quietly.

LANDLADY Good. Anything else?

MS MARCH What about pets? (19) .... you tell me whether you allow cats? You see I've got a small cat – I love cats!

LANDLADY Me (20) ....! I've got three cats! I think we're going to get on really well!

80 Emphatic forms in speech

1 Emphasising verbs

When we want to emphasise a clause/sentence in speech, we stress the auxiliary verb:
Fancy seeing you again. It ***has been*** *a long time!*
Don't beat around the bush. ***Did*** *you or* ***didn't*** *you* ***take*** *it?*
That holiday's done wonders; you ***are looking*** *well!*

In the present/past simple affirmative we insert stressed *do/does/did* before the main verb:
I never drink coffee but I ***do drink tea*** *sometimes.*
I'm very sorry, sir. Our representative ***does try*** *her best to comply with passenger requests.*
The witness is hazy on the details, but she ***did notice*** *a scar on his forearm.*

But if the auxiliary (or infinitive) is preceded by a modal verb then we stress the modal:
That's absolutely ridiculous; you ***must*** *have seen something!*
She wasn't even here – it ***can't*** *be her!*

We can also emphasise imperatives with *do*:
Do be careful! *The path's very slippery.*

We often use this pattern to make polite suggestions or offers:
Do sit down *and make yourself comfortable.*
Do let me help *you with that heavy case.*

Pronunciation ➤ 1.23

2 Emphasising questions

We can add *-ever* to question words (except *whose*) to add a tone of annoyance or surprise to a question. More informally, we can use the question words + *why on earth*:
Whatever *have you done to your hair? It looks terrible!*
However *did they manage to get that ship in the bottle?*
However *did you find it?*
Why on earth *did John decide to study Chinese?*
Where on earth *are you going to put all that stuff?*

We use *else* with question words when we have some information but would like more:
'Elena told me she'd retired last month.' 'Yes, I'd heard that. ***What else*** *did she say?'*

It is quite common to use a question form when we don't really want an answer. We call this a 'rhetorical question' and we use it to express amazement, or irritation with something:
Have you seen the price of fish at that supermarket? It's outrageous.
Are you being deliberately unhelpful? Is this your idea of a joke?

We use *What's the point/use in/of ... ?* to suggest that a course of action is worthless:
What's the point in *writing to your MP? It won't make any difference.*
What's the use of *explaining it all to you if you're not listening?*

3 Emphasising adjectives, adverbs and nouns

We can use *how* + adjective or *what (a/an)* + adjective + noun to make a brief emphatic comment (an exclamation) in conversation:

***How** amazing! **What an** amazing story! **What** lovely shoes!*

We don't use *what* + adjective without a noun:

✗ ~~*What amazing!*~~

We often use *so* and *such* to emphasise adjectives, adverbs and nouns:

so + adjective/adverb	*You should meet Larry. He's **so funny**.* *Time goes **so quickly** when you're having fun.*
such + *a/an* (+ adjective) + noun	*This is **such a lovely place** for a wedding party.* *I had **such a nightmare** last night.*
so much/little + uncountable noun	*I've never seen **so much poverty**. It was shocking.* *There's **so little rainfall** here, almost nothing grows.*
so many/few + plural countable noun	*You must go to the shops. There are **so many bargains** at the moment.*
such a lot of + noun	*There's **such a lot of food** left over – take some home with you.*

All these can be followed by a *that* clause (➤ Unit 59.4). In speech we often omit *that*:

*There was **such a long queue** (that) we decided not to bother.*

*I'm **so tired** I think I'll go to bed.*

Strengthening adjectives with *pretty*, *dead*, etc. ➤ Unit 81.1

so to introduce a result clause ➤ Unit 59.4

4 Using fronting for emphasis

In spoken English we can qualify something in a previous statement by using normal word order (subject + verb + adjective/complement):

'She's <u>such</u> a nice person. <u>So</u> friendly and reliable.'

*'She may be **friendly** but she certainly isn't **reliable**.'*

But to make a strong contrast to the previous statement we bring these elements to the beginning of the sentence (➤ Unit 76.5):

***Friendly** she may be, but **reliable** she isn't!*

We can also put *this* and *that* at the beginning of a response for emphasis. We often use *that* to refer to something the other speaker has said and *this* to refer to something we have said or information/opinions the speaker and listener share:

*'Taxes are way too high in this country.' 'I disagree with **that**.' → '**That** I disagree with.'*

*'And how old is the house?' 'I don't know **that**.' → '**That** I don't know.'*

*'Hurry up. We always get a better seat if we arrive early.' '**This** is true. Let's find a taxi.'*

In this position, *this* and *that* can sometimes replace an adverb or noun phrase:

*It was three years ago. I met her **then**. → **That**'s when I met her.*

*We have to get off **here**. → **This** is where we have to get off.*

*They told me **the same thing**. → **That**'s what they told me.*

Practice

1 Match the sentences 1–10 with the responses A–J. 5.09 Listen and check.

1 Do have a sandwich.
2 Carrie's just told me about Jeff's promotion.
3 I'm going to complain to the store manager.
4 Steve overslept again this morning.
5 Apparently we have to re-apply in August.
6 Jane got upgraded to first class on the flight.
7 Is Mr Granger in the office today?
8 What fantastic photos!
9 Do you think the cancer is going to spread?
10 What did you think of the announcement?

A Yes. That's what they told me.
B I haven't seen him. But I did see his car in the car park.
C That I couldn't say.
D Thanks. I am quite hungry.
E What's the point? They never listen to customers.
F I don't know. There was such a lot of noise we couldn't really hear it.
G I'm not surprised. He's been working really hard recently.
H What else did she say?
I However did she manage to do that?
J I know. Karl took them when we were on safari.

2 Choose the correct or most appropriate words in *italics*. 5.10 Listen and check.

1 Why on earth *you gave up* / *did you give up* that job?
2 If she won't listen, *how's* / *what's* the point in speaking to her?
3 So she told you about her divorce. What *else* / *extra* did she say?
4 It's *so* / *such* a cold night I think I'll stay at home.
5 He says Mandy took it – *what ridiculous* / *what a ridiculous* thing to say!
6 Pretty she might be, but *she young isn't* / *young she isn't*!
7 The salary? *That* / *What* I don't know. Sorry.
8 I'm telling you the truth. I *did leave* / *left* the keys on the kitchen table last night!
9 *Whatever* / *However* did you get her to stay? I thought she was determined to leave!
10 It was at university last year – *that's* / *then's* when I first discovered the truth!

3 GRAMMAR IN USE Replace the underlined words and phrases with a more emphatic equivalent. The first two have been done as examples. 5.11 Listen and check.

What an amazing film!
SALLY (0) That was an amazing film. What did you think of it?
It was so boring that
FRED Rubbish. (00) It was boring and as a result I almost fell asleep.
SALLY Oh. I'm sorry to hear that. Don't you like American films?
FRED Yes, (1) I like them – but I didn't like this one. There were no big stars in it and nothing really happened for two hours.
SALLY I wouldn't say nothing happened. I mean, (2) they visited lots of lovely locations.
FRED (3) I disagree with that. They spent nearly the whole time in Los Angeles.
SALLY They went to the beach …
FRED True. (4) They went there. But (5) what other places did they go to?
SALLY Er. They went to the hills, and the desert.
FRED But (6) why did they go there? That part of the film was really pointless.
SALLY They went to find the boy's father. I thought it was exciting, and very atmospheric.
FRED Well, it might have been atmospheric, but (7) it wasn't exciting.
SALLY OK. (8) There's no reason to continue discussing it – we always disagree about films anyway!

4 **Complete what the people are saying by writing one word in each gap. Use emphatic forms. 5.12 Listen and check.**

'That was .... a great concert! I'm glad they played .... many of my favourites.'

' Please. .... take a seat. The doctor will see you in a minute.'

'.............. is where Anne Boleyn was executed in 1536. It .... look rather gruesome, doesn't it?'

'.............. a stunning outfit! I .... love this designer's evening gowns.'

'What's the .... of complaining? Those boys never listen. Call the police.'

'.............. did you find that? And what on .... made you buy it?'

'Fashionable .... may be, but affordable they certainly ....!'

'Alex? Is it really you? It's years since we last saw you! It .... be you – you look so young! .... did you find us?'

81 Adverbs

1 Modifying adjectives in spoken English

In addition to *really* and *pretty*, expressions such as *nice/good and* + adjective can be used to intensify the meaning of many adjectives:
*The hotel was **nice and clean**.*
*I'll come when I'm **good and ready**.*

In very informal British English, *dead* and a number of slang words (e.g. *well*) can be used as intensifiers:
*The rollercoaster ride was **dead scary**.*

⚠ We can use *a bit* to make gradable adjectives weaker. We don't use *a bit* in front of an adjective + noun:
✗ ~~*It was a bit boring film.*~~ ✓ *That film was **a bit boring**.*

We usually avoid these expressions in formal English:
✗ ~~*The war can be linked to a dead complex series of treaties between various European nations.*~~

2 Using adjectives as adverbs

We sometimes use the adjectives *cheap, clean, clear, good, loud, quick, slow* and *smooth* as adverbs in informal spoken English, although some people consider these incorrect:
*They sell things **cheap** in that place.* (= cheaply) *Congratulations. You did **good**.* (= well)
*This car goes so **slow**!* (= slowly) *Despite its age the engine runs pretty **smooth**.* (= smoothly)

3 Commenting with sentence adverbs, infinitive and participle phrases

In conversation we can use sentence adverbs such as *obviously, surprisingly*, etc. (➤ Unit 78.4) to introduce, extend, or make a comment. We usually put them at the beginning or end of the sentence, separated by a comma:
***Incidentally**, I noticed they were looking for new players down at the club.*
*I thought that film was pretty boring, **frankly**.*

ADVERB	MEANING
anyway, so	I am changing the subject or ending a conversation.
admittedly	This probably qualifies or contradicts what I have just said/heard.
apparently	I have heard this is true, although I'm not certain it is correct.
fortunately luckily	This is something good which contrasts with what I have said/heard.
frankly to be honest	This is my true opinion, although it may be shocking.
incidentally *by the way*	I am changing the subject – this is some information which is not directly connected with the previous information.
understandably	I can sympathise with this.

Some adverbs, e.g. *naturally* and *clearly*, can be used as sentence adverbs and also as adverbs of manner. Note the different meanings:
*Despite being in a zoo, the animals behaved quite **naturally**.* (= in a natural way)
***Naturally**, wild animals behave quite differently in captivity.* (= this is not surprising)
*The teacher answered the question **clearly** and precisely.* (= in a clear way)
***Clearly**, the teacher didn't answer the question.* (= This is obvious from evidence I have.)

We can also use infinitive and participle phrases to add a comment:
*I'm not very keen on it, **to tell the truth**. It wasn't a bad show, **all things considered**.*
***Generally speaking**, they're a pretty friendly bunch of people.*

 Pronunciation ➤ 1.24

Practice

1 Choose the best explanation for each sentence, A or B.

1 We were wearing the same outfit! It was dead embarrassing.
A The experience was slightly embarrassing. B The experience was very embarrassing.
2 Apparently, her children are all going to that expensive private school.
A I know this is correct.
B Somebody told me this and I think it is correct, but I'm not sure.
3 That new computer game is pretty exciting.
A It looks good but it isn't very exciting. B It's really exciting.
4 Make sure you wear something nice and smart.
A Wear something very smart. B Wear something nice.
5 Incidentally, have you seen Roger Baines this week at all?
A I've just been talking about Roger. B This is the first time I've mentioned Roger.

2 Choose the correct words in *italics*. If both options are possible, choose both. 5.13 Listen and check.

1 I haven't seen Sylvia for ages. *Frankly, / Apparently,* she's just remarried.
2 I love my moped but I wish it didn't go so *slow / slowly*.
3 It's a nice restaurant but *it has a bit spicy food / the food is a bit spicy*.
4 And then the show was cancelled. *Luckily, / By the way,* we were able to get a full refund.
5 What a great exhibition! It was *dead / a bit* interesting.
6 Don't play your music so *loud / loudly* – I can't hear myself think!
7 I've never been very keen on football, *telling / to tell* the truth.
8 *Naturally / Generally* speaking, I find the shops here a bit cheaper than the ones in town.

3 GRAMMAR IN USE Use words or phrases from the box to replace each of the expressions in brackets. 5.14 Listen and check.

a bit	admittedly	apparently	by the way	clearly	dead	luckily	naturally	pretty	to be honest

KAREN We had a (1) (really) .... good dinner at Cato's last night. Lizzie was there with her new husband. (2) (This is something I've heard although it may not be true) ...., he's something very high up and important in the civil service.

CLARE Yes, I've heard that too. (3) (This is my true opinion, although it may be shocking) ...., I never really expected her to marry anyone successful. She was always so scruffy and (4) (slightly) .... laid back. She was never into social status or anything like that.

KAREN (5) (This seems clear to me) ...., she's changed her outlook on life. I mean, she kept telling me all about how much money their new house had cost!

CLARE Well she never used to be interested in money at all. (6) (This probably contradicts what I've just said) ...., she did like eating out and travelling.

KAREN (7) (What I'm about to say isn't really related to what we've been discussing) ...., guess who was at the next table? Simon Dell from university!

CLARE Was he? I remember he used to be (8) (so) .... ambitious.

KAREN He still is. (9) (This is not surprising) ...., he's a company director now.

CLARE That's nice. Oh, were the awful Wallace twins there?

KAREN I'm afraid so. (10) (I'm pleased about this) ...., they were right at the other end of the table so we didn't have to talk to them.

82 Hypothesising in speech

1 Imaginary conditions

We can use *imagine, say, suppose/supposing (that)* and *what if* to talk about imaginary conditions. There are several patterns we can use:

+ present simple	to ask about an imaginary situation in the future that we think is likely, or if we want to suggest that it is	***What if*** we **miss** the last train?* ***Suppose/Supposing** he **gets caught** at customs? They can be really tough.*
+ past simple/ past continuous	to ask questions about an imaginary situation in the present or future and its possible results; this is similar to second conditionals (➤ Unit 38)	***Imagine/What if** he **asked** you to marry him, what would you say?* (= If he asked you to marry him ...) ***Say*** he **was stealing** from petty cash, would you report him?*
+ past simple	to make suggestions	***Say/Suppose** we **took** the early train?*
+ past perfect	to talk about an imaginary past situation and its results; this is similar to third conditionals (➤ Unit 38)	***Say/Imagine** your parents **had refused**, how **would** you **have** felt?* (= If your parents had refused ...)

* We often omit the result clause with these conjunctions:
***What if** the money doesn't arrive on time? **Say** he **refuses** to lend us the car?*
We don't use these conjunctions with *will*: ✗ ~~Supposing he will get caught?~~

2 *it's time ...*

In speech we use *it's (high/about) time* + subject + past simple to say that something is not happening and it should be:
***It's high time you found** yourself a job, young man!* (= You should have a job but you don't.)
***It's time we left** for the airport – we don't want to miss the flight.* (= We should leave now.)
***It's about time you defrosted** the fridge.* (= You should defrost it.)

We cannot use a negative after *it's time ...*
✗ ~~It's time we didn't stay.~~

More on *it's time ...* ➤ Unit 40.3

3 *in case ...*

We use *in case* to imagine a future situation. It is not the same as *if*:
*Let's take our swimming things **in case** there's a pool at the hotel.*
(We don't know if there's a pool, but we'll take our swimming things anyway.)
*We'll take our swimming things **if** there's a pool at the hotel.*
(We'll only take our swimming things *if* there's a pool at the hotel)

We often use *in case* to imagine a precaution necessary for a situation:
*I've got the number of a minicab company **in case** we miss the train.*
*Take your mobile phone **in case** you want to call us when you're there.*

provided, as long as ➤ Unit 37.1

Practice

1 Write the second sentence so it has a similar meaning to the first. Use the word in brackets, as in the example. 5.15 Listen and check.

0 What will happen if we don't return the forms on time?
(supposing) *Supposing we don't return the forms on time?*

1 What would have happened if they hadn't got a receipt?
(imagine) ....

2 Use a power breaker when you mow the lawn as you might cut the electric lead.
(in) ....

3 I can't imagine the consequences if the police found out!
(what if) ....

4 How about going to the beach tomorrow?
(suppose) ....

5 I think we really need to have the car serviced now.
(high) ....

6 What will happen if we don't get there in time?
(say) ....

7 Leave me a set of keys because I might need to get in while you're away.
(case) ....

8 What would you do if they refused to give you a visa?
(supposing) ....

2 GRAMMAR IN USE Choose the correct option, A, B or C, for each gap. If two options are possible, choose both. 5.16 Listen and check.

MIKE So, have you thought any more about our holiday? It's time we (1) ..... a decision.
ANITA I'm still not sure. I'm worried about booking something (2) ..... Mr Willets doesn't give me the time off.
MIKE Oh, I'm sure he will.
ANITA But (3) ..... we're really busy in the office? There isn't really anyone to take over my caseload.
MIKE What about Lucy? (4) ..... she took on more responsibility.
ANITA She's still very inexperienced. (5) ..... she messed something up – I'd get the blame and have to deal with the consequences afterwards.
MIKE You're being paranoid, I'm sure she'd be OK.
ANITA All right then. What if we (6) ..... for the last two weeks of July? The weather's sure to be good then.
MIKE Yes, but that's during the school holidays. Everything's bound to be expensive.
ANITA Well, (7) ..... we went for the first two weeks of the month – would that be cheaper?
MIKE Yes, I'm sure it would. Do you still want to go to Florida?
ANITA I'm not sure now. I think we'd better go somewhere closer to home (8) ..... Mum is ill again and we need to get back in a hurry.

1 A make B are making C made
2 A in case B supposing C unless
3 A supposing B in case C what if
4 A In case B It's high time C It's time for
5 A Imagine B It's time C Supposing
6 A had gone B went C go
7 A say B in case C it's high time
8 A imagine B in case C if

83 Other spoken features

1 Contractions

In spoken English and when we represent speech in writing we can combine contracted auxiliaries, e.g. *'ve*, and contracted *not* after modal verbs:
'He shouldn't've done it.' (= He should not have done it.)
'They couldn't've known about it.' (= They could not have known about it.)

In informal speech we can also use contractions when there is more than one subject:
*'Karl and Jenny**'ve** had a new baby.'* *'The boss and her team**'re** going to the conference.'*

2 Ellipsis

If the meaning is clear, we often leave out words in conversation. The most common words to omit are ones that come at or near the beginning of a sentence:

	FULL VERSION	WITH ELLIPSIS
auxiliary verbs	*How are you feeling today?*	*How you feeling today?*
subject + *be*/*will*	*We're fine, thanks.* *I'll see you later.* *I'm not sure about that.*	*Fine, thanks.* *See you later* *Not sure about that.*
question forms*	*Are you joining us later?* *Would you like some coffee?* *Do you want to buy some tickets?* *Have you got the paper?* *Is Henry here yet?* *Have you been here before?* *Do you like it?*	*Joining us later?* *(Some) coffee?* *Want to buy some tickets?* *Got the paper?* *Henry here yet?* *Been here before?* *Like it?*
subject *I*	*I mustn't complain.* *I don't think so.*	*Mustn't complain.* *Don't think so.*
articles	*The taxi's here.*	*Taxi's here.*
it and *there*	*It should get warmer tomorrow.* *Is there anyone at home?*	*Should get warmer tomorrow.* *Anyone at home?*

* We often omit words when we ask questions with the verbs *see*, *hear* and *think*:
Do you think they'll get here in time? → *Think they'll get here in time?*
Have you seen her recently? → *Seen her recently?*

We can also omit words at the end of a sentence, especially in short responses:
*'Will you be at the party?' '**I should be.**'* (= I should be at the party.)
*'Are you going to Italy this summer?' 'Yes, **we hope to**.'* (= We hope to go to Italy.)
*'Did you get the concert tickets?/Did you get them?' 'Yes, **I got four**.'* (= I got four tickets.)

Omissions with modal verbs, infinitives and *wh-* clauses ➤ Unit 74.2/3

3 Inserts

Inserts are words and short expressions that we use in speech but not usually in writing. They fulfil several functions which help conversation to flow smoothly:

INSERT	USE BY SPEAKER	EXAMPLES
well,	to express doubt or to pause before saying you are not sure to start talking about a subject you have just mentioned	***Well,*** *I haven't really decided yet ...* *Do you know Alexei?* ***Well,*** *I was told he's joining our class next term.*
right/all right	to get everyone's attention to seek confirmation or check the listener agrees	***Right.*** *Can you all listen to me, please?* *You're coming tonight,* ***right****?* *I'll call you later,* ***all right****?*
I mean	to explain, or rephrase	***I mean,*** *he wants to do some more tests.* *She plays the violin,* ***I mean,*** *the viola ...*
you know	to ensure the listener understands	*Have you worn that new pullover yet,* ***you know,*** *the one you bought in the sales?*
now	to change the topic or return to an earlier topic	*That was delicious.* ***Now,*** *who wants coffee?*
OK	at the end of a statement, to check the listener agrees	*We'll meet outside the main entrance at six,* ***OK****?*
er, um, like	to pause and to show that you have not finished speaking	*Do you think I've,* ***er,*** *passed the test?* *I didn't buy it because It was,* ***like,*** *really expensive.*

INSERT	USE BY LISTENER	EXAMPLES
mmm/ uh huh[1]	to show the speaker you understand what is being said	*'I'm really fed up with the prices there.'* ***'Mmm.*** *I know what you mean.'*
Really?	to show the speaker you are interested/surprised	*'June's moving to Canada.'* ***'Really?*** *I had no idea!'*
Right/Yeah[2]	to show you agree with the speaker	*'And Lee's the worst player on the team.'* ***'Right.*** *He's rubbish.'*

1 *Uh huh* is more common in American English.
2 We can also use these inserts in an ironic way, to show doubt or scepticism:
'If you buy this new skin cream, you will never have spots again.' ***'Yeah, right!'***

4 Prefaces and tags

A feature of conversation is that we can 'add-on' extra information. For example, we can repeat the subject of a sentence or question using an additional word, either at the beginning (a preface) or at the end (a tag):

Caroline, *she's my best friend now.*

That restaurant, *what's it called?*

Where does he live, ***that student?***

It's a great movie, ***this one.***

We can use prefaces to introduce a new topic. We often use prefaces and tags to make sure that the listener knows which subject we are referring to.

Practice

1 These sentences are taken from informal conversations, but there is one auxiliary verb missing. Rewrite the sentences using a suitable auxiliary verb. Use contracted forms wherever possible, as in the example. 5.17 Listen and check.

0 He could not seen them do it. *He couldn't've seen them do it.*

1 She will not got back by the time the show starts.

....

2 They trying to find a nice hotel for two hours last night.

....

3 He might not known that it was you at the door.

....

4 Alison and Steve taking us out for a meal tomorrow.

....

5 They really should told you about their decision.

....

2 GRAMMAR IN USE In each line of these short informal conversations there is at least one word which can be left out. Find the words and cross them out. 5.18 Listen and check.

1 A Do you see that printer icon?
B No, I don't see it.
A It's at the top of the screen.
B Oh yes. There on the left.

2 A What are you doing, Jim?
B I'm fixing this loose connection.
A Do you need any help?
B I don't think so, thanks.

3 A How are you feeling?
B I'm not so great today.
A Have you got a headache?
B Yes, I have got a headache.

4 A Have you heard the news?
B No, I haven't heard it.

5 A Do you think they'll be here soon?
B I'm not sure. Anyway it's time for me to leave now.
A OK. I'll see you later.

6 A The doorbell's ringing!
B Is there anybody downstairs?
A I don't know.

7 A There are some snacks here. Are you hungry?
B Yes. I am hungry.
A Would you like a sandwich?
B Yes, I'd love one.
A And what about some cake?
B No thanks, I wouldn't want to put on weight!

8 A Do you want to watch TV?
B OK. It should be the football results around now.

3 GRAMMAR IN USE **Choose the correct words in *italics*. 5.19 Listen and check.**

JOSIE Have you got any plans for the weekend, Cara?
CARA Not really.
JOSIE (1) *You know, / Well,* would you like to join us for a barbeque on Sunday?
CARA (2) *Er, / Yeah,* I'm not sure. I've got a lot of work to do, (3) *I mean, / now,* revision for my exams next week.
JOSIE (4) *Well / Really?*
CARA Yeah, these exams are really difficult ones. I'm, (5) *like, / right,* quite worried about them.
JOSIE (6) *Well, / I mean,* why don't you just come for a couple of hours? You'd still have plenty of time for revision.
CARA (7) *You know / Mmm.* I suppose so. But how am I going to get to your place? (8) *I mean, / Well,* my car's in the garage at the moment ...
JOSIE No problem. I can ask Mandy to give you a lift.
CARA Who's Mandy? Do I know her?
JOSIE I think so. She's June's sister; she's very tall.
CARA (9) *Really / Right.* I remember now. She was at your birthday party.
JOSIE I'll ask her to pick you up at four o'clock.
CARA Fine. But ask her to phone first, (10) *OK / like?*
JOSIE Sure. But why does she need to phone you?
CARA (11) *Well, / All right,* the doorbell isn't working. So I don't know when people arrive at the front door.
JOSIE Oh, I see. (12) *Like, / Yeah,* I'll ask her to phone when she gets to your house.
CARA Is there anything you'd like me to, (13) *er, / well,* bring?
JOSIE Not really. (14) *Right, / Well,* I suppose it would be nice if you brought your camera. Mine isn't working.
CARA Fine.
JOSIE See you on Sunday then, (15) *you know / OK?*
CARA I'm looking forward to it!

4 Match the sentences 1–10 with their completions or responses. A–J. 5.20 Listen and check.

1 How you feeling today?
2 That guy,
3 Dennis told me about your pay rise.
4 I love those shoes,
5 We're thinking of emigrating to Australia.
6 Why did you go there in January?
7 How old is she,
8 Seen the news?
9 Alex and Davy,
10 We'll meet up outside the station,

A the ones you bought last week.
B Really? I didn't know that.
C I wouldn't've gone if I'd known about the weather!
D No, not yet.
E all right?
F He shouldn't've told you about it, it's confidential.
G where did you meet him exactly?
H Well, mustn't complain.
I that woman you told me about?
J they're my new flatmates.

Now answer the questions below, as in the example.

Which items contain
A a combination of contracted forms? ....
B ellipsis of the subject and/or auxiliary? 1 H..........
C an insert? ....
D a preface? ....
E a tag? ....

Review MODULE 18

1 **UNITS 79, 80 AND 81** **Choose the correct words in *italics*.**

1 Nobody's been here recently, *have* / *haven't* they?
2 Do you know what *is the answer* / *the answer is*?
3 Incredible! *How* / *What* an amazing coincidence.
4 Expensive it may be, but tasteful *isn't it* / *it isn't*.
5 Hardly anyone turned up for the launch, *did* / *didn't* they?
6 It was a great film but *the ending was a bit sad* / *there was a bit sad ending*.
7 Karl's been falsifying the company accounts, *admittedly* / *apparently*.
8 It was *such* / *so* a hot day we decided to go to the beach.
9 Let's all go out for a Chinese meal, *shall* / *will* we?
10 Could you tell me how *can I* / *I can* replace the battery in this camera?
11 That film actor is *much* / *dead* good-looking!
12 I think the whole lot of them should be thrown in jail, *frankly* / *luckily*.
13 You had a baby last year, *didn't* / *hadn't* you?
14 Nothing survives a nuclear bomb, *do they* / *does it*?
15 That's fascinating. *Else what* / *What else* did the professor talk about?
16 I adore your little boy – he's *so* / *such* cute!
17 There's scarcely enough money to pay the gas bill, *isn't* / *is* there?
18 'I passed my driving test first time.' 'So *I did* / *did I*.'
19 *However* / *Whatever* did you manage to get such a nice suntan?
20 'I love Italian ice cream.' 'Oh, *I* / *me* too!'

2 **UNITS 80 AND 82** **There are mistakes in twelve of these sentences. Find the mistakes and correct them. Tick (✓) the correct sentences.**

1 Why on earth you did invest in that useless company?
2 Do take a seat while I find your records on the computer.
3 Supposing your parents had found out, what would you have done?
4 I'm going to take some warm clothes in case of it's cold when I get there.
5 Marianne doesn't enjoy the theatre but she does going to the cinema occasionally.
6 What else things did the company fail to deliver?
7 The film was such incredibly tedious that I walked out halfway through.
8 This is where we have to wait for the bus.
9 It's high time you throw out all those smelly old trainers.
10 You should meet my new flatmate; so nice is she!
11 Say it Darren invites you to the party, what are you going to wear?
12 What's the point in arrive early?
13 Hard-wearing those boots may be, but comfortable aren't they!
14 Imagine the airline strike continues for another month, how will we get home?
15 I think it's time about you found yourself a job, young man!
16 What if it rains on the day? The party'll be ruined.
17 In case I'd known about the long queues, I would've left home much earlier.
18 You can't get in without a ticket – that's what they told me.

3 UNITS 79 AND 83 **Choose words and expressions from the box to complete the dialogues. There are two extra words/expressions.**

are you coming has she I don't think so like me too not much really right so that what you going to you know

1 A Jane's passed her driving test.
B (1) ....? That's great.
A (2) .... take yours soon?
B (3) .... I haven't had enough lessons yet.

2 A I got a good grade in the test!
B (4) ....! I got a grade A!
A (5) ....? But I thought you didn't do any revision.
B No, (6) .... I guess I'm just super intelligent!

3 A (7) .... to the party tonight?
B I'm not sure. I'm, (8) ...., really busy this evening. I'm still working on that essay.
A (9) ....? I thought you'd finished that.

4 A (10) ...., can I have everyone's attention, please? Have you all filled in your compliance forms?
B Have we filled in our (11) ....?
A Your compliance forms.
C (12) ...., those forms we got last week.

4 ALL UNITS **Read the conversation and write one word only in each gap.**

DAN Excuse me. Could you (1) .... me where the film society desk (2) ....?
TOBY It's over there.
DAN Thanks. ... Hi. Is this the film and video society?
SUE Yeah. (3) .... interested in joining?
DAN I might be. What sort of things do you do?
SUE (4) ...., we show films and discuss them, and we make our own films and videos.
DAN (5) .... you? You make your own films?
SUE Yes. You're interested in making films then, (6) .... you?
DAN Yeah. Actually, I've made a few short films already, I (7) ...., just for fun, not professionally.
SUE (8) ....? That's great. Do you have your own equipment?
DAN (9) ...., I've got a high definition camcorder.
SUE (10) .... you? That would be very useful. What about lights?
DAN I (11) .... have some lights – but no (12) .... was I bringing them to college, they're much too heavy!
SUE Right. (13) .... else have you got?
DAN I've got a camera tripod, but it's not a very good one, to (14) .... honest.
SUE Oh, me (15) ...., but mine's really old! (16) ...., let me tell you a bit more about the society. We meet up every Wednesday at six ...
DAN Oh, I'm not sure. Wednesday – (17) .... isn't (18) .... a good night for me.
SUE OK. Well, what (19) .... you come along next week and see what you think?
DAN All right. Where do you meet?
SUE (20) .... is where we meet, right here in this building, in room 18A.
DAN Great. See you on Wednesday.

Go online for an exit test

APPENDIX 1 Quick checks

QUICK CHECK 1 MODULES 5 AND 6 Verb tenses and forms

TENSE/FORM	USE	EXAMPLE	UNIT
present simple	facts/permanent situations	*Water boils at 100°C.*	20.1
	regular activities and routines	*We always take public transport.*	20.2
	telling stories	*The film takes place in the US.*	20.4
	commentaries (quick actions)	*France kicks off, Vieira passes ...*	20.3
	describing states	*I don't believe that story.*	25.1
present continuous	actions happening now	*I'm just finishing something.*	20.1
	temporary situations	*She's spending the summer with us.*	20.1
	repeated actions in a temporary time frame	*I'm feeding the neighbour's cat every day this week as she's in hospital.*	20.2
	criticising someone	*You're always losing your key.*	20.2
	changes and trends	*The economy is getting worse.*	20.5
	describing pictures/ commentaries	*A woman is coming into the room.* *The teams are entering the field now ...*	20.4
past simple	completed actions in the past	*I passed my driving test last week.*	21.1
	repeated actions in the past	*My brother took the test six times.*	21.1
	sequence of past actions	*We arrived at the airport and took a taxi to the hotel.*	21.1
	past states	*We lived in Oxford for several years.*	21.1
past continuous	an action in progress at a time in the past.	*We didn't hear the intruder because we were sleeping on the top floor.*	21.2
	temporary situations in the past	*We were living in Beijing at the time of the 2008 Olympics. .*	21.2
	repeated actions in a temporary time frame	*For the first three months she was receiving treatment every week*	21.2
	a background situation	*Darkness was falling over the city ...*	21.2
	criticising someone	*They were always borrowing money.*	21.2
	an interrupted action	*He was driving when the car crashed.*	21.3
	unfulfilled plans	*I was hoping to study animation.*	21.4
used to	past actions and states that no longer happen/exist	*They used to get paid weekly.* *Serbia used to be part of Yugoslavia.*	21.5
would	past actions that no longer happen (not states)	*He would be away for weeks at a time in those days.*	21.5
past perfect simple	an action before a time or another action in the past	*Before I found a job, I had been to twenty interviews.*	22.1
	giving reasons for past actions/feelings	*Emily was unhappy because her husband hadn't bought her a present.*	22.3
	unfulfilled plans	*They had hoped to get to the summit but it proved impossible.*	22.5
past perfect continuous	ongoing past actions/states before another time/action	*He had been working for over an hour when the auditors turned up.*	22.1
	focus on duration	*He had been trying to get the film made for more than twenty years.*	22.1
	giving reasons for past actions/feelings	*He was exhausted as he'd been driving all afternoon.*	22.3

TENSE/FORM	USE	EXAMPLE	UNIT
present perfect simple	indefinite past time (to talk about experiences)	*My father has worked for several different companies.*	23.6
	a past action with present results	*He's gone out (so he isn't here now).*	23.4
	with adverbs such as *already, yet, so far*	*We've received over 20,000 entries for the competition so far.*	23.3
	for recent events	*The plane has just landed.*	23.4
	actions in a time period that is still continuing	*I've driven 500 kilometres this week.*	23.2
	situations that started in the past and continue to now	*My family has lived here since 1992/for over twenty years.*	23.1
	giving news	*The Terracotta Army exhibition has opened in London.*	23.5
present perfect continuous	ongoing actions/situations and to focus on duration (often with *for* or *since*)	*Clare's been living with her cousins.* *We've been waiting to see the doctor for three hours/ since two o'clock.*	24.1
	a recent action with present results (focus on cause)	*The hall is in a mess because we've been decorating.*	24.3
future with *going to*	future plans and intentions	*I'm going to be a doctor one day.*	27.2
	predictions (because of something in the present)	*Howard's wife is going to have a baby.*	26.2
future with *will*	certain future	*New Year's Day will fall on a Tuesday next year.*	26.1
	predictions (what we think will happen from previous knowledge or experience)	*He'll be in prison for a long time!* *Don't wait for Alex – he'll be late as usual!*	26.1
	immediate decisions	*I'm tired. I think I'll go to bed now.*	27.1
	to express determination	*I won't believe a word you say again!*	27.1
future with present continuous	future arrangements	*I've got the tickets. We're sitting in row A.*	27.3
future continuous	actions in progress at a time in the future	*Come to the main door – we'll be waiting for you.*	26.3
	a deduction about the present	*She'll be getting ready for bed now.*	26.3
	tactful questions about plans and tactful refusals	*Will you be staying long?* *I'll be working so I can't come.*	27.4
	a routine event in the future	*We'll be having our weekly meeting tomorrow.*	28.2
future perfect	actions completed by a time in the future	*He'll have had the operation by May and should be a lot fitter by then.*	26.4
future perfect continuous	actions in progress up to a time in the future	*By next Friday I'll have been waiting for over two months.*	26.4
future with present simple	fixed future events in schedules after *when*, *as soon as*, etc.	*The Dallas flight arrives at 9.45. As soon as I get there, I'll phone you.*	28.1
was/were going to (future in the past)	something that was in the future at a time in the past	*In 2006 they were going to build a supermarket here.*	29.1
	something we expected to happen but didn't happen	*I was going to study medicine but my grades weren't good enough.*	29.1
be to + infinitive	formal/official future arrangements	*Crash investigators are to release their findings later today.*	27.5

QUICK CHECK 2 MODULE 7 Modal verbs

(pp = past participle)

VERB	USE	EXAMPLE	UNIT
be able to	present ability	*Despite his disability, he is able to drive a car.*	30.1
	future ability/possibility	*After you receive the password you'll be able to log on.*	30.1
	past ability/possibility	*We weren't able to get cheap flights to Malaga.*	30.2
can/can't	present ability	*Can you speak Japanese?*	30.1
	present possibility	*You can use this phone anywhere in the world.*	31.1
	arrangement	*The dentist can see you at 3.30.*	30.1
	general possibility	*Bad weather can cause delays at any time.*	31.1
	permission	*Can I use your bathroom?*	36.1
	prohibition	*Doctors can't give drugs to shorten life.*	34.1
can	offers	*Can I help you with that?*	36.3
	requests	*Can you help me with these bags?*	36.3
can't	present deduction (impossibility)	*It can't be her, she's on holiday in Canada.*	32.1
can't have + pp	past deduction (certainty)	*She can't have fixed this computer – it's still not working properly.*	32.3
could/ couldn't	past ability	*Could the first cameras take colour photos?*	30.2
	past general possibility	*The teachers could be very strict at my old school.*	31.3
	present speculation	*There could be life on other planets.*	32.1
	present deduction (impossibility)	*He couldn't be the senior doctor – he's far too young.*	32.1
	past prohibition	*In those days, women and criminals couldn't vote.*	34.2
could	permission	*Could we stay an extra night in the hotel?*	36.1
	past permission	*In the 1960s you could smoke in cinemas.*	36.1
	unlikely to happen	*We could give up our jobs and live on a desert island.*	31.2
	future possibility	*I could get a part-time job next summer.*	31.2
	suggestion	*We could watch a DVD.*	36.2
	offer	*I could get Lucy's present for you.*	36.3
	request	*Could you help me with this?*	36.3
could + *have* + pp	past possibility	*David could have overslept.*	31.3
	past ability not used/ opportunity not taken	*I could have argued with him, but what's the point?* *She could have paid by cheque but she preferred cash.*	30.2
	weak criticism	*She could have thanked me for the lift.*	34.2
couldn't + *have* + pp	past deduction (certainty)	*Lester couldn't have been driving the car – he doesn't even own a car!*	32.3
had to/ didn't have to	past obligation	*We had to have lots of vaccinations for our trip to Goa.*	33.3
	lack of necessity	*We didn't have to pay for the tickets. They were free.*	33.3
have to/ don't have to	present obligation	*All car passengers have to wear a seat belt.*	33.1
	lack of necessity	*You don't have to pay to visit most museums in Britain.*	33.1
	future obligation	*We'll have to get visas for our trip to the States.*	33.1
had better (not)	advice/warnings (single situation)	*That looks hot. You'd better not touch it.* *You'd better change the locks in case the burglars come back.*	36.4

VERB	USE	EXAMPLE	UNIT
may/ may not	permission	*May I leave early this afternoon?*	36.1
	offers	*May I help you?*	36.3
	specific present possibility	*The manager may be in a meeting. I'll just check.*	31.1
	future speculation	*The tickets may not arrive in time.*	31.2
might/ might not	specific present possibility	*It's a small shop. They might not have batteries.*	31.1
	future speculation	*If we wait a few days, the prices might be cheaper.*	31.2
might (not) have + pp	past speculation (possibility)	*She might have done it – she had the opportunity and the motive.*	31.3
	weak criticism	*You might have told me about the party.*	34.2
must	strong obligation	*All answers must be written in ink.*	33.1
	future obligation	*I really must get to the dentist next week.*	33.1
must not	prohibition	*This appliance must not be used in bathrooms.*	34.1
must	recommendation	*You must try this cake – it's delicious!*	36.4
	present deduction (certainty)	*This must be the place – it's the only restaurant in the street.*	32.1
must + *have* + pp	past deduction (certainty)	*There was a loud bang last night. It must have been an explosion.*	32.3
need to/don't need to/needn't	necessity/ lack of necessity	*He really needs to lose some weight.* *You needn't/don't need to take any food. Lunch is provided.*	33.2
needed to/ didn't need to	past necessity/ lack of necessity	*Javier needed to go to hospital when he broke his leg.* *I didn't need to see a doctor. My cold got better on its own.*	33.3
needn't + *have* + pp	a past action that wasn't necessary	*You needn't have taken a towel. The gym provides them free of charge.*	33.3
ought (not) to	advice	*You look terrible! You ought to see a doctor.*	36.4
	expectation	*The plane ought to be landing about now.*	32.2
ought (*not*) *to* + *have* + pp	past expectation	*I don't know where our main speaker is. He ought to have arrived ages ago.*	32.4
	unfulfilled past obligation	*You really ought to have registered before the term started.*	33.3
shall	suggestion	*Shall we try that new café?*	36.2
	offer	*Your hands are wet. Shall I get you a towel?*	36.3
should/ should not	expectation	*Phone Henry at work. He should be there by now.*	32.2
	advice	*Should I ask my boss for a pay rise?*	36.4
should + *have* + pp	past expectation	*That letter should have arrived by now.*	32.4
	unfulfilled past obligation	*You really should have registered before the term started.*	33.3
	past criticism	*You shouldn't have driven through that red light.*	34.2
will/won't	future certainty/ near certainty	*We'll be able to get a coffee at the airport.* *It'll be cold there at this time of year.*	31.2
	present habits	*The union will always support the staff in a dispute.*	35.3
	(un)willingness	*Jim will act as referee today as Martin can't make it.*	35.1
	offers, promises	*I'll get you a sandwich. Which one do you want?*	36.3
will/won't + *have* + pp	certainty about a past event	*We sent the invitations on Monday, so they'll have received them by now.*	35.2

VERB	USE	EXAMPLE	UNIT
would (*not*)	past habits	*The union would always support the staff in a dispute.*	35.4
	past (un)willingness	*Dad would always help us with our maths homework.* *The shop assistant wouldn't change this coat for me.*	35.6
	request (formal)	*Would you tell the manager that I called?*	36.3

QUICK CHECK 3 MODULE 13 **Linking words**

TYPE	LINKING WORDS	EXAMPLE	UNIT
adds something	*both … and* *not only … (but also)*	*We stock both gas and electric cookers.* *Not only does it wash your clothes, but it also dries them.*	58.1
	also/in addition (to)	*A volcano destroyed the island of Thera. In addition, it destroyed the Minoan city of Knossos.*	61.3
contrasts two things	*while/whereas* *although/though*	*While the food there is very good, it isn't cheap.* *I'm really not tired, although it's very late.*	60.1
	even though *yet*	*We enjoyed our holiday, even though it rained.* *She has experience, yet she lacks confidence.*	60.2
	however, nevertheless	*Credit cards are useful for travellers. However, the interest rates can be very high.*	61.5
gives alternatives	*either … or* *neither … nor*	*We will either meet here or see you at the theatre.* *She can neither sing nor dance.*	58.1
gives a reason	*because* *as/since given that* (formal)	*I don't use trains because they are too expensive.* *As/Since we're late, we'd better get a taxi.* *Given that profits are so low, we won't be recruiting this year.*	59.2
gives a result	*as a result/for this/ that reason* *therefore/consequently*	*There was a hurricane. As a result, the city was flooded* *Trains have become expensive. Therefore, more people are travelling by bus.*	61.4
	so *so (… that)* *such (… that)* *too/enough … to*	*I was awake all night so I'm exhausted today.* *It was so dark (that) I couldn't see her face.* *There was such a noise (that) I couldn't sleep.* *The lake is too cold/isn't warm enough to swim in.*	59.4
gives a purpose	*(in order) to/(not) to* *so as (not) to* *in order that/so that*	*We will hold a sale (in order) to raise money.* *I left early so as not to be late for my interview.* *I'm buying a magazine so that/in order that I'll have something to read on the flight.*	59.3
gives a condition	*if/unless* *as long as* *on the condition that/ provided that* *in case*	*You can't park here unless you have a permit.* *You can go as long as you're home by 11.30.* *She left the money to an animal charity on the condition that her cats were looked after.* *Take some money in case we have to get a taxi.*	59.5
gives a time/ sequences events	*before/after,* etc. *as soon as/once* *the moment/immediately* *by the time* *until*	*We locked the door before we left the house.* *I'll do the letters as soon as I get to work.* *Why didn't you call us the moment you got back?* *The food was cold by the time he arrived.* *We stayed there until the storm had passed.*	59.1
	afterwards, beforehand	*Dinner will be at 8.00. Afterwards, there will be a concert1.*	61.2
gives a sequence of events	*first, then,* *after that, later,* *in the end, eventually*	*First we closed the window shutters. Then we went down to the basement and waited there. Eventually, the storm passed over us and we were able to go back upstairs. Later, we went outside …*	61.2
shows a process	*first, then, next,* *after that, finally*	*First, slice the tomatoes. Then put the peeled potatoes in boiling water. Next, take an onion …*	61.2

APPENDIX 2 Common prepositional phrases

PHRASE	MEANING/USE	EXAMPLE
after all[1]	in spite of expectations	*I thought I'd done really badly at the interview, but they offered me the job after all.*
among other things	one of several things	*The meeting will look at the results of the sales campaign, among other things.*
as a result/ consequence[2]	introduces a result	*Stricter punishments were imposed. As a result, prisons became more crowded.*
as a matter of fact[1]	adds more details	*He was very apologetic. As a matter of fact, he brought me flowers.*
at any rate[1]	anyway	*The deliveries were all delayed. At any rate, that's what he said.*
at hand	close, available	*Don't worry; help is at hand.*
beneath contempt	not deserving respect	*That comment is really beneath contempt!*
by and large	generally	*By and large, the new assistant is working out well.*
by coincidence	not planned	*The three of us ended up working here by coincidence.*
by no means	not at all	*It's by no means certain that he'll take the title.*
by rights[1]	describes what should happen	*By rights, her husband should have custody of the children.*
by the way[1]	to change subject	*It was great. By the way, have you heard from Christine?*
in addition[2]	plus, as well as	*These disturbances indicate the need for more policing. In addition, residents would feel more secure with a greater police presence.*
in any case[1]	whatever happens	*See you later, but in any case, I'll be back before supper.*
in conclusion[2]	giving a summary	*In conclusion, I feel these points entitle me to a refund.*
in fact	adds something surprising	*The final examinations were supposed to be very difficult. In fact, they were easy.*
in hand	under control	*Don't panic! The situation is in hand.*
in practice	to say what really happens	*Theoretically, we have full equality. In practice women earn less than men.*
in short	to summarise	*In short, we can't fund the new project.*
in the event	to emphasise what really happens	*We expected a really long delay. In the event, it was only about three hours.*
in the meantime	between two events	*I'll be back soon. In the meantime, try not to worry.*
off the cuff	spontaneous	*He didn't prepare the speech. It was off the cuff.*
on approval	for a short time, to check sth is right	*I've got the new car on approval for a week. I'll keep it if I like it.*
on hand	close, available	*We have nurses on hand 24 hours a day.*
on the contrary	disagrees with a previous statement	*Arnaud isn't mean with money. On the contrary, he's very generous.*
on the other hand	adds a contrast	*Arnaud is sometimes mean with money. On the other hand, he can be very generous with his time.*
on the whole	generally	*On the whole, it was a good holiday, despite the rain.*

[1] used in speech
[2] used in more formal speech and writing

PHRASE	MEANING/USE	EXAMPLE
out of hand	out of control	*The strikes have really got out of hand now; we need to do something.*
out of practice	no longer skilled in	*I'm out of practice now – I haven't played tennis for years.*
out of the ordinary	unusual, strange	*A pet duck? That's out of the ordinary.*
to hand	close, within reach	*Have you got a needle to hand?*
under age	not old enough	*Kyra can't come to the club with us as she's under age.*
under the counter[1]	bought and sold secretly	*We had strict rationing after the war but a lot of things were available under the counter.*
under the weather[1]	feeling ill	*Brian's staying at home as he's a bit under the weather today.*
without a doubt	certainly	*St Andrews is without a doubt the best golf course in the UK.*
without delay	immediately	*Please advise the director of your decision without delay.*
without exception	nobody/nothing can be exempted	*Each visitor, without exception, must have a valid pass.*

[1] used in speech

APPENDIX 3 Spelling rules

1 Plural forms of nouns and regular present tense endings

most nouns and verbs	add -*s*	*car* → *cars* *argument* → *arguments* *eat* → *eats* *sleep* → *sleeps*
nouns/verbs ending in -*ch*[1], -*sh*, -*x*, -*z* or ending in consonant + *o*	add -*es*	*watch* → *watches* *boss* → *bosses* *fox* → *foxes* *waltz* → *waltzes*[2] *potato* → *potatoes* *hero* → *heroes*[3] *teach* → *teaches* *miss* → *misses* *wash* → *washes* *go* → *goes*
nouns/verbs ending in vowel + *o*	add -*s*	*radio* → *radios* *video* → *videos*
nouns/verbs ending in consonant + *y*	take away -*y* and add -*ies*	*family* → *families* *party* → *parties* *carry* → *carries* *fly* → *flies*
nouns/verbs ending in vowel + y	add -*s*	*enjoy* → *enjoys* *play* → *plays*

[1] If the pronunciation of *ch* is /k/, add -*s* only: *patriarch* → *patriarchs*.
[2] Note these exceptions of vowel + *z*: *quiz* → *quizzes*, *fez* → *fezzes*.
[3] Some words ending in consonant + *o*, especially words from other languages, take -*s* only: *piano* → *pianos*, *photo* → *photos*, *kilo* → *kilos*, *adagio* → *adagios*.

2 Irregular noun plurals

English does not have very many irregular noun plurals. Here are some examples:

nouns ending in -*f* or -*fe*	usually add -*ves**	*leaf* → *leaves* *loaf* → *loaves*
foreign nouns	varies according to origin of word	LATIN *datum* → *data* *erratum* → *errata* *terminus* → *termini* *vertebra* → *vertebrae* GREEK *crisis* → *crises* *phenomenon* → *phenomena*
other irregulars	+ (*r*)*en* change of vowel no change	*child* → *children* *ox* → *oxen* *woman* → *women* *foot* → *feet* *craft* → *craft* (e.g. boat) *sheep* → *sheep*

* Several words ending in -*f* and all those ending -*ff* just take -*s*: *chief* → *chiefs*, *belief* → *beliefs*, *cliff* → *cliffs*.
Some words ending in -*f* take either plural ending: *scarf* → *scarfs/scarves*.
You can check irregular plurals in a dictionary.

3 Possessive *'s*

singular noun: add *'s*	*house* → *house's* *bus* → *bus's*
singular proper noun ending in *-s*: add *'s* or an apostrophe (') only	*Mr James* → *Mr James's house/Mr James' house*
regular plural noun: add an apostrophe only	*boys* → *boys'* *buses* → *buses'*
irregular plural noun (not ending in *-s*): add *'s*	*men* → *men's* *children* → *children's*
one, somebody, everyone, each other, etc: add *'s*	*one's house* *somebody's house* *nobody's house* *everyone's rights* *each other's houses*

4 Comparative and superlative one-syllable adjectives

ADJECTIVE	COMPARATIVE	SUPERLATIVE
most adjectives: *cheap*	add *-er*: *cheaper*	add *-est*: *the cheapest*
ending in silent *-e*: *safe*	omit final -e,add *-er*: *safer*	omit final -e, add *-est*: *the safest*
ending in consonant + *y*: *dry*	change *y* to *i*, add *-er*: *drier*	change *y* to *i*, add *-est*: *the driest*
ending in single vowel + single consonant: *big*	double the final consonant, add *-er*: *bigger*	double the final consonant, add *-est*: *the biggest*

5 *-ing* forms

most verbs[1]	add *-ing* to the infinitive form	*eat* → *eating* *go* → *going*
verbs ending in -e	take away -e and add *-ing*:	*take* → *taking* *use* → *using*
verbs ending in *-ie*	take away *-ie* and add *-ying*:	*lie* → *lying* *die* → *dying*
verbs of one syllable that end in a short vowel + consonant	repeat the consonant and add *-ing*:	*swim* → *swimming* *sit* → *sitting*
verbs with more than one syllable that end in a stressed short vowel and consonant e.g. *begin*[2]	repeat the consonant and add *-ing*:	*begin* → *beginning* *forget* → *forgetting*

[1] In British English, but not American English, we often double the final consonant *-l*: *travel* → *travelling*
[2] We don't double the consonant if the final syllable is not stressed: *visit* → *visiting*.

6 Past tense endings

regular verbs ending in a single stressed vowel + consonant[1] (except *w*, *x* or *y*)	double the consonant	*hug* → *hugged* *pat* → *patted*
regular verbs ending in a consonant + *y*	change *y* to *i*	*copy* → *copied* *tidy* → *tidied*
irregular verbs[2]	do not form past tense with *-ed*	*go* → *went* *sit* → *sat*

[1] In British English, but not American English, we often double the final consonant *-l*: *label* → *labelling*
[2] You can check irregular verbs in a dictionary.

APPENDIX 4 British and American English

Nouns ➤ Unit 1

Some uncountable nouns in British English are countable in American English.
Br E: *accommodation* (uncountable) Am E: *accommodations* (countable)

In American English collective nouns are usually followed by singular verbs only:
Our ***class is*** *studying Dickens this semester.* ***The United Nations has*** *announced a ceasefire.*

Prepositions ➤ Unit 11

Br E: ***at*** *the weekend* Am E: ***on*** *the weekend*

In American English it is possible to omit the preposition before days.
Br E: *Our flight leaves* ***on*** *Tuesday.*
Am E: *Our flight leaves Tuesday.*
Br E: *I'll be staying at the Hilton* ***from*** *Friday* ***until/till/to*** *Monday.*
Am E: *I'll be staying at the Hilton Friday* ***through*** *Monday.*

In American English it is common to use a *quarter/ten/five*, etc. *of* (or *till*) and a *quarter/ten/five*, etc. *after* the hour in addition to the British English use of *to* and *past*.
Br E: *It's (a) quarter* ***to*** *nine. It's ten* ***to*** *seven. It's (a) quarter* ***past*** *nine. It's twenty* ***past*** *seven.*
Am E: *It's a quarter* ***of*** *nine. It's ten* ***till*** *seven. It's a quarter* ***after*** *nine. It's twenty* ***after*** *seven.*

Adverbs ➤ Unit 17

In informal American English *real* and *good* can be used instead of *really* and *well*:
She's a ***real nice*** *girl. That test was* ***real hard****. Congratulations. You* ***did good****!*

Tenses ➤ Units 19 and 23

In American English *have got* is not common; it is used mainly in speech (and not in writing); negative and question forms are not common.
Br E: ***Have you got*** *a pen I could borrow?* Am E: ***Do you have*** *a pen I could borrow?*

In American English the past participle form of *get* when it means 'has become/obtained/received', etc. is *gotten*: *Hollywood movies* ***have gotten*** *more violent in recent years.*

In American English, the past simple can be used after a superlative:
Br E: *This is the worst movie* ***I've*** *ever* ***seen****.* Am E: *This is the worst movie I ever* ***saw****!*

It is common in American English to use the past simple with the adverbs *just, already, yet* and *still*:
'We ***just received*** *the invitation to your daughter's wedding.* ***Did*** *she* ***buy*** *a wedding dress* ***yet****?'*
'No, she ***still didn't make up her mind*** *what style she wants.' 'What about the rings?'*
'Yeah, they ***bought*** *those* ***already*** *– they got them in New York last weekend.'*

Conditionals ➤ Unit 38

It is possible to use *would* in both clauses in American English but NOT in British English.
Am E: *The blockades wouldn't happen if the police* ***would be firmer*** *with the strikers.*
Br E: *The blockades wouldn't happen if the police* ***were firmer*** *with the strikers.*

In American English, it is possible to use *would have* in the *if* clause. This is becoming more common in British English, although many people consider it incorrect.
Am E: *If the play* ***would have finished*** *on time, we wouldn't have missed the train.*
Br E: *If the play* ***had finished*** *on time, we wouldn't have missed the train.*

Question tags ➤ Unit 79

Note the following contrasts:

Br E	*have*	*Oliver* **has** *a lot of friends,* **hasn't** *he?/***doesn't** *he?*
Am E	*have*	*Oliver* **has** *a lot of friends,* **doesn't** *he?*

APPENDIX 5 Word lists

1 Common adverb + adjective collocations ➤ Unit 16

All collocations below are from the British National Corpus.

(sb = somebody sth = something)

ADVERB	+ ADJECTIVE				
bitterly	cold disappointed	divided hostile	humiliated hurt	opposed resented	resentful upset
completely	acclimatised alone different drained	empty/full extinguished immune (from/to sth)	incapable (of sth) incomprehensible lost negative	new open (with sb = honest) overlooked	revised right/wrong untenable
deeply	ashamed attached (to sb/sth = strong feeling for) conscious conservative	depressed disappointed disturbed divided embedded	embittered hurt indebted (to sb) ingrained in love with	involved involved (in sth) lamented meaningful moving	religious rutted
entirely	absent beneficial clear	different false fitting	free global impersonal	loyal new obvious	serious unconvincing unexpected
heavily	armed booked built censored	criticised embroiled (with sb/sth) flavoured	guarded involved (in sth) muscled polluted	populated protected publicised regulated	represented scented soiled taxed
hideously	bad burnt deformed	disfigured disfiguring embarrassing	expensive injured lurid	mangled scarred swollen	ugly unhygienic
highly	commended contagious controversial critical dependent developed educated	enjoyable flexible intelligent mobile paid personal polished	political popular publicised qualified recommended regarded relevant	resistant respected significant skilled specialised technical toxic	trained unlikely valued volatile
painfully	acute aware evocative	learned loud obvious	self-conscious sensitive shy	slow small sparse	thin
perfectly	arranged balanced capable fitting (= appropriate)	formed genuine good healthy	normal placed proper rational	reasonable (all) right safe still	straightforward understandable valid
seriously	damaged exposed	hit (= damaged) ill	impaired rich	undermined threatened	wealthy
totally	abandoned abused alien anaemic decent destroyed	different embarrassed harmless homogeneous honest impervious (to sth)	inadequate incompetent integrated irresistible logical new	normal overpowering stiff surprising unacceptable unbelievable	undefined unjustified wasted
utterly	abandoned alone appalled careless dejected	destroyed devoted (to sb) different disastrous fearless	futile impossible irresistible lacking ruthless	tragic unacceptable unattainable unquestioning useless	wrecked

2 Noun + preposition + noun/*-ing* form ➤ Unit 65

- *advantage of/in*
- *aim of/in*
- *amazement at*
- *anger about/at*
- *annoyance about/at*
- *answer to**
- *anxiety about*
- *apology for*
- *attack on*
- *awareness of*
- *belief in*
- *boredom with*
- *craving for*
- *damage to**
- *danger of/in*
- *decrease in**
- *decrease of* (+ quantity)
- *delay in*
- *delay of* (+ duration)
- *demand for**
- *difficulty in*
- *effect of*
- *excitement about/at*
- *expense of*
- *fear of*
- *gratitude for*
- *hope of*
- *idea of*
- *increase in**
- *increase of* (+ quantity)
- *insistence on*
- *insurance against*
- *interest in*
- *job of*
- *lack of*
- *matter of*
- *matter with**
- *method of*
- *objection to*
- *pleasure of/in*
- *point of/in*
- *possibility of*
- *prelude to*
- *problem of/in*
- *proof of*
- *prospect of/for*
- *purpose of/in*
- *question about/of*
- *reason for*
- *relationship with*
- *satisfaction with/at*
- *sequel to*
- *solution to**
- *success in/at*
- *surprise at*
- *task of*
- *taste for*
- *thought of*
- *way of*
- *work of*
- *worry about*

* nouns that can only follow the pattern: noun + preposition + noun

3 Adjective + preposition ➤ Unit 65

- *absent from*
- *accustomed to*
- *addicted to*
- *afraid* of*
- *amazed at/by*
- *angry, annoyed*, furious*at/about* (+ the cause of this feeling)
- *angry, annoyed, furious with* (+ the person who caused this feeling)
- *anxious about* (= feel nervous/worried about sb/sth)
- *anxious* for* (= waiting impatiently for sth)
- *ashamed* of*
- *astonished at/by*
- *available for* (+ purpose)
- *available to* (+ person)
- *aware of*
- *bad/good at* (= ability)
- *bad/good for* (= effect on health)
- *bad/good to* (= behaviour towards/treatment of the object)
- *based on*
- *bored with*
- *capable of*
- *characteristic of*
- *close to*
- *concerned about* (= worried about)
- *concerned with* (= involved in)
- *conducive to*
- *confident of*
- *content* with*
- *contrary to*
- *convenient for*
- *conversant with*
- *crazy* about*
- *crowded with*
- *curious* about*
- *deficient in*
- *dependent on*
- *devoid of*
- *different than* (Am E)
- *different to/from*
- *disgusted with/at*
- *eager* for*
- *engaged* in* (= working in/involved in)
- *engaged to* (= promised to marry)
- *excited* about*
- *faithful to*
- *famous for*
- *fed up with*
- *fond of*
- *fraught with*
- *glad for* (= pleased for sb)
- *glad of* (= grateful for sth)
- *good at/for/to* (→ *bad*)
- *grateful for* (+ the cause of this feeling)
- *grateful to* (+ the person who caused this feeling)
- *guilty of*
- *harmful to*
- *hopeful of*
- *impervious to*
- *impressed with/by*
- *inclined towards*
- *incumbent upon*
- *inherent in*
- *intent on*
- *interested* in*
- *jealous of*
- *keen* on*
- *kind to*
- *lacking in*
- *late for*
- *made by* (+ the person/company who produced it)
- *made for* (+ its purpose)
- *made from* (+ original material which has been transformed)

* adjectives that can also be followed by *to* + infinitive

made of
(+ original material which is still visible)
nervous of
obedient to
obvious to
opposed to
pleased at/about
(+ something general, e.g. your recovery/the inflation figures)
pleased with
(+ something personal, e.g. my exam results/my new jacket)
popular with
prone to
proud of*

ready for*
related to
reminiscent of
responsible for
riddled with
scared of
shocked at
short of
similar to
sorry about*
(+ the cause of this feeling)
sorry for
(+ the person you feel sympathy towards)
subject to
successful in

sufficient for
suitable for
superior to
sure of
terrified of
tired of
typical of
upset about/by/over
(+ the cause of this feeling)
upset with
(+ the person who caused this feeling)
worried about
worthy of
wrong with

* adjectives that can also be followed by *to* + infinitive

4 Verbs with direct object + preposition + indirect object ➤ Unit 66

*accuse sb of sth**
acquit sb of sth
*advise sb against sth**
advise sb of sth
aim sth at sb
*arrest sb for sth**
*beat sb at sth**
blame sth on sb
bother sb with sth
*compensate sb for sth**
*congratulate sb for sth** (Am E)
*congratulate sb on sth**
*convict sb of sth**
convince sb of sth
criticise sb for sth
cure sb of sth
deprive sb of sth

describe sth to sb
discuss sth with sb
explain sth to sb
help sb with sth
lend sth to sb
make sth for sb
persuade sb of sth
*praise sb for sth**
present sb with sth
present sth to sb
prevent sb from -ing
protect sb from sth
provide sb with sth
provide sth for sb
reassure sb of sth
release sb from sth
rescue sb from sth

rid sb of sth
rob sb of sth
save sb/sth from sth
starve sb of sth
steal sth from sb
stop sb from -ing
strip sb of sth
supply sb with sth
supply sth for/to sb
suspect sb of sth
throw sth at sb
(= in order to hit them)
throw sth to sb
(= in order for them to catch it)
*warn sb about/against sth**
welcome sb to sth

* verbs that can also follow the pattern: verb + direct object + preposition + *-ing* form

APPENDIX 6 Common multi-word verbs

Multi-word verbs which occur at least ten times per million words in the Longman Corpus Network.

(*sb* = somebody *sth* = something)

Prepositional verbs ➤ Unit 66

call for sb *care for sb* *come across sth* (= encounter) *cope with sth* *deal with sb/sth* (= manage) *fall for sth* (= be tricked) *feel like sth* *get at sb/sth* *get over sth* (= recover from) *get through* (= finish successfully) *go into sth* *go with sth* (= match) *lead to sth* *look after sb/sth* *look at sth* *look for sth* (= try to find) *look into sth* (= investigate) *look like sb/sth* (= resemble) *look round sth* (= visit, etc.) *part with sth* *pay for sth* *rely on sth/sb* *run into sb* (= meet by chance) *see to sth* (= organise/manage) *send for sb* *stand for sth* (= represent/mean/tolerate) *stick to sth* (= persevere/follow) *take after sb* *talk about sth* *think about sth* (= consider)

The following prepositional verbs are usually used in the passive:
be aimed at (= intended for), *be applied to, be considered as, be derived from, be known as, be regarded as, be used as, be used in*

Prepositional verb + object + preposition + object ➤ Unit 66

agree about sth with sb *agree with sb about/over sth* *apologise to sb for sth* *complain about sth to sb* *complain to sb about sth* *depend on sb/sth for sth* *disagree with sb about/over sth* *quarrel with sb about/over sth* *rely on sb/sth for sth*

Intransitive phrasal verbs ➤ Unit 67

break down (= stop working) *catch on* (= understand/become popular) *come back* (= return) *come in* *come on* *fall out* (= quarrel) *fall through* *fit in* *get by* (= manage/cope) *get up* *go away* *go on* (= continue) *go out* *grow up* *look out* *pass out* (= faint) *shut up* *sit down* *stand up* *stay on* (= remain) *take off* *turn up* (= arrive) *wake up* *watch out*

Transitive phrasal verbs ➤ Unit 67

act sth out (= perform/demonstrate) *bottle sth up* (= not allow a feeling to show) *bring sth in* (= introduce) *bring sb up* (= rear) *bring sth up* (= mention sth) *carry sth out* (= perform a task) *do sth up* (= restore/redecorate) *fill sth in/out* (= complete in writing) *find sth out* (= discover) *fix sth up* (= arrange) *give sth away* (= reveal) *give sth up* (= stop) *hold sth up* (= delay) *keep sth up* (= maintain) *leave sth/sb out* *let sth out* (= release) *look sth up* *make sth up* (= invent) *pay sb back* *pick sth up* (= collect) *point sth out* (= highlight/explain) *pull sth/sb down* (= demolish) *put sth away* *put sth off* (= postpone) *put sth on* *put sb up* (= accommodate) *run sb down* (= criticise) *set sth up* (= establish/implement/organise) *take sth over* *take sth up* *throw sth away* *turn sth/sb down* (= refuse) *turn sth/sb out*

Phrasal-prepositional verbs ➤ Unit 67

back out of sth *break in on sth* *catch up on sth/sb* *catch up with sb* *check up on sth/sb* *come across as sth* (= appear to be) *come down to sth* (= be essentially) *come up with sth* (= invent) *cut down on sth* (= reduce) *do away with sth* *drop in on sb* *face up to sth* (= confront) *get away with sth* *get back to sth* (= return) *get down to sth* *get on with sth* *get out of sth* *give in to sth* *go out for sth* *go up to sb* (= approach) *keep away from sb/sth* (= avoid) *keep up with sb* *look down on sb* *look forward to sth* (= anticipate) *look out for sb/sth* *look up to sb* (= admire/respect) *make away with sth* *move on to sth* *put up with sth/sb* (= tolerate) *run away with sb* *run off with sth* *stand up for sth* (= defend) *turn away from sth* *walk out on sth/sb*

The following phrasal-prepositional verbs are usually used in the passive:
be cut off from, be made up of, be set out in

Index

(pp = past participle)

A

Diagnostic test answers

MODULE 1 1 chair/chairwoman 2 it's 3 has 4 was 5 have 6 a stone 7 cheese/cheeses 8 sister-in-law's 9 mine 10 wife's expensive car 11 today's local paper 12 cheers of the crowd 13 computer's main component/main component of the computer 14 Graham Greene's collection of short stories 15 to eat 16 one 17 remembering 18 each other 19 you/one 20 something

MODULE 2 **A** 1 an 2 the 3 a, The 4 the 5 – 6 the 7 – 8 the
B 1 an 2 your 3 an/per 4 All 5 both/both of 6 few 7 those 8 of you 9 This/A 10 that

MODULE 3 **A** 1 just behind 2 solicitors getting 3 what they said 4 dismantling 5 that I applied for 6 in 7 into 8 due to
B 1 B 2 B 3 C 4 B 5 A 6 B 7 C 8 A

MODULE 4 1 The maximum sentence was imposed by the judge. 2 people involved 3 seem 4 wonderful Victorian house 5 grey and white 6 in 7 unhappiest/most unhappy 8 far 9 as expensive as 10 the angrier 11 more sweet 12 as 13 much hotter 14 very 15 almost 16 quite 17 faster 18 very carefully opened the old box containing my mother's photographs/opened the old box containing my mother's photographs very carefully 19 Last night I only slept 20 Emotionally, Harriet

MODULE 5 1 has 2 had 3 you're always losing 4 is getting 5 were experiencing 6 was coming 7 was catching 8 used to 9 had taken 10 had been declining 11 had been 12 had finished 13 has increased 14 thought 15 risen 16 rained 17 consists 18 are you thinking

MODULE 6 1 You'll find 2 is going to 3 'll be skiing 4 lived/been living 5 don't think it will be 6 shall we have 7 'm not going to 8 staying/going to stay 9 will be 10 to 11 are not to be 12 takes off 13 have paid 14 will be playing 15 is due to be 16 unlikely 17 hopes to 18 was going to 19 would/were going to 20 open/have opened

MODULE 7 1 can be 2 managed to 3 may 4 might 5 must be 6 will 7 must 8 have to 9 needs 10 didn't need to show 11 are supposed to 12 are not allowed to 13 shouldn't 14 will be 15 won't have 16 always helped us out/would always help us out 17 would not reveal 18 can 19 had better not 20 wouldn't

MODULE 8 1 in case 2 then 3 if the tickets don't turn up 4 If/When 5 charges 6 will be 7 If you were/Were you 8 I'd ask 9 have booked 10 had 11 be living 12 weren't 13 had been 14 you'd stop 15 I wish 16 submit 17 had been 18 high time 19 wear 20 haven't slept

MODULE 9 1 stopped (the train) 2 put a freshly-baked cake on the table 3 an outsider 4 dishonest/a liar 5 us the way to the motorway 6 my father overcome cancer 7 to operate 8 a 9 being 10 it a pity 11 There's 12 It 13 us to pay 14 to find 15 to help 16 dispensing of 17 resigning/your husband resigning 18 making/to make 19 to hurt 20 building

MODULE 10 1 A, B 2 A, C 3 A 4 A, B 5 B 6 B 7 B, C 8 C 9 C 10 B 11 A, C 12 B 13 A 14 C 15 A, B 16 A, C

MODULE 11 1 A 2 A, B 3 A, C 4 A, B 5 A 6 C 7 A 8 A 9 A, B 10 C 11 B 12 A, C 13 C 14 A, C 15 A 16 B

MODULE 12 1 which is the capital city of Scotland, remember to visit the famous castle 2 that has 3 which 4 Hospice, which 5 which 6 which 7 to which it is addressed 8 when 9 up 10 wherever 11 Serviced 12 author 13 opening 14 Because he hadn't / Not having 15 bought 16 for the company 17 to sell/that sell 18 to find 19 what 20 takes less time/doesn't take as long

MODULE 13 1 did 2 immediately/as soon as 3 because 4 so as to 5 light enough 6 if/as long as 7 were 8 even though 9 Ideal though 10 Though 11 In spite of 12 Then 13 before that 14 Consequently/For this reason 15 mind you 16 To

MODULE 14 1 away by the police 2 been 3 be 4 to the eminent scientist 5 has 6 Steve usually has a shower 7 This programme was recorded 8 'The Tempest' is thought to be 9 that carbon emissions are 10 is 11 dress 12 her car repaired 13 had 14 sign 15 got

MODULE 15 1 apologise to them 2 whether 3 of flying 4 demanded 5 for 6 to help 7 her colleague behaving so atrociously 8 the solution to me 9 for 10 for whom 11 into her 12 it down 13 recently brought in 14 reveal 15 turn on 16 to the party 17 up willingly 18 faint 19 doing 20 take

MODULE 16 1 trainer 2 persistent 3 ex- 4 semi-literate 5 record 6 cups of coffee 7 self-service 8 Spanish-speaking 9 made 10 fetch 11 took 12 spoke 13 lie 14 raise 15 stole

MODULE 17 **A** 1 those/the paintings 2 did 3 do so 4 It/This 5 he tore 6 should have done/should have 7 wanted to 8 it was the novelist we had come to see 9 What they're doing is 10 All/The only thing 11 can refunds
B 1 A 2 A 3 A 4 B 5 B

MODULE 18 1 they put 2 does she 3 Are 4 is he 5 they have 6 did turn 7 on earth 8 What 9 so 10 he may be 11 dead 12 Her performance was a bit unconvincing 13 slowly/slow 14 admittedly 15 'd missed 16 left 17 in case 18 shouldn't've 19 I'm fine/Fine 20 you know

Answer key

Module 1

UNIT 1

1 1 is 2 is 3 is 4 has 5 are 6 is 7 is 8 has/have 9 have 10 are/have been 11 a 12 – 13 – 14 a 15 an

2 1 leaded 2 a drama 3 is 4 have 5 were 6 were 7 is 8 great 9 literature 10 a spellbinding

3 1 a stone 2 (the) chair 3 chickens 4 drawing 5 groups 6 a love 7 a drawing/drawings 8 chicken 9 stone 10 love 11 chairs 12 A group

4 *Is* ~~Are~~ art your passion?
Are you interested in ~~a~~ drawing, painting or ~~the~~ sculpture?
Would you like to improve your knowledge and skills?
Would you like to experience the deep sense of satisfaction you get from creating your own original work?
At East Hamley College a team of highly-qualified tutors ~~are~~ is available to help you improve your technique. We run art classes on Tuesday and Thursday evenings from 6.30 to 9.00. Each session costs £15 and lasts for two hours with a 30-minute break. We think you'll agree that £15 ~~aren't~~ isn't a lot to pay for over two hours with the personal attention of our art teachers!
Both the painting and the sculpture classes ~~takes~~ take place in the new annexe on Becton Road. This also has a relaxing café selling ~~a~~ coffee and a range of snacks where you can take a break and socialise with your fellow students.
You won't need to bring anything with you – we supply paint, ~~papers~~ paper and any other materials you need. But wear something that you don't mind covering in paint – ~~a~~ jeans and an old shirt is fine.
Every year, the work of our students ~~are~~ is exhibited in a local gallery. So, if you're lucky, your work might get spotted – you could be the next Damien Hirst!

UNIT 2

1 1 A 2 B 3 B 4 A 5 A 6 A 7 A 8 B

2 SOPHIE Who's coming with us to the exhibition on Saturday?
MAREK Well, apart from me and Kylie, there's Mike and Sandra, my *brother-in-law's* ~~brother's-in-law's~~ nephew, Paul, and Harry.
SOPHIE Harry? Is he a friend of ~~you~~ yours?
MAREK No, he's coming with Paul - he's a cousin of ~~his~~ him.
SOPHIE What's the exhibition about, anyway?
MAREK It's an exhibition by the ~~art's~~ art gallery's new discovery – Stephen Brewer.
SOPHIE Oh yes, I've just read an article about him in the ~~local's paper~~ local paper's culture section.
MAREK Yes, it was written by our next ~~door's~~ door neighbour's wife – she's a well-known art critic, apparently.
SOPHIE OK. It sounds like it might be interesting.
MAREK Great. I thought we might all meet up for lunch first.
SOPHIE Good idea. That ~~French place's in Green Street~~ French place in Green Street's reputation is excellent – a colleague of mine told me about it, although I haven't been there myself.
MAREK Right, let's try that place then. By the way, will you be coming by car?
SOPHIE Why?
MAREK Well, ~~Mike's and Sandra's~~ Mike and Sandra's car is in the garage so they need a lift. Could you take them? They're neighbours of ~~your~~ yours, aren't they?
SOPHIE Yes, they are. OK, I suppose so. Shall we meet at one?
MAREK Fine. I'll tell the others.

UNIT 3

1 1 B 2 A 3 A/B 4 A 5 B 6 B 7 A 8 A/B 9 A 10 A 11 B 12 B 13 A 14 B 15 A/B 16 A 17 B 18 A/B 19 A 20 A

2
1 The British Museum's first edition of *Alice in Wonderland* by Lewis Carroll.
2 Cornell University Library's original copy of the Gettysburg Address by Abraham Lincoln.
3 The National Gallery's painting of sunflowers by Vincent van Gogh.
4 The Museum of Modern Art's statue of Honoré Balzac by Auguste Rodin.

3
1 50 euros'
2 in Uncle Stephen's car.
3 at the top of the hill.
4 the managing director of a major cable TV company.
5 the cries of a girl (who was) trapped under the rubble.
6 Ernest Hemingway's greatest novel.
7 Glenda's description of the party
8 by the flood of 2006.

UNIT 4

1 1 he 2 it 3 him 4 It 5 It 6 it 7 It 8 They 9 one 10 one 11 It 12 he 13 he 14 one

2 1 each other 2 me 3 himself 4 You 5 myself 6 one another

3
1 Alicia and I left the party early; Jane and Marcia stayed longer than ~~we~~ us.
2 ✓
3 You're suffering from too much stress. You should learn to relax ~~yourself~~ more.
4 Do you prefer olive oil or sunflower ~~one~~?
5 I'm afraid these are the best seats I was able to find ~~them~~ at such short notice.
6 Dorinda and Eric have been married for ten years; they met ~~themselves~~ each other at university.

7 They didn't have that spare part I wanted in the local shop but I managed to find ~~a~~ one on the Internet.
8 'Who's that?' – 'Hi Steve. It's ~~we~~ us. We've been ringing the doorbell for ages!'
9 ✓
10 Darren's very good with his hands. He made all the kitchen cabinets ~~of~~ himself.

4 1 A ✗ B ✓ 2 A ✓ B ✗ 3 A ✓ B ✓ b
4 A ✓ B ✗ 5 A ✗ B ✓ 6 A ✓ B ✓ c
7 A ✓ B ✗ 8 A ✓ B ✓ a 9 A ✓ B ✓ c
10 A ✓ B ✓ b 11 A ✓ B ✓ a 12 A ✓ B ✓ d

UNIT 5

1 1 ANDY Why are you so late?
MATT Oh, (1) they're digging up the roads again.
ANDY I know – (2) they're always doing (3) something around here. It's a nuisance because (4) you never know how long it's going to take to get (5) anywhere. It took me two hours to get to the station on Tuesday.

2 SANI (6) Someone called from the office this morning.
RAJ Really? Did (7) they say what it was about?
SANI I think it was (8) something to do with your presentation tomorrow.
RAJ Did (9) they give you their name?
SANI No, but I know it was (10) someone from the sales team.

3 When (11) one looks at the work in detail (12) one can appreciate the superb craftsmanship with which the brushstrokes evoke the shimmering surface of the silks and satins. There is (13) something almost sensual about the lustrous surfaces of these rich fabrics. Every detail is perfect; there is (14) nothing in this painting which is clumsy or ill-thought-out. Of course, Van Dyck's aim is to flatter his sitter, and the accurate depiction of (15) something as luxurious and expensive as silk serves to emphasise the wealth and good taste of the patron.

2 1 somewhere 2 anyone 3 Is 4 anybody
5 something constructive 6 anywhere
7 someone/somebody 8 somehow 9 anything
10 No one 11 something 12 something

REVIEW

1 1 are 2 Steve's 3 has 4 is
5 my boss's secretary 6 us 7 brother-in-law's
8 isn't 9 chicken 10 twenty euros' worth
11 director's depiction of the battle 12 ours
13 is 14 yesterday's local paper 15 were
16 fish 17 the philosophy of science 18 is

2 1 it 2 me 3 one 4 Nobody/No one 5 me
6 I/one/you 7 I 8 it 9 myself 10 one
11 It 12 me 13 me 14 you/one 15 it

3 1 a 2 has 3 of 4 one 5 is 6 painting 7 It
8 it 9 something 10 He 11 it 12 he 13 the
14 of 15 Vinci's 16 of 17 duke's 18 are
19 of 20 has 21 has 22 piece 23 It
24 Vinci's 25 a 26 himself 27 one/we 28 –
29 he 30 his

Module 2

UNIT 6

1 1 1C, 2A 2 1C, 2A, 3B
3 1B, 2A 4 1B, 2A 5 1A, 2B

2 1 the 2 the 3 a 4 – 5 The 6 a 7 – 8 a
9 The 10 the 11 the 12 the 13 the 14 the
15 the 16 The 17 – 18 – 19 the 20 –

3 1 ~~at university~~ at the university
2 ~~a such~~ such a 3 ✓ 4 the unemployed
5 ✓ 6 ~~into a garden~~ into the garden
7 ~~The children~~ Children
8 ~~The Venus flytraps~~ Venus flytraps
9 ~~at the prison~~ in prison 10 ✓

4 The Scout Movement has a rich and exciting history which has led to it becoming the leading global youth movement of today. Here you can find information about the founder of the movement, Lord Baden-Powell, and other interesting facts about scouting.
There are more than 28 million Scouts, young people and adults, male and female, in 160 countries and territories. Some 300 million people have been Scouts, including prominent people in every field.
This is impressive, considering that scouting began with twenty boys and an experimental camp in 1907. It was held during the first nine days of August in 1907 on Brownsea Island, near Poole in Dorset, England.
The camp was a great success and proved to its organiser, Robert Baden-Powell, that his training and methods appealed to young people and really worked.
In January 1908, he published the first *Scouting for Boys*, a book issued in fortnightly parts at four pence each. It was an immediate success.
Baden-Powell had only intended to provide a method of training boys, something that existing youth organisations could adopt. To his surprise, youngsters started to organise themselves into what was destined to become – and is today – the world's largest voluntary youth movement.

UNIT 7

1 1 – 2 – 3 a 4 the 5 the 6 a 7 the
8 the 9 – 10 – 11 the 12 – 13 – 14 –
15 – 16 a 17 – 18 an 19 the 20 –

2 MAC Oh, Carl. I've been meaning to ask you. How did your job interview go?
CARL It was fine. They offered me the job.
MAC Really? That's great. Where's it based?
CARL In their headquarters in the city centre.
MAC Oh, of course. It's ~~the~~ Supersave. You told me last week.

CARL Yes, that's right.
MAC Is it a big organisation?
CARL Huge – over ~~the~~ a hundred thousand employees.
MAC Will you like that?
CARL I think so. In my last job I was a manager in a really small company, but there was nowhere to go from there.
MAC And now you're back to being a salesman again – it'll be a long way up!
CARL All the better! It gives me something to aim for.
MAC Is it an American company?
CARL Well, it's from the Netherlands originally, but it's based here now.
MAC Where did you see the ad for the job?
CARL It was in the *Herald Tribune*, but it was ~~a~~ the smallest job ad I'd ever seen. I could easily have missed it.
MAC Maybe they didn't want hundreds of applicants! Will you have to travel much now?
CARL Yeah, probably. They said in the interview they thought I'd be away two weeks ~~the~~ a month on average.
MAC Janey won't like that ...
CARL No, but she'll like some of the other aspects of the job, like the sports centre membership. She'll be able to play ~~a~~ tennis whenever she wants, free.
MAC That sounds good. Well, congratulations, let me shake ~~the~~ your hand!

UNIT 8

1 1 A 2 B 3 B 4 B 5 A 6 B 7 B 8 A

2 1 This 2 that 3 these 4 That 5 This
6 Those 7 That 8 this 9 those 10 that

3 1 A, C 2 B 3 B, C 4 A, C 5 A
6 B 7 A, B 8 A, B 9 B 10 A, C

4 1 all 2 no 3 some 4 This 5 most
6 many 7 These 8 every 9 both 10 each

REVIEW

1 1 the 2 the 3 – 4 the 5 –
6 the 7 a 8 an 9 a 10 the

2 1 The 2 that 3 each 4 the 5 a
6 little, the poor 7 this 8 The fear

3 1 A + e 2 B + h 3 A + b
4 B + d 5 B + g 6 A + c 7 B + a

4 ~~A~~ The cooperative was founded in 1947 by photographers Robert Capa, Henri Cartier-Bresson, George Rodger and David Seymour. All of them had been involved in the Second World War. Rodger had walked hundreds of miles to escape the Japanese in Burma. And Seymour received a medal for his work in American intelligence.
However, all of the founders of Magnum had been photographers for some time. The photographic work they were famous for dated back further. Capa's photos of the Spanish Civil War were called ' the finest pictures of front-line action ever taken'. They all appreciated ~~an~~ the importance of showing the world what really happens during ~~this~~ these major conflicts and world crises, so they decided to produce the best documentary photography at ~~this~~ that time. Cartier-Bresson once commented, 'Some photographers tell the news step by step as if making an accountant's statement.' He and Magnum, on the other hand, felt that the news had to be shown in ~~that~~ a way that would engage most ~~the~~ people who are unable to experience world-changing events at first-hand. Tragically, within a decade of the start of Magnum, ~~the~~ half of its original founders died while covering other wars. However, the agency had started to employ other top-class photographers and its work was sure to continue.
Today, Magnum is ~~some~~ the goal for many young photographers. It still produces the finest documentary photographs of world events. Recent coverage has included events in the Caribbean and civil wars in Africa, and while Magnum photographers cover these events, we will all be able to appreciate both the best and worst of humanity.

Module 3

UNIT 9

1 1 for hospitals and schools throughout the crisis.
2 from the well by means of a rope.
3 to just under three hours.
4 almost opposite the man with the beard.
5 before calling the mobile phone helpline.
6 in which that actor appeared/which that actor appeared in
7 depended on my agreeing not to reveal
8 except to take off her hat/take her hat off.
9 Who did you lend it to?
10 the standard to which we aspire.

2 1 of which 2 from where 3 having
4 only about 5 it/its
6 with which the houses were decorated/ which the houses were decorated with
7 going 8 to enjoy

UNIT 10

1 2 Champs-Elysées 3 Chaillot Palace (Trocadero)
4 Eiffel Tower 5 Place de la Concorde
6 Tuileries Gardens 7 Musée d'Orsay
8 Louvre 9 Palais de Justice
10 Place du Tertre (Montmartre) 11 City Hall
12 Bastille prison (opera house)

2 1 before 2 at 3 against 4 under
5 in 6 across 7 in 8 up to 9 across
10 on 11 over 12 in front of

3 1 over 2 through/in 3 out of 4 in
5 across 6 along 7 by/next to/beside
8 to/into 9 in 10 on 11 above
12 beneath/underneath/under 13 up to
14 on 15 down/along 16 at 17 between
18 opposite 19 on 20 In/Inside 21 in
22 under 23 to 24 through 25 at

UNIT 11

1 1 from 2 to/until 3 until 4 after 5 by 6 in 7 During/In 8 in/during 9 since/from 10 Since 11 in/during 12 in

2 1 – 2 in 3 on 4 since 5 during 6 by 7 with 8 as 9 Except 10 from 11 beside 12 on behalf of

3 1 by her husband 2 for chopping
3 are made with 4 apart from my brother
5 outside the control 6 According to many experts
7 during take-off or landing
8 Contrary to common belief

4 1 in 2 since 3 as 4 except for 5 Because of 6 of 7 Among 8 during 9 contrary to 10 by

REVIEW

1 1 from 2 across 3 between 4 in 5 According to 6 By 7 to 8 at 9 into 10 behind 11 In 12 under 13 on 14 with 15 during 16 on 17 at 18 against 19 off 20 out of 21 between 22 on 23 in 24 along 25 into 26 to

2 1 from/out of 2 in 3 over 4 as 5 from 6 besides 7 which 8 between 9 providing 10 through/in 11 among 12 During 13 contrary to 14 For 15 behind 16 what 17 In 18 under

3 1 ~~by conclusion~~ in conclusion
2 ~~except from~~ except for 3 ✓ 4 ~~Below~~ Under
5 ~~owing~~ owing to 6 ~~as~~ like 7 ✓
8 ~~before just~~ just before 9 ✓
10 ~~in that~~ in which
11 ~~beyond exception~~ without exception
12 ~~Within the meantime~~ In the meantime

Module 4

UNIT 12

1 1 A ✓ B ✗ 2 A ✓ B ✗ 3 A ✗ B ✓ 4 A ✓ B ✓
5 A ✓ B ✗ 6 A ✓ B ✗ 7 A ✗ B ✓ 8 A ✗ B ✓
9 A ✓ B ✗ 10 A ✗ B ✓ 11 A ✓ B ✓ 12 A ✓ B ✗
13 A ✗ B ✓ 14 A ✓ B ✗ 15 A ✗ B ✓

2 1 comfort and service provided 2 staggering
3 relaxed/relaxing 4 satisfied 5 similar
6 underlying problem 7 researchers involved
8 enhanced 9 somewhere pleasant
10 main concerns 11 Delayed 12 utter boredom
13 Affected passengers/ Passengers affected
14 amused 15 staff who were aloof

3 1 All students interested in the grant
2 There was something inexplicable
3 They gave an involved explanation
4 the only appointment available/ the only available appointment
5 The present state of affairs
6 the person responsible for recruitment
7 in the apartment opposite
8 Anyone sensitive would be
9 the amounts concerned
10 shoes suitable for a rocky terrain

4 Crime is on the rise according to a (1) worried worrying report issued this week by the government's national statistics office.
(2) Concerned citizens are likely to be alarmed by the report's conclusions. Despite promises that the government was tackling serious crime, the report indicates a 6% rise in serious offences over the last year. The largest increase has been in assaults especially those involving knives or other weapons. The (3) factor main main factor in these crimes appears to be the growth of gangs in our inner cities, and many of the crimes are drug-related.
Burglaries and theft have also increased, although by a smaller percentage. The (4) publishing figures published figures show a 3% growth since last year. Government sources claim that the (5) underlying reason for this increase is the economic situation. An opposition spokesman said there was (6) nothing surprising in the figures. He pointed at (7) causes which are social social causes and blamed the rise in crime on the (8) present government's lack of investment in education and training. The chair of the Police Officers' Association placed responsibility for the situation on the shoulders of the Minister of Justice, the (9) responsible politician politician responsible for policing. Reductions in police numbers have been a (10) factor which is principal principal factor in the growth of crime, he contends.
As usual, it is (11) old and vulnerable the old and (the) vulnerable who are most likely to be the victims of crime. More than 38% of the (12) victims identified in the report were over the age of 65. It is certainly true that there is a fear of crime amongst the elderly, and lobbying groups are calling for (13) radical something something radical to be done about the problem. They are asking for (14) sentences which are maximum maximum sentences to be given to those criminals that target (15) the elderly or disabled. They feel the (16) involved criminals criminals involved should be punished more severely than others.

UNIT 13

1 1 red and orange 2 an expensive German
3 brick and stone
4 difficult, demanding/difficult and demanding
5 though 6 large stone 7 oval mahogany
8 boring and sentimental/boring, sentimental
9 and 10 long, detailed/long and detailed

2 1 encrusted enamel and gold
2 beautiful and famous/famous and beautiful
3 celebrated sixteenth-century Florentine
4 simple yet daring/daring yet simple
5 heavy glass 6 shattered glass
7 priceless missing 8 stupid and fatal
9 amazing and fortuitous 10 grainy yet distinct
11 complete(,) undamaged 12 small wooden

UNIT 14

1 1 best 2 the wettest 3 more real than
4 the farthest/furthest 5 looser 6 the worst
7 drier 8 the most keen/keenest 9 prettier
10 more wrong 11 The most scared
12 more bored

2 KAREN Now we've seen all the candidates, what do you think?
TOBY It's a difficult choice, but I thought Steven was the ~~most strong~~ strongest of the three.
KAREN Oh? You couldn't be more wrong! Meera definitely has ~~betterer~~ better experience.
TOBY Well of course she does, she's ~~elder~~ older than the other two.
KAREN Yes, and she's more mature .
TOBY True. But don't you think she's a bit set in her ways? Would she really fit in here?
KAREN I don't see why not. Let's face it, the other two are very young – significantly ~~more younger~~ younger than most of our staff.
TOBY That could be a good thing. I mean younger people are ~~adaptabler~~ more adaptable than older ones.
KAREN OK. What about Ahmed? He was the best qualified ~~in~~ of the candidates.
TOBY I'm not sure. He seemed the ~~less~~ least promising of the three. He was too laid back.
KAREN Yes, he was ~~the easily most~~ easily the most relaxed – people are usually more ~~nervouser~~ nervous at interviews.
TOBY So we come back to Steven. He was ~~one~~ one of the most ambitious candidates I've ever interviewed. I thought that was a positive thing ...
KAREN Yes. But he's very distant. Aren't we looking for someone ~~more friendlier and approachable~~ more friendly and approachable? Let's look at their CVs again.

3 1 further/farther away from the bus stop
2 are tastier than these (ones)
3 one of the most despicable episodes
4 more sentimental than
5 wasn't the worst/was the best
6 was the least expensive of/was the cheapest of
7 by far the most ridiculous story
8 older than her

4 1 a much/considerably/significantly/substantially larger numbers of prisoners than any other country.
2 the highest number of prisoners as a proportion
3 Of (all) the countries in the chart ... the lowest number of prisoners
4 a much/far/considerably/significantly/substantially greater number of prisoners than Russia.
5 by far/easily the highest proportion of prisoners per population apart from the USA and Russia.

UNIT 15

1 1 B 2 A 3 B 4 A 5 B 6 B 7 B 8 B

2 1 not nearly 2 like 3 a film 4 white as
5 like as 6 smaller and smaller 7 more red
8 as 9 such 10 the further 11 like 12 dark
13 than 14 nowhere 15 easy 16 and
17 the colder 18 as 19 as 20 like

3 1 the 2 faster 3 as 4 like 5 not 6 as
7 more 8 as 9 such 10 as 11 like 12 rather

4 1 was nothing like as good as
2 such a bad test score as
3 not so much tired as bored
4 interesting a film as my friends had claimed
5 The more you pick that spot, the worse
6 more disappointed than angry
7 becoming louder and louder
8 get, the less aggressive they become

UNIT 16

1 UNGRADABLE amazing, correct, dead, enormous, extinct, fascinating, freezing, huge, minute, paralysed
GRADABLE attractive, cold, exciting, expensive, good, interesting, large, shy, sick, ugly

2 1 fairly inexpensive 2 a bit stiff
3 virtually indecipherable
4 somewhat bloodthirsty 5 absolutely freezing
6 very interesting 7 fabulously rich
8 highly unlikely

3 1 ✓ 2 ~~very empty~~ completely empty
3 ~~completely full~~ very/almost/nearly/practically virtually full
4 ~~very famished~~ absolutely famished
5 ~~very recommended~~ highly recommended
6 ✓ 7 ✓ 8 ~~very built~~ heavily built
9 ~~absolutely moving~~ deeply moving 10 ✓

4 1 C 2 A 3 A 4 B 5 C
6 B 7 B 8 A 9 C 10 B

UNIT 17

1 1 highly 2 rightly 3 seriously 4 close
5 Roughly 6 freely 7 easily 8 deep
9 easy 10 hard 11 highly 12 right

2 1 started to go faster 2 as quite a
3 happens more slowly 4 there soon enough
5 roughly three-quarters of
6 almost entirely unheard of/unknown
7 was rather a 8 (the) most deeply involved

UNIT 18

1 1 A ✗ B ✓ C ✗ 2 A ✓ B ✓ C ✗ 3 A ✓ B ✗ C ✓
4 A ✓ B ✗ C ✓ 5 A ✓ B ✓ C ✗ 6 A ✗ B ✓ C ✓
7 A ✗ B ✓ C ✓ 8 A ✗ B ✗ C ✗ 9 A ✓ B ✓ C ✗
10 A ✓ B ✗ C ✗ 11 A ✗ B ✓ C ✓
12 A ✓ B ✓ C ✗ 13 A ✓ B ✗ C ✓
14 A ✓ B ✓ C ✓

2 NOTE These answers follow the guidelines for sequence in the unit reference section.

1 Owen kicked the ball skilfully into the net just before half time.
2 Foxes can often be seen scavenging on the streets of London at night.
3 David behaves quite well when he is at home but he often causes trouble at school.
4 The post sometimes doesn't arrive on time in this part of the city.
5 Jennifer didn't immediately recognise the man waving frantically from the balcony at the end of the show.
6 Such losses would normally have been avoided by the use of back-up devices.
7 These children have probably never had the opportunities we take for granted.
8 Unfortunately, access to the Internet is no longer available free of charge at our libraries on weekday mornings.
9 We are usually unable to offer refunds on the spot, but we will examine your claim thoroughly before the end of the week.
10 Many of the old masters had assistants who would prepare the oil pigments by hand in their studios each morning.

3 NOTE Underlined words show spoken stress.

1 'Sorry, I really don't know what you're talking about!'
2 'That place always is full on Saturday evenings!'
3 'Yes, I often have wondered about that.'
4 'I'm not surprised. He never does listen to my ideas.'
5 'That's not unusual; the customs officers here usually are quite thorough.'
6 'I'm sorry but we honestly don't know where he is.'
7 'Come off it. You really can't expect me to just give in like that.'
8 'You absolutely don't have a clue what I'm talking about, do you?'
9 'I'm afraid these programs sometimes do take a long time to download.'
10 'Well, she rarely is in the office before twelve these days.'

REVIEW

1
1 ~~but~~ and
2 ~~a little Persian beautiful cat~~ a beautiful little Persian cat
3 ~~the taken route~~ the route taken
4 ~~the wealthies~~ the wealthy
5 ~~absolutely upset~~ very/extremely upset, ~~boss former~~ former boss
6 ~~afraid~~ frightened, ~~terrified~~ terrifying
7 ~~injuring~~ injured, ~~breaking~~ broken
8 ~~an aluminium and glass-fibre unique hull~~ a unique aluminium and glass-fibre hull
9 ~~very vast~~ absolutely vast, ~~equipment medical~~ medical equipment
10 ~~responsible person~~ person responsible
11 ~~Living in Scotland viewers~~ Viewers living in Scotland
12 ~~Tall anyone~~ Anyone tall

2 1 D 2 G 3 A 4 E 5 B 6 F 7 C

3
1 Financially ruined, the owner of the business rather reluctantly agreed to sell the premises within the month.
2 There is probably nothing better than collapsing lazily onto a sofa at the end of the day. / At the end of the day there is probably nothing better than collapsing lazily onto a sofa.
3 Carefully controlled, this amazingly effective new drug can dramatically reduce blood pressure within hours/can reduce blood pressure dramatically within hours.
4 We rarely seem to get the chance to talk seriously about anything these days.
5 Unfortunately, many of my colleagues thoroughly disapprove of my scheme to update the accounting procedures in the sales department over the next quarter.

4 1 B 2 A 3 C 4 C 5 B 6 A 7 B 8 C 9 A 10 C 11 B 12 B 13 A 14 A 15 C 16 B 17 C 18 C 19 A 20 B 21 B 22 A

Module 5

UNIT 19

1
1 I've been waiting
2 She won't have returned/She won't've returned
3 Protection under this policy does not include
4 He might not have known/He mightn't've known
5 Does their boss not realise/Doesn't their boss realise
6 despite the fact that he hadn't been taking
7 They really should have told you/should've told you
8 have not been received

2 1 were, being 2 have 3 been 4 done, having 5 having, doing, be 6 had 7 doing, being 8 having 9 had 10 done

3
BETH Do you fancy going to the cinema at the weekend? The local Odeon has *has got* a good film on.
SUE I don't really like going to the cinema. I prefer to watch movies at home.
BETH Really?
SUE Yes, we have we've got a fantastic new 3D home cinema system, so the sound and vision are both excellent.
BETH I thought you already had a state-of-the-art TV.
SUE We used to have quite a good one, yes, but our new system has has got much better sound than that had. Why don't you come round on Saturday evening and see it?
BETH I'm having dinner with my parents on Saturday evening. How about Friday?
SUE That's OK, but I've actually ordered the new James Bond film on DVD, and I hope to have got it by Saturday. Let's make it Sunday evening, shall we?
BETH Yes, that's fine, but I need to leave a bit early as I have I've got an interview on Monday morning.
SUE OK, come round about seven. We'll have a snack first, then watch the movie.

4 1 We have a Michelin-starred restaurant …
2 … all of which are from the locality.
3 Would you enjoy having a relaxing swim or sauna?
4 … which has a fully-equipped gymnasium …
5 We have several fully-qualified nannies …
6 Our nannies do this service …
7 … which has a large number of salmon, trout and bream.
8 … as they have been the location for many movies.

UNIT 20

1 1 houses 2 are trying out 3 display
4 are currently showing 5 come 6 brings
7 're always complaining 8 provides
9 'm hearing 10 are becoming

2 1 Do you believe 2 examines
3 is generally getting 4 discovers
5 is continually raining 6 are happening
7 becomes 8 doesn't purport 9 revolve
10 is slowly freezing 11 are continually struggling
12 is currently showing

3 1 A is opening, B opens
2 A arrive, B are just arriving
3 A usually stay, B is staying
4 are generally rising, B rise
5 A often contradicts, B is always contradicting

4 SARAH Welcome to the programme. This afternoon ~~I stand~~ I'm standing in the middle of the northern Black Forest, Germany, with Rainer Sanger, from *Friends of the Forest*, a pressure group which ~~is representing~~ represents people worried about the natural habitat in Europe. Rainer, you're very concerned about this area of the forest. Can you tell us why?

RAINER Yes. Much of the forest was wiped out in the storms last winter, as you can see. Many of the trees are dead, and more ~~die~~ are dying because of the irreversible damage. We at *Friends of the Forest* believe that the authorities ~~don't do~~ aren't doing enough right now to restore this beautiful forest to its former state.

SARAH But they ~~clear~~ are clearing the dead trees away today. I saw some men on the way here …

RAINER Of course, but they ~~are doing~~ do that every year. It's the normal procedure. We need more trees now, but they aren't planting any.

SARAH I see. But you have approached the authorities about this, I understand.

RAINER We have tried but they're always making excuses – usually to do with money. It ~~gets~~ is getting more and more frustrating all the time! Each time, they~~'re telling~~ tell us that they haven't got enough money to restore the forest as quickly as we'd like.

SARAH But it's not just an excuse, is it? They clearly don't have enough money for everything, and the current situation is quite extraordinary.

RAINER Of course, we appreciate that, and the point is that actually, we ~~don't ask~~ aren't asking for much money. We would just like their guidance – we have plenty of volunteers …

UNIT 21

1 1 D 2 G 3 J 4 E 5 B
6 H 7 A 8 C 9 I 10 F

2 1 was 2 allowed 3 was 4 use to allow/allow
5 would/used to 6 was earning
7 was/used to be 8 would always/always used to
9 we'd go 10 was 11 were/used to be
12 would always/always used to 13 were queuing
14 was 15 used to get 16 used to

3 1 was standing, saw 2 was blowing, set off
3 felt/was feeling, collapsed, pressed, settled down
4 spent, were cooking 5 were living, hit
6 soared, announced 7 started, were studying
8 was leaving, decided 9 took, managed
10 ran into, mentioned

4 1 ~~used to be~~ was 2 ✓ 3 ~~would be~~ were
4 ~~while~~ when 5 ~~expected~~ was expecting
6 ✓ 7 ~~didn't use to being~~ didn't use (used) to be
8 ~~were coming~~ came
9 ~~wasn't used to having~~ didn't use (used) to have
10 ✓
11 ~~Would your mother work~~ Did your mother use (used) to work
12 ✓

UNIT 22

1 1 A 2 B 3 A 4 B 5 A 6 B 7 B 8 B

2 1 turned 2 had queued 3 had taken
4 had conquered 5 had eaten
6 had been practising 7 had booked
8 had been working 9 had hoped
10 had been suffering

3 1 had 2 had been doing/had done 3 began
4 had already appeared 5 was studying
6 had been performing 7 accepted 8 did
9 had been competing 10 had been
11 had been 12 continued 13 was promoting
14 had recently directed 15 died

UNIT 23

1 1 B 2 B 3 A 4 A 5 B 6 A 7 A
8 B 9 A 10 A 11 B 12 B 13 A 14 B

2 1 haven't seen 2 've seen 3 've ever seen
4 've already watched 5 've never heard of
6 was 7 did he make 8 won 9 've left
10 haven't finished

3 1 Most of the workers have been/have worked here since 1996.
2 The guest performers have all arrived.
3 We've visited the new theme park three times so far.
4 Kay and I have known each other for twenty years.
5 The latest novel by Chris Cleave is the best he's ever written.

6 The panel has not yet made a decision about the technical irregularities.
7 The government has not increased the rate of income tax recently.

UNIT 24

1 1 1B, 2A 2 1A, 2B 3 1B, 2A 4 1A, 2B 5 1A, 2B 6 1B, 2A

2 1 has just won 2 has been working 3 has been 4 has/'s been directing 5 has directed 6 has/'s also been producing 7 have been 8 have ever been nominated 9 have had 10 has acted 11 has also appeared 12 has/'s been looking

UNIT 25

1 1 1B, 2A 2 1A, 2B 3 1A, 2B 4 1B, 2A 5 1B, 2A 6 1A, 2B 7 1B, 2A 8 1A, 2B 9 1B, 2A 10 1A, 2B 11 1A, 2B 12 1B 2A

2 1 noticed 2 been meaning 3 concerns 4 am having 5 feel/am feeling 6 consisted 7 wanted 8 appears 9 realise 10 promise

3 1 forbid 2 tastes 3 'm watching 4 's been meaning 5 saw 6 hurts/'s hurting 7 're being 8 despises

REVIEW

1 1 are visiting 2 are now thinking 3 is beating 4 hear 5 smell 6 lies 7 invite 8 are currently developing 9 have 10 rise 11 shelters 12 are now showing

2 1 ~~would be much happier~~
used to be/ was much happier E
2 ~~Almost everyone left~~ Almost everyone had left G
3 ~~he continually took~~ he was continually taking F
4 ~~he was running~~ he had been running C
5 ~~was waking up, was getting up, was showering~~
woke up, got up, showered D
6 ~~We used to go~~ We went A

3 1 have unearthed 2 have been digging 3 found 4 contained 5 has been trying 6 existed 7 have been found 8 has discovered 9 has been 10 were discovered 11 has produced 12 has allowed

4 1 has uncovered 2 did not stay 3 had met 4 would get up/used to get up 5 had been enjoying 6 lies 7 has ever been 8 was beating 9 has got 10 has always stimulated 11 is still doing/still does 12 have adapted 13 have been 14 is working

Module 6

UNIT 26

1 1 will/'s going to 2 definitely 3 have been 4 will/'s going to 5 are going to 6 be running 7 is going to/will 8 don't think that will 9 will probably 10 have

2 1 Let's stop playing soon – our opponents are going to win.
2 My great-grandmother will be a hundred years old next year.
3 I don't think (it's possible) that humans will ever be able to live on the moon.
4 My parents will have been married for twenty-five years next Saturday.
5 Come along next Monday afternoon – the band will be practising.
6 Our proposal will certainly be successful.
7 Do you have any idea of when / what time you will be arriving on Friday?
8 That skier is going to hit those trees.

3 1 will have celebrated 2 will soon be/are soon going to be 3 will learn 4 is going to have 5 will fall 6 will have sent 7 will be caring for 8 will help 9 will take/is going to take 10 will be using 11 will almost certainly come 12 will have been

UNIT 27

1 1 A ✓ B ✗, 4 2 A ✗, 1 B ✓ 3 A ✓ B ✗, 3 4 A ✗, 2 B ✓

2 1 B/C 2 A 3 B/C 4 A/B 5 A/C 6 B 7 B

3 1 J 2 E 3 I 4 C 5 G 6 F 7 B 8 H 9 A
A 're having B will be broadcast
C 'm going to complain/'ll complain
E 'll be watching/'m watching
F 'll be looking at/'re looking at G 'll give
H 'll be studying/'s studying I 're filming
J 'll be staying/'ll stay

4 1 are coming 2 are they arriving 3 'm taking 4 won't be 5 'll all be 6 'll be working 7 are going to send/are sending/will be sending 8 'll have 9 'm having 10 'll be picking up 11 'll have to 12 're meeting/'ll meet

UNIT 28

1 1 A ✗ B ✓ 2 A ✓ B ✗ 3 A ✓ B ✓ 4 A ✓ B ✓ 5 A ✗ B ✓ 6 A ✗ B ✗

2 1 begin 2 expect 3 should 4 is likely to 5 is sure to 6 plans to 7 will be 8 anticipate 9 intend 10 hopes to 11 guarantee to 12 due to

3 1 The peace talks are due to take place in Helsinki on 28th–29th July.
2 That music is (so loud that it's) bound to wake all the neighbours.
3 Scientists in Mexico feel that they are on the point of/verge of discovering a new bacterium.
4 Will you swear not to get into debt again this month?
5 We anticipate (that there will be) great interest in this offer.

6 Everyone in the village lived in fear of the impending volcanic eruption.
7 The designer envisages finishing/being able to finish by tomorrow afternoon.
8 I think the examiner is unlikely to accept a handwritten script these days.
9 P D James, recently turned ninety, is about to release yet another novel.
10 The team meeting will be taking place in Meeting Room 4 (as usual).
11 Mr Cooper was on the verge of dying of hypothermia when the paramedics arrived.
12 Given the current media frenzy, the ministers won't be travelling first class for the foreseeable future.

4 1 ✓
2 ~~takes place~~ will be taking place/will take place
3 ✓ 4 ~~is about to~~ is to/will
5 ~~you'll eat~~ you eat/you've eaten
6 ~~We spend it~~ We'll be spending it
7 ~~on the verge to sign~~ on the verge of signing
8 ~~is due to~~ is about to

UNIT 29

1 1 was going to call you
2 was going to help me
3 was due to start/come in
4 would have told me
5 were due to leave/were going to leave/ would have left

2 1 (who/that) I would marry
2 weren't going to reveal
3 was to have made/would have made
4 was due to be increased
5 we'd still be living/we were still going to be living
6 was about to start
7 the ceremony would have finished

REVIEW

1 1 You won't need/ You won't be needing
2 'll be sailing 3 I won't have finished
4 he's going to shoot …

2 The Management of Broadbank Hotel wish to remind you that the hotel ~~might close~~ closes on 5 December for the usual year-end vacation. It is ~~about to~~ due to reopen early next year, but as part of the Value4U chain of hotels.
As you know, the Lister family has been involved in Broadbank Hotel for over twenty years now and ~~the closure impending~~ the impending closure is a blow to all of us. We had recently started to look at ways of finding extra financial support: we anticipated ~~to work~~ working with an investment company to upgrade the hotel with the addition of a gym, swimming pool and sauna complex. We were on the verge of ~~sign~~ signing a contract, which ~~will allow~~ would allow/would have allowed us to retain control of the hotel, but we were unable to complete the deal on time. We were ~~bound to~~ about to send our annual newsletter as usual to all our regular clients, with information about offers for the spring, but of course, that is now not possible. Unfortunately, ~~we are likely to be not able~~ unlikely to be able/likely not to be able to set up another hotel in the near future.
The Value4U chain envisages ~~reopen~~ reopening the hotel by 1 March; you will be advised of the exact date. It just remains for us to thank you for all your support in the past.

3 1 expects to 2 plan to 3 will be joining
4 imminent 5 has taken place 6 will extend
7 definitely 8 will attempt 9 sure to
10 will have spent 11 'll be able to
12 'm going to 13 was going to
14 will be paying

Module 7

UNIT 30

1 1 managed to/was able to
2 wasn't able to/couldn't/(didn't manage to)
3 could 4 'll be able to
5 managed to/were able to 6 could have
7 can/'ll be able to 8 be able to 9 succeeded in
10 being able to 11 were unable to/weren't able to
12 couldn't have been

2 1 were only able to 2 can/are able to
3 couldn't have 4 could hardly
5 are able to (can) 6 managed
7 to be able to 8 won't be able to

UNIT 31

1 1 could have been 2 could 3 can
4 might/could 5 won't 6 might 7 could/might
8 Do you think they might/Might they

2 1 The service in this restaurant can be quite surly.
2 Ten years ago I could have bought my neighbour's apartment for $30,000.
3 We could issue the tickets today if you gave us your credit card number.
4 When I was at university, students could generally have a good lifestyle.
5 Do you think (that) the disparity in the figures could/might be due to a computer error?
6 The shuttle bus may/might not be operating at the moment – it is the low season.
7 Jim may/might have taken it; he was in the office all day yesterday.
8 My sister could well become an opera star – she has a lovely voice.

UNIT 32

1 1 can't 2 must 3 might/could
4 should 5 Could/Might 6 will
7 be 8 won't 9 may 10 shouldn't

2 1 She must have missed it.
2 She might be the baby's mother.
3 She can't/couldn't have phoned her parents.
4 It must have been raining.
5 The man must have fallen off his bike.
6 The woman can't be his wife.
7 Someone must have called the ambulance.
8 There might/could have been an explosion.
9 There can't/couldn't have been an earthquake.
10 It must have been terrifying.

3 1 E 2 F 3 C 4 A 5 B 6 D

4 1 A/B 2 C 3 A (C is too colloquial)
4 B 5 A/C 6 A 7 B 8 C

UNIT 33

1 1 A 2B 3 A 4 A 5 B 6 B 7 B 8 B

2 1 required/obliged 2 should
3 don't have to/needn't 4 must/have to
5 ought 6 needn't/don't have to
7 required/obliged 8 should/ought to

3 1 do I have to 2 have to 3 should
4 will have to 5 obliged to 6 has to
7 supposed to 8 need to 9 having to 10 needs
11 must 12 had to

4 1 A Should I
B You have to/ You are obliged/required to
2 A do I need to/do I have to/ must I
B You'll need to/You'll have to/You must
3 A Did you have to/Did you need to
B I/we had to/needed to
4 B we needn't have (done)/we didn't need to

UNIT 34

1 1 may not 2 should 3 won't 4 cannot
5 may 6 must not have competed
7 may not 8 were not allowed to join

2 1 should have paid for
2 were not allowed to own
3 might have asked me
4 mobile phones is (strictly) forbidden/not allowed
5 ought not to be punished
6 must not have applied for
7 could not leave
8 shouldn't have/ought not to have left

UNIT 35

1 1 B 2 A 3 B 4 B 5 A 6 B 7 A 8 A

2 1 will/'ll be 2 won't work 3 would (always) say
4 will (easily) hold 5 'll be having
6 will have prepared 7 would (always) argue
8 will stop 9 won't have started
10 would come out 11 will go out 12 will check

3 1 they will do
2 they won't do
3 She'll do light cleaning
4 she'll get the shopping
5 she won't do anything heavy
6 she would prepare supper
7 She will say exactly what she thinks
8 she wouldn't eat it.
9 they will pop in
10 he won't ask them for help
11 the car wouldn't start
12 Would he wait for me?
13 he will try to cope by himself.
14 you'll wait for a moment/you wouldn't mind waiting for a moment

UNIT 36

1 1 B 2 A 3 B 4 A 5 B
6 A 7 B 8 B 9 B 10 A

2 1 we'd better 2 love 3 should/ought to
4 you'd better not 5 to focus 6 could/may
7 I'll 8 could 9 can/might 10 wouldn't
11 will 12 Can/Shall

3 1 Would you pass/give
2 Will you have/Won't you have
3 will do/shall do/will continue 4 Shall I take
5 Will you come 6 I'd like you to show

4 1 should, ought, mustn't/shouldn't 2 Will/Won't
3 ought, You'd 4 could/may, may, will/shall
5 Would/Could, rather

REVIEW

1 1 ✓ 2 ~~should~~ will 3 ~~is able to~~ can
4 ~~can~~ may/might 5 ✓
6 ~~can we~~ will we be able to 7 ✓
8 ~~could~~ managed to/was able to
9 ~~mustn't~~ can't 10 ~~couldn't~~ won't

2 1 Having to observe all the health and safety rules these days is onerous.
2 You/We don't have to get an international licence (in order) to drive in this country.
3 The government should not have tried to break the strike.
4 You might have let us know you were coming.
5 We needn't have booked the table ... / We didn't need to book the table ...
6 The gas must be disconnected before removing the boiler/the boiler is removed.
7 We arrived late at the theatre and (we) weren't allowed to take our seats ...
8 Why are we required to state ethnic origin on official forms these days?
9 Patients must not have eaten or drunk anything for three hours before the operation.
10 The public may not visit the private rooms when the owner is in residence.

3 1 would 2 Can 3 He'd 4 wouldn't
5 would hasten 6 would 7 Wouldn't
8 wouldn't 9 might 10 wouldn't
11 should 12 Shall

4 1 will have 2 could 3 should 4 would
5 succeeded in 6 were unable to/didn't manage to
7 had to 8 couldn't have 9 might
10 didn't manage to/were unable to

Module 8

UNIT 37

1 1 A✗ B✓ C✓ 2 A✓ B✗ C✗ 3 A✓ B✗ C✓
4 A✗ B✓ C✗ 5 A✓ B✓ C✓ 6 A✓ B✓ C✓

2 1 if 2 have 3 unless 4 will run out
5 So long as/If 6 is 7 provide
8 When 9 reaches/can reach
10 goes 11 will be 12 Whether

3
1 Even if Sophie doesn't like her parents-in-law, she keeps it to herself.
2 In case of fire, use the signposted exit at the rear of the building. / Use the signposted exit at the rear of the building in case of fire.
3 After her husband's death, Mrs Jenkins sold the house to her son on (the) condition that he lived in it himself.
4 Unless you request next-day delivery, we will send the goods by normal post.
5 You will be awarded marks for trying to answer all the questions, whether the answers are correct or not/whether or not the answers are correct.
6 Should you wish to apply for shares, there is a registration form on our website.
7 Your membership will only be renewed if you pay your subscription within the next seven days.
8 If you park your car illegally then it will be towed away at your expense. /
If cars are parked illegally, then they will be towed away at the owners' expense.
9 You may enter the ruins providing you put on protective footwear.
10 We will not achieve the deadline unless you provide all the resources we have requested.
11 I can play my music as loud as I like as long as my parents are out of the house.
12 The library computer can tell you whether you have any books out on loan or not/whether or not you have any books out on loan.
13 You'd better take your passport in case you need proof of your identity.
14 You may not enter the country unless you have a valid visa issued by the consulate.
15 Should we fail to deliver within fourteen days, we will deduct twenty-five percent from our invoice.

UNIT 38

1 1 are, didn't miss 2 hasn't, doesn't
3 didn't take, have to 4 giving advice 5 is
6 unlikely 7 had to, don't 8 present

2 1 A✓ B✓ C✗ 2 A✗ B✓ C✓ 3 A✓ B✗ C✗

3 1 G wouldn't be/might not be,
L wouldn't have broken/might not have broken
2 H would/might never have been developed,
J wouldn't have
3 C would not have been destroyed,
K would/might be
4 A might not be/would not be, I would not be
5 D would not have become, F would be

4
1 If it were to rain, the crisis would/might/could be averted.
2 The tourist industry might have suffered if the government hadn't stopped releasing pollution levels in June/had continued to release pollution levels.
3 If the governments involved had taken positive action, the current crisis might not have happened/would not have happened.
4 There might be more serious environmental protection if more of the countries affected had a Ministry of the Environment.
5 Current attempts to fight the fires would have been more effective if the governments hadn't failed to build reliable water supply networks in rural areas.

UNIT 39

1
1 I wish you'd told us that you were leaving.
2 If only I was/were as agile as I used to be.
3 I wish she would stop criticising me.
4 If only/I wish I had gone to university when I was younger.
5 She wishes she had a more responsible post.
6 If only/I wish I could speak a foreign language really well.
7 If only we'd taken (some) photos at that amazing party.
8 I wish/If only I didn't have straight hair.

2 1 only 2 would 3 wish 4 you 5 wish
6 'd 7 were 8 had 9 wish 10 could

UNIT 40

1 1 ~~is submitted~~ be submitted 2 ✓
3 ~~receives~~ receive
4 ~~We hope the President will have a long life!~~
Long live the President!
5 ✓ 6 ~~assumes~~ assume

2
1 You look as though you've been unwell.
2 I think we'd rather sit near the front.
3 It is essential that each new client provides proof of identity.
4 It's time we paid the bill.
5 I'd rather you didn't wipe your feet on the carpets.
6 She acts as if she was/were a member of the club.
7 It's about time you gave your parents a call.
8 It was proposed that all members of the sales team be given a ten percent pay rise.

3 1 was finally resolved 2 be kept clear
3 were 4 stop 5 is 6 hadn't agreed
7 kept 8 was/were able to 9 haven't told
10 demand 11 be put
12 not have to refer/we didn't have to refer

REVIEW

1 1 E 2 G 3 F 4 D 5 A 6 H 7 C 8 B

2 1 A 2 M 3 T 4 A 5 A 6 T
7 M 8 T 9 M 10 M 11 T 12 A

3 SAM Did you watch that documentary on global warming last night?
CARL Yes, it was terrifying. I almost wish I ~~didn't see~~ hadn't seen it.
SAM If we ~~would~~ go on destroying the atmosphere like this, the effects will be catastrophic.
CARL You're right. It's high time the government ~~does~~ did something about it.
SAM Well, they have set targets for reducing carbon emissions, haven't they?
CARL Yes, but they're pretty feeble. I think the government should insist that each person ~~to take~~ take (or takes) responsibility for their own carbon footprint.
SAM That's a bit sweeping. I don't see what individual people can do.
CARL What about turning down the central heating by a few degrees?
SAM A good idea – if only the winters ~~aren't~~ weren't so cold in this country!
CARL Well, what about cars, then? If everybody used smaller cars, there ~~was~~ would be a huge reduction in carbon emissions. Take your car, for instance – don't you think it's time you ~~sell~~ sold that big four-wheel-drive thing?
SAM No, absolutely not! If I ~~won't~~ didn't have that car, I wouldn't be able to take all the kids to school. And it's useful to have a big car in case ~~of~~ some of their friends need a lift.
CARL I guess so. Things must be pretty tough with four children ...
SAM Yes. Life would be a lot easier ~~unless I had~~ if I didn't have so many kids!

4 Model answers
1 I'm afraid you can't view the exhibition *unless you have a ticket.*
2 *I wish/If only I was/were* taller!
3 *It's (high) time you* changed your phone.
4 *I'd rather go* somewhere less expensive and more friendly.
5 *I wish you would* tidy up this room!
6 You have to put on your scarf and gloves, *whether you* want to or not!
7 We wouldn't *be in this queue if you'd bought* the tickets in advance on the Internet!
8 They treat their garden *as if it was/were* a rubbish dump!

Module 9

UNIT 41

1 1 A✗ B✓ 2 A✓ B✗ 3 A✓ B✗ 4 A✓ B✓
5 A✗ B✓ 6 A✓ B✓ 7 A✓ B✓ 8 A✗ B✓

2 ... ~~Flights as a safety precaution~~ [As a safety precaution flights] have been grounded, leaving thousands of passengers stranded. This couldn't have happened ~~it~~ at a worse time as this is the final week of the Easter holidays and holidaymakers across the continent have been trying to fly ~~them~~ home.
The source of the cloud of ash is the Eyjafjallajökull volcano in Iceland. A few days after the eruption started ~~it~~, the ash cloud arrived over Europe. At first the cloud was confined to the skies over the British Isles and Scandinavia, but it ~~over the European mainland has now spread~~ has now spread over the European mainland.
The fine particles of ash can enter jet engines and damage the internal parts, leading to catastrophic results.
Fortunately, flights to airports in southern Europe are continuing ~~them~~. Some intercontinental flights originally destined for London, Amsterdam or Frankfurt have been re-routed to Madrid, which is still open ~~the airport~~. Passengers arriving ~~them~~ there will be able to travel on to their final destination by road or rail.
The aviation industry is hoping that the wind direction will change ~~it~~, taking the ash away from Europe. In the meantime, scientists are running test flights to assess the density of ash in the clouds. Depending on their findings, certain flight routes ~~in the next few days may be reopened~~ may be reopened in the next few days.

UNIT 42

1
1 The couple named their first daughter Samantha.
2 His Excellency expects visitors to stand when he arrives.
3 Amanda brought all her expertise to the team.
4 Amanda brought the team all her expertise.
5 A very inexperienced salesman has become the Sales Manager.
6 Tim took his grandmother to the hospital for therapy.
7 Susan liked the bracelet so her daughter bought it for her.
8 The trainer recommended trying an easy programme first/recommended first trying an easy programme.
9 The scenes of destruction in the film made us all sick.
10 The regulations require all athletes to take a drugs test before the competition.

2 1 seemed OK 2 it unsafe 3 us any information
4 to be anyone 5 us when we would be leaving
6 any food or drink to you 7 us 8 you sitting
9 us to go 10 the plane to divert to Bucharest
11 us waiting 12 me mad

3 1 When he made out his will, Mr Smithson refused to leave his estranged son anything.
2 We require all passengers to supply photo identification before check-in.
3 The Management recommends that you keep your valuables safe by handing them in at Reception.
4 The invitation doesn't tell us what we should wear at the reception.
5 Mrs Henderson has been elected the new head teacher.
6 Prizes can be claimed by sending us the form and proof of purchase, at the address below.

4 1 D 2 C 3 G 4 K 5 H 6 O 7 I 8 E

UNIT 43

1 1 Was there really such a long wait between trains?
2 We always have lots of visitors but there tend to be more in the summer months.
3 The director leaves it to the viewer to decide who is guilty and who is innocent.
4 They assured us that there would be no trouble getting a refund if the goods were faulty.
5 You know, it really gets on my nerves when she talks like that.
6 What's incredible is that there might have been so many more fatalities.
7 I find it impossible to believe that someone with his track record would be so careless.
8 In 1666 there was a fire which destroyed a large part of London.
9 We would appreciate it if you submitted your estimate to our head office.
10 Grandpa loves it when the children ask for his advice.

2 1 There are more than a million species of insects in the world.
2 There was a grandfather clock ticking in the background.
3 I find it outrageous that they didn't give you a refund.
4 It was thrilling meeting/to meet that movie star in person.
5 There now follows/There will now be a statement by the Prime Minister.
6 They regard it as inevitable that the currency will eventually collapse.
7 There were two forms of amino acid present in the compound./Present in the compound there were two forms of amino acid.
8 Is there an underground railway in Osaka?
9 There are thought to be at least two leading politicians involved in the scandal.
10 It isn't clear why the landing wheels failed to descend.
11 It is possible that you left your cash card in the machine.
12 Is there nobody here to help us?

3 Model answers
1 *But it comes as a shock to discover that, far from being the source of contentment and inner fulfilment that he expects, the beach turns out to be a place of savage violence, terror and death.*
2 *It is difficult not to be impressed by the author's skill in describing the unfamiliar oriental locations and his ability to empathise with the obsessions of today's young backpacking 'new-age' travellers.*
3 *It is the author's unique blend of these disparate elements which gives the novel its haunting sense of unease and horror.*
4 *There are all the traditional ingredients that make up a successful thriller …*
5 *There is a strong sense of good and evil in the book*
6 *but Garland leaves it to the reader/ but it is left to the reader to decide who is right and who is wrong.*
7 *There are few moral certainties in this exotic corner of the world.*
8 *it is impossible to put this book down once you have started it.*

UNIT 44

1 1 There is bound to be a bad reaction to the news.
2 There will be no difficulty getting a visa. / It won't be difficult to get a visa
3 There is likely to be a massive sell-off of high-tech shares in the next few days.
4 It's no surprise (that) Carol left/has left/is leaving her job.
5 In this bad weather there is certain to be a poor turnout for the election. / There is certain to be a poor turnout for the election in this bad weather.
6 It's no secret that Brian dislikes his mother-in-law.
7 There was no reason to question her motives.
8 It seems as if/though we've got a lot in common.

2 1 there 2 supposed to be 3 seems as if
4 no point in 5 looks as though 6 no need
7 no longer 8 no good 9 sure to be 10 bound

UNIT 45

1 1 Tourists are not permitted to take photos in the museum.
2 Mrs Grimble threatened to call the police if the boys didn't stop.
3 The doctor urged Henry to go on a diet immediately.
4 Alison arrived at the station only to find (that) the train had already left.
5 We promise to reduce taxes radically in order to help small businesses.

2 1 I daren't ask my boss for a pay rise.
2 You aren't fit enough to join the army.
3 He was anxious not to arrive late.
4 I'm not able to give you an answer right now.
5 The government closed the borders in order to catch the criminals.
6 The manager made the decision to close the office this morning.
7 I was surprised to learn that Amanda was going to marry Ronald.
8 They didn't publish the news so as not to frighten the public.

9 I visited the bank this morning to check the balance on my account.
10 We got there only to find they had already closed the store for stocktaking!

3 ... The cabin crew were *to* shocked find the previously healthy 28-year-old in a state of collapse at the end of a long-haul flight from Australia to London ...
Farol Khan, director of the Aviation Health Institute, claims to have evidence that more than 6,000 passengers a year die of deep-vein thrombosis (DVT) as a result of long-haul flights. Unfortunately, as symptoms often take some time to appear, the link between the condition and flying is not always apparent. But there seems to be a clear relationship between the occurrence of DVT and the steady reduction in the amount of legroom between seats in economy-class cabins. In a bid to increase the number of passengers carried and their consequent profitability, many airlines have squeezed more and more seats into their planes, at the cost of comfort and legroom. And our willingness to put up with these uncomfortable conditions is simply based on the fact that we know more seats means lower prices. But with limited opportunities to stretch or move around, the blood circulation in passengers' legs tends to slow down, and blood clots can easily develop. Most at risk are elderly people, sufferers from heart conditions and smokers. But as Emma Christofferson's case shows, even the young and healthy can do little to prevent blood clots occurring under these circumstances.
Promoting a 'caring, sharing' image is something many airlines are keen on, and some of these have finally promised to take the problem more seriously, for instance by issuing health advice to passengers 'trapped' on their long-haul flights. They usually recommend moving the legs and feet regularly, and advise taking walks up and down the aisle at least once an hour. But, as any experienced traveller knows, the aisles on most planes are only just wide enough for the trolleys to get through. It is often impossible to walk down the aisle to get to the toilets, let alone allowing enough space to take any exercise.
The truth is that until we are all prepared to give up paying rock-bottom prices for long-distance travel, the airlines will have no incentive to improve conditions. And a return to exclusive and expensive air travel is something nobody would contemplate advocating.

UNIT 46

1 1 B 2 A 3 B 4 A 5 A 6 B

2 1 to pack 2 leaving 3 pressing 4 to enter
5 washing 6 to get 7 to announce
8 seeing 9 to put 10 to get

3 1 I regret having given up/giving up my job
2 Don't forget to top up your mobile phone credit
3 isn't capable of driving 4 The laying of flowers
5 went on working 6 advised Pedro to give up
7 means taking on a lot of responsibility.
8 needs retyping/to be retyped
9 mind my brother coming
10 burst out laughing when she heard

4 1 to see 2 taking 3 to wear 4 coming
5 heard 6 The over-fishing 7 exploiting
8 installing 9 closing 10 to catch

REVIEW

1 1 ~~broke thousands~~ broke into thousands
2 ✓
3 ~~remain to be tenants~~ remain tenants
4 ~~appears some mistake~~
appears to be some mistake
5 ✓
6 ~~unacceptable your manager's comments~~
your manager's comments unacceptable
7 ~~showed to their gathered fans their trophy~~
showed their trophy to their gathered fans
8 ~~explained us the problem~~
explained the problem to us
9 ~~tell me to go?~~ tell me where to go?
10 ~~placed back in its correct position the gold watch~~ placed the gold watch back in its correct position
11 ✓
12 ~~drives absolutely wild my cats!~~
drives my cats absolutely wild!

2 1 The organisers didn't anticipate there being such an overwhelming demand for tickets.
2 It seems (as if/as though) she's going to marry him. / It seems she may marry him.
3 There are thought to be many other top executives involved in the fraud. / It is thought that there are many other top executives involved in the fraud.
4 I would appreciate it if you would/could send me your up-to-date retail price list/if you sent me your up-to-date retail price list.
5 There were fifty applicants for the scholarship.
6 It is said he hates publicity.
7 It isn't surprising that their children are so badly behaved.
8 In this paper it will be demonstrated that DNA strands can be replicated.
9 There are twelve detached houses with double garages for sale on this estate.
10 It is a great honour to be nominated for this award.

3 1 to call 2 avoiding 3 to exceed
4 to notice 5 keeping 6 to swim
7 to leave 8 feeling 9 to like 10 passing

4 1 forced me to stop
2 asked to see my driving licence and passport
3 to bring them with me
4 a police station to get a receipt
5 it was/had been a hoax
6 there are dishonest taxi drivers everywhere
7 a taxi driver to take me
8 put my bags in the boot
9 remember asking the taxi driver
10 denied doing anything wrong

Module 10

UNIT 47

1 1 C 2 B 3 A 4 B 5 B 6 C 7 A 8 B

2 1 A, C 2 B 3 C 4 A, B 5 B, C
6 B 7 A 8 C 9 A, B 10 C

3
1 We hope that the soldiers don't experience
2 not to give big pay increases
3 is usually no different/isn't usually any different
4 he didn't try to repair the TV himself
5 Not many songbirds/Not a lot of songbirds
6 you get no impression of life/you don't get any impression of life
7 I wasn't willing to help the children/I was unwilling to help the children
8 neither commonplace nor accepted
9 The estimated fee for the project was not unreasonable
10 I don't think that our company will be offering aid/I think our company will not be offering aid
11 she's no guitarist/she's not a good guitarist
12 isn't especially powerful

UNIT 48

1
1 Doesn't/Didn't she (already) belong to it? A, B
2 Aren't you taking your holiday in that week? A, B
3 Haven't you done it yet? B, C
4 Why don't you join us? D
5 Why didn't you tell me earlier? / Couldn't you have told me earlier? C
6 Oh, haven't you bought them/any then? B
7 Don't you think those hair extensions look awful on older women? A
8 Isn't she (the one) giving the opening talk? A

2 1 incredible 2 uncovered 3 illegal
4 unusual 5 discourteous 6 impossible
7 inconvenience/disadvantage
8 disadvantage/inconvenience
9 unintelligent 10 unavailable

3 1 Hasn't 2 hardly 3 Doesn't 4 Why
5 isn't 6 few 7 not 8 hardly/not
9 doesn't/didn't 10 unfair

4
1 Phil denied (having/having had) any involvement in the pensions scam.
2 If no payment is forthcoming, we will be obliged to disconnect you from the electricity supply/disconnect your electricity supply.
3 Few (people) from the housing cooperative showed any interest in joining the Neighbourhood Watch scheme.
4 It's hardly possible to understand what the parents of seriously ill children must go through.
5 It appears that the director deliberately misinformed the investigators.
6 It's best to avoid topics like politics at dinner parties.
7 Singers rarely make it as actors, but Christina Aguilera has done so.
8 Illegible applications will be automatically rejected.

UNIT 49

1
1 who told you
2 Which one are you going
3 Why don't we put
4 who are you going to complain to
5 which ones/comedians did you see?/ who did you see?
6 the point in/the use of

2
SEAN I've just joined the local wildlife trust.
GILL Is that some kind of club ~~and~~ or is it a society?
SEAN Well, neither, really. It's a charity. The idea is that it protects local wildlife.
GILL What's the point ~~to join~~ in joining that?
SEAN What's the point? Honestly! What a crazy question!
GILL Why do you think it's crazy?
SEAN Well, we're in danger of losing a lot of our wildlife as the area becomes more built-up. So we need to create safe spaces for local species.
GILL Oh, I see. And who ~~create~~ creates the spaces?
SEAN The people who run the charity.
GILL How much does it cost to join?
SEAN Oh, it only costs a few pounds ~~much~~.
GILL ~~To who do you pay that~~ Who do you pay that to, then?
SEAN To the charity, of course.
GILL Can you visit the safe spaces they create?
SEAN Yes, we went to their main one last weekend.
GILL ~~How~~ What was it like? / How was it?
SEAN Interesting, very peaceful, just a nice, large wooded area. In fact, they held an introductory barbecue for new members.
GILL Who ~~did organise~~ organised that?
SEAN The people who run the charity. It was great, a lot of people came.

3 1 Which 2 looks 3 else 4 What 5 How
6 whom 7 What 8 Whose 9 about 10 did

4
1 Which applicant/Which of the applicants do you think is (most) suitable?
2 How long have you been giving the cattle that type of feed (for)?
3 Who told you about the divorce?
4 What else did you do on (the/your) holiday?
5 Could/Couldn't you have persuaded David to stay in the team (any longer)?
6 What's the point in complaining about faulty goods?
7 Which watch/Which of the watches is better for scuba-diving?
8 For whom did the accused steal the getaway car? / Who did the accused steal the getaway car for?

REVIEW

1 MARTIN … ~~No~~ Yes, I did. I went last week, but my doctor ~~doesn't know nothing~~ doesn't know anything/knows nothing . I asked for that new flu drug – what's it called?

LOUISA You mean Relenza?

MARTIN That's it. I asked but he wouldn't give me ~~none~~ any .

LOUISA Why?

MARTIN He said that the tests ~~haven't hardly~~ have hardly proved that it works. Not ~~for~~ only did he refuse to give me Defrenol, but he wouldn't give me ~~none~~ any other medicine. I think it's because the surgery is over-budget and he doesn't want to spend any more money!

LOUISA If that's the case, it's really ~~unhonest~~ dishonest ! Have you thought about complaining?

MARTIN No, what's the use? Complaints about doctors rarely have an effect, ~~don't they~~ do they ? Anyway, I suppose there's not much you can do about a virus. He said I should drink plenty of fluids and ~~he didn't tell me to go out~~ he told me not to go out until I felt better.

LOUISA How are you feeling now?

MARTIN Well, I've still got chest problems. It might be from the fumes at the factory, though they're meant to be ~~no-toxic~~ non-toxic .

LOUISA ~~Have~~ Haven't you left that place? I thought you'd moved to a different job.

MARTIN No, not till next month.

LOUISA I see. Anyway, it lasts a long time, this flu. Not many people ~~don't~~ appreciate that. You think it's gone and you try to get back to normal, then it hits you again.

MARTIN Yes, you're right. I still can't taste anything …

LOUISA Look, I must be going. ~~I don't hope it lasts~~ I hope it doesn't last much longer. Bye!

2 1 the point 2 what 3 Have/Haven't 4 Which 5 the use 6 hardly/barely/scarcely 7 which 8 Why don't 9 did 10 What about/How about

3 1 How long has it been in existence?
2 who founded the Society?
3 who belongs to the Society today?
4 How does the Society contribute to science?
5 What else does it do?

4 A Hardly anyone/anybody knows
B not unlike/not dissimilar to
C it didn't receive its royal status until
D not only British scientists but
E a not insignificant number
F non-scientists/people who aren't scientists/ people who aren't involved in science

Module 11

UNIT 50

1 1 The photographer informed us that she was ill.
2 Everyone assumed the young man to be Gemma's brother.
3 Inspector Stanford vowed to bring the guilty person to justice.
4 The leaflet said that the collection would be on Thursday.
5 Sally admitted having taken the biscuits from the cupboard.
6 The guide did not tell us we'd have to pay extra for lunch.
7 We did not imagine that the museum would be closed today.
8 Our director thanked us for working so hard through a difficult year.

2 1 My friend Tina warned me never/not to tell anyone about her problems again.
2 My manager blamed me for losing the Siemens contract.
3 The art critic considered Picasso the most exciting artist of the twentieth century.
4 The reporter apologised for getting the Minister's name wrong.
5 The police officer accused me/him/her of making threatening phone calls.
6 My friends encouraged me to do the marathon with them.
7 The team manager regretted contradicting Julie in front of the team.
8 My wife reassured me that the arrangements were all under control.
9 My mother reminded me that I had had my tonsils taken out at the age of nine.

3 1 thanking A for B that C to 2 explained D would 3 insisted 4 promised E to 5 denied F that 6 added 7 encouraging G to 8 urged H not

4 1 ~~reminded me to not~~ reminded me not to
2 ✓
3 ~~shouted he wanted~~ shouted that he wanted
4 ~~actually said that's a lie, Minister.~~ actually said, 'That's a lie, Minister.'
5 ~~advised to me keep~~ advised me to keep
6 ~~regret not to have gone~~ regret not having gone
7 ✓
8 ~~demanded being shown~~ demanded to be shown
9 ~~answered "it was all sourced locally"~~ answered that it was all sourced locally.
10 ~~congratulated the new champion winning~~ congratulated the new champion on winning

UNIT 51

1 1 has/had 2 could 3 isn't/wasn't 4 he'd made 5 left 6 must/had to 7 could 8 intends/intended 9 came/had come 10 may/might 11 would 12 us

2 1 that she hadn't got to Spanish the night before as she'd been out all day and had got home late. She said she'll ring/she'd ring again to find out what the homework is/was.
2 she was phoning to find out the results of her blood test. She said she's/she was going on holiday tomorrow morning so she'd be grateful if you could ring her back later.
3 he was sorry (that) they couldn't fulfil our/your order as we/you hadn't included credit card details on our/your website order form. He said they must/had to have the/those details, or payment in advance, to fulfil an order. He said he'd await our/your instructions.

3 1 he's decided to stay another week as the research is going so well there.
2 they had got tickets for the opera that weekend.
3 that the smaller islands were mostly uninhabited and very peaceful.
4 her mother is/was really ill. She said she wished they didn't live so far away from her.
5 the house was in a very pleasant cul-de-sac, and there weren't many children here.
6 the accused had first met the Wilsons when he decorated their living room.
7 we switch/switched to an online banking system.
8 that I/we mustn't leave my/our car in the/those parking bays for more than twenty minutes.

4 1 admission, left/had left 2 denial, accepted
3 allegation, stalked/had been stalking
4 explanation, had been suffering/suffers
5 response, had been applied

UNIT 52

1 1 if/whether we'd had
2 if/whether we'd like to freshen up
3 whether we liked spicy food or not/whether or not we liked spicy food
4 what was going on
5 complained
6 for them to be brought
7 asked Lousia to call
8 asked where he was going
9 begged him not to go
10 asked him if he realised how worried she got
11 offered me/asked me if I would like
12 asked me to take/offered me a seat
13 if I had considered
14 if/whether (or not) I'd like

2 1 ~~if could he~~ if he could
2 ~~to draft~~ to be drafted
3 ~~told us let~~ told us to let
4 ~~if or not~~ whether or not
5 ~~where I'd been all night?~~
where I'd been all night.
6 ~~how possibly could she get away~~
how she could possibly get away
7 ~~what is the problem with the new fax machine~~
what the problem with the new fax machine was
8 ~~begged to her landlord~~ begged her landlord
9 ~~didn't beg us to tell~~ begged us not to tell
10 ~~asked whether the bride looked lovely~~
exclaimed that the bride looked lovely

REVIEW

1 A thanking 1 was B added C joke
2 owns/owned 3 couldn't/hadn't been able to
D assertion 4 had learnt E explained
5 had always invited F quoting 6 meant
7 would continue 8 had given

2 1 The student wanted to know if/whether the university library opened on Sundays or not. / The student wanted to know whether or not the university library opened on Sundays.
2 Julie's mother urged her not to talk with her mouth full because it really isn't/wasn't polite.
3 The manager asked for the minutes to be taken and typed up afterwards. / The manager asked for someone to take the minutes and type them up afterwards.
4 Becky begged Mike not to let the children leave the garden, whatever he did.
5 Jeremy complained that the meal was/had been awful because it was/had been cold and had (had) far too much salt in it.

3 1 'Age only matters when one is ageing. As I've arrived at a great age, I might just as well be twenty.'
2 'The liar's punishment is not that he is not believed, but that he cannot believe anyone else.'
3 'Please accept my resignation because I don't want to belong to any club that will accept me as a member.'
4 'Ask not what your country can do for you, but what you can do for your country.'

4 1 C 2 A 3 A 4 C 5 C
6 B 7 C 8 A 9 C 10 A

Module 12

UNIT 53

1 1 B 2 A 3 A 4 B 5 B 6 A

2 1 F The body of a man who jumped off the Severn Bridge has been found in the River Severn.
2 D In Bangkok, protesters who oppose the current prime minister have brought the city to a standstill.
3 C The global warming conference, which was held in The Hague, has ended without agreement.
4 G The president of the United States has visited the area of the Louisiana coastline which is threatened by oil from the leaking underground well in the Gulf of Mexico.
5 A Flights across northern Europe, which were grounded by the cloud of volcanic ash, have resumed.
6 E London Zoo, which was in danger of closing through lack of funds, has remained open.

3 1 refused to discuss our grievances, which (I think) is outrageous.
2 made him marry a distant relative (whom/that) he'd never met before.
3 to stay with my brother who lives in Los Angeles.
4 the pieces of furniture we bought which wouldn't fit in the car.
5 at the shops trying to find a great dress (which/that) she'd seen in a magazine.
6 who used to work in our London office, has started her own Internet company.

4 Arthur Wellesley, first Duke of Wellington, is a leading military and political figure of the nineteenth century. He is best known as the commander of the British forces (1) which helped to defeat Napoleon Bonaparte at the battle of Waterloo in 1815.
Wellesley, who was born in Ireland, joined the British army in 1787. At first he worked for the Lord Lieutenant of Ireland, (2) who was a friend of his brother Richard Wellesley. He also began a political career when he was elected as a member of parliament for Trim, (3) which was a constituency in Ireland, two years later.
Wellesley saw his first active military service in 1794 in the Netherlands. In 1796 he went to India to fight in the fourth Anglo-Mysore war, which culminated in the battle of Seringapatam. But the most significant phase of Wellesley's career began in 1808, when he sailed to Portugal to lead the British army in the campaign against the French occupation of the Iberian peninsula. In 1813 he defeated Napoleon's brother Jacob, the man (4) who had proclaimed himself king of Spain, at the battle of Vitoria. It was a significant victory (5) which effectively liberated Spain from French occupation. As a reward for this success, Wellesley was given the title of Duke of Wellington by the British government.
Wellington's greatest victory came in Belgium in 1815. Together with Gebhard von Blücher, who was the general leading the Prussian forces, he finally defeated Napoleon at Waterloo, in Belgium. The victory brought an end to the war (6) which had ravaged Europe for almost twenty years. Wellington returned to London as a national hero and resumed his political career, serving as prime minister from 1828 to 1830.

UNIT 54

1 1 in which/where 2 who 3 who had/with 4 on which/when/that 5 for whom 6 whose

2 1 whichever towels/ones you like.
2 (the reason) why she disappeared?
3 where Lady Jane Grey was executed.
4 none of which were suitable.
5 into which their curiosity would lead them.
6 when everybody has a party
7 whenever you want
8 many of which are quite inexpensive

3 1 which 2 where 3 who/whom/that 4 whose 5 which 6 whom 7 who 8 when 9 which 10 which/that

4 Tourism today is an industry which has grown so much in recent years that in many countries it provides the greatest single contribution to the country's revenue. But is it always a good thing? Mass ~~tourism which~~ tourism, which is a relatively recent phenomenon, brings with it a whole raft of problems. First, it means that a country's economy may rely on an industry ~~who~~ which/that is wholly seasonal, with the consequence that the huge numbers of people who work in tourism during the season have no income during the rest of the year. Some find ~~wherever work~~ work wherever they can, but others may look for support from a government that/which is already receiving lower revenues/ already receiving lower revenues.
Second, it is true that in many countries tourists are destroying the very sights ~~where~~ that/which they flock to see. They take home pieces of an ancient monument or of a coral ~~reef which~~ reef, which will gradually result in erosion of the attractions and therefore of the industry.
While this kind of destruction may be wholly unintentional, a certain type of tourist ~~which~~ who wants only a 'good time' can be very destructive in a different way: they behave badly, pick fights and often damage the hotel rooms ~~where they are staying in~~ where they are staying/in which they are staying/they are staying in. Obviously, it is then ~~this behaviour by~~ by this behaviour that the local community judges all members of that nationality, creating enmity rather than fostering empathy, ~~whose~~ which should be one of the main advantages of tourism.
Finally, there are many places where tourism is threatening a well-established way of life: people ~~that~~ whose livelihoods traditionally come from older industries, such as agriculture or fishing, are finding new jobs and wealth in the overdeveloped tourist regions, but at what cost? It is sometimes difficult to understand the reasons ~~which for~~ for which/why countries become involved with tourism.

UNIT 55

1 1 D 2 G 3 A 4 F 5 E 6 B

2 1 Not being very fit, I was unable to finish the marathon.
2 Having left my keys at the office, I couldn't get into my flat last night.
3 Not having (got) a visa, Manuela can't travel to the USA.
4 Arriving home early, they found the place had been burgled.
5 Having been restored by experts, the old house regained its former glory. / The old house had been restored by experts, regaining its former glory.
6 Their children having left home, Dave and Maria felt they should move to a smaller house.

3 1 She fell asleep, sitting in the armchair. / Sitting in the armchair, she fell asleep.
2 Being able to speak Finnish, I managed to follow their conversation.
3 So far nobody has claimed the money discovered under the floorboards.
4 Having moved out, Danny found it difficult to find a nice place to stay.
5 Left for too long, oil paint will form a skin.
6 The sea was very rough, making me feel sick.
7 Not being very good with figures, I'll let you do the accounts.
8 This is a house built to last forever.

4 1 working as a nursing assistant
2 wounded in World War I 3 having recovered
4 who had moved there 5 Visiting an airfield
6 Working as a photographer
7 becoming the first woman 8 who received them
9 landing at Culmore
10 having bought a Lockheed Electra 10E
11 heading south-east
12 having covered about 35,000 kilometres
13 Leaving New Guinea 14 having run out of fuel

UNIT 56

1 1 to forgive 2 not to be 3 to be done
4 to live 5 not to have taken

2 ... Louis XIV decided to build a vast new garden *to surround* ~~surround it~~ his new palace at Versailles. The first person to be ~~asking~~ asked to look at the site was his favourite architect, Andre Le Nôtre. Le Nôtre arrived at Versailles only ~~he discovered~~ to discover a thick forest with uneven ground and an inadequate water supply. It was a great honour to ~~had been choose~~ have been chosen for such a task, but it is not difficult to understand Le Nôtre's reluctance to take on such a challenge – the main water basin alone is 1.5 kilometres long, and there are dozens of fountains, statues and avenues. It was the first garden ~~that designed~~ to be designed on such a large scale, and took more than forty years ~~for building~~ to build/to be built. When Le Nôtre died, in 1700, the garden was still incomplete.

3 1 the first person to arrive
2 to have made more of her musical abilities
3 launched an advertising campaign (in order) to increase
4 a great shock to find the old house
5 to sell first/to be sold first.
6 buildings not to have been destroyed

UNIT 57

1 1 less 2 where 3 fewer 4 What
5 why/when 6 how 7 more 8 least

2 1 what he wanted 2 what he'd seen
3 why this happened
4 how different objects moved 5 what he wrote

3 1 It's raining so there are ~~less~~ fewer children in the park than usual.
2 I couldn't believe the ridiculous reason ~~what~~ (that) they gave for their behaviour.
3 ✓
4 We weren't very close so we didn't hear ~~that~~ what she said very clearly.
5 ✓
6 It's quite a good novel, but very similar to the one ~~what~~ (that) he published two years ago.
7 ✓
8 Darren won because he took the ~~fewest~~ least time to complete the task.
9 The explanation (that) the suspect gave didn't convince the detective.
10 ✓

REVIEW

1 1 Emperor Charles V, who ruled over Spain in the sixteenth century, had only one son.
2 That's the vintage car she's spent so much on ~~it~~.
3 I've thrown away most of the clothes (that) I wore when I was a teenager.
4 Do you know the woman ~~who her~~ whose children are always playing football in the street?
5 That's a question ~~which for~~ for which the company has no answer, I'm afraid.
6 The director refused to take my call, which was really annoying.
7 What you need is the cable ✗ that connects the computer to the printer. (no comma)
8 You can collect the new bag, ~~when you see my sister, which cost a lot of money~~ , which cost a lot of money, when you see my sister.
9 It isn't very clear to ~~who~~ whom you are referring in this recent correspondence.
10 Do you have any idea ~~for~~ why she hasn't responded to our various offers?

2 1 directed by Francis Ford Coppola
2 Lasting almost three hours, the film is Shakespearean
3 headed by Marlon Brando as the 'godfather'
4 playing his troubled son and heir Michael
5 Struggling to reconcile his distaste for crime and brutality with his sense of family honour and duty
6 To achieve his aim of taking the audience on an emotional rollercoaster ride, the director intersperses long scenes of family life with shorter sequences of extreme violence.
(OR The director intersperses long scenes of family life with shorter sequences of extreme violence to achieve his aim of taking the audience on an emotional rollercoaster ride.)
7 Shot in explicit detail
8 prepared to put up with this
9 (to have been) made in the 1970s

3 1 Being so charming, Martin is 2 not to charge
3 Having graduated (from college), I took
4 What I saw that night
5 said Mary, throwing open
6 less traffic, there wouldn't be

4 1 C 2 B 3 B 4 A 5 B
6 C 7 A 8 B 9 A 10 C

Module 13

UNIT 58

1 1 that F, M + S 2 although A, M + S 3 if G, M + S 4 after H, M + S 5 or C, M + M 6 and D, M + M 7 unless E, M + S

2 1 although 2 because 3 Before 4 neither 5 and 6 While 7 as soon as 8 both 9 so 10 or 11 as 12 unless

UNIT 59

1
1 for fear that she will be asked difficult questions.
2 except if a deposit is paid.
3 so it was awarded first prize.
4 provided that you undertake not to reveal the sum agreed.
5 after we see/have seen the details.
6 such restrictive conditions that I couldn't accept the job.
7 as if you've had legal training.
8 so much noise in the meeting that I missed the most important announcement.

2 1 as long as 2 Given that 3 the moment 4 in order that 5 except that 6 that 7 as though 8 so much that

3 1 B 2 H 3 A 4 D 5 I 6 E 7 G 8 C

4
1 ~~so~~ because 2 ✓
3 ~~a so violent scene as~~ such a violent scene that
4 ~~as though you've been~~ as though you'd been
5 ✓ 6 ~~enough early~~ early enough
7 ~~so ridiculous as to~~ so ridiculous that 8 ✓

UNIT 60

1 1 A 2 B 3 A 4 B 5 A 6 B

2
1 People didn't leave their homes, in spite of the advance warnings of the flood.
2 Very little of the remaining stock sold, even though the prices were low in the sale/the sale prices were low.
3 Although the magazine had tried introducing several new features, (the/its) circulation continued to drop.
4 The Scots won the battle, despite having a far smaller force/despite their far smaller force.
5 Though this may seem difficult now, you'll soon wonder why it caused so many problems.
6 Much as I adore children, I can't accept that kind of behaviour from any child.

UNIT 61

1
1 Most people who haven't had training in typing start out by using two fingers only. Eventually, they/They eventually learn how to touch type purely by practice.
2 Rob wants us to visit his sister in Canada later this year , though I'm still not sure that I want to fly after all the problems with the volcanic ash , though .
3 He does what novelists have always tried to do , namely to depict the world in which they live.
4 *The King's Speech* was a low-budget British film. Nevertheless, it won four Oscars at the 2011 ceremony , nevertheless .
5 We recognise that all of our clients have different and individual needs. Therefore, we/We therefore offer a tailor-made programme at no extra cost.
6 We were really hoping that we'd have good weather for the day we visited the golf tournament, but it poured down. Still, we made the most of it and enjoyed ourselves as much as we could.

2 NOTE Other adverbs may be possible.
1 B After that/Following that/Afterwards
2 A also B In addition/Furthermore/What is more
3 A All the same/Still/Mind you
B Nevertheless/Nonetheless/However/Even so
4 A so B Consequently/As a result/Accordingly
5 A such as/like/for instance B namely,
6 A though, B However

3 1 However 2 Furthermore 3 Nevertheless 4 As a result 5 in addition 6 first 7 following that 8 consequently

4
1 ~~than though I expected~~ than I expected, though
2 ~~in addition~~ also
3 ~~but came to a unanimous decision after four hours finally~~ but finally came to a unanimous decision after four hours
4 ✓
5 ~~Mind you~~ However
6 ~~as a consequence~~ so
7 ~~We'd rather all the same not.~~ All the same, we'd rather not. / We'd rather not, all the same.
8 ✓
9 ~~nearly one in every two, that is to say~~ that is to say, nearly one in every two.
10 ~~and wait for the menu to appear on the screen then~~ and then wait for the menu to appear on the screen.

REVIEW

1 1 either 2 while 3 had 4 As/Since 5 apologised 6 in order not to 7 if 8 so sad/such a sad sight

2 1 However 2 Nevertheless 3 consequently 4 Despite 5 While 6 though 7 firstly 8 secondly 9 For these reasons 10 Moreover

3 1 S 2 D 3 D 4 D 5 S 6 S 7 D 8 D

4 1 A 2 C 3 A/C 4 B/C 5 A/B 6 B/C 7 A 8 A/B

Module 14

UNIT 62

1 1 I don't like being phoned late at night.
2 The form should be completed in black ink.
3 This product has not been tested on animals.
4 The tickets having been paid for, we had no choice but to continue.
5 Ibrahim regrets not having been sent to a better school.
6 Those sheets need washing.
7 It was the first palace to have been built/to be built on the east bank of the Nile.
8 He ought to have been sent to prison for life.

2 1 to have been 2 had 3 arrived 4 having been
5 to be 6 he decided to help Theseus
7 soldiers were sent to arrest him 8 they had
9 held 10 plunged

3 NOTE ✓ = passive not appropriate
1 ✓ 2 B The bridge was built in 1450. 3 ✓ 4 ✓
5 C The information is collected from retail outlets and entered on the database.
6 A The lift in our block has been vandalised.
7 ✓
8 A/B Foxes are hardly ever seen in daylight.
9 ✓
10 B The man was convicted (by the jury) and sentenced to fifteen years in jail (by the judge).
11 C Milk is heated to 110°C and then rapidly cooled to produce the final pasteurised product.
12 A The twins have been given a kitten for their birthday.
13 ✓
14 C Application forms must be signed and submitted by the end of January.
15 ✓
16 D China is said to be the world's fastest growing economy.
17 B/C An invoice will be sent after the final consignment of goods has been delivered.
18 A An investigation of the circumstances surrounding the kidnapping is being carried out.
19 ✓
20 C The tips are divided up and shared equally amongst the staff.

UNIT 63

1 1 was made to open my suitcases by
2 were given permission/were allowed to park in
3 is felt that the government is
4 is considered to be unworkable.
5 was seen to hide something
6 getting taken over by a large multinational.

2 1 thought 2 to be 3 have criticised
4 forced to make 5 has been suggested
6 it is reported that 7 think 8 They say
9 got criticised 10 made to cut down on
11 be taken over 12 interested

UNIT 64

1 1 B 2 D 3 C 4 C 5 A 6 A 7 A 8 C

2 1 had 2 had 3 got 4 had 5 made 6 got
7 copy 8 had 9 made 10 had 11 buried
12 get 13 had 14 buried

REVIEW

1 1 LINE 4 <u>a French officer discovered a strange stone</u> a strange stone was discovered by a French officer
2 LINES 6/7 <u>the British seized the stone and the British moved it to the British Museum in London</u> the stone was seized by the British and moved to the British Museum
3 LINES 8/9 <u>somebody asked a French scientist named Jean François Champollion to look</u> a French scientist named Jean François Champollion was asked to look
4 LINES 12/13 <u>hieroglyphs, a type of writing in which pictures represent sounds and meanings</u> hieroglyphs, in which sounds and meanings are represented by a type of writing.
5 LINE 14 <u>somebody had solved the puzzle of their written language</u> the puzzle of their written language had been solved
6 LINES 14/15 <u>it became possible for scholars to decipher the inscriptions on all the great monuments.</u> it became possible for the inscriptions on all the great monuments to be deciphered.
7 LINES 15/16 <u>Thus people finally unlocked the mysteries of Egypt's fabulous history and culture.</u> Thus the mysteries of Egypt's fabulous history and culture were finally unlocked.

2 1 1B 2C 3A 2 1C 2A 3B
3 1B 2C 3A 4 1C 2A 3B

3 1 get your travel agent to arrange
2 had the palace built
3 It is believed to have been constructed/that it was constructed
4 is surrounded 5 It is said 6 was abandoned
7 can be purchased 8 have your hotel arrange

4 1 is said that the new government
2 unruly football fans got (themselves) arrested
3 regret not having been given
4 Have/Get this mess cleaned up/Make sure (that) this mess is cleaned up
5 to have been accepted
6 weren't allowed/permitted to take photos
7 I'm getting someone to drive
8 having been completed, the company

Module 15

UNIT 65

1 1 E 2 H 3 C 4 J 5 B
6 G 7 I 8 D 9 F 10 A

2 1 for 2 of 3 for 4 of 5 for 6 in
7 to 8 of 9 with 10 with 11 of
12 to 13 of 14 of 15 of

UNIT 66

1 1 deal with it 2 takes after you 3 go with it
4 get through this course 5 get over this cold
6 call for an ambulance 7 look round it

2 1 aimed 2 rely 3 the fact that 4 for
5 the researchers with 6 across 7 worry
8 for 9 with 10 the public from

3 1 convince, of 2 prevent, from 3 cure, of
4 present, with 5 blame, on 6 explain, to
7 accuse, of
8 disagree with/agree with, over/about
9 depend on/rely on, for
10 agree with, about/over
11 rely on /depend on, for 12 quarrel with, about

UNIT 67

1 1 It was set up by our IT engineer.
2 turned the old barn into a beautiful house.
3 held them up for several hours.
4 put it off until tomorrow.
5 Can you help me work it out?
6 can put him up in the spare room.
7 how to turn it off.
8 will fill it out automatically.

2 1 Would you mind sorting it out yourself?
2 I ran into him by chance at the supermarket this morning.
3 I've fixed it up for ten o'clock tomorrow.
4 You're always running them down.
5 I'm sure the police will look into it.
6 The builders carried it out very professionally.
7 Could you pick them up from school tonight?
8 Has Perry got over it yet?
9 They really take after her, don't they?
10 Would you point them out for me?

3 1 deal with 2 aimed at 3 points out
4 look into 5 face up to 6 fill in/fill out
7 find out 8 act out 9 cover up
10 keep away from 11 running down
12 let down 13 cut down on 14 comes down to

4 GAVIN Is that a new laptop?

ANDY Yes, my old one ~~broke it down~~ broke down a few weeks ago.

GAVIN It looks like a good one. How are you ~~getting with on~~ getting on with it?

ANDY Not great. It's completely different from my old one.

GAVIN Let me have a look. Oh, I think it uses a different operating system. They should have ~~pointed out it~~ pointed it out to you when you bought it.

ANDY Well, they didn't. It's so confusing – the manufacturers are always ~~coming over with~~ coming up with new systems for computers. Why don't they stick to the ones everybody's familiar with?

GAVIN It all ~~comes down with~~ comes down to economics, I suppose. If they didn't keep changing the systems, nobody would spend money on new software!

ANDY That's true. Look, I hate to ~~bring up it~~ bring it up but didn't you say you were a bit of an expert on computer programs? Could you give me a hand with this one?

GAVIN Of course. No problem. But I'm a bit busy right now. I have to ~~get back of~~ get back to the office in a few minutes.

ANDY Sorry. I don't want to ~~hold up you~~ hold you up. Can we fix up another time?

GAVIN Sure. I'll be here for lunch tomorrow. We can ~~catch up each other with~~ catch up with each other then and ~~set up it~~ set it up. Well, I ought to be going.

ANDY Yes, I'd better ~~get down at~~ get down to my work. I've got a big report to finish ...

UNIT 68

1 1 do 2 make 3 have 4 weak 5 stronger
6 light 7 made 8 poor 9 take 10 in
11 make 12 run 13 heavy 14 have 15 light

2 1 make 2 take 3 make 4 do 5 have 6 have
7 have 8 make 9 has taken 10 take 11 have
12 having 13 do 14 doing 15 will make

3 1 make a decision 2 took a chance
3 made a/the journey 4 take hours and hours
5 done some research 6 taken place
7 made a mistake 8 having problems
9 laundry to be done 10 make a charge
11 make a fuss 12 made a promise 13 have a go
14 do me good 15 have/take a stroll
16 do some shopping 17 make trouble
18 made a bad job of it

REVIEW

1 1 depend/rely 2 taken 3 from 4 at
5 about 6 accused 7 in 8 succeed
9 of 10 make 11 strong 12 risk

2 1 turn the radio down 2 finished off
3 doing up 4 turning it into
5 put the wallpaper 6 stay up 7 goes with
8 sorted out 9 putting her up 10 get on with
11 put up with her 12 talk about
13 looks down on me 14 takes her coat off
15 sits down 16 looking at everything

3 1 Lizzie's going to use her inheritance to set up a charity.
2 We were astonished at/by the quality of her singing voice.
3 It's important to stand up for the rights of minorities.
4 Can you keep an eye on the children while I'm at the shops?
5 Do you think his behaviour had an effect on the outcome of the election?

6 I've got no objection to your sleeping on the sofa.
7 The new legislation is concerned with deregulation of the airline industry.
8 Have you taken account of your parents' reaction?
9 The daily swim seems to be good for him/ do him some good.
10 I couldn't see the details until the guide pointed them out.
11 My brother is engaged in an exciting renewable energy project.
12 She took pity on all the homeless children.
13 Ramon has difficulty in coping with stress.
14 The current political situation is fraught with danger.
15 Looking up to sports stars is a common trait amongst teenagers.
16 I take pleasure in helping people less fortunate than myself.

Module 16

UNIT 69

1 SAMMY ~~suitable~~ suitable
JOSH ~~voluntor~~ volunteer, ~~persistant~~ persistent, ~~permanous~~ permanent
DELLA ~~ridiculent~~ ridiculous, ~~subvalue~~ undervalue, ~~successible~~ successful
ALEX ~~differant~~ different, ~~pre-flatmate~~ ex-flatmate, ~~overnational~~ international

2 1 economists 2 underclass 3 elusive 4 employees 5 bilingual 6 Persistence 7 dependence 8 Intermarriage 9 closure 10 solidify

UNIT 70

1 1 filing cabinet 2 database 3 make-up 4 highway 5 outbreak 6 upkeep

2 1 Eleanor is an attractive and self-confident person.
2 The Midlands is Britain's main car-manufacturing region.
3 They were soon engulfed by the fast-moving water.
4 Each new member of staff must take part in a three-hour training session.
5 Northumberland is a rarely visited part of England.
6 The home-made desserts are the main feature of our restaurant.

3 1 genetically-engineered 2 animal lovers 3 asthma sufferers 4 Research scientists 5 carefully-extracted 6 allergen-free/hypoallergenic

UNIT 71

1 1 fetching 2 take 3 speak 4 stolen 5 risen 6 laying 7 talking 8 done 9 arise 10 bring 11 rob 12 made

2 1 rises 2 Taking 3 have been brought/are brought 4 bring 5 are stolen/are taken 6 take/steal 7 lying 8 robbing 9 lied 10 done 11 Speaking 12 raise

3 1 ~~laying~~ lying 2 ~~arising~~ rising 3 ~~arose~~ arisen 4 ~~talked~~ spoke 5 ~~robbed~~ stolen 6 ~~stolen~~ robbed 7 ~~raising~~ rising 8 ~~laid~~ lain 9 ~~done~~ made 10 ~~Talking~~ Speaking 11 ~~fetch~~ bring 12 ~~Arising~~ Rising 13 ~~make~~ do 14 ~~rise~~ raise

REVIEW

1 1 infections 2 unsuitable 3 beneficial 4 severely-disabling 5 Continuous 6 lowered 7 dependence 8 considerably-improved 9 psychological 10 remarkable 11 heightened 12 responsibility 13 self-confidence 14 overstate 15 enable

2 1 A 2 B 3 A 4 A 5 B 6 A 7 B 8 B 9 A 10 A

3 1 fetch 2 raise 3 selling 4 laziness 5 speak 6 autobiography 7 stolen 8 made 9 lain 10 carefully-controlled 11 trainer 12 closure 13 brought 14 arise

4 1 substandard 2 endurance 3 consultant 4 low-maintenance 5 mathematician 6 outsourcing 7 laid 8 walk-in 9 differentiate 10 repay 11 high-status 12 spiteful

Module 17

UNIT 72

1 1 the door 2 the train 3 Tessa 4 kilometres 5 bags 6 bag 7 bag 8 the job opportunity 9 Warsaw 10 birth 11 the job 12 train

2 1 ~~Alice and Jasper~~ them 2 ~~the backpack~~ it 3 ~~Alice~~ She 4 ~~The step back~~ This 5 ~~Jasper's~~ His 6 ~~his face~~ it 7 ~~Alice's~~ her 8 ~~that look~~ it 9 ~~Her wrist~~ It 10 ~~the doors~~ them 11 ~~Alice and Jasper~~ they 12 ~~On the first floor landing~~ Here 13 ~~the chairs~~ them 14 ~~no other room~~ none

UNIT 73

1 1 done that 2 does 3 did so 4 thought so 5 did 6 do it 7 If not 8 That 9 so do 10 do

2 1 <u>that he had had no involvement</u> it/that
2 <u>If he/she doesn't answer the question correctly</u> If not, / If he/she doesn't,
3 <u>they hurt</u> they do (a human)
4 <u>applauding during play</u> doing so
5 <u>pushed myself too hard</u> done that/done so/done it
6 <u>The increased number of burglaries</u> This
7 <u>it would be a one-sided match</u> (thought) so
8 <u>do not agree</u> do not
9 <u>helped them</u> did so
10 <u>held a referendum</u> done it/done so

3 1 If so 2 did 3 doing (just) that
4 it/this 5 doing so/doing that 6 so
7 doing that/doing so 8 do this
9 do so 10 doing it

UNIT 74

1 1 A ✓ B ✓
2 A ✓ (B would be acceptable if rewritten as: '… better that the usual pianist does.')
3 A ✓ B ✓ 4 B ✓ 5 A ✓ 6 A ✓ B ✓

2 1 The students could ~~either~~ take the exam in June or ~~they could take it in~~ December.
2 The children were delighted with the party lights and ~~they~~ wanted to see them turned on again.
3 We enquired whether the new restaurant would be open on Sunday evenings, like the one it replaced, but the new owners could only tell us that it might be ~~open on Sunday evenings~~.
4 The casual labourers didn't earn much money during the summer, though they had expected to ~~earn some~~.
5 The young woman plays the violin superbly and her brother ~~plays~~ the cello equally well.
6 Baxter's sick tonight, which is unfortunate as he can play better than all the others ~~can~~.
7 We thought that the old woman had been looking after the house, but she can't have ~~been looking after it~~ as she was in hospital at the time.
8 The task states that candidates should not write more than the number of words given, but it doesn't state how many ~~words~~ that is.

3 This popular course examines literature from the last twenty years and ~~it examines literature~~ from a variety of countries across the English-speaking world. It was due to be replaced this year, but because of its popularity it has not been ~~replaced~~; instead, it will run for two more years.
• The course is a compulsory Level 3 component in Literature degrees and ~~the course~~ forms an optional part of the English language degree.
• For this course you are required to have studied at least two previous literature courses at Level 2 and ~~you are required~~ to have passed them with Grade 3 minimum. If registering for this course from another educational institution, you may be asked to provide proof of previous study and ~~you may be~~ required to take an internal test.

UNIT 75

1 1 L 2 B 3 F 4 A, J 5 D 6 H

2 1 No, it was because he got stuck in a traffic jam that he was late.
2 No, what Nick did was (to) call his manager from his hands-free phone.
3 No, it was on Monday morning that he was late.
4 No, what she did was (to) reschedule the meeting for the afternoon.
5 No, not the town centre; it was on the ring road that he got stuck.
6 No, it was because Nick was late that she had to reschedule the meeting.
7 No, it was because he was (going to be) late that he rang her.
8 No, she didn't feel a little annoyed. What she felt was furious!

3 1 The person who/that called the strike was the union representative.
2 It isn't his dedication that political analysts question.
3 What these criminals are is totally ruthless.
4 The place around the corner is where Dickens used to live.
5 The one who complained was the next-door neighbour.
6 The only thing the children did not inherit was the house.
7 It was at six o'clock that the climbers reached the peak.
8 What they did was to engage two au pairs to look after the children.
9 The last thing we did (before leaving) was (to) switch off the power supply.
10 What the company has done is imposed a ban on private emails.
11 All the customers wanted was to get their money back.
12 It was the managing director who/that informed the staff of the news.
13 All our mechanics need to change the tyres is just five minutes.
14 The thing that led to the loss of the American colonies was the introduction of stamp duties.

UNIT 76

1 1 B 2 A, C 3 A, B 4 C 5 C 6 A 7 C 8 B

2 1 ✓
2 ~~Little we knew~~ Little did we know
3 ~~as most of the marketing team~~
as are most of the marketing team
4 ✓ 5 ~~so it be~~ so be it
6 ~~put they on a great display~~
put on a great display they did
7 ✓ 8 ~~Now the time is~~ Now is the time
9 ~~Rarely the early explorers had encountered~~
Rarely had the early explorers encountered
10 ✓ 11 ~~as those are~~ as are those
12 ~~did the old city walls run~~ ran the old city walls
13 ~~he managed to escape~~ did he manage to escape
14 ~~No doubt didn't he realise~~
No doubt he didn't realise

3 1 Exhausted though he was, he managed to reach the finishing line.
2 To make the pilgrimage to Makkah is Selim's life's ambition.
3 Boyd's most complete work is *The New Confessions*.
4 That proposal the school governors really can't accept.
5 On the table was placed an enormous flower display.
6 Much more challenging for the dedicated skier is the Cresta Run.
7 Also included in the report were several sharp criticisms of ministerial conduct.

8 Lying in the shop doorway was an elderly man.
9 To get to the bottom of the mystery proved impossible.
10 So severe was the damage that the pilot couldn't regain control.

UNIT 77

1 1 C 2 E 3 B 4 A 5 D 6 E

2 1 A 2 B 3 B 4 A 5 A 6 A 7 B 8 A

3 1 At this height, the light from space is not affected by interference from the Earth's atmosphere.
2 This makes it the most useful tool in our search for distant stars and planets.
3 the American astronomer used his close observation of the Andromeda Galaxy to develop the theory that the universe is expanding.
4 Only two months after it went into orbit, scientists at NASA discovered that the main mirror had become distorted and could not be used with any accuracy.
5 The name of the solution was COSTAR (corrective optics space telescope axial replacement).
6 The repairs were completed in January 1994 and/The repairs being completed in January 1994, the Hubble Space Telescope is now working correctly and sending its astonishing data back to Earth.

UNIT 78

1 1 D Despite being commercially successful
2 B to write a third is near impossible!
3 A The selection of Arnold Makepeace as the new Professor of Literature
4 B it's also a gripping story.
5 D Apparently,
6 A The publication of several biographies of Princess Diana very soon after her death was
7 C customers are requested not to bring food and drink into the shop.

2 1 ~~We've heard that~~ Apparently
2 ~~to fall asleep to~~ falling asleep to
3 ~~The crowd and the riot police~~ The situation
4 ~~You ought to press~~ Press/Then press
5 ~~Professor Mills explained at length the principles~~ Professor Mills' lengthy explanation of the principles behind the theory of gravity ~~to the students, which made them~~ made the students
6 ~~really special~~ exceptional
7 ~~with exceptional punctuality at ten, and an exhausting period of three hours was spent unloading~~ on the dot of ten,/right on time at ten, and we spent an exhausting three hours unloading

3 1 outbreak
2 the town's residents/the town's population
3 (spokesperson's) statement 4 full investigation
5 conclusion 6 unsurprisingly 7 outcome
8 suggestion 9 call 10 Financially

REVIEW

1 ... where ~~childless couples~~ they must undergo a series of intrusive interviews and examinations and, if ~~they are~~ successful, they will then be put on a waiting list for an unspecified period of time. An Inuit couple wanting to adopt simply makes ~~the fact that they want a child~~ it known and soon enough ~~the couple~~ they will receive a call from a woman who is prepared to give up her child. ~~She may want to give up her child~~ This may be because she already has too many children and ~~she~~ does not want another ~~child~~ one, or the call may come from a relative or friend who wishes to help someone less fortunate than themselves. Traditionally, the couple would be asked if ~~the couple~~ they would like the child and, if ~~they do~~ so, a simple handover would take place. Today, however, ~~the handover system~~ this has been replaced by bureaucracy in the form of civil registration, although the tradition itself has not ~~been replaced~~. ~~The tradition~~ It survives even in the twenty-first century.

2 1 sooner had Rick entered the room
2 all that any aspiring actor wants
3 so sparse was the vegetation
4 it was the chief inspector
5 Much more interesting were
6 It was the decadence
7 seldom had we been treated
8 The last thing Anastasia wanted was

3 1 B 2 C 3 A 4 F 5 E 6 D

4 1 thing 2 neither/nor 3 those/the ones
4 one 5 what 6 they 7 Not 8 so
9 do 10 It is/It's 11 may 12 so

Module 18

UNIT 79

1 1 I'd like to know why it took you so long to deliver this parcel.
2 Can you tell me whether Harriet has finished the minutes of the meeting yet or not?
3 Please let me know when the new curtains for the hotel suites will be ready.
4 Does the brochure say how often the bed linen in the villas is changed/how often the bed linen is changed in the villas?
5 Do you know which metro station we should go to for the Eiffel Tower?
6 I wonder whether or not Vettel won yesterday's race/whether Vettel won yesterday's race or not.

2 1 were there 2 need we
3 will you/could you/would you 4 have you
5 were they 6 will you/can't you 7 hasn't it
8 can you 9 didn't she 10 was he

3 1 C 2 H 3 E 4 G 5 B
6 J 7 I 8 A 9 F 10 D

4 1 if/whether 2 Did 3 won't 4 Isn't 5 what
6 so 7 are 8 so 9 haven't 10 could 11 really
12 shall 13 they 14 think 15 didn't 16 Did
17 it 18 neither/nor 19 Could/Can 20 too

UNIT 80

1 1 D 2 H 3 E 4 G 5 A
6 I 7 B 8 J 9 C 10 F

2 1 did you give up 2 what's 3 else 4 such
5 what a ridiculous 6 young she isn't 7 That
8 did leave 9 However 10 that's

3 1 I do like 2 they did visit 3 That I disagree with
4 They did go 5 where else did they go?
6 why on earth 7 exciting it wasn't
8 What's the point in/use of discussing it?

4 1 such, so 2 Do 3 This, does
4 What, do 5 use 6 Wherever, earth
7 they, aren't 8 can't, However

UNIT 81

1 1 B 2 B 3 B 4 A 5 B

2 1 Apparently, 2 slow/slowly
3 the food is a bit spicy 4 Luckily, 5 dead
6 loud/loudly 7 to tell 8 Generally

3 1 pretty 2 Apparently 3 To be honest
4 a bit 5 Clearly 6 Admittedly 7 By the way
8 dead 9 Naturally 10 Luckily

UNIT 82

1 1 Imagine what would have happened if they hadn't got a receipt.
2 Use a power breaker when you mow the lawn in case you cut the electric lead.
3 What if the police find/found out!
4 Suppose we go to the beach tomorrow?
5 It's high time we had the car serviced.
6 Say we don't get there in time? (What will happen?)
7 Leave me a set of keys in case I need to get in while you're away.
8 Supposing they refused to give you a visa? (What would you do?)

2 1 C 2 A 3 A/C 4 B 5 C 6 B/C 7 A 8 B

UNIT 83

1 1 She won't've got back by the time the show starts.
2 They were trying to find a nice hotel for two hours last night.
3 He mightn't've known that it was you at the door.
4 Alison and Steve're taking us out for a meal tomorrow.
5 They really should've told you about their decision.

2 1 A ~~Do you~~ see that printer icon?
B No, I don't ~~see it~~.
A ~~It's~~ at the top of the screen.
B Oh yes. ~~There~~ on the left.
2 A What ~~are~~ you doing, Jim?
B ~~I'm~~ fixing this loose connection.
A ~~Do you~~ need any help?
B ~~I~~ don't think so, thanks.
3 A How ~~are~~ you feeling?
B ~~I'm~~ not so great today.
A ~~Have you~~ got a headache?
B Yes, I have ~~got a headache~~.
4 A ~~Have you~~ heard the news?
B No, I haven't ~~heard it~~.
5 A ~~Do you~~ think they'll be here soon?
B ~~I'm~~ not sure. Anyway, ~~it's~~ time for me to leave now.
A OK. ~~I'll~~ see you later.
6 A ~~The~~ doorbell's ringing!
B ~~Is there~~ anybody downstairs?
A ~~I~~ don't know.
7 A There are some snacks here. ~~Are~~ you hungry?
B Yes. I am ~~hungry~~.
A ~~Would you like~~ a sandwich?
B Yes, ~~I'd~~ love one.
A And ~~what about~~ some cake?
B No thanks, ~~I~~ wouldn't want to put on weight!
8 A ~~Do you~~ want to watch TV?
B OK. ~~It~~ should be the football results around now.

3 1 Well, 2 Er, 3 I mean, 4 Really 5 like,
6 Well, 7 Mmm 8 I mean, 9 Right 10 OK
11 Well, 12 Yeah, 13 er, 14 Well, 15 OK

4 1 H 2 G 3 F 4 A 5 B
6 C 7 I 8 D 9 J 10 E
A 3F, 6C B 1H, 8D
C 5B, 10E D 2G, 9J E 4A, 7I

REVIEW

1 1 have 2 the answer is 3 What 4 it isn't
5 did 6 the ending was a bit sad 7 apparently
8 such 9 shall 10 I can 11 dead 12 frankly
13 didn't 14 does it 15 What else 16 so
17 is 18 did I 19 However 20 me

2 1 ~~you did invest~~ did you invest 2 ✓ 3 ✓
4 ~~of~~ 5 ~~going~~ go 6 ~~things~~ 7 ~~such~~ so 8 ✓
9 ~~throw~~ threw 10 ~~so nice is she~~ she is so nice!
11 ~~it~~ if 12 ~~arrive~~ arriving
13 ~~aren't they~~ they aren't! 14 ✓
15 ~~time about~~ about time 16 ✓
17 ~~In case~~ If 18 ✓

3 1 Has she 2 You going to 3 I don't think so
4 Me too 5 Really 6 not much
7 Coming 8 like 9 Are you 10 Right
11 what 12 You know

4 1 tell 2 is 3 You 4 Well 5 Do 6 are
7 mean 8 Really 9 Yeah 10 Have 11 do
12 way 13 What 14 be 15 too 16 Right/Now
17 that 18 such 19 if 20 This